The handbook of child and adolescent psychotherapy

Focusing on the development and practice of psychoanalytic psychotherapy with children and young people, this handbook provides both an introduction to this specialist profession and an insight into recent developments in technique and practice.

It includes:

- history, development and training
- theoretical underpinnings
- the process of work and the varied contexts in which it is carried out
- the application of psychoanalytic approaches to different settings and client groups
- in-depth expert overviews of current areas of specialist clinical interest
- a review of research
- an overview of international developments in the profession.

The Handbook of Child and Adolescent Psychotherapy: Psychoanalytic Approaches is an essential resource for all professionals interested or working in Child, Adolescent and Family Mental Health, as well as those working in counselling and adult psychotherapy. Students of psychoanalysis will learn much from the detailed accounts of this specialised application of psychoanalytic thinking and technique.

Monica Lanyado helped to found the Child and Adolescent Psychotherapy training in Scotland and remains involved with training issues at the British Association of Psychotherapists in London. **Ann Horne** was Head of the Child and Adolescent Psychotherapy training at the British Association of Psychotherapists. She works at the Portman Clinic, London, where she is co-editor of the Portman Series.

Contributors: Chriso Andreou; Dilys Daws; Sira Dermen; Judith Edwards; Denis Flynn; Barbara Gaffney; Viviane Green; Trevor Hartnup; Jill Hodges; Juliet Hopkins; Ann Horne; Carol Hughes; Margaret Hunter; Monica Lanyado; Meira Likierman; Sheila Melzak; Niki Parker; Marianne Parsons; Pat Radford; Sandra Ramsden; Susan Reid; Paulina Reyes; Margaret Rustin; Valerie Sinason; Elizabeth Urban; Peter Wilson.

The handbook of child and adolescent psychotherapy

Psychoanalytic approaches

Edited by
Monica Lanyado and Ann Horne

London and New York

First published 1999 by Routledge
11 New Fetter Lane, London EC4P 4EE

Simultaneously published in the USA and Canada
by Routledge
29 West 35th Street, New York, NY 10001

Routledge is an imprint of the Taylor & Francis Group

Typeset in Garamond by
J&L Composition Ltd, Filey, North Yorkshire
Printed and bound in Great Britain by
St Edmundsbury Press, Bury St Edmunds, Suffolk

British Library Cataloguing in Publication Data
A catalogue record for this book is available
from the British Library

Library of Congress Cataloguing in Publication Data
The handbook of child and adolescent psychotherapy/[edited by]
Monica Lanyado and Ann Horne.
    p.   cm.
Includes bibliographical references and index.
1. Psychodynamic psychotherapy for
children.   2. Psychodynamic psychotherapy for
teenagers.   3. Child analysis.   4. Adolescent
analysis.   I. Lanyado, Monica, 1949–   . II. Horne, Ann,
1944–   .
RJ505.P92H36   1999
618.92'8914–dc21   98–48880
                                                          CIP

ISBN 0–415–17258–6 (hbk)
ISBN 0–415–17259–4 (pbk)

Contents

    refugees from political violence**   405
    SHEILA MELZAK

27 **Autism: clinical and theoretical issues**   429
    JUDITH EDWARDS AND MONICA LANYADO

28 **The psychotherapeutic needs of the learning disabled
    and multiply disabled child**   445
    VALERIE SINASON

    Appendix: Further information   457
    Index   461

Contributors

Chriso Andreou is a founder member of Nafsiyat, an intercultural therapy centre in London. She has undertaken clinical research into sexually abusive behaviour in young adolescent boys at Great Ormond Street Hospital, and worked at the Adolescent Unit in Wandsworth, London.

Dilys Daws is a consultant child psychotherapist at the Tavistock Clinic, London, where her work includes being part of the Under Fives Counselling Service. She has also for the last twenty years visited weekly the Baby Clinic at the James Wigg Practice in the Kentish Town Health Centre, London. She was Chair of the Child Psychotherapy Trust and is founding Chair of the Association for Infant Mental Health.

Sira Dermen is a child psychotherapist and a Member of the British Psycho-analytical Society. She has a private psychoanalytic practice, and also works at the Portman Clinic, London, where her special interest is in violence.

Judith Edwards is a consultant child and adolescent psychotherapist in a Family Centre and teaches child development at the Tavistock Clinic. She is currently joint editor of the Journal of Child Psychotherapy. She has published in professional journals and contributed chapters to books including *Autism and Personality* (Routledge 1999).

Denis Flynn has worked as Head Child Psychotherapist at the Cassel Hospital, London, and is now Head of the Adolescent In-patient Unit at the Cassel Hospital. He is a psychoanalyst in private practice.

Barbara Gaffney trained as a child psychotherapist with the British Association of Child Psychotherapists having previously worked with deprived and abused children at the Mulberry Bush Residential School. She worked at the Gender Identity Development Clinic, St George's Hospital, South London (which subsequently moved to the Portman Clinic) from 1992–7. She currently works in the Child and Adolescent Mental Health Service within Pathfinder NHS Trust, London.

Viviane Green is head of Clinical Training at the Anna Freud Centre, London. She is a visiting lecturer at the University of Padua in Italy and also works in private practice. She is Extraordinary Member of the Board of the Child Clinical Training, Genootschap, Utrecht (Netherlands Psychoanalytic Institute) and is particularly interested in children with learning difficulties.

Trevor Hartnup trained at the Anna Freud Centre and worked at the Cassel Hospital until 1984, before taking up his present post as Head of Child and Adolescent Psychotherapy in Wandsworth, London. He has published papers in the UK and France on in-patient psychotherapy and the psychotherapy setting. He is currently Chair of the Association of Child Psychotherapists. He is also a member of the British Association of Psychotherapists and an adult psychotherapist in private practice.

Jill Hodges is a consultant child psychotherapist in the Department of Psychological Medicine, Great Ormond Street Hospital, London, and an honorary senior lecturer in the Behavioural Sciences Unit, Institute of Child Health, London. In her research work she has studied adoption and the impact of early adversity on later development.

Juliet Hopkins is a consultant child psychotherapist on the staff of the Tavistock Clinic. She also trained as an adult psychotherapist with the British Association of Psychotherapists and sees adults in private practice. She specialises in working with children under five and their families and has a special interest in infancy and attachment.

Ann Horne trained at the British Association of Psychotherapists where from 1994–8 she headed the Child Psychotherapy training. A previous joint editor of the Journal of Child Psychotherapy, she works at the Portman Clinic, London, where she is co-editor of the forthcoming 'Portman Series'.

Carol Hughes trained as a child and adolescent psychotherapist with the British Association of Psychotherapists. She is Principal Child and Adolescent Psychotherapist employed by the Maudsley and Bethlem Royal Health Service Trust at the Belgrave Department of Child Psychiatry at Kings College Hospital, London and also by the East Kent Health Authority in Canterbury. She has worked for many years with children in care at ISP and Heath Farm in Kent as well as in consultation to Social Services. She is co-author of *So Young, So Sad, So Listen*, on childhood depression, and Reviews editor of the Journal of Child Psychotherapy.

Margaret Hunter is the Head Child Psychotherapist for the Maudsley NHS Trust, London. Her special interests include fostered children and recovery from abusive experiences in childhood. She is currently writing a book about psychotherapy with young people in foster care.

Monica Lanyado helped to found the Child and Adolescent Psychotherapy training in Scotland and remains involved with training issues at the British Association of Psychotherapists in London. She has worked for many years within the NHS and carried out clinical research on sexually abusive behaviour in young adolescent boys at Great Ormond Street Hospital, London. She is former co-editor of the Journal of Child Psychotherapy and is currently in private practice in Blackheath, London.

Meira Likierman works at the Tavistock Clinic where she is leader of the Psychoanalytic Psychotherapy Doctoral Programme in the Child and Family Department. She also teaches part-time for the Lincoln Centre and the University of Oxford. She has lectured widely in Britain and abroad and published in leading professional journals. She is currently writing a book on Melanie Klein for the Tavistock Clinic Series.

Sheila Melzak works as Principal Child and Adolescent Psychotherapist at a human rights charity, The Medical Foundation for the Care of Victims of Torture where she co-ordinates a child and adolescent treatment team. She has a particular interest in trying to understand the external and internal factors involved in the development of resilience in children who have experienced violence, loss and exile.

Niki Parker is Head of Child Psychotherapy at Bexley and Greenwich Child and Adolescent Mental Health Service. She trained at the British Association of Psychotherapists (BAP), is an active member of the BAP Child and Adolescent Psychotherapy Training Committee and also teaches on the course. She has special interests in eating disorders and working with young children.

Marianne Parsons is a child psychotherapist and a child and adult psychoanalyst. She was Head of the Clinical Training at the Anna Freud Centre and Joint Editor with Ann Horne of the Journal of Child Psychotherapy. She has a private practice and also works at the Portman Clinic, London.

Pat Radford was a teacher and social worker before training as a child psychotherapist at the Anna Freud Centre. She has worked in a variety of NHS settings and published papers on many different aspects of her work. She teaches and supervises trainees on the child and adolescent training at the British Association of Psychotherapists and at the Anna Freud Centre.

Sandra Ramsden trained at the Anna Freud Centre and has worked in hospital and community settings since qualifying. In particular she has worked at the Middlesex Hospital, London (now UCLH) developing a clinical specialisation in growth problems, working particularly with Paediatric Endocrinologists. She retains a strong interest in Child Psychotherapy training and has been active at a senior level in the Association of Child Psychotherapists.

Susan Reid is a consultant child and adolescent psychotherapist at the Tavistock Clinic with a major involvement with the training of child psychotherapists. She founded the group psychotherapy workshop at the Tavistock in 1985 and has two books on psychoanalytic group psychotherapy in preparation. She is founder of the Autism Workshop at the Tavistock and editor of *Developments in Infant Observation: The Tavistock Model* and with Anne Alvarez, editor of *Autism and Personality: Findings from the Tavistock Workshop.*

Paulina Reyes trained at the Tavistock Clinic, and is Senior Child Psychotherapist at Pathfinder Child and Adolescent Mental Health NHS Trust. She also does freelance work for Social Services. She worked at the Gender Identity Clinic, St George's Hospital from 1992–5.

Margaret Rustin is Consultant Child Psychotherapist and Organising Tutor of Training in Psychotherapy with Children, Young People and their Parents, at the Tavistock Clinic, London. In 1993 she was elected Dean of Postgraduate Studies at the Tavistock. She has published widely in professional journals and is joint author of *Narratives of Love and Loss* (Verso 1987), and joint editor of *Closely Observed Infants* (Duckworth 1989) and *Psychotic States in Children* (Duckworth 1997).

Valerie Sinason is a widely published poet, writer and author, Director of the Clinic for Dissociative Studies, Consultant Research Psychotherapist at St George's Hospital Medical School Psychiatry of Disability Department, London, and Consultant Child Psychotherapist at the Tavistock Clinic. Books include *Mental Handicap and the Human Condition* (Free Associations 1992), *Treating Survivors of Satanic Abuse* (Routledge 1994), *Night Shift* (Karnac 1996) and *Memory in Dispute* (Karnac 1998).

Elizabeth Urban is a professional member of the Society of Analytical Psychology where she undertook the child and adult analytic trainings. She is in private practice and also works as a child psychotherapist in the South Brent Child and Family Service. Her special interest is early development and Michael Fordham's model of development, and she has taught and published papers in this area.

Peter Wilson trained as a child psychotherapist at the Anna Freud Centre. He worked in Child Guidance clinics in South London and was Senior Clinical Tutor at the Institute of Psychiatry and Maudsley Hospital Children's Department. He became Director of the Brandon Centre in 1984 and was Consultant Psychotherapist to Peper Harrow Therapeutic Community. Since 1992 he has been Director of Young Minds, the National Association of Child and Family Mental Health.

Foreword

It is with pleasure and professional pride that we welcome this *Handbook of Child and Adolescent Psychotherapy*, which puts psychoanalytic child psychotherapy firmly on the map with other professions in the Handbook series. As the editors of *The Child Psychotherapist and Problems of Young People* (Daws and Boston 1977), this probably places us as grandparents to this book! When our book was first published, child psychotherapy was a relatively young profession, only recently recognised by the NHS. It was very much a first attempt to introduce our work to the general public and it felt quite exciting to put these ideas into print.

Since that time *Extending Horizons* (Szur and Miller 1990) has given an account of increasingly varied work, and the way in which the originality of many members of our profession has flourished.

In this book, the creative ideas by Lanyado and Horne's 'quiet experts' are stunning. In spite of this quietness, the passion and commitment of the work is evident. Child psychotherapy is about close work with children and families in emotional turmoil, often giving them a 'voice' and ways in which to reflect on themselves. Years ago a young patient told his teacher that, in psychotherapy, 'you learn why you cry'. Other children who have suffered abuse may have become so emotionally frozen that crying is out of reach. Through psychotherapy some of these children get back in touch with their feelings (Trowell and Kolvin 1999).

Over the years, knowledge about children's emotions gained through psychotherapy has helped to inspire other professions deeply involved with the welfare of children. This however is a two-way process, and our colleagues' experience has equally stimulated child psychotherapy to respond to new challenges. Just as intensive experience with a few children can generalise to useful thoughts about clinical populations, so, in reverse, can general ideas inform individual work. Many of the chapters in the book reveal courage by child psychotherapists in tackling new areas of concern. This bravery both reflects a move in our society to take responsibility for our fellow beings and may be one part of its inspiration.

The last ten years have seen a further expansion of child psychotherapy, this time geographically. No longer is it restricted to the area of the original training schools. Life can exist outside London! New schools have been established in Scotland and the Midlands and there is a gradual spread of child psychotherapists to other parts of the country.

The Child Psychotherapy Trust was set up in 1987 to promote ideas about children's emotional development and their mental health needs. The Trust has been able to back local enterprises and to stimulate our own profession and our colleagues to think about the provision of child and adolescent mental health services throughout the country.

Another sign of growing confidence has been the establishing of links with universities, enabling students to attain master degrees and doctorates in conjunction with their training. Such initiatives have started in many places, not simply in London.

The profession can now be considered to have achieved maturity and the fiftieth anniversary of the establishment of the Association of Child Psychotherapy is to be celebrated in 1999. The production of this well-referenced and comprehensive handbook, with contributions from senior, experienced members of the profession, is therefore timely. It continues the tradition of describing in jargon-free English the wide scope of child psychotherapists' activities and will be useful to interested lay readers as well as to child and adolescent mental health professionals. Those considering child psychotherapy as a career will find it an invaluable source of information. When we first edited *The Child Psychotherapist*, we were told that students gave it to their parents, or spouses (or even their own children) to explain their new profession! The present book will do this even better.

Similarly, the parents of children in therapy will have the opportunity to understand the background to the work with their children and with themselves. The book is part of a generally more open approach and willingness by psychotherapists to engage in discussion with their patients and clients.

In the twenty-eight chapters, many areas of specialist work, full of originality, are described. Of great interest is the discussion on how much therapy is 'good-enough'. In the current climate of economic pressure, it is vital to discriminate whether various kinds of brief intervention can bring to life deep enough clinical energy to effect useful change, or whether children and their families are being deprived of longer-term work that they really need. The overview of research contributes to this debate.

Through this book we can see fifty years of the growth of a profession that is now confident, wide-ranging and coherent. The editors are to be congratulated on its portrayal and we wish the handbook every success.

Mary Boston
Dilys Daws

References

Daws, D. and Boston, M. (1977) *The Child Psychotherapist and Problems of Young People*, Wildwood, reprinted London: Karnac, 1988.

Trowell, J. and Kolvin, I. (1999) 'Lessons from a psychotherapy outcome study with sexually abused girls', *Clinical Child Psychology and Psychiatry* 4(1): 79–89.

Szur, R. and Miller, S. (1990) *Extending Horizons*, London: Karnac.

Acknowledgements

Following the request by our publishers that we undertake editing this handbook for an ongoing Routledge series, and after a mild combination of euphoria and panic, we approached Dilys Daws to discuss producing a new work and its relation to the now seminal *The Child Psychotherapist and the Problems of Young People*. Our prime thanks, therefore, go to Dilys, Juliet Hopkins and Eric Rayner for their early and continuing encouragement and support – and for a lovely summer evening meal in the garden. We are very grateful, too, to Dilys and to Mary Boston for providing a Foreword, thus fostering a sense of continuity with their text of 1977.

The individual contributors to this work have spent much time in communication and discussion with colleagues and many mention those to whom they are indebted. We would additionally like to thank Domenico Di Ceglie, Ricky Emanuel, Tammy Fransman, Heather Howard, Mary Lightfoot, Dorothy Lloyd-Owen, Graham Schulman, Inji Toutounji, those who responded to Sandra Ramsden's request for case material, and the many colleagues and overseas representatives of the *Journal of Child Psychotherapy*. Especial thanks to Judith Edwards and Marianne Parsons for their generous help, advice and support throughout the preparation of the handbook. At Routledge we have been fortunate to have had access to editors with confidence that all will be well and who have taken a light approach to our occasional obsessionalities.

Finally, Saul and Chris may be in the business world (we both 'married out') but their common sense, humour and ability to deal with our prolonged co-habitation with the handbook have been a major contribution to this effort. We can only inadequately thank them.

1 Introduction

Ann Horne and Monica Lanyado

The psychoanalytic tradition, with its emphasis on the importance of childhood experience, is now just over one hundred years old. Early papers on work with child patients began to appear about eighty years ago (Hug-Hellmuth 1912; Sokolnicka 1920; Freud, A. 1926; Klein 1927). Trainings in child and adolescent psychotherapy began in the UK in the 1930s and 1940s, consolidating in 1949 in the formation of the Association of Child Psychotherapists, which today accredits courses and sets standards for membership of the profession. As a young profession, operating mainly within the National Health Service in the UK, child and adolescent psychotherapy has not only survived but has reached a maturity.

Nevertheless much of what child psychotherapists actually do remains a matter for specialist professional journals, *The Child Psychotherapist and the Problems of Young People* and the later *Extending Horizons* being notable exceptions here (Daws and Boston 1977/81; Szur and Miller 1991). There are at least three important influences that have encouraged this phenomenon. Behind such a reality there lie concerns about maintaining confidentiality while writing about troubled and vulnerable young people – an issue addressed at the end of this chapter. There has also been the development of a variety of approaches to working with children, adolescents and their families – the initial understanding of the child's internal world and the unconscious processes at work in the positions he adopts in relation to his environment, very much the keystone of early child guidance work, came under pressure in many clinics with the advent of family therapy and behavioural and cognitive approaches. Although psychoanalytic work continued to develop in child and family mental health settings (especially in London), it was of necessity slower, longer-term work than that of other interventions, and (until fairly recently, see Chapter 9) less amenable to the research instruments then available. Publication in other than specialist psychoanalytic journals was therefore rare. Finally, one has to consider the impact of numbers and geography: child and adolescent psychotherapists are not numerous, there being less than 300 practising or in training in the UK. These are unequally spread across the country, most being not only in London but in north-west London, within reach of the four London training schools and the psychoanalytic world of that area. The actual influence, in terms of consultation, teaching and the continuing evolution of applied work and ideas has, in contrast to the numbers of practitioners, been surprisingly great.

It seemed, therefore, timely to respond to our publisher's invitation to join their handbook series at a point when debate within the profession has become more open, when research tools are more sophisticated, when the availability of child psychotherapists and psychoanalytic thinking about children grows, both in the UK and internationally, and when public outrage about violent and disturbed children lives uneasily in a society that still gives its children few rights and finds it difficult to take seriously child mental well-being.

The handbook

This handbook is designed for several types of reader. For those who are already training or working as child psychotherapists the value will probably lie mainly in the chapters on work of specialist interest, although many of the other contributions will offer creative ideas and sparks to further thinking. For the reader in allied professions, we hope at the same time to offer an introduction to the profession that not only helps to locate it in its historical and present context but also enables an appreciation of some of the practices involved in a psychoanalytic approach to understanding and working with distressed and 'stuck' children and young people. Some chapters are therefore deliberately written to be accessible to a general audience and the authors have responded to that brief – this is especially true of the section introducing the theoretical foundations.

While we recognise that there can be dangers in pitching a book at several levels, we felt it important to use this opportunity to present the profession of Child and Adolescent Psychotherapy as it is now. Our year of publication, after all, marks the fiftieth anniversary of the establishment of the Association of Child Psychotherapists. It is frequently the case that practice moves ahead of theory, and practitioners are at times reluctant to share *what they actually do* outside (or even within) the profession, as innovations may be viewed as radical or not conforming to established theoretical tradition. We have been fortunate in our contributors: many, like the authors of Chapters 22 and 24, are quiet experts who, in writing for the first time together on their subject, present important developments in theory and practice. Our hope, therefore, would be that the more generalised introduction will then make accessible some of the excitement and potential in recent thinking about practice, and that the general reader will also find much in the more specialised chapters to enhance practice in other professions as well as to facilitate understanding of why and how the child psychotherapist is working in a specific field.

We have also included writers from a variety of theoretical backgrounds:

Contemporary Freudian, Independent, Jungian and Kleinian. Although there has in recent years been much movement away from the bitterness of argument and theoretical polarisation experienced in the 1940s (King and Steiner 1991; Daws 1987), there remain important differences amongst theoretical schools, leading to divergence in technique. A by-product of the handbook may therefore be the explication of approaches taken for granted in a particular training school but possibly less available in others. In general, however, we have gathered experienced writers with proven interest and expertise in specific areas. This multi-authored approach should give the reader a sense of the diversity within the profession, and of a vibrant profession able to discuss, differ and develop, while sharing clear underlying principles.

Structure

The book is structured in five main parts but each chapter, particularly those in the final part, can be read in its own right. The first part introduces the theoretical foundations of the work and is the most generalised section of the entire book. Throughout, authors have used straightforward language to introduce important ideas and concepts. Most useful for the non-psychoanalytic reader who may wish to follow up the suggestions for further reading, these introductory chapters also provide plentiful references for those readers who wish to have more detailed knowledge.

The theoretical section is followed by five chapters about the child and adolescent psychotherapist in practice. These comment on family and cultural context, explore the nature of the relationship between child and therapist and the clinic setting in which this occurs, and includes an overview of research. Psychotherapy is a particularly difficult area to research. An increasing number of highly relevant and useful studies are now being conducted, partly because qualitative research, which allows for the complexity and interactive nature of what is being studied in psycho-therapeutic terms, is becoming more generally acceptable in research circles. This is an increasingly important area of development for the profession. The varied settings for direct and applied work are outlined in Part III and set the context for later chapters. The importance of membership of the multi-professional team is stressed in descriptions of the role of the therapist in the community, in residential settings, in hospital in relation to physical illness, and when children are in specialised in-patient therapy units. Child and adolescent psychotherapists in different parts of the world have also been approached to present as accurately as possible the international spread of this work.

The fourth part of the book describes the diversity of treatment models offered by child and adolescent psychotherapists. The tradition of intensive psychoanalysis (of four- or five-times weekly duration) with which the profession began retains its rightful place; the principles, however, have become applied and developed in once-weekly work, probably the norm for most treatments. In addition, consultative work applies psychoanalytic principles to enable colleagues in a variety of settings to make sense not only of the young people with whom they work but also of their own responses and feelings. Psychoanalytically informed group work is also a developing area for the profession. The fascinating new area of parent–infant psychotherapy is another arena in which there is a great increase in interest, bringing together the advantages of early intervention, the skills of careful observation which are central to our training, and research in parent–infant developmental psychology.

The final section of the book describes areas of special clinical interest: trauma, deprivation, delinquency, violence, sexual abuse and sexually abusive behaviour, gender identity problems, eating disorders, work with refugees, autism and disability. These chapters provide a mixture of an overview of ways of working with these specific problems as well as some of the theoretical thinking behind them. They are rich in case illustrations as well as thought-provoking, and provide an intimate and impressive view of how far the profession has come in adapting classical psychoanalytic practice, originally developed for the treatment needs of mainly neurotic patients, to the more complex nature of a child and adolescent psycho-therapist's work today.

Historical developments

Although the lasting impetus to the establishment of the profession of Child and Adolescent Psychotherapy comes from the theoretical interest and practice of both Anna Freud and Melanie Klein (Daws 1987), there are other influences, both earlier and parallel, which helped found the structure for psychoanalytic work with children and young people. In Vienna, Hermine Hug-Hellmuth (or Hug von Hugenstein) combined her experience as a teacher with her growing interest in psychoanalysis, publishing her first monograph in 1912 and a paper on child analysis in 1921 (MacLean and Rappen 1991). Indeed, in a masterly account of the history of child analysis (or of psychoanalysts working formally with children), Geissman and Geissman elaborate Hug-Hellmuth's early contributions, concluding: 'Her work, buried for sixty years, is being unearthed at last: and that work was the invention of child psychoanalysis' (Geissman and Geissman 1998: 71).

MacLean and Rappen interestingly delineate, in Hug-Hellmuth's approach, factors adopted by Anna Freud (work with latency children; the educational role of the analyst; the preliminary period establishing a therapeutic alliance) and decried by Klein; and points developed by Klein (interpreting the negative transference; the use of play; distinguishing the educational from the analytic role) and criticised by Anna Freud (MacLean and Rappen 1991). Her influence on both is rarely acknowledged.

Other psychoanalysts engaged in thinking about and working with children and young people at much the same time as Anna Freud and Melanie Klein were Eugenie Sokolnicka in France and, slightly later, Sophie Morgenstern (Geissman and Geissman 1998). The tradition of 'child analysis', however, remains in a slightly contentious relationship to psychoanalytic psychotherapy, and the reader wishing to explore the former further is directed to Geissman and Geissman for an excellent history.

In the 1920s the child guidance movement, begun in the USA, reached the UK. The first specially trained psychodynamic workers with children in the child guidance multi-professional teams were the psychiatric social workers (PSWs). Following the establishment of the first child guidance clinics in the UK (by Emanuel Miller and Noel Burke in London and the Notre Dame Clinic in Glasgow) the 'Mayflower ladies' – the first PSWs – went out to the USA to be trained by colleagues there. This interest in gaining particular expertise in work with children and young people grew amongst the early professions in the new clinics – psychologists, psychiatrists (originally specialists in Psychological Medicine) and social workers. Although there was a stimulating ethos of interest in applying psychoanalytic and child development understanding to children, many clinics remained voluntary, reliant until the advent of the National Health Service in 1948 upon jumble sales and donations to keep going. This picture of committed enthusiasm by professionals, yet a backcloth of it being difficult for society to take seriously child mental health issues, remains with us.

At University College, London, the 1920s saw the first courses in child development and observation, run for social workers and teachers. Cyril Burt was appointed to the experimental post of Child Psychologist by London County Council (Urwin and Hood-Williams 1988). It was during this period of early excitement that Dr Margaret Lowenfeld established in 1928 the Children's Clinic for the Treatment and Study of Nervous and Delicate Children:

> Here Lowenfeld's wartime experience and research observations had already led her into the belief that, in addition to environmental considerations, there were processes inherent in children themselves which would enable them to find more adaptive solutions. For Lowenfeld the key to these possibilities was play.
>
> (Urwin and Hood-Williams 1988: 42–3)

This developed in 1931 into a one-year training course and, in 1935, into a three-year 'training in psychopathology and psychotherapy with children and leading to a diploma' (ibid.: 89). The first child psychotherapy training was thus established at Lowenfeld's Institute of Child Psychology.

Melanie Klein's move to England in 1926 greatly influenced the British psychoanalytic world not only through her theoretical exploration of the internal world of the infant and the very early mother–infant relationship but through her practice of child psychoanalysis and her belief in the availability of very young children to psychoanalysis through the analytic play technique that she developed (Klein 1955). The 'symposion on Child Analysis', held by the British Society in 1927, demonstrates the split already evident between the followers of Klein and those of Freud's daughter, Anna, in Vienna (Klein 1927). Klein's influence led the Psychoanalytic Society to develop its own criteria for training in child analysis, beginning with the supervised analysis of two adult patients, and followed by supervised work with a pre-latency, a latency and an adolescent, all while the candidate was in full analysis.

In her Preface to *The Psycho-analytical Treatment of Children* (1946), Anna Freud makes apparent her hurt at the 1927 Symposium's criticism of her approach. Originally perceiving a psychoanalytic approach as of benefit only to latency children (perhaps influenced by her career in education), and arguing for an introductory phase of treatment, she established an on-going discussion group with Viennese analysts (later including colleagues from Budapest and Prague) as a result of which, 'The age range to which the technique was found applicable was lowered from the latency period, as originally suggested, to two years, and extended at the other end to pre-adolescence and adolescence' (Freud, A. 1946: x).

By 1936 her work on defences and defence mechanisms had also led her to modify her position on an introductory phase: 'In a study of the defence mechanisms of the ego, the author described ways and means to uncover and penetrate the first resistances in the analysis of children, whereby the introductory phase of the treatment is shortened and, in some instances, rendered unnecessary' (ibid.: xi–xii).

Notable at this time, however, was the work undertaken by Anna Freud and colleagues in applied psychoanalysis in relation to children: the establishment of the Jackson Day Nursery (forerunner of the Hampstead War Nurseries) and the use of systematic, detailed observation of children; two child guidance clinics in Vienna for children and for adolescents; work with Aichhorn on juvenile delinquency; the establishment of a school, run by Eva Rosenfeld, to give disturbed children an appropriate learning environment; lectures for teachers and the development of a growing relationship between teaching and psychoanalysis. All changed in 1938.

The final scene in the pre-war setting for post-war developments in child psychotherapy, therefore, was that of the Freud family's arrival in London in 1938. Daws gives a singular insight: 'It is characteristic of Anna Freud's directness and the practicality of her interest in children that her luggage included 10 little stretcher beds – a foreshadow of the War Nursery she later helped create' (Daws 1987).

Anna Freud and Melanie Klein, as psychoanalysts, provided a rare combination of the close observation of children with psychoanalytic theory. Despite important theoretical differences, harshly disputed in the Psychoanalytic Society's 'Controversial Discussions' (King and Steiner 1991), these two principles remained central in the development of that application of psychoanalysis which was child psychotherapy.

Multiple influences arose from the experiences of the Second World War: evacuation of children which, for the first time, probably alerted the middle classes to the conditions of the poor and especially of the inner-city child; loss of parents in war; the work of John Bowlby on maternal deprivation and on separation, foreshadowing his thesis on attachment (Bowlby 1969); an Army Medical Corps, influenced by leadership from the Tavistock Clinic, taking seriously issues of war neurosis, mental health and trauma; and the influence of the child guidance movement on the establishment of the National Association for Mental Health. Together with the climate of change heralded by the Beveridge Report and the advent of the Welfare State, it seemed an atmosphere in which development could be nurtured.

In 1947 Anna Freud established at the Hampstead Clinic (now the Anna Freud Centre) a child psychoanalytic training based on her approach and accepting lay and analyst candidates. The following year the Tavistock, where John Bowlby was Director of the Children's Department, instituted a psychotherapy training under the joint auspices of Bowlby and Esther Bick (who developed the Infant-Observation model that was to become a central part of all analytic trainings (Bick 1964)). As Urwin and Hood-Williams note: 'It was Bick's initiative that was responsible for the distinctly Kleinian theoretical orientation of the training' (Urwin and Hood-Williams 1988).

Doris Wills has described the processes leading up to the establishment of the Association of Child Psychotherapists (Wills 1954, 1978) – initially the Provisional Association of Child Psychotherapists (non-medical). The parenthesis rather glides over the critical reaction of some doctors to the idea of a lay profession. The active involvement and support of doctors committed to this work was therefore vital: John Bowlby, Ethel Dukes (a colleague of Lowenfeld), Margaret Lowenfeld, Kenneth Soddy and Donald Winnicott helped draft standards and engaged in successful negotiation. In 1949 the Association of Child Psychotherapists (ACP) was born. It took a little longer, however, before the parenthetic 'non-medical' could, 'with confidence be lost' (Daws 1987).

Although many graduates of the ICP (Institute of Child Psychology) had Jungian analyses, it was not until the late 1950s that the first moves towards a Jungian child training began at the Society of Analytical Psychology (SAP) in London, under the guidance of Michael Fordham. Davidson (1996) gives a personal insight into this process, which culminated in the arrival of the first trainees in 1974, and: 'In 1979 the training was finally granted accreditation and our members were entitled to membership of the ACP' (Davidson 1996: 45).

The contribution of Michael Fordham to work with children is, for a profession where theoretical differences can sometimes assume large dimensions, both an immense and an integrative one. Astor writes:

His innovative researches into childhood gave a genetic basis to Jung's ideas about the importance of the self as both an organizing centre and the thing being organized within the personality. He connected it both to Jung's work on the self in the second half of life and to emotional development as described by psychoanalysts (the depressive position), while making clear what was distinctive about his 'Jungian model'.

(Astor 1996)

In the 1980s and 1990s three further training schools have been established and gained accreditation from the ACP. The London-based British Association of Psychotherapists, established in 1951 and training psychoanalytic psychotherapists and Jungian analysts in work with adults, set up a child and adolescent training in 1982, gaining full accreditation in 1986. The theoretical emphasis is that of the British school or Independent Group in psychoanalysis (Kohon 1986), an object-relations-based training. Equally independent is the Scottish Institute of Human Relations which also now runs a fully accredited training in child psychotherapy from its bases in Edinburgh and Glasgow, although trainees come from all over Scotland and the north of England. Finally, the Birmingham Trust for Psychoanalytic Psychotherapy training marks a further welcome development in the establishment of training courses beyond the London nucleus. The Tavistock has played an important part in fostering this last extension of Kleinian training in child and adolescent psychotherapy to the regions.

In addition, there has been a spread of analytic influence in a number of ways: most schools now run introductory courses in observational studies (for a fuller account see the Appendices) for a range of participants from a wide variety of professional backgrounds; around the country there are groups of both trained and interested people, meeting for theoretical discussion and clinical supervision, and which may at some future point develop into trainings proper; and each training school is noticeably involved (as evidenced in Chapter 14) in trainings abroad.

The role of the ACP today, in setting standards for the profession, in accrediting and reviewing trainings, in appointing assessors for interviews for Child Psychotherapy posts, and in acting on behalf of the Department of Health in assessing the qualifications, for work in the UK, of EU nationals, has expanded greatly since the days of the Provisional Association of Child Psychotherapists (non-medical). There remain tensions, however, in this integrative and monitoring role – tensions outlined in the history of the demise of the ICP as a training school in 1978 (Urwin and Hood-Williams 1988). Although economic reasons finally led to the closure of the ICP as a clinic, the search for comparability across trainings was felt to have been an influence as the ACP and its Training Council consolidated around a more purely psychoanalytic approach than the holistic Lowenfeld one was felt to be. It is somewhat ironic today that many admired senior members of the profession are ICP graduates and some of the most stimulating and creative writing on children and psychoanalysis comes from that stable. The awareness of the quest for high standards of training and practice, but that this does not preclude the capacity to embrace difference, is a very live issue in today's Association of Child Psychotherapists.

Training

The content of present-day training has built on the base of the original trainings, with the caveat that there now is more – a growing and wider body of theory, tremendous expansion in child development and attachment theory, greater variety in individual children helped, and a broader experience of different ways of working within the multi-professional team. Rustin compares training cases over a 25-year span:

> I can clearly recall the explanations my generation was given about the unsuitability for psychoanalytic treatment of severely deprived children who lacked experience of continuous parental care or its equivalent. They were felt to be unable to form a transference relationship of a sort open to psychoanalysis.
>
> (Rustin 1991)

This gradual move from the neurotic to deprived and traumatised child patients marks further development in the application of psychoanalytic theory to the therapy of children (Boston and Szur 1990). Work with psychotic children, not featured in this volume, has also been cultivated (see Rustin *et al.* 1997) and Rustin is probably right in her assessment of the importance of Bion's work on primitive states in helping make this possible (Rustin 1991). Amongst recent developments there is work with children presenting with attention-deficit disorder/attention-deficit hyperactivity disorder (ADD/ADHD): the *Journal of Child Psychotherapy* has contained interesting correspondence on this (Vol. 22, Nos 1 and 2) and the reader is also referred to articles by Orford (1998) and Widener (1998).

The core of training remains fourfold:

- personal psychoanalysis (preferably 4/5-times weekly)
- psychoanalytic theory and practice
- training in Child Development and Parent–Infant Observation
- clinical work under supervision.

All trainees are required to be in four- or five-times weekly personal psychoanalysis, although this may exceptionally be three-times weekly where there are access/ geographical pressures. The ACP regulates strictly the qualifications required of those who become training analysts. 'This is an essential and central requirement of training' (ACP 1998). Such a requirement is not, simplistically, to give an experience of analysis and 'being a patient': it is vital that the child psychotherapist explores his or her own unconscious motivations, defences and anxieties and is as 'grounded' as possible before engaging with the inner world of children. The trainee is in analysis throughout training and most continue after qualification.

For trainees who enter training without adult mental health experience, a supervised placement is required by some Training Schools. Trainees should be aware of adult psychopathology, of the roots of that in childhood, and of the particular predicament of the child with a mentally ill parent.

All trainees undertake a Parent–Infant Observation. A newborn infant and carer are visited for an hour a week for a two-year period. The trainee records these observations, bringing the recordings to a weekly seminar group (no more than five members, to allow frequent discussion and presentation) where an experienced seminar leader enables the group exploration of the material. A final paper is required and assessed. The importance of this cannot be stressed too highly: it marks the development of skills in close, detailed observation that will be necessary professionally, and begins the integration of child development theory and psychoanalytic theory into a framework combining what is observed, what one knows and what one thinks. Bick, who established the approach, describes the development of this part of training (Bick 1964) and it is now a feature of all child psychoanalytic trainings in this country. For a fuller and fascinating view, the reader is directed to Miller *et al.* (1989). In addition, sustained observation of young children is also a requirement. These observations may be undertaken as part of training or may form part of a pre-clinical Diploma or Master's Course in Observational Studies.

Throughout training, trainees attend both theoretical and clinical seminars. Areas to be covered include:

- human growth and development (including non-psychoanalytic perspectives and particularly including developmental psychology and attachment theory)
- developmental disturbance and psychopathology
- psychodynamic theories (each school will differ in emphasis, according to its theoretical stance, but 'this should be set in the context of other theories' (ACP 1998))
- psychotherapeutic techniques
- the range of treatment techniques is taught and trainees are encouraged to explore other approaches
- research, outcome studies and evidence-based methodologies.

In their clinical settings, trainees must see at least three intensive (*at least* three-times weekly) cases under weekly supervision by an approved supervisor. These are an under-five-year-old, a latency child and an adolescent, and the group must include both boys and girls. At least one must be in therapy for not less than two years and the others for a minimum of one year. Additionally, at least six children and young people must be seen once or twice weekly on a long-term basis for which the trainee is offered regular supervision. These should include a range of presenting clinical problems, levels of disturbance, ages and both sexes. Trainees also undertake weekly work with the parent(s)/carer of a child in therapy with another psychotherapist: this is not adult psychotherapy but aims to hold the child in mind and address the parents as carers of the child. An assessed report is written on this work. Assessments are also undertaken, both with the trainee as colleague in a multi-professional assessment process and with the aim of making appropriate recommendations to the team, parents or outside agencies. In their work settings, trainees are expected to learn the structure and management of the NHS (especially as it operates in that workplace), current legislation and child protection procedures, and to keep appropriate records and write appropriate reports. These structures are taught by the training schools but local systems differ.

Towards the end of their training, trainees will explore aspects of brief work, family work, group work and parent–infant counselling. Contact with children 'accommodated' in the care system, in residential establishments, and in paediatric in-patient settings is also an expected part of the trainee's experience. Consultation to other institutions and other professionals working with children and young people is a later feature of the training.

Such an intensive training requires a minimum of four to five years to complete. It is also expensive, the major cost being the personal psychoanalysis, and for many trainees it is self-funded. Recently North Thames region in England has begun to establish fully funded trainee posts, following much hard work by child psychotherapists, the Child Psychotherapy Trust (established to support trainees financially where possible) and a key group of dedicated managers. It is to be hoped that this initiative will spread and that the iniquitous anomaly of one professional training, out of the whole multi-professional Child Mental Health team, having to operate on a voluntary training basis, will be a thing of the past.

The ACP has established a Code of Ethics. Concerns about the practice of any child psychotherapist are referred to the Ethics Committee of the ACP.

Legal and social context

Although Freud originally thought that a certain level of intelligence was a prerequisite for analysis, it will be evident from this introduction and from the range of chapters in the 'Specialist Interest' section that this is known not to be the case. Indeed, we work with underachieving, inner-city children from areas of multiple deprivation more often than with neurotic, intelligent, 'middle-class' young people. Sinason's comments on 'emotional intelligence' (Chapter 28) give a truer picture. Given the increasing referral rate to Child and Family Mental Health agencies

(Trowell and Bower 1995: 4), the seriousness of most cases and the high prevalence of emotional disturbance in childhood (Kurtz 1992), one often despairs of help being offered early enough to the less-demanding child with neurotic problems.

The backcloth to the increase in serious referrals is woven in part from the breakdown in voluntary co-operation between funding departments responsible for multi-professional teams and from the impact of discrete change in one governmental department on others – an unthought-out domino effect. Changes in education, for example, with the introduction of league tables for achievement at a range of ages and for attendance/truancy have led to a climate of exclusion and expulsion at a time when off-site units are being closed and funding reallocated. The Education Reform Act 1988 and the 1993 Education Act together have moved power from the Local Education Authorities down to the individual school level, with little monies allocated for children with Special Educational Needs (SEN) and schools reluctant to grasp the nettle of emotional disturbance as a key factor. Trowell and Bower contrast the 2 per cent of children budgeted for SEN help with the 20 per cent affected by emotional and behavioural difficulties (Trowell and Bower 1995: 6).

With the Children Act 1989 came hope of progress and co-operation. The Department of Health, indeed, produced guidance in a series of publications culminating in *Working Together* (DoH 1991), a proposal for joint practice. Yet the emphasis on partnership with parents has led to a vast drain of resources into a few cases where constant recourse to law is entailed and social workers find that child protection work engulfs most of the departmental budget. The flexibility to fund posts for conjoint child mental health work has, in many areas, vanished.

Health, too, has been reorganised. A culture of competition and individuality, with a split into 'purchasers' and 'providers', leaves little time for more than survival. Accountability is all too often to someone ignorant of child mental health needs and an ethos of negotiating contracts for psychotherapy – to be argued and renewed annually at best (one *has* heard of three-monthly) militates against in-depth long-term work.

Such changes occur in a framework where poverty (a factor in mental ill-health) has increased, where children's rights appear to be few and disturbed children as young as ten are not understood but simplistically branded 'evil monsters', where the individual effort is rewarded and the common good appears to have been lost. It seems vital, therefore, that child psychotherapists are not only politically aware but use their psychoanalytic understanding to help change this climate. Indeed, the Child Psychotherapy Trust (see Appendix (i)) has been in the forefront of creating a climate of educated awareness, as has the Child Mental Health charity Young Minds. As Trowell and Bower stress:

> We do not need only specialist services. We need a framework for
> understanding extreme emotions – love, hate, jealousy, envy, destruc-

tiveness. This is something that psychoanalysis can provide. It also helps us understand how these emotions come to be violently evoked and enacted and how they can be modified and channelled more constructively. We believe that psychoanalysis can function as a shared framework of understanding between professionals from a variety of disciplines, even if they are not using it as a therapeutic tool.

(Trowell and Bower 1995: 4)

A note on confidentiality

At the very heart of any therapeutic contact is the need to protect the privacy of the client – adult or child. When working with an adult, the boundaries of privacy are usually fairly straightforward as contact between the therapist and other people in the patient's life is likely to be minimal. However with children, there is often an equally important need for the therapist to be in regular contact with the key adults in the child's life – parents and foster parents in particular, but also teachers, social workers, residential workers and medical staff. The multidisciplinary team plays a very important role in the child's treatment (Chapter 10) as does the work with the parents and the rest of the family (Chapter 7). In practice, issues of confidentiality are worked out within the guidelines of the Code of Ethics of the profession for each child who is seen, as appropriate. The complexity of therapeutic work with children means that a wise and flexible balance has to be found between the child's need for confidentiality and the need to communicate helpfully with the child's parents, carers, family, and the multi-professional team.

The experience of a private and protected therapeutic space is so central to the child and adolescent psychotherapist's work that the question of how to write publicly without compromising this privacy raises many issues. As with any other profession that needs an ever-evolving theoretical and experiential base, we have to share our clinical experience with each other and outside the profession if we are not to become moribund. The problem is how best to achieve this without sacrificing our relationship with our patients. This issue is very alive within the profession, particularly as we become more 'public' and venture out of the consulting room to share our work with colleagues in the multidisciplinary team, at conferences and lectures, and in the increasing numbers of books written by child and adolescent psychotherapists.

The first consideration is how to disguise the case illustration. This can be achieved by giving no more historical or biographical information than is absolutely essential to the particular aspect of the case that is being discussed. In addition, some 'red herrings' may be added, to further disguise the case as long as they do not detract from coherency in the process. For example, if the relationships with or positions of siblings are not a key feature of the illustration, the ages and sex of the siblings might be altered to conceal possible identification. It is always tricky to know how much to disguise a case before it begins to sound unconvincing. This has been a matter for much discussion between the editors and the individual authors in this handbook and we believe we have arrived at sensible solutions in each case.

Some of the children and families discussed in this handbook will have been directly approached by their therapists asking for permission to write about their treatment. Depending on the individual circumstances, they may or may not have seen the actual text and given their agreement to it. There can be a problem with this direct approach when treatment is ongoing, or where, as can often be the case, it is possible that the patient may want to return to the therapist for further help as he or she grows up. The fact that the therapist has spent so much additional time thinking and writing about the patient, indicating that in some respect the patient has a 'special' status for the therapist, can interfere with and possibly disrupt any ongoing or future therapeutic contact. This is not necessarily a problem, but it can be and has to be carefully thought about before any patient is approached for permission to publish. In many respects, because of the possibility of disrupting or distracting from the therapeutic relationship by showing the patient and/or the family what has been written, some therapists ask for permission to use disguised material for teaching or publication at the outset of treatment. This request is made in the spirit of advancing knowledge, training and practice, so that, should it be helpful to share what has been learned from a particular treatment, permission has been given.

The way in which the rich variety of clinical examples throughout this handbook brings the work alive is perhaps the best testimony to the value of grappling with such difficult issues. As editors, we have found it a pleasure and a privilege to collate this overview of the profession of child and adolescent psychotherapy.

References

Association of Child Psychotherapists (ACP) (1998) *The Training of Child Psychotherapists: outline for training courses*, London: ACP.

Astor, J. (1996) 'A tribute to Michael Fordham', *Journal of Child Psychotherapy* 22(1): 5–25.

Bick, E. (1964) 'Notes on infant observation in psychoanalytic training', *International Journal of Psychoanalysis* 45: 558–66.

Bowlby, J. (1969) *Attachment and Loss: Vol. 1 Attachment*, London: Hogarth.

Boston, M. and Szur, R. (eds) (1990) *Psychotherapy with Severely Deprived Children*, London: Karnac.

The Children Act (1989) *Guidance and Regulations V1, 2 and 3*, London: HMSO.

Davidson, D. (1996) 'The Jungian child analytic training: an historical perspective', *Journal of Child Psychotherapy* 22(1): 38–48.

Daws, D. (1987) 'Thirty years of Child Psychotherapy: the psychoanalytic approach to children's problems', Tavistock Clinic Paper, No. 48, London: Tavistock Clinic.

Daws, D. and Boston, M. (1977/81) *The Child Psychotherapist and the Problems of Young People*, London: Wildwood House.

Department of Health (1991) *Working Together under the Children Act 1989: a guide to arrangements for inter-agency co-operation for the protection of children from abuse*, London: HMSO.

Freud, A. (1926) 'Introduction to the technique of the analysis of children', in *The Psychoanalytical Treatment of Children* (1946), London: Imago.

—— (1927) *The Psychoanalytical Treatment of Children*, London: Imago, 1946.

Geissman, C. and Geissman, P. (1992/8) *A History of Child Psychoanalysis*, London: Routledge.

Hug-Hellmuth, H. (1912) 'Analyse eines Traumes eines Fünfeinhalbjahrigen', *Zentralblatt für Psychoanalyse und Psychotherapie* 2(3): 122–7.

—— (1921) 'On the technique of child analysis', *International Journal of Psychoanalysis* 2: 287–305 (Abstract printed in the same journal (1920) 2: 361–2).

King, P. and Steiner, R. (eds) (1991) *The Freud–Klein Controversies 1941–45*, London: Routledge.

Klein, M. (1927) 'Symposium on Child Analysis', *International Journal of Psychoanalysis* 8: 339–70.

—— (1932) *The Psycho-analysis of Children*, London: Hogarth.

—— (1955) 'The psychoanalytic play technique: its history and significance', in *Envy and Gratitude and Other Works 1946–63: The Writings of Melanie Klein*, Vol. III, London: Hogarth 1975.

Kohon, G. (1986) *The British School of Psychoanalysis: The Independent Tradition*, London: Free Association Books.

Kurtz, Z. (ed.) (1992) *With Health in Mind: Mental Health Care for Children and Young People*, London: Action for Sick Children.

MacLean, G. and Rappen, U. (1991) *Hermine Hug-Hellmuth*, London: Routledge.

Miller, L., Rustin, M., Rustin, M. and Shuttleworth, J. (1989) *Closely Observed Infants*, London: Duckworth Press.

Orford, E. (1998) 'Wrestling with the whirlwind: an approach to the understanding of ADD/ADHD', *Journal of Child Psychotherapy* 24(2): 253–66.

Rustin, M. (1991) 'Psychotherapy pure and applied: some reflections on current practice in work with individual children', in S. Ramsden (ed.) *Psychotherapy Pure and Applied*, Occasional Papers, No. 6, London: Association for Child Psychology and Psychiatry.

Rustin, M., Rhode, M., Dubinsky, A. and Dubinsky, H. (1997) *Psychotic States in Children*, London: Duckworth.

Sokolnicka, E. (1920) 'L'analyse d'un cas de névrose obsessionelle', *Revue du Neuro-Psychiatric et d'hygiène mentale de l'enfance* 16: 477–87.

Szur, R. and Miller, S. (eds) (1991) *Extending Horizons: Psychoanalytic Psychotherapy with Children, Adolescents and Families*, London: Karnac.

Trowell, J. and Bower, M. (eds) (1995) *The Emotional Needs of Young Children and their Families: Using Psychoanalytic Ideas in the Community*, London: Routledge.

Urwin, C. and Hood-Williams, J. (eds) (1988) *Child Psychotherapy, War and the Normal Child: Selected Papers of Margaret Lowenfeld*, London: Free Association Books.

Widener, A. M. (1998) 'Beyond Ritalin', *Journal of Child Psychotherapy* 24(2): 267–81.

Wills, D. M. (1954) 'The Association for Child Psychotherapists (non-medical)', *Bulletin of the British Psychological Society*, May.

—— (1978) 'Fifty years of child guidance: a psychologist's view', *Journal of Child Psychotherapy* 4: 97–102.

Further reading

Astor, J. (1995) *Michael Fordham's Innovations in Analytical Psychology*, London: Routledge.

Freud, A. (1992) *The Harvard Lectures*, J. Sandler (ed.), London: Karnac.

Hodges, J. (1992) 'Outside the therapy room: the varied contributions of child psychotherapists', *Newsletter of the ACPP* 14(3): 109–13.

Klein, M. (1955) 'The psychoanalytic play technique: its history and significance', in *Envy and Gratitude and other works 1946–63: The Writings of Melanie Klein*, Vol. III, London: Hogarth 1975.

Ramsden, S. (ed.) (1991) *Psychotherapy: Pure and Applied*, Occasional Papers, No. 6, London: ACPP.

Segal, H. (1973) *Introduction to the Work of Melanie Klein*, London: Hogarth.

Urwin, C. and Hood-Williams, J. (eds) (1988) *Child Psychotherapy, War and the Normal Child: Selected Papers of Margaret Lowenfeld*, London: Free Association Books.

Part I

Theoretical foundations

2 The roots of child and adolescent psychotherapy in psychoanalysis

Meira Likierman and Elizabeth Urban

This chapter provides a brief historical overview of psychoanalysis, the body of thought that underpins the practice of child psychotherapy and that equally informs a wide range of therapies that are practised today.

Psychoanalysis is a clinical and theoretical discipline that is only a century old and yet has accumulated a body of knowledge that is substantial and complex. Having started as a single theory, it has branched out into several substantial schools of thought around the world, each with its distinctive culture, training institutions, favoured techniques and theoretical contributions. Whilst traditionally these schools have competed for a monopoly on the 'truth' about mental life, many contemporary psychoanalysts are able to sustain a pluralist position whereby they accommodate a theoretical diversity in their clinical approach.

Psychoanalysis began with the efforts of Sigmund Freud shortly after he completed his medical training in Vienna in 1885. Before deciding on the area in which he should specialise, Freud obtained work experience in Paris under the tutoring of Jean Martin Charcot who was making ground-breaking discoveries in the treatment of hysteria.

Hysteria was a major public health concern throughout the nineteenth century, afflicting women with symptoms such as paralysis of the limbs or loss of vital functions such as sight or speech. The symptoms would strike suddenly and would typically baffle medical experts, which even led some to dismiss it as no more than a female excuse for opting out of responsibilities.

Charcot was among the progressive medical scientists who viewed the condition as a genuine neurological disorder and, while he assumed that it indicated a degeneration of the nervous system, he also hypothesised a possible traumatic trigger for it in the patient's life circumstance. In order to substantiate this, Charcot began to hypnotise hysterical patients, managing to demonstrate that in an altered state of mind some of their symptoms could vanish.

Freud was impressed by witnessing these experiments at first hand and, furthermore, had an immediate intuition of the implications of what he saw. If indeed ideas had agency and could affect the body to such a degree, then

there was a whole region of human experience, which was as yet un-
discovered, as were the scientific principles that governed it.

Freud returned to Vienna to set up his own practice for nervous disorders.
He continued to hypnotise his patients, trying to use this as a means of
uncovering the possible traumatic triggers of their condition. Hypnosis,
however, proved too clumsy a method for eliciting the detailed information
that Freud soon found he required. He gave it up for a new method of
introspection that he taught his patients – free-association. He asked his
patients to follow their natural train of thought using as guidance their
spontaneous associations. They were to relinquish the normal self-critical
standard of their speech and to narrate to him in full what their minds led
them to, whether this seemed trivial, irrational, rude, embarrassing or
otherwise.

His patients had some success with this method. Furthermore, the narratives that emerged from their attempts to disclose thoughts without self-
censorship uncovered a hidden world of human mental activity. This was
governed by secret desires and urges that often conflicted with the patient's
self-approval. The method of free-association revealed that one's everyday
mind, far from being occupied mainly with intellectual content, was close
to the life of the body with its primitive pleasures and urges. Patients often
felt at odds with their intimate bodily states and found the force of their raw
sexuality obtrusive and threatening. The result was a distressing psychological conflict which patients tried to end by fending off unacceptable
ideation.

Their unease led Freud to what he thought was his first clinical discovery,
for he assumed that it pointed to the traumatic trigger of hysteria hypothesised by Charcot. Thus in his first theoretical model Freud suggested that
the trauma at the root of hysteria was a sexual one and that his patients had
all been the victims of childhood sexual abuse. The reason that his patients
could not tell him this directly was that their minds had never been able to
assimilate the traumatic event and store it as an ordinary memory. The
patient 'forgot' or repressed the event without dealing with its forceful
impact. Unbearable traumatic tension thus remained trapped within the
patient, and this now found an outlet via neural pathways into the body –
hence extreme physical symptoms.

It did not occur to Freud at this early stage that human subjective
experience was, in itself, a worthwhile object of study. He regarded his
work as essentially medical, hoping to demonstrate the organic processes at
the root of nervous illness. He believed that neurological psychic energy,
though still not fully understood, justified attempts at a scientific quanti-
fication and investigation.

However, psychoanalysis was to take a different turn from a purely
neurophysiological direction, and this coincided with a change of mind
in Freud about his 'seduction theory' that attributed all neurotic illness to
childhood sexual abuse. This theoretical revision resulted from his new and

hitherto most ambitious project of research. Freud decided to put his method of free-associations to a rigorous test via an analysis of his own mental life, specifically an area of it that seemed the most free of his conscious control – his dreams. Since he did not suffer from a major nervous disorder he was not expecting to discover a trauma in his own background, but what he did discover surprised him.

His dream material revealed to him the almost equally powerful impact of apparently ordinary life frustrations. Each night his dreams resurrected fragments of the previous day, which were connected with areas of failures, anxieties, disappointments and hurts. His frustrated professional ambitions, his envy of successful colleagues, his anxiety about promotion, his small jealousies of his wife and his pain when he thought she was slighting him, all surfaced again at night, but not as he had actually experienced them. Rather, his dreaming mind transformed the reality of his daily lacks, made good his frustrations and presented to him his wishes as fulfilled.

Freud was struck by how insistently his mind wished to compensate him for the frustrations of living. Further exploration led him to realise that ordinary daily disappointments had accrued a traumatic-like force because they were underpinned by hurts that had accumulated over an extended period, dating all the way to childhood. The sorrows and resentments of childhood lived on in his unconscious, infusing each new disappointment in his life and influencing his mental well-being.

In this new understanding, the helplessness of the human child with its unfulfilled needs itself seemed traumatic, and this led Freud to realise that the needs and wishes of the child were far more acute than had been suspected. The childhood memories that linked with his dreams revealed that, far from desiring a simple care regime, the child has powerful cravings for love and physical pleasure, as well as an intense primitive sexuality. Freud thus realised that it was not necessarily actual sexual abuse that had been at the root of his patients' disturbances. Nervous illness was not a sudden phenomenon with a single traumatic cause, but a condition that developed over time and was intimately bound up with the life history of the human individual. It seemed to Freud that the most delicate and formative area in this history was childhood, dominated as it was by the unruly forces of infantile sexuality.

It was thus that Freud reached one of his theoretical milestones, which was his theory of infantile sexuality. Along with this achievement, Freud's exploration of his dream life had a further crucial outcome, and this was an updated and newly understood version of the unconscious mind. Freud had made use of the term 'unconscious' from the very beginning of his psychological researches, but did so initially in a purely descriptive sense. In other words, he used the term as an all-purpose label for a range of mental states in which the individual was not aware of certain ideation. This now seemed too superficial to Freud. His dream life had just provided a 'royal road to the unconscious', suggesting to him that it was far more useful to view the unconscious as a separate mental system which was subject to its own, distinct patterns of logic, and which had a complex relationship with the very different system of consciousness.

Freud noted that the dreaming mind offered a first-hand knowledge of unconscious processes because its activity was not restricted to a mere gathering and reproducing of portions of reality from the preceding 'dream day'. Rather, the dreaming mind subjected such portions to alterations which followed typical patterns; unconscious activity either condensed disparate fragments of reality so as to create multiply determined symbols, or else it did the opposite, breaking apart what should have remained together, for example, by shifting the appropriate feeling stirred by an event to a trivial substitute. It is thus that an individual can dream of the death of a loved one without feeling appropriate grief, or that the person who appears to us in a dream is often a condensed creation which combines features drawn variously from family members, friends, colleagues, each selected because it contributes to the symbolic meaning of the dream.

Freud reasoned that such manipulations of the truth had a function, which was to enable the nightly processing of those of the day's thoughts which had been too unbearable to own during waking hours. The sleeping mind used stratagems to conceal the full impact of the meaning which it was addressing so as not to raise levels of anxiety and awaken the individual. The very intricacy of the mind's stratagems led Freud to realise that unconscious content causes anxiety precisely because, once repressed, it refuses to lie still and continues to press for discharge. Unconscious wishes continually press to reach the conscious mind, which alone commands the body's movements and thus the route to need-fulfilling action.

These insights led Freud to further realisations. Whilst awake, the mind was surely equally under a continual pressure from unconscious impulses. And even when this does not result in neurotic symptoms, repressed unconscious impulses keep returning to hound consciousness in various large and small ways. Freud was to explore how this happens in our every-day life, manifesting as slips of the tongue or built into the comic moment in jokes. These explorations highlighted for Freud the need to discover why the human mind needs to repress wishes to such an extent, and he found the answer in his conception of infantile sexuality.

Childhood sexuality was not a new idea in the late nineteenth century, but Freud's originality consisted in his ability to draw on pre-existing theories and integrate them in a unique way with his own findings. This culminated in a groundbreaking theory of psychosexual development that accounted both for normal development and for neurotic illness.

In this vision, childhood psychosexual development was posited as the biological underpinning of human mental development. Freud described the infant as bringing with it into the world elemental aspects of its sexuality which infuse every facet of its existence. Sensations, sights, smells, tastes and sounds all carry some sexual charge with a potential for excitation and arousal. Of particular intensity are sensations in the body orifices of mouth and anus where the internal membranes are sensitive, hence becoming focal sexual centres.

As the infant develops and its experiences cohere, the still immature components of its sexuality find a more intensified expression. Since the small child is not self-conscious or ashamed, it expresses its developing sexual trends uninhibitedly in its family circle, much like an adult afflicted with perversions. For example, in its normal daily routine the child derives sexual pleasure from activities that variously enable elements of voyeuristic, exhibitionistic, fetishistic, sadistic or masochistic excitement. Its oral and anal experiences mingle with these to create particular 'pre-genital' configurations of sexuality.

In this thinking Freud's interest shifted to an 'instinct theory' in which sexual instincts underpinned human urges and were the prime motivational energies in mental life. Freud felt that normal development requires a gradual subsuming of infantile sexuality with its 'perversions' in a normal reproductive adult sexuality, leaving only symbolic traces in the sexual activities of fore-pleasure. But if this process is disrupted for some reason, the child becomes fixated to a particular primitive sexual urge in a damaging way. This results in later pathology, with the individual either taking the path of perversion or else of neurosis, depending on whether the fixated sexual activity is retained in its explicit, primitive form, or whether it is repressed at the cost of developing symptoms.

Tying the theory of mental development to biological sexuality seemed promising, as it appeared to ground psychoanalysis in an established branch of science. However, one aspect of Freud's thinking on infantile sexuality intruded on this purely scientific aspiration, inserting the perplexing topic of human subjectivity into an otherwise watertight biological theory. This aspect was Freud's (now widely familiar) concept of the Oedipus complex. It was this concept that obliged Freud to recognise that biology, along with the mental life, which it underpins, does not take place in a vacuum. Human sexuality and its instincts are inseparable through their very aims from interactions with others, initially caregivers and eventually sexual partners. The social behaviours of seeking, and interacting with, love objects are inherent in psychosexual development.

Taking the male child as an example (but suggesting an analogous female experience) Freud delineated an intimate psychosexual bond with the mother from the time of conception. The mother not only carries the foetus in her body and feeds the newborn from her body, but also continues, through her physical proximity, to cater to basic infantile needs. She is thus the natural recipient of her infant's nascent sexuality. By the time the boy develops into a small child, his primitive component instincts give way to a new focus of pleasure, which is his penis. But the boy is not mature enough to understand the significance of this event. Since his mother has always looked after all his bodily and emotional needs, and apparently regards herself as responsible for satisfying these, he assumes that she will similarly continue to be responsible for satisfying his growing genital desires.

Normally the boy's open expression of desire meets with disapproval in the family. Not only are his attempts to induce his mother to witness or touch his genitalia rebuffed, but he is now cognitively mature enough to make sense of her disapproval. His growing awareness has bred in him self-consciousness, enabling him to experience shame, disgust and guilt for the first time in his life. As well as this, the boy is much more perceptive in registering obstacles to his desires. He realises that the genital pleasure refused to him by his mother is nonetheless awarded to his father. In referring to this stage in life Freud did not use the term 'complex' lightly. He realised that it raised emotional storms of desire, pain and rage that lead to extreme conflicts between love and hate in the boy. It thus amounts to the first life crisis or infantile neurosis.

Freud suggested that, as with earlier stages of infantile sexuality, the Oedipus complex needs to be outgrown. However, this event is a developmentally complex task. It is not enough for the boy to surrender his desires uncomprehendingly, as this only leaves him feeling defeated and 'castrated'. A genuine resolution requires a fundamental psychical change which expands the boy's mental horizons, enabling an altered and developmentally broadened perspective on his situation.

Freud visualised this psychical change in structural terms. The mind acquires a new and qualitatively distinct extension, and this happens when the child absorbs into itself aspects of parental authority. These are internalised to create an intra-psychic agency of a 'super-ego', enabling the boy to find a more mature perspective on the procreative sexual roles of his parents. The boy identifies with this newly understood family structure, internalises parental values and instates his father in his mind as a role model which points the way to his own future sexual aspirations.

In his last 'structural model' Freud put much more emphasis on mental life as the product of subjective human experience – that is, of the child's mode of interacting with its caregivers and family. However, Freud also wanted his structural model to absorb his lifelong scientific interest in instinctual energies that propel the human organism. He thus hypothesised a tripartite structural model which accommodated a 'super-ego' internalised from the external world, an 'id' which consists of raw instinctual activity, and an 'ego' – the mind's central organising agency which mediates between the id and the super-ego (instincts and the world), thus negotiating an optimal developmental route for a growing 'self'.

From Freud to ego psychology and object relations

Freud's final theory attempted to bring into dialogue two aspects of his own thinking – his scientific concern with the organic, biological energies that propel the individual from within, and his humanistic concern with subjective, narrative meaning that emerges from the individual's relationship with his human environment.

This synthesis was not straightforward, at least not in the sense of bequeathing to the psychoanalytic movement a single theory that could be agreed upon. Freud's followers found it easier to focus on partial aspects of his structural model, giving prominence either to its interpersonal aspect as exemplified in the relationship of ego and super-ego, or else to its biological-instinctual aspect as exemplified in the relationship of ego and id. One crucial result for psychoanalysis was a cleavage between an 'object relations' school favoured in Britain and an 'ego-psychology' school favoured in North America.

Two thinkers who were instrumental in influencing this division were the pioneers of child psychoanalysis, Anna Freud and Melanie Klein. It is important to stress that neither saw herself as dispensing with Freud's tripartite structural model. Their differences emerge from subtle but crucial shifts in emphasis onto different aspects of it.

Anna Freud

Anna Freud focused on the id–ego aspect of the model, exploring the effects of instinctual pressures on the ego's development. She realised that the ego is unlikely to fend off id impulses in simple, easily distinguishable ways. Rather, defences infuse the ego's entire mode of functioning and are integrated into its very life. Whilst the ego's healthy survival does indeed depend on its ability to master turbulent id functioning, if defences are too entrenched in the ego's habits, instinctual impulses are stifled rather than processed and mastered, hence continuing to overwhelm the individual with pathological manifestations.

Anna Freud's thinking led to emphasis on the ego's complex tasks in its move towards an adaptation to reality, and this theme was taken much further by an 'ego-psychology' school which included among its thinkers Ernest Kris, Edith Jacobson and Heinz Hartmann. A further dimension of Anna Freud's influence was evident in the work of Margaret Mahler, who demonstrated how the complex task of separating from the mother and loosening the most primitive psychical ties with her paved the way to ego autonomy and a coherent sense of self.

Melanie Klein

Unlike Anna Freud, Melanie Klein explored the interpersonal aspect of the structural model. She believed that it was not helpful to view the super-ego as a mere conceptual abstraction because its internalisation is experienced subjectively in a highly anthropomorphic manner. Contradicting Freud, Klein suggested that the infant could relate to its mother from birth, even though it possesses only a rudimentary capacity to apprehend aspects of her nurturing. However, these are qualitatively distinguished as 'good' or 'bad' and internalised as archaic 'part-objects'. An archaic phantasy life thus emerges in the infant, infusing its perceptions of, and interactions with, caregivers. Growth and cognitive development enable the child to internalise increasingly understood, realistic objects which complete and refine its formerly internalised primitive ones.

Klein felt that the internal world created through these processes is the key to mental health, provided that it isn't populated with disturbing, persecuting objects but is, rather, a domain in which objects emit benevolence and continually infuse the personality with warmth and security.

Divergencies between Anna Freud and Melanie Klein

Anna Freud and Melanie Klein proceeded from the same significant starting point, which was their study and treatment of children. And since this was a new field of enquiry, its principles needed to be established even as it was being used as a research tool. It was thus that they both became engaged in pioneering a psychoanalysis for children, and at the same time utilised this process to investigate and discover the nature of earliest mental life. Yet theirs was not a joint venture; quite the contrary, they did not perceive any complementarity in their respective findings and conclusions, and in fact engaged in a lifelong professional debate.

Melanie Klein's belief that the infant relates to others from the beginning of life required her to assert that an ego exists from birth. Although she felt that the infantile ego was not unified or coherent, she nonetheless assumed that it could carry out a few essential operations such as a limited registering of reality, an ability to welcome or fear its impact and also an ability to defend against this. Such thinking led her to conceive of an array of archaic defence mechanisms and, in a further controversial step, to link these to the kinds of defences employed in adult schizophrenic and manic-depressive disorders. This threw light on the infantile origin of adult mental illness, but it also portrayed early ego activity as strangely destructive to the very process of growth which it was supposed to promote.

Anna Freud felt that such thinking was negative and also that it attributed too much complexity to the early psyche. Like her father, she continued to believe that the infant is unlikely to arrive in the world with a psyche that is sufficiently formed to possess a clearly differentiated entity such as the ego. The infant's post-natal existence amounted to an undifferentiated, foetal-like state of 'primary narcissism', and he only emerged from this gradually and in response to environmental impingements. In this view, identity and mental structure were shaped during the process of early acculturation, and were thus constructs which did not exist outside of this process. Anna Freud suggested that in keeping with this, defence mechanisms develop later and express a broader and more diverse relational repertoire than that expressed by the limited archaic defences which Klein envisaged.

Anna Freud and Melanie Klein might have continued to develop their views separately and to have their thinking go by unchallenged were it not for circumstances which brought them into the same professional organisation. The war in Europe obliged them to settle in London and join the British Psychoanalytic Society, where it was difficult to find a mode of professional co-existence. This was to lead, in 1941, to a theoretical confrontation between the two of them which was popularly referred to as the 'controversial discussions', and which also drew the entire British Society into a debate on early mental life and the origins of the psyche. In spite of the discussions being careful and lengthy, no consensus was reached and members of the British Society were obliged to accommodate a greater diversity. This gave rise to three schools of thought, since to the classical Freudian group were now added a Kleinian and a further 'independent' group. It was this last which provided the foundation for a distinct British object relations school, the members of which chose to draw on the thinking of both Anna Freud and Melanie Klein, and to add further original discoveries to this mixture.

Object relations theorists

Klein's theories gave rise to an 'object relations' school, which included among its thinkers Donald Winnicott, Michael Balint, Ronald Fairbairn and Wilfred Bion. However, while these thinkers agreed with Klein on the activities of the early ego, they also, unlike Klein, and with an awareness of Anna Freud's insights, emphasised the utter helplessness of this ego in the absence of external support from the mother. Winnicott noted that, viewed philosophically, the newborn's ego exists only in a potential sense, since it is activated and brought into being only in the context, and through the agency, of maternal handling.

In spite of areas of disagreement, the object relations group which Klein inspired were at one with her on a crucially significant issue. They underscored the fragility of the newborn psyche at moments of distress, and outlined a range of archaic defensive manoeuvres which it employs to break down and disperse portions of disturbing reality that impinge on it. Bion, for example, pointed out that repeated and excessive deflections of reality can damage an individual's capacity to absorb and process experiences and hence to mature mentally. Anna Freud and her followers were sceptical about the suggestion of a very early onset of defence mechanisms, but they did agree that defensive functioning begins in childhood and should be explored with the child where appropriate.

With this thinking Melanie Klein, Anna Freud, and the schools which they inspired, made a unique mark not only on psychoanalysis, but also on the broader canvas of twentieth-century thinking. Their legacy is evident in the degree of sensitivity which our culture, to this day, considers as appropriate for infants.

While Anna Freud and Melanie Klein exemplify some of the ways in which creative thinking extended and refined the foundation provided by Freud, it is important to remember that psychoanalysis had other important strands which enriched it and which therefore need to be taken into account.

Fordham and the influence of Jung

Another major contributor to child analysis was Michael Fordham. Although he drew upon Freud and Klein, his central concepts were derived from Jung, especially Jung's idea of the self. This idea needs to be distinguished from that used by self psychologists, such as Kohut, and requires further explanation.

After six years of close collaboration, Freud and Jung parted, leaving Jung to develop his own school of thought, analytical psychology. Jung had all along held that the energy of libido was neutral, rather than exclusively sexual. The theoretical dispute between the two men rested on this and the nature of psychic contents. Jung thought that the mind was made up not only of repressed sexual wishes, but also an innate psychic endowment. This endowment is expressed in typical and universal structures and images, such as myths, religions and rituals common across cultures, which Jung termed 'archetypal'. He spent most of his life investigating these patterns within patients, including those with psychotic features, but especially those in mid-life, and studying analogies between various cultures and religions. Thus his investigations drew upon anthropology and ethnology as well as biology.

When the split with Freud came, Jung had a severe breakdown. Part of his recovery involved observing his dreams and fantasies. He sketched a series of circular patterns, or mandalas, which reflected his inner condition and eventually helped him to see psychic changes from day to day. Later he concluded that these mandalas represented the whole of his self, conscious and unconscious, changing over time yet having continuity and overall individuality. He observed that the self had a centralising, organising and integrating function, thus making Jung's concept of the self similar to Freud's notion of the ego; however Jung's concept goes beyond this. For Jung the self is the basis and organisational centre of the whole personality, of which the ego, the perceptual centre, is only a part and a secondary, although important, organiser.

Jung's ideas arose from experiences with adults, and it was Fordham, a child psychiatrist, who integrated archetypal theory with clinical and observational experiences with children and infants. Fordham drew upon Jung's concept of the self to postulate a primary integrate capable of relating to the environment, called the primary self. The primary self exists from before birth and represents the psychosomatic whole of the organism and its potential. The potential unfolds through the complementary processes of deintegration and reintegration, lifelong processes that involve coming into relation with the environment and then assimilating these experiences. These processes are structured by the self, which organises them in distinctively human, archetypal ways – for instance, the over-arching patterning and timing of the complex experiences of infancy, Oedipal development and adolescence. The mental contents that are built up do not simply represent external experiences that are internalised. They also are influenced by archetypal shaping of contents, for instance, into good and bad objects, and reflect intensities associated with the self, such as feelings of grandiosity and omnipotence and their opposites.

According to Fordham, individuality, adaptation and continuity of being are expressions of the self. This notion of the self is more comprehensive and extensive than that in psychoanalysis, in which the self tends to refer to the ego, or the ego and the id. The id is a concept that has no meaning in analytical psychology because in Fordham's theory instinctual activity is essentially organised, not chaotic.

Despite this difference, Fordham's work brought archetypal theory much closer to the instinctual phenomena that is the focus of psychoanalysts. Fordham recognised that Klein's concept of unconscious phantasies were virtually the same as that of primitive archetypal images. Both refer to mental images of instincts and to early processes, which indicate that the infant is object related at birth. Fordham, in contrast to Klein, did not consider mental contents or processes to be innate, however he believed the potential for them is. Fordham thought the contents and structures of the psyche were built up through interactions with the environment both before and after birth, eventually leading to symbolisation and imaginative activity.

What Anna Freud, Klein, Fordham, and the schools which they inspired, all had in common was a strong belief in the importance of the child's imaginative life as developed in the matrix of family relationships and as expressed symbolically through play. Understanding how play could be used clinically took time to develop. Freud had indirectly treated a 5-year-old, 'Little Hans', through the boy's father, and Jung wrote a paper concerning observations of his daughter. Other early psychoanalytic practitioners had attempted some direct work with children, but it was Klein who worked out a technique that combined the rigorous technical tools in work with adults with the child's natural expression in play. This technical development proved an effective way of reaching the child's unconscious, and others, like Winnicott and Fordham, drew upon this. Thus play, as the crucial idiom of childhood, remains the medium through which child analytic therapy is conducted.

Conclusions

To conclude, divergencies between the psychoanalytic schools described in this chapter have produced conflicts but have also been advantageous, as they have led to the development of psychoanalytic theory through the collective effort of gifted practitioners.

Further reading

Astor, J. (1995) *Michael Fordham's Innovations in Analytical Psychology*, London: Routledge.

Gay, P. (1988) *Freud: A Life for Our Time*, London: Dent.

Grosskurth, P. (1986) *Melanie Klein*, London: Hodder and Stoughton.

Hinshelwood, R. (1994) *Clinical Klein*, London: Free Association Books.

King, P. and Steiner, R. (eds) (1991) *The Freud–Klein Controversies 1941–1945*, London: Tavistock/Routledge.

Kohon, G. (ed.) (1988) *The British School of Psychoanalysis: The Independent Tradition*, London: Free Association Books.

Sandler, J. *et al.* (1997) *Freud's Models of the Mind*, London: Karnac.

Petot, J-M. (1991) *Melanie Klein*, Vols I and II, Madison CT: International Universities Press.

Sidoli, M. and Davies, M. (1988) *Jungian Child Psychotherapy: Individuation in Childhood*, London: Karnac.

Wollheim, R. (1991) *Freud*, 2nd edn, London: Fontana Modern Masters.

Young-Bruehl, E. (1988) *Anna Freud*, London: Macmillan.

3   Normal emotional development

Ann Horne

Introduction and context

Child and adolescent psychotherapists are constantly aware of the developmental processes at work – or obscured and obstructed – in the children and young people whom they see. In simple terms, the normal capacity of the child to adapt to and embrace growth and change, both physically and emotionally, is an ally of the therapist. Given that our caseloads today, however, tend towards children who have experienced severe and often very early trauma, where the survival of any sense of self seems an amazing achievement, it has become even more vital that we retain as part of our repertoire a clear sense of the normal developmental tasks and processes which lead to 'good enough' emotional health and functioning.

Each psychotherapist, in considering emotional development, will tend to use the constructs and vocabulary of his or her own theoretical orientation (see Chapter 2). In practice, one integrates this with what is found to be clinically useful and valid. This chapter will inevitably present the author's view of key developments but attempt to incorporate major theoretical positions. A workable brief overview is the aim.[1]

The reader should also keep in mind Stern's dictum that developmental progress does not take place at a smooth, even pace. Rather, the infant and child is subject to quantum leaps in physical, emotional and cognitive achievement (Stern 1985). One would add that it is also important for the therapist to keep in mind that, although each sign of progress represents a gain for the child, it also contains a loss: the infant who achieves walking has made a step (or several!) which leaves behind the perhaps comfortable dependency of the pre-mobile nursing state. The child's world, moreover, has suddenly become a very different place. It is not unusual for sleep problems to be associated with such developmental gains as mobility, as separation anxiety sets in (Daws 1989). Developmental achievement thus incorporates loss and the child can feel a regressive pull to earlier states at times of anxiety and uncertainty. Anna Freud gave probably the clearest early model of normal development from which pathological diversion could be assessed, with the emphasis on normality (Freud, A. 1965).

Early infancy

The development of the infant's psychological sense of self paradoxically begins, for the psychotherapist, with the development of the 'body ego' or sense of physical boundariedness in the baby. The first defence mechanisms – ways of protecting and enabling the growing 'self' (see Chapter 5) – are physical: crying, kicking, using the body and the musculature to cope with internal anxiety or external intrusion. An experience of the body as potent, to be enjoyed, therefore, is important for the developing baby, as is the mother/carer's capacity to meet, understand and enjoy the communication involved. Where the communication is one of distress, the infant needs the mother to make sense of this and respond in a way which both alleviates the distress and does not leave the baby with an overwhelming feeling of uncontainment and 'falling to pieces'. A colleague who observed Sikh friends with a new baby boy noted that part of his care involved his mother oiling his body and lovingly massaging his limbs and torso – an interaction clearly delighting both. While this example may be culture-specific, the need for the baby to feel that his body, and therefore his person, are wanted, understood and valued is an important one. The quality of touch in containing and confirming body boundaries can be seen in this vignette, as can the mother as *active* participant with her infant, calling forth and 'meeting' his capacities and ventures.

This sense of omnipotent functioning, of expecting and receiving a caring experience in line with one's needs, is described in different ways by various commentators: the caregiving mother of attachment theory (see next chapter), the 'dance' of the mother–infant dyad outlined by Daniel Stern (Stern 1977), and probably most famously the in-tune 'good-enough' mother of Winnicott's writings (Winnicott 1965). The critical experience for the infant is of being protected, kept safe, of maternal containment (Bion 1962). The corollary is to leave the infant with overwhelming anxieties that have to be coped with by pathological means: avoidance/denial/a recourse and retreat to the bodily self as the only available resource.

Freud termed the first stage of infant psychosexual development the 'oral stage': the infant uses the mouth to test objects, to gain pleasure, and a major focus of that pleasure is in the feeding relationship with the mother. Although the concept of infantile sexuality (see Chapter 2 for a fuller account) is one of Freud's most important legacies, it is important to keep in mind that this sexuality or 'proto-sexuality' of the infant is *not* the adult sexuality of equals. Thus total physical and emotional satisfaction can be engendered by a good experience, such as a good feeding relationship where the infant's sensuality is met and encouraged by the touch and holding of the mother as the infant feeds.

Winnicott describes the gradual move into reality made by the baby as the mother, in careful accordance with what the baby can manage, allows gentle frustration and 'an experience of disillusionment' (Winnicott 1953). Should the lessening availability of the mother occur at a pace with which the infant cannot cope, the immature sense of self is overwhelmed and a range of early defence mechanisms is called into play to deal with the primitive anxieties of annihilation, disintegration and abandonment. These, if they persist into childhood and adolescence, augur badly for peer relations and the capacity for independent functioning.

Although the focus of most commentators on the first months of child-hood has been on the mother–child relationship, the work of attachment researchers has made us very aware of the infant's capacity and drive to engage and communicate with others in his environment. The role of fathers thus becomes important early on, not simply as the 'facilitating environment' described by Winnicott (1979), but also as an alternative to the intensity of the mother–infant dyad with its potential fears of merging and over-closeness. Wright (1997) has developed an elegant thesis about the father's place in the development of creativity: that the receptive, good-enough Winnicottian mother meets the infant's primary creativity and encourages it, while the father's role is to help the infant direct that creativity towards the outside world and to take advantage of what that world offers. The different nature of the father's relationship with his child is also outlined by Colarusso (1992), who finds that task-achievement, setting limits and looking outwards to being a socialised person in the world are part of the paternal function.

Toddlers

With mobility and further development of sensorimotor functions, the infant takes a major leap forward. In Chapter 22 the authors describe the growing independence and assertiveness of the toddler. Ambivalence in the relationship with the mother who has to refuse his demands, the place of magical thinking ('I hate her therefore she has been made to go or been killed off by me'), and the growing capacity to integrate love and hate in the same person are features of this stage (Klein 1937). The child by two has a primary sense of gender (see Chapter 24) and a sense of agency that is constantly exercised and tested. The anal stage of Freudian theory contains this sense of wilfulness, taking control for oneself, and the ability to enjoy saying 'No!' In the temper tantrum of the toddler can be seen a real sense of disbelief and acutely-felt insult to the omnipotent self that is now being challenged. The toddler begins to explore leaving mother, making sorties with her in sight, but returning to the secure base for reassurance and congratulations. This develops into the capacity to make the adults pursue the child, another significant sensation for the toddler. Games of escape and capture create high excitement but are not always tactfully located: the queue at the supermarket is an all too frequent venue. Language is develop-ing and, with it, the capacity to symbolise rather than to enact – to use words rather than the body of earliest childhood. Crucial progress lies in the affirmation of identity, now internalised, demonstrated in the appropriate use of 'I'. Play at this stage is still very much interactive with mother, but an ability to be 'alone in the presence of the object', engaged in his own fantasy, has developed (Winnicott 1958). Play with objects has not yet acquired symbolic content but seems to focus on tactile exploration of basic concepts – shape, sensation, hardness, softness – and on motor competencies of stacking and knocking over, pulling and pushing, as 'What can I do with this?' is investigated.

Finally, progress towards the use of 'transitional objects' (toys or materials like a comfort blanket, which can contain aspects of the mother–child relationship and so help in the tolerance of independence and absence) should be mentioned (Winnicott 1953). Such objects, often from very early infancy and treated with both attachment and contemptuous disdain, provide a space that is transitional between infant-and-mother and infant-alone, an 'intermediate area of experience' (ibid.: 2). They can remain important to the child for many years.

The child's preoccupation with his anatomy is a feature of genital stage development: theories of difference between boys and girls emerge along with fears of castration in boys and reactions to male potency in girls. The sense of an internal space for babies in girls can be paralleled by an envy of this child-bearing capacity by boys. A more narcissistic, self-centred child appears, almost in preparation for the integrated identity that is consolidated after the Oedipal resolution.

Play

The ability to play is important for the growing child. Early creativity and curiosity depend greatly on the mother's attunement to her infant. Responsive playfulness and the potential to initiate play appear even before the infant is mobile, although mobility adds to the possibilities. The capacity for symbolisation is linked, psychoanalytically, to the perception of separateness from the mother and the need to bridge that gap. Although this differs from the inborn drive for engagement and communication seen by the attachment researchers, both approaches contain the inherent element of the need to attract and engage the primary person in the infant's life.

As the toddler grows, so does his ability to endow toys and play materials with genuinely symbolic meaning and his competence in using others in this play: the child who begins nursery may at first 'play alongside' others, but develop the ability to 'play with' as he advances. Earlier experiences of 'good-enough' attachments and separation of a non-overwhelming kind will obviously play a role in allowing the growing toddler the internal security that enables him to explore how he can interact with others safely and with curiosity (Furman 1992).

The purpose of play is diverse: a rehearsal for future life; dealing with anxiety and conflict; exploring the space between fantasy and reality; and cognitive and social experimentation. As one three-year-old reportedly said to Winnicott, 'Play is work, of course!' All toddlers at some time engage in play which copies the roles and tasks they have observed their parents undertake. This is not necessarily gender-specific and can be very fluid in the possibilities thus entertained. One may see precursors here to the use of day-dreaming in the adult, trying out possibilities and exploring dreams and hopes (Freud 1908; Rycroft 1974). Perhaps less obvious is the play which helps the child make sense of things which cause anxiety – the visit to the dentist repeated with a teddy bear as the patient or using dolls to re-enact a family quarrel or trauma. This ability to symbolise what has been feared and to place it outside, for perusal and hence to acquire control, is important for later adolescent and adult capacities to think, to gain mastery and not be overwhelmed, and helps in the process of not having to act out what might otherwise feel uncontainable (see Chapter 23). This is patently of importance in child psychotherapy where the child's capacity to symbolise anxiety through play is a route to unconscious conflicts (Klein 1955). When a child cannot play, it is the task of the therapist, through work on the immature ego and early attachments, to help the child's abilities develop safely.

Oedipal resolution and parental sexuality

In classical theory the importance of the Oedipal phase and its successful resolution cannot be overstressed. This involves the renouncing of the intense emotional relationship with the mother (most parents of boys will recall the stage where their child was certain that 'When I grow up I am going to marry Mummy'). Winnicott's description of the Oedipal child as 'all dressed up and nowhere to go' gives a succinct picture of infantile sexuality and passion (Winnicott 1964). For the boy, ambivalence in the relationship with the father, admired and feared as possessor of the mother and a potentially castrating rival for her, becomes gradually replaced by a developing closeness to an available father-figure, allowing identification with him and the outward-looking described earlier. For girls, the intensity of the maternal relationship is replaced with passion for the father who, equally unavailable as a sexual object, has to be renounced as partner. As the girl turns away from parental partners, identification with the mother becomes possible.

Most modern commentators would now view the significant parts of the Oedipal resolution as those centring on the realisation of parental sexuality and partnership, three-person relationships, and on the boundaries between adults and children, parents and offspring. For the child in a single-parent family, as for the child with two parents available, the *idea* of a parental relationship matters – that the parent living with the child does not decry adult partnership but can keep the possibility benignly in mind for the child. The child, therefore, turns from the parents and infantile amnesia sets in ('Did I use to do that? No I didn't!' and embarrassment at family myths and stories are common). The normally developing child will focus with relief on external peer relations and the continuing acquisition of skills and competencies as his cognitive development grows.

Hamilton (1993) in her eloquent reassessment of narcissism and the Oedipus complex offers an important and wider reinterpretation:

> The resolution of the Oedipus complex entails a renunciation; not only must the child give up the fantasy that he can have an exclusive relation-ship with the parent of the opposite sex, he must also accept that there is an objective order of things which he will never completely understand or control. In *some* cases this realisation is experienced as a castration or narcissistic blow. The blow is to the child's budding feelings of power and curiosity and to the satisfactions gained by learning.
>
> (Hamilton 1993: 273)

It is useful here to think a little further about the role of the parents immediately post-Oedipally. For the girl, identification with the mother and engaging in play as a rehearsal for her future as a woman is a feature. It is also vital, however, in the consolidation of her sense of femininity to have a sense of being valued as a girl by her father. For many of the girls who present with gender dysphoria (see Chapter 24), the emotional or physical absence of the father seems to play a part. The opposite process, with the mother, is important for boys. For parents it is vital that this affirmation of the opposite-sex child does not become sexualised and confusing.

At this point, one finds the presence of the capacity for guilt and shame: the child has an 'ego ideal', a sense of who he is and who he would like to be, based on internalisations of his parents and the 'self' they reflect back to him, and is aware when he falls short of achieving this internal ideal.

Psychoanalytic theoreticians differ as to the age at which such develop-ments occur. Perhaps one could say that, while seeing development in absolute stages to be achieved by a particular age may not be helpful, to see a spectrum of development on which the child takes up a changing position, according to nature, environment, growth and internalisation, is useful. Indeed 'most of the processes that start up in early infancy are never fully established, and continue to be strengthened by the growth that continues in later childhood, and indeed in adult life, even in old age' (Winnicott 1963).

The primary-school-aged child

With the move into school, other identifications not only become more available to the child but can also be useful in separating from and challenging the parents. 'But my teacher said . . .' is not unheard in families with latency children, as 'greater' external authority becomes internalised into what is initially a fairly rigid conscience or super-ego. 'Latency' (in psycho-sexual terms) or primary-school age is par excellence the time of rules, fairness and the acquisition of self-control, as the child struggles to leave behind the conflicts and embarrassing desires of the Oedipal stage and focuses on internalising mechanisms of competence and control. As the years go by, the severity of this conscience eases and an autonomous, non-persecuting super-ego should be established before the child has to deal with the changes and regressive pull of the pre-pubertal period.

This is the time of the 'family romance', the sense that one has been taken home by the wrong parents from the hospital or that there has been a dreadful mistake and really there are a 'princess' and a pop star some-where waiting sadly to find their real child. Such fantasies aid the necessary distancing of the child from the passion of earlier inter-familial feelings.

Children at this time tend mostly to play with their own sex. Clubs, groups and games with clear rules are important; new rules will be created but must be adhered to. A clear and rigid perception of right and wrong is at work. Nevertheless, there is also a delightful sense of subversion at this time – a glance at children's literature will show children defeating or being cleverer than the adults, and a gentle mocking of adult roles, hypocrisies and pretensions (Lurie 1991; Allen 1993). Indeed, few would now agree with the idea that sexuality has disappeared in a 'latency' phase. Although the intensity of parentally directed passion has lessened, children of this age are still developing theories about sex and explore these with peers, away from adult view. 'Doctors and nurses', with all its variations, is an early latency game, after all. Curiosity about the sexuality of others (outsiders, not family members who are simply embarrassing when they make children aware of sexuality and towards whom a certain prudishness can often be found) is ongoing and a rehearsal for adult wishes and possibilities. Identifications with heroes and idols are a feature of this age range – it is always interesting to note which pop stars appeal to pre-pubertal girls with a glossy but safely packaged sexuality and which become the heroes of the adolescent, when individuality of choice and discrimination are coming to the fore.

The rhythmic games of girls in the playground have long been seen as a sublimation of sexual feelings, enacted safely and physically. It is also possible to see the rough and tumble of boys' play, and the intrepid rush towards contact sports, as an affirming rehearsal for their adult sexuality as they establish a sense of boundary to their bodies in preparation for an adult penetrative role.

Puberty and adolescence

> Adolescence begins with biology and ends with psychology. It is kick started by puberty and cruises slowly to a halt at adult identity, the point at which the petrol is getting low and we need to think about saving it for the long, straight road ahead.
>
> (Van Heeswyk 1997)

This wry comment comes as the author notes the tendency of our profession to list developmental tasks as absolutes. For the child approaching puberty, comparison in any kind of straight-line physiological way with his peers may be the source of more anxiety than consolation. There is a gulf between the girl who reaches her menarche at nine and the one who desperately hopes that menstruation will start now that she is sixteen. Indeed, a rapidly changing body with its overture to adult sexual roles can be more difficult for the younger girl to encounter without the parallel experiences of her peers to support and confirm her feelings (Orford 1993). Similarly, the boy whose growth spurt comes later than his peers can find the idea of ever coping as an adult a terrifying and bizarre prospect. Shifts in the body self in pre-puberty (Tyson and Tyson 1990) can often be accompanied by regression in relationships with key adults: a swing back to the safety of previous experience in the face of the inevitability of adolescence.

Although puberty can often be presented as '*Sturm und Drang*', most young people make their way successfully through adolescence despite the projections of adult envy and adult fears that accompany every step. That said, there *are* important psychological negotiations to be made. 'Who will I be?' is the sub-text as the adolescent faces external, physiological and internal pressures about future role and identity.

Intimacy once more becomes an issue, but intimacy of *mind* as well as of the body. This can be perceived as finally taking over from the parents responsibility for and ownership of one's body at a time when the earliest sexual feelings of infancy are revived, but with the addition of a sexually functioning body: no longer 'all dressed up and nowhere to go' but potent. Adapting emotionally involves somehow making the parental intimacies less intense – a reworking of the Oedipal experience. This occurs in the realm of ideas and opinions, too, where separation from parental assumptions and family values can feel shocking to suddenly disparaged parents. The silent adolescent is not a myth: keeping quiet keeps fantasy, thought and internal life private (the use of a personal diary is not uncommon), and helps with finding the optimal safe intimate distance as the adolescent seeks to accommodate change. The reluctance to care for the body – often a contentious issue in families in early puberty and perhaps an attempt to ignore the imperative of physiological and sexual changes – gives way to great attention and concern in later adolescence. Family pressures refocus on ownership of the bathroom. Acting via the body – discos, flirtation with drugs, alcohol and nicotine, sports, sexual exploration – takes the teenager back to early mechanisms for dealing with what might feel unmanageable and rehearses possible futures. The capacity to tolerate this new, fluid body-self is crucial: adolescence is not surprisingly the risk time for eating disorders (see Chapter 25) and suicide in those who find the move towards establishing an adult, sexual self too impossible a task.

The availability of peers and alternative adults takes on even greater priority in early and mid-adolescence than at earlier ages. This can be the time of the 'crush', of passionate feelings for same- and opposite-sex grown-ups and young people. Identifications are part of these, as is exploration and integration of aspects of others into a modified ideal, hoped-for self.

The use of the group in mid-adolescence provides a similar function to the relationship with a close, same-sex friend in early adolescence. The mirroring obtained from peers is important at this stage and is based on the early identity formation of infant years. The group, moreover, offers a variety of roles and the opportunity to share responsibility and irresponsibility, trying out different aspects of the self and perceiving these in others. The risk-taking that can be indulged in during adolescence has in it qualities of the omnipotence of the toddler stage, a heady disregard for danger that, it is assumed, will never ever strike personally. Failure in friendships and relationships with peers leaves the adolescent developmentally very handicapped in his resources for trying out himself in the world. Family pressure moves to 'Where were you?' or 'Where are you going?' and to the size of the telephone bill.

Mid-adolescence is also the time at which we place heavier educational burdens on the young, when intellectual challenge becomes serious and achievement or failure is seen in stark terms, incorporated into the fluidity which is the emerging identity. As with all aspects of adolescent development, there is a danger that this can polarise and the whole sense of self be felt to be bound up with progress in one single area. One can be left with a dramatic sense of 'all or nothing'; it is hard to keep open the transitional space so creative in early childhood (Hamilton 1993).

Theoretically, but not always in practice, by late adolescence 'stability of identity' (Tyson and Tyson 1990) has been achieved. No longer conflicted over parental relationships, the young person can find a disengaged intimacy with family, which allows rapprochement and appreciation. This occurs from a position of security as a separate, functioning young adult.

Approaching adulthood: conclusions

There is, in psychoanalytic theory, an assumption that one achieves adulthood by about twenty-five years of age. This entails a developed capacity for intimacy, responsibility and autonomy. Perhaps this is so. Perhaps, on the other hand, it is also important for us, in adulthood, to retain something of the fluidity of childhood and adolescence: the tolerance of states of not-knowing, the curiosity to engage with the world, a sense of playfulness linked to the aptitude to be creative with ideas (Winnicott, after all, in 1971 described psychotherapy as 'done in the overlap of two play areas, that of the patient and that of the therapist') and the ability (however muddled the prospects might seem) to greet change as an indicator of further potential in our lives as social beings. In adulthood, we should not lose the developmental strengths of childhood.

Note

1 At the time of writing there are in preparation or in print several books of relevance. Emotional development from pregnancy and birth onwards is covered in *Lectures on Personality Development* edited by Hindle and Vaciago Smith; the Tavistock has several series including *Understanding Your ( ) Year Old*; Margot Waddell has written on development; and in Australia Ruth Schmidt Neven has brought out a text on this area.

References

Allen, N. (1993) *The Queen's Knickers*, London: Red Fox.

Bion, W. R. (1962) *Learning from Experience*, London: Heinemann.

Colarusso, C. A. (1992) *Child and Adult Development: A Psychoanalytic Introduction for Clinicians*, New York/London: Plenum Press.

Daws, D. (1989) *Through the Night: Helping Parents and Sleepless Infants*, London: Free Association Books.

Freud, A. (1965) *Normality and Pathology in Childhood: Assessments of Development*, New York: International Universities Press.

Freud, S. (1908) 'Creative writers and day-dreaming', *SE* 9: 141–53.

Furman, E. (1992) *Toddlers and their Mothers*, Madison CT: International Universities Press.

Hamilton, V. (1993) *Narcissus and Oedipus: The Children of Psychoanalysis*, 2nd edn, London: Karnac.

Hindle, D. and Vaciago Smith, M. (1999) *Lectures in Personality Development: A Psychoanalytic Perspective*, London: Routledge.

Klein, M. (1937) 'Love, guilt and reparation', in (1975) *Love, Guilt and Reparation and Other Works 1921–1945: The Writings of Melanie Klein*, Vol. I, London: Hogarth Press.

—— (1955) 'The psychoanalytic play technique: its history and significance', in M. Klein *et al.* (eds) *New Directions in Psychoanalysis*, London: Tavistock.

Lurie, A. (1991) *Not in Front of the Grown-ups: Subversive Children's Literature*, London: Sphere Books.

Orford, E. (1993) *Understanding your 11 Year Old*, Tavistock Clinic series, London: Rosendale Press.

Rycroft, C. (1974) 'Is Freudian symbolism a myth?', in P. Fuller (ed.) *Psychoanalysis and Beyond*, London: Hogarth Press, 1985.

Stern, D. (1977) 'Mis-steps in the dance', in *The First Relationship: Infant and Mother*, London: Fontana/Open Books.

—— (1985) *The Interpersonal World of the Human Infant*, New York: Basic Books.

Tyson, P. and Tyson, R. L. (1990) *Psychoanalytic Theories of Development: An Integration*, New Haven: Yale University Press.

van Heeswyk, P. (1997) *Analysing Adolescence*, London: Sheldon Press.

Waddell, M. (1998) *Inside Lives: Psychoanalysis and the Growth of Personality*, London: Duckworth.

Winnicott, D. W. (1953) 'Transitional objects and transitional phenomena', in *Playing and Reality*, Harmondsworth: Penguin, 1971.

—— (1958) 'The capacity to be alone', in *The Maturational Processes and the Facilitating Environment*, London: Hogarth Press, 1979.

—— (1963) 'The development of the capacity for concern', in *The Maturational Processes and the Facilitating Environment*, London: Hogarth Press, 1979.

—— (1964) 'The child and sex', in *The Child, the Family and the Outside World*, Harmondsworth: Penguin.

—— (1965) *The Family and Individual Development*, London: Tavistock.

—— (1971) 'Playing: creative activity and the search for self', in *Playing and Reality*, London: Tavistock.

—— (1979) *The Maturational Processes and the Facilitating Environment*, London: Hogarth Press.

Wright, K. (1997) 'Stories of creation', paper given at Annual Conference of British Association of Psychotherapists, November 1997.

Further reading

Brazelton, T. B. and Cramer, B. G. (1991) *The Earliest Relationship: Parents, Infants and the Drama of Early Attachment*, London: Karnac.

Colarusso, C. A. (1992) *Child and Adult Development: A Psychoanalytic Introduction for Clinicians*, New York/London: Plenum Press.

Furman, E. (1992) *Toddlers and their Mothers*, Madison CT: International Universities Press.

Solnit, A. J., Cohen, D. J. and Neubauer, P. B. (eds) (1993) *The Many Meanings of Play: A Psychoanalytic Perspective*, New Haven/London: Yale University Press.

Tyson, P. and Tyson, R. L. (1990) *Psychoanalytic Theories of Development: An Integration*, New Haven: Yale University Press.

van Heeswyk, P. (1997) *Analysing Adolescence*, London: Sheldon Press.

Waddell, M. (1998) *Inside Lives: Psychoanalysis and the Growth of the Personality*, London: Duckworth.

Winnicott, D. W. (1964) *The Child, the Family and the Outside World*, Harmondsworth: Penguin Books.

4   Some contributions on attachment theory

Juliet Hopkins

Attachment theory developed from the pioneering work of John Bowlby (1907–90), a British child psychiatrist and psychoanalyst. At a time when many psychoanalysts were focusing their attention on the role of internal factors, such as instinct and fantasy, in the development of psychopathology, Bowlby turned his attention to the role of external factors which he believed to be of more significance. He intended, following Freud, that psychoanalysis should be respected, not only as a method of psychotherapy, but as a reputable science, 'the science of unconscious mental processes'. Since scientific research begins with observation, Bowlby decided to study the responses of young children to separation and bereavement, for these could be accurately observed and were thought likely to be of pathogenic significance.

Bowlby's early observations of young children, separated from their parents in hospitals or institutions, revealed that they characteristically passed through three phases of response to their loss: protest, despair and detachment. Each of these phases could be seen to be linked to a particular psychoanalytic concept: separation anxiety (threat of loss), grief and mourning (acceptance of loss) and defence (protection from the pain of loss). To these central concepts, Bowlby added another: the nature of the child's tie to the parent (or main caregiver) which could be disrupted or lost. This tie he termed attachment. In the course of his study of attachment and loss Bowlby found it necessary to reformulate psychoanalytic theory in terms compatible with modern scientific thinking and with empirical findings. His aim was to develop hypotheses which could be tested by research. His trilogy *Attachment and Loss* (1969, 1973, 1980) combines ideas from ethology, systems theory and cognitive psychology.

This chapter aims to introduce the biological basis for attachment theory and to describe some of the findings from subsequent attachment research which are of value for child psychotherapists.

Evolution and the need for attachment

Bowlby approached the early mother–child relationship from the standpoint of a biologist concerned with the central biological theory of our time:

evolution. Our hunter–gatherer ancestors inhabited an environment in which only the fittest survived to reproduce and our instinctive behaviour must have evolved to increase our chances of survival in these conditions. Bowlby avoids Freud's use of the term 'instinct' with its outmoded concept of some internal driving force, and prefers the term 'instinctive behaviour'. This, in accordance with modern ethology, is conceived as a pattern which is activated or terminated by particular internal or environmental conditions.

Attachment behaviour is an excellent example of such instinctive behaviour. Bowlby conceives of it as being separate from the instinctive systems subserving feeding and sexual behaviour. Its aim is proximity or contact and its subjective goal is felt security. It is activated in infancy by the internal conditions of fatigue, hunger, pain, illness and cold, and by external conditions indicating increased risk: darkness, loud noises, sudden movements, looming shapes and solitude. When it is activated the child seeks contact with one of his particular attachment figures whom he has learned to discriminate.

Babies are clearly pre-programmed at birth to learn the specific details of a few caregiving adults. They show their capacity to discriminate by their preference for their caregiver's qualities. Although clear preferences develop from birth, the full intensity of the baby's attachment behaviour is only manifest from the latter half of the first year.

When attachment behaviour is activated at low levels it is possible for parents to calm their infants by voice and proximity alone; but when infants are very upset, only close physical contact can terminate distress. Anxiety is experienced throughout life when we are threatened either by a hostile environment or by the withdrawal or loss of our attachment figures. As adults, we still need attachment figures and we still seek physical contact at times of acute anxiety, trauma or loss.

Bowlby's evolutionary perspective offers us a simple explanation of the development of infants' fears. In the second half of the first year, babies become increasingly afraid of strangers, heights, the dark and solitude. This development can be understood as a maturational concomitant of the baby's new capacity for independent locomotion, a capacity which clearly increases the risk of encountering danger. Natural selection has equipped infants with a behavioural repertoire which increases their tendency to seek proximity to their mother at times of increased risk. There is no need to postulate the irrational projection of hostility to explain infantile fears, although of course such fears can be increased by projection. Typically, the very timid, fearful baby is one who has learned to expect that his attachment figure will not be reliably available when he is distressed; this is certainly a realistic cause for both fear and anger.

Bowlby's initial research focused on the effects of physical separation of young children from their parents. Later attachment research has focused on the nature of the mother's availability when she is present – her sensitivity and responsiveness. Evidence shows that the toddler who knows his mother is physically and emotionally available when he needs her can use her as a secure base from which to venture to explore his environment. He can concentrate well and play independently because he feels safe. Further research has also shown a strong positive correlation between the security of children's attachments and their capacity to co-operate with adults, to concentrate on play, to persist at problem-solving and to be popular with peers.

The central feature of good parenting, Bowlby (1988) believed, was 'the provision by both parents of a secure base from which a child or adolescent can make sorties into the outside world and to which he can return knowing for sure that he will be welcomed when he gets there, nourished physically and emotionally, comforted if distressed, reassured if frightened'. In order to provide this care parents must have an intuitive understanding of, and respect for, the child's attachment behaviour and treat it 'as an intrinsic and valuable part of human nature'. Parents must also be well supported themselves. As children and adolescents get older they venture steadily further from their secure base and for increasing lengths of time. The more confident they are that their base is secure, the more readily they take it for granted.

The concept of security is not entirely new to psychoanalysis. In 1959 Sandler suggested the notion of safety as a feeling state quite distinct from sensual pleasure. He went on to describe how patients might thwart analytic work by regressing to childhood relationships associated with punishment or pain, because the security associated with these relationships made them more rewarding than the insecurity and isolation belonging to new ventures and not associated with familiar parent figures.

Abuse

Attachment theory is able to shed light on the powerful attachment which an abused child can develop to an abusing parent. When the source of a child's security is also a source of pain and danger, the child is placed in a position of irresolvable and self-perpetuating conflict. The situation is irresolvable because rejection by an established attachment figure activates simultaneous and contradictory impulses both to withdraw and to approach. The infant cannot approach because of the parent's rejection and cannot withdraw because of the intensity of its own attachment when afraid. The clinical outcome is an intense anxious dependency which may lead the child to resist separation from the parents and so deceive professional workers into believing that all is well.

Security of attachment: the observed infant

Since biologists have found each organism to be highly adapted to its environment, Bowlby always supposed the infant to be more influenced by real aspects of parenting than by internal fantasy. This assumption has been supported by Ainsworth's research (e.g. 1985) which reveals that certain characteristics of a mother's parenting are more important for determining the infant's security of attachment at a year, than any innate quality of the infant that has yet been assessed.

Ainsworth *et al.*'s (1971) 'strange situation test' has been widely used to provide an assessment of infant security. In this standardised test the infant is left briefly alone in a strange room and then reunited with his mother: his reactions on reunion are considered indicative of the nature of his security with his mother, since they reveal the expectations he has developed about her physical and emotional availability when he is afraid.

Secure attachment

In general, patterns of behaviour on reunion with mother fall into two broad categories. The exact proportions of babies falling into each category vary with the sample (several nationalities have been assessed), but roughly speaking nearly two-thirds of babies are rated as securely attached. On reunion these babies immediately seek contact with their mother: on being picked up they are quickly comforted by her and they soon ask to be put down so that they can pursue their exploration of the toys provided. They may express some anger with mother, especially if she tries to interest them in the toys too soon, but their crossness is easily assuaged.

These babies can be said to have developed basic trust.

Insecure attachment

The remaining third of babies are classified as anxiously attached. These babies have developed either of two major strategies: avoidance or resistance. Psychotherapists are clinically familiar with the distinction between these two solutions to insecurity: the self-sufficient avoidants who seek safety in independence and the clinging resistants who rely on physical proximity to feel safe, but never feel satisfied. The revelation of Ainsworth's research is that these defensive patterns of response to stress are clearly established by the first birthday.

The avoidant infant

The characteristic response of these babies on reunion in the 'strange situation' is not to greet their mother, and, in some instances, not even to look at her. Any approaches tend to be abortive. If picked up they may lean away or squirm to get down. Frequently they divert their mother's attention to a toy or distant object. However, it is clearly perplexing that stressful events which normally heighten attachment behaviour apparently diminish it. Bowlby (1988) interprets the avoidant response to indicate that 'already by the age of twelve months there are children who no longer express to mother one of their deepest emotions, nor their equally deep-seated desire for comfort and assurance that accompanies it'. Fearfulness, dependency and hostility are not expressed. Defensive strategies are already active.

The ambivalent or resistant infant

These babies are intensely upset by the separation and are highly ambivalent to the mother on her return. They want to be close to her but are angry with her and so are very difficult to soothe. They cling, resist being put down and are slow to return to play.

As Ainsworth has pointed out, the psychological significance of the three patterns of attachment behaviour which she described rests upon their close association both with mother–infant interaction observed in the home, and with their persistence over time.

Observations in the home

Observations in the home reveal that the reaction of babies in the 'strange situation' is closely related to the nature of the mothering which they have received during their first year.

(a) Briefly, babies with a secure response have mothers who have proved responsive and accessible. These mothers are able to read their babies' signals and to respond to them sensitively and reliably. They easily accept their babies' bids for close physical contact. At home their babies are observed to be happier and more co-operative than babies who manifest an insecure attachment.

(b) Babies with an avoidant response have mothers who are restricted in their range of emotional expression and who exhibit an aversion to close physical contact; these are babies whose bids for comforting have been consistently rebuffed. Their mothers hold and carry them less comfort-ably than other mothers do, tending to avoid close ventro-ventral contact. Their babies have been found to be no less cuddly at birth than other babies are, but by a year they neither cuddle nor cling but are carried like a sack of potatoes.

An avoidant attachment does not necessarily result in manifest pathology. Avoidant adaptation ranges from the self-contained and emotionally distant personality to the severely schizoid.

(c) Babies with an ambivalent attachment have mothers who enjoy physical contact, but who provide it erratically, often in response to their own needs rather than in response to their babies' needs. They are in general inconsistently responsive. Their babies' anger towards them can be understood as an attempt both to express frustration at their inconsistent handling, and to force their mothers to provide the care and comfort of which they know they are capable.

The insecure disorganised-disoriented attachment pattern

This additional and infrequent attachment pattern is normally found in conjunction with infant behaviour characteristic of one of the other major attachment categories. Whereas the purely avoidant and ambivalent infants have developed consistent strategies for dealing with stress, the disorganised-disoriented infants have not. In the 'strange situation', they reveal their inability to cope in a variety of individual ways. For example, the infant may freeze motionless, fall prone, exhibit tic-like stereotopies or a simultaneous display of contradictory behaviour patterns, such as approaching with head averted. Much research remains to be done, but early findings indicate that the parents of these babies are either frightened or frightening; some have been abusive. Other parents of these babies are suffering from unresolved grief and mourning. As these infants grow up they are liable to cope with their helplessness by becoming very controlling of their parents, in either a caregiving or punitive way. They form the majority of children referred for child guidance.

Fathers

Another major finding has emerged from attachment research. Contrary to psychoanalytic expectation, the infant's relationship to his father (or other major caregiver) cannot be predicted from the nature of his relationship to his mother. It is independent of it and reflects the qualities which the father himself has brought to the relationship. This means, moreover, that the nature of the infant's security is not a function of his general temperament but depends on the history of interaction which he has had with each caregiver.

One common division of functions between parents is that father becomes the preferred play partner while mother is the preferred attachment figure. This means that when the baby is lively and happy he will seek out his father for play and entertainment, but when he is tired, ill or frightened he will want comfort from his mother. However, it should not be forgotten that when the child's relationship to his mother is insecure, father may well be the preferred attachment figure, even when he spends less time in childcare than mother does. It is the quality of adult availability which determines security of infant attachment, not merely the quantity. This also means that babies' attachments are not dependent upon biological related-ness. The term 'psychological parent' has been used to describe the adult to whom the child is most attached and who is now recognised in law to have rights when in dispute with the biological parent.

Changes in attachment pattern

Attempts to predict the course of child development from individual characteristics assessed during the first year have always failed, but the nature of the child's attachments both to mother and to father at the first birthday have emerged as factors with significant predictive power. This must be because the attachment pattern is an aspect of a relationship, not just of the child himself, so as long as the child continues within the same relationship, the stability of the attachment pattern is high.

However, changes in attachment patterns do occur and they are found to be a function of the availability of the parent concerned. For example, with regard to mothers, attachments are likely to become more secure if mother gets more support, whether from her husband, her mother, a friend or a professional worker. Attachment to mother may become less secure when mother goes out to work, gives birth to a sibling, is depressed or bereaved. However, as the child grows older his attachment pattern becomes increasingly a property of himself, and is less responsive to changes in parenting. Individual psychotherapy may then be needed to increase the security of an insecure child. Before this, therapeutic work with the family or with the parents is likely to be the treatment of choice.

The infant's contribution

What part do individual differences between babies play in the development of their security at a year? Infant temperament is not a significant factor in the development of security, as shown by the findings that security with mother and with father are independent of each other, and that either can change with changes in parental availability. Indeed the overall findings of attachment research are firmly weighted in favour of the overriding influence of parental care in determining infant security.

However, statistical generalisations can be misleading when it comes to the consideration of individual cases. Attachment research has been carried out on samples of normal, healthy, full-term babies. Ainsworth herself has acknowledged that the effect of infant behaviour on the mother might be much greater among infants thought to be developmentally at risk.

As attachment research expands more will be learned about the infant's contribution. Already a few studies have reported positive findings. For example, the neonate's ability to orient towards a face has been found to be correlated with secure attachment at a year while babies whom neonatal nurses found difficult were more likely to develop insecure attachments.

Intergenerational transmission

Further research (Main *et al.* 1986) has revealed that there is a significant correlation between parents' representation of their own childhood attachments and the nature of their child's attachment to them. When interviewed about their childhood experience, parents reveal as much by the nature of their communication to the interviewer as they do by the content of their replies. Parents of both resistant and avoidant infants are alike in giving accounts which typically are characterised by unrecognised inconsistencies and contradictions, but their accounts also differ from each other's in predictable ways (Main *et al.* 1986). Parents of resistant infants generally give a lengthy account of unhappy, entangled relationships, with ample evidence that they have remained entangled with their own parents or with memories of them. Parents of avoidant infants give much briefer accounts, partly because they minimise the importance of relationships and partly because they tend to have forgotten childhood experiences. They are likely to make generalised statements about having had happy childhoods, but to be unable to support this with evidence, which is either lacking or contradictory.

In contrast to the parents of insecure infants, parents of secure infants give a fluent, consistent and coherent account of their childhoods in which they treat relationships with significance and recall events with appropriate affect. The vast majority of these parents have had secure childhoods themselves, but among them are a number who recall childhoods of extreme unhappiness and rejection. They have thought and felt deeply about their experiences and have tried to understand them. Some of them have remained very angry with their own parents while others have achieved forgiveness.

The outcome of this research clearly supports the clinical finding that the repetition of adverse childhood relationships can be avoided when adults come to terms with their unhappy past. It seems that this can happen when they recognise what happened to them, acknowledge how they felt about it and are aware that their parents contributed significantly to their unhappiness, which was not entirely of their own making. For example, a father who remembers with resentment being thrashed by his father is much less likely to beat his own child than a father who says, 'He only thrashed me when I asked for it'. The work of child psychotherapists aims to help children gradually become more self-aware and self-reflective, which not only enables them to make more secure and trusting relationships in the present, but may also help them to break the intergenerational cycle of insecurity when they become parents.

Conclusion

Attachment research has proven the importance of the baby's first year in establishing defensive patterns of relating to parents which are likely to persist. The research has also demonstrated the significant role played by parents in shaping their children's ongoing attachments and has shown how parents' capacity to parent depends both on the current support they have and on the way in which they have come to terms themselves with their own childhood experiences of being parented. Attachment research continues to present us with new findings. Bowlby's development of Freud's 'science of unconscious mental processes' has provided the base from which a new science of developmental psychopathology is growing.

References

Ainsworth, M. D. S. (1985) 'Patterns of infant–mother attachments: antecedents and effects on development', *Bulletin of New York Academy of Medicine* 61(9): 772–91.

Ainsworth, M. D. S., Bell, S. M. V. and Stayton, D. J. (1971) 'Individual differences in strange situation behaviour of one-year-olds', in H. R. Schaffer (ed.) *The Origins of Human Social Relationships*, London: Academic Press.

Bowlby, J. (1969/82) *Attachment and Loss, vol. 1: Attachment*, London: Hogarth.

—— (1973) *Attachment and Loss, vol. 2: Separation*, London: Hogarth.

—— (1980) *Attachment and Loss, vol. 3: Loss, Sadness and Depression*, London: Hogarth.

—— (1988) *A Secure Base: Clinical Applications of Attachment Theory*, London: Routledge.

Main, M., Kaplan, N. and Cassidy, J. (1986) 'Security in infancy, childhood and adulthood: a move to the level of representation', in I. Bretherton and E. Waters (eds) *Growing Points of Attachment Theory and Research*, Monograph 50, Society for Research in Child Development, pp. 66–104.

Sandler, J. (1959) 'The background of safety', in *From Safety to Superego*, London: Karnac Books, 1987.

Further Reading

Goldberg, S., Muir, R. and Kerr, J. (1995) *Attachment Theory. Social, Developmental and Clinical Perspectives*, Hillsdale NJ: Analytic Press.

Holmes, J. (1993) *John Bowlby and Attachment Theory*, London: Routledge.

Karen, R. (1994) *Becoming Attached. Unfolding the Mystery of the Infant–Mother Bond and its Impact on Later Life*, New York: Warner Books.

Part II

The child and adolescent psychotherapist in practice

5 The therapeutic relationship and process

Monica Lanyado and Ann Horne

The constantly evolving relationship between the therapist and patient lies at the heart of all psychoanalytic work and is the main vehicle for psychic change. In some respects this statement may seem surprising. The child comes to see the therapist with all manner of difficulties in his or her relationships with family and peers, and talks and plays around these themes, and yet in psychoanalytic work the most important insights which lead to deep change in the patient's relationships and internal world are gained from what is happening in the consulting room, in the 'here and now' of the meeting of two people, the therapist and the child.

We have chosen in this chapter to write about the concepts that are central to the therapeutic relationship and process in a discursive manner as we hope to demystify them a little for the general reader and to demonstrate their roots in ordinary forms of development and communication. The case illustrations in this handbook show how we work in a vivid and straightforward way, whilst providing many references for the reader who wishes to explore in more detail. For those who are new to psychoanalytic thought, this chapter will serve as an introduction to important concepts; for our colleagues who are very familiar with these ideas, there may be value and stimulation in revisiting one's theoretical and technical roots.

In selecting the most important concepts about the therapeutic relationship and process to introduce at this stage in the handbook, we have had the great advantage of reading and discussing the contributions of other authors, thus gaining a picture of contemporary clinical practice and thought across the profession. In addition, colleagues from a range of theoretical positions have read this chapter to help us to create as representative a picture as possible of current practice. We are aware, however, that there will inevitably be debates around these concepts, their understanding and use: this is healthy and to be encouraged.

It is not surprising that the concepts of transference and countertransference, interpretation, anxiety and defence, containment, internal and external worlds, and specific defences such as projection and introjection arise again and again in the text. Indeed most psychoanalytic practitioners would agree that these concepts provide the main tools for our work. In addition, particularly when working with children and young people, there is the leitmotif throughout the therapeutic process of facilitating normal emotional development, as described in the previous chapter. Indeed, Winnicott draws attention to the parallels that exist between the way in which ordinary parents provide the facilitating environment within which their children can develop emotionally, and the therapeutic relationship which facilitates emotional growth in areas where development has become stuck or has not developed adequately (Winnicott 1965, 1971).

Psychoanalytical psychotherapy does not involve specific treatment programmes for particular kinds of presenting problems as in, say, behavioural or cognitive therapy – although therapists working as part of a team may well provide psychotherapy as one part of a broad treatment plan. Psychotherapy, indeed, may be offered when another treatment has not, or has only partially, worked. Good systemic work may have produced change in the family system, but somehow one is still left with a 'stuck' child, unable to take up a more creative and developmentally appropriate position in relation to himself and his world. It becomes the task of the therapist, then, to explore with the child the sense which he makes of himself in his world, and how and why this has come to be so, based on the features of the particular relationship he establishes with the therapist.

What is it that makes a relationship 'therapeutic'?

In normal caring relationships we listen to and share time with friends and family when life offers its pains and setbacks. This wish to help and protect those we care for when they are in physical or emotional pain is a capacity which some would argue is a basic human instinct, the counterpart of the instinctual need to form attachment relationships (Bowlby 1969, 1973). On a slightly different level, the good general practitioner will, in his role as family doctor, offer to a distressed patient a listening relationship which may obviate the need to refer that patient for more specialised help. The everyday caregiving components of ordinary relationships become highly refined and further concentrated within a specialised professional therapeutic relationship.

Yet the therapeutic relationship is also very different in important respects from relationships outside the therapy room. First, it is not a reciprocal relationship: in psychoanalytically informed treatment the therapist's personal and emotional life is not shared with the patient. The therapist makes every effort to be emotionally available and thoughtfully attentive to the patient, whilst retaining this privacy. Second, it is not a spontaneously available relationship: the child patient attends, whether once or five times weekly, at a fixed appointment time on a set day for a set length of time – usually fifty minutes. Third, the location is neither home nor surgery but a special room set aside for such work as described in Chapter 8.

What is it that the psychoanalytic psychotherapist brings to the unique-ness of each therapeutic encounter? Experienced therapists develop their own individual style and 'way of being' with their patients as a result of training and clinical experience, as well as their own individual person-ality. (In addition it is a feature of the profession that supervision, consultation and discussion is sought by child psychotherapists at many stages throughout their development, even when they are senior practi-tioners.) As a result, each therapeutic encounter is the unique product of this very particular meeting of the mind and emotions of therapist and patient. The only 'equipment' (apart from the toys that aid communica-tion for the child) is the therapist's emotional receptivity and ability to maintain a space for thinking about what is being communicated by the patient and what is being experienced within the session. Additionally, the ACP has a code of ethics which protects members of the public from incompetent or unethical practice. In many respects the difficulties and demands of the lengthy psychoanalytic training, usually at least five years of post-graduate study, result in all trainees' work and personal qualities being very well known by senior members of the profession before qualification, so that any difficulties are likely to be noticed and appropriately dealt with during training. We make these points because psychoanalytic work relies so heavily on the interaction between therapist and patient.

Some discussion of the importance of all psychoanalytic psychotherapists undergoing a training analysis as an intrinsic part of their training is relevant here. All psychoanalytic trainings require that trainees undergo psychoanalysis four- or five-times-weekly (exceptionally three times a week) with an approved training analyst throughout the period of time that they are in training. In practice, analysis may have started well before commen-cing training and may continue for a considerable time after it ends. This lengthy period of personal psychoanalysis means that the therapist should come to know his or her own internal world in depth and detail, recognising characteristic emotional responses and ways of relating to others. Indeed, a training psychoanalysis became a training requirement as a result of the early psychoanalysts' recognition of how their own internal worlds could affect their perceptions and understanding of their patients' internal worlds and relationships. Such requirement was first agreed at the Budapest Congress of the International Psychoanalytical Association in 1918 (King and Steiner 1991: 14).

Key concepts

The basic assumption of all psychoanalytic work is the concept of the unconscious, 'that part of the mind which is inaccessible to the conscious mind but which affects behaviour and emotions' (Concise Oxford Diction-ary). Indeed psychoanalysis is defined in the same dictionary as 'a therapeutic method of treating mental disorders by investigating the interaction of conscious and unconscious elements in the mind and bringing repressed fears and conflicts into the conscious mind'. Although separating out the components of the therapeutic relationship and process may seem a somewhat artificial device, it is important to be clear about them because they offer an interlinking framework for understanding in the therapist's mind. Particular concepts will have more significance in work with certain patients than with others.

Ideas about the way in which the therapeutic relationship and process operate have been discussed, debated and developed, often with great heat (King and Steiner 1991), since Freud first realised that the transference relationship, rather than being a nuisance factor that got in the way of what he was trying to communicate to his patients, was in fact the essence of therapeutic work. The process of development through debate, indeed, is vital in any field where thought is not to become a creed: just as practice, technique and theory evolve within professions like teaching and medicine, so too do they continue to evolve within psychoanalysis.

The transference–countertransference relationship

The child's sense of who he is and how others will react to him is very much affected by expectations based on his past and present family relationships. It is the 'transferring' of these expectations onto the new relationship with the therapist which constitutes the transference–countertransference relationship (often abbreviated to the 'transference relationship'). In some ways the transference relationship becomes rather like a representative sample of the child's ways of relating to those who are important to him. As a result of this, specific anxieties and painful conflicts come alive and can be worked with, in the first instance, within the contained context of the transference relationship. The emotional changes resulting from the working through of these issues gradually become more generalised and a part of the child's repertoire in everyday relationships. The child's fantasies and imaginings about the therapist as a person are the medium through which past and present relationships are transferred into the therapeutic relationship. If, for example, the therapist gives personal information too readily, some of this transference may be forestalled and the scope for exploring the child's ideas, fantasies and expectations limited.

All patients can at times feel that their therapist is too impersonal, and may accuse the therapist of 'not caring' or 'only doing it for the money'; but if the therapist's way of being with the patient is one of compassionate attentive listening, these accusations can be understood as containing important information about the way in which the patient experiences many people – that is, as not really caring about them or being interested in them, or only being interested because this meets their own needs.

The countertransference is the therapist's response to the transferred aspects of the patient's ways of relating – that is, the feelings aroused in the therapist by this, as opposed to the therapist's own customary way of being. The particular qualities of the transference–countertransference relationship help the therapist to know more about the patient's fantasies, relationships, functioning and expectations in the past (as well as the present). There can also be aspects of countertransference that indicate mostly unconscious personal difficulties and blind spots of the therapist – hence the need for a lengthy and in-depth personal training analysis, to enable the therapist to separate out what belongs to the patient's communication and what to the therapist.

There are many different aspects to these transferred relationships. Possibly the most important distinctions are between the *positive and negative transference*. As these terms imply, the positive transference embodies those friendly, loving, trusting feelings which enable the patient to feel invested in the therapeutic process and come to his sessions, even when the sessions are painful and distressing. The negative transference contains feelings such as anger, hatred, rejection, envy and mistrust, which may make the patient feel at times that he hates the therapist who is experienced as causing all the misery that he feels in his life.

The *infantile transference* is a way of describing those aspects of relationships that have remained active in the patient from infancy. The understanding of how these relationships, internalised during infancy, can still operate powerfully in the patient's everyday life is one of the most important aspects of the transference to be understood and interpreted before internal change can take place.

In addition, many other aspects of ordinary developmental processes come alive within the therapeutic relationship, both as a part of the ongoing development of the child during treatment, and as a result of past developmental conflicts being expressed within the transference relationship. Oedipal conflicts, to take one example, may be expressed through intense jealousy and sensitivity in the patient about the fantasised adult sexual relationships of the therapist. The child may feel this particularly when there are holiday breaks in therapy, when the therapist may be imagined to be totally involved in a sexual and emotional relationship with a partner without a thought or care for the child patient. Sibling rivalry may similarly be expressed through painful feelings of jealousy and envy towards other patients or the fantasised children of the therapist. Similarly, a patchy pattern of attendance at therapy sessions, in which helpful and fruitful sessions are interspersed with sessions missed without explanation, may express the ordinary adolescent need to develop independence and a separateness from parental figures, as well as the adolescent tendency to act rather than verbalise.

It is important to bear in mind that, alongside the transference relationship, there will always be to some degree a 'real relationship' with the therapist. The therapeutic relationship encompasses both the transferred relationships of the past, and this 'real relationship' of the present. It is the gradual realisation in the patient, in his external reality, that past relationships are not always repeated in the present which is part of the untangling process. This fluctuates, depending on how ill the patient may be or how intense the transference relationship is at any particular point in time.

When working with children the real relationship is particularly apparent when, for example, one has to help a small child in going to the toilet or stop an angry older child from being physically violent. In addition, the therapist may need to be actively involved in management issues that support the child's therapy – such as attending meetings or being available to the parents in a thoughtful way.

It must be emphasised that, whilst the relationship with the therapist is likely to become extremely important to the child for all the reasons described in this chapter, the relationship is not intended in any way to undervalue or become rivalrous with the child's relationships with his parents. The therapist is not trying to be a 'better parent' to the child than the parents themselves are, although at times parents who are feeling demoralised may express this view. These feelings need to be known about and recognised by the therapist, not only to disentangle possible misapprehensions, but also because they may indicate that the child is splitting his feelings into idealising the therapist whilst denigrating the parents – a form of primitive psychological defence which needs to be tackled and understood as relating to the child's difficulty in facing the fact that those closest to him can be both 'good' and 'bad', and loved and hated at times. Working towards the developmental and therapeutic achievement of being able fully to express positive and negative feelings towards loved ones, and to make reparation when loved ones have been hurt by negative actions and feelings (known as the 'depressive position' in Kleinian thinking (Klein 1952) or the 'capacity for concern' by Winnicott (1963)) is a very important part of the process in a child's therapy.

Similar mechanisms of splitting and projection can operate within the staff group in multi-professional teams making it very necessary at times to keep in mind the child's transference to the entire clinic. Thus all team members need to be aware of these processes at work – and at times the dangers of splitting (for example the 'good, kind receptionist' contrasted with the 'bad, uncaring therapist') that relate to the overwhelming feelings which the child unconsciously projects into the clinic team, sometimes destructively and at other times in the hope of being understood. Recognition and discussion of the team conflicts thus engendered, which can be an externalisation of the child's internal conflicts, leads to further understanding that can aid the therapist in containing the child's anxieties and conflicts.

Anxieties and defences

Psychoanalytic therapy can be painful when distressing feelings become alive within the therapeutic relationship. Nevertheless, children come to value the personalised attention and thought that their therapy provides, even though entering this therapeutic space raises many anxieties and discomforts as well as many characteristic defences. The dynamic interplay and conflict between *anxieties* and *defences* needs to be experienced within the therapeutic relationship so that it can be witnessed and thought about first-hand by the therapist and patient as it occurs in the session, as well as explored in the patient's relationships in everyday life.

The problem of how to deal with anxiety – the fantasised or real threat of some form of loss, or otherwise deeply feared experience – is central to the concept of neurosis. This is a complex issue, and indeed Freud offered different formulations about anxieties and defences at different phases of his career (Freud S. 1894, 1917, 1926). The way in which clinicians think about and work with anxieties and defences depends considerably on their theoretical backgrounds and clinical experience. For example, in Freudian theory anxieties and conflicts relating in the main to aggressive or sexual feelings can lead to the use of defences such as repression, regression, displacement, identification with the aggressor and idealisation, to name but a few. From a Kleinian perspective, clinicians are more likely to think in terms of the defences of splitting and projective identification, particularly in the paranoid-schizoid position, and manic and omnipotent defences, together with reparation in the depressive position (see Chapter 2). The central human dilemma of how to express love and hate within close relationships is the essential source of conflict, with the inherent need to find ways of restraining destructive aggressive or sexual feelings at its core.

In addition, arising from the first days of life when the capacity to form relationships is rudimentary, there are the very primitive and early fears of abandonment, annihilation, disintegration and merging – all fears about the survival of the infant self. As will be apparent in the clinical examples in this handbook, in practice there is little evidence of theoretical demarcation lines and many child and adolescent psychotherapists use their knowledge of different theoretical perspectives to provide as broad an understanding as possible of the anxieties and defences that they encounter in their patients.

In ordinary life we all learn mechanisms of coping with anxiety (that is, defences) and these hopefully become more adaptive and flexible as we grow. Particularly for the infant and child, however, anxieties of a primitive and, at times, terrifying nature need the helpful presence of an attentive adult if they are not to become overwhelming. Night terrors are a prime example, known to most families with toddlers; separation anxiety in its various forms is another.

However, anxieties are also a very important part of life, giving realistic warnings when there is physical or emotional danger, as well as giving the kinds of 'false alarms' which are so characteristic of anxiety driven by unconscious forces. In the latter case, which is typical of neurotic anxiety, the sufferer can be highly aware of the irrationality of the fears that he or she cannot consciously control, such as phobic anxiety of spiders, lifts or heights. The interaction between the way in which ordinary anxieties have been contained or exacerbated by parents and carers as a child grows up, as well as the presence or absence of real anxiety provoking situations – such as, for example, severe childhood illness, physical or sexual abuse, or actual loss of an attachment figure – are likely to affect how anxious a person becomes in life and how they try to cope with these anxieties. (For further introductory discussion of these concepts, see Brown and Pedder (1991) and Trowell (1995).)

Defences are developed and utilised by the ego (the functioning psychological self) to protect itself at times of anxiety. For example, one of the features of the primary-school-aged child is the development of appropriate defences which enable the Oedipal drama to be left behind and the acquisition of control and competence to proceed. Without defences, we are vulnerable in our interactions with others and may respond inappropriately or be hurt very readily (Freud, A. 1936; Klein 1952).

At times of intense fear or anxiety, we all use the most effective defences available to us. A legacy of earlier and therefore primitive defences, however, leaves the child with a repertoire which can be less effective or even destructive to other parts of the personality. As time goes on, these same defences can become less effective or even destructive to other more developed parts of the personality and yet, because they have been so helpful in the past as a protection against anxiety, they may be held on to quite fiercely. This may be despite the fact that the child has other more sophisticated and less self-destructive means of protecting him or herself emotionally.

When working with the defences in therapy there are two aims: to explore the defences that are neither age-appropriate nor helpful and to increase the range of defences available to the patient for coping with unbearable anxiety or emotional pain. In addition, the anxiety in all its irrationality needs to be faced gradually, without raising further defences. This becomes possible through the medium of the therapeutic relationship in which the therapist stays with the patient in articulating and facing the fears so that he is no longer on his own with them, and so that the infantile anxieties can be named and made sense of within an attentive, holding relationship. The processes of projection and introjection described later in this chapter are crucial here.

It is a matter of experience and training whether the therapist decides to try to interpret the anxiety or the defence first; indeed this may vary within the same treatment depending on how integrated the patient is and how mature the ego is at any particular stage of the treatment. Therapists can often find themselves both acknowledging to patients the existence of high levels of anxiety whilst recognising their need to maintain some levels of less appropriate defence as they do not yet feel safe enough to let these go. Particularly for very vulnerable patients, such as deprived and abused patients, defences always need to be treated with great respect as they may be the only way that the patient can hold him or herself together. If defences are tackled without this respect, breakdown, suicide and collapse may follow, or patients may feel unable to face continuing with therapy.

The process of waiting to see what deeply concerns the child can be puzzling to referring agencies who often ask, 'Have you tackled X with him?' By following the dynamic interchange between anxiety and defence within the child, psychotherapy can clear a way for later 'real world' exploration. But primitive anxieties and defences do not disappear in a brief few sessions – time and space are needed for the psychotherapeutic process to develop.

The interaction of the internal and external world

Why is it that a perception of other people as callous and uncaring can persist in the face of quite contradictory evidence? In psychoanalytic thought, this perplexing observation is understood in terms of differences between the individual's very personal experience of his *internal world* and the *external world* of experiences which can be observed by other people. The dynamic interaction between these two worlds and areas of experience is pivotal in psychoanalytic theory and practice.

The internal world is made up of several components and could be described as the place where we live most intensely within ourselves, particularly when not communicating with others. It is a private world of thoughts, fantasies and feelings, many of which we would find it very difficult to articulate to ourselves, let alone to others – inchoate half-thoughts and fleeting fragments of feelings. It is a world where ordinary social values and relationships can be suspended, where it is possible in fantasy to love or hate whomever we want with impunity. It is also a world of many layers, some more subtle than others, in which conscious thoughts and fantasies mingle with the barely conscious, as in day dreams, and where unconscious thoughts and fantasies surface in dreams in ways which can surprise and at times shock and embarrass the dreamer.

The way in which the internal world and external world interact with and affect each other is the subject of much debate in terms of the 'balance of power' that exists between them. Our external world is perceived through the eyes of the internal world filter, which in turn will have been affected by what has actually happened in our external world experience. The earlier in life that these experiences have taken place, the more powerfully but often irrationally they seem to hold sway in the internal world.

To return to the example of the patient who feels that the therapist and others in his life do not really care about him or only care as much as this suits their own needs: there may have been a time, possibly very early in the patient's life, when perhaps his mother really was emotionally unavailable to her baby and not responding well to her baby's needs. This could have been for many reasons – maternal depression, marital tension, financial worries, bereavement. It may not even have gone on for long or have been severe, but for a baby who perhaps found it particularly hard to cope with the feelings of frustration and anger, or even abandonment, arising from his mother's lack of her usual patience in trying to understand his communications, these feelings of persecution could remain long after the mother actually became emotionally available again. In other words, the baby might continue to perceive the mother as unavailable, or might have internalised the idea of an unavailable mother in his mind. He may actually have become harder to comfort as a result of this brief period of difficulty and not have been able to recover from the experience. Such a scenario can be further compounded by the mother's expectation of retribution from the infant for her emotional absence, which could be one response to her concerned guilt about her earlier unavailability. This can happen despite the reality that the 'good' mother had actually returned in the external world. The internal world and the external world can thus become very out of kilter (Klein 1952).

Some babies and young children do have an unfortunate number of negative and hostile experiences, in which case their internal worlds, if very persecuted, are in fact a fairly accurate representation of what they have experienced in the external world. Even in these instances, therapists are often amazed at the genuine fortitude, resilience and hope that some of these children demonstrate, suggesting that, despite awful life experiences, in their internal worlds they have managed to keep alive those few experiences that have been good and internalise them into their constructs of 'self'. This raises the important question of the role of the child's 'constitution' and its influence on emotional life. There is considerable debate about which factors can be considered constitutional; we would include individual differences in the capacity to tolerate frustration and express anger, to love and to hate, to feel guilty, to show gratitude (Klein 1957) and to be resilient in the face of hardship. This whole topic is very complex; we have simply tried to give a flavour of what is meant when we think about the interaction between the internal and external world and how this affects functioning and relationships.

During therapy, access to the patient's internal world is sought by the therapist through free association, dreams and, with children, through play. Freud's original dictum – when he abandoned hypnosis as a means to reach into his patient's past – was that his patients should simply say whatever came into their thoughts when they lay on the couch, making every effort to overcome embarrassment or shame about what was in their minds. This non-directive method of working is vital for the painstaking exploratory nature of psychoanalytic work, which does not attempt to lead the patient in particular directions but chooses to follow the patient's conscious and unconscious thoughts and feelings. Imaginative play offers the same insights as Freudian 'free-association' into the child's internal world.

Communication and interpretation within the therapeutic relationship

Communication between the therapist and patient is both verbal and non-verbal. The child patient talks and plays when with the therapist but may also, for example, be silent and resistant, communicating non-verbally a range of feelings by processes such as projection. In addition, many children, and particularly adolescents, will unconsciously 'stage' situations in the therapy by 'acting out' conflicts which they cannot put into words. For example, a child who cannot believe that the therapist is prepared to accept hostile as well as more friendly feelings without rejecting him may behave in a very challenging and difficult way in sessions, needing to experience that, however awfully he behaves, the therapist is still there to see him again at their next session.

The therapist is likely to respond to these various forms of communication in a variety of ways. Sometimes the therapist may make a simple comment which clarifies the meaning of the child's play – this may be as straightforward as putting a name to a feeling. At other times the therapist may be able to identify a common or recurring theme in the child's feelings or thoughts (as unconscious processes gradually come into relief in the child's conscious life) and comment on this to the child, watching to see how the child responds to this idea. In accordance with non-directive psychoanalytic technique, the emphasis is always on following the child's train of thought or feelings, not on introducing or suggesting issues that the therapist feels the child *should* be tackling, other than in very special circumstances.

The therapist starts with careful observation and reflection about the child on all levels, and, having commented on what has been observed, waits to see how the child responds in words, play or action. These comments should not be dogmatic, but offered more as something to think about that might be helpful or even interesting to the child. Developing a sense of curiosity and capacity for reflection in the child becomes an important part of the process, internalised through identification with the therapist. It is always important for the therapist to bear in mind how able the child is to listen to or understand what is being said. Naturally the language must be in tune with the child's ability to comprehend.

In addition, there can be many times in therapy when the therapist suddenly understands a particular dynamic within the child or in the child's relationships, but is aware that it is too soon to try to share this understanding with the child because it may be too painful, or raise too many anxieties and defences. Such insights have to be very carefully put to the child, sometimes almost in stages over time. Meanwhile an important first stage in understanding and interpretation has been reached in the therapist's mind. This understanding may be offered at the time to the child, but it may equally well have to lodge in the therapist's mind for a considerable time without being shared with the patient – contained by the therapist for the patient until he is able to take in and digest the idea (Bion 1962). Once again the emphasis is on *how* to communicate in such a way that the communication can be received. It can be surprising to find that there are times when the understanding remains with the therapist and is never put into words, and yet there is a significant change in the child's relationships and level of disturbance.

Interpretations made by the therapist, particularly interpretations about the transference relationship, can, if well timed, lead to real breakthroughs in therapy. However, interpretation is no longer seen as the only, or most important, way of bringing about significant change. Interpretation is the process of putting into words – making conscious and known to the patient – fantasies, aspects of relationships, anxieties, conflicts and defences, and insights into the way the patient's mind works, which previously could not be known because they were unacceptable, and thus had remained repressed in the unconscious mind. For Freud, this process of making the unconscious conscious was the main route to psychic change. Nowadays we are aware that there is often a lengthy build-up to such pivotal transference interpretations, of which there may be surprisingly few in many treatments.

This build-up includes what may be lengthy periods of the therapist containing painful feelings and thoughts projected onto them by the patient, without understanding what they are about. Tolerating *not knowing* what is happening within the therapeutic relationship may be a very important experience which the patient needs the therapist to have, as this 'not knowing' and confusion may be the state of mind that the patient finds the most impossible to deal with. Premature attempts at knowing may detract from this. Thus, when insight finally comes to the therapist and it is possible to make an interpretation to the patient, the interpretation itself is the final product of what may be weeks or even months of verbal and non-verbal communication between patient and therapist. This is what gives it its power.

With adolescents in particular, but also with children where shame may be a factor, it can be helpful to take up the anxieties *in the displacement*. Adolescents may talk of 'a friend who . . .' and may need the vehicle of 'the friend' for several weeks before they can own the anxieties disclosed as their own. The younger child may focus on 'the angry crocodile' or the abusive doll and explore the emotions in the activities of the toys before rage can be personally owned. Although the process of therapy aims for an integration and personal ownership of feelings, such strategies are useful. Equally, the therapist may differentiate the patient's infantile behaviour and feelings from his age-appropriate competencies. This can allow the patient to examine such feelings from a position which offers the possibility of control and lessens humiliation: 'that sounds like the two-year-old bit again' is more bearable and helps engage the patient's curiosity about himself. Again this can be particularly helpful when working with adolescents.

Finally, the therapist has to give thought to the timing of interventions. With verbal interpretation the child tends to let one know if this is right – although few will be like the eight-year-old who said to a psychiatric registrar of our acquaintance 'Gee, Doc – that's right!' hitting the heel of his hand to his forehead for dramatic effect. The lessening of anxiety in the room, a fleeting smile or a development in play are more usual cues. It is important for the therapist, however, to keep in mind the sometimes paradoxical impact on the child of being understood: Alvarez has commented thoughtfully on the child's need to adjust to and integrate the good experience, as well as to deal bravely with the terrifying or depriving one (Alvarez 1988). This is of particular importance when working with deprived children for whom the 'good experience' and being understood may in themselves be overwhelming for the child and need time to be internalised.

Containment and emotional holding – when words are not enough

As already indicated, interpretation and other forms of understanding are sometimes not possible when a child is in a very anxious state – whether this is driven by actual external events or a general state of mind. The child may be so highly on the defensive that the therapist's words are drowned out by the noise the child makes or by general overactivity. Or the child may be so clearly distressed and barely holding himself together that words seem woefully inadequate – or, indeed, the therapist cannot immediately find words to express the pain the child is communicating. At other times a child can express enormous anger (sometimes out of panic and anxiety) and become destructive of toys or furnishings in the room, or even attack the therapist. Adolescent patients can become deeply depressed and extremely fragile so that they feel quite unreachable.

When these kinds of feelings threaten to boil over or overwhelm the patient, the therapist is likely in the first instance to try simply to 'contain' the feelings that are experienced by the child or young person as overwhelming, before exploring ways of talking about what is being communicated. The distinguishing feature of containment as a process is that, at the same time as empathically responding to the patient in a non-judgemental and non-retaliatory way, the therapist is attempting to understand and reflect on the process of what is happening between them, by listening carefully to and accepting the patient's *projections* of intense feelings which often cannot be verbalised. This is more than an absorption of the patient's pain; it is an attempt by the therapist to use his or her mind to think about what feels almost unthinkable and to be in touch with feelings communicated by the patient that feel unbearable to the patient. This can help to bring these feelings and thoughts down to size, or at least make them gradually more tolerable. It is the way in which the therapist receives – that is, *introjects*, tolerates and survives, and tries to think about and understand these feelings – that is the key to containment. In time, the patient becomes able to own the feelings again when these have been received, modulated and, wherever possible, finally articulated by the therapist, when they can be fed back in manageable form.

This model of non-verbal communication derives from observation of and theories about communication during the earliest days of life. A mother has to be prepared to be emotionally available to her baby by attempting to understand what he needs, particularly when crying, by the same processes of projection, introjection and containment described seminally by Bion (1962). These processes are at their most intense in mother–baby interaction and are studied in depth by all child psychotherapists in the two-year observation of a baby growing up in a family, which forms a central part of their training. As any parent will testify, the power of these non-verbal communications is astonishing. The baby's cries can mobilise great emotional and practical activity in parents until they feel they have understood and responded appropriately. The baby's smile can, in just as powerful a way, wipe away hours of tiredness, anxiety and frustration in parents, helping them to feel loved and loving, and 'good-enough' as parents.

The therapist also offers confidentiality and the possibility of talking about issues that cannot be talked about elsewhere for fear of shocking, distressing or angering the listener. This is one of the more obvious ways in which the therapeutic experience provides *containment* of the patient's anxieties. For children, in particular, fear of rejection and abandonment by those they most depend on and need is common, especially where aspects of the self that they feel to be ugly, shameful and unacceptable are concerned. This fear of rejection then comes into therapy where it can be noted and thought about, rather than feared. The therapist's continued commitment to being reliably available for the patient during his regular session times, and the ways in which this interweaves with the frustrations of the other times that the therapist cannot be available, help to provide both a growing sense of containment and a growing awareness that the patient is increasingly known and accepted as he truly is – beauty spots, warts and all.

Ending therapy

When patients and therapists have been involved in such intense therapeutic relationships, often for lengthy periods of time, the question of how and when to end the therapeutic process is complex and sensitive. Ideally, the consideration of a number of criteria would inform any decision on the therapist's part about the timing of the end of a child's therapy. Amongst these are: a lessening of anxiety and less of a need to resort to extreme and self-defeating defences; the establishment of a healing process with respect to traumatic experiences; the re-establishment of appropriate emotional development including more age-appropriate functioning; an improvement in the child's relationships with family and peers; a sense of self that allows feelings to be integrated and a future to be contemplated; and, under-pinning all these achievements, an increased capacity to think about his or her feelings and the feelings of others. All of these criteria are compara-tive, not absolute, and highlight the need to think about the realistic aims of each patient's therapy.

As described later in the handbook, there are many forms and applica-tions of psychoanalytic psychotherapy offered to children, ranging from occasional consultations to intensive five-times-weekly psychotherapy. Some children with severe problems can be in therapy for a number of years. However, the norm within the public sector in the UK is likely to be once-weekly therapy for between eighteen months to two years. Where the child is well supported by his parents and family or carers, and where they have also been able to engage in therapeutic work and to develop their understanding of and responses to their child during the time of his treatment, the therapist can feel reasonably confident that the child's healthy ongoing development is well-enough established and supported within the family for therapy to end – and indeed for the parents or the child to consult with the therapist if there are difficulties at later stages of development. A date for ending therapy can then be agreed by therapist, child and parents, ideally allowing enough time for the child to experience and explore his feelings of sadness and loss about therapy coming to an end. Depending on the form of treatment, the date for ending could be many weeks or even months ahead. Again, taking the norm of once-weekly work in the public sector, a period of three to six months would allow for a thorough exploration of feelings about ending to take place. These feelings of sadness and loss, as well as possibly anger, abandonment and jealousy of new patients, can arouse further memories of past losses in the child's life. This can provide a renewed opportunity to explore past losses in the context of the anticipated loss of the therapist in the present. In addition, the planned ending of therapy offers the important experience of learning that loss and letting go can be valuable developmental experiences in their own right.

Unfortunately, there can also be times when children end therapy with-out the therapist feeling they are ready. This can be the result of practical issues in the child's life – difficulties in getting to therapy sessions because of the problems of trying to balance all the needs of the family members, or moving away from the area. Therapy can also end because funding has run out or there is disagreement between professionals about therapeutic priorities in a child's life. Although these practical issues are explored carefully at the start of treatment so that the limitations of what can be achieved are worked within, it is not always possible to anticipate the external changes which can affect a child's therapy. This can lead to what, from the therapist's and possibly the child's point of view, feels like a premature end of the therapeutic relationship. In such circumstances, the sadness and anger of premature ending have to be faced in the final therapy sessions, and therapists will struggle to have as many sessions as possible in which to try to help the child to cope with the ending of a relationship they are not ready to let go, in as positive a way as they can. Often, in these circumstances, the therapist has a very difficult task in the countertransference, not only because of the feelings expressed by the child that the therapist is abandoning them – or indeed the defensive opposite of this, that the child doesn't care about therapy ending – but also in relation to the therapist's personal anger and dismay at decisions being made which she (the therapist) feels are not in the best interests of the child.

Disagreements about when to end treatment can also arise when there has been a clear symptomatic improvement in the child's problems – for example, soiling has stopped or nightmares have ceased – but the therapist is aware that the child still has many unresolved anxieties that are being held within, and worked on in the transference relationship. The therapist's concern would be that, if the child stopped treatment at that time, the anxieties would become unmanageable again in the child's everyday life and, without treatment, the original symptoms would reoccur or new ones replace them. In other words, the process of recovery and growth started by the therapy would not yet be able to continue on its own when therapy ended. This is one of the risks when treatment in the public sector is defined by budgets rather than the individual child's needs; in such instances, it is rather like trying to 'fit a gallon into a pint pot' or only taking half the course of prescribed antibiotics. The consideration of the need to consolidate and 'work through' important psychic changes, so that they become a deeply established part of the patient's personality, affects the therapist's views about the timing of termination of therapy.

The ending of therapy is also a real separation and loss of the new relationship with the therapist. The way in which the child approaches this real loss is likely to emerge in many ways in the sessions leading up to a planned ending. Just as, throughout therapy, the child's ability to cope with breaks between sessions and holiday gaps in treatment can reflect the ways in which the child is internalising the therapeutic process, so the approach to the end of therapy gives an indication of how much of the therapeutic experience the child will carry within himself when he no longer comes for his therapy sessions. This partly relates to very clear memories of what has been said and shared between the child and therapist, but, more importantly, it relates to the change within the child's internal world that has taken place during the course of treatment. The child may simply express this in terms of feeling happier, more relaxed and 'different' or 'better' than when the treatment started.

There are varied views about what kind of contact is appropriate between therapist and child when regular therapy has ended treatment. Certainly some form of follow-up meeting is often offered a few months after ending treatment.

Some patients and their families want to keep in touch, and others do not. It is important for children to feel that the therapist has not forgotten all about them, even if they choose not to come to a follow-up session because therapy already feels such a thing of the past. Some children or their parents keep in touch with the therapist for many years – possibly by an occasional letter or phone call. The very individual nature of each therapy and each ending, combined with the increasing need to provide research evaluation studies on psychoanalytic psychotherapy, has led to much more thought being given in the profession to the post-therapy relationship between therapist and child: what is helpful for the child needs to be balanced with what is helpful in research terms.

It is important to note that, whilst the last sessions of a child's therapy can be poignant for child and therapist, there is of course also a real achievement for the child in being ready to move on from therapy and start a new chapter in his or her life. It is a truism to say that, in order to move on and forward in life, it is necessary to let go of experiences and relationships that are no longer necessary. In many ways, at the end of therapy, when all has gone well, the child has outgrown the need for therapy at that stage of his life and is ready to move on. This is the very nature of emotional development. In some respects, the therapist could be thought of as being used rather like the special teddy or blanket that many children are so deeply attached to in early childhood and which is imbued with a rich and varied fantasy life (Winnicott's transitional object, Winnicott 1971). At the height of its powers, the child cannot be parted from the transitional object, yet, as life moves on, it gradually fades in importance. Years on, the previously treasured transitional object is remembered with fondness, and sometimes amazement or even embarrassment that it once meant so much to the child. It has simply been outgrown and is no longer needed. Although ending therapy is hard, the therapist must be seen in this context – as a very important figure in the child's life at the height of the therapeutic relationship, but inevitably to be left behind when his purpose has been served and therapy ends.

References

Alvarez, A. (1988) 'Beyond the unpleasure principle: some preconditions for thinking through play', *Journal of Child Psychotherapy* 14(2): 1–13.

Bion, W. (1962) *Learning from Experience*, London: Heinemann.

Bowlby, J. (1969) *Attachment and Loss, Vol. 1: Attachment*, London: Hogarth Press.

—— (1973) *Attachment and Loss, Vol. II: Separation, Anxiety and Anger*, London: Hogarth Press.

—— (1988) *A Secure Base: Clinical Applications of Attachment Theory*, London: Routledge.

Brown, D. and Pedder, J. (1991) 'Psychodynamic principles', in D. Brown and J. Pedder *Introduction to Psychotherapy*, 2nd edn, London: Routledge.

Freud, A. (1936) *The Ego and the Mechanisms of Defence*, Rev. edn, London: Hogarth Press/Institute of Psycho-Analysis.

Freud, S. (1894) *The Neuro-Psychoses of Defence (1)*: *Complete Works of Sigmund Freud*, *SE* vol. 3, London: Hogarth Press/Institute of Psychoanalysis.

—— (1917) 'Mourning and Melancholia', in *SE*, Vol. 14.

—— (1926) *Inhibitions, Symptoms and Anxiety*, *SE*, Vol. 20.

King, P. and Steiner, R. (eds) (1991) *The Freud–Klein Controversies 1941–45*, London: Tavistock/Routledge.

Klein, M. (1952) 'Some theoretical conclusions regarding the emotional life of the infant', in J. Riviere (ed.) *Developments in Psychoanalysis*, London: Hogarth.

—— (1957) *Envy and Gratitude*, London: Tavistock. (Reprinted 1975 in *The Writings of Melanie Klein. Volume 3: Envy and Gratitude*, London: Hogarth.)

Trowell, J. (1995) 'Key psychoanalytic concepts', in J. Trowell and M. Bower (eds) *The Emotional Needs of Children and their Families*, London: Routledge.

Winnicott, D. W. (1963) 'The development of the capacity for concern', in D. W. Winnicott *The Maturational Processes and the Facilitating Environment*, London: Hogarth Press, 1965.

—— (1965) *The Maturational Processes and the Facilitating Environment*, London: Hogarth Press/Institute of Psycho-Analysis.

—— (1971) *Playing and Reality*, Harmondsworth: Penguin.

Further reading

Brown, D. and Pedder, J. (1991) 'Psychodynamic principles', in D. Brown and J. Pedder *Introduction to Psychotherapy*, 2nd edn, London: Routledge.

Sandler, J., Dare, C. and Holder, A. (1973) *The Patient and the Analyst: The Basis of Psychoanalytic Process*, London: Allen and Unwin.

Sandler, J., Kennedy, H. and Tyson, R. (1980) *The Technique of Child Analysis: Discussions with Anna Freud*, London: Hogarth.

Segal, H. (1986) *Introduction to the Work of Melanie Klein*, London: Hogarth Press.

Trowell, J. (1995) 'Key psychoanalytic concepts', in J. Trowell and M. Bower (eds) *The Emotional Needs of Children and their Families*, London: Routledge.

6   Some intercultural issues in the therapeutic process

Chriso Andreou

Child and adolescent psychotherapists today are much more aware of the importance in emotional life of the different cultures their patients and themselves come from, than they were in the past. In parts of Great Britain, and particularly in London, there is a tremendous social mix of cultures – including Afro-Caribbean, Arabic, Bosnian, French, Greek, Indian, Irish, Italian, Jewish, Muslim, Nigerian, Somali – each of these cultures bringing their own traditions, customs and histories with them when they come to Great Britain. As immigrants, their histories may be full of terrible experiences of war, torture, loss and oppression. Others have come to Great Britain for better work and educational opportunities than they would have had 'at home'. Some have found true refuge, safety and prosperity in their new home. Others find that they must face daily prejudice because of their colour. Some find that they can make important contributions to British society, with many opportunities open to them on their personal merit, others find the same doors to opportunity firmly closed because of prejudice.

In addition, when the family's immigration experience was in past generations, the complexities of how the new generations integrate their cultural heritage with the customs of their host country, and the balance that they strike between assimilation and keeping their cultural identity, can become the source of tremendous conflict within families, particularly during the adolescent years. When, for example, a Greek family, or an Afro-Caribbean family are in need of help for a child or teenager, where should they go? They may wonder whether a therapist who is not of their culture can fully understand their problem and, in addition, there may be significant language problems where English is the second language. They may fear covert racism in the therapist – particularly if that is their daily experience elsewhere. These are very complex issues which need to be a conscious aspect of any therapeutic encounter between therapist and child-family where there are obviously different cultural and racial backgrounds. The clinic and therapist may be in the patients' mind, the same as the racist world outside, hostile and critical of them.

Because of the difficulties of these issues, there are now a number of counselling and therapy centres that specialise in treating members of particular communities – often with therapists of the same cultural background on their staff. There are, for example, some specialist centres specifically for black children in care, where only black workers are employed to encourage a positive black identity. There are Jewish counselling services where traumatisation related to the Holocaust is understood as part of the presenting problems of many families – the second and third generation being affected in their own ways, but all living with the impact of anti-Semitism on their family. There are specialist Catholic services . . . and so on. For many people, engaging in a psychotherapeutic encounter with a therapist from the same culture can be very valuable. Since much that would otherwise need to be explained can be taken for granted and a trusting therapeutic relationship may be established more readily. However, there can also be pitfalls in these assumptions, and it would be unfortunate and severely limiting if this view of how to tackle intercultural issues in therapy were the only one.

For example, for the therapist who is working with people from his or her own background there is sometimes a pressure not to break ranks in case they will seem to be, and may even feel themselves to be, traitors to their own people. A family may choose to see a therapist from their own culture in the unconcious hope that this will mean that they will not be challenged in areas where, for example, paranoid fantasies are intertwined with real persecution. The therapist may find him or herself colluding with unduly paranoid perceptions of a hostile outside world, instead of exploring the internal world and family relationships of the patient with which the possibly exaggerated view of the outside world interacts. This pressure to collude can be very strong as there may well be some reality-based identification with the patient's problems which may cloud the therapist's judgement when thinking about the transference–countertransference relationship.

Two case illustrations

A six-year-old Greek Cypriot boy was referred to me because other efforts to engage the family in treatment had failed and it was hoped that a therapist from his culture might be more acceptable. He was very disruptive in class and the school had exhausted all their usual efforts to help him. The situation had reached a crisis and he was hitting and kicking other children for no apparent reason. When asked why he was doing this, he said he was just protecting himself. When I met the parents, they were angry and upset, saying their son was very good at home and they couldn't recognise the school's description of him. The only problem they could see was that he kept telling them that he could see monsters in his room and would wake up with nightmares. They had taken him to see someone in the community to 'take the fear away from him' but, although he was all right for a week, the nightmares had returned. They now just hoped that he would grow out of this.

One could see that although the parents were in touch with the fact that their son was troubled and frightened, they did not see it as a disturbance coming from within the boy, but as something which had been put into him by someone with an 'evil eye'. This is a cultural issue and is very difficult to question, particularly at the start of a therapeutic contact.

When I asked the parents why they thought the teachers were so worried about their son, the father suddenly became very angry with me, shouting and accusing me of being just like the teachers and not wanting to help him. He felt I just believed what the teachers said, and that it was all the fault of the school because they were not good at discipline. He felt that the English schools were no good, and that there was nothing wrong with his son. The teachers simply did not like him and the family because they were foreigners. I think that by asking the parents what they thought the teachers were worried about, I broke the illusion that I was one of them. Dispelling this collusion brought out the father's perceptions of the school, the teachers as being racist and his feeling that his son was a victim of his teacher's racism. If a person thinks that an institution is racist, whether this is true or not, it has to be acknowledged and talked about, because racism is a reality for many people in a multi-cultural society, and these suspicions must therefore be taken seriously if any kind of therapeutic alliance is to be formed.

The mother then started to talk about how the teachers frightened her and she did not know what to think any more. The teachers said that her son was fighting and hurting other children, but he came home with bruises saying other boys had beaten him up. Maybe this was what was causing his nightmares. I was able to talk to her about how confused and hurt she was feeling and also how criticised she felt as a mother by the teachers. This related to how she would feel if I saw her son – would I also criticise her as a mother. These very difficult dynamics, based on the family's real experiences of being 'foreign', needed to be wisely disentangled from the boy's anxieties, which the parents could recognise in his nightmares and fears. Otherwise, the cycle of mis-understanding that had set in, with fears of racism interacting with feelings of persecution which are common to all human beings at times, was likely to escalate. In the midst of all this was a troubled child in school who clearly needed help, but who was getting more and more confused and angry at what he perceived to be the very mixed messages he was receiving from his teachers and family.

By contrast, some specialised therapy centres choose to be less culture specific, concentrating on establishing a reputation for cross-cultural psychotherapy where cultural and racial factors will be taken into consideration. The ways in which these factors can be taken into consideration in therapy are complex, subtle and, at times, very prone to misinterpretation. There are no clear formulae and there is a pressing need for the therapists to be able to unpick the interrelationship between emotional distress resulting from individual/family dysfunction that would be individual/family dysfunction in any culture, and cultural issues that are specific to that particular cultural group.

Present-day trends in conceptualising personal and social difficulties can at times become confusing for therapists in their efforts to work cross-culturally. For example, sometimes simplistic sociological explanations can be used to understand behaviour without understanding how, in order to avoid mental pain and conflict, human beings of all cultures adopt various defensive mechanisms. This is not to imply that social and cultural factors are unimportant, nor to diminish in any way the great need to explore the way in which our values and culture predispose our way of thinking. It is not an intellectual luxury for professionals to include cross-cultural considerations in their work – it is essential. All therapists, whether working in special cultural treatment services or in general NHS or social services settings, need to be aware of the cross-cultural currents in their work.

Racial and cultural differences between the therapist and patient involve issues of unconscious meanings at many levels, and at times this can activate very primitive defences in patients and therapists. This must be recognised and utilised in therapy. There are serious hazards in overestimating or ignoring them. To ignore them is to avoid a large part of the patient's and the therapist's everyday reality. To be over interested in them can represent an effort to deny and negate other deeper intrapsychic conflict.

Very often for children and adolescents the question of identification is a continuous shift between their own culture and the main culture where they have been bought up. Often they are able to accommodate this shift. When there is an interpsychic conflict things are not straightforward, as for example, in the case of Nela.

Nela was referred by her General Practitioner. The referral simply stated 'Please see this sixteen-year-old girl who appears to be depressed and is asking to see a psychotherapist'.

The therapist's initial impression of Nela was of a pretty Asian girl who appeared to be very self-composed. She spoke with a flat emotionless voice, her eyes sad and diverted from the therapist, and articulated how she perceived her problems and the root of their cause.

I have an English surname but I am not English. I was adopted when I was eleven. My father and mother have always been good to me and I don't want to do anything to hurt them but they are not my real parents. My real parients don't want to know me, nobody in my family did . . . well, not after I was beaten by my father very badly and I was taken into care. He beat me because he said I was bad – a liar. I said my uncle sexually abused me to my mother. When I was in the children's home nobody came to see me. My mother came once. She said she was coming back but she never did.

I thought I had forgotten what happened, the abuse I mean. I mean I get frightened again for no reason and I want to run away and leave home. I feel all alone then. I get angry when they keep asking me what's wrong. My adoptive mother keeps telling me she loves me; that makes me feel guilty. Sometimes when I see an Indian woman in the street for a moment I think it's my real mother. I panic and I run.

Transracially adopted children, such as Nela, who have once lived with parents they no longer have and now live with parents who are not their biological parents, have not only migrated from one family to another, but also from one race and culture to another. Like Nela, they bring with them memories and traumas of their past that, in some cases – as in hers – remain intrapsychically unresolved. She told her therapist that she was seven years old when she was received into care – old enough to remember her biological parents and extended family and to have internalised aspects of her culture and its values and suffer from their loss.

During the second and third sessions, she spoke in more detail about the continuous flashbacks of her sexual abuse and her sense of abandonment and grievance against her biological parents. It also became evident that she was very attached to her adopted parents and expressed her love and gratitude to them. She felt horror at the negative feelings she harboured towards them at times and the voice inside her that kept telling her to leave them. She was academically gifted but was finding it increasingly difficult to concentrate on her work and at times felt too depressed to go to school.

Concluding remarks

There is a vast literature on the impact of racist attitudes on modern society. The complexity and subtlety of how this affects intercultural therapy, and indeed therapy where therapist and patient are from the same social community, has been outlined in this chapter and needs to be present in the larger therapeutic context of this handbook. When the reality of racism and prejudice can be talked about in the consulting room, black youngsters, for example, become able to describe the impact that racism has on their state of mind. One aggressive and unhappy youngster said, 'You know, racism can drive you mad'. Another challenged his white therapist saying, 'How would you feel if each time someone looked at you, you could see that they were scared you were going to mug them?' Thought about the impact of such everyday experiences on the internal world of children and young people has to be part of any psychotherapeutic relationship in which cultural issues are significant.

People who are clearly different in their culture to the larger community that they live in, are often the receptacles of all the negative, unwanted and unacceptable feelings of the larger community. They can become perceived as 'non-persons' and become hated by some sections of the community quite simply because of the colour of their skin, or their unfamiliar social customs and language. To be hated for no reason other than this can have profound effects on developing minds.

Acknowledgements

I would like to thank Koulla Mikellides and Monica Lanyado for their help in preparing this chapter.

Further reading

Adams, V. A. (1996) *The Multicultural Imagination, Race, Colour and the Unconscious*, London/New York: Routledge.

Curry, A. (1964) *Myth, Transference and the Black Psychotherapist*, International Review of Psychoanalysis 1945.

Fanon, F. (1967) *Black Skins, White Masks*, New York: Grove.

Frosh, S. (1989) 'Psychoanalysis and racism', in B. Richards *Crisis of the Self: Further Essays on Psychoanalysis and Politics*, London: Free Association Books.

Grinberg, I. and Grinberg, R. (1989) *Psychoanalytic Perspectives on Migration and Exile*, New Haven: Yale University Press.

'Inter-cultural social work and psychotherapy', *Journal of Social Work Practice* 3(3) November 1988.

Kakar, S. (1985) 'Psychoanalysis and non-western cultures', *International Rev. of Psychoanalysis* 12: 441–8.

Kareem, J. and Littlewood, R. (eds) (1992) *Intercultural Therapy: Themes, Interpretations and Practice*, Oxford: Blackwell Scientific.

McGoldrick, M., Pearce, J. K. and Giordano, J. (eds) (1982) *Ethnicity and Family Therapy*, London: Guilford.

Stein, H. F. (1987) *From Metaphor to Meaning: Papers in Psychoanalytic Anthropology*, Charlottesville: University Press Virgina.

7 The child and adolescent psychotherapist and the family

(a) The family context

Juliet Hopkins

The decision to refer a child for psychological help is usually taken within the family. The cultural values of each family may determine what sort of childhood difficulties are considered serious enough to merit intervention. These values may also determine whether intervention is primarily welcomed, resented or feared. In order to seek a referral, a child's problem must first be faced and the need for psychological help accepted; this usually means that some significant communication has taken place within the family, leading to determination to make a change, which the referral represents. It is this development in family dynamics which probably accounts for the common finding that a child's problems have somewhat diminished between the decision to refer and the child's arrival at the clinic. Such a remission, even if only partial and temporary, illustrates how sensitively a child's problems can respond to changes in the family climate.

Because the family context is crucial in determining a child's attitude towards psychological help, an increasing number of child psychotherapists like to meet the whole family together as part of the initial assessment. Family meetings not only provide a useful opportunity to discuss the whole family's attitude towards referral, but are also usually a more reliable way of learning about family relationships than anything the parents or children can individually report. Such meetings frequently prove to be the first occasion that all the family members have been able to pursue a sustained discussion of their difficulties. Often the family gains immediately from becoming enabled to broach painful or even taboo topics, which, once openly voiced, can continue to be discussed at home. Thinking about the history of the children, and sometimes of the parents too, may lead to the recognition of disturbing events whose pathogenic significance may previously have been overlooked. Siblings of the referred child are usually glad to be present, to understand what is going on, to contribute their opinions and, if necessary, to be included in further plans for help.

When a psychological assessment includes the possibility of a child being offered individual psychotherapy, the child psychotherapist will plan to meet the child alone on one or more occasions. These individual meetings provide an opportunity for the therapist to understand some aspects of the child's internal world, his pre-dominant pattern of relationships, his out-standing anxieties and his means of coping with them. Family meetings help to illuminate what sort of experiences, past and present, within and without the family, have contributed to the child's particular difficulties and may be maintaining them. Sometimes, it emerges that these difficulties were a function of conflicts which are spontaneously resolved by the assessment meetings, so that no further help is needed.

Case example: Emma

Emma, aged six years, was referred for daytime wetting at home and at school; she had had this symptom for about a year. Emma had a younger brother, Tom, aged four years. Her older sister, Cicely, had died six months previously at the age of nine years, after a year's illness with a brain tumour. In the first family meeting at the clinic, the parents described how they were still 'in shock' about their loss. They realised that Emma's wetting had begun soon after the serious-ness of Cicely's illness was recognised. They explained how they had kept their pain and grief to themselves in order to protect Emma and Tom from their loss. With support from the therapist, Emma and Tom became able to voice their feelings about their loss too. Emma angrily protested that her parents had kept her away from the hospital when Cicely was dying and Tom muttered that his parents 'only love Cicely'. Emma burst into tears. After she had been comforted by her mother, Tom created an attention-seeking diversion by climbing onto the window sill. Both parents became aware that their children had felt rejected by their protection of them and by their private preoccupation with their own grief. Their children had never seen them cry. Emma had become withdrawn, while Tom had become aggressive and attention-seeking. In the course of family meetings, the whole family's response to their loss was voiced and shared. They left feeling united in their mourning which no longer pervaded the whole of the parents' lives. Emma's wetting stopped after the first meeting and did not recur.

Another possible outcome of a family assessment may be a decision to offer help primarily to one or both parents rather than to the referred child.

Case example: Rory

Mr and Mrs S referred their six-year-old son, Rory, because he was aggressive and hyperactive at home, though not at school. They said that they had never felt able to have another child because they were so exhausted by his behaviour. During the family assessment meetings, it was observed that Rory could be quiet and self-contained as long as his parents were in harmony, but he became restless, irritable and attention-seeking as soon as there was the slightest friction or dis-agreement between them. Although Rory was not consciously aware of any reasons for his annoying behaviour, it soon became clear that it had the predictable effect of uniting his parents against him. His problem behaviour seemed to perform the function of preserving his parents' marriage while expressing his anger at their rows and testing the limits of his capacity to break up the home. Mr and Mrs S admitted that they constantly threatened to leave each other but felt bound to stay together because neither of them could manage Rory alone. Family meetings helped them all to recognise that Rory's problem behaviour was linked to the parents' own difficulties. Mr and Mrs S decided to seek couple-counselling and reported that Rory's behaviour steadily improved.

Unfortunately, most referred problems are not easily resolved and a choice may need to be made between continuing family meetings or offering individual therapy to the referred child and possibly to the parent(s). Child psychotherapists have not traditionally carried out long-term family work, and although this situation is changing, in many clinics, long-term family work will be undertaken by a specialist family therapist, or by a child psychotherapist in conjunction with a colleague. Family therapy is often the treatment of choice when the whole family has undergone the same crisis or trauma, such as bereavement or immigration. It is also the natural approach with toddlers and pre-school children who are too young to separate easily from their parents. In addition, it may sometimes be the only approach available to offer teenagers whose behaviour may be causing their parents great distress, but who have no awareness of personal difficulties themselves; adolescents like this may agree to come with their family because they believe the problem to be their parents. And finally, family therapy is usually the initial treatment of choice when children are deeply enmeshed in family relationships or are so omnipotently controlling that their parents need to be helped to bring them down to size before individual therapy can begin.

Case example: Patrick

Patrick was fifteen years old when he stopped going regularly to school and often spent his days at home, listening to music and playing his guitar. On the advice of the school's educational psychologist, his worried mother referred him for psychological help. However, Patrick resolutely insisted that there was no point in attending the clinic since there was no point in going to school. His father, who lived separately following his divorce from Patrick's mother, refused to be involved and Patrick's older brother, John, did not know whether to encourage Patrick to attend the clinic or not. Patrick's mother went to the clinic alone where it was suggested that Patrick might attend if he and John were both invited to come with her in order to discuss, not Patrick's problems, but his mother's worries. Patrick agreed. In the four family meetings which followed, it emerged that both boys felt burdened with the needs of their father, who was living alone, unemployed and drinking heavily. John had recently refused to visit his father any more, leaving Patrick to bear the worry alone. Patrick had not even allowed himself to know how worried and depressed he felt about his father, but found himself staying at home as his father did, feeling that life was pointless. Father refused to come to the clinic and although his worrying situation did not change, the family meetings provided Patrick with sufficient support to face his anger and grief about his own and his father's situation. He returned to school and refused an offer of individual therapy, saying that he would prefer to continue with occasional family meetings.

The family work presented in these three case examples was undertaken by a child psychotherapist. Such work is primarily psychodynamic in approach and does not normally aim to give advice or to set the family tasks. As in individual therapy, the aim is to provide a safe and reliable setting with definite boundaries in which it is possible to feel increasingly secure. Within this setting, the therapist aims to provide what is termed 'containment'. This is a dual process in which the therapist has to tolerate and contain her own anxiety and frustration, as well as the family's, and to wait until she can see how to verbalise her experience of the family's conflicts in ways that make them bearable to acknowledge and so to think about. As also happens in individual therapy, the therapist monitors the family's feelings about herself and the clinic, and may need to explore this aspect of the transference with them, especially if the family feels blamed or threatened.

There are also, of course, major ways in which family therapy differs from individual therapy, most notably in the opportunity it offers to work directly with family relationships and, in particular, to study transference as it occurs between generations. Inter-generational transference is evident when parents are seen to project onto their children unrealistic attributions and expectations which derive from their own past experience with their families of origin. Parents commonly identify themselves too closely with their children, assuming them to have the same needs or attitudes as they had themselves, but more subtly may identify their own children with their parents and so repeat a childhood relationship by putting their own child in their parent's place. Mr S did this when he experienced Rory as constantly showing him up and making him feel inadequate as his own father had done to him. In the course of couple work, when Mr S was enabled to see how he expected and unwittingly invited Rory to treat him as his father had done, he was able to free himself from this repetition and to become more confident and authoritative with his son.

The three case examples cited have illustrated the significance of the family context in which childhood problems occur and the possibility, in some cases, of providing help with family work alone. However, individual therapy for children is often the treatment of choice, and, when this is so, the therapist will need to assess whether the family can support individual treatment for their child. Is it practical to attend for regular appointments, or are there conflicting family needs? Can the parents allow their child to develop an intimate relationship with another adult, or will their curiosity, jealousy or envy lead them to interfere? And, most importantly, can they allow their child to change? Although it may seem obvious that change is what parents want, there is no guarantee that the child will change only in the direction which the parents desire. For example, in her recovery from her symptom of wetting, Emma expressed a lot of anger and grief which were painful for her parents, though happily they could understand and tolerate her feelings. Successful therapy of any kind is liable to stir up turbulent and painful feelings which, until they are integrated, may sometimes make parents wish that treatment had never begun. In extreme cases, for example, a parent's actual sanity may depend upon a child's support, and, if therapy should lead the child to withdraw uncritical loyalty, the parent might break down. Possibilities such as these need to be considered so that therapy can be provided for parents to enable them to allow and support the recovery of their child. This is the focus of the following section.

Further reading

Byng-Hall, J. (1995) *Rewriting Family Scripts*, New York: Guilford Press.
Scharff, D. E. and Scharff, J. Savege (1987) *Object Relations Family Therapy*, New Jersey: Aronson.

7 The child and adolescent psychotherapist and the family

(b) The place of consultation with parents and therapy of parents in child psychotherapy practice

Margaret Rustin

Child psychotherapists have in recent years developed the range of work offered to parents who refer their children for psychological help. The previous chapter outlined a way of working with the whole family which draws on a psychoanalytic frame of reference to understand family relationships, and this chapter will describe other current modalities.

Consultation with parents

The traditional role for the child psychotherapist limited contact with parents to meetings, held from time to time, to review a child's progress in therapy. Their purpose was to sustain a co-operative relationship between therapist and parents, to give the therapist a sense of the child's development in the family, at school and in the wider social world, and the parents an opportunity to enquire about the therapy and test out their confidence in the therapist's capacity to help their child. At their best, such meetings can offer a real chance to integrate diverse perspectives and to enrich the understanding of both parents and therapist, but they can also be difficult occasions in which divergencies in aim between therapist and parent may erupt. Such reviews remain an important part of good practice.

Two examples will serve to illustrate these points.

> ### Case example: Jacob
>
> Jacob is a ten-year-old boy referred by divorced parents, who remain very angry with each other, but who have managed to co-operate in supporting Jacob's therapy. He was referred for extremely aggressive and disruptive behaviour at school, which was threatening to lead to his exclusion, and for his very difficult and unrewarding family

relationships. His rigid defences made him rather inaccessible to help and his therapist found it hard to sustain hope in the face of a barrage of contempt from Jacob. Termly review meetings were held with each parent separately as neither felt able to sustain parental concern in company with the other. When the issue of choice of secondary school arose, parental conflict flared up, and there was potential for Jacob's much improved behaviour at school (his problems now being gathered, and more or less contained, in his relationship with his therapist) to be undermined. The review meetings could be used to support the more adult aspect of the parents' personalities and thus enable them to think about Jacob's needs at school rather than be drawn into another fight at his expense. The therapist's observations about Jacob's vulnerability to being upset by changes, his need for careful preparation and explanation, and his well-concealed panic about what secondary school would be like, helped them to hold back and work out their differences less flagrantly.

Case example: Elizabeth

Elizabeth is an adopted girl, aged nine, with a very sad and disrupted early life. She attends for intensive psychotherapy. Review meetings often provided rather crucial opportunities to test out realities. Elizabeth would often give a very convincing account to her therapist of external events which would interfere with her clinic appointments, leaving the therapist in doubt as to what was going to happen. Her parents, similarly, would hear disturbing stories about school and therapy whose reality they could not assess. Exploration suggested that Elizabeth was not telling lies in any ordinary sense, but rather conveying both just how hard it was for her to distinguish between reality and fantasy (this was the conundrum she set her listeners to solve) and how doubtful she was that adults could co-operate and stick to arrangements made for her benefit. In her first five years, she had very little experience of consistent adult care and she continued to recreate opportunities to be let-down, when her conviction that people did not really care would be confirmed. Helping Elizabeth's parents not to be pulled into rejecting behaviour was facilitated by the exploration of the details of her difficult behaviour. For example, Father complained at her tendency to scream right into his ear, but was helped to think about this symptom when we could identify the painful intensity and shock which she was forcing him to experience on her behalf. Perhaps this might be likened to the ordinary behaviour of a crying infant, but when the baby gets no response the screams stay lodged in the baby's head in an unbearable way. Seeing the baby within the nine-year-old helped Elizabeth's parents to find ways to cope with her.

Individual work

The supportive work with parents, very often provided in the past by psychiatric social workers, is now more frequently undertaken by child psychotherapists themselves. This may be alongside a child's therapy taken on by another therapist, or sometimes as an intervention in its own right, because the most helpful input is deemed to be work aimed at changing parental functioning. A considerable variety of approach is required in this work. The spectrum includes support for quite disturbed parents whose own mental state may impinge in damaging ways on their children, support for deprived and vulnerable parents (for example, bereaved families, mothers abandoned by their partners, refugee families), and work which attempts to explore ways in which parental functioning is disturbed by unconscious aspects of the parents' own ways of seeing things. The balance of listening and receptiveness on the one hand, and insight-giving interventions on the other, will depend on what a particular parent seems likely to be most helped by. Some fragile parents may be able to take in very little reflective comment and have urgent need for a relationship within which they can express their confusion, depression, despair and self-doubt, and feel that they can be accepted as they are. Others, with some source of greater hopefulness within their personality, will respond to the opportunity to think in-depth about their own contribution to their children's problems, and to consider their own family history as part of an attempt to understand the current family difficulties more fully.

In working with parents, the therapist offers a model of how to respond to emotional distress which has some core elements. The first, is attention to establishing and maintaining a reliable setting in which it is possible to talk about very upsetting things. As with a child's treatment, sessions for parents have regularity in time and space, and this helps to contain the infantile elements which are aroused. The second, element is the creation with the parent of some shared language to describe painful emotional states. Finding words for anguish is a help in itself, because it provides the comfort of feeling understood and therefore not alone with one's pain. Many lonely or emotionally deprived parents discover resources for understanding their own children through the experience of feeling understood and acquiring ways of thinking about feelings which may be very new to them. Third, is the valuing of boundaries and differentiation: the differences between parents and children, and between adult and more infantile aspects of the personality, can be clarified within a structured therapeutic setting. For example, an emotionally deprived parent can find it very difficult to distinguish between need and greed in herself and her child: if primary needs have never been met adequately, setting limits which are not arbitrary is almost impossible. Fourth, is an adequately complex understanding of human emotion and intimate relationships. This involves exploration of the internal world and of the constraints and creative possibilities of external reality. To support the development of genuine parental functioning, attention has to be given not only to the individual but also to the marital relationship – where there is a partnership – to the role of work in the individual's identity, to the full range of family relationships across the generations, and to the community setting. Last, and most important, there is the focus on giving meaning to behaviour. The urge to blame and reject aspects of ourselves and others is most helpfully modified if our destructive impulses can be given meaning.

Case example: Mrs D

Mrs D was a divorced woman of fifty with two sons. The older, aged twenty-five, was on the edge of a third schizophrenic breakdown when Mrs D referred herself and her younger boy, Sam, aged thirteen for help. It quickly became clear that the help Sam wanted was that someone should take care of his troubled mother and relieve him of a very heavy burden of anxiety. Mrs D began once-weekly psychotherapy. Her concerns for her two sons were deeply interwoven with the overall pattern of her life. She had had two significant sexual relationships and each had produced a child, but neither father had a reliable relationship to his son or with her. Mrs D's struggle to find an identity of her own and emerge from compliance with what she felt had been an authoritarian and rather loveless family had contributed to her choice of partner, as each of them had represented a counter-cultural protest against the restrictions she so resented. Now she was struggling with two enormous anxieties: her schizophrenic son exploited her ruthlessly, stealing from her and taking a very unfair share of the emotional and physical space she tried to provide. How could she stand up to him? As she became more in touch with the anger she had never expressed to her own parents, whose work abroad had resulted in her being sent to a boarding school from age five, she developed a capacity to challenge him. Her second concern was her own health. She had had two life-threatening illnesses in the last five years and was anxious that her younger son might have to cope with her early death. Thinking about this meant facing all her own painful losses. The depression this precipitated took her deep into herself. Gradually Mrs D became more able to acknowledge and value her feelings, including those that made her feel guilty, and less prone to see them in others. Her creative capacities began to re-emerge.

Case example: Mr J

Mr J was a father of two boys, the older of whom was autistic. He was troubled by his own deep passivity in the face of his son's regressed behaviour. He and his wife were initially seen jointly to talk about their children's difficulties: the younger son's omnipotent and manic behaviour seemed to complement his brother's autistic withdrawal from life, and the parents became aware that the division of labour between the boys and between the two of them was at the expense of all of them as individuals. Mr and Mrs J were each offered individual help to understand this destructive process. As Mr J talked, he began to see that his two sons were confused in his mind with himself and his younger brother. This brother had a heart condition from birth, and Mr J had given up much of his ordinary childhood desires to take care of him. This had evoked hatred of which he had been unaware, and when his brother died he had been left with a burden of guilt which lay heavily on his early adult years. His own child's autism and consequent need for special care had been experienced as just punishment. The younger son was left to express the ambition and longing for life and the anger which Mr J had had to disown.

Group work

Some parents are more responsive to group therapy. The group offers the comfort that others, too, share a sense of failure, whether it be losing one's temper, failing to get a child to school on time or to bed at a reasonable hour, or trying to bear a child's failure at school, quarrelsomeness with siblings or antisocial behaviour. Group work seems to be helpful when there is a sense of social isolation, strong feelings of failure and an absence of supportive partners. The group culture, as long as the group does not contain deeply disturbed and destructive individuals, can create a place for each person's vulnerability and a sense of continuity over time as each member feels kept in mind by others. By and large, group work with parents builds on the constructive potential mobilised by the parental role and does not address so successfully negative factors, which can be better tackled in the more protected space provided by individual work. This is because the members' identity as parents cannot be set on one side, as it might be in individual psychotherapy where their more infantile aspects can be contained. Parents do, however, challenge each other's evasions of responsibility, often with the help of humour.

Conclusion

Child psychotherapists bring some special capacities to work with parents. The place of infant observation and the broad study of child development in their training, together with their own analysis, put them in touch with the changing pressures on parents as their children grow and change, and the intensity with which parents' own infantile difficulties are stirred up by their children's emotional lives. This knowledge and sensitivity can be used well in responding to parental anxieties, but of course it can also be a source of trouble. A degree of competition, jealousy and envy is likely to be evoked by professionals who try to help when parents feel themselves to have failed. Tact, humility and a real belief in the shared nature of the task are essential. The direct use of transference and countertransference and interpretation are only appropriate when there has been explicit agreement that the parents wish to become patients in their own right. However, the understanding available through observation of the relationship made with the therapist can inform other kinds of conversation which have therapeutic potential. It is the capacity to empathise with both parental and child perspectives which is so valuable.

Further reading

Harris, M. (1987) 'The child psychotherapist and the patient's family', in *Collected Papers of Martha Harris and Esther Bick*, Strath Tey, Perthshire: Clunie Press.

Tsiantis, J. (ed.) (1999) *Working with Parents of Child and Adololescents who are in Psychoanalytic Psychotherapy*, EFPP Clinical Monograph London: Karnac Books.

Klauber, T. (1998) 'The significance of trauma in work with the parents of severely disturbed children, and its implications for work with parents in general', *Journal of Child Psychotherapy* 24(i): 85–107.

Tischler, S. (1979) 'Being with a psychotic child: a psychoanalytical approach to the parents of psychotic children', *International Journal of Psycho-analysis* 60(i): 29–38.

8 The therapeutic setting
The people and the place

Trevor Hartnup

Introduction

Wilson (1991) has this to say about the setting:

> The primary task of a psychotherapist is to ensure conditions of work that facilitate communication, and enable both psychotherapist and patient to observe and think about what is happening within and between them. The concept of a therapeutic setting refers to everything that forms the background in which psychotherapy takes place.

Before a child or adolescent and a child psychotherapist start work together the ground must be prepared. The child and the parents have often sought help from friends and relatives, from teachers, doctors or social workers, who have eventually helped put them in direct touch with a child psychotherapist, or, more probably, with a clinic offering a team of professionals with different specialties. Depending upon the clinic's resources, there will be a range of interventions available (see Chapter 10). Child and adolescent psychotherapists may offer one-off consultations, brief (see Chapter 16) or longer-term interventions, may work with children or adolescents individually, with parents only, with parent and child, or join colleagues in working with the whole family. As a result of assessment and sometimes lengthy preparatory work, it may be agreed that, amongst all the possible interventions, longer-term individual psychotherapy for the child or adolescent represents the treatment of choice. This agreement between parents, child or adolescent and the professionals lays the foundation for the setting to be described in this chapter. To be a secure foundation, it must be based upon a sound enough assessment of what psychotherapy can achieve for the young patient (see Chapter 16). When difficulties have a long history, the treatment itself may be long. This may have serious implications for those who have to manage in the meantime, caring for the child and/or providing his education. If they feel unable to manage, then thought must be given to a child's care and education *as well* as to his or her treatment.

The practicalities

Children usually come between one and five times per week as agreed with their parents or carers and the child or adolescent themselves. Sessions take place at the same times and in the same room each week, and parents are usually seen at the same time by another member of the professional team, in order to liaise about the treatment and support their efforts to help the child at home (see Chapter 7). The length of treatment varies and is difficult to predict, but is counted in months and sometimes in years, unless a brief intervention is explicitly agreed. Arrangements to review progress are automatically built in, if the parents are also being seen regularly.

The practical arrangements to bring a child regularly over a period of months are a crucial part of the setting, but they can affect the life of the whole family. However, the journey itself can become an enjoyable and helpful activity for parent and child, and the life of the whole family can be enhanced when a child with problems becomes ordinarily happy as a result of the co-operation between family and professionals.

Consent, trust and confidentiality

The psychotherapist needs to be properly authorised by the child, the parents, colleagues and society at large to undertake the work. This requires the psychotherapist to gain the trust of parents and professional colleagues. The accountability of the profession with regard to ethical practice and training standards provides a framework for this. However it is ultimately the patient's, parents' and professional colleagues' direct experience of their relationship with the child psychotherapist that establishes a feeling of trust. Informed consent, consistency and confidentiality represent important elements in the relationship between all Health Service professionals and their patients. In the case of psychotherapy, the relationship itself is especially important as the means through which the treatment takes place. Patience may also be required to explore problems which sometimes cannot be expressed directly in words in any clear way, because the meaning is cut off or associated with strong emotion, anxiety and pain.

Psychotherapists offer children and adolescents confidentiality in order to maximise the chances of their regarding the session as their own treatment setting, separate from everyday life and the normal rules of social behaviour. They may say, by way of explanation, something like, 'confidentiality means I won't tell your parents or your teachers or anyone else about what you do or say in sessions'. However, nowadays children have been warned about grown-ups who want to do things with them in secret, so that it can be helpful to add, 'but *you* can if you like'. Psychotherapists in the NHS work within a framework of local child protection regulations governing a wide range of public services for children and young people. Confidentiality is intended to protect the patient, not the therapist, and carers are reassured to know that the rule of confidentiality is waived if a child's safety is at risk. When children and young people reveal in psychotherapy real dangers to which they are exposed in their lives, either from self-harm or at the hands of others, it is helpful if the young patient can be involved in working out with the psychotherapist what to do and whom to tell.

The room

The setting provides three things: a place for the problems to present themselves 'live', a place where they can be observed and thought about and the means to convey new possibilities into the live interaction of the session. The setting is the room within the clinic or institution, and the ground rules are agreed with the child or young person and their parents; it is also the therapist's empathy, informed by professional training and experience and bound by accountability and an ethical code. The 'live interaction' consists of talking and/or playing together, and the accompanying feelings or emotional charge. The new possibilities arise within the patient as a result of the relationship with the psychotherapist within the setting of the room and the framework of ground rules outlined below.

Ideally the room provides both a sense of space and a sense of containment, where young patients can bring whatever is on their minds without objective reason to feel crowded or unsafe, where they can feel recognised for who they are, become able to think about what goes on between themselves and others. Because of their relative immaturity, children do not have the same capacity as psychologically mature adults to report verbally on what is going on inside them. For younger children especially, play is an important means of communication. Therefore, the psychotherapist aims to provide a setting that is safe for free play. Toddlers may feel at home with small chairs, toys, room for action. Older children may need facilities for creative activities and for exploring. Facilities for water and/or sand play can be very helpful for some children and a mixed blessing with others. It is helpful if there is not a host of personal items in the room that excite curiosity and require protection: pictures drawn by other patients, coats and brief-cases, or computers and such like. Adolescents need a more comfortable adult environment, with the space to look around so they are not eyeball to eyeball with the psychotherapist. They may feel insulted by the presence of 'babyish' things in the room. Wilson (1991) devotes considerable attention to the setting for adolescents.

The patient's free play and talking, verbal and non-verbal engagement with the psychotherapist is the starting point of the 'live interaction' between them. The psychotherapist attempts to provide an atmosphere of acceptance which does not intrude upon the child's opportunity to structure the interaction. (For this reason, some psychotherapists prefer a bare room without books on shelves or even pictures on the wall. Others feel that the room can be made more homely provided that it remains consistent and does not interfere with the child's freedom to play.) Children's own initiatives can then be seen as reflections of their inner world, the 'templates', as it were, which the child uses to interpret his or her experiences of the world. The way the child relates to the psychotherapist is an especially rich source of knowledge about the child's conception of human relationships (see references to transference in Chapter 5). Thus the child's 'inner world' is understood to represent the space in the patient's mind which finds expression in the space in the room. It can then be thought about in the *therapist's* mind and articulated in words which convey the psychotherapist's empathy and ideas. The psychotherapist's mind itself is part of the therapeutic space. When children experience their psychotherapist as thinking about them, it is equivalent to having a place in the therapist's mind. The theory behind this description of the process can be found in the writing of D. W. Winnicott, who developed some fascinating and illuminating ideas about the function of play in development, and the development of a space (a mind) within the child, for the (inter)play between internal and external reality (see Winnicott 1971).

Practice varies, but it is usual to provide children with their own box of play material containing, for example, family dolls, a range of model animals (wild and domestic: crocodiles and monsters prove popular!), soldiers, cars, drawing materials, glue, scissors, paper, plasticine, etc. Available every session, this box often carries, in a concrete way, the order and disorder, the rigidity and fluidity, the creativity and destructiveness, the linking threads and the tangled knots of the child's inner world, and of the ongoing work between child and psychotherapist. When the children ignore the box for long periods of time, the psychotherapist may wonder whether the appropriate play material has been provided or whether, for example, this represents the children's anxiety about giving expression to their inner world, or a feeling that they have never been given what they needed. Child psychotherapists know that what children feel does not necessarily correspond to the objective truth. Nevertheless, what children feel is itself a *psychological* truth, and when the child's psychological truth is getting in the way of their growing up, it is the specialist function of the psychotherapist to attend to it.

Other equipment may be available in the room for general use, such as a doll's house, a bag of bricks, etc. The child's spontaneous play and developing relationship to the psychotherapist provide insights into the child's experience and imagination. The children's use of these materials helps the psychotherapist understand how they use their minds to represent their life events and transform them into emotional events, a personal version of the truth. The psychotherapists convey in words and play their understanding of what is going on (see Chapter 4).

Consistency

When changes are made to the room or the arrangements, it is important to pay attention to the possible meaning of this to the child. Consistency itself can represent a therapeutic factor for children whose lives have been disrupted (see Chapter 20). But impeccable consistency represents rigidity and 'no change' and is unachievable anyway. What is important is that children's feelings about past disruptions arise in the treatment room in a context of sufficient consistency for them to be talked about. This helps the child to see that the inconsistencies in the treatment are not the same as those in the past, even though sometimes it may feel the same. This ability to have a feeling rather than be taken over by it means that things can be thought about.

If the setting is consistent, variations in the child's play, behaviour, and mood can be more clearly seen to derive from inside the child on any particular day. Different parts of the room and the play material come to stand for themes which can be explored, left, and returned to as children gradually work on and work out, with the psychotherapist's help, what is bothering them. One girl's washing-up play at the sink led on to her behaving as if the room and the psychotherapist were dirty and needed cleaning up. When she herself linked this supposed dirtiness to sex, it became possible for the psychotherapist to talk to her about her wish to get all her thoughts about her sexual abuse out of her mind. First she had to develop the idea that it was the room and the psychotherapist which were dirty.

'Bad behaviour' in psychotherapy

Sometimes children display in sessions what their parents and teachers might call 'bad behaviour'. It is no part of a child psychotherapist's role to encourage good behaviour, or discourage bad, for its own sake. That is the proper concern of parents and teachers. The psychotherapist's task is to understand. If the 'bad behaviour' represents the child's way of letting people know about the bad things that are really happening in his or her life, then perhaps something can be done to change those circumstances. If, however, children are showing how bad they feel about themselves, then the reasons for that can be understood, and the children helped to see things differently. At times children do treat their psychotherapist in unpleasant and denigrating ways as a method of expressing their awful feelings about themselves, or set out relentlessly to provoke, apparently determined to enrage the psychotherapist. This may represent a first step to knowing their own rage and what it is about as a move towards feeling better about themselves, eventually to feeling recognised for what they feel and who they are (See references to transference and countertransference). When the work of the psychotherapist is successful the child or adolescent becomes better able to benefit from the good things that are on offer from other adults, including their teaching about good behaviour.

Psychotherapists establish rules with their young patients, sometimes from the beginning and sometimes over a period of time, as the need arises. These rules are intended to support the treatment setting. The general purpose is that children are free to express themselves in ways that do not harm the child, the room and its furnishings, or the therapist. If a child's behaviour in a session leads to understanding, it is one thing. If it prevents understanding, it is another and may lead to a session being ended early because the behaviour in question is making it impossible for the psychotherapist to work. At difficult periods of treatment, a parent may be asked to wait in the clinic for just such a contingency.

Edgcumbe (1971) explains clearly why different children need different kinds of help in relation to their aggressive behaviour (see also Chapter 22). Some may need help with socialisation (adult guidance on how their behaviour affects other people). Child psychotherapy is not the best way to address this, because the psychotherapy room is not a social setting. Some may be aggressive because of excessive anxiety. For instance, they may be afraid of other people, either because they feel guilty about their own aggression and therefore fear punishment, or because they feel rejected or threatened with rejection in a serious way in their real lives. Others may have identified with an adult who has behaved aggressively towards them. These children may be able to benefit from psychotherapy, i.e. from the experience of being held in a space in the mind of a therapist who can differentiate between different subjective experiences underlying apparently similar behaviour. As Edgcumbe observes, we expect children, in the course of their development, to give up direct physical attacks in favour of using words, or games, or legitimate forms of competition. One of the tasks of the psychotherapist is to facilitate normal development. The way the psycho-therapist thinks about the child's behaviour and motivations helps in several ways – for example, suffering is relieved by feeling understood, and the therapist's thinking directly and indirectly helps the child find new ways of dealing with things.

Case example: Susan

Six-year-old Susan was clingy and whiny with her mother, nervous and shy at school and suffered from nightmares. As a result of treatment, her unacknowledged anger became apparent. It emerged that she tricked her mother in contemptuous ways. Although she felt guilty about this, she was unable to stop herself. She was the oldest child of a couple who were in chronic, unhappy conflict with one another and she witnessed their ongoing quarrels. She did not know whom to side with. Because of their conflict the parents tended not to notice when she played one off against the other. Susan was loved by both parents and in some respects indulged. Her mother believed in a permissive approach to parenting and 'laughed off' Susan's naughtiness with tickling games. Her mother had a medical condition which restricted her ability to pay attention to Susan's behaviour. Indeed she herself had to rely on Susan in certain respects. Mother's real, though limited, dependence upon her daughter seems to have interfered with Susan's ability to separate from her mother and the child would cling to her. She found it hard to make friends at school and her learning appeared to be inhibited.

Susan had not long begun psychotherapy before she became disinhibited in the room, both as regards her sexual and aggressive behaviour. (Domestic violence and sexual abuse were not factors in this case.) Susan would demand to go through the drawers of the desk, and when frustrated, would throw water over her therapist, stick plasticine on the walls of the room and on the plants, and threaten to draw on the walls. When she became angry or anxious, she frequently left the room to return to her mother in the waiting room. This seemed to mirror her experience of being between her two parents (transference), but she drowned out her psychotherapist's attempts to talk to her about this. She tried to engage her male therapist in 'physical education lessons' which involved undressing. He declined to play this game. The guilt which prevented her from expressing crossness *directly* towards her mother did not prevent her from attacking her therapist when he would not comply with her demands. However, it was also plain that Susan felt that the psychotherapist frustrated her because he did not like her. She engaged the psychotherapist in repeated 'classroom' scenes in which she allotted the psychotherapist the role of a naughty boy who was constantly told off and treated as stupid by his teacher, played by Susan. This was understood as an enactment of Susan's relationship with her own super-ego. She instigated games in which she tricked her psychotherapist, for instance, by asking him to close his eyes, and then throwing a wet flannel in his face or spitting. It seemed as if Susan had an all-or-nothing super-ego. Either she suffered from extensive inhibition, or became uninhibited. In the latter case, her super-ego seemed easily tricked. It was no help to Susan in finding more acceptable ways of expressing her feelings, but came in heavily and too late leaving her feeling bad and unlovable afterwards. Susan's low self-esteem arose partly from her attempt to avoid feeling bad by tricking her super-ego, rather than by finding age-appropriate ways of expressing her aggression and sexuality. The task was to bring the angry part of her into a more constructive relationship with her conscience in order to free her development. In his role as the naughty boy, the psychotherapist began to express (on Susan's behalf) his wish to be good and his wish for a strict teacher who could help him with that. In the next session Susan made the naughty boy into a monitor who could help the teacher. This was understood as her unconscious relief that her problem had been recognised, but she now became excited and naughty again, possibly because an improvement in her relationship with her male therapist made her feel disloyal towards her mother (transference). However it remained impossible to talk to Susan about this.

She continued to trick her psychotherapist in sessions. One day she started kicking the wall of the treatment room. The psychotherapist said Susan really felt like kicking a person. She made as if to kick him and then continued to kick the wall. The psychotherapist said she wanted grown-up help to stop herself. Susan tried to wipe the marks off the wall. The psychotherapist commented that this was a sign that she could be the grown-up for herself. She began to see how high she could jump, pretending not to know that she was kicking the wall at the same time. The psychotherapist pointed out what she was doing. Susan stopped, saying, apparently about something else, 'What a relief!'. Her therapist's non-condemnatory recognition of her aggression seems to have enabled her at last to recognise it and take responsibility for it herself. Thus she was relieved that her angry feelings towards adults had been recognised because it helped her to stop her secret attacks, and so feel better about herself.

Work undertaken concurrently with the mother (father refused to attend) helped her to become stricter with her daughter, much to Susan's evident relief. Susan became able to make friends and she became free to learn. However, the daily reality of the chronic marital difficulties seemingly made it impossible to address Susan's loyalty conflicts and misplaced guilt about her parents' relationship, as manifested in her transference relationship to her psychotherapist. She could not bear to think about it, and could not allow her therapist to get his mind around it in her presence. Nevertheless, it remained in the setting of the room in the form of Susan's *behaviour*, her frequent trips to the waiting room to see her mother and her continuing denigration of her therapist. Under these circumstances it was not useful for the treatment to continue. It was brought to an end gradually, with a reduction in the frequency of sessions and a term's notice, to enable Susan and her psychotherapist to do some work on the ending.

Adolescents tend to talk rather than play, and the freedom to express their thoughts, no matter what, is an integral part of the setting. But words, too, can be attacking and destructive of the work of treatment. Sometimes adolescents may use the permission to say what they like in a way that is destructive to the treatment rather than helpful to it. Then the psychotherapist may usefully distinguish between thoughts and dogmatic assertions by saying something like, 'You can say you *think* I'm a xxxxxxx idiot but you can't say I *am* one.' The statement that the psychotherapist *is* an idiot represents an attack on the setting in the form of the therapist's mind. The psychotherapist defends the setting by drawing the young person's attention to his/her *thoughts,* which is the subject of the work, and not identical with objective reality. Second, this demonstrates that the psychotherapist, as the human aspect of the setting, is still alive and thinking in the face of relentless denigration. The integrity of the setting reassures young people about the limits of their destructive power and may enable destructive thoughts and feelings to be thought about.

Beginnings and endings

Discovering that we are individuals in our own right, separate from parents, is an important part of human development which progresses gradually from the earliest beginnings through to adulthood. For the infant, birth is perhaps the first ending and beginning, though, especially with the first baby, parents experience endings and beginnings throughout the pregnancy or adoption. At birth, the umbilical cord is replaced by a psychological and emotional attachment which grows and changes over months and years. This new attachment exists between the child and others. Normally people think of attachment as being about love, but it is about hate and survival too. Fundamentally, it is probably the expression of an innate capacity to attach or relate (see Chapter 4; also Holmes's (1993) account of Bowlby's attachment theory). Relationships involve discovering the extent and limitations of one's own being, one's powers and responsibilities, knowing what belongs to one and what belongs to others (feelings as well as things), having a good-enough sense of where one begins and ends. This requires young children to tolerate giving up the idea that they can maintain a feeling of safety by controlling their parents. The relinquishment of power over others requires the establishment of trust, a feeling of relative safety inside, which enables us to relate to others in a mutually satisfying way. The problems which bring children into psychotherapy interfere with this ordinary process of growing up and achieving psychological separation. Beginnings and endings in psychotherapy, are moments of separation when children may get in touch with feelings of unsafety.

Case example: Linda

Linda was an attractive six-year-old daughter of good-looking parents. They were at their wits' end because Linda was literally pulling out her hair. At the first meeting she was brought wearing a pretty floral dress with her hair in wisps with bald patches. Both parents were smartly dressed. Mother had shoulder-length, black curly hair, well cut and cared for, a striking feature of her appearance. The parents travelled abroad frequently for business and pleasure and made proper arrangements for the care of their children in their absences.

In her first session on her own with the psychotherapist, Linda heard a car start up outside. She rushed to the window in a panic. The psychotherapist said she seemed frightened and perhaps she thought her parents were leaving her there. Linda looked relieved, left the window, and was able to play for the rest of the session although she remained wary, which was appropriate for her first meeting with her psychotherapist. In the treatment, her hidden fear and her anger about her parents' absences appeared in her play and was verbalised by the psychotherapist. After some months her hair pulling ceased. Once her fear that her parents did not want her had been understood, she could recognise that it was not true in the way she imagined it. Her parents' absences had been only part of the problem. The core of it was that she had not had the help she needed with her feelings about it. One might imagine that, for Linda, her mother's hair symbolised what she did not have. It remained physically attached to her mother, received a great deal of attention and went everywhere with her. By pulling her own hair out Linda expressed perhaps her unconscious experience of having no place in her mother's head. In spite of the work undertaken with the parents, they could not recognise Linda's problems around attachment and physical and psychological separation. They 'pulled her out' of psychotherapy abruptly, soon after her symptom disappeared.

Different children experience loss in different ways and react to it differently. It may be feared as abandonment, or experienced as a loss of part of themselves (as for example, in Linda's case), or as a substantial loss of safety. At such moments some children just 'lose it', that is, they are overwhelmed with anxiety or fury, whereas others become very controlling, or very cut off and controlled. Treatment itself has a beginning and an end, as does each session, and there are breaks for holidays, illness, etc. These moments may trigger existing fears about there being no space for them or no boundaries to their bad feelings. (Linda seemed to feel that her parents were leaving her *for ever*.) Children who are trying to shut everything out (like Susan) may be terrified of the space and time provided in psychotherapy at moments and may not want to come back after a break, or may run out of the session. Children who fear rejection may not want to leave at the end, may wish to take control of endings by refusing to leave, by leaving early, or by reluctance to return after a break.

The same issues are faced at holiday times. Psychotherapists like to give children and parents good notice of when they are taking their holidays. This allows children to experience the ending at their own pace, and gives time for the feelings to emerge and be understood in sessions. It is equally helpful to the treatment if parents give good notice of their intended holidays and of missed sessions, if possible. Sometimes psychotherapists prepare calendars for younger children to give a pictorial idea of what 'a few weeks' means. Psychotherapists tend to place emphasis on the possible distress to a child of such breaks in order to help parents recognise and deal with it when it occurs. Whereas some children may overtly express their worst fears of loss and abandonment during these breaks, others may not, especially if the situation is handled with ordinary sensitivity. Copley and Forryan (1987) have a whole chapter on endings in their book, and many useful remarks on the setting.

Summary

Parents and professional colleagues sometimes feel that child psychotherapists are too particular in the detailed attention they pay to the setting. Sometimes it is misunderstood as an attempt to provide children with some kind of ideal environment in which they will not have to suffer the frustrations of the real world. However this is not what the child psychotherapist has in mind. This chapter attempts to describe how the setting helps with a very difficult task. The setting is a place for a meeting of minds. It starts out as the child psychotherapist's place, with the intention that it will become the child's, invested with the child's own meanings. Thus it provides conditions in which the invisible inner world of the young patient can become visible to the psychotherapist, and the child or adolescent can allow the psychotherapist into that world, both as a transference figure, and as a professionally helpful human being in his or her own right.

This highly structured setting, integrated into the treatment itself, enables the young patient and the psychotherapist to focus and work safely on the confusion, aggressive and sexual impulses, guilt, anxiety, fear, and distress which underlie the symptoms of the troubled child or adolescent.

References

Copley, B. and Forryan, B. (1987) *Therapeutic Work with Children and Young People*, London: Robert Royce.

Edgcumbe, R. M. (1971) 'A consideration of the meaning of certain types of aggressive behaviour', *British Journal of Medical Psychology* 44: 373–8.

Holmes, J. (1993) *John Bowlby and Attachment Theory*, London/New York: Routledge.

Wilson, P. (1991) 'Psychotherapy with adolescents', in J. Holmes (ed.) *Textbook of Psychotherapy in Psychiatric Practice*, New York: Churchill-Livingstone.

Winnicott, D. W. (1971) *Playing and Reality*, Harmondsworth: Penguin.

9 Research in child and adolescent psychotherapy

An overview

Jill Hodges

Introduction

This chapter will survey two fields of research developments. The primary one is research into the outcome or effectiveness of child psychotherapy. An additional area is research in which child psychotherapists are using concepts or techniques based in child psychotherapeutic work to enrich investigation of particular kinds of disturbance by more conventional empirical means. Chapters elsewhere in this book will provide more detail on some of these areas. Though clinical case studies have the potential to play an important role in generating and guiding other research, I have not tried to encompass these – both to limit the scope of the chapter to a manageable area, and to orient it clearly towards objective systematic research.

In general this chapter confines itself to recent or ongoing research. There are obvious difficulties in getting to know of research where the results have not yet been published, let alone that which is still ongoing or in the planning stage. However, I have included both categories wherever I have known of them, on the basis that one aim of this chapter is to alert people to others who may be carrying out studies relevant to their own particular fields of interest.

My efforts will not have produced exhaustive coverage; and studies outside the UK are very likely to be left out. If a recent or current study is omitted from this survey, this is because I am unaware of it, not because it has been intentionally excluded.

Research into outcome

In a recent report commissioned as part of the Department of Health's Strategic Review of Psychotherapy Services, Target and Fonagy (1996) contribute an excellent chapter reviewing studies on the treatment of children and adolescents. The chapter is a detailed, rigorous overview of the research evidence on treatment effectiveness of all forms of therapy, and I have drawn very much upon it. Target and Fonagy note that research on the effectiveness of therapies for children has continued to lag far behind that on adult treatment. They also point out, as did Shirk and Russell (1992), that there are many more systematic studies of behavioural and cognitive-behavioural treatment of children than there are of non-behavioural therapies, including individual psychodynamic treatment.

However, although evidence on adult treatment is still ahead of that on children, there are some recent studies, and some currently in progress, beginning to make up the gap.

Problems of earlier research studies

Before surveying these new developments, it is worth making a brief detour and summarising some of the problems which in past research have contributed to a very poor showing for psychotherapeutic treatment, and have also made the findings of many outcome studies more or less meaningless in terms of assessing the effectiveness of actual clinical practice. It is encouraging that as better designed studies are done, which more closely reflect actual practice, they tend to show better results for psychotherapy than the earlier studies and the meta-analyses based upon them. This is consistent with a finding by Shirk and Russell (1992). They examined existing studies containing twenty-nine non-behavioural treatments, based on the study by Weisz *et al.* (1987), and found that the studies which were more seriously flawed methodologically yielded estimates of treatment effects which were substantially smaller than in more adequately designed studies.

Some of the main problems are as follows:

- *Mode* 'Psychodynamic' treatment as evaluated in outcome studies has often been group treatment, while individual treatment is the norm in clinical practice. Shirk and Russell (1992) found that twenty of the twenty-nine treatments (69 per cent) in their sample of research studies were administered in group format. However, in practice, surveys of child psychiatrists and psychologists showed that they did not regard group therapy as particularly useful, and individual therapy was by far the most commonly used treatment modality. They also note that the average effect size for group treatments was significantly less than that for treatments which had individual therapist–client contact.

- *Duration* In most research studies, treatment tends to be very brief. Shirk and Russell's research showed that non-behavioural treatment in over 20 per cent of the studies consisted of ten sessions or less, and less than one-third had over twenty sessions. This is obviously far fewer than the clinical norm. The sessions themselves also tend to be shorter than is usual clinically.

- *Therapeutic training and practice*   Therapists in research studies are not necessarily experienced; 'psychotherapy' in research studies has not necessarily been carried out by someone with any recognised training in psychotherapy. Nor can it be assumed that whatever 'psychotherapy' was intended, it was actually delivered, or delivered in a recognisable form, since in very few studies was there a treatment manual or review through supervision. To give a flavour of what such studies may describe as 'psychotherapy', here is an example from a critique by Barrnett *et al.* (1991):

  > The second study . . . is remarkable for the fact that this is one of the few studies that used clear diagnostic criteria. The 20 subjects were randomly assigned to either analytic play therapy or operant conditions for 50 sessions followed by 50 sessions of the other treatment. Individuals were chosen and matched on a variety of variables, and then each pair was assigned to one therapist and randomly assigned to begin either treatment. The major flaws in this study are that it appears that the outcome measurements were biased in favour of examining the effect of the behavioural treatment, and there is virtually no description of the psychoanalytical play therapy. Lastly, the therapists were described as 'aides', with no description of their training. The use of these therapists biases the results in favour of the behavioural treatment.

  In other words, the same 'aides', qualifications unknown, carried out both the operant training and some unspecified form of 'analytic play therapy'.

- *Bias in outcome measures*   As mentioned in the example above, a problem with some studies of behaviourally oriented treatment compared to psychotherapy is that the outcome measures may be so closely related to treatment procedures, or bear so strong a resemblance to tasks practised during the course of behavioural treatment, as to render meaningless any finding of greater effect size.

- *Non-referred or otherwise unrepresentative subject populations*   Evaluations of therapy tend to focus on treatment for a specific problem, while generally in child psychiatry children referred for treatment are likely to show more than one problem at referral. Related to this issue of co-morbidity, many research studies use samples which have not been referred for treatment at all, but are specifically recruited for the research because they meet criteria for one given problem and one alone (Weisz and Weiss 1989). Though this makes for tidier evaluation of a given treatment approach to the given problem, it obviously reduces the relevance of this evaluation to real-world applications.

- *Investigator allegiance* Another problem of some outcome studies is that the theoretical allegiance of the researcher influences how effective the therapy is found to be. Most outcome research on psychotherapy with children has been carried out by behaviourally oriented researchers, and these studies demonstrate a markedly smaller effect size than the few studies carried out by psychodynamically oriented researchers. Conscious or unconscious bias and self-fulfilling prophecies may play a part here. But likely to be important too is that the psychotherapy tends to be set up as the 'control' condition for a trial of behavioural treatment; it is therefore designed to be comparable with the latter in terms of duration, frequency, etc., rather than being a treatment thought out and set up in its own right and within its own parameters.

Target and Fonagy (1996) provide the wry summary: 'Thus far, then, psychodynamic therapy has been judged mostly (for want of better evidence) on studies of brief group therapy conducted by behaviourally oriented clinicians.'

The Anna Freud Centre retrospective investigation

By using the Anna Freud Centre clinical archive, Fonagy and Target (1994; Target and Fonagy 1994a, b; Target 1993) were able to avoid these pitfalls. They used the closed treatment files of 763 children seen at the Anna Freud Centre – about 90 per cent of the cases treated – in an extensive and detailed series of studies. However, since this research concerned treatment at one particular centre of training and treatment, the results cannot necessarily be generalised to other settings.

The closed treatment files contained very detailed diagnostic and clinical records of the individual treatments of clinically referred children. The average length of treatment was two years, with 75 per cent of children seen 4–5 times weekly and 25 per cent 1–2 times weekly. About 40 per cent of these treatments were carried out by very experienced staff. The main drawback of the study was the lack of a comparison group, and also, since it was retrospective, follow-up data were not systematically available. (An ongoing follow-up, described below, will remedy the latter and, to some degree, the former problem.)

Outcome was indicated by diagnostic change and by clinically significant change in adaptation. Diagnostic change was measured by DSM-III-R Axis I and II diagnostic classifications, at referral and termination, and general adaptation by referral and termination scores on the Children's Global Assessment Scale (CGAS) (Shaffer *et al.* 1983). These classifications and scores were not made at the time of referral, but retrospectively using the extensive detailed referral and clinical material available for each case.

Target and Fonagy (1994a) found that over four-fifths of children referred with anxiety disorders, including phobias and depression, no longer showed symptoms by the end of treatment, and general adaptation improved in a great majority of cases. As regards depression, intensive treatment (4–5 times weekly) showed greater gains than non-intensive, when other variables were controlled for. (Strikingly, this was so despite most of the depressed referrals being adolescents, who in general did not do better with intensive as opposed to non-intensive work (Target and Fonagy 1994b).) Follow-up data would be necessary before this could be taken as a decisive demonstration of effectiveness in treating depression, since major depression tends to follow an episodic course, and might recur after improvement and the end of treatment.

More frequent sessions were also associated with greater improvement where symptoms were severe or where children showed several different disorders. In the absence of a comparison group, these rates of improvement for anxiety disorders cannot be compared with untreated controls, but they are certainly greater than expectable on the basis of longitudinal studies of childhood psychiatric disorder (see Target and Fonagy 1996).

The same series of studies also examined treatment outcome for 93 children with disruptive behavioural disorders who remained in treatment for at least one year. Children with oppositional disorder improved the most, those with full conduct disorder the least, with those showing attention-deficit/hyperactivity disorder intermediate. Overall, by the end of treatment, 69 per cent improved to a point indicating no diagnosis of any type of disturbance. Again, although a control group is lacking, comparison can be made with childhood longitudinal studies of the usual course of such difficulties, and suggests that treatment produced considerable improvement. The presence of an anxiety disorder in addition to the disruptive disorder, and persistence with the treatment, were both associated with improvement, while the presence of school difficulties meant it was less likely that a child would do well in treatment. Younger children improved more than children over nine. They were also helped more than older children by more frequent therapy sessions.

This study concluded that children with mental retardation, or with severe, pervasive developmental disorders, such as autism, showed little change on the diagnostic or adjustment outcome measures used, even with prolonged intensive treatment.

Replication

Following the Anna Freud Centre study, the Child and Adolescent Ambulatory Psychiatric Clinic in Heidelberg carried out, independently, a similar retrospective study (reported in Target 1998). They found similarly that intensive treatment showed greater effectiveness, and that the younger the child, the more marked this was. They also found, as Fonagy and Target had done, that there was also a separate benefit from longer treatment. Unlike the Anna Freud Centre study, which found no gender difference, they found that girls were more likely than boys to benefit from intensive treatment, once the effect of age had been controlled for.

Continuing follow-up

An extensive follow-up to the Anna Freud Centre study, based on the same group of cases and carried out by the same research team, is under way at present (Target 1997). This research follows children into adulthood, so adjustment and resilience can be examined in the long term. Also, and importantly, it compares individuals treated in childhood with two control groups. The first group consists of people referred for treatment as children with similar problems, but who did not receive treatment. This provides the standard form of comparison group to examine treatment effects: did children with problems improve more with treatment than with time alone? The second control group is an interesting choice, being siblings of the treated children, who were not themselves referred for treatment. Although each individual child in a family has a different experience of that same family, this sibling comparison controls for social and emotional family environment (not to mention any genetic influences) in as good a way as could possibly be achieved. This comparison should provide:

> an intriguing glimpse at the complexities of individual development, at the questions of whether the particular child referred from a family was really the most disturbed, whether psychoanalytic treatment offers the possibility of restoring that child to the path of normal development as Anna Freud believed, and to what extent the two siblings then follow comparable pathways through life.
>
> (Target 1997)

In this study, great effort has gone into ensuring that the adult picture is as far as possible uncontaminated by knowledge of the picture in childhood. The assessment covers present functioning and adjustment in detail, using a range of established measures to look at personality functioning, physical health, attachment relationships, coping with stressful life events, attainment of life goals (such as separation from parents, establishment in work), psychopathology and mental health service use since treatment, and social adversity over the lifespan.

This study will be of the greatest importance, both in that it examines *long-term* outcome, and in the scope of the outcome measures used. There are a number of longitudinal studies which indicate a poor long-term outlook for disturbed children (Rutter 1994). The measures planned for this study mean that the outcome will be examined not just in terms of symptom removal, but will encompass something much more akin to what we might aim for in psychoanalysis. This will enable individuals to function better in all domains of life, including 'love and work', social relationships, resiliency, and capacity to shape their own lives as they choose. We need to know if the poor long-term prognosis for disturbed children can be improved by psychoanalytic treatment, which sorts of childhood disturbances respond, and where intensive treatment is necessary as opposed to non-intensive. As noted above, there are very few pieces of research which examine the outcome of intensive child psychoanalytic treatment, even in the short term, and detailed follow-up studies of adult psychoanalytic treatment are also rare (see Bachrach *et al.* 1991). Only this kind of study will tell us whether psychoanalytic treatment of children really achieves what we aim for it to achieve – not just symptom relief but much more fundamental changes. Has psychoanalytic treatment restored children to the path of normal development, such that individuals who have had treatment as children subsequently show a life course and development comparable to their siblings? Have they managed the tasks, relationships, challenges and adversities of life as well as their siblings, and better than those who as children were seen as having difficulties but who received no treatment? Does non-intensive treatment, as expectable, provide less benefit than intensive where children showed severe, pervasive disorders?

Treatment frequency

The Anna Freud Centre study is unusual in being able to include a very large number of cases treated intensively (4–5 times per week) for comparison with non-intensive treatment. Heinicke (1965) and Heinicke and Ramsey-Klee (1986) had earlier shown a greater response to intensive treatment than non-intensive in 7–10-year-old children with reading difficulties linked to emotional disturbance, but there is little other evidence on the relative effectiveness of intensive, compared to non-intensive, treatment.

Intensive treatment in 'brittle' diabetes

One of the very few studies of the effectiveness of intensive psychoanalytic treatment with children and adolescents is the work on diabetic control in 'brittle' diabetes carried out by Moran *et al.* (1991). Among chronic illnesses, diabetes particularly lends itself to the study of effectiveness of psychotherapy, in that the outcome measures are very clear-cut. This research showed clearly that intensive (3–5 times weekly) psychoanalytic therapy led to improved diabetic control in young adolescents whose previous control had been so extremely poor as to be potentially life-endangering, and likely to have severe physical consequences in the long term.

Based on this work, a planned study centred at the Middlesex/UCH hospitals (Viner, personal communication) will be investigating whether very much less intensive psychotherapeutic treatment – more consonant with scarce psychotherapeutic resources and limited treatment budgets – can also produce worthwhile improvement in a similar population of diabetic adolescents.

Psychotherapy with fostered and adopted children

One recent study is especially interesting for its efforts to devise clinically appropriate and valid methods of examining 'internal' change during treatment, as well as external indicators of change or progress (Boston (1989), Lush *et al*. (1991); Boston and Lush (1994)).

This was a naturalistic, prospective study of all the adopted, fostered and in-care children aged 2–18, referred to the Tavistock Clinic within a three-year period, who entered and continued psychotherapy – thirty-one children in all. The range of symptoms at referral was very wide; half the children were under ten years old, and nineteen were girls; thirteen were adopted, thirteen were fostered and five were in children's homes. Except for four children adopted very early with minimal disruption of care, all had suffered abuse or trauma as well as discontinuity of care. Twelve received treatment two or three times per week, the rest once-weekly. Most continued treatment for at least one year. All the therapists (twenty-three in all) were trained in the same training school of psychoanalytic psychotherapy, though some were more experienced than others.

The main measures of change used were therapists assessments. At the outset of therapy, a wide range of observations on the child's behaviour and personality were elicited from the therapists using a semi-structured interview/questionnaire format (see Lush *et al*. (1991) for details). Therapists were asked to state the aims of the psychotherapy with this specific child, to specify the criteria, internal and external, which would define improvement, and to make a rating of predicted progress on a 5-point scale, ranging from 1 (considerable progress anticipated) to 5 (poor expectations). Two years after the start of treatment or at termination, whichever came earlier, comparable information was gathered and therapists were asked to rate the degree of actual progress made. (No case was rated 'worse', though this possibility was added to the scale at this point.)

Because there are no readily available existing measures of psychodynamic change, these measures were developed specially for the study. They were of unknown validity and reliability, and efforts were made to address this difficulty. Two researchers independently assessed the internal consistency of the information from the therapists, and also gave independent ratings of progress, finding good agreement in all cases. The therapists material was compared with reports from parents, teachers, social workers and referrers where available; although standardised parent and teacher scales would have been preferable, their use would have altered routine clinical practice, and would have been more difficult to implement. A particularly interesting form of validation of the therapists assessments of internal change was attempted in which an experienced child psychotherapist, external to the study, made a blind assessment of the raw data of sessional material from early and later stages of treatment for a sub-group of twelve cases. This external clinical rater was blind to the children's history, referral problems and placement, and to information and ratings given by the therapists.

The findings regarding outcome were encouraging. In terms of 'external' change, fourteen of the total were agreed by all raters to have made considerable progress and another eleven showed some progress. The accounts given by parents and others agreed with the ratings by the therapists and researchers. In most cases, all aspects of relationships improved, including depth. Although the small numbers make comparisons difficult, it appeared that progress was greater where treatment had continued longer, and that external support for the treatment, by parents, carers and colleagues, was essential.

Although it was not expected that substantial inner change would be brought about in two years or less of therapy, in fact twenty-five of the children were said to show some degree of inner change, mostly in the direction of increased strength and supportiveness of internal figures, leading to greater security, trust and confidence and less depression.

Current and planned comparative studies of treatment

Group and individual treatment of sexually abused girls

A comparative study carried out by Trowell and colleagues, on the treatment of sexually abused girls, is now beginning to report findings (Trowell and Kolvin 1998; Trowell *et al.* 1998). This was a multi-centre study, based at the Tavistock Clinic, the Maudsley Hospital, the Royal Free Hospital, Camberwell Child Guidance Clinic, and Guy's Hospital (Trowell *et al.* 1995). As the authors make clear, a multi-site project such as this imposed huge difficulties over and above the considerable administrative and therapeutic tasks involved in any psychotherapy outcome study. They felt too that the complexity of the work was increased by the nature of the referral problem; the dynamics of abuse and power had an impact upon clinicians and research team, and the management of these stresses within the professional networks and the host institutions was crucial.

The subjects of the study were girls aged between six and fourteen, who had suffered contact sexual abuse, who were symptomatic, and who had disclosed the abuse within two years of referral. A small number were excluded if assessed as too disturbed, or where out-patient psychotherapy was not considered suitable. Seventy girls were allocated at random either to individual therapy, or to group therapy. A comprehensive multidisciplinary initial assessment of each child, including information about the carer, was followed by a reassessment one year after therapy began, and a two-year follow-up is on the point of completion.

This was not a comparative study in the sense of comparing two treatments on a single dimension of 'effectiveness'. Rather, the researchers hypothesised that the different forms of treatment would lead to differences in outcome. Their hypotheses were that group treatment would produce more short-term benefit and individual treatment more long-term benefit; and that group treatment would be particularly helpful to social skills and social relationships while individual therapy would produce change in the girls' relationships, attachments and views of themselves and improve their academic and general social functioning. A modified version of the Adult Attachment Interview (George *et al*. 1985) was used as part of the initial assessment and at the two-year follow-up, and one aim of the research was to explore whether this can be used to measure change, and whether it can be used to predict which children will benefit from psychotherapeutic intervention.

Individual therapy consisted of up to thirty sessions of focused work, guided by both a manual of agreed statements of the aims and objectives of the work, and by clinical supervision. Most individual therapists were qualified or senior trainee child psychotherapists from one school of training, but some had less formal training. Group therapy consisted of 12–16 sessions, depending on age, with older-girl groups receiving more sessions; again, these were guided by a manual. The group therapists were Senior Registrars in Child Psychiatry and other senior members of Child Mental Health teams. All were experienced in this area of work. The number of sessions, for both individual and group work, was based on the minimum felt by experienced therapists to be useful.

For both forms of therapy, the girl's carers were offered guidance and counselling in parallel with the girls, but less frequently. This work was generally done individually because, given the random allocation of the girls to treatment groups, the attempted parent/carers groups turned out to be very heterogeneous. Different carers had very different needs – for instance, the needs of a professional foster carer were very different from those of a distressed single mother whose ex-partner had abused the child.

It became evident that the girls had extensive difficulties at referral; the initial assessments diagnosed post-traumatic stress disorder in the majority, and reactive attachment disorder, major depressive disorder and anxiety disorder in over half.

Individual psychotherapy and cognitive-behavioural therapy

Cognitive-behavioural therapy, a symptom-focused form of treatment, has been better researched than other forms of therapy with children, and has been found effective in a sizeable proportion of cases with emotional disorders without other associated diagnoses (Roth and Fonagy 1996). A planned comparative study by Fonagy, Target, and the University College London/Anna Freud Centre research team, in collaboration with service providers and other researchers, aims to compare cognitive-behavioural therapy with psychoanalytic treatment for children referred for help with severe emotional problems, where the anxiety or depression is accompanied by other forms of disorder such as disruptive or attachment disorders, learning difficulties or psychosomatic disorders. Children will be randomly allocated to one of four comparison groups: intensive (3–4 times weekly) or non-intensive (once-weekly) psychoanalytic therapy; cognitive-behavioural treatment; or treatment or management as usual at the referral centre. Both forms of psychoanalytic therapy include parent work, and similarly the cognitive-behavioural treatment includes parent training. Each group will consist of forty children, and both psychoanalytic therapy treatments, and the cognitive-behavioural treatment, will offer at least one year of treatment. The two different forms of therapy, psychoanalytic and cognitive-behavioural, will be carried out by different therapists, so that each form of treatment is provided by therapists trained and experienced in, and committed to, their particular therapeutic approach. The study includes careful procedures of manualisation, training and monitoring of treatment process, to ensure that the treatment provided adheres to the approach it represents. Outcome measures include both standard measures, and others developed for the study, more closely attuned to the kind of changes which may be especially relevant in treatment. It is also intended to examine treatment costs, savings to other services, and satisfaction of children and their families or carers.

Some contributions of child psychotherapy in other research

This next section will point to some areas in which child psychotherapists have brought their specialist skills to bear as part of a wider research effort. My aim in this section is not to give full coverage to these varied projects, but to provide a 'noticeboard' so that interested practitioners may be aware of studies relevant to their own particular interests.

Work with refugee children and families

A current project based at the Medical Foundation for the Care of Victims of Torture, London, and run by a child psychotherapist and a group analyst, should be mentioned. This specialist project is primarily clinically oriented, but is developing ways of assessing therapeutic change in refugee families – for instance, in enabling parents who have themselves suffered trauma and displacement to recognise and respond helpfully to their children's own difficulties. The work with the children is more fully described in the chapter by Melzak (this volume).

Children who sexually abuse others

One recently completed study at the Institute of Child Health/Great Ormond Street Hospital, London, uniquely included research child psychotherapists as members of a multidisciplinary investigation of young adolescent boys who sexually abused other children. This was a hypothesis-generating study, resulting in a number of indicators of risk, the generalised validity of which is now being tested out in a large longitudinal follow-up study on a separate population (Hodges *et al*. 1994; Lanyado *et al*. 1995; Hodges *et al*. 1997; Skuse *et al*. 1997, 1998).

The initial study examined 11–15-year-old boys, using a four-group design – boys who were both victims and perpetrators of sexual abuse, boys who were victims but not perpetrators, boys who were perpetrators but not victims, and antisocial boys who were neither victims nor perpetrators of sexual abuse. Full background assessments were carried out, which included cognitive and psychiatric assessments, interviews with the mothers about their own personal histories and sociometric assessment of the boys' peer relationships.

A sub-group of forty-eight boys entered an extended psychotherapeutic assessment. This consisted of twelve once-weekly individual psychotherapeutic sessions with an experienced child and adolescent psychotherapist. Half of these sessions included structured or semi-structured material, some standard questionnaires or interviews, and others designed especially for the study. In this way additional detailed quantitative data could be gathered and qualitatively explored in the therapeutic context. The focus of the other six sessions was determined jointly by the concerns of the child and by the clinical and research concerns of the psychotherapists. The sequence of sessions containing semi-structured material was constant, and the form in which sessions were recorded provided a standard framework for recording themes and aspects of psychotherapeutic process.

The task of the psychotherapists was to provide a clinically informed, integrative view of all the clinical and research information available about the individual boy, his developmental history and current functioning. The aim was to clarify the mechanisms which led to, or protected against, the development of sexually abusive behaviour in each individual. The three psychotherapists involved met weekly to discuss work with those boys who were in the process of intensive assessment. As recurrent themes began to emerge, and particular individual mechanisms became clearer, these were fed back and discussed in regular meetings of the whole research team, providing hypotheses which could then be operationalised for statistical analysis.

The result of the study was a risk index, identifying a series of factors which appeared to increase the risks of a boy becoming an abuser. These differed somewhat between boys who had been sexually abused and those who had not, but included a history of discontinuity of care, exposure to domestic violence, exposure to other forms of abuse, and a sense of rejection. The identified factors are now being tested out through follow-up of a different and much larger sample of sexually abused boys. If validated, there will be obvious implications for primary prevention in boys known to have been sexually abused who may be at risk of developing an abusive orientation.

Psychotherapeutic process

In 1988 the Erica Foundation in Sweden, in collaboration with a British academic, began a programme aiming to stimulate the staff to greater understanding of the need for research and development in psycho-therapeutic work with children. This programme, which continued for several years, considered several areas; one was an analysis of 'turning points' in child psychotherapy (Carlberg 1997), and another used a focus-group approach with approximately ten therapists of pre-school children diagnosed with pervasive developmental disorders – psychotic and borderline conditions. This focused upon characterising four phases of work with these children: assessment, beginning psychotherapy, the main process and the termination phase (Nilsson 1997).

Effects of earlier maltreatment on children placed in new families

Child psychotherapists have long been interested in work with this group of children, and the Fostering and Adoption workshop at the Tavistock Clinic and the Adoption Research Group at the Anna Freud Centre reflect this interest. Assessment work with these children is often requested, and interest has developed in the use of narrative-stem assessments as one way of gaining some picture of the child's mental representations of attachment relationships, self and parental figures. Similar assessments are becoming more widely used within an attachment-theory framework. The narrative stems technique presents children with the beginning of a story, with some dilemma or situation which requires resolution, both spoken and simultaneously played out with small toy figures. The child is then invited to 'show me and tell me what happens next in the story'. It has the advantage of providing an indirect and displaced form of investigation with children who have suffered maltreatment within their families of origin.

A study by child psychotherapists based at Great Ormond Street Hospital and the Anna Freud Centre compared a clinical series of 4–7-year-olds who had been removed from their parents following abuse or neglect, with a matched group of children living with their families where there had been no child protection concerns (Hodges and Steele 1995). The narrative stems were found to be useful as a part of individual clinical assessment, but in addition meaningful differences between the groups emerged in the prevalence of certain themes and defensive manoeuvres, rated in accordance with a manual of definitions. These differences both supported the validity of the clinical use of these assessments, by showing that differences within the stories were associated with known differences in previous actual experience, and confirmed the usefulness of the technique as a research tool.

Building in part on this work, a prospective investigation of children in adoptive placements is under way, based jointly at Great Ormond Street Hospital, the Thomas Coram Foundation for Children Adoption Service and the Anna Freud Centre. This study examines attachment representations in the adoptive parents prior to placement (using the Adult Attachment Interview) and in children shortly after placement (using narrative stems) alongside other assessments. One aim is to track changes in the children's representations of attachment relationships between themselves and their new parents by repeating the narrative assessments at one and two years post-placement. A second is to examine the relationship between the attachment organisation of adoptive parents, and changes in the child's attachment and adjustment. The attachment organisation of adults is strongly related to that of their birth children, but there has so far been no research on adoptive families where the child already has a complex and difficult attachment history.

Some comments on the field of research in child psychotherapy

To begin with research on outcome, there are still very few adequate studies of psychoanalytic psychotherapy with children and adolescents. However, the position has begun to shift significantly since Graham's (1993) assessment that 'The evidence for the effectiveness of individual psychotherapy is weak, and with the decline in the predominance of psychoanalytic techniques in North America, there has also been a marked reduction in the number of scientific studies evaluating its efficacy'. The studies published since this assessment have, at the very least, encouragingly reopened the question of effectiveness, and done so in ways which point to the need for further research in clinically relevant form.

It also seems a significant step, at least at a symbolic level, that among the studies about to begin, there are two which could be described as second-generation, in that they are based on evidence of effectiveness from earlier studies. Viner's study on diabetic control will examine the dimension of intensiveness of treatment, based on the evidence from Moran *et al.* (1991) that intensive treatment provides effective help for children with dangerously poor diabetic control. The Fonagy–Target comparison of cognitive-behavioural treatment with psychoanalytic therapy, intensive and non-intensive, draws on the information from their study of the Anna Freud Centre data, which showed the effectiveness of psychoanalytic treatment with emotional disorders and examined the effects of other variables including age and treatment intensiveness.

Why has psychoanalytic work with children engaged in so little scientific evaluation of its effectiveness? Increasingly, child psychotherapists working in some areas of the NHS are under pressure to give evidence of the usefulness and cost-effectiveness of their work, and so such evaluation becomes important in practice as well as in principle. It may also be worth reminding ourselves at this point that the fact of assessment, and the criteria decided for assessment, inevitably have effects upon what is assessed. It is better, obviously, to be able to ensure a good fit between criteria and what we want child psychotherapy practice to achieve, than to find practice measured against criteria which are irrelevant or unhelpful.

There are at least three sorts of reason, I think, why so little research has been done: ethos, problems of operationalisation, and reasons to do with the position of psychoanalytic training and work in institutional structures. In part, the lack of research reflects an ethos – a feeling on the part of psychoanalytic therapists that their work cannot be appropriately evaluated in these terms. There is a fear that the nuance of process and transference will be lost, that the codification necessary for research loses the essence of what psychoanalytic work is about and how it operates; while case studies can go some way to capturing this and retaining the individual complexity of cases. Ironically, the shortcomings of previous research bear out the view that it grossly misrepresented psychoanalytic therapy; but it would be very hard to argue that the ethos of psychoanalytic distrust of research was based on actual familiarity with the research studies.

These concerns obviously lead on to the second question, that of appropriate operationalisation. On this subject, Boston and Lush (1993) comment:

> A central issue to be addressed in the evaluation of the effectiveness of psychotherapy concerns the relationship between the concepts and aims of psychotherapy, and the scope of currently available research techniques. Psychotherapists have placed considerable emphasis on change in the structure of the personality with fundamental implications for perceptions, internalised relationships, and sense of self, and have argued that these are only loosely related to symptomatic change. Symptoms may be lost without substantial internal changes, and may remain or increase whilst profound change is taking place. In the past this may have appeared to be a bid to deny research access to the phenomena, but now that the measurement of internal processes such as social perceptions (Dodge, 1990), self concept (Harter, 1986) and attachment status (Main et al, 1985) are available, their relationship to symptomatic change may be studied. The role of transference, both as therapeutic tool and technique of assessment does still present difficulties. Therapists may be reluctant to allow researchers into the clinical team, because of anxieties that this might lead to transference

complications, and where transference observations are to be included in the assessment, these will not by definition be available from control groups.

Boston and Lush note Stevenson's (1986) view that the problem lies in establishing 'outcome measures that would do justice to the therapists' multiplicity of aims. It is the articulation of outcome objectives and the development of indicators that they have been achieved that represents the main hurdle'. Their own study, described above, attempted to address this difficulty, examining the psychotherapists' aims for their particular patients and developing ways of assessing to what extent those aims were achieved, paying particular attention to qualitative, internal changes.

There is a strong argument to be made that whether or not the outcome indicators do justice to the specific characteristics of psychoanalytic treatment, psychotherapy should nonetheless be able to demonstrate its effectiveness in the same, albeit simpler, terms appropriate to simpler therapies. It may achieve more, but it should be able to show itself at least equivalent on appropriate measures, even if these measures do not adequately reflect its specific characteristics (Target 1998).

Not all child psychotherapy research is outcome research. This review has mentioned studies where other forms of research have been informed by, and sometimes initiated by, child psychotherapist's work. However, there is little multidisciplinary research work involving child psychotherapy. The ethos of child psychotherapists and the attitudes of other disciplines may both be involved here; and issues of appropriate operationalisation are just as important in this form of research as in outcome research. For child psychotherapists to work as an integral part of a research team, they have to be able to consider clinical material in ways which can render it into data which are research-friendly. Equally, the other professionals in the research team must be open-minded enough to value the specific material which psychotherapists may be able to provide, and to help devise ways of using it in research terms.

Beside the issues of ethos and the problems of operationalisation, there is also a likely structural, institutional reason for the lack of research compared to some other psychological treatments. Child psychotherapy training has not been based in academic departments, unlike clinical psychology or medicine. Institutionally, it has thus had no research skills base, and (until some recent changes) has taught none. Unlike university lecturers, those engaged in teaching child psychotherapy are under no expectation that they will also be pursuing research, especially conventional forms of empirical research.

There has, in contrast, been a strong tradition of case-study based scrutiny of areas of particular interest, as evidenced by the many specialist workshops at the Tavistock Clinic, and the research groups at the Anna Freud Centre, to take the two longest-established training schools. These have also produced a large number of publications. Despite the important role of case studies, with few exceptions (e.g. Moran and Fonagy 1987; Lush *et al.* 1998) these studies have not made use of the single-case designs often used in studying behavioural techniques. Though not all such designs lend themselves to cases treated by psychoanalytic psychotherapy, some are more appropriate (Fonagy and Moran 1993). Treatment cases studied and presented in this way, with a degree of methodological rigour, may have an important role in building bridges with other disciplines and establishing the credibility of psychoanalytic psychotherapy alongside other modes of treatment. They are, evidently, neither equivalent to, nor a substitute for, psychoanalytic case studies.

The way in which training institutions have developed, historically, seems to have worked against the development of more academic forms of research whose methodology is shared with related areas of medicine, psychology or the social sciences. This may begin to change with the present development of clinical doctoral programmes linked to child psychotherapy training, and the increasing links between child psycho-therapy training schools and university departments. Change will be slow, if only because child psychotherapy training is long and few child psychotherapists are trained relative to most other clinical specialisms. However, if I were writing not now but in fifteen years time, the research landscape this chapter surveys could be a very different one.

References

Bachrach, H. M., Galatzer-Levy, R., Skolnikoff, A. and Waldron, S., Jr (1991) 'On the efficacy of psychoanalysis', *Journal of the American Psychoanalytic Association* 39: 871–916.

Barrnett, R. J., Docherty, J. P. and Frommelt, G. M. (1991) 'A review of child psychotherapy research since 1963', *Journal of American Academy of Child and Adolescent Psychiatry* 30(1): 1–14.

Boston, M. (1989) 'In search of a methodology for evaluating psychoanalytic psychotherapy with children', *Journal of Child Psychotherapy* 15: 15–46.

Boston, M. and Lush, D. (1993) 'Can child psychotherapists predict and assess their own work?', A research note, *ACPP Review and Newsletter* 15(3): 112–19.

—— (1994) 'Further considerations of methodology for evaluating psychoanalytic psychotherapy with children: reflections in the light of research experience', *Journal of Child Psychotherapy* 20(2): 205–29.

Carlberg, G. (1997) 'Laughter opens the door – turning points in child psycho-therapy', *Journal of Child Psychotherapy* 23(3): 331–49.

Dodge, K. A., Bates, J. E. and Pettit, G. S. (1990) 'Mechanisms in the cycle of violence', *Science* 250: 1678–83.

Fonagy, P. and Moran, G. S. (1993) 'Selecting single case designs for clinicians', in N. E. Miller, L. Luborsky, J. P. Barber and J. P. Docherty (eds) *Psychodynamic Treatment Research: A Handbook for Clinical Practice,* New York: Basic Books.

Fonagy, P. and Target, M. (1994) 'The efficacy of psychoanalysis for children with disruptive disorders', *Journal of American Academy of Child and Adolescent Psychiatry* 33: 45–55.

—— (1996) 'Predictors of outcome in child psychoanalysis: a retrospective study of 763 cases at the Anna Freud Centre', *Journal of American Psychoanalytic Association* 44: 27–77.

George, C., Kaplan, N. and Main, M. (1985) 'The Berkeley Adult Attachment Interview', unpublished manuscript, Dept of Psychology, University of California at Berkeley.

Graham, P. J. (1993) 'Treatment of child psychiatric disorders: types and evidence for effectiveness', *International Journal of Mental Health* 22: 67–82.

Harter, S. (1986) 'Cognitive-developmental processes in the integration of concepts about emotions and the self', *Social Cognition* 4: 119–51.

Heinicke, C. H. (1965) 'Frequency of psychotherapeutic sessions as a factor affecting the child's developmental status', *Psychoanalytic Study of the Child* 20: 42–98.

Heinicke, C. M. and Ramsey-Klee, D. M. (1986) 'Outcome of child psychotherapy as a function of frequency of sessions', *Journal of American Academy of Child and Adolescent Psychiatry* 25: 247–53.

Hodges, J. and Steele, M. (1995) 'Internal representations of parent–child attachments in maltreated children', paper to Thomas Coram Foundation conference 'New Developments in Attachment Theory', September 1995.

Hodges, J., Lanyado, M. and Andreou, C. (1994) 'Sexuality and violence: preliminary clinical hypotheses from psychotherapeutic assessment in a research programme on young sexual offenders', *Journal of Child Psychotherapy* 20(3): 283–308.

Hodges, J., Williams, B., Andreou, C., Lanyado, M., Bentovim, A. and Skuse, D. (1997) 'Children who sexually abuse other children', in Justice Wall (ed.) *Rooted Sorrows: Psychoanalytic Perspectives on Child Protection, Assessment, Therapy and Treatment*, Family Law, Bristol: Jordan Publishing.

Lanyado, M., Hodges, J., Bentovim, A., Andreou, C. and Williams, B. (1995) 'Understanding boys who sexually abuse other children: a clinical illustration', *Psychoanalytic Psychotherapy* 9(3): 231–42.

Lush, D., Boston, M. and Grainger, E. (1991) 'Evaluation of psychoanalytic psychotherapy with children: therapists assessments and predictions', *Psychoanalytic Psychotherapy* 5: 191–234.

Lush, D., Boston, M., Morgan, J. and Kolvin, I. (1998) 'Psychoanalytic psychotherapy with disturbed adopted and foster children: a single case follow-up study', *Clinical Child Psychology and Psychiatry* 3(1): 51–69.

Main, M., Kaplan, N. and Cassidy, J. (1985) 'Security in infancy, childhood and adulthood: a move to the level of representation', in I. Bretherton and E. Waters (eds) *Growing Points of Attachment Theory and Research*. Monographs of Society for Research in Child Development.

Moran, G. S. and Fonagy, P. (1987) 'Psychoanalysis and diabetic control: a single-case study', *British Journal of Medical Psychology* 60: 357–72.

Moran, G. S., Fonagy, P., Kurtz, A., Bolton, A. and Brook, C. (1991) 'A controlled study of the psychoanalytic treatment of brittle diabetes', *Journal of American Academy of Child and Adolescent Psychiatry* 30: 926–35.

Nilsson, W. (1997) 'The child psychotherapists view of therapy with severely disturbed children', English summary of Ericastiftelsen report no. 9, Stockholm, Sweden: Erica Foundation.

Roth, A. and Fonagy, P. (1996) *What Works for Whom? A Critical Review of Psychotherapy Research*, New York: Guilford Press.

Rutter, M. (1994) 'Beyond longitudinal data: causes, consequences, changes, and continuity', *Journal of Consulting and Clinical Psychology* 62: 928–40.

Shaffer, D., Gould, M. S., Brasie, J., Ambrosini, P., Fisher, P., Bird, H. and Aluwahlia, S. (1983) 'A children's global assessment scale (CGAS)', *Archives of General Psychiatry* 40: 1228–31.

Shirk, S. R. and Russell, R. L. (1992) 'A re-evaluation of estimates of child therapy effectiveness', *Journal of American Academy of Child and Adolescent Psychiatry* 31: 703–9.

Skuse, D., Bentovim, A., Hodges, J., Stevenson, J., Andreou, C., Lanyado, M., Williams, B., New, M. and McMillan, D. (1997) *The influence of early experience of sexual abuse on the formation of sexual preferences during adolescence*, Behavioural Sciences Unit, Institute of Child Health, London; submitted to the Department of Health.

Skuse, D., Bentovim, A., Hodges, J., Stevenson, S., Andreou, C., Lanyado, M., New, M., Williams, B. and McMillan, D. (1998) 'Risk factors for the development of sexually abusive behaviour in sexually victimised adolescent males: cross sectional study', *British Medical Journal* 317(18 July): 175–9.

Stevenson, J. (1986) 'Evaluation studies of psychological treatment of children and practical constraints on their design', *ACPP Newsletter* 8(2): 2–11.

Target, M. (1993) 'The outcome of child psychoanalysis: a retrospective investigation', unpublished PhD thesis, University of London.

—— (1997) 'The long-term outcome of child psychoanalysis', research plan, unpublished manuscript, Anna Freud Centre.

—— (1998) 'Research and audit', in R. Davenhill and M. Patrick (eds) *Rethinking Clinical Audit: The Case of Psychotherapy Services in the NHS*, London: Routledge.

Target, M. and Fonagy, P. (1994a) 'The efficacy of psychoanalysis for children with emotional disorders', *Journal of the American Academy of Child and Adolescent Psychiatry* 33: 361–71.

—— (1994b) 'The efficacy of psychoanalysis for children: prediction of outcome in a developmental context', *Journal of American Academy of Child and Adolescent Psychiatry* 33: 1134–44.

—— (1996) 'The psychological treatment of child and adolescent psychiatric disorders', in A. Roth and P. Fonagy *What works for whom? A critical review of psychotherapy research*, New York: Guilford Press.

Trowell, J. (1997) 'Attachment in children: developments from a study with sexually abused girls', unpublished manuscript, Tavistock Clinic.

Trowell, J. and Kolvin, I. (1998) 'Lessons from a psychotherapy outcome study', *Journal of Clinical Child Psychology and Psychiatry* (in press).

Trowell, J., Berelowitz, M. and Kolvin, I. (1995) 'Design and methodological issues in setting up a psychotherapy outcome study with girls who have been sexually abused', in M. Aveline and D. Shapiro (eds) *Research Foundations for Psychotherapy Practice*, Chichester: Wiley.

Trowell, J., Ugarte, B., Kolvin, I., LeCouteur, A. and Berelowitz, M. (1998) 'A psychopathology of child sexual abuse', *European Journal of Child and Adolescent Psychiatry* (in press).

Weisz, J. R. and Weiss, B. (1989) 'Assessing the effects of clinic-based psycho-therapy with children and adolescents', *Journal of Consulting and Clinical Psychology* 57: 741–6.

Weisz, J. R., Weiss, B., Alike, M. D. and Klotz, M. L. (1987) 'Effectiveness of psychotherapy with children and adolescents: a meta-analysis for clinicians', *Journal of Consulting and Clinical Psychology* 55: 542–9.

Part III

The child and adolescent psychotherapist in different therapeutic environments

10 The child and adolescent psychotherapist in the community

Margaret Hunter

The majority of child psychotherapists work within the National Health Service in community child and adolescent mental health teams. There is no single formula for the composition of these teams which have developed at the local level according to the priorities of health, education and social service departments of that area. These services were traditionally joint-funded with health, education and social service departments all putting money into the service which would then employ childcare professionals from each agency. Education funded education social workers, psychiatric social workers, educational psychologists, educational therapists and, occasionally, special needs teachers. Social services funded social workers who had statutory casework training and sometimes retained statutory responsibilities in the mental health team. Health services funded child psychiatrists, child psychotherapists, clinical psychologists and nurses. The particular mixture of different professionals was variable and so were their priorities. For example, if a team was funded by education there would be a greater concentration on school problems and expectation that the team be responsive to difficulties such as bullying and school refusal. Where social services departments funded the service, greater concentration on child protection, accommodated and fostered children, treatment of abused and neglected youngsters and support to residential homes was expected. Health departments, which are always one of the fund providers, have their own priorities in screening and treating mental illness, depression, para-suicides and rarer conditions such as childhood psychosis or eating disorders.

Child psychotherapists in these community mental health teams are therefore involved in a very wide range of childhood problems. Just as some of the teams specialise in certain problems, so it is common for child psychotherapists to develop their own clinical experiences and speciality – for example, in autism or in the treatment of child sexual abuse. A child psychotherapist's training is broadly based, however, and the concentration on normal child development, the child's emotional growth and primary relationships form the backdrop to any later specialist experience. Child psychotherapists are the only professionals whose four to five years of training concentrates specifically on children and their emotional growth.

The understanding of mental handicap, trauma or mental illness is always placed in the context of the feeling and developing child so that the child's view of themselves and of their world retains a central place. The phenomenology of any medical condition or social problem – that is to say the experience of the child – remains the core of the child psychotherapist's approach.

According to the team in which the child psychotherapist is based, working practices will follow the priorities set by that team. In a predominantly health setting, the team is likely to be led by a child psychiatrist and informed by psychiatric research. Referral to the service may come by the general practitioner, community medical officer or school doctor. Some teams, based for example in hospitals, may only accept referrals through GPs especially where fund holding of practices are involved. Other community services, perhaps situated in a large building in a residential area or as part of a health service building on a council estate, are open to families within a certain geographical area to walk in or phone for an appointment. Referrals commonly come to the team from schools, from social workers, from health visitors and from other professionals working with children in the community.

Referrals from schools[1]

The Child and Adolescent Mental Health Service (CAMHS) receives a letter, often from the Special Educational Needs Coordinator (SENCO) or from the headteacher. Attached to the letter is the CAMHS's own referral form which it has made available to all the local schools and which it sends routinely to any telephone enquirer. The form asks for basic information about the referred child and the problem.

Case example: Jimmy

Referral

In this case, Jimmy Marlowe, aged six and a half, is presenting great difficulty at school. The referral reads:

Jimmy is moody and irritable. While he can sometimes produce work which gives evidence of his intelligence, he easily flies into a rage at his teachers' requests and has tantrums over minor things. He swears and shouts at the teacher. He can spend play time fighting with other children but, more often, is solitary and unwilling to go out to play. His mother says he's just as bad at home. He won't get ready in the morning and makes her late for work. He hates his little sister Jenny and recently pushed her over. His mother recently split up from her partner, this is Jenny's father, not his. Mrs O'Farrell would like some help with him because he is just getting worse and worse. He wrecked his trainers deliberately last month by cutting them with scissors. His mother says he's made her so depressed she has had to have tranquillisers from her doctor. Please see them urgently!

The multidisciplinary meeting

All referrals to the CAMHS team are brought to a meeting of the whole team. This gives the different members of the team, including the child psychotherapist, the opportunity of hearing about all the week's referrals and discussing them with all the different professionals in the team. If there is reason to believe that a particular discipline will be appropriate the case will be allocated to them. But often it is not clear what skills may be needed and team members will be equipped to assess the needs of the child in a preliminary way referring back to colleagues if particular skills are needed. In this instance the child psychotherapist takes the case although she has not decided that individual child psychotherapy is needed. She will use her generic casework skills to get a clearer picture of the difficulties and her initial role will be an exploratory one.

At the team discussion of Jimmy's case, members wondered how depressed mother was and what effect that may have on Jimmy. They noticed that the initial tendency was to blame him for mother's state of mind although it seemed likely that the separation from her partner would also have affected her. Jimmy sounded quite depressed and unhappy himself as he was isolating himself from friendships at school. His cutting up his trainers with scissors was an unusually destructive and defiant act, especially given his age. The team thought that it might be important to get further details about this.

Fact finding and liaison work

The GP is informed of every child who attends a CAMHS clinic. In this letter, the doctor is given an outline of the referral and asked for any relevant information. A GP may inform the team, for example, that the child has long-standing enuresis problems, or that mother or father have a mental health problem, or that the child has had several episodes in hospital, or the GP will commonly have nothing to report but would like to be kept informed of treatment and progress.

> In this case, the school, as the referring agency, will be informed of the acceptance of the referral, given an indication of the extent of the waiting list, and then advised of allocation.
>
> Later the psychotherapist may speak to the child's teacher, or set up a meeting at the school with mother and teacher, or visit the school to see Jimmy in the classroom context. First though he or she will want to see Jimmy's mother so that any liaison work is approved by the parents and done in partnership with them.

In this case example, no other agencies were indicated as being involved, but where the child has seen other professionals such as an educational psychologist, or has a past history with Social Services, information will also be sought from these by the allocated child psychotherapist.

At the same time, or before this flurry of requests for information, the therapist will write to the parent or parents – in this case Mrs O'Farrell – telling them that the clinic has received a referral for their child and will be sending an appointment. Where there is a waiting list, some indication of waiting time will be given. Many NHS trusts specify a time limit between referral and first appointment. However, most Child and Adolescent Mental Health Services have suffered staff cuts by education and social services departments who have tightened their budgets year on year. Some CAMHS therefore have waiting lists of months rather than weeks and it is rare to find a CAMHS without a waiting list.

Seeing the family

It is common practice to ask to see all family members living together at the first appointment or at some time early in the assessment process. This enables the child to be seen in their family context and is useful because observations of the family's interactions can be gathered, as well as different family members' views of the child's problems. Frequently, however, mother and the child in difficulty will be the ones who present themselves at the first appointment.

Mrs O'Farrell and her two children come to this first appointment. Jenny is three and a rather sturdy, fearless girl who commandeers her chosen toys with gusto and settles to some vigorous playing at the dolls house. Jimmy is a well-groomed, morose-looking boy. Both children are 'mixed race', their fathers are Afro-Caribbean and mother is 'White British'. The details that the psychotherapist collects from mother allow her to describe their ethnicity in her own way, so this is the parent's description. Mother is angry and harassed at having to take time from work for this appointment. She expresses resentment and humiliation that the school complain of her son. She is worried that she cannot control him because he does not seem to listen to her. His father was violent and she wonders if he has inherited this? The therapist gets her to explain that Jimmy rarely sees his own father but he did like Jenny's father. Since they split up Jenny spends Saturdays with her dad but he doesn't take Jimmy. The therapist asks Jimmy about his likes and dislikes, his friends. He answers cautiously and complains that other children at school get him into trouble. It emerges that he cut his shoes because he had been promised new ones which he did not receive. It was Jenny's father who had promised them, but he left before the promise could be fulfilled. His irate mother, faced with a child who had cut open the toes of the old trainers, had telephoned his own father and eventually he bought him the new pair Jimmy was now wearing.

The child psychotherapist reflects that the shoes have certainly become a powerful symbol. Somehow they have reconnected Jimmy to his rarely seen father after the sudden loss of his sister's father. Mother and son are gently offered the suggestion that the problem is about meaning and misery rather than simply an act of vandalism and attack on mother. Mrs O'Farrell softens when she considers that she was not the target of Jimmy's rage and sympathises with her own feelings of loss and abandonment. Her own depression surfaces and she admits that she has had little time for Jimmy, having buried herself in work to overcome her despair. She subsequently begins to under-stand her excessive blame of Jimmy as a way to get rid of her self-blame at the ending of her relationship.

Jimmy meanwhile is helped to stop attracting punishment to himself and to find other ways of ensuring his mother's attention.

Individual child work in this case was only a few exploratory sessions with Jimmy. Away from his mother's depression and anger he was able to reveal that he felt himself to blame for driving away his sister's father. He revealed his wish to see his second father again and, fortunately, this could be arranged. Jimmy was able to be less jealous of his sister and other children at school who, in his mind, seemed well cared for by their fathers. The trainers which he had so vehemently attacked in his rage at being abandoned were the nearest he dare come to an attack on his fathers for failing him and deserting him.

In this case, the child psychotherapist worked to bridge Jimmy's feelings with his mother's concern. Mother was enabled to feel that she now understood what had gone wrong between them and turned her attention to supporting rather than blaming her son. She no longer felt that the therapist was likely to blame or punish her and became able to use the therapist for support.

The therapist also took on an advocacy role for Jimmy and his mother at the school. At a school meeting, teacher, mother, Jimmy and therapist worked out a way in which Jimmy could be assisted through this difficult period in his life. He was allowed to go and seek help from the SENCO when he felt that things were getting too much for him in class. Mother voiced her concern that she felt overwhelmed by the teacher's daily reports on Jimmy's naughtiness and these were modified to weekly reports and the school clarified that mother should not punish Jimmy for these.

After four months the family seemed to have recovered well from this adjustment difficulty and treatment ceased.

Had Jimmy's difficulties been more entrenched, or had mother been chronically depressed, longer-term individual psychotherapy for son or mother may well have been indicated. This example has been chosen however to illustrate an aspect of the child psychotherapist's work which receives little attention, though it is very common − namely, short-term focused interventions where the therapist uses her psychodynamic skills to inform and to guide a family's understanding of each other.

Referrals from Social Services

Social Services departments have a legal, statutory role in child protection. They also have wide-ranging duties to 'children in need'. Given the severe limits on expenditure and the historical legacy of under-funding for children's services (Berelowitz and Horne 1992), it is not surprising that some of the neediest and more complex referrals come from social services departments seeking help for their clients. I have advocated elsewhere (Hunter 1993) that Social Services departments employ their own child psychotherapists because of the inordinate amount of work necessary to 'network' these cases as well as engaging in often intensive psychotherapy − that is, two to four times weekly. Mental health services, with a steady flow of referrals that must be allocated to their mental health workers, soon grow impatient with cases that are so greedy of resources. Nevertheless, it is for these young people that individual psychotherapy is most often the treatment of choice, easily justified in terms of the necessity of 'repair work' to children who are typically multiply disadvantaged and often multiply traumatised. In economic terms, too, the cost of even the most intensive psychotherapy – i.e. five times a week – amounts to an annual cost of only about £6,000 (at 1997 prices) whilst residential care costs the same amount for six weeks – and annual costs for most therapeutic communities are at least £50,000. There is a clear gap in the provision of psychotherapy to support children either in their own homes or in foster homes where this could prevent the need for the expensive residential option. As a practitioner who specialises in psychotherapy with fostered children, I find that children whose placements are under threat of disruption can often be well held by the extra provision of psychotherapy, together with supportive work with the foster parents. Children and young adults who have a weight of emotional baggage that they cannot carry through their days end up throwing it in every direction. These young people are undoubtedly helped by regular visits to a psychotherapist who assists them to sort it through instead of telling them to put it away and attend to another task. In general such young people find the attentiveness of a psychotherapist irresistible and, despite a tendency to act in rejecting ways, there is a surprisingly high chance that they will engage in therapy.

A referral from a Social Services department to a CAMHS is usually of the 'tip of an iceberg' variety. By this, I mean that it will detail a problem that is one amongst many. It will be wise for the therapist to begin the work by meeting the social worker, if there is an allocated one, and gathering a history which is usually extensive.

Case example: Leroy

Leroy is a ten-year-old boy referred by his social worker for help with a severe episode of sexual assault. Leroy has been found roaming the streets having run away from his mother, a 'crack' cocaine user. On trying to contact his mother the police find that she has disappeared from her home address. As she is wanted for questioning on suspicion of theft it appears that she has gone into hiding on that account. Leroy is accommodated with temporary foster carers. He discloses to these foster parents that he has been sexually assaulted by a friend of his mother's and that she is implicated in the abuse, having accepted money for letting this happen to him. It is this event that has precipitated Leroy's running away and his mother's disappearance.

A child psychotherapist receiving this story has to struggle with her own reactions as well as sharing the response of the foster carers and the social worker. Working with the network in this and similar cases is not simply time- and energy-consuming, it is emotionally taxing. Having a colleague who sees the child in psychotherapy whilst the therapist deals with the network is one tried and tested way to set up the work. However, it is also possible for both tasks to be performed by one child psychotherapist. There is some benefit in both the social worker and foster parents relating directly to the therapist as they can all feel more involved in the work with the child, but for the therapist this is emotionally strenuous.

In this case, it was Leroy's good fortune to have been placed with foster carers who extended their initial short-term commitment to long-term care. He could eventually therefore look forward to staying with them until maturity. Getting him to sessions more than once weekly was not acceptable to foster mother however. Often a balancing act between the needs of the child and the needs of the carers must be taken into account. Many foster carers are devoted 'rescuers' who will give a great deal to a needy child. This can clash with their view of psychotherapists whom they fear may upset the child and his settledness in their home. They may also feel disempowered by a psychotherapist, or rivalrous, envious, or afraid. Making a good working relationship with a carer is not incidental or additional to a child psychotherapist's task, it is the 'sine qua non' of treatment. Compromise, even in the form of fewer sessions than is ideal, is a better working contract than the use of professional power to override the foster parents. Foster carers are very much a 'Cinderella' service, poorly paid, poorly supported, and rarely allowed to have proper recognition in the decisions made around children in their care. Yet they are the closest adults to the child; it is they who pick them up when they fall, who put them to bed each night. If a foster carer is opposed to treatment, it is better to work with and through them rather than overrule them.

For Leroy, foster mother's reservations were not too antipathetic and, over two years of treatment, a respectful alliance was made between therapist and carer for once-weekly psychotherapy.

The major part of Leroy's therapy concerned his relationship to a mother he both idealised and denigrated. In the early stages of therapy he found relief in letting his therapist know that secretly he longed for his mother's return. These feelings are commonly difficult for an accommodated child to share with his foster carers. Partly, it is a problem of consistency where the child has initially allied himself with the foster parents against the abusive parent, and partly, it is a problem of loyalty to the rescuing carers; but it is also a problem of pain, where denial of the past and how much it haunts him seems to the child to be a better strategy for survival. The foster family may therefore be genuinely unaware how much these children recapitulate the past: the child takes good care to keep these feelings hidden. In Leroy's therapy, the traumatic components of his rape came out in a barely perceptible, piecemeal fashion: a hint here, a memory there, a worry confessed and lots of diversionary banter. It was not simply a matter of 'post-traumatic stress syndrome', though many of those symptoms appeared. It was also the years of neglect, of loneliness, of mistrust, preceding the sexual trauma. Gradually, these events subsided and Leroy looked to the future with some trepidation. He insisted that his psychotherapist attend his 'Child in Care' reviews and advocate his point of view about practical but deeply felt issues. He wanted it to be clear that, if mother returned, he would be allowed to see her. He wanted to be able to stay overnight with a friend from school without a 'police check' of the family. He wanted to stay in therapy for two years, but have review appointments from time to time once it came to an end.

It may be clear from these details that child psychotherapists working with children 'in care' have to play a role in the 'loco parentis' network as well as working with the inner world. A different orientation to confidentiality is often needed. It is important that the child feels that the adults form a 'parental couple' even if this is composed of several adults. To this end, the child psychotherapist can play a useful role as a representative of some of the child's feelings; she can also advocate decisions which will help the child and can share her understanding of the child's situation with social worker and foster parents as well as sometimes with judges and courts of law. In all this difficult terrain of what to share and what to keep quiet, the criterion used is the best interests of the child. Inevitably this is work where child psychotherapists are still formulating the codes of practice. This is new terrain for psychoanalytic work and it will take time to determine what is best practice. Nevertheless, we should trust to the traditional analytic tools – calm reflection, analysis of need, logic, predictable consequences and learning through experience.

Consultancies to agencies

Some referrals to child psychotherapists are essentially requests to use their psychodynamic skills for understanding a child's difficulties without the child necessarily being seen.

Case example: Tina

Tina, a fifteen-year-old girl resident in a local authority community home, is referred by a residential social worker for 'counselling'. Tina's problems are multiple and she is proving difficult for staff to manage as she reacts to any enforcement of boundaries, such as being in by a certain time, by running away for a day or two. It emerges during the initial stages of exploring this problem that residential staff have had strong disagreements about how to handle this behaviour. One group of staff thinks a tough policy of removing privileges should follow any episode of absconsion. Other staff fear that Tina will simply stay away longer if she faces what they perceive as reprisals when she returns.

The referral of Tina to a child psychotherapist at this point is more interesting than practical. Tina openly stated that she would never go to see a therapist. The child psychotherapist judged Tina was unlikely to comply with appointments when she already ran away regularly. What did the staff hope the therapist could do that they could not? It is likely that staff were seeking help with their difficulty in parenting Tina and keeping themselves from being 'split' in the process. Working with the staff group was the 'treatment' that the child psychotherapist suggested. When staff were seen together they came to reflect that perhaps they were acting out Tina's dilemma for her. Parental boundaries were being felt to be either useless, ineffectual and unprotective or, alternatively, cruel, disempowering and punitive. In discussion staff noted that this exactly mirrored Tina's upbringing. Her alcoholic mother who raised her to the age of thirteen was preoccupied with drink and therefore ineffectual and neglectful, whilst her abusive father was strict, angry and punishing when he forced her to obey him. Once the staff could think about these themes, and their reflection in staff behaviour, it became possible to act in a significantly different way. The staff group agreed a common set of responses to Tina. They emphasised that her safety was their prime concern and negotiated sanctions that reflected her need to be protected when she showed she could not protect herself. This involved one-to-one care when Tina was most vulnerable, but allowed a negotiated series of ways in which she could demonstrate that she was able to look after herself for increasing lengths of time. Although Tina did not respond immediately to these changes, the staff group held on to their cabinet-style decisions and were no longer split or critical of each other. Tina found it harder to play off one staff member against another and the highly emotional dramas that had surrounded Tina's absconsions calmed down. A sense of containment and control steadily grew and, over a six-month period, Tina's running away was half the rate it had been six months earlier.

This staff group had found the consultation with a child psychotherapist helpful enough that they twice requested further consultation sessions concerning other residents in their care.

For some residential homes, schools and special schools, consultation sessions focused on individual children or a series of children can be a service provided in its own right. Child psychotherapists thus frequently work with staff or professional groups helping them to understand more clearly the meaning of difficult or challenging behaviour. Child psychotherapists offer, in consultancy work, a time for busy and burdened staff to pause and focus on the meaning of behaviour. Their psychoanalytical skills can be used to bridge the child to the worker, or to alert staff to symbols or patterns of interaction that may reflect an inner drama of the young person. Being caught up in countertransference responses is an everyday event to child psychotherapists however careful or experienced they are. Therefore insights are offered from the basis of joining with the staff's worries and struggling with them to bring some emotional clarity to what is happening. Sometimes simply helping to bear the confusion and hostility which is directed toward staff is the main task. Professionals can easily feel that they must be wrong or to blame when things go badly for very damaged young people. It is often a great reassurance for project workers to find that it is not their lack of skills or expertise that is necessarily at fault: rejected and abused children reject and try to abuse their carers. It can be an extremely enabling insight to learn that feelings of anxiety, bewilderment, anger, rejection have been evoked or provoked by the child and therefore should be unravelled and understood with some care. To return to my example. The staff who wanted to punish Tina for running away were in many senses being provoked into being a punitive parent. The helpless feelings that some staff felt towards constraining her destructive behaviour had similarly been deposited in them by Tina's own despair and that of her mother's before her. Tackling emotional obstacles is a real event that allows behavioural approaches to be well founded. These staff were very skilled in their application of a wide range of sanctions and rewards, but what was needful was the message behind the behaviour, both for themselves and for Tina that 'we care and this is how we are trying to show it'.

Most child psychotherapists spend at least part of their professional lives in consultation work. More senior practitioners may spend as much time in this way as seeing children individually. As part of the NHS directive for 'cascading' skill sharing, this work is clearly significant as it involves colleagues in acquiring psychodynamic insights as well as helping young people.

Private practice

Many child psychotherapists spend at least some proportion of their time in private practice.

Referrals

The Code of Ethics which binds all members of the Association of Child Psychotherapists states that we may not advertise for clients. This policy however is currently under review, and there are feelings that this stricture, which is aimed at protecting the public, may in effect serve to keep them uninformed. Traditionally, child psychotherapists have received their private referrals via GPs and other agencies such as social services departments. Parents who may be aware of psychoanalytic treatment often refer themselves, finding a therapist by personal recommendation or by contacting the Association of Child Psychotherapy. Nevertheless, it is clear that there are many parents who have not heard of child psychotherapy, and GPs and social service departments who are poorly informed. In recent years, the profession has sought to enhance its public profile and the Child Psychotherapy Trust (see Appendix) a charitable organisation, has taken on this role as one of its central functions.

A private referral usually goes to an individual child psychotherapist. There is no central or clearing system. The psychotherapist therefore has to embark on a preliminary exploration of the child's suitability for treatment and then an assessment process. A typical intervention may look like this:

1   Meeting with parents to identify their concerns about their child.
2   Meeting with parents together with child and rest of family.
3   A full child's history can be taken from the parents.
4   The GP will be informed and asked for relevant information.
5   The school may be informed and asked for information.
6   Three meetings with the child alone will explore the child's current preoccupations and willingness to use therapy.
7   A meeting with the parents to discuss the child psychotherapist's findings, her formulation of the problem and her recommendation for treatment.

This therefore is very similar to what happens in a CAMHS referral except that here it is focused on the possibility of psychoanalytic treatment. Alternative treatments or recommendations will result here in advice to approach more suitable services. Some, but not all child psychotherapists may offer short-term or focused work in a private setting. It is best practice to separate the assessment process from treatment and to allow a clear decision-making time for the parents as to whether to embark on psychotherapy for their child. A treatment contract has then to be negotiated, whether written or verbal, for it is important that the parents commit to a treatment plan that will not lead to the child being suddenly withdrawn. A regular review procedure and supportive meetings for the parents will be negotiated at this time also.

Child psychotherapy practised privately can be a quieter process; it is not so much in the public domain with its demands of reports, case notes and dilemmas of confidentiality. The child and therapist can in many cases simply get on with it. It is useful, and usually wise, for a colleague to see the parents privately at regular intervals. The therapist will also want to meet with parents at regular intervals, usually between 6–12 weeks, i.e. half-termly or termly.

All child psychotherapists are bound by the rules of the Association of Child Psychotherapists to carry personal indemnity insurance of a regulated amount in order to work privately. They are also bound by a Code of Ethics and Rules which include a formal complaints procedure. A sub-committee of the Association, the Private Practice Sub-Committee, works to support best practice and gives advice and guidance to fellow practitioners. Therefore, although there is little formal organisation of private practice, the field is not under-regulated. One of the current concerns of child psychotherapist private practitioners is the lack of regulation of non-qualified therapists who can offer their services to the public through advetisements and claim any amount of competency without check. The public are little aware of the difference. The Association of Child Psychotherapists has been active in the process of registration, not only having long held its own register of members, but joining with other accredited therapists in joint registers. Child psychotherapists are therefore listed in the Register of the British Confederation of Psychotherapists (BCP) – all psychoanalyticlaly trained therapists – and in the Register of the United Kingdom Council for Psychotherapy (UKCP). These registers only list therapists whose training and practice adhere to strictly laid down criteria and to professional codes of rules and ethics.

To summarise then, child and adolescent psychotherapists working in the community carry out a wide spectrum of interventions with a range of young people who present with different problems. They liaise with schools, with GPs, with the social services and with parents. Psychodynamic principles always underpin their skills, as does their focus on the child, but the range of application is very wide.

Note

1 All names are fictitious and examples derived from an amalgam of several cases.

References

Berelowitz, M. and Horne, A. (1992) 'Child mental health and the legacy of child guidance', *Association for Child Psychology and Psychiatry Newsletter* (commissioned review) 14(4): 161–7.

Hunter, M. (1993) 'The emotional needs of children in care', *Association for Child Psychology and Psychiatry Review* 15(5): 214–18.

Szur, R. and Miller, S. (1992) *Expanding Horizons: Psychoanalytic Psychotherapy with Children, Adolescents and Families*, London: Karnac.

11 The child and adolescent psychotherapist in a hospital setting

Sandra Ramsden

Introduction

Child and adolescent psychotherapy is a newcomer amongst the professions, becoming firmly established after the Second World War. In hospital settings child psychotherapy has increased in the last two decades. However, the specific theoretical and clinical foundations for this hospital work date back to the beginnings of child psychotherapy. John Bowlby and his work not only gave an impetus to the foundation of the Association of Child Psychotherapy and to the establishment of formal trainings, but also his early work on maternal deprivation (Bowlby 1951) and subsequent work on attachment (Bowlby 1971) had immediate effect on the development of the theory and practice of child therapy.

James and Joyce Robertson, child psychotherapist collaborators with Bowlby in the 1950s and in the 1960s, produced four films on the impact on young children of separation. Three of these films were set in hospitals. The work of Bowlby and the Robertsons was strongly instrumental in altering paediatric practice. The influence of Bowlby on the contents of the Platt Report (HMSO 1959) had a primary impact on changing health policy by advocating the admission of parents together with their young children to hospital.

The action research of another distinguished child psychotherapist, Isabel Menzies Lyth, throughout the 1960s, '70s and '80s, provided a further essential dimension for hospital-based work: a psychoanalytic view of the social system of the hospital (Menzies Lyth 1959/1961/1970; 1973/1982, revised 1987).

Anna Freud, too, had a noticeable interest and influence in the area of paediatrics. As well as employing a paediatrician to run a Well Baby Clinic within her own child analytic clinic, she took part in regular case-based discussions with prominent consultant paediatricians and wrote, amongst other texts, 'On the interactions between paediatrics and child psychology' (Freud, A. 1971) and 'The role of bodily illness in the mental life of children' (Freud A. 1952).

There now exists a large literature on the psychological aspects of illness and hospitalisation in relation to children, young people and their families, based both on research and clinical practice. Child psychotherapists work in many different hospital settings now, and make their contribution to our knowledge of the difficulties and needs of both patients and staff.

This section will endeavour to represent an overview of child psychotherapy work in hospital, at the same time drawing particularly on the author's twenty-five years' experience at the Middlesex Hospital in London (now part of the UCHL – University College Hospitals, London). The actual focus will be on the *liaison work* in the hospital setting rather than referrals into the child psychiatric team in hospitals of community cases.

The hospital setting

Most child and adolescent psychotherapists are based within departments of Child and Adolescent Psychiatry (departments of Psychological Medicine) in the hospitals. In one unusual arrangement a child psychotherapist is employed within the Paediatric Directorate and not based in a child psychiatry department. Child psychotherapists are members of multi-professional teams that include psychiatry, psychology, social work and sometimes family therapy and/or specialist nursing.

The hospital, in its wards and clinics, represents an 'applied setting', taking the practice of psychotherapy far outside its consulting room base. The hospital represents a complex and potentially confusing system for the child, young person and family. It is likely that physical illness, occasional or chronic, severe psychosomatic disorder or serious psychological dysfunction (such as an eating disorder or an hysterical conversion) would have brought the family to the hospital. Few have specifically sought the aid of a psychotherapist for their problems and few will understand what contribution a psychotherapist might make to their difficulties. Most child psychotherapists working in this hospital context underline the singular importance of their relationship with colleagues in the hospital. This support is practical and reciprocal and operates at all levels of the system from consultant to student nurse. Thus the photograph of a child psychotherapist may figure in the photocall on the notice board in the paediatric ward; his or her name may appear on the out-patient clinic notice board of staff in attendance. The introduction of the child psychotherapist, whether direct or indirect, by phone call or letter, is made carefully, with some appreciation of its meaning for child and family. This meaning itself may emerge gradually – as in the work with the mother of a diabetic ten-year-old admitted to hospital for a second opinion review of poorly controlled diabetes. When the therapist first met mother and child, the mother had 'forgotten' that the consultant endocrinologist arranging the admission had told her that this would include consultation with a child psychotherapist, myself. As I spoke to mother and daughter, I learned that the mother had been dissatisfied with her daughter's earlier medical care, that she herself had been called 'a neurotic mother' because she was so anxious about poor diabetic control. Later in the contact she told me that she 'remembered' being told about me but had thought it might mean she was being 'fobbed off'. As she became satisfied with the new medical advice, and diabetic control improved, she became fully co-operative and communicated with me about difficulties in the family history and problems that she and her daughter had struggled with.

Physician, nurse and psychotherapist in the hospital setting will hold a view of the bio-social-psychological function of children, young people and families, a view that embraces individual development, the family and the wider system in which the child lives, and the nature and impact of illness and its treatments. Whether illness is primarily physical or psychological in aetiology and in appearance, its effect is most likely to be both. Treatments by this author of children who were failing to grow were undertaken initially at the insistence of a referring paediatric endocrinologist who was convinced that the aetiology of their growth failure was primarily psychological and that psychotherapeutic treatment, including that of the family, was the treatment of choice. The author's experience of successful psychotherapeutic intervention in these cases provided a basis for her occasionally to make a *negative diagnosis* to the referring doctor – that is, it appeared that psychological factors were insufficient to account for growth failure. Such an opinion in some cases would result in further endocrine investigation and, for example, successful treatment by growth hormone. This illustrates the importance of a clinical dialogue over time, a basis of a working clinical relationship between physician and therapist, which becomes an essential feature of the hospital context. Context is not simply a place or a set of structures but a complicated set of professional interrelationships and attributions.

The hospital context, similarly, for the child, young person and family is both actual and subjective, influenced by fears and fantasy as well as by knowledge and real experience. Each individual during development has experiences of illness, medicine and doctors. Some will have previous occasional experience of hospital and a few will suffer chronic disease or severe illness. Active and information-seeking styles of coping, family support and appropriate preparation positively influence the outcome of the individual's contact with this medical system. It is important and encouraging that successful coping within the inherent difficulties of hospitalisation may leave child and family more resilient in facing future stresses (Rutter 1987): that is, that hospital experiences do not inevitably damage children and young people.

Context, too, is changing and evolving: one thinks of changes in medical practice and in health policy; of the moving of care away from hospitals towards primary care settings. At the same time it is known in London that hospital A & E (Accident and Emergency) departments are often used by patients in preference to more appropriate primary care settings. There has been a move from hospital-based midwifery to community midwifery practice. Hospital admissions grow shorter and day care more frequent. In contrast, evidence-based medicine indicates that specialist centres for some serious medical conditions such as cancer and cardiac problems produce better outcomes. Specialist centres move children and families *away* from their own local communities for their care. Specialist centres are also likely to be involved in treatment trial programmes. The hospice movement and the development of home care teams have moved some palliative and terminal care away from hospitals.

Child psychotherapy work in hospitals

There are no national guidelines in the UK for the provision of psychosocial care for children and young people using hospital services, either in terms of levels or type of provision. There is now considerable evidence of the effects of illness and of hospitalisation on young children, their siblings and on family functioning. (The effects of hospitalisation on young children were recently reviewed by Sylva and Stein (1990).) A literature review, 'The psycho-social aspects of childhood cancer', has been published by VanDongun-Melnen and Sanders-Woodstra (1986). Increased vulnerability in emotional and behavioural development in children with chronic illness has been demonstrated by Garralda *et al.* (1988). The vulnerability of siblings has similarly been shown by Lavigne and Ryan (1979). There are also accumulating indications of problems among staff working with sick children: high staff mobility associated with 'burn-out' is one index.

In the face of this considerable need, several questions arise including: 'What *can* be done by mental health practitioners; what *should* be done that is known to be effective; what is *actually* done by mental health professionals and what is done by child psychotherapists?'

Mercer (1994), in a recent review of psychological approaches to children with life-threatening conditions and their families, helpfully distinguishes between 'in-breadth approaches' and 'in-depth approaches'. In-breadth approaches may include self-help groups, facilitator-led groups, outings, holidays and information giving. Mercer cautions therapists against missing participation at this level, which may either be all that some of the most resilient families require, or may provide a positive experience base from which less resilient families can move towards more in-depth approaches. This background of in-breadth approaches, involving mental health professionals, may reduce the anxiety and possible stigma experienced by some patients and families who actually need more help from professionals.

In-depth approaches need to be delivered with a flexibility that is guided by children's and families' current needs and fluctuating capacities. A variety of therapeutic approaches and modalities will be required. These may all be available to a single mental health professional such as a child psychotherapist, but are more likely to be held within a multiprofessional group. The psychological task for a child and family varies greatly with the nature of the medical problem: for example, a diagnosis of diabetes in childhood implying lifetime insulin injections, medical supervision and long-term risks; or growth hormone deficiency, diagnosed in childhood, with daily injections, medical supervision and the treatment not completed until late in puberty; a childhood leukaemia with acute illness, intensive treatment and good prognosis but with some danger of recurrence; or a scoliosis operation in puberty with one- or two-stage surgery, well prepared for, with immobilisation and some pain immediately post-surgery and a full recovery.

Interventions in such cases would be directed at child and family, possibly also including the extended family. They would involve staff, and occur while patients are in-patients or out-patients. Indications from research indicate that those most vulnerable while hospitalised are those with severe or chronic illness with frequent hospitalisations, particularly early in life. Individual factors in the child or the family – temperament, family constellation, family histories, family functioning – may all add dimensions of vulnerability. Indications are that many interventions may be helpful, especially those that *prepare* children and families, and those that *strengthen coping styles*. There is little specific indication about which type of intervention may be maximally effective with which type of difficulty, and still less is known about what precisely are the mutative factors in interventions. But here all patients look for early and accurate medical diagnosis and appropriate treatment. Most ask for access to information and want a part in planning and decision-making. The statutory framework, which allows access to medical information and requires informed consent to treatment, supports them. Some may need psychological help in understanding, processing or coping with information. They may need or ask for help with shock at the given information – for example, the shock of premature birth, the shock of a child born handicapped, the shock of medical diagnosis, the grief of bereavement. Some (probably a minority) may ask for 'counselling'; some may retrospectively complain that counselling was not offered, when needed. Some ask for access to other patients coping with the same condition: this may be offered in support groups or, where they exist, by national associations. In the hospital setting it may involve other patients who have recovered, for example, from an amputation or a transplantation of an organ. Recovered patients may volunteer to be available to meet others undergoing the same experience. Some professional 'steering' of these arrangements can be helpful.

In some cases children or families may not be coping with their illness and this may show in a variety of ways – most commonly in non-compliance or difficulty in compliance with unpleasant regimes and in overt distress. This is picked up by medical and nursing staff, through their contact with child and family, from behavioural difficulties in children, learning problems or deterioration in sibling relationships or child–parent relationships. Help may then be offered.

The child psychotherapist is likely to modify his or her methods in the

hospital setting, although patients referred as out-patients during or subsequent to hospital treatment may be treated in traditional ways. Emanuel,
a child therapist working at the Royal Free Hospital London, in his paper
on psychotherapy with children with leukaemia (Emanuel *et al.* 1990) gave
a very clear exposition of the child psychotherapist's aims as 'attempting to
receive and contain the conscious and unconscious communications of the
children, or elucidating the meaning of the experience of the child. Naming
feelings and emotions which the child is communicating to us remains an
integral part of this work'.

Emanuel and his co-authors, and Vas Dias (1990), agree that transference
interpretations are rarely used in the work undertaken in the hospital
settings. Transference itself is complicated, as a therapist is part of a large
group of people looking after the child. The child's contact with a therapist
is discontinuous, according to the pattern of hospital admissions or appointments. The contact with the therapist may be interrupted by medical
procedures. The psychotherapist working with child or family directly
will have a particular role: representing the child's understanding and
experience of illness and of treatment; representing a psychological perspective; and he or she may have a responsibility to try to modify possible
iatrogenic effects of medical treatment. These roles and responsibilities
require that particular consideration be given to parameters of confidentiality, the contract between child, family and family member and the therapist. Without the responsibility for medical treatment, the child therapist
can have the child's overall developmental needs in perspective. The therapist will be aware of the inevitable dependency or possible over-dependency
a child and a family may have on the doctor and others in the face of illness,
and may have an active role in working with patient and doctor in helping
patients assume possible and appropriate responsibility for their own monitoring and care. The therapist may have a similar role when dependency and
responsibility become too fixed between parent and child, for example, in
the administration of injections for the treatment of diabetes. The aim is to
help the child to be a 'child-with-diabetes' rather than a 'diabetic child'.

In-breadth interventions

These encompass individual one-to-one consultations or supervision given
by the child psychotherapist to a staff member, teaching or training
activities such as lectures or seminars to medical students and nursing staff,
or the supervision of clinical case studies undertaken by medical students.
They may include group supervision – for example, the child's therapist
working with a group of play specialists in a ward setting, or with a group
of domiciliary midwives. Group work may be therapeutic or supportive in
intention, as in parent groups led by child psychotherapists or in staff
support groups similarly led. There are inherent difficulties in running
such groups in high stress environments: in parent-support groups there

are times when parents may find experiencing the stress of other parents not helpful to them, and too much to bear whilst they are bearing much already in relation to their own child. The group itself may be avoided and badly attended. Sometimes, staff groups which aim to anticipate and understand feelings and reactions in a stressful situation become over-identified with the source of the distress itself (group = upset) and are also avoided.

There are, however, examples of successful staff support groups conducted by child psychotherapists. Linda Winkley quite vividly illustrates her experience in such a group in the children's ward of a renal dialysis unit (1990). Sandy Stone wrote to me of her experience in conducting a long-running staff support group in the children's ward at the Middlesex Hospital, which is a regional centre for the treatment of bone tumours and which had and continues to run a mixed patient group:

First of all, the more people working on the ward who participate, the more effective is the group. In an ideal world the consultant in charge would co-run the group. Although multidisciplinary groups are hard to run they accomplish more and I think the benefit is very clear in terms of ward function and patient care. The group is especially important with oncology patients, who may be treated over several years, because it provides a continuous picture of the patient experience but facilitates continuity of care. Hence it reduces patient distress about change-overs in staff and staff distress about coming in on the middle of a case. The group runs for one hour each week. Although this may look expensive in terms of staff time it actually saves time. People are not duplicating each other's efforts during the week as happens when there is not such a forum, or retrieving situations in which people have acted individually. Problem solving takes place collectively and then solutions get implemented; everyone feels better with consistency – patients, parents and staff. By containing anxiety the group lessens the scramble and shooting-off in all directions that occurs in response to the fact that working with patients with cancer is like working perpetually on a major disaster.

The Middlesex group has a dual purpose; to look after the well-being of patients and their families and the well-being of people working on the ward. It is not a teaching seminar. It differs from the ward round or the nurses' report as there is no specific agenda. The focus is clinical. Cases are bought up by participants because they are worrying, upsetting, puzzling, hopeless or infuriating. As the feelings of the people working on the ward are responsively intertwined with the feelings and personalities of the people undergoing treatment, it is essential for the group leader to untangle this complex weaving. Strong feelings are contagious. They spread and turn up in surprising places causing people to behave in unusual ways. They interfere with communications, decision-making and treatment.

Adolescents who have cancer are faced with two psychological tasks that are diametrically opposed. They must move towards independence, but the cancer forces them to become dependent. Staff support groups struggle in each case towards accepting this dilemma and the feelings it produces in all involved.

The child psychotherapist may have some advantages in attempting this in-breadth work as he or she is a kind of 'inside-outsider', not directly responsible for medical care or nursing nor for the training of junior staff. He or she will need to become knowledgeable about illness and its treatment, remaining never the expert, although able to attempt to identify the positions of both staff and patient. Child psychotherapy training is founded on knowledge of normal development and an appreciation of the unconscious influences upon behaviour. A child psychotherapist may contain the anxiety of patient, the staff or the parents, process it, reflect on it and sometimes make sense of it with the group. For example, Sandy Stone writes about just one meeting of one staff group:

The group began with an intense discussion of child abuse sparked off by the discharge from the ward of an adolescent with a miserable long history of abdominal pain for which no organic cause had been found. In his background was an abusive alcoholic father. People struggled to understand why parents abused. Although this discussion was useful it seemed to me to be partly maintained by a wish not to look at the presence of so many children with poor prognoses receiving last-ditch treatment on the ward.

Eventually we got around to discussing denial in parents: it came up in context of Paul and his family. Paul had died peacefully at home; many of the staff had been to the funeral. Back at the house his mother told the ward sister she never really believed Paul would die. Mother confessed she knew she had been horrible whenever they came up to the ward but she could not help it. I linked the parents' need for denial with our need for denial. This was resisted strongly, as if I had made a criticism. But as I spoke of the investment all of us made in the kids, how we cared as the parents did, the idea seemed more acceptable. I went on to say that this week we specially needed it because of the awfulness of what was happening to 'our' kids on the ward. Reflecting afterwards, it seemed to me that on an unconscious level 'child abuse' was like the catalogue of horrors we impose on the children to try to get them better or keep them alive. What we do also hovers on the edge of abuse. Some children plead, 'No more chemo, no matter what!' To be involved in this means that staff take a terrible battering too. The child in each of us suffers 'abuse' by continually being exposed to pain and loss over and over again.

In-depth work

The single consultation

Jamila, a thirteen-year-old Bangladeshi girl with five siblings, was referred during a busy out-patient growth clinic that the author attends. She was accompanied by her father. She had complained of a hoarse voice. This had no endocrine basis and had also been investigated in ENT where it was found to have no organic basis.

During a short exploration of the family situation by the child psychotherapist, the patient revealed (and her father confirmed) that an older brother frequently attacked her, and in particular attempted to strangle her. The father was unable to control this older son; his daughter was frightened and outraged. Further exploration revealed that the father felt that his daughter was too loud and assertive in the family, not helpful enough to her parents: behaviour contrary to their cultural expectations. All the children had been born in England. This consultation revealed the individual psychological, family and cultural dimensions of a problem presenting as an organic one. The child psychotherapist referred the case, with the backing of hospital consultants, GP and family, to a local specialist Asian Family Counselling Service known to her.

Mr and Mrs B, parents of a nine-year-old girl with Androgen Insensitivity Syndrome (AIS) were referred to the author by a Paediatric Endocrinologist for an initial consultation relating to their management of their daughters' care.

AIS is amongst the inter-sex disorders. An inherited deficiency of testosterone receptors causes failure of male external genitals to form in the male foetus. A uterus, Fallopian tubes and an upper vagina do not develop because of the functioning of another hormone, the anti-mullerian hormone. The baby is born appearing female but has male chromosomes (XY). The diagnosis in some cases may not be made until puberty when there is no menarche and no growth of axillary or pubic hair.

Mr and Mrs B had learned of their daughter's condition soon after her birth at the time of a medical crisis-intervention, and had begun to prepare Sally in a low-key way ('not all ladies can have babies') for the fact that she would be infertile as an adult. Now they had to tell her a little more as she needed soon to start oestrogen replacement treatment: her internal male gonads had been removed surgically when she was an infant. The parents were highly anxious about this 'telling', seeing it as irreversible and dangerous. The particular meaning of 'telling', their particular fears associated with it, was the focus of a lengthy consultation that assisted the parents towards some differentiation of their own perspective from their daughter's and some elaboration in their minds of the processes of 'telling' and 'knowing'. The parents drew actively on the therapist's knowledge of the condition, her work with many other parents, and with girls and young women with this condition.

The isolation of patients and parents with a diagnosis such as AIS is related to its rarity and to the high levels of anxiety experienced about inter-sex conditions and their implications. The nature of gender identity is frequently explored by parents in these consultations. A fuller discussion of work with children and gender identity development can be found in Chapter 24.

Longer-term work with child patients

Studies in the 1980s by Moran, a child psychotherapist and psychologist, made a significant contribution to the understanding of the psychological effects of diabetes. These seminal studies demonstrated, using physiological measures of diabetic control, the impact of psychoanalytic psychotherapeutic intervention. The first two case examples illustrate a continuation of child psychotherapeutic work with this condition, its complexity and its effectiveness.

The first is provided by Francesca Bartlett working at St Bartholomew's Hospital, London:

Donna B was a thirteen-year-old diabetic girl, admitted to stabilise her following a dangerous and unaccountable rise in her blood sugar levels. She had a history of similar admissions and there were concerns as to what might lie behind the swings in these levels. This instability had also led to her missing a worrying amount of time from school. The social worker and diabetic nurse had met with Donna and her mother on a number of occasions but remained unsure as to what might account for what was happening. On the ward Donna came across to everyone as pleasant and co-operative. She presented similarly when I met with her in the ward 'Den', a hang out for the adolescent patients. Whilst we talked I was struck by how very responsible and mature Donna was for her age and how immensely accommodating she was of her hard-working mother, a single parent, whose long working hours meant Donna's having to take on much of the responsibility for administering her insulin as well as caring for a younger brother after school. It became clear that Donna felt unable to make direct demands on her mother, who was struggling to do her best for her family after a long period of unemployment. Donna was able to acknowledge how by sometimes failing to administer her insulin correctly she was mobilising the sort of support she really needed at a crucial time in her development as an adolescent. She attended a follow-up meeting once discharged, and through liaison with the diabetic nurse and her mother we managed to instigate a more supportive regime for Donna at home, thereby taking some of the burden of responsibility for her physical care from her shoulders.

The second example is provided by Carol Hughes who works at the Belgrave Department in King's College Hospital, London:

Alan is an adolescent boy with diabetes who had been severely unstable necessitating upwards of fifteen emergency admissions to hospital in the two years preceding our intervention. Given that he was in hospital for an average of a week to two weeks each time, this had a severe impact on his daily functioning. We intervened with a combined package of prescribed admissions at the same rate that he was having the emergency admissions (that is roughly two or three weekly intervals, staying five days), and then twice-weekly psychotherapy when he was in hospital, and once-weekly family therapy. Along with this went, of course, liaison with the hospital staff and the paediatricians treating him. A huge amount of work was done trying to establish and protect treatment boundaries e.g. when the boy or the family could ring up the professor out of hours and when they could not, and what local emergency services could and should be provided in terms of medical emergency. Within six months the emergency admissions for ketosis dropped away to five. It is now absent and it has been almost eight months since there has been an emergency admission. Along with this massive and dramatic reduction in emergency admissions there has been a concurrent improvement in the glycosoated haemoglobin. It is clear that the health service has saved huge amounts of money by an expensive but relatively time-limited intervention.

The third case illustration is provided by Angelina Trelles Fishman from the Middlesex Hospital, London, and reflects contact with an adolescent girl with lymphoma. It shows the moving from child to parent and the connection of the therapist's work with other ward staff.

I went to introduce myself to Mrs B and twelve-year-old Paula, who had recently been diagnosed as having Non-Hodgkin's lymphoma. The doctors had explained to the family that this was a type of cancer that was treated successfully in most patients, and that they could say that it was one where there was about an 80 per cent survival rate. Paula was the only daughter of an engineer (who was at a later stage described as 'anti-talking' by mother), whom her mother had married when Paula was a toddler. Mother (who described herself as 'I just get on with things') had worked mostly in pubs in her youth, and had now stopped working at a health organisation in order to be able to care for Paula.

Paula was lying in bed, apparently asleep, looking pale and tired. Mother presented as calm and composed; perhaps slightly 'cut off'. She invited me into their cubicle. I mentioned that we could talk outside if she wished, so that we would not disturb Paula's sleep. 'Come in, I want to hear what you have to say', said Paula, suddenly opening her eyes and seeming quite alert. I introduced myself to Paula explaining that I had thought she was asleep. She clarified that she believed that people were talking behind her back these days, and that she wanted to hear what everybody had to say. On exploration it emerged that Paula was anxious and upset because she was not sure whether she could trust her mum to be completely open with her about her illness. She added that every time she needed to have a scan or other procedure done, then the doctors took her mother aside to talk to her. I reflected on how such impressions made Paula feel very insecure, that she may have thought I was doing the same, and how worrying it was for her not to know exactly what was being discussed. Mother explained she had told Paula about her treatment and illness as far as she had been able to understand it from the doctors and that she had not agreed to talk to them separately. Paula said her mother had not told her everything: she had not said whether people could die from her illness. Mother thought about the doctors' explanations somewhat anxiously, and finally said she did not know, that she did not understand everything about it either. I said perhaps this was a question that naturally filled them both with anxiety, and wondered if perhaps having a joint talk with the doctors might help. They agreed and said they would raise it when they talked with the Registrar the following day. As if to continue to tell me about how insecure she felt, Paula began to tell me about when she was little and how mum was 'always losing me in the shops'. Mother calmly confirmed this, saying that she was always running off. Paula added some other details of school life in the same vein, and finally said she realised she was only thinking about all the bad things now, and that she was being negative. I acknowledged this was a time when she was naturally feeling very insecure, and perhaps it had stirred up memories of other times when she had felt similarly. I offered Paula some individual sessions to discuss her worries, which they agreed to.

It was interesting that in discussion at the staff meeting the following day, the doctors confirmed that they inadvertently talked to mum while Paula got 'worked up', and that perhaps Paula had good reason to feel suspicious. I fed back the exact nature of Paula's anxiety so that the Registrar would be aware of it when he met her to answer her questions.

Two months later there was a further incident with the family, this time involving mother. The nurses had expressed concern that she looked very tense and anxious, and that she had made comments, almost to herself, about how she felt she 'had to get out of here' while she pressed both hands against the glass of the window. The Senior House Officer had gone to see her that evening, and mother had intimated that she had suffered from claustrophobic anxiety since her college days. At the time this had required hospital appointments and attendance at group therapy sessions. She added that as Paula was getting better, she was in fact feeling worse and that she did not know why. The SHO had offered mother psychological input, which she was reluctant to take up, and tranquillisers which she had refused. They agreed, however, that she would think about these options.

The following morning I went to the ward as usual and saw Mrs B walking down towards Paula's room, looking stiff and tense. We greeted each other and, unaware yet of the situation, I instinctively asked how things were and whether she would like to have a chat. She accepted and I realised she was not feeling well when she started looking for a room as actively as I was doing. As the private spaces were all busy, we ended up in the adolescents' room where she burst into tears. We sat side by side on the couch with Mrs B looking at me out of the corner of her eye as she did not feel able to turn her head and neck in my direction. She explained how she felt a tremendous pressure in her head that went down to her shoulders, and that as Paula had been feeling better now that she was successfully approaching the end of her treatment, she had been feeling worse, and thought she would not be able to cope. On exploration it emerged that Mrs B had a long history of claustrophobic anxiety (to this day she was unable to get into lifts) and she found it difficult to talk for fear of being overwhelmed. However she managed to explain that she was unable to get out of hospital for short breaks when Paula was in, because she would engage into obsessional thinking where she would have visions of Paula being run over by a car, etc. We discussed her fear that Paula could die if she took her eyes off her, and how perhaps paradoxically now that she was able to relax a bit more because Paula had responded well to her treatment, she was having a kind of 'delayed reaction' to all the stress they had been under. She had had to suppress this in order to be able to look after Paula and concentrate on her treatment. We also discussed her worries about having a chance to express her anxiety as she was afraid of being over-whelmed by it all, but that it might be a good thing if we kept in touch. She agreed and was grateful. She left the room and I realised she now turned her head and neck to say good bye.

Work with a sibling

An illustration provided by Francesca Bartlett from St Bartholomew's Hospital:

Jimmie L: Jimmie's younger sister, Ellie, was diagnosed as having leukaemia when Jimmie was three and a half and Ellie was two. Ellie had responded very well to treatment and was in remission but the parents were very concerned about Jimmie, now five, whom they described as acting in a crazy way at home. They were finding him quite unmanageable and he was disruptive and unsettled in school. I saw Jimmie for three assessment sessions and then met with his mother. In the assessment sessions Jimmie had come across as an intelligent and highly imaginative boy but also as very confused and trying desperately to work things out for himself. He had rather cut himself off from his mum, with whom he had been very close prior to his sister's birth. With Ellie's illness and the need for mother to spend a great deal of time with her, this process had been exacerbated, leaving Jimmie on his own, struggling with all sorts of fantasies of the terrible damage he had inflicted on his little sister and terrible fears as to the punishment he would receive in consequence. Jimmie's disturbance and anxiety manifested itself in difficult and maddening behaviour which left his parents exhausted and unsympathetic, their emotional resources already depleted after the very worrying time they had had nursing Ellie through her treatment. I followed up the assessment with a number of sessions for Jimmie and his mum whereby they were able to find their way back to each other and Jimmie was able to find his proper place back in the family as well as to feel settled with his peer group and function better in school.

Work with parents

This excerpt provided by Anita Colloms at the Homerton Hospital illustrates work within a Special Care Baby Unit. It indicates how her chosen focus on parents includes work with staff as well as other family members and siblings:

I make myself available to any parent who wants to speak with me, which also makes me accessible to parents and grandparents, the baby's siblings and any other family members who are visiting, as well as nurses, midwives, doctors, social workers, chaplain and students. I keep very regular hours and think of the ward as I would a patient in terms of the environment in that I try to arrive punctually, leave when I'm expected to and am consistent in warning them about holidays or absences.

My patient is the *mother and baby* together, *both of whom are premature* as Amira Fletcher said (Fletcher 1996, personal communication).

A premature birth interrupts all the natural processes of pregnancy. The development of the mother's fantasy life even from before conception, first about herself and the baby's father, and then, her baby in the family, comes to an abrupt end. The mother's body and her baby's body are separated before either is ready. Mrs M and I are watching her 28-week-old son sleep two days after his birth. He is wearing a cap on his head, which holds the ventilator in place, and his chest is inflated like a little frog's. He is fed through a nasogastric tube and several lines connect to monitors. The muscles stand out in his arms and legs. His face is covered and he is receiving phototherapy.

I notice his mother feels shocked and she agrees. She had no warning at all. 'I did not expect THIS', she says, nodding in his direction. She is still in pain herself.

The baby is very still, but suddenly startles. I ask if he did this when he was inside her. She points to her belly. 'I can feel it. Here.' She still feels the baby as part of her own body.

Parents have to take in the loss of the imagined baby and of themselves as good parents. The absence of any predictability, especially with respect to the baby who hardly ever shows anything approaching linear progress, but also in relation to the loss of control over preparations for the baby and support for the mother (such as her own mother coming from abroad) usually means all plans are awry.

The child psychotherapist has a different role from the medical staff, who need strong defences to care for such small defenceless babies, often with painful and invasive procedures, well aware that many of their charges will die or endure permanent damage. We may observe the baby with the mother, alert to any response to her touch or voice, and help her discover her own special meaning for her baby. We may be the only people to whom it is acceptable to show anger, especially where parents fear the baby's care will be affected if they express their negative feelings.

Other members of the family are usually seriously affected by the early birth of a baby and sometimes young siblings are very traumatised while very young ones may be thought to be unaffected, their trauma missed. The mother of a 25-week-old girl said her five-year-old son had been told by school friends that little babies like his sister die. The boy was not allowed to visit during a flu epidemic and refused to let his mother give his new sister the doll he had bought for her – he wanted to make sure himself that she was still alive. Hearing this with the older child in mind, I could discuss it with hospital staff who were only too happy to find a way the child could visit the new baby. It was, however, more difficult to understand the experiences of his two-year-old sister, quietly sucking her bottle with large all-observing eyes.

Conclusion

The range and diversity of clinical work undertaken by child and adolescent psychotherapists in hospital settings has been growing steadily during the last three decades. Clinically-based research is also a feature now of work by some therapists in hospital settings. As child psychotherapy as a discipline slowly extends, it is likely that the work done in hospital settings will increase similarly and also that increasing numbers of child therapists will have some training experience in the hospital setting. The future will hold a greater emphasis on outcome evaluation and it is possible, where child therapists' work is preventative in intention (as in work with siblings and families of children with life-threatening illnesses), that 'quality of life' measures might be used. Child psychotherapists may follow the organisation of hospital medicine into specialist treatment centres by developing a greater range of specialised clinical skills relating to the hospital specialisations. In District General Hospital settings, which provide a full range of medical and surgical services, child psychotherapists are more likely to remain generalists in their work.

This chapter has provided a framework, including an historical perspective, within which to review this growing range and diversity in an applied field of work.

References

Bowlby, J. (1951) *Maternal Care and Mental Health*, Geneva: World Health Organisation.

—— (1971) *Attachment and Loss*, vol. I, London: Penguin.

Emanuel, R., Colloms, A., Mendelsohn, A. *et al.* (1990) 'Psychotherapy with hospitalised children with leukaemia: is it possible?', *Journal of Child Psychotherapy* 16(2): 21–37.

Freud, A. (1952) 'The role of bodily illness in the mental life of children', in *Psychoanalytic Study of the Child*, vol. VII.

—— (1971) 'On the interactions between Paediatrics and Child Psychology', in Special Issue No 1 1980.

Garralda, M. E., Jameson, R. A., Reynolds, J. M. *et al.* (1988) 'Psychiatric adjustment in children with chronic renal failure', *Journal of Child Psychology and Psychiatry* 29: 79–90.

HMSO (1959) *The Welfare of Children in Hospital* (Platt Report).

Lavigne, J. V. and Ryan, M. (1979) 'Psychological adjustment of siblings of children with chronic illness', *Paediatrics* 63: 616–27.

Menzies Lyth, I. (1959) 'Functioning of social systems as a defence against anxiety', in *Containing Anxiety in Institutions*, London: Free Association Books, 1988.

—— (1987) 'Action research in a long-stay hospital', in *Containing Anxiety in Institutions*, London: Free Association Books, 1988.

Mercer, A. (1994) 'Psychological approaches to children with life-threatening conditions and their families', *Review of the Association for Child Psychology and Psychiatry* 16(2): 56–63.

Rutter, M. (1987) 'Psychosocial resilience and protective mechanisms', *American Journal of Orthopsychiatry* 57(3): 323–56.

Sylva, K. and Stein, A. (1990) 'Effects of hospitalisation on young children', *Review of the Association for Child Psychology and Psychiatry* 12(1): 3–7.

VanDongun-Melnen, J. E. W. M. and Sanders-Woodstra, J. A. R. (1986) 'The psycho-social aspects of childhood cancer', *Journal of Child Psychology and Psychiatry* 27(2): 145–80.

Vas Dias, S. (1990) 'Paediatric psychotherapy: the development of a service in a general outpatient clinic', *Journal of Child Psychotherapy* 16(2): 1–20.

Winkley, L. (1990) 'Living with chronic illness: consultation to a children's renal dialysis unit', *Journal of Child Psychotherapy* 16(2): 49–62.

Further reading

Erskine, A. and Judd, D. (1994) *The Imaginative Body: Psychodynamic Therapy in Health Care*, London: Whurr.

Jacobs, B. and Green, J. (1997) *Psychiatric In Patient Treatment for Children*, London: Routledge.

Journal of Child Psychotherapy (1990) 16(2): Special Issue on work with children with an illness or disability.

Judd, D. (1995) *Give Sorrow Words: Work with a Dying Child*, 2nd edn, London: Free Association Books.

Magagna, J. (1997) 'Psychodynamic psychotherapy in an in-patient setting', in B. Jacobs and J. Green *op. cit.*

12 Therapy and consultation in residential care

Peter Wilson

There are good reasons for some children being in residential care. Despite prevailing concerns about costs, abuse and institutional dependency, it is nevertheless the case that many children need to be resident in establishments of one sort or another, at different times in their lives, in order to be adequately looked after, protected, educated and treated. Children who suffer chronic physical illness, children with severe learning disabilities, children whose behaviour is very irrational and bizarre or whose psychological illness is life threatening, such as anorexia nervosa – all require continuous attention and treatment within a safe environment. Children with serious behavioural problems, sufficient to be a danger to themselves or to others, need to be securely held and helped within the physical constraints of a secure unit or youth treatment centre. Children with emotional and behavioural problems arising from abusive and traumatic family experiences require the sustained understanding and containment provided in special schools and therapeutic communities. Children whose lives have been disrupted by family tragedy, death, separation and loss may need to be accommodated by the local authority residential establishments, either temporarily whilst awaiting foster care placement or on a more long-term basis. And finally, children whose parents live abroad or who prefer their children to be educated in residential establishments require boarding school placements.

Given adequate and responsible residential provision, all of these children can benefit from a greater level of care, protection and commitment than they are likely to receive in their families and communities. This includes specialist assessment and treatment as well as the provision of structured therapeutic and educational milieux.

Whilst in residence the majority of children and young people suffer varying degrees of emotional distress and disturbance. Some manage well enough, though most would prefer to be at home and attend their local schools. Children who are physically ill or have severe physical, mental or sensory impairments contend with much pain and frustration and experience intense feelings of anger, fear and disappointment. Children in local authority children's homes, in secure units, youth treatment centres, therapeutic communities and special education establishments have significant emotional and behaviour problems. In the main, these derive from their inability to cope with either misfortune (e.g. family disruption, following parental death) or maltreatment (e.g. neglectful or abusive experiences) earlier in their lives. They enter residential establishments feeling abandoned and ostracised (some, scapegoated by their families) and carry with them a great deal of anxiety and mistrust. Many cannot relax or settle to any task and feel inadequate and worthless because of their inability to learn or to achieve. In general, they have not received sufficient care or consistency in their lives – and in the residential setting they effectively demand that which they have lacked.

The impact of such distress in the residential establishments in which they live is considerable. Each establishment has its own resources and procedures to cope with the emotional demand; and in different ways, each is held together under the authority and expertise of a lead clinician (e.g. a consultant child psychiatrist or paediatrician), head teacher or director and bolstered by the operation of a multidisciplinary team. A great deal of burden however rests upon the residential care staff, who are responsible for the day and night running of the establishment (Polsky 1962). It is they who provide the fabric of primary care – the feeding, establishing routines, maintaining order and discipline, getting children up in the morning, settling them at night – that constitutes the core of residential therapeutic activity. It is through their behaviour and response, in the close proximity of the living group, that children learn and develop. Much depends on their personal resourcefulness. In the midst of their everyday ordinary exchanges with children they deal with a wide variety of children's feelings, many of which are transferred on to them from past experiences. The residence becomes in effect an arena of transference re-enactment and residential care staff invariably find themselves all too easily perceived inappropriately, for example, as depriving, abusive, neglectful or seductive. 'The essence of residential treatment is that each child projects its inner world against the macrocosm of the residence' (Ekstein *et al.* 1959).

In order to cope with these pressures, most establishments seek additional assistance to supplement and further support their mainstream provision. Child and adolescent mental health professionals are often recruited to provide specialist help both to children directly as well as to staff. Child psychotherapists have a particular contribution to make in this context by virtue of their psychoanalytic training and experience.

The contribution of the child psychotherapist

Child psychotherapists' knowledge of child development and psychopathology, and their understanding of the effects of unconscious processes on behaviour and attitude, are of considerable relevance to the central issues that arise in residential work with children. So, too, is their awareness of the influence of projective mechanisms and transference and countertransference phenomena in human relationships. Their actual clinical practice, predominately based as it is on individual work in clinical settings in the community, is different from that of the residential care staff. Nevertheless, the application of their knowledge and understanding in the residential context is of considerable value. There are different forms that this can take:

(a) providing individual psychotherapy
(b) providing consultation to individual staff
(c) providing consultation to staff groups.

Providing individual psychotherapy

In view of the complexity of children's psychological difficulties, there is a clear argument for employing the specialist skills of child psychotherapists to provide individual psychotherapy in residential settings. For many children, such provision can be very helpful. However, in carrying this out, child psychotherapists need to be prepared to adapt their technique and understand their impact on the residential setting as a whole (Wilson 1986). Unlike in a clinical out-patient setting, child psychotherapists cannot practise with the same degree of privacy or confidentiality. Customary procedures of establishing the boundaries of an individual psychotherapeutic setting need to be modified. In a residential setting, individual psychotherapy is but one part of the overall therapeutic provision. There is a danger that its privacy can be seen as secretive, arousing suspicion and envy, and having a generally divisive effect on the coherence of the community. Children who are seen in individual psychotherapy are also affected; they are often confused and unsure about why they are being selected, whilst those children who are not clearly feel excluded. Furthermore, whilst confidentiality is important in individual psychotherapy, it is not something that can be fully upheld in a residential context. Staff need to know what is happening in individual therapy particularly when children become upset as a result of feelings aroused in sessions, leading possibly to agitated or disruptive behaviour or sometimes self-destructive activity (e.g. suicide attempts, self-harming, absconding). Progress, too, in individual psychotherapy can often be improved if the child psychotherapist is informed of significant events and experiences in the community.

Providing consultation to individual staff

In view of these difficulties and of the general scarce resource of child psychotherapists, it is often more productive that they act as consultants to staff. Residential care staff, in particular, require support to enable them to work effectively and to ensure that they do not become overwhelmed or demoralised by the emotional pressures placed on them. They need the opportunity to reflect on their work in order to understand better the interactions between the children and themselves.

It is important that in carrying out this work child psychotherapists, like all consultants, are clear about the meaning and purpose of consultation, as distinct from other associated activities such as supervision, training or psychotherapy. Caplan (1970) refers to consultation as work that is carried out when one professional (the consultee) involves another (the consultant) to help with a work problem. It is an activity that occurs between professionals as distinct from within a profession or between those who are trained and untrained. Central to the concept of consultation is the understanding that professional responsibility for the work remains with the consultee, as indeed the choice of whether or not to use or do anything that has been discussed in the consultation. This is clearly different from supervision in which the supervisor has managerial responsibility for the work and has the authority to require the supervisee to follow advice and direction.

There are many occasions in the life of a residential unit when staff are challenged and perplexed by the behaviour and attitude of children and confused and alarmed by their own reactions to them. It is not uncommon, for example, for a child to behave for several days in a co-operative and affectionate way only to change suddenly and relate to the residential care worker quite differently. The child may become sullen, withdrawn or tearful; he or she may become secretive, devious and undermining; or at other times obstinate, defiant and antagonistic. These changes and demands are commonplace in residential childcare and, for the most part, they can be adequately dealt with by the staff under effective supervision. However, it is often the case that, beyond this level of management, there arises a need for further thought. There may still be questions about why children are behaving in the way they are and uncertainty about how best to proceed. In this context, the function of consultation has its place.

> Fundamentally the question of consultation arises when someone or some group gets stuck or feels limited working within the mainstream of everyday business. A point is reached when there is a recognition that existing personal or established institutional resources are not enough – and additional assistance is required. It is here that consultation comes in . . .
>
> (Wilson 1991)

The purpose of consultation is to enable the residential staff to think more clearly about their own observations and experiences and to facilitate their greater understanding of the children and of the emotional impact of the children on themselves. Whilst staff may be aware of some of the reasons underlying children's behaviour, they may well miss out on others – not least because of their close involvement. They may see straight away, for example, that a child has become irritable or abusive following a distressing home visit; but they may not recognise the significance of the arrival of a new resident into the unit that exacerbates the child's fears of being excluded. In addition, they may not fully appreciate the extent of their own impatience or of how they themselves are getting drawn into a dismissive mode of response that repeats the child's experience of rejection. In consultation they have the opportunity to gain a wider perspective and catch hold of themselves and of the subtle yet powerful influence of the child's demands and provocations.

Consultations can take place both individually and in staff groups. In the following example, a child psychotherapist met with a residential staff worker in an adolescent unit on an individual basis. The achievement of this consultation was to make sense of a disturbing feeling in a staff member that was interfering with her capacity to respond appropriately to one of the girls in her unit.

> The problem that the staff member presented for consultation was her extreme anger with the girl. In particular, she could not tolerate the way the girl ignored her. The consultation initially focused on understanding the girl's behaviour in the light of her past experience with a domineering and violent mother. In large measure, this could be seen as her way of blotting out potential intrusion, at the same time attacking those who threatened her. With this in mind, the staff member understood her own anger as representing something of the girl's projected fury, as well as the mother's ambivalence. A further, more personal dimension, emerged in the course of the consultation. This related to the fact that both the staff member and the girl shared an experience in common, namely the death of a younger sister. The girl's apparent indifference to this and her tendency to mock the staff member's distress only added to the latter's anger and intolerance.

Providing consultation to staff groups

In a residential setting, staff tensions are inevitable; some may arise from organisational difficulties, others from external pressures, whilst a good deal arises from the emotional demands and expectations of the residential children and adolescents. It is crucial to the development of a coherent therapeutic environment that staff work well together and have the opportunity to discuss these tensions and share their common difficulties. Child psychotherapists, with experience and additional knowledge of organisational dynamics, may help facilitate staff groups to deal with organisational issues. For the most part, however, they are best suited to help staff groups explore the emotional tensions that arise from the residents in the course of their work.

In the following example, a staff group in a therapeutic community for adolescents met to review the progress of one of the residents. This was a 16-year-old boy who had become increasingly violent in recent weeks and whose future in the community was being questioned. The main part of the meeting was chaired by a senior staff member and a formal review was carried out of the boy's family circumstances and progress in the community. To further understanding of the boy's behaviour and address some of the key concerns amongst the staff, the final part of the meeting was taken up in considering the staff's reactions to the boy's behaviour. This part of the meeting was conducted by the child psychotherapist.

To facilitate discussion, the child psychotherapist invited staff members to express briefly in turn their feelings and reactions about the boy during the preceding six months. This was carried out with the clear understanding by management and all concerned that such views were necessarily personal and subjective and not intended to be in anyway prejudicial, but rather to broaden awareness of the boy's predicament.

Two major themes emerged. The first related to the nature of the boy's difficulties; the second to the impact of his behaviour on the staff group. It became clear that the boy aroused intense but varied feelings in different staff members. The men, in particular, were threatened by his violence: some wanted to retreat from him whilst others wanted to retaliate against him. The women staff felt less strongly, but were equally divided: some felt maternal and protective whilst others were frightened by him. The range and depth of feeling was disturbing yet revealing. In experiencing this together in an approved and structured meeting, the staff obtained a context in which to place their own individual reactions and, at the same time, gain a greater insight into the boy's emotional predicament. They could see, for example, the extent to which the accumulation of their feeling represented a group countertransference, reflecting in varying degrees the traumatic experience of this boy's past experience with a violent but often absent father and a mentally ill mother. The second theme related to a particular staff tension that arose from this situation. One of the staff members complained about the burden he felt he carried in confronting this boy's violent behaviour. He felt he was being left by other staff members to act as the 'hard man' in dealing with the violence; this distressed him, not least because of how it reminded him of his strained relationship with his own father.

This was a tense meeting in which a number of different issues were addressed – relating to the particular boy under review, divisions within the staff and the well-being of the community. After much discussion, it was agreed that every effort should be made to ensure that the boy was not excluded from the community. A number of important decisions were also made about staff cover to share more equitably the burden of the boy's violence.

A meeting such as this existed as part of a series that, over time, contributed to the greater understanding of the boy and of the staff group itself. The child psychotherapist had a key role to play, entrusted by the staff and sanctioned by the senior manager to facilitate and contain what was, in effect, a highly sensitive and crucial group learning experience.

Conclusion

In most residential establishments dealing with children and young people, there is a great deal of emotional turbulence amongst the children and amongst the staff. The effectiveness of such establishments depends on how well this is addressed. Establishments that employ well-trained staff who are properly managed can provide good quality care and therapy. Invariably, they value the additional input of specialists, including child and adolescent mental health professionals. Child psychotherapists have a particularly relevant contribution to make through providing individual psychotherapy and consultation to staff. Consultation is of particular importance since it can enable those who have fundamental responsibility for the residential care and therapy to be more effective.

In providing consultation to staff, whether on an individual basis or in groups, it is crucial that child psychotherapists ensure that their work is understood and supported by the management of the residential units. In taking such a significant part in helping staff gain greater understanding of their work and considering various options about how best to proceed, child psychotherapists, as consultants, may well be mistaken for taking responsibility for the staff's problems. Equally, in engaging with the personal issues of the staff in carrying out their work, they may be misperceived as providing psychotherapy for residential staff. It is of key importance that child psychotherapists are clear in their own minds that they are neither managers nor psychotherapists in this context.

Given this clarity, the contribution of the child psychotherapist as consultant in a residential setting can be substantial. Their value resides in their objective and psychoanalytic perspective; and in their capacity to provide an experience in which staff feelings can be expressed and shared. The essence of consultation resides in its capacity to contain (Bion 1962) – to receive feelings and observations, to tolerate uncertainty, to allow for reflection and thought and, ultimately, to empower staff to move forward in their own way. In the two examples given, staff were helped to acknowledge the impact of the emotional pressures of children upon them and the extent to which these pressures impinged upon their own lives. Staff needed time to take stock of themselves in order to gain a greater measure of self-understanding and control and thereby to be more effective in withstanding the dictates of transference re-enactments inherent in residential experience.

References

Bion, W. R. (1962) *Learning from Experience*, London: Karnac Books.

Caplan, G. (1970) *Theory and Practice of Mental Health Consultation*, London: Tavistock Publications.

Ekstein, R., Mandelbaum, A. and Wallerstein, J. (1959) 'Counter transference in residential treatment of children', *The Psychoanalytic Study of the Child*, New York: New York University Press.

Polsky, H. (1962) *Cottage Six: The Social System of Delinquent Boys in Residential Treatment*, New York: Russel Sage Foundation.

Wilson, P. (1986) 'Individual psychotherapy in an adolescent unit', in D. Steinberg (ed.) *The Adolescent Unit: Work and Teamwork in Adolescent Psychiatry*, Chichester: John Wiley.

Wilson, P. (1991) 'Consultation to institutions: questions of role and orientation', in S. Ramsden (ed.) *Occasional Papers No. 6 Psychotherapy – Pure and Applied*, London: Association of Child Psychology and Psychiatry.

Further reading

Caplan, G. (1970) *Theory and Practice of Mental Health Consultation*, London: Tavistock Publications.

Silveira, W. R. (ed.) (1991) *Consultation in Residential Care*, Aberdeen: University Press (reviewed by P. Wilson (1992) *Journal of Child Psychotherapy* 18(1)).

Steinberg, D. (ed.) (1986) *The Adolescent Unit: Work and Teamwork in Adolescent Psychiatry*, Chichester: John Wiley.

13 The challenges of in-patient work in a therapeutic community

Denis Flynn

This chapter looks at how formal psychoanalytic psychotherapy, with its emphasis on the transference and the inner world, takes place within a therapeutic community at the Cassel Hospital and orientates itself to some of the realities of a specialist in-patient treatment setting. Here both adult and child psychotherapists and nurses work closely and intensively together. Although starting from different theoretical backgrounds and using different methods of intervention, the work of each discipline can inform and enrich the other. There is some sharing of information and of thinking so that, in terms of overall aim and purpose, there is a coming together to treat very difficult patients who may not be treatable elsewhere. Despite the complexities of this setting, one can see that there are aspects of the overall work which are distinctively psychoanalytic. We can see that in the therapeutic community there are different issues from elsewhere for the child psychotherapist about the use of information and about the understanding of fantasy and reality. It is important for the child psychotherapist, as it is for other workers, to know and work with the patients' perception, adjustment to and conflict about the in-patient setting, and the affective impact of their experience, in particular, the psychodynamic processes operating amongst the patients and in the staff groups (Flynn 1993). The child psychotherapist needs to understand not just the disturbed child or adolescent as they are seen in the individual psychotherapy session, but to learn to deal with tensions about roles between workers and to tolerate severe infantile projections, often of hostility and despair, as they affect them personally. Such efforts by the staff to tolerate primitive psychological processes parallels the efforts of severely disturbed and traumatised patients to tolerate and to work through their problems.

History

The Cassel Hospital was founded after the First World War to treat patients who suffered conditions in civilian life which were similar to the 'shell-shock' which many soldiers had suffered in the war, but which were distinct from the most severe mental conditions, usually psychoses, that were treated in the old asylums, or psychiatric hospitals. Like other treatment institutions in Britain, such as the forerunners of today's Child Guidance Clinics, in the inter-war years the Cassel Hospital developed types of treatment influenced by developments in psychology and, in particular, in psychoanalysis. There is today a pervasive sense of continuity and history from this time, and indeed one of the units within the Cassel, the Families Unit, is still referred to colloquially as 'Ross', after the pioneering work of the consultant of one of the units in the 1930s. In 1948, when the Cassel Hospital had moved from Kent to its present site on Ham Common, in Richmond, Surrey, Dr Tom Main was appointed as Medical Director and, with Doreen Waddell, who was appointed matron – both of whom became psychoanalysts – there was a creative period of twenty-five years in which psychoanalytic psychotherapy was developed in an in-patient context, alongside psychosocial nursing in a therapeutic community. Since this time there has been a continuous flow of ideas and personnel between the Cassel and the other major institutions involved in psychoanalytical training in Britain. Tom Main, like Wilfred Bion and a number of influential army psychiatrists, who were to become famous subsequently as psychoanlysts, group analysts and social researchers, had worked with soldiers with psychological problems which incapacitated them from active service – problems of morale and of rehabilitation into civilian society, back to work and family. One of the central ideas of this movement of thinking was that individuals, groups and organisations, if given the freedom and responsibility for organising and undertaking work in their own environment, would respond, have more human purpose and fulfilment, and individual problems, including formerly debilitating psychological problems, would be seen in a new light or indeed lose much of their debilitating effect. There are many telling continuities over this time: in how a type of hospital treatment, developed as a 'tool' to help 'shell-shocked' civilians with the devastation of their lives, that reflected the break-ups and devastation of war, is now used with our current problems of the devastating break-ups of family life and relationships, following serious problems of abuse and mental illness; in how rehabilitation of soldiers after war gives way now to rehabilitation of families after family breakdown; in how problems of morale facing the terrors of conflict in war gives way now to problems of morale amongst the staff and patients in a therapeutic community facing the pain, tensions and fears of those suffering severe borderline conditions which affect all aspects of daily functioning and routine.

The setting of in-patient work in a therapeutic community at the Cassel Hospital

Treatment of the severely disturbed patient in an in-patient setting provides particular opportunities for supportive containment of the patient as well as particular dangers of severe regression and intensified disturbance. How in-patient treatment works, whether and why it works, depends on how different aspects of treatment are brought together. At the Cassel Hospital patients are offered psychoanalytic understanding and insight in individual and group psychotherapy, together with intensive psychosocial nursing in a therapeutic community context. But patients receive a range of other types of care. These include some tangible benefits, such as food, an overnight bed, spare time, opportunities for pleasures including recreational time and activities, and the company of other patients in a shared communal living and treatment space. There are indeed, then, other aspects of in-patient treatment apart from what is specifically psychoanalytic. Amongst the most important of these are: (a) real bodily care; (b) levels of protection, from total exposure to the reality pressures of outside life, and, within the hospital itself, from harmful and abusive attacks by others; (c) real sanctions to be invoked to prevent or reduce self-abusive attacks, and (d) supervision and appraisal of childcare issues and individual psychiatric mental state, as appropriate.

Usually psychoanalytic psychotherapy can only take place when the patient's ego is strong enough and the level of motivation sufficient for them to accept the limitations of the psychoanalytic setting, to attend the same place at agreed times, to accept rules of abstinence from actual libidinal relationships with the therapist and rules of restraint from aggressive attacks upon the therapist. For the borderline patient who has failed in treatment elsewhere, who may be caught in a chronic cycle of suicidal or self-abusive attacks, or for the abusing parent who primarily wants the child returned to them from foster care, or for the abused child who is showing disturbance when placed back with the family, such preconditions are rarely there from the outset.

The organisation of in-patient treatment

Psychoanalytic treatment is possible at the Cassel because the patient is held in treatment by the mutually co-operative effort of nurse and therapist, and by the sustained involvement of patients and staff together in a 'culture of enquiry' within the therapeutic community. There are many areas of shared aims and focus, particularly in concentrating attention on the capacity of the patient actively to address his or her problems around what Kennedy (1987) has called the 'work of the day', that is, the emotional issues which arise in the performance of the tasks of everyday life which give a structure to the patient managing the day.

Within the therapeutic community context of the hospital, patients have responsibility for their own treatment and parents have an actual and real responsibility for their children throughout the day and night (Flynn 1987, 1988). Nurses working alongside will help to make emotional sense of what the patients are doing, dealing not just with eruptions of disturbed behaviour, but with the patients' capacities to take on specific responsibilities and tasks.

The day is organised so that there is only one meal, lunch, prepared by hospital staff, which gives time for patients to have therapeutic meetings with nurses, activities, and psychotherapy sessions. The other meals are organised and prepared by patients. There is practical work to be done – cleaning, cooking, ordering food and planning menus and managing the therapeutic budgets. There are the ordinary tasks of the family with children, getting dressed, preparing for school in the Children's Centre, having breakfast, and, after school, finding appropriate leisure activities, evening meals, baths for children, settling down, managing the night-time. In unit or 'firm' meetings, practical and emotional issues are discussed. There are three units: Family, Adolescent and Adult. These come together in three-times-weekly community meetings to discuss the practical and emotional issues affecting the whole community. Some patients become 'firm chair' or 'community chair', each for three months or so, and are actively involved with, and have a special responsibility for, other patients and patient–staff meetings during the day and especially in the evening. From 7 p.m. until 8 a.m. there is only one nurse and a night orderly in the hospital, with duty team back-up, so patients effectively manage their emotional issues together. It is the task of the 'firm chair' and 'community chair', and all the patients, to hear concerns in the 'night meeting', to respond directly, aid the nurse with crises and bring pressing and relevant issues into the more formally structured day meetings. Staff review individuals' progress and the community and firm process in daily staff meetings, and other formal meetings, which involve nurses and psychotherapists together. In a weekly 'Strains' meeting, attended by all the clinical staff, the emotional impact of the work on the staff is examined, including current pressures and strains between staff. In effect this looks at the countertransference processes in the staff working with these patients in a therapeutic community setting. I shall mention nurse–therapist supervisions below.

The role of nurse and psychotherapist

There are essential differences between nursing and therapy and each brings something quite distinct to treatment. Nurses use their own experience of patients as a central guide to their understanding of them individually and in community and institutional processes (Barnes 1976; Kennedy 1987; Griffiths and Pringle 1997). Nurses help the patient to relate, to confront the all-consuming aspects of personal conflict which take them away from a focus or direction in life, and can reduce the ordinary to the superficial or the irrelevant. As such it is essential to work with the underlying narcissistic base of the patient's problems.

Nurse and therapist have separate tasks and separate roles. Yet each will focus on the current processes of the patient's treatment over the last twenty-four hours. The therapist primarily concentrates on an understanding of the patient as it becomes apparent in the individual transference. The nurse primarily seeks to elucidate the nature of the patients' capacities as manifested in their daily activities and relationships, guiding them with plans and stategies for moving forward, keeping in the forefront the emotional meaning, quality and impact of their behaviour and plans of action, using ordinary human reactions and responses. Each, nurse and therapist, will be aware of the work of the other. For the therapist, this provides valuable information to set alongside what is emerging in the individual transference, and may lead to an understanding of wider transferences, including split transferences, for example, to the nurse or to the hospital, or parts of it.

Patients form transferences to both nurse and therapist, and to other important figures and indeed to aspects of the hospital. Nurses also draw the transference around ordinary household issues to themselves, as they work alongside the patients in the kitchen, the pantry, the linen allocation or activities groups, and can more quickly than therapists become the focus of a community or institutional transference (Barnes 1967; Barnes *et al.* 1997; Griffiths and Pringle 1997; Flynn 1993). Some aspects of the transference may be apparent early on, but the patient's transference to therapist and to the hospital, including that of the child with his family, usually only becomes apparent as time goes on, and may come from therapy or nursing, or interestingly from both at once, after the importance of what each has been struggling with has been fully recognised (Flynn 1988).

In cases of primitive attacks and confusions, the staff themselves can begin to lose their own identity and capacity to work in their separate ways, and their effective functioning together may break down (Rosenfeld 1965). As Tom Main outlined in 'The ailment' (1957), the strain of working in what becomes a hostile environment can become manifest in a decline in the health and capacities of the staff. This can lead to failure in individual cases, effective splitting of the staff team and the possibility of retaliatory attacks by the staff upon the patients, or vice versa.

Such work, with its unremitting quality at times, does have its strain. Effective working together of therapist and nurse can however have a supportive and restorative effect for one another, and can produce more ongoing co-operative effort in the work. Work with the destructive, fragmented and depressed sides of the patients may move the patient out of a quagmire of regressions and regressive distortions, and may lead, with some relief, to a recurrent process where steps are taken towards something more lively and restored.

Nurse–therapist supervision

Both nurse and therapist then will have affective contact with the patient and what is most useful in nurse–therapist supervision is to understand how both nurse and therapist fulfil their separate roles and deal with conflicts that come to light. As Tischler (1987) writes, nurse–therapist supervision 'pays special attention to the feelings in the counter-transference which patients evoke in their treaters, and the effect these feelings have on their work'. There can be a 'proliferation of the transference to the institution, not only the transference of the patient, but also the counter-transference of the staff to patients and to each other'. Nurse–therapist supervisions are different and additional to other supervisions of clinical work. A senior therapist and a senior nurse meet with a primary team of workers with a family, including the nurse, the child psychotherapist and the adult psychotherapist. One or other of the workers will elect to speak first, talking of how they find working with the family, how they are working in their role and how they are communicating, or not, with the other workers. Each of the workers will follow, then the supervisors will pick out themes. It is important not to make it into a formal review and to keep it to a degree experiential, so that one may feel and see if there are processes of re-enactment at work in relation to each other or one or both of the supervisors; for example, does one of the workers feel squeezed out, dropped, neglected, and murderous towards the rival? This work requires a degree of freedom and trust of each other to be able to bring out in a group of workers countertransference feelings which may show up how adequately one is working in one's role with the family and how able one is to work with other professionals. Such supervisions augment, for many nurses and therapists, their own experience of personal psychoanalysis. In general, I believe the nurse–therapist supervision is experienced by staff as invaluable in developing working alliances when working with families which have intense disturbance and where there may be hidden severely destructive splitting processes.

Mother–infant sessions

Over the last fifteen years the Cassel Hospital Families Unit has developed a progamme for rehabilitating abused children, including very young children and small babies, with their families. When working with severe child abuse cases where there is a child under three years old involved, mother–infant sessions take place weekly and include a child psychotherapist and sometimes, too, a nurse. They are set up so that the mother can discuss with the child psychotherapist any issues of concern about the infant. The child psychotherapist can observe and work with the here and now of the mother–infant relationship, integrating outside observations from within the hospital or the foster home. When there is a father or stepfather involved, they sometimes also attend. Most of the infants are returning to their mothers after being in foster care. A few toys are provided and the mother is encouraged to bring some of the child's own toys. The sessions are usually very emotionally charged, and in most cases there are contentious legal issues about whether mother and infant should be together. Often, after abuse and neglect, and having lost and indeed missed out on emotional contact with the child, the mothers need to recognise and face up to aspects of their way of relating to the child which are hindering a deepening of their bond. Mothers need to be able to accept responsibility for what happened, and, as treatment goes on, further blame, shame and painful awareness, so the sessions work against the danger of contact with the child being lost and weak links severed. This is especially so if the mother cannot accept responsibility. In effect, the mother does not bond again with the infant unless she can get beyond the abusive behaviour or her part in the abusive experience. If, as often happens, a defensive or protective shell is created around the mother–infant couple, the habitual responses of mother to child may be ignored, along with the infant's attempts at communication and his/her changing developmental needs.

I have described in detail elsewhere some mother–infant work in two cases of successful rehabilitation (Flynn 1998). Following the clandestine poisoning of two children, Mrs A used the mother–infant sessions, over a period of nearly two years, to get to know her next child Joan, aged eleven months on admission, as a real person. She needed also to use them to recognise she could unleash on a child her own disturbed feelings, and that she could be out of touch with her own dangerousness. An incident about giving the child an over-warm bath brought her hidden murderousness into view within the therapeutic community, and, on a smaller scale, in the mother–infant sessions other parallel examples of potentially dangerous behaviour could be faced. Important work too was done in the mother–infant sessions about intense fears over separateness of the mother from the child. Joan was encouraged to develop more as an individual, alongside parallel work in the nursing about developing Mrs A's social and group capacities with others, and, in her own psychotherapy, about the early breaks in her relationship with her parents as an infant, and the false solutions she adopted to cover over her hostile and embittered relationship with her mother.

In another example from mother–infant sessions, work was done with Susan, a mother who had been released from prison after serving a term for neglect, following the killing by her partner of their baby girl. Her older daughter, Ann, now aged three years, was being returned to her from foster care after eighteen months. In the work a new bond had to be formed between them, the positive wishes to be together nurtured, alongside other passive, muddled and negative wishes in both mother and child. The erratic and disturbed behaviour of the mother had to be relived to a degree in the therapeutic community before she could more fully accept the effect it was having and had had within her family. Overall it was Ann's tolerance of individual sessions and her wish to have her thoughts and feelings understood that showed her willingness to persevere through the painfulness of the process. Ann had to be able to know how it could have happened that her baby sister had been killed, in order to overcome her internal trauma, but importantly too, to know how thinking in her internal world could get killed off, and would need to be reformed and found. Susan had to face her own responsibility and some of her failings, and indeed she did do this and was capable of deep and genuine guilt and remorse, which she worked through in her individual psychotherapy. She also needed to be able to allow her child to express her feelings, including her anger with her mother and her acceptance of her stepfather's responsibility, indeed to allow herself to know what had happened. Sufficient support and tolerance was needed in the whole in-patient treatment team to survive negative attacks and to create the space for something new to grow between Ann and Susan.

'Tolerance or survival?' in the child during family rehabilitation

Within the hospital there are a number of elements of treatment for the family as a whole and for each member of it, but essentially relationships are tested not just with others in the therapeutic community but within the family itself, and, importantly, between parents and children. It is important to assess – not only in a narrower sense, in family meetings and mother–child work, but also in a wider sense, bringing together an understanding of all aspects of the work and centrally the intensive individual psychotherapy which the child has during treatment – the impact the treatment is having on the child. This is invaluable for assessing the overall impact of the therapeutic community work (Flynn 1988), and especially what the child can put up with or survive. I shall look at this theme in two cases which involve severe abuse. Children can survive abuse by learning to 'tolerate' too much, causing deep emotional scars. But unless they can tolerate the emergence in a painful way of central issues, attempts at rehabilitation may not survive. There are painful issues about when and what to tolerate or not to tolerate, and about whether this furthers or hinders the child's attempts to develop emotionally and survive psychically.

We know, after the work of Bowlby, that a child in a new foster or adoptive home, having left the family of origin following loss of parents or family breakdown, will face a major task of readjustment on return to the family, and that such experiences can be traumatic and disturbing. The task for an abused child coming back again into the family is that much more difficult, especially in coming to terms with how the abuse has severed family relationships, and when reliving aspects of the abuse. There are crucial questions we need to ask throughout this rehabilitative treatment: namely, is the child surviving emotionally, can the family now provide enough protection and security for the child, has the family survived?

Case example: Stefan

Stefan, aged four years, had suffered repeated physical and verbal abuse whilst in the care of his mother, a single parent who, isolated from her home environment, had had post-natal depression and then drug and alcohol problems. Through neglect Stefan had fallen out of a high window, but survived. In three-times-weekly psychotherapy, Stefan presented as a dull depressed child with a speech impediment, withdrawn sometimes, but with alternating wild out-of-control behaviour – hitting out, hurting himself and scratching me and him – and close clingy contact. In the therapeutic community, although now off unprescribed or hard drugs, his mother seemed locked in on herself as if she were drugged. She was sometimes warm and physically caring, but then hostile and lashing out as she felt he was punishing her. In a preliminary meeting with his mother present, he first drew on paper an outline of a crocodile, then played with fascination with a toy crocodile. When his mother handed it back, he flinched away with terror, as if it were a real crocodile that was going to bite him. I thought his experiences were so powerful that play could become concretely real so that his capacity for symbolic communication in play and speech became very tenuous.

In psychotherapy sessions Stefan occasionally shifted out of his depressive dullness and become a lively and expressive child. He was however often painfully confused, had a speech impediment, and one almost literally had to catch the words from his mouth to understand him. I was better able to do this when he began playing, which he could now do in an energetic and increasingly meaningful way.

In a session early on, an object was pulled out of the window of the dolls' house and fell. Then the biting crocodile pulled the tree-person out of the window. In another version it was pushed and then the building collapsed.

Stefan was pleased that I could make sense of his very bitty play. I indicated I knew he was talking about what happened when he fell. He felt guilt and bewilderment about this and the catastrophic destruction of his time with mother. This linked to earlier when his mother 'fell out of sight' during her depression. In sessions, if I was not fully attentive to him, he re-experienced this as another form of my 'falling out of sight'. Then his fear of catastrophic loss reappeared and with it all his difficulties. Usually he had a devilish streak, which was largely playful, but sometimes it gave way to frenetic repetitive activity. He then subsided into timidity and abject whinyness, which I found had a very wearing effect on me. Basically, however, he thrived on attention to his feelings.

After some months of treatment, Stefan's mother's behaviour became increasingly more disturbed (for reasons I shall not go into), and actively rejecting behaviour towards Stefan in the hospital was observed to increase. His behaviour now worsened. In one incident Stefan got up in the night and poured water over two other small boys. His mother was furious with him and poured a jug of water over him. She refused to change him or do anything, was quite out of control and abusive and threatening to staff. Typically she took a long time to come out of her rage. In brief, this is what happened in Stefan's psychotherapy session next day:

He and his mother had 'made up' and, as I approached the waiting area, he was asking his mother for a kiss and a cuddle in a whiny but playful voice. His mother did not look at me and insisted on carrying Stefan to the door of the room, supposing him not able to come. Inside the room, now his mother had left, he immediately complained there was no water in the bowl. He began impulsively hauling the water container off the shelf and knocking the side of it. I pointed out there was water in the bowl. He took it, put it on the table and began to put pieces from the teaset in it. He then jerked and tipped the bowl forward and poured some of it over his jeans and his shirt. He started whining that he was wet. This developed into a real cry and then sad sobbing. I said he had wet himself and felt I would leave him wet and unhappy, like his mummy had done in the bedroom last night. I said I knew about the incident last night. He said that he had wet the boys because they were 'too hot'. I said I thought he may feel the boys had his hot angry feelings inside them. Stefan did not reply but stood still crying saying he wanted his mum. I was undecided what to do, phone his mother or try to help him myself. I decided on the latter. I acknowledged he did want his mother really to do the drying for him, but for the moment I would see if I could dry him, so that he could continue to stay with me for the rest of the session. After I had dried him and begun to wipe up some of the mess, he became angry with me for doing this and threw over two small chairs in a rage. He cut his box with scissors and threw the toys all over the floor. He clutched his trousers and pulled on his penis, then used the pencil sharpener damagingly on some felt tips and crayons. He tipped the rest of his toys in the bin and then tipped this on the floor. I was left scrambling around, wondering if I could stop the devastation. Stefan clambered on to a small table and managed to fall, hurting himself and he began to cry again. I said again about how he was showing me how mixed up everything was, and how he felt I would leave him to fall and get hurt.

I had to choose in this session whether to help Stefan directly, call his mother to help him, or to continue deeper with interpreting his internal perceptions and conflicts in the transference and in relation to the current reality of life with his mother. My dilemma over this increased over the next weeks as the situation deteriorated further. Stefan then presented either as a very ideal child, quickly collapsing into acute disturbance, or as an openly depressed child, when he was passive and 'floppy', as if he had no effective skeleton. His relationship with his mother became increasingly impoverished, and he became more self-destructive, actually cutting and hurting himself – a disturbing thing to see in such a young child. Stefan was now showing that the continued efforts at rehabilitation were intolerable. Treatment was stopped at this point after nine months. I was left wondering whether in Stefan's interests we should have acted at an earlier point of the deterioration.

Since Stefan's treatment, we have begun to look for earlier signs of whether children find continued family rehabilitation tolerable or not. Careful monitoring is needed so that children do not become the victims of repeated abuse. When children find it intolerable, their psychic survival is threatened and there are open signs of deterioration. This can lead to further reactive disturbed behaviour from the parents towards them.

Case example: Stuart

Stuart, aged nine, suffered physical and sexual abuse (anal abuse) from his father. His mother was extremely deprived, had suffered continuous abuse and humiliation as a child, and came from an horrific, very large, incestuous family where each child barely found a way just to survive. Crucially, too, in the background, Stuart had a history of lack of maternal containment; his birth weight was just four pounds, he was in an incubator for several weeks, and he had a bad pneumonia during his first year.

When the psychotherapy setting was established, Stuart used it to express his vulnerability and his need to build up defences. He was sad and lonely, unsure about his mother and triggered easily into expressing violent feelings towards her. The experience of abuse had represented a physical and a mental threat and in particular was like being psychologically killed off. He tried to placate and fit in with what he thought I wanted of him, which was alarming, and expressed a deep mistrust of being himself. I felt it important to allow him to build up some of his own defences. He could use the sessions as he wanted, and only talk about the abuse if he wanted to.

Even when he knew this, his anxieties shown in his play were very much centred around anal abuse. He covered his toy box with plasticine and various types of covers so that it would be safe. Cups were thrown into a bowl of water to be tested to see if they were clean or dirty. I was tested by being given the dirty one and then observed with glee. The transference developed and he had a number of fantasies about secrets and showed fears that I would harm him. Confused sequences developed in which he would want to barter with me. I would be seen, in the play, to give him money, and he would do things for me. He did however genuinely want to develop a special affectionate relationship with me. I think he found my interpretations about his vulnerability relieving, but even 'being relieved' was a confusing experience, and he frequently had to rush to the toilet after points of anxiety or relief in our interchanges. Clearly he was suffering a number of types of zonal and functional confusions. He attempted to rework his experience and to gain some control over it. One frequent sequence of play was to make masks which he could use to see the top half of people but not their bottom half. Outside the sessions odd behaviour occurred too, for example, when he suddenly stuck a balloon into the nursing officer's face and nose. Going back to the record one discovers that he suffered from having his father's bottom stuck into his face.

From early on Stuart was preoccupied with why he, rather than his brother or sister, was being rehabilitated. He was lonely, guilty and confused about this, and behind it were the questions, why was he chosen for abuse, why was he now with mother, and was he special, or had he managed to push the others out? What now came more into focus was how he could identify with the sexual aggression he had suffered. He frequently poked sharp objects into the playroom wall and damaged it. He had misgivings about his sexual identity – was he a boy or a girl and how should he act to men and to women? At times he was very confiding in me in a genuine way, telling me all sorts of details about life with his mother and father. These periods were when he was settled. But at other times the effects of the abuse showed through in difficulties with other children and staff. Some of these involved reasonable sexual boundaries with other children, and some concerned his excitable and overactive behaviour.

As time went on it was apparent that it was increasingly difficult for Stuart to sustain progress. He became ill at points of stress, and his mother's alliance with me as his psychotherapist progressively lapsed – for example, in not telling me of fights he had had with his brother at the weekend, which at one point explained some of his depression. The accumulated impression was that he was not being thought about. As her alliance and capacity to care and nurture Stuart lapsed, it became impossible for him to talk about the abuse at all in the therapy. In other words he lost all sense of trust that I would be able to think about him. His mother at this point was finding it especially difficult to face the facts of her own abuse, and broke off treatment and her attempts at rehabilitation.

After a long period of time, clinical follow-ups and the ensuing court proceedings, Stuart's mother could accept his need for another family. The work for this had been done in the treatment. Crucially Stuart had learned to trust and understand more of his own needs, and he and mother could agree about her incapacity to meet them now. This recognition of reality allowed for a good placement in a family elsewhere to be made and for a number of years of intensive out-patient psychotherapy to be arranged for Stuart. Stuart's mother has independently made something of her life, and they are still in regular contact with each other.

Conclusion

During family rehabilitation the child's capacity to distinguish internal and external reality is affected. The terror inflicted on the child by abuse continues to affect them internally, through continued persecution and dread. Primitive feelings and emotions connected with the earliest emotional life are stirred, primitive confusion (Rosenfeld 1965), catastrophic anxiety (Bion 1970) and fear of annihilation (Winnicott 1956).

Meltzer (1973) defines terror as 'paranoid anxiety whose essential quality, paralysis, leaves no avenue of action'. A dread develops because of a loss of protection against terror, and a tyrannical internal organisation may build up. This needs to be tackled therapeutically before progress can be made to understanding depressive and dependency needs. Because of this one needs to understand both the child's repetition of abusive contact and confront the tyrannical and omnipotent element within the child which, in my experience, so frequently gives the therapeutic encounter with the severely abused child the quality of a battle. Only after addressing the underlying terror can progress towards rebuilding relationships be made. In family rehabilitation the parents need help to recognise the needs of the child and to understand how the child will react and behave with difficulties after the abuse. Importantly, they need to acknowledge responsibility for their part in causing the abuse, whether they are the actual perpetrator, or whether they have colluded in it. Intense work is necessary to build up trust. They have to recognise that they have duties and responsibilities as parents, including providing clear and safe boundaries for the child, which will determine whether the child finds the family safe enough.

The child psychotherapist has a central role in an in-patient therapeutic community setting to make and maintain contact with the deepest aspects of the child's feelings and emotional responses, to work with and help the child directly and to contribute to the thinking of the other staff. He or she will also face emotional pressures and conflict in the work as different levels of disturbance become manifest, either in a directly understandable form or as painful and irrational forms of enactment by the patients, or indeed amongst the staff struggling in the work. The tolerance of severe infantile projections of hostility and despair and the struggle to maintain co-operative work together, not just the technical changes of the in-patient setting, are what makes work towards successful rehabilitation of such families possible and, in the end, enables both the patients and the workers to survive and to continue to work in a psychoanalytic way.

References

Barnes, E. (ed.) (1967) *Psychosocial Nursing*, London: Tavistock Publications.

Barnes, E., Griffiths, P., Ord, J. and Wells, D. (eds) (1997) *Face to Face with Distress: The Professional Use of Self in Psychosocial Care*, Oxford: Butterworth-Heinemann.

Bion, W. R. (1970) *Attention and Interpretation*, London: Tavistock.

Flynn, C. (1993) 'The patient's pantry: the nature of the nursing task', *Therapeutic Communities* 14(4): 227–36.

Flynn, D. (1987) 'The child's view of the hospital: an examination of the child's experience of an in-patient setting', in A. Heymans, R. Kennedy and L. Tischler (eds) *The Family as In-Patient*, London: Free Association Books.

—— (1988) 'The assessment and psychotherapy of a physically abused girl during in-patient family treatment', *Journal of Child Psychotherapy* 13(2): 61–78.

—— (1998) 'Psychoanalytic aspects of inpatient treatment', *Journal of Child Psychotherapy* 24(2): 283–306.

Griffiths, P. and Pringle, P. (eds) (1997) *Psychosocial Practice in a Residential Setting*, London: Karnac Books.

Kennedy, R. (1987) 'The work of the day: aspects of work with families at the Cassel Hospital', in A. Heymans, R. Kennedy and L. Tischler (eds) *The Family as In-Patient*, London: Free Association Books.

Main, T. (1957) 'The ailment', *British Journal of Medical Psychology* 30: 129–45 (reprinted in *The Ailment and other Psychoanalytic Essays* (1989), London: Free Association Books).

Meltzer, D. (1973) *Sexual States of Mind*, Strath Tay, Perthshire: Clunie Press.

Rosenfeld, H. A. (1965) *Psychotic States: A Psychological Approach*, London: Hogarth Press.

Tischler, L. (1987) 'Nurse-therapist supervision', in A. Heymans, R. Kennedy and L. Tischler (eds) *The Family as In-Patient*, London: Free Association Books.

Winnicott, D. W. (1956) 'Primary maternal preoccupation', in D. W. Winnicott (1975) *Through Paediatrics to Psycho-analysis*, London: Hogarth Press.

Further reading

Bandler, D. (1987) 'Working with other professionals in an inpatient setting', *Journal of Child Psychotherapy* 13(2): 81–90.

Coombe, P. (1995) 'The inpatient treatment of mother and child at the Cassel Hospital: a case of Munchhausen syndrome by proxy', *British Journal of Psychotherapy* 12: 195–207.

Flynn, C. (1993) 'The patient's pantry: the nature of the nursing task', *Therapeutic Communities* 14(4): 227–36.

Flynn, D. (1988) 'The assessment and psychotherapy of a physically abused girl during in-patient family treatment', *Journal of Child Psychotherapy* 13(2): 61–78.

—— (1998) 'Psychoanalytic aspects of inpatient treatment', *Journal of Child Psychotherapy* 24(2): 283–306.

Heymans, A., Kennedy, R. and Tischler, L. (eds) (1987) *The Family as In-Patient*, London: Free Association Books.

14 International developments

Judith Edwards

Introduction

Since child psychotherapy first began in the consulting rooms of our psycho-analytic forebears such as Melanie Klein, Anna Freud, Donald Winnicott and Michael Fordham, there have been many developments in the field, both theoretical and in terms of trainings. Application of the thinking accumulated by the profession has been made in terms of consultation to those in related fields of child mental health and primary health care. This chapter sets out to document some of these developments as they have grown and multiplied around the world. It may well not be an exhaustive list or cover every development in each country, but in the variety of approaches and the geographical span of the work it will show how those beginnings over fifty years ago have seeded themselves worldwide.

I would like to thank the many people who have contributed to this chapter, and also to acknowledge that in a short piece such as this many facets of the work in different countries have of necessity to be represented in a condensed way – one which may not adequately convey the detailed diversity of the work.

Asia

India

In 1974 in Bombay, a group of psychoanalysts founded a public charity trust called the Psychoanalytic Therapy and Research Centre, whose aims were to provide reduced fee treatment for children and families, to provide clinical workspace for students, and to promote the growth and develop-ment of psychoanalytic work with children and families. By the mid-1980s Bombay achieved semi-autonomous status for its training: although the official address of the Psychoanalytic Society is in Calcutta, the thousand-mile distance between the two cities was causative in the birth of the Bombay Sub-Committee Board of Training.

From 1979, however, the emphasis had been more on training than treatment. In 1993 the Child and Family Consultation Centre was opened in order to redress this imbalance. A multidisciplinary team was formed and, in 1995, with the arrival of two more Tavistock-trained child and adolescent psychotherapists, the work expanded rapidly in this the only functioning psychoanalytic psychotherapy centre for the treatment of children and families in Bombay. The centre not only provides a public forum for those working with children, but has also developed a training on the Tavistock model, which is currently being undertaken by eleven students. In 1990 some Bombay analysts decided to promote international links, and this resulted in the bi-annual Indo-Australian Psychoanalytic Conference, which became subsequently the Asian–Australian Psycho-analytic Conference.

Australasia

Australia

Child psychotherapy in Australia would probably trace its roots to 1936 when Ruth Drake, a nursery teacher and speech therapist, worked as a play therapist in the Psychiatric Clinic of the Royal Children's Hospital in Melbourne. She was subsequently appointed as the first child psycho-therapist in the Department of Psychology at the hospital. Since then, developments in this vast country have continued to expand, and the originally 'English thinking' has now percolated down over two genera-tions. This has resulted in innovations as Australian practitioners evolve from those original psychoanalytic models, responsive to the current need to be psychodynamically informed in a climate where the value of short-term early intervention is increasingly in the frame. Australia, equidistant between the United States and Great Britain, has benefited from a combination of thinking from both countries, and 'classic' psychoanalytic models have combined with theories of attachment and the rich thinking that emerged from that concept, through such pioneering work as that of Mary Main, Daniel Stern and Berry Brazelton. Notable developments recently include the setting up of the Child Psychoanalytic Foundation, where the Observation Studies course in Sydney was formally accredited by the Tavistock Clinic in 1997. This course will be expanded to a full child psychotherapy training. In addition, a two-year part-time Graduate Diploma in Psychodynamic Psychotherapy will be established at the University of Wollongong in New South Wales in 1998, covering work with infants, children, adolescents and adults. Also in 1998, the University of Melbourne will be running a Masters course in Parent and Infant Mental Health: this will include a clinical training in infant–parent psychotherapy. A Graduate Diploma in Child Psycho-therapy by Distance Education will also be offered by Monash University in Melbourne from 1998. The training in Brisbane is developing, although as yet without university links.

Despite this, there is virtually no establishment of child psychotherapy posts within the public sector. In the State of Victoria, for instance (which has about 4 million of Australia's total population of 17 million), there are only four full-time equivalent posts in the public sector, located at the Royal Children's Hospital. While the term 'child psychotherapist' is not a protected title, there have been recent moves towards setting up an Australian Confederation of Psychotherapists, and the Victoria Child Psychotherapists Association would seek to be included in this.

North and South America

Canada

The first psychoanalytically-based initiative for children was set up in Toronto in 1976, inspired by Dr Gordon Warme, a psychiatrist and psycho-analyst who had become interested in training child psychotherapists while engaged in his own training in the 1960s at the Menninger Clinic in the United States. The training was based on the combined models of the Anna Freud Centre, the Tavistock Clinic and the Cleveland Centre for Research and Child Development. By 1997 this had evolved to become an autono-mous educational institute, with forty graduates to date. A professional association was formed in 1981, and this has developed a code of ethics and standards of practice. In 1991 the Child Psychotherapy Foundation, a charitable organisation, was founded in order to raise funds for the psycho-analytic treatment of children. The training now comprises four years of academic course work including theory, child development, diagnosis and psychopathology, the principles and practice of psychotherapy, and contin-uous case seminars, in addition to infant and young child observation and a course on working with parents.

Here as elsewhere, at a time of increased budget cuts and with severe stresses increasingly found in children and their families, the goal of the TCPP and the Foundation is to promote awareness of the value of this kind of treatment, and to make the thinking accessible to as wide an audience as possible.

United States

The United States has no federally or state funded psychoanalytic psycho-therapy services for children and adolescents, although a very limited amount of support (soon to be further curtailed) is available through Medicaid, which helps the poorest and most handicapped. Private insurance varies from state to state, but few policies support anything longer than once-weekly work for two or three months. There is, at the moment, no formal training comparable with that which exists elsewhere – for instance, in Europe and Great Britain – although there are many schools of professional psychotherapy, in clinical psychology and social work for instance, which contain components related to the treatment of children and adolescents. There have been, however, some initiatives which have offered and continue to offer psychoanalytic treatment to children and young people.

The Hannah Perkins Centre in Cleveland, Ohio was founded in 1951, and remains today devoted to the provision of psychoanalytic treatment, training, research and application. Its founder, Erna Furman, was a close collaborator of Anna Freud, and this spirit has been perpetuated in the therapeutic school, which consists of a mother–toddler programme, a nursery school and a kindergarten. In addition, the Child Analytic Clinic provides therapeutic services from infancy to adolescence, and this is indeed the only facility in the United States where for forty-five years treatment has been carried out, as intensive as needed, with a liberal sliding scale of family contributions. The Child Analysis Course began in 1958, and until recently was the only facility for non-medical professionals in the country, offering a seven-year intensive training and a modified two-year course for psychologists, psychiatrists and social workers. The centre also undertakes an enormous range of applied and consultative work.

In Los Angeles, the Hilda Karsh Centre was founded in 1978 from an endowment from Hilda Karsh, who had worked with Jung and was one of the founders of the Los Angeles Institute. The centre provided ongoing case discussion and supervision, becoming increasingly influenced by Michael Fordham's ideas on transference and countertransference. Today, this also includes an ongoing study group for trainees and analysts, with lectures on various aspects of Jungian child psychotherapy.

San Francisco offers infant observation seminars and also seminars related to work with children and adolescents, with plans to develop training in parent–infant psychotherapy and infant research in Palo Alto, in conjunction with the School of Infant Mental Health in London.

Argentina

Developments in the field over the past twenty-five years have been prolific, from the efforts of the first pioneers to promote the dissemination, teaching and practice of child psychotherapy and the organisation of the first course set up and taught by Arminda Aberastury in 1948 under the aegis of the Argentine Psychoanalytical Association. Since then until today, the APA and later the Buenos Aires Psychoanalytical Association have been involved in training, while there are in addition numerous independent associations which teach psychoanalytic theory according to different orientations such as the British, French and American schools.

The first hospital service available for psychoanalytic work with children in a Spanish-speaking country was created in Buenos Aires in 1934. The

Psychiatry and Psychology Centre was part of the paediatrics chair at the Hospital de Clinicas Jose de San Martin. Subsequently psychoanalysis was incorporated into the understanding and treatment of children's disorders in many national and municipal hospitals. In the 1980s Kamala Di Tella, who had trained at the Tavistock Clinic, generated a space in the Hospital Italiano for the psychoanalytic treatment of children with autism. At the same time she started Infant Observation seminars, and her work has been carried on by colleagues since her death. During recent years there have been greater obstacles to the implementation of psychoanalytic theory and practice because of health policies which focus on seeing a larger number of patients in as short a time as possible.

Brazil

Child and adolescent psychotherapy has been established and developed in the main cities in Brazil such as Rio de Janeiro, Porto Alegre and Coritiba, with training centres established in São Paolo and Rio. Most notable of recent developments is the establishment in 1987 of the Centro de Estudos Psicanaliticos Mae-Bebe-Famila in São Paolo which runs Tavistock–Martha Harris Courses in Infant Observation and in Child and Adolescent Psychotherapy. Recently the Latin-American Congress on Child and Adolescent Psychoanalysis was organised in Brazil, and there is a thriving and growing list of publications which reflect and extend the work in terms of thinking and practice.

Chile

Child psychotherapy training began unofficially in Chile in 1960, and has been going on there since then, but without the recognition of a formal qualification, although it is recognised by the Institute of Psychoanalysis. After slow beginnings, psychotherapy has been available as a treatment mainly in the psychiatric clinic of the medical school at the University of Chile. While for a time there was a Mahlerian orientation, an influence which was introduced by those who had trained and worked in the United States, the orientation of the work is now largely Kleinian. Currently there is an initiative to reorganise the training and to establish it gradually in a more formal way, whereas work with children has until now been undertaken principally by psychoanalysts.

Africa

South Africa

Although currently there is no systematic training available for child and adolescent psychotherapists in South Africa, there are many clinical and educational psychologists as well as social workers who work in a psycho-analytically oriented way. The Parent and Child Counselling Centre, established as the Johannesburg Child Guidance Clinic in 1944, has retained a strong psychoanalytic tradition, and the influence has been predominantly from Tavistock-trained child psychotherapists, both historically and today. Several of the Tavistock-model Observation Course modules are now taught on a monthly course in Durban, and plans for a full training are being formulated.

The visits by Henri Rey in the 1970s and '80s to Capetown were influential in spreading psychoanalytic thinking: the Capetown Child Guidance Clinic and the Red Cross Child and Family Centre have been centres of excellence for many years. Since 1995 pre-clinical components of the Tavistock Observation Course have been available. Generally it is not easy for child and adolescent psychotherapists with overseas qualifications to obtain registration in South Africa unless they have a psychology background. However, in the light of the country's urgent need for clinical skills to address the needs of South Africa's children, this situation is under review.

Middle East

Israel and Palestine

While there is in Israel no formal training in Child and Adolescent Psycho-therapy, in-service training and work with children is undertaken in child and adolescent clinics, supervised by child analysts. In recent years, initiatives by Tavistock-trained psychotherapists have led to several developments: these include opportunities to follow Tavistock-model courses in observational studies and a programme, 'Parents in Transition', which has been set up to develop skills and expertise in Israeli and Arab professionals from multidisciplinary backgrounds who work with infants, children and their parents. In the West Bank of Israel, now under the rule of the Palestinian National Authority, workshops have been given to Palestinian childcare workers in order to develop the psychological skills that are required to address the immediacy and urgency of child mental health problems in an area of considerable political turbulence. A course in 'Counselling and Psychoanalytical Observational Skills' for childcare professionals is planned for 1998.

Europe: Central Europe

Czech Republic

During the period between the two world wars, child psychotherapy was virtually non-existent in Czechoslovakia. Some tentative beginnings were further interrupted by the post-war discouragement of existing initiatives so that, in effect, while adult psychoanalysis survived principally on an illegal basis, work with children disappeared completely. In 1971, the Children's Psychiatric Clinic in Prague was established under the leadership of Dr J. Spitz, and a space for psychotherapeutic approaches was created, mainly with families, and later developing into a systemic family therapy training. It was not, however, until 1993 that the Society for Psychoanalytic Psychotherapy was founded, connected with the European Federation of Psychoanalytic Psychotherapy, and as part of this society a child psychotherapy section came into existence. At present this section has fourteen members with psychoanalytic experience, who are now in their second year of training, led by colleagues from the British Association of Psychotherapists in Great Britain. Between their weekend visits to Prague, individual work and peer groups extend the thinking and practice, and it is hoped that this will eventually build up to become the basis of a more formal training.

Hungary

In 1970, the mainly psychoanalytically oriented Child Psychotherapeutic Outpatient Clinic of Budapest set up theoretical seminars on child psychoanalysis for interested professionals. Two years later, technical seminars became available for all child guidance clinics and in 1982 intensive short-term training began. In 1986 child psychotherapy became a part of the systematic psychotherapeutic training for psychiatrists and psychologists, and in 1990 the Ego Clinic, a private out-patient clinic for children and adolescents, became the training centre for child and adolescent psychotherapy. While it can be said that training in Hungary is largely concentrated in Budapest, there are private theoretical and technical seminars led by trained psychoanalysts and supervision is available outside Budapest. In 1992 'On One's Own Way' came into being, under the auspices of the Psychoanalytic Institute, as a centre for training and work with adolescents.

Hungarian child analysts have, since the 1970s, been in regular contact with both the Anna Freud Centre and the Tavistock Clinic, and there has developed a two-way link with, for instance, members of the Tavistock's Young People's Counselling Service travelling to Hungary to exchange ideas with colleagues. Hungary has also been a regular participant from the inception of the EPF Standing Conference on Child and Adolescent Psychoanalysis.

Yugoslavia

It was in Belgrade in the early fifties that the first initiative specifically for children was set up: the Medical–Educational counselling service for children and adolescents, where psychoanalytically oriented psychotherapy was practised, although there was at that time no formal training. At present in Belgrade at the Faculty of Medicine, psychologists and psychiatrists can pursue a specialisation in work with children and adolescents, and also at the Institute for Mental Health there is a four-term child psychotherapy module. There is a sub-section of child and adolescent psychoanalytic psychotherapy in the society founded in Belgrade. It is hoped that the Jugoslav Society will join the European Association of Psychoanalytic Psychotherapy in the near future.

For years the professionals practising child psychotherapy have participated in conferences throughout former Yugoslavia and Europe, and the two main journals for publication of papers are *Psychiatry Today* (Belgrade) and *Psychotherapy* (Zagreb). Strong international links were forged in the 1980s, specifically with France, and also now with London, from where a senior colleague travels regularly to Belgrade to supervise the work. In spite of the fact that the training and work of child psychotherapists has developed in Yugoslavia over the past thirty to forty years, there is still no formal training, and personal analysis is as yet not part of the requirements for those pursuing a specialisation in the area of work with children and adolescents.

Russia

It was in the 1960s that the first non-drug-related therapies were introduced in Russia, and the term 'psychotherapy' entered professional language, although at that time psychotherapy was the prerogative of medical doctors only. As the Soviet Union's communications with the West have opened up, so too have notions about treating children psychotherapeutically, but initially there was no specific training for the work which began at the Bechterev Institute in St Petersburg (formerly Leningrad) and the Serbsky Institute of Psychiatry in Moscow. In 1990 the course in child and adolescent psychotherapy was established in the Department of Psychotherapy of the Medical Academy for Postgraduate Studies in St Petersburg. The majority of students remain medical doctors, but there is an increasing intake of psychologists. As a consequence of the opening up to Western influences, there was an undifferentiated explosion of ideas following previous deprivation, and this has yet to be rendered coherently. One of the most important events recently was the one-year course in psychoanalytic concepts taught by staff from the Anna Freud Centre. The twenty-five professionals who took the course are carrying on with the work and aim to establish an Association of Child Psychoanalytic Psychotherapy. There is, in the country, a feeling of wanting to catch up with mainstream development: for instance, personal analysis has yet to be included in training. Longer-term trainings are being considered but economic constraints put a brake on these aspirations.

Psychoanalysis, long prohibited in Russia, was simply neglected during the time of perestroika. It was only in 1997 that the President's Decree was issued to support psychoanalytic work both morally and financially. Again, this opening up of a previously closed door brings its own difficulties in terms of a huge influx of ideas and initiatives, and time is needed to ground many differing approaches in appropriate structures for training and treatment. One of my correspondents has thought of the present situation as one where 'post-totalitarian stress syndrome' has released a new set of conflicts as old structures change and anxieties are released.

Europe: Scandinavia

Denmark

Interest in the practice of psychoanalytically oriented child psychotherapy has grown during the past few years, with practice mainly based in schools' psychological services, hospitals and child guidance clinics, and a small amount of private work also developing. The Danish Association for Psychoanalytic Child and Adolescent Psychotherapy was founded in 1992, and a training programme is currently being set up, dependent however on subscription and funding. Following government legislation a few years ago, one can obtain authorisation after two years' supervised work following a first degree in psychology to work as a specialist in the field of psychotherapy: as this is a relatively new arrangement, there is as yet no difference in requirements for work with adults and children. At the Institute of Clinical Psychology, founded in 1950 as a training school for psychoanalytically oriented work with children, inspired by the old child guidance movement and by the work of Anna Freud, there is now a full-time post-graduate two-year training programme. The Centre of Infant Studies of the Institute of Clinical Psychology has a professional link with Harvard College in the United States, and it is also developing a similar link with the Tavistock Clinic in Great Britain. While there is not as yet a Danish academic journal specifically linked to work with children, such psychoanalytic work finds space for publication in the Scandinavian journal of psychology, *Nordisk Psykologi*, or in the journal of the Danish Association of Psychologists, *Psykolog Nyt*.

Finland

In 1976 members of the Finnish Psychoanalytical Association and of the Therapeia Foundation formed together the Finnish Association of Child and Adolescent Psychotherapy, with the aim of beginning a training which then started as a three-year course in 1978. The students were doctors, psychologists, social workers and psychiatric nurses. In 1987, when 32 students had qualified, the two societies separated, and since then the Finnish Psychoanalytical Association has continued a child psychotherapy course organised by the Helsinki Psychotherapy Society. In 1993 this became a four-year course, treating children up to 14 years of age, following the EFPP criteria. Infant Observation on the Tavistock model is part of the training requirements. In addition the Therapeia Foundation began its own longer training, aiming to qualify child psychoanalytic psychotherapists for independent intensive psychotherapeutic work. The course has an observation component and lasts five years. Two additional trainings are now established in Northern Finland at Monasteri, and in 1994 the first European training in group psychotherapy for children was set up. Working with adolescents entails a separate training, and some therapists have dual training, although generally in Finland they are separate professional categories. The first training for those working with adolescents began in 1980, and since that time about 100 students have qualified. In addition, in Northern Finland at Oulu, training in work with adolescents was established in 1994 with the help of Marianne Parsons and the Anna Freud Centre.

Altogether there are about 80 child psychotherapists and 100 adolescent psychotherapists in Finland, mostly working in the public health sector, with some private practice developing. Private treatment for children and adolescents can be subsidised either totally or in part by the government, for up to four years of treatment. (This picture is markedly different from that in other countries where, as has already been mentioned, treatment per se is becoming squeezed because of lack of funding and by the requirement to do short-term work as a budget-led decision rather than as the treatment of choice.)

Norway

The history of psychoanalytic work with children in Norway began in effect with the establishment of the Institute for Child and Adolescent Psychotherapy in 1952. The Institute (later to be renamed the Dr Waals Institute, after its founder) inaugurated a three-year psychoanalytic psychotherapy training, with a particular emphasis not only on treatment but on the multidisciplinary framework which holds it. Subsequently this training and service has spread throughout the country, and there are now about sixty out-patient psychiatric clinics providing treatment to children and families. About 2 per cent of the population under eighteen receives some service, and of this 9–10 per cent receive short- or long-term psychoanalytic psychotherapy. In addition there exists some private work. The goal is to double the numbers of those in receipt of treatment, but this of course has budget and training implications. The child psychotherapy training as such has not been formalised, and training within the National Health system varies in quality. In 1991 the Norwegian Association of Psychoanalytic Psychotherapy was formed (and is now a member of the EFPP) with 70 members, and their emphasis has been to stimulate post-graduate training. For the past fifteen years senior practitioners, beginning with Martha

Harris, have been visiting teachers, with a series of Infant Observation seminars also running since that time. There has also been a steady stream of Norwegian visitors to the Tavistock Clinic, and with international links increasingly being promoted, with the EFPP a central focal point.

Sweden

In a climate where the mental health and welfare of children had already been on the agenda from the beginning of the twentieth century, the child guidance movement in Sweden began in 1933, following a previous initiative some ten years before. It was not, however, until the 1950s that specialists in child psychology and psychiatry were introduced, earlier work having largely focused on parents.

The Erika Foundation, an independent institution providing treatment, training and opportunities for research, was established in 1934, modelled on Margaret Lowenfeld's Institute of Child Psychology in London. Since then about 300 psychotherapists have been trained at the Foundation, where research and treatment are seen both as essential in terms of increasing knowledge and also in attracting government funding.

Since the start of the 1990s there have been other training programmes – one, for instance, at the University of Gothenburg, although this is only open to psychologists.

Most work is done in the public sector, but a decrease in government financial support has led to fewer opportunities for children to receive intensive treatment and a call for short-term initiatives.

Europe: Western

France

While direct work with children has been relatively slow to develop in France, with the psychoanalytic community favouring direct work with parents rather than focusing on the child's contribution to pathology, in recent years there have been some encouraging developments. In 1990 the first French Observation course on the Tavistock Clinic model was set up in Larmor-Plage (Lorient, Morbihan), followed in 1994 by the creation of the Martha Harris Centre of Studies. Since 1996 these initiatives have been further developed by the addition of a clinical course for the training of child and adolescent psychoanalytic psychotherapists, again following the Tavistock model.

The Caen group began in 1993 and now has twenty-five students. Also affiliated to the EFPP is the Bordeaux group, established in 1996 along the same lines. The next step will be the setting up of a French Federation for Psychoanalytic Psychotherapy.

Germany

The first association of German child and adolescent psychotherapists was founded in 1953 (the Vereinigung Deutscher Psychagogen), and in the 1960s this association called into existence the Standing Conference of the dozen existing training institutes in order to standardise and safeguard requirements for training. In 1975 the association was given its present name: Vereinigung Analytischer Kinder-und-Jugendlichen Psychotherapeutien (VAKJP), and it has at present over 1,000 members. Since 1971 practitioners registered with the association have been recognised by health insurers and therapy is paid for according to health company guidelines: this as a rule may be up to 150 sessions for children and 180 for adolescents.

In spite of its membership numbers, there is still a shortage of trained practitioners on a federal level. The training is costly and trainees tend to have to retain their previous work commitments, thus making the training itself longer in duration. As elsewhere, the training is open to teachers, social workers, psychologists and medical doctors between the ages of 25 and 40 (generally) and it takes five years to complete. The training includes, alongside the usual components, specific psychiatric experience with very disturbed children or adolescents. The VAKJP publishes a journal, which appears four times a year, and a substantial newsletter twice yearly. At the European Federation of Psychoanalytic Psychotherapy in the Public Sector, the VAKJP is represented by two delegates in the child and adolescent section, and takes an active part in EFPP conferences.

Ireland

Since the 1980s, there has been a huge upsurge of interest in psychoanalytic psychotherapy with children and adolescents, and 1995 saw the publication of the first issue of the *Irish Journal of Child and Adolescent Psychotherapy*, currently published annually.

It had been in the early eighties that concern was expressed about the relative neglect of intrapsychic processes in children, with an emphasis solely on family therapy and systems approaches. The Irish Forum for Child Psychotherapy (IFCAP) was established in 1986, and in 1990 the first diploma course began, which was subsequently converted into a master's degree in Child and Adolescent Psychoanalytic Psychotherapy. The course is now a part of the Faculty of Health Sciences at Trinity College, Dublin. In response to a demand for wider discussion and dissemination of psychodynamic thinking, IFCAP has run a series of introductory courses for interested colleagues in related professions. It has also strenuously pursued a policy of promoting international links, and there is now a steady two-way flow of ideas, in terms of lectures and seminars, and strong links both with the Anna Freud Centre and the Tavistock Clinic. IFCAP, in its role as part of the Irish Standing Conference on Psychoanalysis founded in 1990, has been monitoring the issues of accreditation and harmonisation in Europe, as well as issues of registration and practice in Ireland itself. A voluntary register of psychoanalytic psychotherapists already exists, and a statutory register is in the offing. The most recent development was the setting up in 1996 of the Irish Association of Infant Observation to monitor and promote the understanding and development of the work.

Italy

During the years of the fascist regime in Italy the practice of psychoanalysis was forbidden, but in the late 1940s the Centri Psico-Pedagogici (Psycho-Pedagogic Centres) were established with the aim of preventing anti-social tendencies in children and adolescents. There were 200 centres in all throughout Italy. It was not until the 1970s, however, that the emotional problems of childhood became to be seen not only to have organic origins, but very often to be rooted in family and society.

While continuous changes of government during the last twenty years have hindered the development of child and adolescent psychoanalytic psychotherapy in the public sector because of an absence of coherent policies for children, there have nevertheless been enormous developments in the field. The most severe consequence, however, of the lack of planning for children and adolescents in government policy has been that the role of child psychotherapists, for political and trades union reasons, has not been specifically included in the organisation of provision for child mental health. Notwithstanding this hurdle, since the 1970s there has been a steady growth in opportunities both for preclinical and clinical training, hitherto predominantly on the Tavistock model, but with both Freudian and Jungian trainings about to be made available. The first Observation Course began in Rome in 1976, and the students from the first two courses, thanks to the pioneering help of a senior teacher at the Tavistock Clinic, set up a structure for clinical training. The training follows the Tavistock model originated by Martha Harris, and indeed was set up with her help and support. Subsequently the Observational Studies component has spread to other centres – in Trapani, Palermo, Bologna, Milan, Pisa, Florence, Naples, Pescara and Venice. These developments led to the foundation of the AIPPI and the association Centro di Studi Martha Harris, both in Rome, to offer a support structure for the training. Since then the AIPPI has organised ten clinical courses to date. Also in 1976 a training began at Rome University's Institute of Child Psychiatry: this is still operative, and regularly welcomes key international figures to give seminars and courses. Apart from this flourishing network, private associations in Rome, Turin and Monza-Milan have played an important role, promoted by university teachers in the faculties of child neuro-psychiatry.

Together with the AIPPI and the Centro di Studi Martha Harris, these institutions are represented in the child and adolescent sections of the EFPP (European Federation of Psychoanalytic Psychotherapy), with 150 qualified psychotherapists to date. While this represents a huge development, it is concentrated mainly in the north of the country, with the south of Italy and the main islands still having little or no provision.

Afterword

What becomes apparent when reading this chapter is the sheer scale and diversity of the work. There has been a ripple effect that is still increasing, and the map is being redrawn yearly with the initiation of new structures to promote the growth of our work and also its application to related professions. It is fascinating to note how political shifts impact on the work, and how these are opening up new avenues as we approach the millennium. Budget constraints can restrict potential, but they have also spurred the growth of thinking around new ways to apply our skills, and to systematise our results (see Jill Hodges' chapter on research). Development in the area of our professional growth and training, as in any developmental form, is a complex and multi-factorial process, but in the last twenty-five years, just as our own theoretical spaces have expanded and developed, so we have also seen external developments in parallel. Perhaps it is not too fanciful to liken this process to that of the ancient navigators whose journeying was so facilitated when the discovery of a way to map longitude emerged. One can only speculate, given the expansion of the last twenty-five years, where the fourth dimension of time will lead both the external and internal spaces over the next quarter of a century.

Part IV
The diversity of treatments

15 Traditional models and their contemporary use

(a) Intensive psychotherapy

Viviane Green

Introduction

A primary aim of this chapter is to focus on the different types of developmental difficulties that would indicate the need for an intensive therapeutic intervention. I also hope to convey a qualitative feel of what intensive psychotherapy offers as a form of treatment and to delineate something of the psychic, mental and affective processes involved in a therapeutic relationship: what sort of experience does intensive therapeutic contact offer a particular child and how, too, does a therapist reflect on his or her part in the therapeutic engagement in order to understand the child.

For the purposes of this chapter, and in line with the Association of Child Psychotherapists' definitions for training purposes, intensive work (in terms of frequency) is a minimum of three-times-weekly sessions. When indicated and practicable children can also be offered sessions on a four or five times a week basis. In demarcating a line between intensive and non-intensive work, I do not wish to suggest that there are necessarily a series of ensuing differences between the two, nor that there is a neat fit between quantity and quality or depth. Many children are able to make very good use of non-intensive psychotherapy – indeed, this is the principal approach offered by child psychotherapists working in the NHS (National Health Service) today. Greater frequency is not always more appropriate. Conversely, there are children for whom intensive work is both positively indicated and also may be considered the sine qua non in order for them to begin to engage in a therapeutic process. In such circumstances it will be considered the necessary level of contact required to bring about some process of psychic change.

The transference relationship

In any form of psychotherapeutic treatment the therapist uses her sentient and reflective psychoanlaytic self to attempt to understand and make sense of the child's emotional world. Through the therapeutic relationship the therapist will try to understand the internal figures that inhabit a child's emotional and mental life and, in conjunction with this, the ways in which the child feels and thinks about himself. Alongside this the therapist also tries to grasp the ways in which the child seeks to protect himself against the pain, hurts, anxieties and confusions engendered by his inner life. Attention is also given to aspects of the child's experiences that are sources of pleasure, self-esteem and satisfaction, which promote resilience. The medium through which this is expressed in a clinical setting is the transference and the countertransference. The term transference refers to the way in which new and current relationships are coloured by past and ongoing experiences. The new person, in the form of the therapist, is related to in a way that conveys the child's internal sense of the important figures in his life. The child also conveys the ways in which he has incorporated and shaped a sense of himself through these relationships. In short, the therapist lends herself as a person on to whom the child's wishes, thoughts and fantasies can be transferred. It is an 'as if' phenomenon where the therapist can be responded to as if he or she were a mother, father, grandparent, sibling or other significant figure. The corollary of the transference is the therapist's own countertransference, by which is meant particular aspects of the therapist's responses to the child. In keeping a vigilant analytical reflective watch on her reactions to the child, the therapist seeks to understand the many varied, subtle and sometimes not so subtle ways in which the child unconsciously evokes a response in his therapist. This is particularly evident when a therapist finds herself experiencing a reaction which she recognises as not normally hers (role responsiveness) that has arisen specifically in response to something that has happened within a session.

When eight-year-old Laura, a child with learning difficulties, issued a stream of incomprehensible maths questions to her therapist, the therapist became overwhelmed with a sense of frustration, shame and confusion as she remained unable to unravel what she was expected to do. Laura was conveying vividly her own daily experience of feeling horribly muddled and humiliated when she could not understand something. Another therapist was given a vivid account by Peter, an adolescent boy, of his various risk-taking activities. He was engaging in promiscuous, unprotected intercourse and took various drugs when he went clubbing. The therapist noted how she found herself feeling increasingly alarmed and somewhat disapproving whereas Peter was apparently unconcerned. The therapist concluded that, in order to remain free of any conflict and to sidetrack thinking about the implications of what he was doing to himself, he had psychically 'handed over' this part of his capacities to the therapist. She then had to take it up as his internal conflict.

Transference and countertransference are thus the therapist's tools for increasing her understanding of the child's conscious and unconscious life. The precise course of any treatment differs widely according to each child and the particular 'story' as it unfolds in the course of a given therapeutic relationship. This also occurs in non-intensive work, but inten-

sive treatment does provide the optimal conditions for fostering the intensification and growth of the therapeutic relationship. For some children it
secures the necessary conditions for its very establishment.

Advantages of intensive work

From the therapist's point of view there are some distinct advantages in
intensive work compared to, say, once-weekly treatment. Knowing that
contact is frequent, the therapist can give herself full permission to relax
into an unhurried pace, thus freeing her to be with the child in a frame of
mind allowing free-floating attention. It is the framework which gives the
fullest possibility for the intricate revelation of the child's concerns and
allows a gradual process of elaboration to take place. Whilst ideally once-
weekly work is also approached with a similar attitude, it is inevitably
constrained by a sense of pressure and curtailment. It comes from the feeling
that unless very close intense attention is paid then something might be lost
irretrievably or for a long time to come. There is also the clinical question of
whether certain material should not be taken up, given the long gap
between sessions, particularly if the child may be left in an 'unsealed' state
during the interval. When the child is due to return the next day, and
where there is a stable holding environment for the child at home, the
therapist can leave themes and anxieties looser without the need to 'parcel
up' at the end of the session. Intensive work is, paradoxically, the necessary
luxury of knowing that if at any given moment something is only barely
expressed or manifested by the child, or only partially glimpsed or discerned
by the therapist, then it is possible to wait until it re-emerges again in a
more crystallised form in another session.

Criteria for intensive work

The criteria indicating the need for intensive help will be based on an
overview of the many different aspects of the child's overall functioning.
Children and adolescents referred (or who self-refer) for psychotherapeutic
help have diverse developmental difficulties of varying degrees of severity
and complexity. The precise developmental 'story' is different for each child.
The underlying assumption is that the child's inner emotional landscape has
been wrought from a dynamic interplay between forces from within and
without and these forces are themselves subject to growth and change.
Development is a complex weave and synthesis of many strands. The threads
are woven together in a series of intricate interdependencies between maturational sequences, experiences afforded or withheld by the environment and
developmental steps reflecting the growing internal psychodynamic organisation. At the heart of a child's emotional development lies the relationship
between the child and his primary caregivers. To a large extent this will be
experience-dependent but the picture is additionally fleshed out in the more

idiosyncratic ways a given child has built up an affective sense of relationships with others and, in turn, a sense of himself. The particular manner in which the self and others are experienced will also be coloured by the child's level of development and his own psychic make-up.

The difficulties of any given child 'can only be evaluated against a concept of age-appropriate developmental status in many areas of psychological growth' (Edgcumbe 1995: 3). Many parents and professionals working with children hold a working model of what age-appropriate means and will calibrate their responses and expectations accordingly. It is against this background sense of 'age-appropriateness' that we can see where a child's current and future emotional development is in jeopardy. Within this overall framework the child psychotherapist will try to gauge the child's level of development and nature of the difficulties along different dimensions.

How 'stuck' is the child?

It is important to evaluate whether a difficulty is transient or fixed with repercussions for future development. Sometimes, the move into a new developmental phase can in and of itself bring a period of strain for an otherwise well-functioning child. At other times, a child's development may seem to grind to a halt, or even regress, in the face of specific events such as divorce, hospitalisation, the birth of a sibling. However, given the child's own resilience and previous experiences, with sensitive and appropriate parental handling these waters are navigable or require minimal intervention. If, however, alterations in parental handling and the child's own resources are insufficient to alleviate the child's distress then psychotherapeutic help may be recommended. Fonagy and Target pinpoint the child's experience of anxiety as a significant indicator for a positive outcome for intensive psychotherapy (Fonagy and Target 1996). The child's anxiety will feed into what is referred to as the therapeutic alliance, the galvanising force for a wish for help and change. However, difficulties are not always consciously experienced as a state of internal distress within the child, but can be manifest as ongoing conflictual relationships between the child and his parents or others in whom concern is generated. Where these difficulties have been of a particularly longstanding or intractable nature, dogging the child at each stage in development, then intensive psychotherapy may well be necessary. Intensive treatment can also be indicated where a child or adolescent becomes noticeably fixed or stuck at a given point in his development and becomes unable to move forward to engage with the psychic tasks of the stage. Intensive psychotherapy may be the least level of contact necessary to free up the development process.

The following case of Paul, a late adolescent, illustrates when there is an unequivocal need for intensive treatment due to acute longstanding difficulties.

Paul had severe restrictions in his capacity to relate, first evident in early childhood and continuing throughout his development. At each step of the way he found it hard to steer a course through age-appropriate development. Paul's difficulties in forming relationships with others had arisen despite adequate parenting. He had originally received and benefited from once-weekly psychotherapy. This had successfully allowed him to gain a degree of self-confidence. Nonetheless, the severity of his difficulties meant that, by late adolescence, both the NHS clinic Paul had attended and his parents continued to feel serious concern about his future. As a late adolescent his life had effectively ground to a halt. He was extremely withdrawn, suffered incapacitating self-consciousness and was socially isolated. He described himself as feeling depressed and physically tired most of the time. He felt cut off from other people, ashamed of his body, and oppressed and frightened by what family members might say about him. He continued to live at home where he mostly spent his time in his own room or addictively watched horror films on television, often until the early hours of the morning. He had no plans for the future. Relationships with his family were strained; he had little contact with anyone else. He had never had a girlfriend. His current life was the outward expression of his con-strained, immobilised internal state indicating that intensive therapy was the least that was needed if he were to have any chance to move forward in his emotional life. The alternative would have been a residential psychiatric placement. Paul was offered three-times-weekly help. Initially he was intensely anxious, constricted in his speech, thoughts and associations. Through the therapeutic relationship he gradually became able at times to be more open, lively, spontaneous and thoughtful, and to communicate more freely and clearly with his therapist. He was also able to allow himself to feel some hope. The therapist took up with him the ways in which his fear of change pre-vented him from making any real progress in his life. In turn, he was enabled to begin talking about previously denied aspects of himself. For the first time he could acknowledge that he had sexual thoughts and feelings about women and that he regretted actively cutting himself off from other people. He could also look at the ways in which he played a part in the difficulties with his parents. He began to perceive that many of the thoughts and feelings he ascribed to others were in fact his own. The door opened to reveal Paul to himself: that he had a whole range of feelings from which he had cut himself off. By the end of the first year of intensive psychotherapy Paul reported a number of changes. He had given up his addictive watching of television. His relationship with his family had improved and he was doing a job one afternoon a week, which involved working in pairs. He was considering starting a part-time training course, and overall he felt consistently better within himself.

The nature of the child's relationships and sense of self

A crucial dimension in assessing emotional development is the nature and quality of the child's object world – i.e. how does the child relate to others and feel about him or herself? Here there is a useful notion of the capacity to relate to others as a progressive developmental line, moving from the child's initial necessary self-absorption growing gradually into an ever increasing capacity and wish to relate to others as people with their own and different feelings, wishes and thoughts. The outward expression of this is the difference between a two-year-old's outbursts of grabbing toys from another in pursuit of an interest to an eight-year-old child's wish to engage in friendships with other children built on an understanding that friendships entail reciprocity. The qualitative way in which a child relates to others is built up by the mainly conscious, unconscious and experiential forces that have fed into his development.

The child's internal object world is inextricably linked to the manner in which he will negotiate the path towards separation and individuation. This refers to the incremental steps taken that lead from a state of total dependency on a caregiver, to a gradual shaping of an internal feeling of separateness with a growing wish for increasing independence. Sometimes children want to rush precociously ahead before they are fully able to take care of themselves appropriately, and in some cases a child might hanker for the state of early childhood and not want to move on. Acceleration, stasis or regression along this continuum can spell difficulties for both child and parents, impairing the capacity to take gradual steps towards carving out a sense of self as a different and separate person who can gradually move away psychically. This process is contingent upon the quality of the relationship with primary caregivers and their own unconscious conflicts.

For Simon, referred at the age of twelve years and six months, his difficulties in separating from his mother left him feeling very ashamed and distressed. If she went out he would feel unduly anxious and would need to cling to her. His difficulties had originally been fuelled from early on by his mother's impatient annoyance at his clinginess. Her impatience reflected an intergenerational difficulty in her own family of origin whose members had suffered severe losses. Simon's parents had altered their handling of him but his anxieties persisted. He made it abundantly clear that he felt internally restricted when he told the therapist: 'I mean I want to be able to leave my mother one day. It would look stupid to be still at home when I am thirty.' He then went on to reveal many fantasies about his fears which he recognised as irrational, confessing that every time his parents went out he was dogged by the thought that they would sneak away permanently. Simon was able to articulate his inner anxieties and to link them to his specific worries around separation which he recognised militated against his progressive wishes. He, too, was offered intensive psychotherapy where the close regular contact rapidly enabled him to bring into treatment his fears around separation and loss evoked by the gaps between sessions, the weekend and holiday breaks in treatment.

The inevitable breaks in treatment, coupled with the frequency, regularity and consistency of the renewed contact with the therapist, facilitate the emergence of the child's feelings and fantasies. Intensity of contact is particularly indicated where a child's history of inconsistent or discontinuous caregiving may leave him unable to engage safely or invest sufficiently in once a week contact in order to get to the point where separation from the therapist is meaningful. For some children, it is only where there is a great enough sense of trust and safety fostered by frequent contact that they can dare to begin to allow themselves to know what it is to miss someone, to rage against them for their absence and to experience that survival of self and other is possible.

Mastery of the self

In the course of early development children are gradually enabled to take steps towards regulating and mastering their inner impulses. In order to do so, they are dependent upon the continued presence of a consistent caring attuned adult. The route to mastery can be impeded in different ways: the absence of a caring consistent caregiver, discontinuities in care and traumatic impingements or losses.

Intensive treatment was offered to Davey when he was four and a half years old. This was supplemented by regular work with his father who, following the death of his ex-wife in a car crash when Davey was four, remained Davey's principal caretaker. Mr S felt that his own conflicts around aggression (his father had been violent) did not allow him to manage Davey with firmness. Thus, when Davey, uncomprehendingly distraught at the loss of his mother, would rage at his father and lash out at other children in his nursery class, Mr S felt powerless to intervene firmly. In other respects Davey's development had progressed well. However, his attachments were marked by a prickly aggressiveness. Underneath this were his anxieties about feeling he was an unlovable, dirty, messy boy who had caused his mother to desert him by dying. The corollary was his anxiety about daring to allow himself to experience closeness to another who might also leave him. Growing feelings of affection had to be strenuously fought off.

The nature of defences and anxieties

In the course of psychic development children build up ways of defending themselves against pain, worries and wishes they feel are unacceptable. These psychic mechanisms are part of normal development and we all use them. However, sometimes the nature or intensity of the use of certain defence mechanisms may ultimately be restricting for the child in certain areas of his life. Less frequent contact may not be enough to loosen up a child who has erected strong or rigid defences. A long gap between sessions may enable them to seal up again so that the psychic work is three steps forward, two steps backwards.

Jane was fourteen when she referred herself for help. She was able to articulate her fantasy that her mother would one day just wander off in the supermarket when they went shopping, and in so doing captured her emotional reality that her mother, who had episodes of mental illness, was not really able to keep her consistently in mind or indeed attend to her needs. Her own unconscious hostility and destructive wishes towards her mother were vividly captured in a dream she recalled. In that dream, a pane of glass had crashed down on her sleeping mother. Shortly after telling the therapist this dream, she distanced herself and became lost in her own thoughts. When the therapist asked what she was thinking about, she replied that she had been counting the numbers of squares on a picture in the room. Her obsessional type of defences, alongside a tendency to intellectualise, indicated the ways in which she protected herself from her frightening rage at her mother who, at the same time, she felt was vulnerable.

There are also children who have a fragmented sense of themselves and others, and who may not even have begun to build up sufficient coping defences against their anxieties. Such children can be prey to overwhelming and disorganising anxiety and need the containment of knowing and feeling they will not be left too long in an unmanageable state.

Ego development

Environmental onslaughts, inadequacy in the provision of care, or reasons intrinsic to the child can result in impairment in the child's ego development. By this is meant the range of capacities that help the child orient himself towards reality. Ego capacities also refer to a range of cognitive abilities such as the ability to think, communicate verbally, reason. The ego is also the agency which enables the child to develop internal means of managing and regulating his internal world through the use of defence mechanisms. Children with impeded ego functioning experience various types of difficulties that often manifest at school. During the primary school years well-functioning children are developing peer group relationships and there is a rapid growth of their interests both in and outside school. This is in contrast to the child who has poor ego functioning. The causes for ego impairment are manifold. Often the roots will lie partly in the subtle dynamic interplay of the child's early emotional relationships which provide the matrix within which ego capacities can or cannot fully unfold. Where there are marked ego difficulties there will often be concomitant difficulties in the area of relationships. In addition to this, a child will also find defensive ways to adapt to the original difficulties in order to protect himself from further humiliation and exposure. The defensive adaptation may then compound the problem. Teachers are well acquainted with the class clown who plays up when he cannot do a piece of work or the child who omnipotently professes to know everything or conversely rubbishes everything, claiming it is not worth knowing. A feeling of damage, worthlessness, or a sense of confusion and disorientation may be the underlying experiential reality for the child. Intensive treatment offers a chance for children whose ego potential has not been able to unfold or has become arrested in the course of development.

John F was offered five-times-weekly intensive treatment at the age of seven years. The need for this was established on the grounds of his longstanding difficulties with his mother, which had resulted in impaired ego development. He was flooded with unmanageable levels of anxiety and terrifying fantasies against which he had not been able to erect sufficient defences. He was not free to use his mind to learn and in the context of the classroom was unable to concentrate or take in anything.

John had developed within a not quite safe enough environment where he had been exposed to overstimulation. His wish for a continued early bodily intimacy with his mother was fuelled by her difficulties in setting appropriate relational boundaries. His mother was invested in maintaining his vivid fantasy life, unable to recognise that this frequently left him overwhelmed and over-excited. For John, the boundaries between his fantasy life and reality were barely established. Since the age of two, at mother's instigation, a social worker and psychologist had been involved with the family. At just over two years of age he had been placed in day foster care. His mother, having herself had a chequered history of inadequate mothering marked by long separations interspersed with care from a mentally ill mother, poignantly confessed to having little internal sense of how to mother her son.

John was a confused child who presented as much younger than his chronological age in terms of all the above dimensions. His fragmented world was one where no safe acceptable distance had been created between himself and his mother. Intimacy was embroiled with mutual threats of attack and seduction. He had made little progress at school, finding it hard to manage his frustration or regulate his impulses. He was flooded with exciting and dangerous fantasies of destruction, which he expressed in his play with dolls. He attempted to draw the assessing therapist into a frightening and seductive relationship. He experienced her as a terrifying witch who needed to be simultaneously placated, seductively engaged and attacked. He expressed his chaotic inner feelings of helplessness and disintegration when he described the toy robot he had sent crashing to the ground as 'alive in his body but not in his spirit'.

In the course of his intensive psychotherapy his vivid fears, rage and helplessness were apparent. It was only after a year in treatment that he could begin to experience protracted periods of a sense of safety and going-on-being in the presence of his therapist, who knew how to remain empathically unintrusive. In order to get to this point he had repeatedly to experience that his fears about what he and his therapist might do to each other were contained through her steady frequent presence, a continually renewable reminder that they had both survived the feared onslaughts. His underlying fears of mutual destruction could be reflected on through her verbalisations, clarifications and interpretations of the transference relationship. In turn this inscribed the means by which he could begin to discover that his internal horrors could be named, shaped and thought about safely without the danger of the therapist falling into the role of the over-excitingly involved retaliatory witch-like figure of his worst imaginings. Through this mutual process of making sense of his world John began to be able to develop a more structured sense of himself and others. His mind was freer to engage in more age-appropriate activities requiring attention and to use his ego capacities to think, plan and sublimate in creative ways, particularly through the medium of imaginative and complex lego constructions.

In summary, thinking about a child's development involves taking into account these many different aspects. A prime organiser for the child's overall way of being will depend on the qualitative nature of his internal object world. Integrally related are the ways in which he has been enabled to manage his developmental tasks within the overarching continuum of separation and individuation, his capacity to regulate and modulate his inner feelings and impulses and the growth of his ego capacities. The greater the number of realms in which a child has difficulties that affect his overall functioning the greater the need for intensive work. The introduction of a new person, who through an intensive therapeutic relationship can impact on the shape and course of the developmental stream offers the child a chance to move forward and to make better use of positive experiences offered by others outside the clinical setting. The younger the child at the age of entry into treatment the better the outcome. The research by Fonagy and Target (1996) confirms the common sense assumption that the age at entry into treatment, given the greater fluidity of the child's representational world, is a factor for a good outcome. Ultimately, it is hoped that such a relationship enables the child to tolerate rather than fend off the painful aspects of his world through the internalisation of a capacity for toleration, reflection and understanding of the self by means of a new self and object representation. This becomes part of the child's way of being and can continue after the treatment has ended.

Intensive treatment: some considerations

There are many issues involved in setting up intensive psychotherapy, the main one being working with the child's parents or caregivers to ensure that it can be practically maintained and psychologically supported. The therapist should also consider whether there is a need to spread the sessions evenly through the week to provide the maximum holding. This may be particularly important where a child's overall functioning is fragile as a result of overwhelming fantasies and worries. Whatever the pattern, the therapist will be alert to the meanings evoked for the child as they manifest within the therapeutic relationship. The affective meanings vary enormously be it a sense of abandonment, loss of love, a sense of disintegration of the self or a feared mutual destruction.

Intensive treatment can be set up as such from the outset. However, it can also be paced by intensification from non-intensive treatment. The building up of a sense of basic trust and a wish to explore further may be a delicate matter requiring a longer initial period of engagement. This may be particularly true for adolescents where intensive treatment cuts across the developmental grain, the wish and the need to move away from childhood dependency towards increased independence.

After a period of intensive treatment, where the therapeutic relationship has been well established and certain difficulties worked through, it is possible to cut down to less frequent sessions. There is also the question of how to work in the termination phase of an intensive treatment. In the course of therapy, hopefully, the child will have built up a capacity to integrate and hold on to the therapist as a new developmental object. Nonetheless, this period will herald strong feelings about separation, relinquishment and loss. Some children need a 'weaning period' by reducing the frequency of sessions. Others may need the continuing intensity of contact to face and manage their acute feelings and fears.

Implications for the network

When a family or a support agency such as Social Services does agree to commit themselves to supporting intensive treatment they are taking a significant step. A great deal of thought and care needs to go into the initial stages leading to such a decision. Often it is preceded by a preparatory period involving a therapist or a social worker working with the family to reach the point where the child's need for intensive help can be fully acknowledged. Stable arrangements need to be put into place to ensure that the child can be brought regularly by a parent, involved professional or escort. The investment of time and effort made needs to be weighed in relation to the impact this will have on the rest of the family's life.

Once intensive therapy is underway the therapist, or another professional, will work with the parents or caretaking adults to support the treatment. They, too, need a person with whom to weather the vicissitudes of change that will occur. Parents also need help in reflecting on how their understanding and handling of a child promotes or holds up their forward moves. When the transference relationship unfolds and intensifies the child may start to respond differently to his parents. A classic occurrence is when the transference becomes split. By this is meant the process whereby the child's positive feelings are concentrated on the idealised therapist and the parents receive the child's more negative feelings. At certain points in treatment parents can feel that their child is actually getting worse. Conversely, when the therapist is in the midst of the child's negative transference the child can be all sweetness and light at home: the parents may unwittingly collude with a changed child who refuses to go to therapy. The child can also prove resistant to attending sessions and need parental encouragement to express the resistance to the therapist. At points of apparent improvements at home, the parents may conclude that the change is permanently for the better. Understandably, this is particularly tempting if the child has relinquished a troublesome symptom such as bedwetting, nightmares or school refusal. Parents may need to come to terms with the uncomfortable reality that treatment should not end simply because there has been symptom relief or a period of improved relationships within the family. Both positive and negative feelings towards others need to be analysed within the therapeutic relationship until they can coexist in a more fully integrated way within the child. All this takes time. The length of treatment can vary enormously, but on the whole a minimum of a year is required and very often treatments can continue for much longer depending on the nature and severity of the difficulties. In some cases it is arguable that a shorter period of intensive help may be more productive than a longer period of non-intensive work.

The context

Intensive work can take place within a variety of institutional contexts. It can also be sought privately. From a Health Service perspective there is little doubt that need and demand outstrips provision. Not only is child psychotherapy a relatively scarce resource, but the demographics of where it can be accessed point to real dearth in certain areas outside London. Where there is a concentration of NHS child psychotherapeutic resources, as in London, the mental health profile of the population means that need remains greater than the help available. Clinicians working in child and family mental health teams are faced with the task of attempting to match resources to demand within a framework of operating constraints. There are inevitably occasions when, even if it is agreed that intensive help is the treatment of choice and the least help necessary, it nonetheless cannot be offered.

Conclusion

The therapeutic relationship is one that is created and lived through by two people, the child or adolescent and the therapist. What comes to life through the transference and countertransference is a gradual process of unfolding and elaboration of the young patient's unconscious life. Through the therapist's use of her sentient and reflective self, the child can begin to experience and explore himself and his thoughts and feelings about others in a new and different way.

The considerations that would lead to a recommendation of intensive contact are many and varied. In a sense it is, of course, a reification to separate out the various elements of the child's psychic organisation from the sum totality of how the child experiences himself and others. However, it can offer a useful way of conceptualising to a finer degree the nature of the child's difficulties. The qualitative nature of the child's relationships to others and his sense of himself remain the crucial considerations when thinking about a recommendation for intensive treatment. Where there is a marked curtailment in the child's capacity to relate to others in a satisfying way, or indeed to feel comfortable within himself, allied with the sense that the child's future emotional development is in jeopardy, intensive treatment may be indicated.

The many strands woven into the child's inner psychic organisation can also be thought about when deciding about the intensity of treatment. An overarching consideration is whether, overall, the child's development is moving forwards, backwards, or is stuck. A developmental impasse, suggesting that the child will find it hard to move on to a further stage of development with marked repercussions for his future emotional relationships, is an indicator. For some children there may have been an early developmental curtailment of many capacities.

The way in which the child copes with anxiety and the impact of distressing experiences is another criterion. This would include the nature and degree of the child's anxieties. Difficulties in managing anxiety can occur through over-restrictive use of the defences. Another factor can be fragile ego development where the ego does not have recourse to sufficient or effective defensive strategies. A fragile ego may also create other difficulties for the child, particularly a school-age child. Intensive therapy can sometimes be indicated in order to help children make sense of their experiences and, in doing so, it allows them to make greater use of the ego capacities they do have. For some children it allows those very capacities, especially thinking, to unfold in the first place.

Where there are a large number of domains in which the child is experiencing difficulties, the greater is the need for intensive treatment.

Of necessity, this chapter has expressed in broad brush strokes ways of thinking about children, their development and the need for intensive treatment. Ultimately, each child's developmental story is a complex mosaic. The intensive therapeutic relationship is one within which the particular texture of the child's story, as it exists in his imagination, conscious and unconscious life, can begin to be lived out and expressed.

References

Edgcumbe, R. (1995) 'The history of Anna Freud's thinking on developmental influences', *Bulletin of the Anna Freud Centre* 18(1).

Fonagy, P. and Target, M. (1996) 'Predictors of outcome in child psychoanalysis: a retrospective study of 763 cases at the Anna Freud Centre', *Journal of American Psychoanalytic Association* 44(1): 27–77.

Further Reading

Hurry, A. (ed.) (1998) *Psychoanalysis and Development Therapy*, London: Karnac.

Sandler, J., Holder, A., Dare, C. and Dreher, A.U. (1997) *Freud's Models of the Mind: An Introduction*, London: Karnac.

Tyson, P. and Tyson, R. (1990) *Psychoanalytic Theories of Development*, New Haven CT: Yale University Press.

The reader is also directed to accounts of clinical work in the *Journal of Child Psychotherapy* and *The Psychoanalytic Study of the Child*.

15 Traditional models and their contemporary use

(b) Non-intensive psychotherapy and assessment

Marianne Parsons with Pat Radford and Ann Horne

Introduction

Non-intensive psychoanalytic psychotherapy (usually once, sometimes twice-weekly sessions) forms the bulk of the work of the child psychotherapist – the majority of clinical examples in this book describe this approach – yet surprisingly little has been written about it as a specific form of treatment distinct from intensive psychotherapy, about the technical issues involved or about the particular benefits of non-intensive *vis-à-vis* intensive psychotherapy with children and adolescents. Similarly, the assessment of children and adolescents figures infrequently in the psychoanalytic literature. Much has been written about the very detailed Diagnostic Profile originally devised by Anna Freud (1965), but not about styles of assessment more common within the public sector. Although there is insufficient space in this chapter to address these issues in detail, we hope to offer an overview and encourage others to contribute to these rather neglected but very important topics.

Non-intensive psychoanalytic psychotherapy

The practice of child psychotherapy has its roots in and is informed by the theories of psychoanalysis. Non-intensive psychotherapy is an application of psychoanalytic understanding to a specific situation that requires special skills, training and experience. Child psychotherapists are trained in both intensive and non-intensive psychotherapy, but many find working non-intensively harder and more demanding both technically and intellectually. It is very difficult work requiring a lot of practice. The therapist can feel swamped by large amounts of biographical data and session material, and anxious about being able to hold all this in mind if she is working with a lot of children in once-weekly sessions. The therapist cannot often afford the luxury of waiting until the next session (as one can in intensive work) to pick up on something in the child's material, as it may get lost more easily in the interim. Similarly, there may be felt to be a pressure of less time available in non-intensive psychotherapy for the therapist to think through how to respond interpretatively. Extra vigilance and quick thinking is therefore required on the part of the therapist.

Non-intensive psychotherapy is the treatment most usually offered within the public sector. Some child psychotherapists consider this the most appropriate treatment frequency and feel that intensive psychotherapy is only warranted in very particular circumstances. They believe that there are very few cases where very significant improvements cannot occur in non-intensive work, especially if the transference is a major focus of the work, and that in certain cases non-intensive psychotherapy is the treatment of choice and more intensive work is contraindicated. Others feel that there are definite limitations to non-intensive psychotherapy and that ideally more intensive work would be more beneficial for many children. They suggest that non-intensive therapy is rarely recommended as the preferred treatment of choice – that is, as more beneficial to the child than intensive work – but is usually recommended for more pragmatic reasons, such as scarcity of resources within clinics in the public sector or constraints within the child's family. Some consider that the different treatment frequencies are best suited to particular types of disturbance, whereas others see the difference between intensive and non-intensive work as lying not in the child's pathology, but in the therapist's capacity to identify with the child's inner world and to be not only a transference object for the child but also a developmental object (Hurry 1998) with whom the child can identify to help him to grow.

These differing views have not been widely discussed within the profession, partly perhaps because of controversial 'political issues and value judgements' (Furman 1998) and partly because of historical difficulties in gaining outcome research evidence. Due to the wide provision of non-intensive as opposed to intensive psychotherapy, a large number of children can be offered help: this would seem to offer benefits to the community as a whole. It is also important, however, to try to consider carefully what might be most beneficial for each individual child. Some recent studies (Heinicke and Ramsey-Klee 1986; Fonagy and Target 1996; Furman 1998; Target and Fonagy 1994a, 1994b) have begun to consider this question. However, far more research needs to be done before definitive statements could be made about what one can and cannot expect to achieve in non-intensive psychotherapy with children and adolescents and where it is most likely to be beneficial.

The particular nature of non-intensive psychotherapy and some technical implications

The less frequent contact between child and therapist in non-intensive psychotherapy, in comparison to intensive psychotherapy, can make the therapeutic endeavour more manageable for some children and/or their families. For some it may be all that is necessary to help them to return to the path of normal development; for others it may not offer the depth of experience that is required to affect the severity of their disturbance, and intensive work may be necessary.

Some preliminary findings about the successful outcome of child psychotherapy concern not only the frequency but also the length of treatment. In their outcome research into the detailed records of 763 closed treatment files at the Anna Freud Centre, Target and Fonagy found that 'In children younger than 12, intensity but not duration of treatment was related to good outcome' (1994b: 1140). In contrast, they found that the reverse was true for adolescents: the length of the treatment rather than its frequency seemed linked to the benefit gained. This is of particular importance when one takes into account another of their findings (1994a), namely, that there may be more of a likelihood that once-weekly therapy will be ended prematurely either by the child or the parents. Boston and Lush (1994), in their study of 31 adopted and in-care children in psychotherapy, reported that 12 out of the 19 children in once-weekly psychotherapy dropped out of therapy early, in contrast to only one of the 12 children in twice- or three-times-weekly therapy. Added to this is the well-recognised fact that adolescents have a tendency to drop out of treatment early – often for developmental reasons to which we will refer later.

The tendency for children in once-weekly therapy to drop out of treatment is likely to be affected by their own and their parents' motivation. Sometimes once-weekly psychotherapy is offered to a child when parental motivation is not very strong. In such a case, premature ending of the therapy by the parents would not be very surprising, and the research statistics become somewhat biased: once weekly is not here the *treatment of choice for the child* but the *treatment of compromise for the parent*. Also, the parents, or other caregivers of the child, are far more likely to support the child's therapy if they feel supported themselves by the therapist or another clinician. This support will affect their attitude and motivation towards the child's treatment. The parents of children who are in intensive treatment may not only be more motivated towards the child's therapy in the first place, but may also be more willing to engage in regular work themselves to support the therapy and develop their parenting skills.

Consideration needs to be given to the impact of the longer gap between sessions in non-intensive psychotherapy. How well will the child be able to manage between one session and the next? The therapist needs to take this question into account when assessing the child and deciding on the appropriate treatment frequency. A child with a relatively strong ego will probably cope quite well, but a child who is more fragile and finds it harder to contain feelings of anxiety, aggression, dependency, separation and loss may be thrown severely off balance. Such a child may need more help from the therapist to 'seal' sufficiently by the end of the session in order to feel contained and strong enough to carry on his life outside of the therapy without too much anxiety until the following week. The therapist's sensitivity to the child's need to manage during the gap between sessions, and the child's capacity to do so, is extremely important and will alert the therapist to be careful about how and when to take up anxiety-provoking issues (especially towards the end of the session) and about how to support the child's appropriate defences and capacity for healthy mastery, whilst at the same time conveying to the child acknowledgement and understanding of the feelings of rejection, anger, fragility, loss, etc. that may feel over-whelming in the absence of the therapist. The supportiveness and sensitivity of the child's home environment is another factor in enabling the child to manage the gap between psychotherapy sessions. This emphasises again the importance of establishing a good working relationship with the child's caregivers.

Assessment of the range and flexibility of the child's defences is crucial in terms of considering the appropriate treatment frequency. If the child's defences are very restricted and rigid, non-intensive contact with the therapist may be insufficient to help the child to loosen them, because defences become consolidated between sessions. Similarly, there may be less opportunity for thorough 'working through' and there can sometimes be a tendency for a 'stop-go' process in once-weekly psychotherapy. However, many children will be able to maintain a flow in the therapeutic work and make excellent use of non-intensive psychotherapy. This is so, especially, if the transference is a major focus of the work, if they are motivated to want help and are able to establish a treatment alliance with the therapist, if they have the capacity to contain their anxieties and feelings between sessions, and if they have a relatively strong progressive developmental push.

Thinking about assessment

Careful assessment of the child is essential to any form of treatment. We would underline the importance of assessment of the whole child in guiding the child psychotherapist towards a recommendation for the intensity of treatment that is in his best interests. (For further elaboration of what follows and of assessment in general, see Colarusso 1992; Edgcumbe and Baldwin 1986; Freud, A. 1965; Furman 1992; Hayman 1978; Heinicke and Ramsey-Klee 1986; Laufer 1965; Yorke 1978.)

The aim of an assessment is to consider the nature and extent of the child's disturbance and then to decide on the most appropriate form of treatment. This is normally done within the multi-professional child and family mental health team. It is important to take into account all aspects of the child's internal and external world, the developmental stage he has reached, and the child's problems as perceived by the child himself and by significant adults in his environment (such as parents and teachers), as well as his strengths and capacities.

A theoretical framework for assessment

The child psychotherapist needs a theoretical framework which will help her to make use of all the material obtained during the assessment process: the external material (from meetings with the family, parents and/or social worker and from school reports where appropriate), as well as the material about the child's internal world obtained in individual assessment meetings with him. Projective testing by a clinical psychologist can also offer valuable insight into the child's internal world. If other psychological test results are available, they can indicate whether the child is realising his intellectual potential or underachieving, perhaps due to anxiety or trauma, and whether there are specific difficulties in particular areas of his cognitive functioning that may be addressed by psychologist and school together.

One theoretical framework, the Diagnostic Profile devised by Anna Freud (1965, Chapter 4), helps the diagnostician to focus attention on the many different facets of the child's personality, and on the effects of the child's development and problems on his mental, emotional and social functioning. In addition to considering the external environment of the child (his family, friends, school, and the impact of actual experiences on his development), the Diagnostic Profile pays special attention to assessment of the child's internal world. It considers:

(a) his ego capacities and ego strength (including the range, flexibility and effectiveness of his defences, his capacity to tolerate and contain anxiety and frustration, and his capacity to differentiate between reality and fantasy and between self and other);

(b) his capacity for attachment and for relating, the quality of his relationships and identifications, and his capacity for concern;

(c) the nature and extent of his anxiety;

(d) his narcissistic vulnerability, the relative strength or fragility of his sense of self, his level of self-esteem and his means of regulating it;

(e) the development of his super-ego (i.e. his conscience and ideals);

(f) the nature of his conflicts, wishes and fantasies;

(g) his tendency for regressive or progressive development, his developmental level overall and the evenness or otherwise of his progress along specific lines of development.

The Developmental Lines (Freud, A. 1965, Chapter 3; 1979), which are supplementary to the Diagnostic Profile and which are particularly useful in the assessment of young or very severely disturbed children, provide a picture of the child's evenness or unevenness of development at the time of referral and help the diagnostician to be specific about which areas of development are delayed, age-appropriate or precocious. Although it is usually not practical to carry out a full Diagnostic Profile when assessing children and adolescents in the public sector, it is extremely useful to have in mind the kind of diagnostic thinking that informs the Profile in order to be alert to all the different aspects of the child's internal and external world that need to be assessed.

When undertaking an assessment of any child or adolescent, the child psychotherapist looks for deviations in the child's behaviour from the generally expected norm for his age, gender and culture. She uses her knowledge of typical development to pinpoint the deviations, irregularities and deficiencies shown in such aspects as relationships, behaviour patterns and symptom formation (Freud, A. 1965, 1974).

The assessment process

In most Child and Family Mental Health teams today, assessment begins with family meetings. These are not only useful in gaining insight into the views of all family members about what is problematic, but enable the symptoms the child presents to be seen in the context of the emotions, expectations, defences, myths and anxieties of the family system. A scape-goated child may gain more from a recommendation of family work than from individual work that perhaps maintains his scapegoated position. One can, however, still be left with a 'stuck' child – and individual work would then be considered.

Sensitively handled meetings with the parents/carers by a social worker, child psychotherapist or other team member during the assessment process are extremely important for a number of reasons. They give the parents a chance to talk about their concerns for their child and to feel listened to and understood. This encourages the parents to think about the issue of parenting a child in difficulties and to consider engaging in ongoing work with a colleague during their child's psychotherapy and to support it, if this is recommended. They provide an opportunity for the clinician to build up a picture of the child's psychosocial history, developmental background and family setting and of the parents' perceptions of the child – all very important material for the assessment. They help the diagnostician to assess the strengths of the parents and their capacity to co-operate in what might be recommended to help the child. They allow the clinician to discuss the assessment procedure with the parents and to think with them about how best to talk about it with the child.

It is helpful for the child psychotherapist to see the child two or three times. This gives time to build up a picture of the child and of his internal world, and it is often informative to notice how the child presents himself in the different meetings. For example, familiarity with the setting and the diagnostician in a second meeting may help the child's initial anxiety to decrease, or it may increase perhaps as the result of an intensification of transference phenomena. It is always of interest to compare a psychologist's report and/or a school report with the child psychotherapist's impressions of the child. If the impressions of the child are very different, this may be due to the nature of the child's anxiety – does the child feel safer and more contained in a structured setting (such as school or doing a psychological test); is the child very fearful of getting things wrong, causing an increase in his anxiety in the school setting or the psychological testing; is the gender of the different professionals relevant in terms of the child's feelings about himself and ways of relating?

When setting up an assessment, the diagnostician is careful to find appropriate tools in relation to the child's problems and age to facilitate the expression of his inner world. Verbal communication is more difficult than symbolic expression through play for the younger child, so some toys should be available. These could include: family figures (ideally corresponding to his actual family in terms of number and gender of siblings), toy animals (including some which are usually thought of as fierce, like a crocodile or tiger, that could act as a means of communicating fear, anger and aggression), plasticine, drawing materials, a cuddly toy. With older children, other age-appropriate small toys can be included. For the adolescent, drawing materials are probably all that is necessary. Some child psychotherapists feel it is important to offer a fairly limited number of toys so that the child remains more focused and does not either feel overwhelmed by the variety or use the range of toys for defensive purposes. Other therapists consider that whatever the child does with a wider variety of toys available will be illuminating in terms of assessing his defences and his capacities to relate, play, and express his conflicts. The same goes for treatment itself:

> Eddie, an eight-year-old who was confused and frightened about growing up as a boy, was able to express and work through his conflicts by using the girl-specific toys and toys usually used by much younger children that were available for everybody's use in the main toy cupboard – items which one would have hesitated to provide for Eddie specifically.

An assessment is a limited and closed process and is therefore different from treatment. The child psychotherapist has a unique role – attuning to and exploring the child's inner world and considering how best to help him – but, unlike treatment sessions, she can make wider use of the outside information which has been supplied at the time of referral. The technique used in an assessment is usually also rather different from what happens in treatment sessions. While the transference may be recognised by the therapist during the assessment, many therapists do not consider it helpful or wise to make explicit transference interpretations because the assessment process is time-limited and there will be no room for exploring the child's feelings in an ongoing relationship in a way that will feel safe for him. However, since it is likely that some transference relationship will be established during the assessment, it is very important to let the child know from the beginning if he will be meeting the therapist only a few times, so that the child is prepared for the probable loss of the diagnostician at the end of the assessment. If therapy is not immediately going to follow the assessment, it is also important to recognise that the child's defences need to be kept intact or reinstated in order to help him to contain his anxiety and reduce the possibility of harmful acting-out.

The diagnostician will usually aim for a free flow of material from the child. By following what the child brings through words and play and accepting the role assigned by the child, the diagnostician gains insight into the child's fantasies:

> Mary, an eight-year-old, was very inhibited in her play in the assessment. She toyed rather aimlessly with the wild animals for a long time, but eventually began to put fences around them. When the therapist commented on the fences keeping the animals inside, Mary began to enact a furious battle between the tigers and the lions, thereby freely expressing aggressive feelings against which she usually needed to erect strong defences.

However, there are a number of simple techniques which can be useful in helping the child to engage with the diagnostician and communicate his concerns, especially if he is having difficulty in feeling safe enough to express himself either through play or words – for example, if his anxiety arouses defensive inhibition. Most importantly, the diagnostician will relate to the child in a friendly way, acknowledging that it probably feels rather nerve-racking to talk to a stranger. If the child has already been seen by a number of other professionals, the sense of 'Oh, no, not another one!' can be verbalised by the therapist in an empathic tone that might relieve the initial anxiety and resistance, help the child to feel more ready to engage with the assessment and feel freer to express his resentment. It is helpful for the diagnostician to ask the child if he understands why mum (or his social worker) brought him, and to suggest he might have been worried about what kind of person he would meet. This gives an opportunity to explain to the child about the assessment process ('to get to know what it is like to be you', 'to see if we can think how best to help you'), and to prepare the child for seeing the diagnostician just a certain number of times. It also helps the child to feel that the diagnostician understands he feels anxious and gives him the opportunity to express his fantasies about her and the assessment: some children worry that going to a clinic for an assessment will be like going to the hospital and that something horrible will be done to their bodies; other children, especially those who have been abused or who have got into trouble because of their behaviour, will worry about being asked a lot of invasive questions, and may fear that they have been brought because they are bad and will be taken away. It is important to show interest in the child's positive achievements and in the things he likes doing, as well as what worries and frightens him. In fact, many children and adolescents are unable to feel safe enough to communicate their concerns about themselves until they have experienced the therapist's positive interest in their strengths and in the things they enjoy.

One useful technique in an assessment, especially with children who find it hard to express anything pertaining to their inner world, is to invite the child to imagine that he has three wishes to do or have whatever he would like. This can provide valuable insight into, and open up discussion about, the child's fantasies. However, some children are so anxious and heavily defended that they cannot allow themselves to reveal anything in their three wishes. They may reply with 'don't know' or simply use their wishes for new toys or 'lots of money!' One of us stumbled on an elaboration of the three wishes idea out of desperation, when assessing a particularly anxious and heavily defended boy:

Darren, aged fourteen, had sexually abused his nine-year-old sister, had been stealing money and cars, and had become so aggressive and out of control that his mother had placed him in local authority care. It was clear that he felt enormously ashamed and also afraid of being told off. Although the diagnostician verbalised this anxiety, he remained silent with his eyes averted throughout the meeting. The diagnostician was unable to help him to experience sufficient safety to talk to her, and even the three wishes didn't help him to engage. In desperation she suddenly had the idea to suggest a variation of the three wishes – namely, not what he would like to have but what he would like *not* to have had. She wondered if he could imagine having a time machine so that he could go back to the past and change three things that had already happened. To her surprise he said, 'For the thing with my sister never to have happened', and 'For my dad not to have kept beating me, and to have been a nice dad who wouldn't have left us'. It then became possible for Darren to communicate more freely.

Drawing a family tree with the child – and, with younger children, perhaps also using the symbolic family figures – can help him to feel freer to talk about the important people in his life. One can then ask 'who is the best at', for example, keeping people safe, helping you if you're cross or sad, understanding how you feel. This often leads on to discussion of whom the child does not feel safe with, helped or understood by. Family and personal difficulties can also be explored: 'Who is the family expert at being grumpy?' and who resembles whom with different family traits – all offer important information about the child's sense of self and which attachments are bearable for him. It can also be useful to ask who the child would want to have with him on a desert island. Attachments, merging and despair can all emerge.

During an assessment, the diagnostician observes how the child relates, plays, communicates, protects himself from anxiety. By observing and agreeing to participate in the play, the therapist will become aware of the underlying anxieties and fantasies. In addition to wondering about the possible meanings underlying the material and how he relates to her, the diagnostician will also be alert to the specific relationship between the child's psychic structures. This facilitates a dynamic under-standing of the child's conflicts between instinctual and relationship needs and the defences and prohibitions against them. The previous history and experience of the child may well be affecting this balance, and may be illustrated in his play. The defensive structures may have attempted an economic distribution of the ego's resources to deal with the anxiety arising from these conflicts, and the child may have found a compromise solution through his symptoms.

As well as being alert to the child's conflicts and difficulties, the therapist should also aim to assess the child's underlying strengths and his capacity for sublimation, mastery and progressive development. An important factor in working with children is their capacity for growth and development. In so far as the problems and symptoms have delayed progress and, perhaps, have presented a picture of regression, the therapist should be able to clarify from the child's material to what extent he can show a wish to move forward.

The diagnostician will also be alert to the child's ability to tolerate frustration and to contain anxiety – factors important in the choice of treatment. The child's feelings about himself (e.g. loving, hating, turning aggression against himself, feeling a failure, respecting himself) are of importance in his relation to his capacity to make use of therapy. The diagnostician will be particularly interested in the child's relationship to the most significant people in his life (especially his parents and siblings), both in terms of his actual observable relationship with them and also, most importantly, as perceived in his inner world. His belief or fantasy about how much he is loved and loveable and how much he is able to love will have a bearing on his capacity to relate to his therapist and on the use of trans-ference as a tool in the therapy. In the assessment this will be evident in how the child relates to the therapist, particularly between one session and the next:

Sam, aged five, reluctantly left the first session feeling inappropriately angry towards the therapist. The therapist thought that he might well be very reluctant to come to the next session because she had become a 'witch' in his eyes. How far his reality strength would enable him, in the second meeting, to overcome his fear and hostility and thus recognise the benign aspects of the therapist would be invaluable in deciding on the most appropriate treatment frequency. If his fantasy held sway and his anxiety increased, this would demonstrate the inadequacy of his defences against his aggressive impulses and the need for greater frequency of sessions.

Making a diagnostic formulation and recommendation

Following the assessment sessions, the material from the meetings with the child and the information from the parents, school and other sources should now be brought together. On the basis of these the child psychotherapist and team can make a diagnostic formulation (Freud, A. 1965, Chapters 4, 5). Does the child have a neurotic conflict, a developmental disturbance, a borderline or atypical disturbance, a psychotic disturbance, is the disturbance due to trauma? Are the conflicts internalised or are they a consequence of ongoing environmental factors? How severe is the disturbance? The diagnostic formulation will take into account the nature of the child's past and current environment, his strengths and weaknesses, the nature and intensity of his conflicts and anxiety, his capacities for relating, for coping with anxiety and frustration, for defending himself age-appropriately and for progressive development. All this will enable the child psychotherapist to consider the most appropriate treatment. This may well be non-intensive or intensive individual psychotherapy for the child, often with a recommendation of concurrent work with the parents, but this is not always the case. Sometimes it may be appropriate to recommend remedial teaching, work just with the parents, family therapy, supportive counselling, a behavioural programme, or an environmental intervention such as a change of school or foster placement. Whatever recommendation is chosen – sometimes a combination of interventions will be appropriate – it is important to try to validate the assessment by follow-up in order to enhance a high standard of diagnostic skills.

If the recommendation is for psychoanalytic psychotherapy, the child psychotherapist can begin to consider the frequency of therapy that is likely to be best suited to the child's needs. Consideration should be given to the parents' motivation towards therapy for the child and their willingness to engage in thinking with a professional about their own and their child's difficulties. The nature of the parents' relationship and the situation of the family as a whole should also be taken into account. How will these be affected by a recommendation for non-intensive or intensive psychotherapy? How much support for the child's psychotherapy can one realistically expect the parents to provide?

The question of non-intensive or intensive psychotherapy

Very significant work can be done in non-intensive psychotherapy as the many case examples in this book vividly illustrate. It is an appropriate form of help for a large number of children and adolescents, enabling them to gain considerable benefit. However, there are some children for whom non-intensive psychotherapy is insufficient to address the depth and extent of their disturbances. It is very hard, for example, to tackle the widespread disturbances evident in borderline and atypical children in non-intensive psychotherapy (Tustin 1973), and children with severe narcissistic disturbance need the long, slow process of intensive work to achieve internal change. Fonagy and Target suggest that children with severe or multiple pathologies require intensive treatment, and that 'children with generalised anxiety disorders, depressive disorders, or concurrent disruptive disorders responded significantly better to intensive therapy' (1994a: 370). Furman considers that some children need the framework of the consistent investment and availability of intensive psychotherapy to feel 'held' and contained enough to tolerate, explore and ultimately master the primitive states manifested by children with severe ego weakness, arrest and regression. She suggests that intensive work is necessary to help such children to

> face and tame their primitive unfused aggression. This applies to aggression against the analyst, helped by the built-in assurance that he or she survived the patient's attack and remains available, as well as to aggression against the internal representation of the analyst which often can 'survive' the day to day interval between sessions but is in danger of being destroyed during intervals of several days. Such primitive aggression is usually too threatening to face in psychotherapy or can interfere with its usefulness or continuity, whereas in daily analysis it has a chance of being fused.
>
> (Furman 1998)

Non-intensive psychotherapy is particularly effective for children whose disturbance is not too severe or global. Having said this, child psychotherapists can and do bring about considerable change in non-intensive psychotherapy even with extremely difficult cases. The research results quoted are also open to debate: retrospective research in institutions where intensive work is the norm and non-intensive a second best alternative *may* be tainted by difficulties in perceiving non-intensive work as a positive choice.[1] We really lack prospective research in this area. It is also a feature of our work today that we often take children into therapy after some freeing-up has occurred in family work: non-intensive therapy may be a more realistic choice following shifts in the family system, in the parental view of the child and in the child's view of himself-in-family. Perhaps, too, the important question is: how much change is necessary to help the child get back on a developmental path and to move onwards? When working with children we do not aim for 'cure', any more than can be aimed for realistically by those who work with adults. As Anna Freud often said, we aim to help the child return to the path of normal development.

The debate about which children have most need of intensive psychotherapy appears to centre around the following issues:

The nature and extent of the child's disturbance

The child who has developed a transient developmental disturbance with the appearance of symptoms and considerable anxiety, but who does not have a deep-seated emotional disturbance, will respond well to being offered help through a difficult time, especially via the therapist's understanding and verbalisation of the child's feelings of shock, anger, sadness, grief. Non-intensive therapy may be indicated for such a child.

The child with mostly adequate functioning, but with a delay in a limited number of aspects of development, or with a relatively mild form of neurotic disturbance can benefit well from non-intensive psychoanalytic help. Fonagy and Target (1996) suggest that a child suffering from a simple phobia, separation anxiety, or an obsessive-compulsive disorder gains as much benefit from non-intensive as from intensive psychotherapy. It needs to be stressed that they are referring to the kinds of disorder that fall within the range of neurotic disturbance and not those which are part of more pervasive and severe psychopathology such as borderline, narcissistic or psychotic disturbance. We would add that many people agree that it is very hard to treat an obsessional child successfully in non-intensive psychotherapy, because of the rigidity and restricted nature of the child's defences.

Non-intensive work may be appropriate for the child who is not too severely disturbed and who is engaged in other activities/interests (after-school clubs, important exams ahead, friendship groups and clubs) that, if he had to forego for the sake of intensive psychotherapy, would undermine a centrally important aspect of his development. It may be very important, for example, for a child with somewhat precarious self-esteem, but not a severe narcissistic disturbance, to continue with certain activities that enhance his feelings of achievement and self-worth. For some adolescents who need to focus on important exams, non-intensive psychotherapy may be an appropriate treatment, at least to begin with; more intensive work may be possible later. We have already noted how, in assessing any child or adolescent, it is important to recognise fully the healthy and adaptive areas of his life and to acknowledge these with him. We can become so used to the need to be alert to damage, anxiety and disturbance that we sometimes pay insufficient attention to adaptive and healthy aspects of functioning and instead have a tendency to 'pathologise'. However, a word of caution – the balance of the child's healthy and pathological functioning needs extremely careful consideration. We are certainly not advocating collusion with the child's or the family's omnipotence or resistance towards therapy, and we want to stress the importance of assessment of priorities. It is not worth the risk of sacrificing the chance to effect lasting change to the young person's mental and emotional health and of alleviating severe distress in the long term in order to give him short-term relief. A very disturbed young person can always sit exams or start college later, when he is on a more healthy development track and will be able to make good use of his improved state of mind and of his capacities for making healthier relationships.

A very disturbed child may feel so frightened, anxious or humiliated about having psychotherapy that he is quite unable to countenance the idea of intensive work, which, ideally, he needs. But such a child may be able to accept the offer of non-intensive psychotherapy. Intensive psychotherapy may become possible at a later stage, if appropriate and available, if the child is able to experience therapy and his therapist as safe enough.

The child's developmental stage

Adolescents who are actively engaged in the adolescent process of separation-individuation from the parent figures may benefit well from non-intensive work. Fonagy and Target's outcome study research found that adolescents did equally well or better in non-intensive treatment, in contrast to younger children who improved far more with frequent sessions. 'The age of 12 marked a threshold beyond which children were somewhat less responsive to treatment, particularly on an intensive basis' (1996: 51). However, it should be noted that this research did not differentiate between the different stages of adolescence. It is generally well-recognised that youngsters in early and mid-adolescence (roughly 12–15 years of age) are especially hard to engage in the therapeutic relationship, whatever the treatment frequency. This is due to the developmental process and tasks of adolescence itself (see Chapter 3). If therapy starts before they have begun to engage with the developmental tasks of adolescence, they are more likely to become emotionally involved in the therapeutic process and then be able to continue during early to mid-adolescence. If they start therapy in later adolescence (having either succeeded in accomplishing some of the age-appropriate developmental tasks, or having recognised their failure to do so and experiencing anxiety about this), they are also far more able to feel motivated to engage in the work and in the therapeutic relationship.

In some cases it may be more possible to engage an adolescent in non-intensive therapy where the intermittent contact with the therapist allows the adolescent more easily to 'go with the flow' of the adolescent process. The young person who is age-appropriately engaged with the developmental tasks of adolescence struggles against the regressive pull to childlike dependence on his parents, and makes use of a typically strong progressive developmental push towards independence and separation from parents and other authority figures, towards taking ownership of his sexually mature body, and towards searching for a satisfying sense of identity, including a more stable sexual identity. In order to accomplish all this, the adolescent will swing between periods of intensely self-absorbed reflection and periods of sometimes quite dramatic action, including risk-taking and other potentially self-damaging behaviours. Anna Freud had such adolescent processes in mind when she expressed her caution about intensive therapy in adolescence: 'To try and analyse an adolescent in his phase of successful detachment from the past seems to be a venture doomed to failure' (Freud, A. 1958: 270).

However, Anna Freud saw intensive psychotherapy as both 'indicated as well as urgent' in cases where the adolescent had withdrawn from engaging with the developmental process of adolescence. For example, there are those who have broken down during the strain of struggling with the age-appropriate developmental tasks; there are some with severe narcissistic disorders who require the long slow process of intensive work to be able to feel safe enough to address their difficulties; and there are some who are so developmentally delayed that they have not yet been able to enter the developmental phase of adolescence, even though chronologically they would be called adolescents. Such young people have the level of disturbance that requires skilled intensive intervention, although this should only be recommended if the young person's environment is sufficiently containing and supportive to 'hold' him during periods of intense distress, regression and acting-out.

Where non-intensive psychotherapy is what the network can manage

As well as assessing what is the most appropriate treatment frequency for a child and what he can manage, one also needs to take into account what is manageable for the child's parents and family, and, if he is in local authority care, what is feasible for the network of professionals responsible for him.

Intensive psychotherapy may not be manageable for a child whose parents face too many obstacles in trying to combine bringing the child to his sessions and caring properly for the rest of the family. There may be other children in the family whose needs also have to be considered, and the parents' relationship may be undergoing a great deal of stress. The length and awkwardness of the journey, and the long working hours of some parents often make anything more than once-weekly therapy practically impossible. If the parents are very ambivalent about the child's therapy because of the strain it puts on them and the family, it will be hard for the child to feel free to express negative feelings about his therapy to them, because they might then feel justified in ending it. Also, the child's capacity to feel free to build up a good-enough relationship with the therapist will be undermined, and the parents are likely to be less supportive of the therapy – a very important factor for not prematurely ending treatment and for a favourable outcome.

Non-intensive psychotherapy may thus be indicated for a child in the context of his particular family. However, if the child urgently needs intensive help, it is important to try to talk with the parents in a way that is sensitive to their needs and the needs of their family to see if there are any means by which to make it possible for the child to have the frequency of therapy necessary to help him.

Conclusion

We have emphasised the importance of the child psychotherapist's careful assessment of the child and his family situation in order to arrive at the most appropriate recommendation for the frequency of sessions. Non-intensive psychotherapy will often be considered the most suitable and appropriate option; but where it is assessed that intensive psychotherapy would be the treatment of choice, it may still be that non-intensive work is the only available possibility because of scarce resources or environmental constraints. It remains highly important to consider what is in the best interests of the child in the context of what is also manageable for his family. It is also important to keep alive the possibility of arranging intensive psychotherapy in those cases where it is clearly indicated, but we should also be alert to the need for flexibility of movement between treatment frequencies in working with any particular child. A child in non-intensive psychotherapy may reach the point where he (or his carers) could manage more frequent sessions and where he would benefit from this. Or it may become appropriate for a child in intensive psychotherapy to reduce to less frequent sessions.

The lack of prospective research remains an issue that the profession must address. The debate about the choice or efficacy of intensive vis-à-vis non-intensive work will otherwise remain theoretical or a matter of personal assumption.

Finally, until we have trained more child psychotherapists, until more of them work in areas outside London, and until the NHS is able to put more resources into the provision of child psychotherapy, non-intensive psychoanalytic psychotherapy will continue to be the norm. This, for many children, represents an adaptation of classic psychoanalysis that is enabling and helpful. It would be unfortunate, however, if resources rather than knowledge determined its use, especially in those cases where more intensive help is clearly indicated.

Note

1 Two small prospective studies by Heinicke and Ramsey-Klee (1965, 1986) showed that children in once-weekly therapy made quicker initial progress in reading than those in four-times-weekly sessions. However, progress in the child's flexible adaptation, capacity for relationships and rates of reading improvement was sustained two years after the end of treatment by those children seen in four-times-weekly therapy, but not in those seen for once-weekly sessions. These results did not appear to be affected by the therapists' attitude towards the different treatment frequencies.

References

Boston, M. and Lush, D. (1994) 'Further considerations of methodology for evaluating psychoanalytic psychotherapy with children: reflections in the light of research experience', *Journal of Child Psychotherapy* 20(2): 205–29.

Colarusso, C. A. (1992) *Child and Adult Development: A Psychoanalytical Introduction for Clinicians*, New York: Plenum.

Edgcumbe, R. and Baldwin, J. (1986) 'The use of Anna Freud's developmental profile in the differential diagnosis of a young severely handicapped child', *Bulletin of the Anna Freud Centre* 9(1): 35–49.

Fonagy, P. and Target, M. (1996) 'Predictors of outcome in child psychoanalysis: a retrospective study of 763 cases at the Anna Freud Centre', *Journal of American Psychoanalytic Association* 44: 27–73.

Freud, A. (1958) 'Adolescence', *Psychoanalytic Study of the Child* 13: 255–78.

—— (1965) *Normality and Pathology in Childhood: Assessments of Development*, London: Hogarth Press.

—— (1974) 'Diagnosis and assessment of childhood disturbances', in *Psychoanalytic Psychology of Normal Development*, London: Hogarth Press.

—— (1979) 'Child analysis as the study of mental growth, normal and abnormal', in *Psychoanalytic Psychology of Normal Development*, London: Hogarth Press.

Furman, E. (1992) *Toddlers and Their Mothers: A Study in Early Personality Development*, Madison CT: International Universities Press.

—— (1998) 'Child analysis and psychotherapy: a comparison based on clinical experience', paper presented at annual meeting of Association for Child Psychoanalysis, 3 April 1998, Boston, Mass.

Hayman, A. (1978) 'The Diagnostic Profile: II Some clinical and research aspects of the developmental profile', *Bulletin of the Hampstead Clinic* 1(2): 75–85.

Heinicke, C. and Ramsey-Klee, D. (1965) 'Frequency of psychotherapeutic session as a factor affecting the child's developmental status', *Psychoanalytic Study of the Child* 20: 42–98.

—— (1986) 'Outcome of child psychotherapy as a function of frequency of session', *Journal of the American Academy of Child Psychiatry* 25(2): 247–53.

Hurry, A. (1998) 'Psychoanalysis and developmental therapy', in *Psychoanalysis and Developmental Therapy*, London: Karnac Books.

Laufer, M. (1965) 'Assessment of adolescent disturbance: the application of Anna Freud's Diagnostic Profile', *Psychoanalytic Study of the Child* 20: 99–123.

Target, M. and Fonagy, P. (1994a) 'Efficacy of psychoanalysis for children with emotional disorders', *Journal of American Academy of Child and Adolescent Psychiatry* 33(3): 361–71.

—— (1994b) 'The efficacy of psychoanalysis for children: prediction of outcome in a developmental context', *Journal of American Academy of Child and Adolescent Psychiatry* 33(8): 1134–44.

Tustin, F. (1973) *Autism and Childhood Psychosis*, New York: Jason Aronson.

Yorke, C. (1978) 'Notes on the developmental point of view in the diagnostic assessment of adults and children', *Bulletin of the Hampstead Clinic* 1(4): 163–80.

Further reading

Boston, M. (1989) 'In search of a methodology for evaluating psychoanalytic psychotherapy with children', *Journal of Child Psychotherapy* 15(1): 15–46.

Freud, A. (1972) 'The widening scope of psychoanalytic child psychology, normal and abnormal', in *Psychoanalytic Psychology of Normal Development*, London: Hogarth Press.

Kaplan, A. (1988) 'Choice of treatment versus treatment of choice', *Journal of Child Psychotherapy* 14(2): 47–60.

Rustin, M. (1982) 'Finding a way to the child', *Journal of Child Psychotherapy* 8(2): 145–50.

Wilson, P. (1987) 'Psychoanalytic therapy and the young adolescent', *Bulletin of the Anna Freud Centre* 10(1): 51–79.

Yorke, C. (1976) 'A developmental view of anxiety: some clinical and theoretical considerations', *Psychoanalytic Study of the Child* 31: 107–35.

The Journal of Child Psychotherapy regularly publishes papers where non-intensive work is demonstrated. The interested reader is encouraged to browse.

16 Brief psychotherapy and therapeutic consultations

How much therapy is 'good-enough'?

Monica Lanyado

The eminent psychoanalyst D. W. Winnicott coined the heartening phrase 'good-enough mothering' in an effort to provide a realistic perspective on what mothers can hope to provide for their children. He felt that mothers (and nowadays we would add fathers to this description) do not need to be perfect, indeed should not even try to be 'perfect'. But he did emphasise that they do need to be 'good-enough' if their child is to have a reasonable start in their emotional life. Good-enough parenting reflects the physical and emotional care given to the child, in thoughtful response to what the individual child needs. As individual needs differ so much, even from birth, what is good-enough mothering for one child may be inadequate for another. There is therefore no absolute pass or fail line when it comes to what constitutes a good-enough parent (Winnicott 1989).

A similar issue relates to the question of how much therapy is required for a child. This question arises at the very start of therapy when it is not clear what form of therapy to offer the child or how best to help the family as a whole, as well as when deciding at what point to end once-weekly or intensive psychotherapy. On first responding to a referral, there are many ways of setting up a treatment plan (see Chapter 10). Will the child be unable to recover unless they have twice-, three-, four- or five-times weekly therapy for several years? Should the child be offered once-weekly sessions which are open ended, and will continue for as long as the therapist and the child's family agree? Should the child be seen for a fixed number of consultations – maybe three or four times followed by a review of their progress? How should these sessions be spaced out – weekly, fortnightly, or pragmatically according to the therapist and family's availability? What kind of help needs to be offered to the parents, carers and school?

Within the public sector, quite apart from these important decisions about the best form of treatment for a particular child and their family, there is now often a clear directive from the managers of the treatment service that in order to cut down child mental health waiting lists and offer as broad a service to the community as possible, a limited number of consultations, often well under ten, should be the norm of any treatment plan. Open-ended, weekly or more intensive treatments may then only be offered to a small number of extremely carefully selected children, and there is likely to be a considerable waiting list for this kind of psychotherapeutic treatment.

However, when thinking about consultation work, economic and pragmatic arguments can obscure the fact that for some children a fixed number of consultations, a clear focus for the work, or a clear date for ending the therapy, may be the best form of treatment plan for their problems at the time of referral. This chapter will give some examples of this way of working and how consultation work is becoming an increasingly important part of the range of treatments offered by psychoanalytic psychotherapists.

A case illustration

Nine-year-old Joanne's parents contacted me because she had recently been having powerful nightmares in which she became very angry, thrashing around in her sleep, fighting off her parents and not letting them comfort her. She was upset and disorientated by these dreams and she had also started to sleepwalk. During the day, she seemed well. Her parents felt that the sleep disturbance connected with a very unfortunate accident that Joanne had had when she was six years old, from which she had physically totally recovered. She had been playing in an ordinary way with another child who had pushed her over, but she had fallen awkwardly, causing a complicated fracture of her wrist, which over the course of the next eighteen months had required seven operations and in total twenty weeks in plaster. During this time, she had to be very careful about any energetic play (which singled her out from other children, particularly at school), because she was at risk from the rough and tumble of the playground. For many months she had a rigorous daily routine of physiotherapy which she carried out with little protest. She had coped very stoically and sensibly with this whole experience, as had the parents in their management of what became a very complicated and upsetting phase of their family life.

We arranged that I would see Joanne for four consultations and then meet with her parents to discuss how to proceed. It was clear from the outset, that I would see Joanne for as few consultations as possible, as she had had enough of being a patient and just wanted to go back to being the same as other children. The parents' account of what had happened gave me good reason to believe that this was a family which had a lot of strengths which would enable them to make good use of a few consultations.

In the first few consultations Joanne and I talked a lot about the accident and operations. This included Joanne showing me the small physical scars from her operations, and, unprompted, bringing to the consultations one of her plaster casts and some of the pins that had been in her wrists. It soon became apparent that rather than there being a profound sense of physical pain or fear surrounding these memories, there was a deep, unspoken sense of sadness and loss. I tried to talk to her about what these feelings might mean.

It gradually emerged that she had badly wanted her mother to be with her literally all the time when she was in hospital for operations, or in pain at home, but that her mother for a variety of reasons had been unable to do so. Her father had always been with her when her mother could not, but this was just not the same and Joanne was able to admit to feeling angry with her mother, as well as bereft and pining for her during these times. There were good and ordinary reasons why her mother could not be there all the time which Joanne fully understood, but this in turn led to intense feelings of guilt because nevertheless she still felt so angry with her mother.

Clinical experience suggests that in many cases of trauma such as Joanne's accident, the trauma victim on an unconscious level feels not only that her mother did not actively protect her from the dangers of the world when the trauma occurred, but that her mother actually stood by and passively allowed the traumatic event to take place (Laub and Auerhahn 1993). Joanne's parents, in a way which seemed to reflect the parental counterpart of this fantasy, irrationally blamed themselves for what had happened. Many parents of children who have been traumatised, experience intense feelings of guilt about what happened to their child. Whilst this fantasy may well reflect ordinary but deeply unconscious aggressive feelings, they are also a powerful reflection of the biological caregiving role emphasised in attachment theory (Chapter 4) which in situations of trauma may be experienced as having failed to protect the child from danger.

Joanne agreed that I could talk to her parents about her feelings of anger and sadness, which I did when I met them (without Joanne present) to discuss how to proceed after her first four consultations. I met them on their own as I felt that they needed to explore their feelings, about how they had handled the accident and the acute phases of

Joanne's hospitalisations and treatments, without her being present. Joanne's mother was able to talk about her conflict and distress over how to balance the needs of her other two children and her invalid mother at the time of the accident and during all that followed. Both parents were relieved that Joanne was finally able to talk in her consultations about how hard it had been to share her mother with others when she had needed her so much. They reported that the nightmares and sleep disorder had stopped, but they did not want to end the consultations at this point as they could see that Joanne needed further help to consolidate this improvement and understand more about the feelings that lay behind her symptoms. We agreed that I would see Joanne weekly until the end of the school term – a further seven consultations, including one family consultation which Joanne's brother and sister would also attend.

Themes of rivalry and jealousy of my other patients started to emerge during the next few consultations and we were able to relate these to Joanne's growing awareness of her anger with her mother for sometimes choosing to look after her siblings or her grandmother instead of her. Joanne became irritated with me for seeing other patients when she was not there, and played the amateur sleuth noting when the small signals that she deliberately left in the therapy room to detect the presence of other patients, had been moved. She was annoyed that the planned family session was to include her brother and sister. This gave further opportunity to talk about the ways in which the attention her parents had needed to pay to her during all the problems with her wrist had affected the whole family – and how her brother and sister had felt fed up with all the attention Joanne was getting.

During the family consultation, which again deliberately focused on the impact of the accident on the family, I was able to talk about how it was still hard for Joanne fully to forgive her mother for the pain and distress that surrounded the accident and all that followed. Their relationship seemed to get caught on a rather difficult dynamic, in which Joanne seemed deliberately and successfully to be making her mother suffer and feel unduly guilty about the accident, as well as about many everyday issues. As we talked about this Joanne's mother was able to show how upset she felt knowing that Joanne was still distressed and angry such a long time after the accident and operations had taken place. Joanne was then able to go and sit next to her mother, cuddling up to her and sucking her thumb, and there was a sense of some rapprochement between them.

As Joanne was clearly getting quite involved in her relationship with me – seen in her possessiveness and rivalry with other patients – and I did not wish to encourage this in view of the limited number of consultations that we had left, it became particularly important to focus on what it meant to her to be ending her consultations with me in a few weeks time. She knew that she did not want or really need to continue but found it hard to let go of me – rather similar to her difficulty in letting go of her anger with her mother. However, we could talk about this characteristic of her way of being – that she was someone who found it hard to let go of feelings. This helped her to move towards her last consultation at which we agreed to meet again in three months. At this follow-up meeting she remained generally less angry with her mother and siblings and was coping well with school and family life. On enquiry when writing this chapter, two years after the consultations took place, there had been no recurrence of the sleep problems and she is developing well. As there may be a concern that consultations do not have a lasting impact on emotional life, this kind of follow-up is helpful in demonstrating how effective this way of working can be.

One of the factors that helps consultation work to be brief is a clear focus for the treatment. In Joanne's case, the focus suggested by her parents' account of the problems – the accident and operations – made sense when I met with Joanne. There is often a fear that, in selecting a treatment focus, other important issues for the patient may be neglected. However, as work with Joanne illustrates, the chosen focus can have a 'tip of the iceberg' quality in that many other significant issues lie beneath the surface and can be associated with the chosen focus. Balint *et al.* (1972) describe what they term 'Focal psychotherapy', with adult patients. They view this treatment as being a form of applied psychoanalysis and helpfully discuss the way in which a focus for brief work can be chosen and worked with. They emphasise that once chosen it is important to stick to this focus and not to be diverted on to other interesting paths of enquiry unless they look likely to supersede the existing focus by becoming a new focus. This idea of *applied* psychoanalysis remains central to psychoanalytically trained psychotherapists' approach to consultations and brief work (Daws 1989; Edwards and Maltby 1998; Lanyado 1996; Winnicott 1971).

From this example it can be seen that by exploring the focus of Joanne's accident and all that followed, themes of separation and loss, sibling rivalry, and angry feelings and fantasies about her parents leading to guilt and conflict could all be explored. These themes are ongoing life issues for everyone and would be very much a part of any open-ended therapy. In consultation work they are approached in a different way, the principles of which will be discussed later in this chapter. Many other themes which could have been taken up – such as Joanne's feelings of disfigurement because of scarring, or Oedipal feelings as expressed through her longing for her mother, and minimisation of her father's contribution to her care – were not taken up as they were not foremost in her conscious mind at the time of the treatment.

Joanne's relationship to me was not discussed other than very lightly – in the form of comments or observations about how she didn't like the fact that I saw other patients. If Joanne had been in open-ended therapy, I would have worked much more with her feelings towards me and they would have formed a core part of the transference relationship that needed to be interpreted over the course of the treatment. Finally, a good deal of attention was given to how Joanne felt about coming to the end of her consultations and her clearly expressed wish to make me feel bad about not seeing her for longer. Simultaneously, she was also quite clear that she resented the time spent on her consultations and felt that she no longer needed to come! As already mentioned, this was very similar to the way in which she attempted to make her mother feel bad about the accident.

Who is most likely to benefit from therapeutic consultations?

The term 'therapeutic consultations' was coined by Winnicott (1971) to describe one form of the work described in this chapter. It is a term I find helpful as it emphasises that the consultations are therapeutic in their own right, and not solely a precursor or assessment for more open-ended regular therapy.

It is probably easier to say who is unlikely to get sufficient help from therapeutic consultations than to give a list of the types of problems that will respond well to this type of treatment. Broadly speaking, the earlier in life that relationship problems developed, or traumatic events took place prior to referral, the more intensive and long term treatment will need to be. For example, severely deprived children who are in care, autistic children, and abused children are very likely to need long-term relationships with their therapists if they are to establish or recover their mental health. However, there are many children of all ages who come from essentially sound and loving homes, but where there are nevertheless relationship problems which the family is unable to resolve.

Joanne is a good example of how therapeutic consultations can be the appropriate and effective way to help such a child even when there are quite worrying symptoms. There were a number of factors which helped this treatment to work so well, such as the clear focus already mentioned and the fact that this was a well-motivated family who were open to change. The ripeness of a patient for therapy may well play an important part in whether consultations are effective or not. If therapeutic consultations can be offered reasonably promptly when help is sought, they may be more potent than a lengthier intervention offered to a family that have waited for nine months for consultations or for weekly psychotherapy. This is an important aspect of the 'demand feeding' aspect of consultation work and the flexibility of approach it implies (see 'Nancy' in Chapter 19) .

When parents come to a psychotherapist asking for help for their child, they often do not have a clear picture in their mind about what form this help is likely to take. It may come as a surprise — at times a rather unwelcome surprise at that — for parents to hear that they will need to make a significant commitment to the child's treatment in terms of their own openness to change and willingness to engage in some therapeutic work (Chapter 7). The frequency or regularity with which the child and parents will need to come for help is something the psychotherapist has to advise about, but it is important to bear in mind that many families who attend public sector clinics are unfamiliar with the idea of weekly or intensive long-term treatment. It may be that the kind of treatment model that many parents have in mind is more closely related to an out-patient medical model than open-ended weekly therapy sessions. The child and family may be surprised to be offered so many 'long' (forty-five minutes to one hour) consultations. In other words, to return to the ideas at the start of this chapter, consultation work may very well feel as if it is 'good-enough' and sufficiently helpful from the child and family's perspective, providing a treatment programme to which they feel they can make a realistic commitment. If this is the case, the therapist's task is to be a catalyst for change in the family's emotional life, rather than the more constant companion for change that she becomes in weekly or intensive work.

In this time-pressured world, so-called 'brief' psychotherapy or therapeutic consultations offer a significant experience in time, of being attentively listened to and thoughtfully and compassionately responded to within a secure and confidential setting. The skill for psychotherapists is in judging how big the gaps between consultations can reasonably be and whether the work can realistically be time-limited. Consultation work builds on the strengths and coping mechanisms of the child and family, and their abilities to work through their problems with no more professional help than is required to help them move on from a 'stuck' period in their family life.

What kinds of consultation work are available?

Preparing this chapter provided the opportunity to talk with a number of child and adolescent psychotherapists in Great Britain who are working 'briefly' with children and their families. The model provided by parent–infant psychotherapy (Chapter 18) is being used and developed further by therapists all over the country. Work with 'under-fives' is generally flourishing as more and more therapists combine the depth of understanding and experience from their intensive and weekly work, with the brief model as described by Daws, and the approach to family work as described by Hopkins (Chapter 7).

Some therapists have taken this encouraging experience into a more general consultation response to many, or even all of their new referrals across the age range. Edwards and Maltby (1998) describe their work in a family consultation service in which they offer a series of up to five consultations to families to explore their difficulties. They describe their work which they see as an alternative choice for families, making links with colleagues and professionals in the community and including the use of telephone contact which is seen as central to the referral process.

This approach differs from the principle of assessing new cases for suitability for psychotherapy as there is increased emphasis on the value of the consultations in their own right as a therapeutic experience for the child and family. Judith Edwards' researches of work going on internationally (Chapter 14), indicate that, comparatively, there may be more consultation work going on outside Great Britain and certainly a search of the literature on the subject raises many non-English references. Having said this, Hunter (Chapter 10) gives a clear example of the type of consultation work many therapists now consider an intrinsic part of their work. This aspect of the work may simply not yet have been written about as much as weekly and intensive work.

However, Epstein (1997) gives a fascinating account of her telephone counselling for Childline, a twenty-four-hour free telephone service for children and young people. She argues that 'far from being an inappropriate medium, the telephone can actually offer some children and young people an ideal way to access therapy; it allows them to be heard, to feel safe and to retain control of the therapeutic process'. Hopefully, this growing versatility in applying psychoanalytic training to many forms of therapeutic help will be written about and debated more in the profession over the coming years.

When I asked the therapists who offer consultations how they felt their work differed from that of a family therapist, they tended to emphasise that at the heart of the consultations was a focus on the internal world of the child within the context of observable and internalised family relationships. This is in contrast to the emphasis of a family therapist who would tend to concentrate on the interactions between family members. The stimulation of working together with family therapists in inter-disciplinary teams within clinics, has bought about a useful cross-fertilisation of ideas and techniques encouraging psychotherapists to develop new applications of psychoanalytic principles, and thus new treatment models.

Adolescence is a time in life when consultations may be much more acceptable than an open-ended long-term psychotherapy commitment. For many years, specialist adolescent services in schools, universities and the wider community have used this approach. The success of this way of working seems to relate to the ordinary age-appropriate need in adolescence to become independent and self-sufficient, which pulls in quite the opposite direction to the intimate emotions of the transference relationship that are stirred in regular open-ended therapy. Many teenagers are more prepared to enter into some thinking and feeling about their difficulties if they know that there is a clear point of separation decided at the outset that helps them not to feel trapped into a commitment which they feel unable and unwilling to make. The aim of these consultations in psychoanalytically oriented treatment centres is not to select patients for regular therapy, although this can be one of the outcomes, but to offer sufficient help for the youngster to feel somewhat clearer about the distress that bought about their referral (and this can be a self-referral in this age range) and to be more able to bear and understand his or her painful and confused feelings and thoughts (Bronstein and Flanders 1998). This can often help to free log jams in adolescent development and lead to a spurt of energy and growth that can be so typical of the peaks and troughs of the teenage years.

With this type of treatment structure, the adolescent can dip into and out of the consultations without feeling they have reneged on a therapeutic commitment when they feel well enough to manage without consultations for a while. He or she can also then feel more able to approach the service for further help when the need arises. This whole process feels much more in touch with adolescent process and is reminiscent of Ainsworth's concept of exploration from a secure base (Chapter 4). The adolescent seeking help may have a very shaky 'secure base' in their relationships with their parents, or may be unable to acknowledge or develop from this base. As a form of acceptable displacement so common in adolescence, where teachers and other adults are consciously much more acceptable figures for identification and open communication than parents are acknowledged to be, the clinic and therapist can come to represent the place to return to when in trouble. This can be so despite the conflict which may also be a crucial part of the therapeutic relationship. An open-door policy can help many a troubled youngster to find a way through the difficult transitional years of adolescence.

So far I have described those treatment situations in which consultation work is likely to be helpful. I would now like to look at a much more disturbed group of patients where consultations can also prove helpful, but for entirely different reasons.

Brief work with young offenders

Child and adolescent psychotherapists are all too familiar with the ways in which deprivation and abuse in childhood can lead to violence and anti-social behaviour in young people. The whole question of whether it is possible to rehabilitate young offenders so that they are not inevitably set on a life of crime and imprisonment is a matter of public debate. There is a conflict between those who are unrealistically naive about how difficult it can be to turn around a young person's life when they have started to offend, and those who feel that offering treatment, instead of punishment, to those who create such trouble in society is a waste of valuable resources and a foolishly soft and indulgent attitude. Consultation work can be valuable in differentiating those youngsters who are able to respond to longer-term therapy and who are capable of change, from those who cannot. This can be very helpful in the allocation of severely limited specialised treatment resources for young offenders.

A multidisciplinary hypothesis-generating research project at Great Ormond Street Hospital into sexually abusive behaviour in young adolescent boys incorporated twelve consultations with a child and adolescent psychotherapist in which it was possible to explore the boys' emotional life. This work has been written about in more detail elsewhere (Hodges *et al.* 1994; Lanyado *et al.* 1995) and work with one of the boys is described in Chapter 19, from the point of view of the role of traumatic experience on his offending behaviour. I would like to focus here on the consultation work itself and the factors which helped us to enable some of the boys to accept more intensive treatment.

The boys had little motivation to seek help and were, in the main, reluctant to come for the research consultations at the start of contact. They were also a very unpromising group to work with psychotherapeutically because of the high level of acting out behaviour they indulged in (abuse and anti-social acts) – indicating a limited ability to think before they acted – and because of generally poor verbal skills, in addition to the ordinary difficulty of putting thoughts and feelings into words which is typical of early adolescence.

Despite these contra-indications, and although the consultations were there to explore their emotional lives for research purposes, some of the boys nevertheless found themselves getting drawn into the consultations and attracted by the attention to their feelings that was being offered. As psychotherapists we were not surprised to find this and gradually learnt to maximise the possibilities of developing this involvement in the boys. It was not that we thought it possible to adequately treat the boys in this context, but we did find that small but significant change could be bought about during the consultations. Sometimes a turning point could be reached in which utter hopelessness and unavailability for change could be alleviated enough for the youngster to see that there could be a different and more encouraging path ahead for them (Lanyado 1996).

Billy came from a large family in which there was a long-established pattern of inter-generational sexual abuse. He and all his siblings had been sexually abused by their father who had eventually been imprisoned. Despite the abuse, and his anger with his father, he also missed him greatly and possibly this had led to him identifying with his father and taking his place as eldest male in the family by sexually abusing two of his younger siblings. He was sixteen and living in a good and caring children's home when he came for his research consultations. Billy could not bear to think about what he had done to his siblings, particularly as he feared that they must now hate him as he had hated his father. He tended to blank off whenever his abusive behaviour was mentioned in the consultations, as if he hadn't heard the therapist and was miles away in his thoughts. When he could no longer blank off his feelings, he would go on mind-numbing drinking sprees, becoming violent to others and smashing up the children's home. By contrast, he was also able to express real affection and concern for his brothers and sisters who were by now all in care because his mother had had a breakdown and could not look after them. He was also very remorseful about all the trouble he caused the children's home staff and this sometimes influenced his behaviour in a positive way.

As with other boys who found themselves increasingly involved with the consultations, the lessening of his sense of despair seemed to follow an experience during a consultation when I had felt acutely and painfully aware of what a terrible life he had lived and how much he was suffering underneath his nonchalant way of being with me. Other authors (Bergman and Jucovy 1982) have described this moment in their work when it feels as if an arrow has pierced their hearts and given them an intense awareness of the distress their patients are in. This is more than ordinary compassion or empathy and inevitably deeply moves the therapist, often staying within them for a long while – even years – after the session. It is possible to have this experience in consultation work, as in weekly or intensive therapy, and when it happens it is a sign of a highly significant process taking place between therapist and patient. This process can be described as a kind of desperate non-verbal communication, an SOS message from deep within the patient, who just briefly believes that there is some point in sending out this message in a world that has, in the main, not heard all his or her previous cries for help. Paradoxically, it is probably only when the consultations have been established within boundaries that are very clear, safe and secure that youngsters such as Billy can dare to risk this type of communication. In this respect, consultation work can be very emotionally demanding for therapists as they must be highly attuned to the patient all the time, since the SOS can be weak and is not always easily recognised.

It is not that therapists are not highly attuned to all their patients. However, with the time pressure implied by consultation work, there is more of a need for the therapist to dare to use their countertransference response and informed intuition gathered from clinical experience, to be more ready to explore therapeutic hunches and to be generally 'less non-directive' than in weekly or intensive work. With experience this can make consultation work a very exciting and rewarding way of working, particularly when despair turns to the first glimmerings of hope, as it did for Billy.

Whereas he had previously tended to deny that there was any risk that he would ever sexually abuse again, he was able to face courageously the fact that, because he had no idea why he had abused his siblings, he also had no way of stopping himself doing this again. This is an odd kind of hope – but it became possible to think this way in the context of appreciating that the children's home and the research project were trying to understand him and his actions in all their complexity and felt that he was worth listening to and feeling for. The offer of helping him find regular open-ended psychotherapy did not therefore fall on deaf ears and a closed heart. Following the research consultations he was able regularly to attend therapy for a considerable period of time.

It is still too early to tell whether Billy will be able to avoid reoffending and further research is needed to evaluate to what extent treatments of young offenders such as Billy are effective. However, without the consultations and the turning point that took place in them, Billy would not have accepted any treatment and therefore had much less of a chance of changing his behaviour, and ultimately his future. Whilst there were only a small number of boys within the research project who were able to respond in this way, with treatment resources as limited as they are, it was possible to have a conviction that these boys were worth struggling with in the difficult treatments that followed.

The importance of 'beginnings and endings' in therapy have long been recognised, and many have noted the way in which the first consultation with a patient contains, in a highly condensed form, so many of the major therapeutic themes which gradually unfold during subsequently lengthy treatments. Similarly, the way in which therapy ends, as discussed in Chapters 5 and 8, is likely to involve many important emotional issues for the patient. Beginnings and endings are highly emotionally charged and one could argue that brief psychotherapy deliberately draws on this, both in the care and attention that must be paid to separation issues in the last few sessions, and in being particularly alert and responsive to the anxieties present in the first session. As already mentioned, therapists experienced in brief work have learnt that careful exploration of their 'therapeutic hunches', can be particularly helpful when examining the clues about the child and family's internal worlds as seen at these crucial junctions in family life.

In attempting to give the flavour of consultation work with all its time pressures, opportunities, and intensities of contact, it is important to bear in mind how far child and adolescent psychotherapists have come in terms of working 'briefly' and extending the applications of their psychoanalytic training. Psychoanalysts writing about brief work with adults, have a very different timescale to those described in this chapter (Malan 1976; Davanloo 1994; Molnos 1995). They are usually talking about thirty to forty sessions, which is a very far cry from the work I have just described. So how 'brief' is brief? For many children, thirty or forty sessions is probably close to the median number of sessions in weekly therapy – about one year of once-weekly therapy including holidays. This suggests that child and adolescent psychotherapists have already made major applications of their psychoanalytic training as a clinical response to the readiness of children, young people and their families to change when offered appropriate treatment. A year is a long time in family life. Recent publications, and a general interest and wish in the profession to respond to the time pressures of busy clinic life indicate a confidence in being able to offer a variety of treatments which can be helpful to patients and their families, all of which are based on psychoanalytic principles and training,

Acknowledgements

I am grateful to Maria Pozzi, Michelle Stern, Paul Barrows and Judith Edwards for the helpful discussions we have had about their consultation work.

References

Balint, M., Ornstein, P. H. and Balint, E. (1972) *Focal Psychotherapy: An Example of Applied Psychoanalysis*, London: Tavistock.
Bergman, M. S. and Jucovy, M. E. (eds) (1982) *Generations of the Holocaust*, New York: Basic Books.
Bronstein, C. and Flanders, S. (1998) 'The development of a therapeutic space in a first contact with adolescents', *Journal of Child Psychotherapy* 24(1): 5–35.
Davenloo, H. (1994) *Basic Principles and Techniques in Short-term Dynamic Psychotherapy*, New Jersey/London: Jason Aronson.

Daws, D. (1989) *Through the Night: Helping Parents and Sleepless Infants*, London: Free Association Books.

Edwards, J., and Maltby, J. (1998) 'Holding the child in mind: work with parents and families in a consultation service', *Journal of Child Psychotherapy* 24(1): 109–33.

Epstein, C. (1997) 'You can do therapy on the telephone', London: *Young Minds Magazine* 29.

Hodges, J., Lanyado, M. and Andreou, C. (1994) 'Sexuality and violence: preliminary clinical hypotheses from psychotherapeutic assessments in a research programme on young sexual offenders', *Journal of Child Psychotherapy* 20(3): 283–308.

Lanyado, M. (1996) 'Winnicott's children: the holding environment and therapeutic communication in brief and non-intensive work', *Journal of Child Psychotherapy* 22(3): 423–43.

Lanyado, M., Hodges, J., Bentovim, A., Andreou, C. and Williams, B. (1995) 'Understanding boys who sexually abuse other children: a clinical illustration', *Psychoanalytic Psychotherapy* 9(3): 231–42.

Laub, D. and Auerhahn, N. (1993) 'Knowing and not knowing massive psychic trauma: forms of traumatic memory', *International Journal of Psycho-Analysis* 74(6): 287–302.

Malan, D. H. (1976) *A Study of Brief Psychotherapy*, London: Tavistock, Plenum/ Rosetta.

Molnos, A. (1995) *A Question of Time*, London: Karnac.

Winnicott D. W. (1971) *Therapeutic Consultations in Child Psychiatry*, London: Hogarth and Institute of Psycho-Analysis.

—— (1989) *The Family and Individual Development*, London/New York: Routledge.

Further reading

Edwards, J. and Maltby, J. (1998) 'Holding the child in mind: work with parents and families in a consultation service', *Journal of Child Psychotherapy* 24(1): 109–33.

Lanyado, M. (1996) 'Winnicott's children: the holding environment and therapeutic communication in brief and non-intensive work', *Journal of Child Psychotherapy* 22(3): 423–43.

Winnicott D. W. (1971) *Therapeutic Consultations in Child Psychiatry*, London: Hogarth and Institute of Psycho-Analysis.

17 The group as a healing whole

Group psychotherapy with children and adolescents

Susan Reid

This book outlines the wide range of psychoanalytically informed work undertaken by the child psychotherapist: it quickly becomes apparent that most child psychotherapists prefer to work with individuals rather than with groups. Whilst all child psychotherapists do some group work, this primarily takes place within the natural group of the family. However, group psychotherapy began with the support of Martha Harris, in the Children and Families' Department at the Tavistock Clinic in the early 1970s (Reid *et al.* 1977). The establishing of the Group Psychotherapy Workshop in 1985 has provided a forum for ongoing developments in thinking about theory and practice as a result of which there is a book in preparation with contributions from many members of the workshop (Reid 1987, 1991; Reid and Kolvin 1993). Outside the Tavistock, other child psychotherapists, notably John Woods, for example, have contributed to thinking in the field (Woods 1993). However, group psychotherapy is not practised as widely as might be expected when one takes into account the advantages of group work, particularly for reaching those children, adolescents and their families who would never attend a child guidance clinic. Whilst there has certainly been much more interest in psychoanalytic group psychotherapy with adults, and an accompanying literature, it is also true to say that group psychotherapy has never equalled the interest given to individual work. Interestingly, this seems to be the case not only in Great Britain but around the world.

In this chapter, I discuss why group psychotherapy might be a treatment of choice for some children and some of the particular benefits it offers.

The use of groups for therapeutic interventions

The idea that social life begins at birth has long been accepted. Freud himself viewed the family group, and the patterns established therein, as the foundations for individual and group relationships. Recent research has revealed that the foetus, as many mothers had already intuited, interacts with the environment, both intra- and extrauterine (Prechtl 1989; Piontelli 1992). From four months, the developing human foetus reacts to noises from outside; the mother's voice – its pitch and rhythm – and the voices of others. The baby also responds to the mother's state of mind, for example, as reflected by her heartbeat. As soon as the foetus begins to perceive, it seems then that it perceives itself as not alone but in the company of others. Infants are born with some preconception of the existence of others, and this is met by the reality of the family group into which they are born. Even at the time of birth itself, there are usually others present.

The rest of human life is spent in various social groups. In ordinary development these gradually extend out from the family base to include the wider family and family friends and, in Western society, to playgroup or nursery and then school, through to the adult work groups and the various leisure groups we join throughout life. Even the hermit who could be said not to be a member of a group, is only a hermit because he has excluded himself from the society of others.

The psychoanalytic understanding of the group recognises that man is a social animal and lives all his life in groups, but that there is another sense in which we may accurately be described as members of a group. This group is the most basic of all – the 'group of ourselves'. None of us has only one 'self'. This is evident from the different ways we behave; we are one self with our parents but show a rather different side of ourselves at work or with peers. Different 'sides' of ourselves appear with different friends – take thinking alone. When we think alone it could be described as a conversation in our minds – but with whom? With other aspects of ourselves and with our version of other people in our external worlds – who might then be said to form another sort of group inside us. Creative artists, of course, are particularly in touch with this; writers can create numerous characters as if they knew them in detail, which indeed they do since they are based, at a conscious or unconscious level, on aspects of themselves.

Some advantages of group psychotherapy

- Many of the children who are referred to us have, among their present-ing difficulties, problems in making and keeping friends. They may be bullies or bullied, overwhelming in personality or withdrawn, but something about them means they do not engage in, or cannot sustain, the ordinary friendships which are so much an essential part of ordinary childhood development. These children experience intense loneliness and often the depression which accompanies it. For such children and adolescents a psychotherapy group can offer a safe, supportive and empathic setting where boundaries and limits are determined by an adult, the therapist. There is an opportunity for immediate acceptance, first by the therapist(s) and then, in time, by other group members. The safe setting provides an opportunity to learn how to make friends and, for many children and adolescents, their first experience of feeling wanted and essential to the life of a group.

- Child psychotherapists particularly enjoy and value multidisciplinary work; group psychotherapy offers just this possibility as it is always desirable to have groups co-led and, where possible, to have a male and a female therapist working together. A child psychotherapist with appropriate experience in group psychotherapy might work with a special needs teacher, a nurse, a paediatrician or residential social worker. Each discipline's training brings its own particular skills and these can often complement each other in a particularly helpful way when working with groups. It is also possible for those with training and experience in group work to work with those who wish to learn by functioning as co-therapists.

- Unlike adults in therapy, children are dependent on others for attendance at therapy sessions. Hence, there are many children who would not attend as out-patients for regular psychotherapy sessions because their families are unwilling, or unable, to provide the necessary support. However, it is possible for group psychotherapy to be 'taken to the child' in other settings, such as those enumerated below.

- Psychotherapy groups can be run in many settings that may not easily provide the conditions necessary for individual psychotherapeutic work – for example, in children's homes, ordinary schools and remand homes. For instance, it has proved possible to run groups in what might be considered rather unpromising circumstances in normal junior and even senior schools, by restructuring the environment available, setting sensible limits and working within the timetable constraints of the host institution.

- Some children and adolescents find being in a one-to-one situation overwhelmingly persecutory. Careful and rigorous assessment indicates those who would make more progress in a group. They may then subsequently be able to accept and engage in individual therapy.

- Within the group children are enabled to see the consequences of their own behaviour and to see the impact of others' behaviour upon themselves. This is because the group experience is shared; children have an opportunity to see not only the consequence of their own projections, but also how they may be vulnerable to the projections of others. For example, the bullied child may be helped to see how and why they may subtly provoke others to bully.

- Being in the company of children with different personalities, and seeing their weaknesses and strengths, enables children to rediscover aspects of themselves that have been suppressed, and to value the positive qualities they already have, thus enhancing a feeling of self-worth.

- Each member of the group will acquire a memory of all those events that have a significant impact on the life of the group. This is particularly helpful for those children who have been traumatised psychologically by their own life experiences and seem able to retain or learn little, and those children who deny responsibility for their actions at all – the psychopathic personalities. In individual therapy, experiences and events can be denied and responsibility refused, but in the group it is more difficult, over time, to deny experiences that the rest of the group insists have occurred.

- The group facilitates the exploration of a number of relationships and offers different models of behaviour and different perspectives on situations. This is particularly helpful for many deprived children, and for all children who have little capacity for self-reflection. Similarly, with older children, group processes and the appreciation that personal problems are not unique may facilitate self-disclosure.

- Some parents are unable to tolerate the suggestion that their child needs therapeutic help because they perceive this as their child being singled out, and for these an offer of group psychotherapy is often less threatening. Some adolescents find the label 'patient' intolerable and prefer the 'safety in numbers' of a group experience. In society, the view that only 'crazy' people need therapy is still widely held and a group can seem more innocuous.

- Where assessment indicates that group psychotherapy is the treatment of choice, then it may be a more economic use of the therapist's time.

Composition of groups

As suggested above, groups can be conducted in many settings and the nature of the group is often determined by the nature of the setting. In non-clinical settings the children will already have some prior knowledge of one another outside of the group. Groups can be broadly split into six categories:

The mixed group in a shared setting

Here the children share the setting, perhaps a school or a children's home, but something about their behaviour has brought them, particularly, to the attention of those adults with responsibility for their care (Flynn 1992). They are experienced as in need of, and/or able to make use of, extra help.

The group focused on a traumatic event

It can sometimes happen that children, even when they are not in the same family, can nonetheless share a traumatic experience. The children may all have suffered a sudden bereavement of a parent, or the death of a sibling, or be caught up in some catastrophic event such as the Abervan disaster many years ago, or, in more recent times, the horror of Dunblane in Scotland.

The sibling group

It often makes good sense to treat siblings in a group setting. This is both an economic use of time if several children in one family are all felt to be in need of help, but it can also be the treatment of choice. Seeing the siblings together can facilitate the exploration of the ways in which they see one another, their parent or parents, and the ways in which one may be a carrier for particular feelings or experiences for the others. It can be particularly helpful when one child has been 'scapegoated', enabling the exploration of projective mechanisms and allowing a healthier redistribution of feelings and even cognitive capacities. The group also offers the opportunity for further diagnostic exploration which may indicate where additional help may be needed and for whom, and what treatment modality would best meet those needs.

The shared traumatic event in a family

Following upon the sudden death of a parent or sibling, or the removal into care of all the children in a family, working with the siblings as a group would seem to be the initial treatment of choice. At the Tavistock Clinic, Sheila Miller has pioneered working with families where one parent has murdered the other. It is clear in these cases that the traumatic impact is shared by all of the children, but that each is likely to have a different reaction, depending upon personality and family position. It can happen that one sibling, in any traumatic situation, can carry all 'knowledge' about the event, giving that child an unbearable burden, but also preventing each of the children from engaging in a process of working through. They then need the support of one another, and also the opportunity to explore the similarities and differences in their responses, and perhaps to discover that each of them holds some pieces of the jigsaw, but only together can a clearer picture emerge.

The homogeneous group

Working with single 'populations' of children and adolescents has been quite popular in recent times. Many clinics and hospitals run groups for sexually abused children or anorexic girls. Here there can be a danger of seeing the child as a 'symptom' rather than as a complete and complex human being. Focusing on a particular symptom, too, does not allow the child the same freedom to explore and discover, or rediscover, different aspects of their personality. Such groups can be experienced as restrictive rather than expanding. One child, who had been in a group for sexually abused girls, complained, when she was subsequently in individual treatment, 'all they talked about was sex abuse, sex abuse, sex abuse, that's not the only thing that's happened to me!'

The heterogeneous group

Here, the children will not have met prior to the setting up of the group. They are brought together only because they are all experiencing emotional difficulties with which they need help and because the group therapist has assessed that their personalities, presenting problems and strengths are complementary and therefore likely to facilitate psychoanalytic group processes.

The composition of the heterogeneous group

The composition of a group is critical to its success or failure. Experience suggests that 'mix' is the essential element. The most successful groups seem to be where there is an observable spread of ages amongst the members. Children of one age grouped together can often become very stuck; they also can become very competitive. The very knowledge that they are the same age seems to surmount any other knowledge in importance and does not allow the same flexibility of behaviour which can be observed when the children are of chronologically different ages. Similarly, a mix of sexes seems to be helpful and avoids stereotypical 'boys' games' or 'girls' games'. A group, if it is to be therapeutic, needs to provide an atmosphere in which it is possible for boys to discover the feminine aspects of themselves, and vice versa.

A wide range of personalities and presenting problems increases the possibilities of different identifications for each child. It may be evident that to put several young children between the ages of four and eleven together who all have been described as aggressive will be unlikely to allow for therapeutic work to be done. Similarly, a group of very timid children together is likely to become flat in its emotional atmosphere.

At the Tavistock Clinic, these groups are run for one year – a realistic period in which sustainable development is possible. Many children make enormous progress within this period of one year, and it is therefore not reasonable to expect those children to continue for a longer period because other children in their group might need further help. We have a preference for closed as opposed to open groups for the 4- to 11-year-old children.

Group size

Group psychotherapy with children and young adolescents encompasses two distinct sub-groups: those who are in the 4–11-year-old range (equivalent to primary school) and those in the 11–15-year-old range. Most children are sensitive about the issue of age and, once at secondary school, may see themselves as beyond childish things, even if this may not in reality be reflected by their developmental level; they can become persecuted and resentful being grouped with 'kids'. The younger children's groups are most successful when composed of five children. This seems to be the maximum that children, up to eleven years of age, can relate to in a therapeutic way, and, very importantly, the most that can also be contained by the therapists, as children need to be kept safe as well as thought about. The young adolescents in the 11–15-year-old range, however, seem to need a larger group of six to nine people; absenteeism is not uncommon in young adolescents and it is wise not to expect that all members will arrive for each and every session. Young adolescents also seem to find smaller groups too intimate and, except with severely abused or neglected and deprived adolescents, it is reasonable to expect that their feelings can, by and large, be expressed verbally.

How do psychoanalytic therapy groups work?

The psychoanalytic therapy group explores relationships as they appear in the here and now of the group setting between members of the group, between individuals and the group leader or leaders, and between the group as a whole and the leaders. These are treated as indicative of other levels of relating, for each member of the group. All communications from the individual to other group members and to the group therapists are understood to have significance at the transference level. The therapists focus not only on *what* is said and done but *how,* and all in the service of understanding *why.* The whole *raison d'être* of the therapy group, as in individual therapy, is meaning. An interest in meaning by all members of the group is its aspiration. All communications, miscommunications and non-communications are treated as having significance and are therefore of interest to the therapist. The aim is that within the life of the group they will become of interest to the individual members and to the group as a whole (Bion 1961; Foulkes and Anthony 1984; Muir 1985).

The more heterogeneous the group, the more representative it will be of other groups to which each member belongs. But also, and very importantly, it gives access for each individual to models of other ways of being and of relating, and of strengths and weaknesses other than his or her own. Each member thus brings potential richness to the group because she or he is unique in many ways. In watching others each may discover unknown, unwanted, split off, repressed or projected parts of the self. In doing so each child has the possibility of standing back and observing another child's impact on other children and on the group therapists. Each child can explore their impact on each other person in the group and vice versa. Thus it comes to be understood that each member of the group has an essential and important part to play in the group. Someone may be absent one week, but they will always be a member of the group even in their absence. For some children this will be their first experience of being needed and missed and, eventually, wanted by the group.

Clinical example

Jack: a child who was helped by group psychotherapy

Jack, aged nine, was referred for group psychotherapy by a colleague, a social worker, who had been working with Jack's parents. He was described as a very worrying little boy who had been excluded from school because of his uncontainably violent behaviour and was awaiting a placement at boarding school. Meanwhile his parents were at their wits' end as they felt that he was completely out of control; one of the many troubling incidents they reported was that he had set fire to his bed which had then gone on to cause a serious fire in his family's home. He had made suicidal threats and seemed in as much despair about himself as was everyone else.

Following upon my individual assessment of Jack it was agreed that he would join the group for 4–11-year-olds which was about to begin. The group was to be run by me on my own as a co-therapist was not available, and to be of a year in duration. In addition to Jack there was one other boy who was younger and two girls, one older and one younger. As I had discovered for myself how little control he had over his violent impulses, I agreed to take Jack into the group only if his mother would agree to stay in the waiting room during the sessions. I anticipated that it would be impossible, in the early stages of the group, for Jack to stay in the group throughout a session. We therefore agreed that if, and when, Jack became out of control within the group, I would return him to the waiting room, but with the clear understanding that he could try again the following week.

In the first session, shortly after introductions had been made and the other children had begun to play, Jack erupted. He sent objects flying from the table and began kicking out at anyone who approached him, screaming and yelling. He was a frightening sight to behold. I tried to calm him but failed, my interpretations did not reach him. I therefore explained to him and to the other children that I was going to hold him to see if that helped; if it did not then I would return him to his mum in the waiting room, but he could come back next week and try again. I explained to the rest of the children that I could see that they were feeling frightened and, indeed, what Jack was doing was dangerous, but that I felt that *today* he was unable to stop himself. I also added that, although it was probably impossible for them to see it, I thought that

Jack was also very frightened of all of them. (I had observed that he had begun to throw things and panicked when one of the other children got too physically close to him.) I therefore told them that I thought Jack was frightened of people getting close and that throwing things was the only way he knew, so far, to get people to keep their distance. With some difficulty I returned Jack to the waiting room and, as we had agreed, his mother was not angry nor punitive but confirmed that she would return with him next week.

Week after week, for the first five weeks, Jack erupted. Sometimes it was possible to take him out for a little while and for him then to return later. At other times that was clearly it for the day – I always had to balance his needs with the needs of the other children in the group. This was interpreted to all of them. My colleague was working in parallel with Jack's mother to help her to hold on to hope that, in time, Jack would really manage to stay in the group like the other children. What was noticeable to all of us was that Jack managed longer in the group each time; his outbursts became less ferocious; he made attempts to be friendly and to sustain this friendliness, and his desperation to come to the group and his need for it was evident, even to the other children. The other children in the group moved from fear and resentment, followed swiftly by relief when he'd gone, to genuine sympathy and growing support for him in his efforts.

The other children meanwhile watched me very closely to see how I dealt with Jack. Jenny, for example, a seven-year-old girl, was a particular beneficiary of this. She was a very depressed little girl, in care, who was subdued to the point of almost complete withdrawal. She hardly ever spoke and showed little emotionality, either positive or negative. Her social worker was concerned that she should have an opportunity to have this thought about since, within her children's home, Jenny was only too easy to overlook, leaving staff feeling both guilty and resentful. Initially, when Jack exploded, Jenny would withdraw, both emotionally and physically, turning her back on him. However, even with her back turned, she could continue to hear my comments, Jack's shouts and screams and the other children's comments. Week by week she became subtly emboldened until she allowed herself to show openly her intense interest in the proceedings. I spoke about the group's interest in how I would deal with Jack: would I get angry back, did I disapprove, what would I tolerate and what would I not tolerate? I noted their different responses on each occasion. When

Jack left the room the children now began to talk about their experiences of their own anger and of that of others and, over the weeks, as Jack calmed down, Jenny, Michael and Elizabeth warmed up.

Jack's parents reported improvements at home. For the sixth session, Jack managed to stay in the group room throughout the session. This was a source of considerable pride for him and his achievements were noted and respected, not only by me, but by each of the other children too. The next session he missed through illness and genuine disappointment was expressed when I informed the group at the beginning that he would be unable to come that day. The next week, on his return, Jenny said quietly 'Oh good, Jack's here'. Jack looked first surprised, then turned pink and hurriedly sat down at the table and began to draw, but he chose to sit next to Jenny. Jenny smiled shyly – no one in the group had ever chosen to sit next to her before. I welcomed Jack and said that the group had missed him last week. Jack's face was open and soft. He looked me in the eyes before turning shyly to look at each group member. Then he smiled and nodded. I added that I thought that Jenny had also been pleased that he had chosen to sit next to her. Jack and Jenny smiled shyly at one another and taking a piece of paper, began spontaneously to draw together.

Jack did not go to boarding school but, after the group, and at his own request for further help, he went into individual psychotherapy. However, at the time of the initial referral, group psychotherapy was the treatment of choice for him. He was a very persecuted little boy with very little capacity to symbolise or reflect, who dealt with his feelings by projecting them before he even knew what they were. Within the safe setting of the group, the presence of other real children reacting to him, and to whom he could react, helped him to develop some insight. He had been a very lonely little boy and the group became the high spot of his week. He desperately wanted to be with other children and it was they whom he expressly wished to see.

The other children became effective assistants in the therapeutic process. They did not like his violence and said so, and in time he realised that he cared. It became possible for him to see that not only were there consequences to his actions but also that his own behaviour had some meaning. It became possible for him and the other children to understand that the close physical proximity of another human being felt to him like a violent attack and intrusion. Once the other children understood this, they could be helped and supported in 'giving him his space'. It also became possible to understand that this seemingly powerful little boy actually felt extremely impotent. Jack had been unable to judge the quality of another child's advances towards him but always assumed that they would be violent in intent. Having his own violence met with firmness but a wish to understand its cause, gave him an experience that whilst his violent outbursts would not be tolerated when they became dangerous, he was a member of the group and therefore was always welcome (initially of course only by the group therapist) to return the following week. This seemed to give Jack some confidence that, just as the group therapist would not allow him to hurt others, similarly she would protect him from those intrusions he feared from other people.

Acceptance is a basic pre-requisite for healthy mental life. Children need to feel welcomed and accepted from birth and, for this to happen, a mother and father need to be able to tolerate disappointment if the baby of reality is not the baby they had fantasied. Acceptance within the group means accepting, without criticism, the children as they are when they first join and with a wish to understand them. Acceptance means accepting the individual, it does not mean putting up with realistically intolerable behaviour. It is astonishing how therapeutic the experience of acceptance is. An accepting atmosphere seems to be infectious and the degree to which children begin to find previously unacceptable behaviour something which can be thought about so that it becomes tolerable, is impressive.

From acceptance grows the sense of belonging 'come what may'; with trust it becomes safe and possible to be one's self. To see Jack's obviously anti-social behaviour thought about, accepted but limited, seemed to embolden the other children to show those aspects of themselves which they sensed were least likeable, as well as those aspects of themselves which were also their strengths. Out of this grows the sense of group cohesion. In group psycho-therapy, becoming a group is the therapy. What starts out each time as a number of individuals, moves towards the experience of THE GROUP as a psychological whole, with some modification of self-centred behaviour in recognition of the needs, wishes and feelings of others.

In the emotionally fluid atmosphere of the group the children discover new dimensions to their own personalities. Jack, for example, who hadn't a friend in the world when he joined the group, and who seemed to have been disliked by adults and children alike, became respected and liked within his group for the good qualities which emerged when his aggressiveness no longer dominated. This volcanically violent little boy, when his violence was contained, revealed a passionate, spontaneous gratitude and generosity.

Although his outbursts continued for some time into the group, they no longer dominated his experience of the group nor other's experience of him. Both he and the other children, when he lost his temper, had some trust, hope and belief that a recovery could be made. It was also of interest to him to see in the course of the group that other children could be nasty, explosive and out of control too.

Having other children present as part of the therapy experience was a great support to Jack; initially he did not like or trust adults. In individual therapy, we have probably all had experience of the child who becomes stuck: behaviours repeated session after session with the therapist apparently the only one who holds conscious memory of previous events. Within group psychotherapy, it is much harder for the individual to deny their involvement in previous events. Each member of the group holds a memory since each and every person's feelings and behaviours within the group must have an impact on everyone else. Each event becomes inextricably woven into the fabric of that group's experience and memory. This group would not allow Jack to deny and repress the knowledge of the havoc he wreaked in the group room in those early sessions, and apparently he had consistently denied any responsibilities or even knowledge, both at home and at school, for his outrageous behaviour. His inability to show any remorse had further aggravated his teachers leading to his exclusion from school.

Conclusion

Group therapy can enable children and adolescents to discover at first-hand the impact they have on others and how other people function. Because the children are accepted by the group for who they are and what they are and, because their strengths are recognised as well as their vulnerabilities and weaknesses, the individual's capacity to be more self-reflective is supported. Being together with their peers, within the safe setting of the therapy group, creates a 'laboratory' for experimentation with new ways of thinking, feeling and behaving which can then give the child the confidence to approach other people outside the group in a new way. Because the therapy takes place in the company of their peers, there is often a rapid carry over in terms of improvements into their school lives. For many children, group psychotherapy is sufficient to get them on the pathway of healthy and happy development.

Children who have been in group psychotherapy often, like Jack, become able to recognise for themselves when they need further help. They then become partners in a new therapeutic endeavour. Many of those children who have used the group as a stepping stone to individual therapy seem, in my experience, particularly able, not only to make good use of individual work, but also to need individual therapy for a shorter time.

References

Bion, W. R. (1961) *Experiences in groups and other papers*, London, Tavistock Publications.

Flynn, D. (1992) 'Adolescent group work in a hospital in-patient setting with spina bifida patients and others', *Journal of Child Psychotherapy* 18(2): 87–107.

Foulkes, S. H. and Anthony, E. J. (1984) *Group Psychotherapy: The Psychoanalytic Approach*, 2nd edn, Harmondsworth: Penguin.

Muir, E. (1985) 'The Kleinian concept of position and group therapeutic process: an experience in group psychotherapy with emotionally disturbed boys aged 6 to $9^{1}/_{2}$ years', *Journal of Child Psychotherapy* 11(2): 97–109.

Piontelli, A. (1992) *From Fetus to Child: An Observational and Psychoanalytic Study*, London: Tavistock/Routledge.

Prechtl, H. F. R. (1989). 'Fetal behaviour', in A. Hill and J. Volpe (eds) *Fetal Neurology*, New York: Raven Press.

Reid, S. (1987) 'The use of groups for therapeutic interventions', *Educational and Child Psychology* 4(3/4): 171–9. Special issue J. Thacker and R. Williams (eds) *Working with Groups*.

—— (1991) 'Group work with children in schools', in Maureen Fox and Liz Kennedy (eds) *Proceedings of the 1991 Conference for Educational Psychologists in Training*, London: Tavistock Clinic.

Reid, S. and Kolvin, I. (1993) 'Group psychotherapy for children and adolescents', *Archives of Disease in Childhood* 69: 244–50.

Reid, S., Fry, E. and Rhode, M. (1977) 'Working with small groups of children in primary schools', in D. Daws and M. Boston (eds) *The Child Psychotherapist and Problems of Young People*, London: Wildwood House.

Woods, J. (1993) 'Limits and structure in child group psychotherapy', *Journal of Child Psychotherapy* 19(1): 63–78.

18 Brief psychotherapy with infants and their parents

Dilys Daws

'Do babies have problems?', I am often asked in a puzzled sort of way. The implication is perhaps, that psychotherapists can see trouble anywhere, and even infancy is not sacrasant from this tendency to pathologise.

Well, yes babies *do* have problems, but even more, parents have problems about getting their relationship with their baby going. Recognising these early difficulties can be an optimistic process, and being involved therapeutically with parents and infants can be effective in helping them to make a good start with each other. The attachment process can be greatly enhanced, and there is a good chance that strengthening the relationship at this early point will help prevent future difficulties (Fonagy 1998). This work is flourishing around the world; various writers have conceptualised it, and described their own style of therapy: Barrows (1997), Cramer (1995), Hopkins (1992), Lieberman and Pawl (1993), Stern (1995) and Watillon (1993).

Under-fives counselling services respond to this opportunity. I work within such a service of the Tavistock Clinic and also at the baby clinic of the James Wigg practice (Daws 1999). In both these places, I see families who come with problems about their infants. These may be sleeping, or feeding, or excessive crying. Sometimes parents will come openly worrying about their problems in 'bonding' with their baby, and, now that post-natal depression is so much more easily recognised, many mothers come for help about their state of mind and its effect on their relationship with their baby. With older babies and toddlers another range of problems are presented – those of weaning and separation difficulties, toilet training and behaviour problems.

In this chapter I shall describe the two settings in which I work and something of the style of the work itself and the meaning of the nature of the problems.

An under-fives counselling service

The ease of referral is a striking aspect of the service offered; parents can self refer by telephone or letter, though contact is then made with the GP. Because of a strong belief that problems with infants should be responded to quickly, appointments are usually given within two weeks. Up to five meetings are offered, and therapist and parents discuss the time-frame within which these are used. The philosophy behind this service is that parents come to consult a professional about the problems *they* feel they and their baby or young child are having. Sometimes, of course, this leads to a realisation by the therapist and the family that more serious disturbance is at issue. The brief work may then prepare the way for a referral for longer-term therapy.

Baby clinic

In the baby clinic accessibility is even more a feature of the work. I have been visiting this baby clinic once weekly for over twenty years, discussing families that health visitors and GPs are worried about, and also seeing some families myself. By having the therapist available in a room at the family's own doctor's premises, the worry of an outside referral is avoided. To some extent local families feel that the health centre belongs to them, and to see a child psychotherapist there keeps the referral located in the friendly ambience of the baby clinic. However, there is some formality in the referrals in that they are always made by letter from the GP or health visitor and with discussion about the suitability of the case. The service is not a drop-in one, and appointments are always made for a time at least a week ahead or as soon as possible after that. My belief is that there needs to be a quick response, but also a space between the referrer, health visitor or GP offering the idea of seeing the child psychotherapist, and the first meeting. In this time, there can be some mental preparation, which is just as important in brief work as in long-term work. There is more chance of fathers as well as mothers being involved if there is time at home to discuss the referral. This natural kind of mental preparation involves some thinking about the problem, and the meaning of its urgency now: it also allows parents to marshall their appropriate defences, as well as accessibility to the therapeutic situation.

Clinical work

In both places, an assumption is made by the therapist that having a baby, as well as being one of the most important events in anyone's life, can also be disturbing and upsetting. It is well known that post-natal depression can follow closely on giving birth. When parents are themselves distressed it often seems that echoes of painful childhood experiences have been stirred up by the birth of the baby. It also seems that many of the problems that parents describe in their infants, such as severe sleep disturbance, may similarly be a symptom of a *difficulty between parent and baby* rather than just a problem in the baby.

Although this work is brief, often one or two meetings only, the method is psychoanalytically based. Problems are thought of in the context of both the baby's history and that of its parents. I tell the parents that in order to understand problems in the present, I need to know what has happened in the past. I ask for memories of the pregnancy and birth, for details of how the parents established their own relationship and how they get on with each other now. I also ask for information on what they feel is relevant about their own childhoods and their relationships with their parents now. In describing all this, links between these ideas often emerge and parents seem strikingly relieved to make these connections.

Advice is rarely given; it seems to me that most parents have access to much advice from family or friends, and from books or the professionals they have already consulted. They often come preoccupied with specific advice they feel unable to take. 'Don't tell me to leave her to cry', they tell me about a sleepless infant. My task often seems to be to think with them about what the advice represents for them. I assure them that I agree that 'leaving a baby to cry' could be a cruel and neglectful act, but that 'allowing' a baby to protest as she settles need not be. Crucially, I look at the personal trauma that underlies this dilemma. When asking parents if *they* were left to cry, surprisingly often some painful history of separations or abandonment in the parents' own history comes up. It may be in their childhood; it may be a recent bereavement such as the death of a parent, or a miscarriage or stillbirth. But where 'common sense' action by the parents to deal with a problem in their child's development seems to be impossible, one almost always finds some unbearable event in the family history. Discovering and understanding all this strengthens parents' ability to change things in the present (Fraiberg *et al.* 1980).

Observation

Child psychotherapists' training begins with infant observation – seeing an ordinary baby in its own home, with its mother and perhaps other members of the family, for an hour a week, for at least one year (Miller *et al.* 1989). Through these observations, the trainee learns about an infant's normal development – physical, emotional and social. The trainee can also experience at first-hand the emotions stirred up by this exposure to the intensity of being with a tiny baby, and the dramas of the mother–baby relationship (Miller 1992). Learning to observe is a difficult art in itself; it is also a particularly appropriate way of learning how to start being a therapist. Observing what is going on for others in a heightened situation, while at the same time noting the feelings stirred up in oneself, is one of the basic tools of a therapeutic relationship. It is then necessary to learn how to manage these feelings, and to use them as a source of information, *not* as a key to action.

With this approach, I look at the baby carefully and tell the parents what I notice. The meetings are packed with emotion and action. I take in and reflect on what the family tells me and shows me so that an understanding and integrative process that begins in my mind can then take over in theirs. Solutions are as much the province of parents as of myself; my task is to restore their ability to think effectively so they can provide the answers for their child.

Observing what is actually happening in front of one's eyes is valuable information. It may illustrate what the family is telling the therapist about the problems at home, or about traumatic events in the past. Sometimes indeed, it can be even more informative by filling in the gaps of what is *not* being told in words. It can provide the therapist with convincing material to help the parents think about the situation between them and their baby. However, it does need to be used with caution: it can feel very persecuting to some parents who may feel judged or even 'spied on' by the observing therapist. At best, the observation can become a shared activity where the family become able to observe themselves and reflect on what they notice.

In the clinic I work in, a large imposing building, long corridors with fire-doors provide a diagnostic obstacle course in themselves. I often feel that I know a great deal about a family's functioning by the time we have negotiated our way from the waiting room through these doors to my therapy room. I have seen something of how the parents are able to work co-operatively with each other, or not – who is most responsible for toddlers, who holds the baby or pushes the buggy, who carries the nappy bag, how they make use of me, the outsider to the family.

Similarly, as in all family therapy work, the use of the space of the therapy room may illustrate relationships, and the process of the work. One very simple example was two parents coming about a weaning and separation problem in their year-old baby. At first both parents sat stiffly next to each other on the settee, the mother clutching the baby on her lap. As they all relaxed, talking to me, the baby was allowed to slip down and crawled along the floor. She pulled herself up by the table, and then approached me, putting a small toy in my lap, a very usual way for babies this age to introduce themselves. This moving away by the baby from the parents to make use of me, the interested outsider, was a very neat symbolisation of the parents' readiness to let their baby start to become unstuck and make use of more of what the world has to offer. It does seem that in the presence of a therapist, who is empathising with conflicts, things can start to open up. In this case, perhaps, the parents had to deal with two irreconcilable feelings – that weaning felt like an unbearable loss, and that they knew the baby was being kept back from 'making friends' with the wider world. The physical action of the baby crawling across the room was, of course, only one little moment, perhaps playfully seized on by me. The real 'work' of the session was in the painful exploration of the meaning of separation to this mother and father, of hearing from them of serious losses in their lives which meant that the very ordinary 'loss' of the breast-feeding relationship had particular meaning for them. The next week they talked more about their experiences, and the baby was ready for exploring from the beginning of the session. She again crawled towards me, and then moved further afield to the chair beyond mine. She got her hand stuck behind the chairleg, turned to her parents and called out. They looked over to her, and instead of rushing to swoop her up, father said, 'Are you stuck?' Reassured by his words, the baby sorted out the spatial problem and got her hand out. It seemed to me that her parents were demonstrating their new respect for their baby's individuality and thus, her ability to solve her own problems in their supportive presence.

In the case just described, it was satisfying to observe the parents and baby's relationship progress. Other times what I observe is much more painful. In one family, two parents were at war with each other. Their baby, on the floor, looked ready to crawl. I mentioned this, they acknowledged my remark saying that, yes, he would be crawling soon. They barely glanced at him and continued engrossed with each other. I watched with distress as the baby actually crawled a few feet, unnoticed. It was a very miserable confirmation of how neglected this baby was, but at least gave me specific 'evidence', rather than just theoretical ideas, of how the baby's needs were being ignored. The parents did shortly after split up and, fortunately, the mother, on her own, was able to be more available to her baby.

Sometimes there is a remarkable connection between what parents talk about, and small babies' actions and vocalisations. Babies are often in tune with the emotional atmosphere, and may cry when painful matters are being talked about. This can in fact be a clue to why some babies cry excessively; it may connect with some inconsolable experience in the parent's own history. When the parents are able to talk about this with the therapist, they may then be able to console the baby (Hopkins 1994).

The parent's reaction to a baby crying in the session may, in itself, be useful material for the work. Some mothers or fathers may seize the opportunity to take the baby out for a walk in the corridor, and it may seem as though this is an attempt to get away from painful issues stirred up in the room. Persuading the family to stay in the room can sometimes enable parents to share difficult feelings with each other for the first time. Similarly, toddlers' urgent requests to be taken to the toilet need to be thought about. Balancing the reality of the need – of toddlers' natural preoccupation with such matters, with the excuse for parent and child of getting away from difficult subjects by leaving the room – is an interesting subject in itself, and you can get it badly wrong!

Going back to crying babies, mothers who have difficulty in soothing their baby may be trying to do so silently. When pointing this out to one mother she said, 'If I did say anything to him, it would be too horrible'. The opportunity to put into words to the therapist the 'horrible' thoughts that she had about the baby came as a release to her. Once these thoughts were said, and acknowledged, they perhaps became bearable.

A therapist who is genuinely able to be there non-judgementally for parents and baby can allow parents to own their hostile feelings towards the baby. In this case, it enabled the mother to have a different range of feelings towards her baby. She was able to hold him close to her and to put into words what *he* might be feeling: she was no longer preoccupied with the force of her own impulses. The baby sensed this difference and was able to be comforted by his mother's holding of him. In this kind of instance, as in parent–infant work generally, the therapist can be thought of as carrying out a symbolic holding of the emotions crashing around in a family. The experience of this holding enables parents to pass it on to their baby.

Sleep problems

Sleep disturbance often illustrates what is going on in a family and the issues uncovered between parents' and children often lead back to parents own experience in their childhood. Repeatedly, the theme of how to deal with and survive separations comes up (Daws 1989).

The clinical method that I use with sleep problems is in fact similar to that for any presenting problem. The nature of the problem itself must be taken seriously, although I and the family may come to understand it as a symptom of a relationship problem. However, a sleep disturbance is itself a serious matter to a family and sleepless parents are likely to be exhausted, distressed and angry.

I start by letting parents tell me, in their own way, what the problem is, so that I get the particular flavour of what they feel is the problem and its origin, and also get the chance to experience the predominant emotion with which parents begin their story. Once I have begun to ask questions I am, perhaps, felt as looking after them, and intense emotions often subside. Whatever emotion comes out strongly in these first few moments may be the same as what the baby feels is directed towards him during his sleepless nights, be it anger, anxiety or responsible concern. After the parents have told me the problem, I explain that I would like to ask them questions about the baby and the family in general so that we can discover what links there may be.

The method that I use is to combine three different elements. First, a structured questioning about the details of the baby's timetable. As I ask for the precise details of day and night, a vivid picture builds up in my mind of what actually happens in this family, and their assumptions of what should happen. My mental picture also involves the physical placing of cots and beds and the permutations of who sleeps with whom and in which room. The questions themselves sometimes begin to clarify a confused situation as the parent both informs me and thinks about the logical connections of the questions.

Second, is a free-ranging enquiry into memories of the pregnancy and birth, and early weeks. I tell parents that I need to know the baby's lifestory to make sense of what is happening now. Third, are questions about the parents' relationship with each other and with their own parents so that we can see the family context of this particular baby.

The parents I see have usually been offered much advice already and often feel they have 'tried everything'. What I give them in the first place is simply the ordinary psychoanalytic *free-floating attention*. As they tell their story *unconscious threads* draw together and connections emerge. Because I do not at once offer solutions they are less likely to react negatively. They are left able to free-associate – that is, let their minds lead freely from one related theme to another. They may perceive me as interested, receptive and capable of holding on to a great deal of information. In this setting, it is striking how parents can convey economically much focused information. It seems as though all ordinary parents have a story to tell about their baby as dramatic and moving as any work of literature. What is also communicated, and confirmed by my interest, is the uniqueness of each baby and its family.

As this story unfolds, themes emerge about the nature of their relationships, and the meaning of not sleeping may change with the age of the child. But underlying it at every stage seems always to be some aspect of the problem of separation and individuation between mother and baby: in other words, the nature of attachments. Feeding and weaning problems are closely related; bereavements, marital conflict, difficult births, psychosomatic tendencies can all link with sleep problems. Ambivalent feelings are a crucial factor in all this. Making these links enables parents to separate their experience from their infants and frees them to solve the problem.

The setting up of a baby's sleep–wake rhythm is influenced by the interaction between parent and baby. It is also an aspect of the baby's own temperament and personality, and of the stage of development it has reached. Sleep problems are ones that persist after parents have made allowances for many natural, usually transient, causes of sleeplessness.

Separation problems

Simplistically speaking, the problem for a mother in getting a baby to sleep is the basic act of putting the baby down – that is, of separating herself from her baby and the baby from her. It can be as difficult for the mother to be without the baby as it is the other way round. The mother of an eight-month-old said, 'when he closes his eyes, I feel left out'.

I have, however, become aware of how many parents these days keep their babies very close to them, by day and by night, for the first months or even longer. In fact, it does seem that there is a biological imperative for this closeness, which in itself aids attachment. Some of these parents find that their baby has difficulty in getting to sleep; many do not. It seems that there is an ability in some parents and babies to enjoy their closeness, and, at the same time, to let go of each other emotionally – enough for each to be free to go to sleep. Other parents and babies come to experience such closeness as a mutual torment of intrusiveness, and no one is able to sleep long and deeply. They seem also to get caught in the closeness and become unable to think about how to get more separate from each other. There are two important issues here. First, *all* babies need closeness and intimacy with their parents to develop a sense of themselves as individuals, as well as a sense of themselves in relation to other people. Second, all babies need, at appropriate moments, to take steps away from their parents, both literally and metaphorically, in order to begin to grow.

When a family is able to discuss such issues, allowing me as the outsider to have some new ideas of what might be helpful, it shows that the family is ready for a change. One such thought is that the use of 'transitional objects' is part of the process by which babies manage some of the first steps of separation (Winnicott 1971). For instance, when I ask if the baby has a teddy bear, I may be told that she has several cuddly toys. When I suggest that *one* significant toy is important, parents may be able to create a shared idea with the baby, that a particular toy has a job to do. Often, of course, blankets, dummies, or the baby's own thumb may become the source of satisfaction that allows separations from the mother, at the same time as being a link or memory. Parents and babies are able to move on to such solutions when the emotions involved in the original problem have been sufficiently attuned to.

Feeding

Similarly to sleep problems, it is often appropriate to think of a feeding problem within a relationship context. Feeding problems fall into two main categories: 'too much' or 'too little'.

When babies are being fed constantly, whether by breast or by bottle, it does often seem that there is a separation problem (Daws 1993). Parents and babies are able to be close to each other, but cannot manage to pull apart. As with some sleep difficulties, it is common to find bereavements, or significant losses in the mother's or father's lives. Equally important is the impact of ambivalence towards the baby in the mother, and particularly of unacknowledged feelings. Some mothers feel that good mothering involves always being available to the baby, and that saying 'no' means being a 'bad' mother.

In such cases, helping parents to work out the connections between their own experience and their perception of their babies needs can be helpful. Parents' ability to work in partnership is particularly relevant here. Sometimes a mother enmeshed with her baby is also excluding the father's contribution to the relationship. His attempts to help them be a bit more separate may be dismissed as 'male insensitivity'. Work on the need for three-person relationships and the value of a father introducing the baby into the excitement of what is new outside the close mother–baby duo can help this situation. Babies with a little distance between themselves and their mother can then enjoy the memory of a feed, and the anticipation of the next one.

The therapeutic work, therefore, needs to take account of family relationships in the past and present. It also must deal with interactions which can be observed in the room. Parents may be helped to recognise babies' signals in a more varied way: at its simplest this means that an approach by the baby to the mother may not always be for feeding; it may be for an interaction through speech or playing. In one family meeting about an eight-month-old who was being fed constantly the father was holding the baby. When he started to cry father was about to hand him to his mother. I asked, 'What would happen if you went on holding him?' Father did try this, and was able to soothe the baby himself. Patterns of response can be thought about with an interested outsider, and altered.

When babies are fed 'too little' this is a much more serious problem. Here again, the relationship aspects of when babies are failing to thrive can be significant. It does seem that very often there has been a real experience of neglect, deprivation and hunger in the parents' own lives. Depression in the mother can derive from this, and make her feel she has no resources to give her baby. Therapeutic work that feels like symbolic parenting may release ability to parent the baby. This therapeutic work has to be able to take account of the seriousness of the negative feelings towards the self, baby and any helping professional (Daws 1997).

Post-natal depression

It has recently been realised what a large number of new mothers suffer from post-natal depression – at least 10 per cent become seriously depressed. The depression can have an effect on the baby which may last after the depression in the mother itself has lifted. Father and other members of the family are also involved. Post-natal depression can cause relationship difficulties; it may also be the result of them. Furthermore, the cure to it is also through relationships, professional and other (Murray and Cooper 1997).

There are no direct causes of post-natal depression, any more than in depression generally, but there are vulnerability factors and precipitating events. These include a lack of confiding partner or other supportive person (Brown and Harris 1978) and the death of the mother's own mother, especially before she was eleven. A difficult relationship with the mother's mother is also relevant.

Other key factors can include a difficult birth, including unexpected caesareans. The anxiety, humiliation and misery of births that are felt to have gone 'wrong' can leave a mother too exhausted to make the first steps of getting to know her baby, and mother and baby can find it difficult to learn each other's rhythms.

In fact, there is a connection between one causation of post-natal depression – the lack of empathic mothering – and its treatment, which can be a professional as a reliable supportive parent substitute. This professional can be a psychotherapist; more appropriately, it can be a health visitor. It has recently been discovered that a limited number of therapeutic meetings with the health visitor can prevent or cure many cases of post-natal depression (Holden *et al.* 1989). However, this work is not simple. To be truly therapeutic, the worker needs to listen to what a mother really feels about herself, her partner and her baby. The content of this can be quite shocking: anxiety, anger, self-hatred, hatred of the baby or partner, disturbing dreams, fear of damage that has happened, or might happen. Of course, many non-depressed mothers go, perhaps more briefly, through these same feelings.

Consultative work in a baby clinic

This takes me to what may be the most helpful role of the psychotherapist in the baby clinic – of consulting to the team. This aspect of the work may be less intrinsic when families refer themselves away from primary care to a service such as the under-five's service in a Child and Family Consultation Centre. However, there are many occasions when consultations to the primary care network are possible.

In the primary care team at the baby clinic, there is the opportunity to talk about the feelings stirred up in professionals by patients. I try to help the team to recognise these feelings, to manage them, and indeed use them as a source of information about feelings the patient might have and be unable to deal with.

Post-natal depression is a good example of this process; it is a condition hard to diagnose. Some mothers are only really depressed when alone with the baby; in the presence of a concerned health visitor, they may feel cared for and not at all depressed. On the other hand, women who are most severely depressed can be so flat, elusive and dismissing of an approach that it is easy for the health visitor to feel unwanted and unneeded. These parents can perplex the health visitor, or even, more likely, irritate or anger them. I would hope to be able to discuss where these feelings come from. Vulnerable new parents may elicit in a receptive health visitor feelings that really belong within parents' unresolved relationships with their own parents. By understanding this, they are more likely to be tolerant, and the mother may start to feel understood and supported at a crucial emotional moment in her life. Feeling supported herself, the mother, in turn, manages her own baby's feelings better.

So, one outcome of this consultative work is in helping members of the primary care team, GPs, health visitors and others, to be 'braver' – to follow the clues to the emotional and relationship issues behind the requests for help with developmental problems or even some physical symptoms presented to them. There is a body of work now on how doctors can respond in a wider way to their patients requests for help (Elder 1996). Similarly, many health visitors interact with their clients on an appropriate emotionally supportive level (Daws 1995). This does not need to lead into endless time spent. In fact, more satisfying interactions may lead to more focused use of time. A psychotherapist can be a helpful back-up to this approach to the work.

Parent–infant work has the satisfaction of getting in early – though when listening to families' historics, there is almost always the wish to have started at least one generation earlier! There are three strands to this work: first, the direct clinical work with parents and their infants. Second, is the use of the insights gained from this clinical experience by talking with primary care workers about the connections between problems and symptoms and the underlying emotional issues. Lastly, is the consultative work – of helping these primary care workers themselves to grapple more directly with patient's and client's feelings. This work can be painful and, without support workers, can become stressed. The psychotherapist can have an ongoing role in backing up colleagues brave enough to take on this compellingly interesting work.

References

Barrows, P. (1997) 'Parent–infant psychotherapy: a review article', *Journal of Child Psychotherapy* 23(2): 255–64.

Brown, G. and Harris, T. (1978) *Social Origins of Depression*, London: Tavistock.

Cramer, B. (1995) 'Short-term dynamic psychotherapy for infants and their parents', in K. Minde (ed.) *Child and Adolescent Psychiatric Clinics of North America*, 4(3): 649–60 (July 1995).

Daws, D. (1989) *Through the Night: Helping Parents and Sleepless Infants*, London: Free Association Books.

—— (1993) 'Feeding problems and relationship difficulties: therapeutic work with parents and infants', *Journal of Child Psychotherapy* 19(2): 69–83.

—— (1995) 'Consultations in general practice', in J. Trowell and M. Bower (eds) *The Emotional Needs of Young Children and their Families*, London: Routledge.

—— (1997) 'The perils of intimacy: closeness and distance in feeding and weaning', *Journal of Child Psychotherapy* 23(2): 179–99.

—— (1999) 'Child psychotherapy in the baby clinic of a general practice', *Clinical Child Psychology and Psychiatry* 4(1): 9–22.

Elder, A. (1996) 'Moments of change', in H. Stewart (ed.) *Michael Balint: Object Relations, Pure and Applied*, London: Routledge.

Fonagy, P. (1998) 'Prevention: the appropriate target of infant psychotherapy', *Journal of Infant Mental Health* 19(2): 124–50.

Fraiberg, S., Adelson, E. and Shapiro, V. (1980) 'Ghosts in the nursery: a psycho-analytic approach', in S. Fraiberg (ed.) *Clinical Studies in Infant Mental Health*, London: Tavistock. (Now in paperback as *Assessment and Therapy of Disturbances in Infancy*, New York: Aronson, 1989.)

Holden, J. M., Sagovsky, R. and Cox, J. L. (1989) 'Counselling in a general practice setting: a controlled study of health visitor intervention in the treatment of postnatal depression', *British Medical Journal* 298: 223–6.

Hopkins, J. (1992) 'Infant–Parent Psychotherapy', *Journal of Child Psychotherapy* 18: 5–17.

—— (1994) 'Therapeutic interventions in infancy: two contrasting cases of persistent crying', *Psychoanalytic Psychotherapy* 8: 141–52.

Lieberman, A. and Pawl, J. (1993) 'Infant–Parent Psychotherapy', in C. H. Zeanah Jr. (ed.) *Handbook of Infant Mental Health*, New York: Guilford.

Miller, L. (1992) 'The relation of infant observation to clinical practice in an under fives counselling service', *Journal of Child Psychotherapy* 18(1): 19–32.

Miller, L., Rustin, M., Rustin, M. and Shuttleworth, J. (1989) *Closely Observed Infants*, London: Duckworth.

Murray, L. and Cooper, P. J. (1997) *Post-partum Depression and Child Development*, London: Guilford.

Stern, D. (1995) *The Motherhood Constellation*, New York: Basic Books.

Watillon, A. (1993) 'The dynamics of psychotherapeutic therapies of the early parent–child relationship', *International Journal of Psychoanalysis* 74: 1037–48.

Winnicott, D. W. (1971) 'Transitional objects and transitional phenomena', in *Playing and Reality*, London: Tavistock.

Part V
Special clinical interests

19 The treatment of traumatisation in children

Monica Lanyado

Traumatic experience, is by its very definition shocking, unexpected and not part of everyday predictable life. In the medical terminology from which the term originates, trauma refers to a wound or injury which is a consequence of external violence. Laplanche and Pontalis point out that

> in adopting the term [trauma], psycho-analysis carries the three ideas implicit in it over to the psychical level: the idea of violent shock, the idea of a wound and the idea of consequences affecting the whole organisation.
>
> (Laplanche and Pontalis 1988)

Traumatic experience has an essentially overwhelming impact on the mind, emotions and soul, after which the sufferer often feels that he or she will never be the same again. There can be a distinct sense of 'before' and 'after' the trauma, suggesting that the sense of safety and security which existed before the traumatic event has been lost or severely shaken, to be replaced by an abiding sense of fear together with raised or high levels of anxiety – often in the clear absence of any true external threat (unless there is repeated experience of trauma). The extreme levels of anxiety aroused are likely to be countered by desperate and extreme levels and types of defence (see Chapter 5). Traumatic experience encompasses the idea that the protective shield, which the person felt kept him or her safe in the world, has been shockingly breached and the pre-existing emotional means of facing fear, danger and loss have been swept away. This is a severe emotional wound which can be experienced as, and may in reality have been, life-threatening, rather than an emotional illness of the type that may be caused by difficult family relationships.

Clinical material from the psychoanalysis of adults is rich with examples of fantasies, thoughts and memories of past traumatic experience in which the balance between real traumatic events, fantasies that relate to these experiences and the vagaries of memories are all interwoven. This complexity has led to heated disagreements in the 'false memory' debate about adults' memories of childhood sexual abuse, which may not be very far removed from the controversy Freud encountered over his early theories about the role of sexual seduction in childhood and its importance in the aetiology of neurosis (Freud, S. 1898). The way in which traumatic memories are stored and recovered is pivotal to the treatment of trauma because the balance between remembering and forgetting is such a constant underlying theme in treatment. There is often a large grey area in which the sufferer may be very unsure about whether 'remembered' traumatic events happened or not.

In the course of treatment a reconstruction of 'what happened' may emerge, but this narrative may be rewritten many times in the patient's and therapist's minds. Reconstruction is not an end in itself in psychoanalysis, as is often portrayed in the movies, but improving the coherency of the narrative and trying to make sense of traumatic experience may be central to recovery. (This has interesting links to developments in attachment theory in which research has shown that emotional security is powerfully related to the coherency with which adults tell their life stories as opposed to the actual disruptions of attachment that they have suffered (Main *et al.* 1985).) It is what the traumatic experience has done to the sufferer's mind and emotions that is crucial. Traumatic experience, as child psychotherapists often see in multiply abused and traumatised children, can 'blow the mind'. Even in single event traumas, the effect on the internal world can be deeply destabilising.

By contrast to adult psychotherapists, child psychotherapists can work with children who are known to have suffered well-documented traumatic experiences – such as physical and sexual abuse, abandonment, the violent death of a parent, and serious accident or illness. Whilst many of the treatment issues are similar to those relating to adult patients, the impact of external reality is much more alive in child treatments because there is less doubt about what has actually happened. Perpetrators of abuse may have been imprisoned following carefully collected evidence from social workers, solicitors and the police; parents and doctors can describe the operations and painful treatments children have endured; teachers can confirm the child's emotional fragility following traumatisation. This can then be more readily responded to and distinguished from the way in which these external experiences have been perceived and processed (or importantly, often *not* processed) in their internal worlds.

Part of the debate that has taken place about trauma within psychoanalysis reflects the fact that 'traumatisation' can be used to describe a wide continuum of psychological states. These may range from mild to severe, the result of a one-off experience or of an accumulation of experiences, either acute or chronic. A traumatised child will usually be affected to varying degrees by a complex interaction of the following key factors:

1   *the impact of a shocking external event* such as the sudden death or threat of death of a parent, or a violent assault by an adult in which injury, real danger, and excessive fear are experienced by the child

2 *the personal and unique meaning* that this shocking event has for the child
3 *the pre-disposition of the child* to cope with the particular traumatic event(s), depending on his or her state of emotional well-being and resilience before the traumatic event
4 *the range, quality and intensity of the psychological defences* that have been used to cope with life following the traumatic event(s)
5 *the quality of past and current, external and internal relationships* that may help or hinder the child in living through the repercussions of the traumatisation.

Later in this chapter, the impact of trauma on two children will be described: $3\frac{1}{2}$-year-old Nancy who was witness to an armed robbery in her home (an example of an isolated acute traumatic event and its effects on Nancy's inner world and family life), and twelve-year-old Tony who was physically abused for many years by his father (an example of cumulative and chronic trauma and the unfortunate defences that can be used to survive it). Their treatments illustrate and contrast the influence of the developmental stage of the child at the time of the trauma, how the effect of the trauma can change as the child grows up, and the implications of the pre-existing attachment relationship between the child and the person who victimises him or her, on subsequent development. The question of early intervention and the possible limitation of the long-term effects of traumatisation is also raised. Nancy was seen by a psychotherapist a week after the armed robbery took place, whilst Tony did not have any therapy until he had suffered years of physical abuse and emotional cruelty.

It is possible that different forms of treatment intervention suit different periods of time after the trauma has taken place. For example it is possible that early treatment intervention may stop biochemical responses, which are appropriate for survival at the time of the trauma, becoming perpetuated into a more chronic and unneccesarily raised state of neural hyper-alertness to danger when the dangerous situation no longer pertains (Pynoos 1996; Perry *et al.* 1995). Links with neurophysiology are providing important information with regard to how to treat severely traumatised patients, as discussed later in this chapter. In some referrals, there may have been a number of distressing experiences which, whilst manageable on their own, build up to an intolerable and overwhelming degree that becomes traumatising (Khan 1963). In other referrals, children have suffered one awful traumatic event after another (see Chapters 20, 22, 23 and 26 in particular). Child psychotherapists may be involved with the immediate aftermath of large-scale traumatic events, such as war situations or natural catastrophes. They also see children and adolescents who suffered trauma many years before referral. For detailed examples of the treatment of traumatised children, see Almqvist and Broberg (1997), Grunbaum (1997), Hindle (1996), Hopkins (1986), Lanyado (1985) and Mendelsohn (1997).

Brief historical background

The impact of trauma on emotional life, has been a central consideration for psychoanalytic clinicians and theoreticians, since Freud started to develop his ideas together with Breuer, over one hundred years ago (Breuer and Freud 1893–5). The idea that traumatic childhood experience (which Freud came to believe to be of a sexual nature) could lead to neurotic disturbance in adult life was one of the factors that led to the direct treatment of children by Anna Freud and Melanie Klein amongst others. In 1905 Freud revised his view that real sexual seductions had taken place in his adult patients' childhoods, coming to the conclusion that these seductions were a product of conscious or unconscious fantasy life. This was stated clearly in 'Three essays on the theory of sexuality' (1905), in which the theory of the Oedipus complex was first expounded and the reality of sexual seduction in childhood was abandoned.

Influenced by this view, to some extent it would be fair to say that the psychoanalytic treatment of traumatisation in children from the 1920s through to the 1970s emphasised the 'internal world' of the child, and what the trauma had meant to the child as influenced by his fantasies. Whilst the importance of the external event that had prompted the child's disturbance was naturally recognised, it was what this meant in the child's internal world that was the key to treatment and, indeed, in many respects this remains the case. It was rare, at this time, to have a child referred for treatment because of sexual abuse or incest, or to work with a child who was known to come from a family in which generations of incestuous relationships were clearly established. In the 1990s, this is sadly no longer the case.

The type of referral started to change with the growing clinical recognition in the 1950s and '60s of the impact of physical abuse on babies and children (Kempe and Kempe 1978). During the 1980s, adult sexual interference with children became recognised as being much more widespread than had previously been thought probable. Interestingly, in Great Britain the public awareness of this issue was largely due to campaigning investigative journalism, which convinced not only the general public that sexual interference and abuse of children was in varying degrees a terrible and fairly common occurrence, but also stimulated debate and a great deal of anxious soul-searching within the Child and Family Mental Health services, where the verifiable external reality of actual sexual trauma had to be recognised, *in addition to* the internal reality of sexual fantasy. In the 1990s, services for the victims of trauma recognise the importance of fully acknowledging the reality of traumatic events (working through what actually happened to the child whilst taking care not to traumatise the child further in the process) as well as the internal world significance of the trauma.

From the 1980s onwards, as a result of the growing recognition of the verifiable nature of sexual abuse in particular, Child and Family Mental Health resources were transformed into centres where severely physically and sexually traumatised children claimed a high proportion of the therapeutic resources. Another very significant dynamic started to emerge. A young child would become known to a clinic or social services department because he or she had suffered appalling physical and sexual abuse, drawing great compassion from those who worked with him or her. But then as time went on, quite often as he or she entered puberty and adolescence, some of these victims of abuse would start to behave abusively towards others. Without a full understanding of the manner in which traumatic experience becomes transformed into traumatising behaviour, it is very difficult to make any sense of this dynamic. (Chapter 23 discusses this dynamic in greater detail.)

As the number of trained child and adolescent psychotherapists grew during the 1980s, a number of specialisations started to develop as a direct result of seeing the impact of trauma on child patients and a concern to lessen the impact that this had on healthy emotional development wherever possible. For example, some children who had been born prematurely or had been seriously ill during the neonatal period, resulting in hospitalisation at the start of life, were found to require treatment for the emotional repercussions of these experiences in later years (see Chapter 11).

Case study: Christine

A two and a half-year-old girl, Christine, was referred to the psychotherapist because of severe eating difficulties. Her mother said she barely ate unless mother literally dropped tiny offerings of specially prepared highly nutritious food into her mouth whenever she could catch her unaware. Christine had had severe feeding difficulties ever since a few days after her birth when she had nearly died because of an undiagnosed medical condition which had required several lengthy operations to correct. She had been tube fed (having previously been breast fed) for a number of weeks during her recovery and was now medically healthy. However, the impact of the trauma of her near death experience on Christine, and on her parents, had left deep-seated traumatisation concentrated around the area of feeding. Christine powerfully resisted eating and drinking in an ordinary way, and her mother remained terrified that she would die, this time from starvation because of her refusal to accept her food. The memory of how Christine had nearly died, which had initially become evident to her mother as she became weaker and weaker in her breast feeding, remained as vivid in the mother's mind as if it had only recently happened. This is a powerful indication of the traumatisation which had become deeply embedded in the mother–child relationship. This was further complicated by the ordinary battles for power and control which go on between many two-year-olds and their parents. Christine needed eighteen months of three-times-weekly treatment (during which time her parents had once-weekly help from a colleague) before her resilience and capacity to live could be believed in by her parents, and the battles over food subsided.

This type of clinical experience has led child psychotherapists working with babies, parents and staff in Intensive and Special Care Baby units to attempt to mitigate as much as possible the far-reaching effects of the traumatic physical and emotional experiences that the vulnerable baby, and its parents, have had to cope with at the start of their relationship (see Chapter 11). This has included trying to help mothers and babies cope with the consequences of separation in the first days of life, which research has suggested could at times lead to the 'battered baby' syndrome (Kempe and Kempe 1978; Klaus and Kennel 1982).

Children suffering from serious illnesses such as heart disease, diabetes and leukaemia have been recognised as sometimes developing psychological problems, often after the physical dangers have subsided, which are clear sequelae of the painful and frightening effects of their illnesses and the necessary treatment procedures (see 'Joanne' in Chapter 16). As a result of this recognition, child and adolescent psychotherapists now work in paediatric units (see Chapter 11). Importantly, in all cases where the parents have not contributed to the child's traumatic experience it has become clear that the parents have often also been traumatised by the events and need help to recover, both for themselves as individuals and in their capacity to parent and help their child to recover from the trauma.

In the following more detailed examples only the essential minimum of personal information will be given and the identities are deliberately disguised to protect the anonymity of patients and their families.

An armed robbery: Nancy and her family

The Smith family were referred for help one week after experiencing a robbery in the middle of the night by an armed gang in their home. Nancy was three and a half at the time and had been held at knifepoint by the gang to force her parents to open a small safe which contained jewellery. In the days that followed the robbery she kept bursting into prolonged and terrified screaming, from which her parents found it enormously difficult to comfort her. She was particularly upset each time she remembered her father's feet being tied up, and had become terrified of falling asleep, and of letting her father out of her sight. Not surprisingly, Nancy's parents were also very shocked by what had happened. The family had turned the home into 'Fort Knox' but still could not feel safe, particularly at night, and had great difficulty sleeping. Every little noise was felt to be an indication of a further attack.

During the first phase of treatment, which took the form of three lengthy (one-and-a-half to two-hour) consultations within days of each other, part of the time spent with the family as a whole and some time with Nancy on her own, the most intense fears relating to personal safety and the sleep disturbance started to abate. In her sessions, Nancy spontaneously spoke and played about her nightmares and other dreams, in which ghosts and monsters featured prominently. It was possible to connect her pre-existing age-appropriate dreams and nightmares with the terrifying reality of the night-time attack, and this seemed to help her.

A recovery process started and her parents regained some of their previously sound parenting ability to help their daughter when she was severely distressed and frightened. They felt they had received enough help in the three lengthy consultations to overcome the immediate impact of the robbery. However they also understood that there could be longstanding repercussions from the trauma which needed to be monitored, so we agreed that we would be in touch again in a few months' time.

By this time, Nancy had successfully started at nursery school and was felt to be a bright and normal child by the staff. She was still having difficulty sleeping through the night, although she was now able to go to sleep in her own bed again. In addition, because their home had become so associated with the robbery, the family decided to move house and this led to Nancy's father being temporarily without work. Nancy, although affected by all these changes, was nevertheless generally happy and settled and had not had any screaming attacks. As a result, there was intermittent phone contact with her parents but no further consultations for a number of months.

Fourteen months after the robbery, Nancy started to wake during the night, severely distressed in a way that she had not been since the robbery took place. However, rather than going to her parent's bed as she had done in the past, she got out of bed and stood rooted to the spot, screaming, biting and scratching herself in distress, and seemingly unable to move. Her parents phoned requesting another consultation. Although Nancy had not seen me for many months, she immediately told me about the dreams that she was having of terrifying ghosts that came to eat her. She described their disgusting faces and bodies in great detail and said that in the dream she could not run away from them. She knew there was a link with the robbery which she connected to her visits to me, but she didn't know what. She just knew that she needed to tell me about her dreams, as she stated clearly that she didn't want to tell mummy and daddy because she was worried they'd get upset by her memories of the robbery. Because of my previous knowledge of the family, I was able to connect Nancy's inability to run away in the dream, with my memory of how terrifying it had been for her when the robbers threatened her with the knife and she had had to keep absolutely still. In addition, I was able to link the terrifying, helpless sensation of not being able to move, with the immense distress Nancy had shown when she first came to see me whenever she thought of her father's feet being tied during the robbery.

I was then able to explain to her parents that when she was rooted to the spot, screaming at night, she was actually stuck in her nightmare and not just being demanding (as she could be in ordinary everyday life). Although it took a little while for these screaming attacks to stop, their intensity diminished following the relief of sharing the dream with me, and Nancy's parents became more able to comfort her and help her again. It was never clear what had triggered the renewed terrors relating to the robbery.

After the next follow-up appointment, eighteen months after the robbery Nancy and her parents decided to come for fortnightly therapy sessions to help them deal with further repercussions of the robbery on their family life. Nancy was very clear that whenever she felt unduly frightened she needed to see her therapist, and she seemed to arrive with her own agenda of what she needed to talk about relating to the robbery. She felt safe knowing that I was there for her if she needed to talk in this way, as did her parents, although, as time went on, she had less and less of a need to talk about dreams, feelings and memories related to the trauma and often simply used the sessions to play in an age-appropriate way. Because of the episodic and long-term nature of this particular treatment, therapy is effectively still ongoing and seems to offer the family a form of encapsulation of their residual thoughts and fears about the trauma which enables them to 'get on with life'.

In this example, Nancy and her family were helped through the acute stage of traumatisation by three lengthy consultations within days of each other. This improvement may well have been a result of the closeness in time to the trauma that treatment was offered – one week after it had happened, as well as the fact that the whole family directly experienced the trauma and could try to process the experience together. In addition, the healthy family relationships, and Nancy's sound emotional development prior to the robbery, contributed to the family's resilience.

The way in which the consultations became spaced out in the second, more long-term phase of the treatment was the result of a constant concern in the treatment of the traumatisation, for trying to work out a balance between how much to remember and how much to forget. Talking too much about what had happened threatened to disrupt the healing processes that were taking place, but *not* talking about the connection between the robbery and Nancy's later nightmares would have deprived her of the opportunity to understand and think about her terror, rather than be swept away by it. In therapy, this is a constant clinical and ethical issue (for further discussion of this, see Alvarez 1992 and Lanyado 1985). This ebb and flow of traumatic memories and overwhelming feelings often leads to treatment of traumatisation being episodic because it is so prone to being reactivated by chance associations, major life events and, particularly in children, each new stage of emotional development.

Trauma is inevitably experienced through the filter of the child's current stage of development. For Nancy, the traumatic experience came when she had a limited command of language and was in the midst of an ordinary three-year-old's fears of monsters and ghosts – fantasies from her internal world, which were vividly present in her dream world before the robbery, and unfortunately confirmed by external reality when the robbers attacked in the middle of the night.

In some instances, the full implications of trauma may not be perceived until the child becomes an adolescent or even an adult. It can be bewildering when traumatic experience resurfaces, having been thought to be long 'forgotten' or dealt with. Often it is not clear what has triggered the re-evoking, or even first clear memories, of past traumas. In other cases, possibly particularly with sexual abuse, there are some clearly vulnerable life stages such as the first adolescent sexual relationship, childbirth – or simply seeing a baby's genitals when changing the nappy. In situations such as these, parents who have been traumatised before their child was born, can be greatly affected in their ability to care for their children. This is one of the mechanisms for the inter-generational transmission of traumatic experience.

A mother, who was severely sexually abused by her mother as a child, could barely tolerate changing her baby's nappy. She was conscientious in many respects, wanting to overcome her unhappy childhood experiences and to give her daughter a happier childhood than she had had, but when it came to potty training she became excessively punitive with her daughter, screaming at her and hitting her when she could not use the potty. The mother did not understand this, and could not stop herself, although she felt very guilty about her behaviour. The daughter remained incontinent well into adolescence, became very disturbed and had a deeply troubled relationship with her parents. Fortunately this mother was able to seek help for her daughter, but it was only well into the daughter's intensive treatment that the mother was able to talk about her own childhood sexual trauma to her therapist. This information helped the whole clinical picture to make sense, and the daughter was freed from her mother's projections and was able to start to make a recovery, whilst the mother was offered more intensive help with the repercussions of what had happened to her so many years before.

'Second generation traumatisation', as it is known, may lie behind a number of otherwise incomprehensible emotional disturbances in children. The children do not know the nature of the traumatic memories they evoke in their parents, but may nevertheless be aware of their parent's fragility through glimpses of traumatic or incomprehensible fragments of behaviour in their everyday interactions. The children may be aware of 'no go' areas in otherwise communicative parents' emotional lives. Therapists are often aware of a 'missing link' that would help them to make sense of a confusing clinical picture. This has been written about with regard to traumatic experience in general (Pynoos 1996), as well as specifically in accounts of second generation holocaust survivors (Bergman and Jucovy 1982), and in relationship to sexual abuse (Welldon 1989).

The traumatic impact of physical abuse leading to violent behaviour: Tony

Tony grew up in an atmosphere of marital violence and was often severely beaten by his mother and father. The degree of violence within the family was so awful that when he started treatment, as a twelve-year-old he spoke about clear memories of trying to cut his wrists in the middle of a row between his parents, in the hope of diverting them from their physical fighting – he had been five years old at the time. As well as there being concerns that he had been physically abused and cruelly treated, he had become very aggressive and this was causing increasing concern at his school.

In his therapy sessions, it gradually emerged that he had been extremely vicious towards his three-year-old brother. He described in a casual throwaway line, that when his brother 'bugged' him, he would throw him across the room against the wall. He thought it was funny that his brother was severely bruised and then screamed and yelled, getting into trouble with his mum for all the noise and fuss he was making. Tony saw nothing unusual in his behaviour, as he was, after all, only doing what had been done to him so often by his parents, and was now big enough to do it in turn to someone more helpless than himself. His parents had also minimised the impact of their violence on their son, and in this as well he was merely identifying with their behaviour.

This callousness and cruelty stood in stark contrast to his painful and distressed accounts of his fear of being hit and punched by his parents, and how deeply rejected and unloved he felt by this. In therapy he had even been able to reflect on how he thought proper parents ought to bring up their kids, and that when he was a Dad he would never do to his kids what his Dad had done to him. He was unable to see how his actions towards his younger brother could be the antecedents to hitting his own children. He was already attributing blame to his brother for 'bugging' him. When stating that he (his brother) was only getting what he deserved in punishment, he was using the same words he had heard his parents use when they said that he (Tony) deserved the beatings he got because he was 'bad'.

After a particularly difficult therapy session, Tony started to see that he had got a problem with controlling his aggression, and that he was already in danger of enacting exactly what had happened to him. He was stunned and shocked when he eventually was able to see what he was doing. This was a big step forward in his therapy, involving the expression of a great deal of anger and hostility towards his therapist for daring to suggest that he could possibly resemble this despised aspect of his father.

An important dynamic when working with patients who have started to traumatise others is the preparedness of the therapist to recognise the trauma victim behind the traumatising behaviour. Indeed, a number of authors stress that until the therapist has experienced their patient's trauma 'in an attenuated form' (Bergman and Jucovy 1982; Hodges *et al*. 1994) within the context of the therapeutic relationship, and felt genuinely shocked by what the patient has experienced, the patient cannot start to work on the problem of their own traumatising behaviour. This is not an excuse for a patient to avoid taking responsibility for his or her actions; indeed this is one of the issues at the heart of how to metabolise the traumatic experiences in a manner which is not an anti-social 'acting out' or discharging of the trauma into and onto other people, but does not then alternatively remain intolerably and painfully stuck within the self.

The process of 'identification with the aggressor' is central to the conversion of traumatic experience into behaviour that becomes traumatising for others. It is a combination of a defence against overwhelming anxiety and distress due to the traumatic event, and the tendency that traumatic events have of repeating themselves in an uncanny way in traumatised people's lives. For example, for Tony, being sadistically beaten by his parents and witnessing marital violence was traumatising. He might have found a similar situation kept recurring in his life, possibly by being physically abused and beaten up, or cruelly treated in his adult relationships, or he could have suffered from terrible nightmares about his mistreatment as a child in which he felt he kept reliving the horror he had gone through. As it was, he defended himself against his anxiety about the trauma by reversing the roles and identifying with his abusive parents. He told himself that they were 'right' and he was 'wrong'. In this way, rather than passively experiencing the trauma, he actively perpetrated it. Bentovim (1992) argues that males are more likely to 'externalise' trauma, by this form of identification with the aggressor, whilst women are more likely to 'internalise' their distress, leading to problems such as severe depression, suicidal acts and eating disorders. (For further discussion of this process, see Chapter 23 and Hodges *et al*. 1994.)

This, in turn, links with another important dynamic in the therapeutic relationship with traumatised patients, in which the therapist is at times perceived by the patient in the transference relationship as becoming traumatising or even abusive. In the above example, by pressing the point about Tony's violent behaviour towards his brother, the therapist trod a narrow line between putting too much pressure on Tony to face his actions, or letting him avoid an issue which he was nevertheless tangentially and importantly bringing to therapy. When the therapist chose to press the point, Tony did initially feel attacked by her and became very angry and potentially aggressive (see Hodges *et al.* 1994 for a fuller account of this issue). However, he was at a stage in his therapy where he was starting to trust his therapist and listen to her and so he was able to work through this 'abusive' aspect of the transference relationship, which seemed to repeat on a verbal level what he had gone through when his parents attacked him physically. This aspect of the transference relationship can be particularly challenging for the therapist and requires careful work in the counter-transference to ensure that the therapist is not reacting to the patient, as opposed to thinking through the difficult abuser–abused/persecutor–victim transference process. This uncomfortable dynamic is similar to the therapist's concern not to retraumatise the patient by encouraging too much discussion and remembering of the trauma, whilst being aware that too little awareness of the trauma can become an unhelpful avoidance of therapeutic responsibility.

It is important to note that identification with the aggressor is more likely to take place if there is, however flawed, an attachment relationship with the aggressor (mother and father), as in Tony's case, than when there is no relationship with the aggressor, as in Nancy's case. All trauma involves threats to survival, or the feared loss of an attachment figure, which in itself is a threat to a child's emotional, as well as physical, survival (see Chapter 4). When the child victim is also dependent on the adult aggressor, there is a clear conflict in the child's mind because anger towards the aggressor cannot be expressed for fear of abandonment by the attachment figure as well as fear of further attack. It may be pragmatically safer and more life preserving in the short term to identify with the aggressor as being in the 'right', with the child victim in the 'wrong', than to allow oneself to be in touch with the victimisation that is taking place in the relationship.

Whilst there are some traumatised people who feel they cannot get the trauma out of their minds, there are others who have been traumatised and who find it strange that they can barely remember highly significant life events – such as the sudden death of a parent when they were a child. They seem to have been able to avoid the invasion of their internal world by overwhelmingly painful memories, but possibly at a different cost to their emotional life – such as a general restriction of emotionality in key areas of mental life, or sudden eruptions of odd behaviour which, if explored in therapy, have a root in the traumatic past which cannot be thought about. These people have used the defence of 'dissociation' from the traumatic event so that it almost feels as if it did not happen to them at all, and yet they know that in reality it did. They have managed to absent themselves from their minds and bodies by creating a form of split within their mental lives.

The form of defence that an individual uses at the time of experiencing trauma is likely to be related to their characteristic ways of defending themselves against anxiety prior to the traumatic event – hence the significance in the process of recovery of the comparative healthiness of emotional life before trauma takes place – as seen in Nancy's treatment. This helps to explain why different people will respond to the same external trauma in different ways. Here, we again have the complex interaction between the external traumatic event and the internal world, as coloured by the individual's characteristic defensive strategies against emotional pain and their pre-existing object relationships (see Chapter 5). It is for this reason that treatment is likely to be lengthy with children such as Tony. His poor relationships with his natural parents on a day-to-day basis (which would in any case have adversely affected his emotional development) made him less able to recover from the trauma of their physical attacks on him.

'Tony' is similar to many abused youngsters at puberty who are at a pivotal point in their aggressive and social development. Hopefully, treatment helped him to work through his traumatic experiences of violence so that he did not become fixed in his own violent behaviour through identification with the aggressor, but it is probably too soon to be sure of this at present. Many young offenders who commit crimes of violence have histories of severe physical abuse. There is a point in their development when they have turned from victim to aggressor, and this is most obvious during puberty and adolescence. Where does moral responsibility enter into the equation and how should the courts wisely deal with young offenders who have been so severely offended against such a short time before their convictions?

The implications of neurophysiological research on the treatment of trauma

The growing body of neurophysiological research is a timely reminder of the connection between brain function, physiology and traumatic experience. Fear and terror produce clearly measurable physical responses. Memories of terrifying traumatic experience in the absence of any external danger can produce the same effect (Perry 1993). The impact of such intense neurophysiological responses on a baby or young child's immature body and mind when they experience the terror of attack or threatened attack, sometimes from the people that they simultaneously look to for protection, is now being recognised. Particularly when a child such as Tony lives in an environment which is frequently dangerous, a heightened state of alertness and sensitivity to danger can become perpetuated within the child's brain and bodily functioning, even when the external threat finally ceases. These important findings provide a neurophysiological basis for the extremes of violent reactivity seen in traumatised children in therapy (see Chapter 22). Perry *et al.* (1995) describe in detail how these neurophysiologically recordable states of mind, can become established character traits in children and in adults.

This fascinating connection serves to remind us that we are body and mind inextricably working together, and that we are propelled into our most primitive survival responses of fear, fight or flight when faced with real danger. Neurophysiological research gives some important pointers for the treatment of traumatisation in children. If children have become neurophysiologically hypersensitised and over-reactive to danger as a result of traumatic events, this suggests that unnecessary stimulation of memories related to the event will further stimulate or reinforce these states. This, in turn, suggests that patients who feel that they do not want to be *'unnecessarily'* reminded of the trauma by their therapist, may be absolutely right in this insistence. But the crucial issue is how to judge what is *'necessary'* remembering of traumatic events. Without the courage to face these terrifying memories and feelings, no connection can be made between overwhelming fear and its causes, and the consequences of trauma in the past cannot be defused in the present. Perhaps the wisest policy is for the therapist to be highly responsive and sensitive to the eruptions of traumatic memories as they inevitably occur in ongoing treatment, but not actively to search for them without some indication that the patient is already approaching them on a pre-conscious level – as with Tony when he spontaneously described how he attacked his younger brother.

The only way in which it is possible to recover from trauma is when, gradually, the traumatic past can be let go of – which is *not* the same as forgetting – so that the child can live as much as possible in the present and feel that he or she can have a more hopeful future. The painful memories and feelings will come of their own accord and must be fully encountered within the therapeutic relationship as they occur. But in the periods which are comparatively free of these terrible shadows, it is vital that as much development as possible, of emotional life and positive family relationships, is encouraged. This emphasis within the therapeutic relationship enables the child gradually to recover and discover new, hopeful and enjoyable experiences and relationships which are not overshadowed by the past.

References

Almqvist, K. and Broberg A. (1997) 'Silence and survival: working with strategies of denial in families of traumatised pre-school children', *Journal of Child Psychotherapy* 23(3): 47–35.

Alvarez, A. (1992) *Live Company: Psychoanalytic Psychotherapy with Autistic, Borderline, Deprived and Abused Children*, London: Routledge.

Bentovim, A. (1992) *Trauma Organised Systems: Physical and Sexual Abuse in Families*, London: Karnac.

Bergman, M. S. and Jucovy M. E. (1982) *Generations of the Holocaust*, New York: Basic Books.

Breuer, J. and Freud, S. (1893–5) *Studies in Hysteria, Standard Edition*, Vol. 2, London: Hogarth Press.

Freud, S. (1898) 'Sexuality in the aetiology of the neuroses', *Standard Edition*, Vol. 3, London: Hogarth Press.

—— (1905) 'Three essays on the theory of sexuality', *Standard Edition*, Vol. 2, London: Hogarth Press.

—— (1914) 'Remembering, repeating and working through', *Standard Edition*, Vol. 7, London: Hogarth Press.

Grunbaum, L. (1997) 'Psychotherapy with children in refugee families who have survived torture: containment and understanding of repetitive behaviour and play', *Journal of Child Psychotherapy* 23(3): 437–52.

Hindle, D. (1996) 'Doubly bereaved', *Journal of Child Psychotherapy* 22(2): 261–78.

Hodges, J., Lanyado, M. and Andreou, C. (1994) 'Sexuality and violence: preliminary clinical hypotheses from the psychotherapeutic assessments in a research programme on young sexual offenders', *Journal of Child Psychotherapy* 20(3): 283–308.

Hopkins, J. (1986) 'Solving the mystery of monsters: steps towards the recovery from trauma', *Journal of Child Psychotherapy* 12(1): 61–71.

Kempe, R. S. and Kempe, J. H. (1978) *Child Abuse*, London: Fontana.

Khan, M. M. R. (1963) 'The concept of cumulative trauma', in M. M. R. Khan (1974) *The Privacy of the Self*, New York: International Universities Press.

Klaus, M. H. and Kennel, J. H. (1982) *Maternal-infant Bonding*, 2nd edn, St. Louis MD: Mosby.

Lanyado, M. (1985) 'Surviving trauma: dilemmas in the psychotherapy of traumatised children', *British Journal of Psychotherapy* 2(1): 50–62.

Laplanche, J. and Pontalis, J. -B. (1988) *The Language of Psychoanalysis*, London: Karnac/Institute of Psycho-Analysis.

Main, M., Kaplan, K. and Cassidy, J. (1985) 'Security in infancy, childhood and adulthood: a move to the level of representation', in I. Bretherton and E. Waters (eds) *Growing points of attachment theory and research: Monographs of the Society for Research in Child Development* 50: 66–104.

Mendelsohn, A. (1997) 'Pervasive traumatic loss from AIDS in the life of a four year old African boy', *Journal of Child Psychotherapy* 23(3): 399–415.

Perry, B. D. (1993) 'Medicine and psychotherapy. Neuro-development and the neurophysiology of trauma 11: clinical work along the alarm–fear–terror continuum', *The Advisor, American Professional Society on the Abuse of Children* (Summer 1993) 6(2): 15–18.

Perry, B. D., Pollard, R., Blakley, T., Baker, W. and Vigilant, D. (1995) 'Childhood trauma, the neurobiology of adaptation and "user-dependent" development of the brain: how "states" become "traits"', *Infant Mental Health Journal* (winter 1995) 16(4): 271–91.

Pynoos, R. S. (1996) 'The transgenerational repercussions of traumatic expectations', paper given at 6th IPA conference on psychoanalytic research, UCL, 8–9 March 1996.

Welldon, E. (1989) *Mother, Madonna, Whore*, London: Heinemann.

Further reading

Grunbaum, L. (1997) 'Psychotherapy with children in refugee families who have survived torture: containment and understanding of repetitive behaviour and play', *Journal of Child Psychotherapy* 23(3): 437–52.

Hopkins, J. (1986) 'Solving the mystery of monsters: steps towards the recovery from trauma', *Journal of Child Psychotherapy* 12(1): 61–71.

Lanyado, M. (1985) 'Surviving trauma: dilemmas in the psychotherapy of traumatised children', *British Journal of Psychotherapy* 2(1): 50–62.

Perry, B. D., Pollard, R., Blakley, T., Baker, W. and Vigilant, D. (1995) 'Childhood trauma, the neurobiology of adaptation and "user-dependent" development of the brain: how "states" become "traits"', *Infant Mental Health Journal* (winter 1995) 16(4): 271–91.

20 Deprivation and children in care

The contribution of child and adolescent psychotherapy

Carol Hughes

What is believed to be essential for mental health is that the infant and young child should experience a warm, intimate and continuous relationship with his mother (or permanent mother-substitute) in which both find satisfaction and enjoyment.

(Bowlby 1952)

Joanna is a thin, pale, seven-year-old who comes too readily, too easily with me into the therapy room. At the same time she is wary and suspicious. As therapy progresses I learn the full extent of her distrust and the measures she takes to protect herself, and to persuade herself that she does not need to be close to anyone. She is often angry, breaks all the rules, swears volubly and profanely and sometimes shouts in rage that she hates me and could not care less about me, her foster parents or her social worker. At school she is unable to concentrate or settle to school work. At playtime she is often to be found scrapping with other children or bullying them. Parents of the other children have been to the school to complain. The foster parents despair, feeling that she does not seem to respond to their love and concern. Their attempts to provide a caring home are met with abuse, rebellion and outright scorn by this tiny child.

They begin to question whether they are the right family for her. Maybe there is a better family more able to meet Joanna's needs 'somewhere out there'? They feel they are failing as parents and are bewildered and hurt by Joanna's rejection of them. They, in turn, become angry and rejecting.

Joanna has already had two foster family breakdowns. The last family also felt rejected and hurt by her. The family before that were found by Social Services to be neglectful and even possibly abusive of Joanna.

The story does not end there, however. As one goes further into Joanna's past one finds a long history of neglect by her natural parents, marital discord and breakdown, and frequent periods in care as her very young mother struggled to cope with three little children on her own. Joanna's mother spent years in care, herself, and has never had a steady adult relationship. Despite her avowed intentions to give her children the care and consistency lacking in her own childhood, she was unable to care for her three children. When they were with her she would find herself shaking and hitting the children in frustrated rage. Joanna spent her early years shuttling between her mother and father, short and then longer periods in foster homes and a brief spell in a children's home. There were numerous attempts by Social Services to provide sufficient support to either her mother or her father to enable her to live with her natural family. Father disappeared from Joanna's life when she was four. There were many failed attempts to return her home to her mother, until Social Services took out a care order, and sought an alternative substitute family for her.

The details describing 'Joanna' have been changed to protect her identity, but her story is one which is replicated over and over by all too many children in care.

The story illustrates the complexity of the term 'deprivation'. Certainly Joanna was deprived of the 'warm, intimate continuous relationship' with her mother. There was little (but some) mutual satisfaction and enjoyment. However, Joanna was also deprived of a similar relationship with her father or siblings. She suffered abuse and neglect, a multiplicity of carers and the consequences of well-meaning but misguided attempts to rehabilitate her home. Even before the actual physical disruption of attachments, there were evident distortions in the attachment to her mother, who herself has a tragic attachment history.

As with so many children in care, Joanna presents with distrustful, shallow, easily broken or anxious avoidant attachments. Her activity level is fuelled by chronic, unfocused anxiety, leaving her overactive, with poor concentration and attention. She has an aggressive need not to be dependant on or close to anyone. To be close feels much too dangerous for her. She comes across as tough, not caring. She challenges carers and teachers, often deliberately flouting rules, provoking confrontation with adults and children. Children like Joanna may often be actually aggressive or violent. They arouse strong feelings of hatred, despair and rejection in carers – projections of their own powerful feelings of hopelessness and sense of rejection.

Clinical aspects of psychotherapy with children in care

A recently published summary of research into family placements for children states:

> it is . . . difficult to reverse the harmful effects of early adverse experiences on children themselves. Long-term . . . therapy is likely to be needed by children who have suffered early harm, wherever they are placed. . . In one of the studies reported in Messages from Research, Gibbons (1995) conclude from an evaluation of children eight years after they were physically abused or neglected when under the age of 5,

that on average their well-being was lower than that of a matched sample of children who had not been abused . . . It cannot be assumed that when the abuse has stopped and adequate parenting is provided, early harm will be reversed.

(Sellick and Thoburn 1996: 25)

That is, provision of alternative families and the opportunity for security and new attachments is not sufficient to reverse the damage of early experiences. There will be long-reaching effects on an individual's emotional life and ability to form relationships and in turn to provide secure parenting for their own children. Individual psychotherapy will often be necessary to address deep-seated consequences of disturbed attachments, abuse and neglect.

Boston and Szur's book *Psychotherapy with Severely Deprived Children* (1983) remains a definitive text for child psychotherapists working in this area. The book arose from the findings of the psychotherapy of eighty children, discussed at the Fostering and Adoption workshop at the Tavistock Clinic. Many of the clinical insights remain as relevant today as when it was first written in 1983. 'Feelings aroused in working with severely deprived children' (Chapter 15) is just one example. In this chapter Hoxter states that emotional reactions to severely deprived children are

likely to be very strong and whether we be therapists or substitute parents, we are liable to find aroused in ourselves defenses which are not dissimilar to those of the . . . children. Full awareness of the child's loss and suffering is very often nearly as intolerable to us as it is to the child and, like the child, we are tempted to use many ways of distancing ourselves . . . or to diminish the significance of loss . . . We require to be vigilant that we are not drawn into playing a part in the 'cycle of deprivation'.

(Hoxter 1983: 126)

Many carers and workers with deprived children have found it a relief to be able to acknowledge their painful and often negative reactions to the children in their care. Gianna Henry describes how many deprived children prevent closeness within current relationships through rejecting, aggressive behaviour. As such, they are doubly deprived – deprived both in their families of origin, and, later in life, through defensive mechanisms which distance or alienate people who try to become close to them (Henry 1988).

Children are in care for many diverse reasons. These experiences will always include an element of parental deprivation, whether from inadequate and/or abusive parenting or tragic circumstances, loss or death. Very often the precipitating events leading to reception into care are only the end of a lengthy experience of neglect, trauma or abuse. In virtually all cases there will be severe impairments of attachment on both the natural parents' as well as the child's part.

The therapist's relationship with the care network

Here, as in no other area of psychotherapy with children, the therapist needs to be constantly aware of both the internal world of the child and his or her current external reality. It is crucial that the child's needs for a permanent and stable family placement are constantly kept in focus.

The work with children in care demands a particular ability from the child psychotherapist to keep in mind both the internal psychodynamics of the individual child as well as the often complex dynamics of the care network. This is so, even if the therapist is fortunate enough to have a dedicated co-worker to work directly with the child's family and care system. This latter remains the best possible practice. Such a co-worker provides the link between the work of psychotherapy and the child's day-to-day life, and helps to manage the ramifications of the child's care situation. This allows a thinking and working space for the child and therapist to address the internalised aspects of the child's experiences. Unfortunately such valued co-working is becoming a rarity in these days of public sector cut-backs and scarce resources.

For the child in care, the effectiveness of the liaison between the therapist and what is often a very complicated care network can be crucial to the viability of the psychotherapy, as well as being extremely important in the overall care plan of the child, to prevent further traumatisation and unnecessary loss. It may be axiomatic, but it is worth stating and restating that a child's primary needs are for a permanent, stable family. As therapists we have to be aware that psychotherapy cannot provide all the emotional needs for the child. However, many children have the unfortunate (if not tragic) experience of frequent moves from foster family to foster family with the only emotional continuity in life being provided by the psychotherapist.

I have found it important for the child psychotherapist to place herself strategically within the care network in order to have the best possible impact on decision-making about the child, so that permanency needs are not obscured and lost. Many children experience 'care' as a prolonged state of transition – drifting from one temporary placement to another for most of their childhood, never given the chance to form permanent attachments. One of the factors which can muddy long-term thinking is the belief (and subsequent relief) within the child care system that the child's emotional needs are being met through psychotherapy. As therapists we need to guard against this – children need families first and psychotherapists second.

Margaret Hunter (1993) describes her practice of working over many years in a local authority with children in care. She insists on attending Child in Care Reviews for all the children in psychotherapy in order to keep the question of permanency of placement alive. She makes the point that sometimes, with changes of social workers and a lessening of anxiety about the child's difficult behaviour, the long-term perspective of the child's placement needs can get lost and that it may be the therapist's role to keep this alive and in focus during the child's treatment.

A related question is that of the timing of psychotherapy for children in care. It has long been conventional wisdom that a contra-indication for therapy is the placement of a child in short-term foster care. Hunter found, in her experience over ten years, that refusal to treat a child in short-term foster care does not lead to earlier placement in a permanent family. She found little difference in the length of psychotherapy between those children in temporary or long-term placements. In a breakdown of thirty cases, the average length of therapy for those in temporary care was one year ten months; for those in permanent care it was two years six months. She makes the point that children in care may spend a third of their childhood waiting – waiting for their permanent families, waiting for therapy. Much of their life goes by in this state, as if what is happening now is not reality. She argues for the provision of psychotherapy even if a child is placed in temporary care in order to help them with this uncertainty and limbo state and to make the best use of current relationships and opportunities.

It is important to be aware of both the internal psychodynamics of the individual child and the complex dynamics within the care network. It is all too easy for the child's unique perspective to be lost in the complexities and conflicts inherent in legal and care issues.

The child psychotherapist offers a unique contribution to the overall picture. The internal world of the child will be both impinged upon and, in turn, act on the care system. In my experience, I have found that the child's view and unique perceptions and experiences are not directly sought and are quite often missing in psychiatric consultations which focus solely on the network issues. An understanding of the often active contribution of a child's distress, defences and acting out can facilitate better functioning of the care network.

At the point of referral for psychotherapy it is important to ask the question 'Why? Why therapy and why now?' Unless one addresses this question in a way which takes account of the whole system one may enact system difficulties in a way that can make things more difficult for the child. Sandra's social worker was insistent on psychotherapy for this distressed seven-year-old who had recently been placed in foster care, after some excellent social work input. The social worker was the one who had removed Sandra from her drug abusing, chronically neglectful mother. Because of this she was the recipient of all Sandra's rage and distress. She felt overwhelmed by the child's distress and began to doubt whether her decision really was best for the girl. She wanted therapy to alleviate this distress. The foster mother acquiesced to the referral, but it soon became clear that she was deeply suspicious of therapy. She wished Sandra to settle into the family, and believed that a good stable home would be sufficient to help the girl. In addition, she was worried that raking up the past would make things worse for Sandra. She did not express this – foster parents are felt to be of lower status in the Social Services' hierarchy than social workers.

It was helpful for the social worker to realise just how much she was being blamed by the child for all the previous neglect and failures of parenting in the child's life. She was helped, through consultation, to work through her responses to the child and answer what were, after all, questions properly addressed to her by the little girl. We also worked with the two adults on the anomaly that while the social worker was the legal parent of a child on a care order, it was the foster mother who undertook the actual care of the child and who has a parental investment in the child's future (and psychotherapy). After these pieces of work were done, a psychotherapy assessment was undertaken, during which the foster mother was relieved to find that not only did Sandra value the chance to talk to the therapist about her mother, it helped her be more open and trusting of her foster mother.

In child psychotherapy in general, the issue of liaison with parents and carers has undergone major change. Child psychotherapists are increasingly working in flexible and creative ways with parents and carers (Klauber 1998). It is no longer considered good practice for child psychotherapists to be solely closeted away with a child behind closed doors with little or no contact with parents. This earlier model of psychodynamic work was probably based upon the model of psychoanalytic practice with adults where there is a singular relationship between the therapist and the patient. In adult work, the adult patient is left to negotiate the external world in his or her own right. Increasingly, however, this is felt to be inappropriate with child work and we are working very much more with the child's context of care, whether it is with the natural family or a wider social or care network surrounding the child. This is particularly so for children who are in care and who are surrounded by extremely complex systems which need to be understood and taken into account at every stage of the child's therapy.

Monica Lanyado (1998) describes the combination of individual and family work she undertook with a five-year-old child who made the move from foster care to adoption during psychotherapy. In the course of psychotherapy she came to understand the depth of the hurt he experienced through rejection. This hurt was very powerfully conveyed through his rejection of his foster mother and, later, adoptive parents. Without the therapeutic input to help the adults understand and bear this projection of his most painful feelings his family placements would have broken down, as others had done before.

Some themes in psychotherapy

Jill Hodges (1984) talks of the two central questions of adopted children: 'Who were my first parents?' and 'Why did they give me up?' A third question for children in foster care is 'Where do I belong?' Or, all too often, 'Will I ever have a family of my own?'

Hodges points to the wish of adopted children to know about their origins – a wish often kept secret, with consequent elaborate fantasies constructed around this. The child may keep quiet, sensing reluctance on the adoptive parents' part to discuss the matter, or because of a joint wish by both child and parents to foster the illusion that the child does not have a different background from the adoptive parents – to ensure belonging to a new family. Because of the secrecy, these fantasies cannot be tested out against reality and the fantasies may become elaborated, sometimes in bizarre ways. A wish for knowledge about one's origins, about one's natural parents is, in part, a search for identity. Hodges quotes from child and adult adoptees 'a girl who didn't know who she was because she didn't know who her parents were' and 'if I had some description of my birth parents it might help me to recognise myself' (Hodges 1984: 51).

So many children who *have* known their birth parents have to struggle with unwelcome or painful knowledge and memories. Many children I have worked with in psychotherapy struggle to keep accurate knowledge at bay. If a parent is a sexual abuser, or has mental illness, or is cruel and neglecting, what kind of identification is possible for the child? All too often abused children identify with the aggressor and become violent and abusive themselves (see chapters on trauma, sexual abuse and abusers).

Wesley was a nine-year-old boy who had been severely physically abused – from as young as two months of age. He had spent years in and out of his natural family, and was finally placed in foster care at seven years old. His younger brother had never been abused and remained with the natural parents. Wesley had experienced repeated foster family breakdowns because of his aggressive and violent behaviour. In therapy he maintained that the abuse was all his fault. He had taken responsibility for, and identified with, his parents' cruelty so as not to lose them emotionally. He had a very strong, ambivalent attachment to them and a fierce loyalty towards them. As with so many children, he wished to protect idealised memories of his natural parents. This prevented him from making any emotional investment in foster carers. He acted the part of a difficult and unlovable little boy – this was preferable to facing the loss and emotional separation that would be entailed if he should acknowledge his parents' cruelty towards him. At the same time he was consumed with barely conscious rage and a sadistic wish for revenge against his parents – often displaced and enacted against other children or foster parents.

One day in therapy he told me a 'true story' that he had heard, which illustrates his complex identifications. That week two new, smaller children had been placed in his foster family. In the 'true story' a woman lives in a cottage with two babies. She answers the telephone to a man who says he is coming to kill the babies. She rushes upstairs to find them already dead, with blood everywhere. She goes downstairs to telephone the police, only to come upon the man on the stairs. She drives a knife into his head and kills him. In the story Wesley is identified both with the killer (he wishes to destroy the new children, and his brother left at home) and with the victims. As such he feels he is entitled to take violent revenge, as did the woman in the story.

Some time later in therapy a somewhat more realistic and hopeful scenario ensues. He tells the story of a puppy dog that is badly beaten by its owners. It cannot get away. It is too little and too frightened. It is kept in a cupboard, the door blocked by the broom handle, with which it is beaten. One day, someone forgets to replace the broom handle and the little dog runs free. 'It runs away across green fields to find a new family.' Sometimes there is much work to be done to enable such children to begin to believe that new non-abusive families and relationships are available to be run towards.

Psychotherapy with such children is demanding and distressing. So much of the work entails containing the child's projections of hopelessness – projections also forcibly felt within the wider care network, and which are frequently at the root of foster breakdown. There are frequently massive projections by the child of hatred and despair: a deeply-held belief that human relationships are intrinsically cruel, violent and destructive. These projections are very hard to bear both for therapist and family; it can be difficult to retain a belief in the value of relationships.

Psychotherapy with Wesley needed to disentangle his defensive identification with the aggressor (he could feel less terrified and vulnerable in the face of abuse if he believed that he, too, was a cruel, powerful figure), and his acceptance of parental projections that he was a bad, unlovable boy.

Typically, children of mentally ill parents also struggle with establishing a sense of themselves in the face of very powerful projections from their parent. These children in psychotherapy seem not to have a separate sense of themselves, their own thoughts and feelings. For example, I worked with a 10-year-old boy of a schizophrenic parent who had presented with autistic traits. He had no friends and there was a question of special education. We spent a year in psychotherapy doing what I thought was very little – rather repetitive games of shunting a car back and forth between us.

However, I observed his changing moods very closely and would reflect them back to him. After a year of psychotherapy he came excitedly into the room and said, 'I've just realised that I can think my own thoughts. I can have my own mind!' He then told me in great detail how he had always felt that he and his mother had the same mind, and how much he had hated and feared it. Now two years on in therapy he is doing very well, has plenty of friends and is well thought of in his mainstream school.

Psychotherapy with children in care encompasses a wide range of specific issues – too many to cover fully here, but which are discussed at greater length in other chapters of this book (see chapters on abuse and abusers, traumatisation, delinquency and attachment). For instance, one such issue is the difficulty of working with traumatised children. Those in care may well have suffered multiple trauma over a number of years. Quite often the trauma will have become an organising feature of the child's personality in a way that is complex and impossible to disentangle without long-term intensive psychotherapy. I have found that children who have suffered this type of trauma have had to suppress feelings of rage over the original trauma. The rage becomes transformed into long-term hatred and a wish for revenge. These characteristics can become the hallmark of their later relationships – revengeful and filled with hatred.

In contrast, some children are too quiet, passive and compliant. They have been all too used to a watchful vigilance of unpredictable, rejecting or violent parents. They no longer know what their own wishes, needs or even feelings are. Because these children pose little problem at home or school, they can be easily overlooked. But they often become depressed or self-harming in adolescence. Within psychotherapy, the task is to notice, and help the child notice, their responses and feelings. The therapist may need to take a chance remark, a seemingly throw-away comment, and amplify this, exploring the full impact on the child. For example, I had been working for eight months with a very quiet, withdrawn eleven-year-old who virtually never volunteered any feelings or independent thoughts. The week after the Court granted a full care order for her to remain in care she kept losing things in therapy. She couldn't find her eraser or pencil sharpener. I commented on how things were getting lost today. 'Like me, I'm lost', she said so quietly that I couldn't believe I had heard her. She put her head down and wouldn't repeat it or elaborate. It was so unusual for her to make a comment like this that I spent a lot of time amplifying it: how she must feel lost, now that she wasn't returning to her mother. I then talked at great length about how this was another loss in her life, how she had repeatedly lost her mother who had repeatedly put her in care, or sent her to live with relatives, how her father was in prison and her beloved grandmother had died. I talked about how painful it was to be in care, to have lost her own family. Very quietly she said, 'I feel as if I'm born again' – as if she had been born as another child into her new family, and the old, familiar girl had been lost.

Theoretical and practical considerations

From the 1940s and '50s, Bowlby and others (such as Burlingham and Anna Freud (in Bowlby 1952), Spitz (1946) and James and Joyce Robertson (1952)) drew attention to the adverse effects of institutional care and/or frequent changes of mother figure during the early years of life. For example, Burlingham and Freud and Spitz studied the emotional responses of children placed in residential war nurseries in the Second World War. They found that these children were passive, avoided close personal contact and made indiscriminate approaches to care staff (so-called affectionless psychopathy). Spitz described the anxiety reaction of children and consequent depression following separation from the mother.

In their ground-breaking research, James and Joyce Robertson studied early separation in young children. This research, and particularly their film *A Two Year Old Goes to Hospital* (1952), have had a profound and far-reaching influence on the care of children in hospital. It is thanks to this work that it is now common practice for parents to stay with their children during the child's hospitalisation.

Rutter, in *Maternal Deprivation Reassessed* (1972) challenged much of the concept of maternal deprivation. However, he did state that Bowlby's writing could not be discounted as it was by far the most important contribution on the subject in the preceding twenty years. In the twenty years which followed the publication of Rutter's book, Bowlby's notion of attachment, the psychological consequences of maternal deprivation and that of a secure base for healthy emotional development have continued to be catalysts for extensive research and consequent far-reaching changes in practice in the arena of childcare.

Conduct disorder

There is much current interest in the difficulties of children described as having conduct disorder. The Psychiatric International Classification of Disorders (ICD–10) definition of conduct disorder is of a 'repetitive and persistent pattern of dissocial, aggressive or defiant conduct'. In the 'unsocialised' variant this includes offending and isolation from the peer group (World Health Organisation 1992).

This group of children has been proved difficult to help, and theorising as to aetiology ranges from the organic, to cognitive deficit, ineffective parenting and psychosocial stressors. Teaching of parenting techniques seems to be effective in helping younger children (3–8 years old) (Patterson *et al.* in Routh *et al.* 1995). However, a large group of parents drop out of these schemes, do not show improvement or do not maintain improvement.

Routh *et al.* (1995) posit the need for a multi-factorial model to account for these difficulties. They have turned to attachment theory to provide this model. The outcome of their research study shows the necessity to include an understanding of the security of attachments in conduct disorder. A study into the classification of attachment relationships in conduct-disordered children is currently being undertaken in south London (McCutcheon 1997, personal communication). The pilot study of children with aggression and disruptive behaviour shows a history of severely disrupted attachments.

Deprivation and delinquency

Both Bowlby (1952) and Winnicott *et al.* (1990) have suggested a link between maternal deprivation and delinquency. Bowlby summarises the findings of a number of workers who worked with delinquent children – all with a history of grossly disturbed early maternal relationships:

> Many of the typical features included:
>
> > superficial relationships;
> > no capacity to care for people or make true friends;
> > an [emotional] inaccessibility;
> > no emotional response . . . – a curious lack of concern;
> > deceit and evasion, often pointless;
> > stealing;
> > lack of concentration at school.
>
> (Bowlby 1952: 31)

In the course of his work with children evacuated during the war, Winnicott discovered a group of children who were found to be too problematic to be cared for within alternative families. These children had developed difficulties prior to evacuation, and exhibited many of the features Bowlby had remarked upon, and were established in delinquent behaviour. He postulated a link between this delinquency and maternal deprivation. Claire Winnicott has described how this work with others concerned with the impact of separation and loss on children led to the setting-up of the Curtis Committee, which in turn led to the first Children Act of 1948 (Winnicott *et al.* 1990).

Deprivation and Delinquency, republished in 1990, is a collection of Winnicott's papers on this topic covering a wide range of issues. He explores both the life experiences of children in relation to the effects of the war and evacuation, social provision (schools, prison, Borstal and residential care), as well as the psychodynamic aspects of delinquency. His papers on 'The development of the capacity for concern', 'The absence of the sense of guilt' and 'The antisocial tendency' all describe the early interactions between infant and mother. It is with the loss or distortion of this early relationship that a moral sense is impaired.

Michael Rutter challenged the concept of maternal deprivation because he felt the term was used to cover a vast range of causes and effects. In his view, the term was too broad and inclusive and needed to be broken into constituent aspects for investigation to be of relevance (Rutter 1972). He pointed to extensive literature which showed an association between 'broken homes' and delinquency. However, in some cases the break-up of the home was no more than a minor episode in a long history of discord and disruption, and to differentiate the effects of separation as such it was necessary to consider 'broken homes' according to the various causes of the break. For example, parental death showed only a very slight rise in associated delinquency rate (Rutter 1972: 64). Parental discord, disharmony and quarrelling were found to be more closely associated with anti-social and delinquent behaviour in children. Social deprivation has been shown to be the main factor separating children in care from those not in care (Bebbington and Miles 1989).

Deprivation and childcare

Bowlby's 1952 monograph raised a storm of protest, which Mary Ainsworth addressed in 1962. She made the point that many concepts were subsumed under the heading of 'maternal deprivation' (such as separation, or distortion of the mother–child relationship). She argued for the differentiation of these concepts and outlined the considerable body of research undertaken. A primary area of contention was the misunderstanding of Bowlby's emphasis on continuity of maternal care. It was felt by Bowlby's critics that he was saying that only 24-hour, uninterrupted care by the mother could ensure the infant's mental health. Working mothers and feminists objected. In fact, Bowlby does say, 'It is an excellent plan to accustom babies and young children to being cared for now and then by someone else' (Ainsworth 1962: 100). He also specifies that this maternal care can be provided by a mother substitute. But, crucially, particular care needs to be taken to ensure that alternative arrangements for mothering have regularity and continuity.

These days one seldom hears of maternal deprivation as a working conceptual model. Instead there have been many diverse developments into the various components of what was encompassed under the original broad definition of maternal deprivation. This is particularly so within the fields of attachment research (Ainsworth (1971); Maine and Soloman (1986); Hopkins (1990); Fonagy *et al.* (1991)) and childcare (Berridge and Cleaver (1987); Tizard and Hodges (1978, 1990); Wolkind and Rushton (1994)).

John Bowlby defined attachment as that behaviour activated when the young child or infant experiences stress or anxiety (such as cold, hunger, loud noises, looming shapes, etc.). When it is activated the child seeks contact (often physical contact) with one of his particular attachment figures.

Developments in attachment theory have had a significant impact on our understanding of the nature of attachments. Attachment difficulties are no longer simply understood as physical deprivation of maternal care, but can in fact result from a distortion in the relationship between child and mother (or other attachment figure). Mary Maine illustrated this in the 'Strange Situation', a research experiment which demonstrated both secure and insecure attachment patterns in infants of a year old.

Given the avoidant or ambivalent nature of insecure attachments, carers may feel that a child does not care – is not attached. Hurt, rejection and consequent adverse decisions may result from this misunderstanding. An understanding of insecure attachment can clarify an often bewildering experience for carers. That is, the child may well be attached, but in an insecure manner (such as with avoidant patterns) that the carer cannot recognise.

The nature of the child's attachments in the first year of life have been found to have a significant predictive power. Attachment patterns at one year of age are predictive of attachment patterns at six years of age (Main *et al.* 1986). There is a significant correlation between a parent's representation of their attachment (as elicited in the Adult Attachment Interview, see Chapter 4) and the nature of their child's attachment to them (Fonagy *et al.* 1991). Parents of securely attached infants give a fluent, consistent and coherent account of their childhoods; most of these parents have had secure childhood experiences. However, a number recall extreme unhappiness and rejection; they have thought deeply about their experiences and tried to understand them. It seems that it is not the experiences themselves which determine the quality of the adult attachment, but the processing or sense that has been made of these experiences which matters. For children, the ability to process painful experience is dependent on the presence of an adult who can bear to be in touch with the full range of the child's experience – in Bion's terms, to provide a containing function necessary to facilitate the modulation of pain and distress (Bion 1962). This has obvious implications for psychoanalytic psychotherapy which attempts to help an individual integrate past experiences and make sense of their emotional lives.

Clinically, I have found that those children who idealise their parents and cannot bear to face the possibility of their parents' vulnerabilities or failings blame themselves and have poorer current relationships. It is terribly painful to face the fact of a parent's failings as it leaves the child without a sense of the possibility of reconciliation or reparation.

Childcare practice, fostering and adoption

The impact of the understanding of the importance of maternal deprivation and attachment has had a significant impact on the provision of childcare in the United Kingdom. As a consequence there has been a move away from the provision of residential nursery care and institutional care for children to the provision of care within families. For those children who are in the care of the state, this primarily means care provided by foster families. Only 10 per cent of children in care are placed with a view to adoption. The majority of children are in long-term care, mainly in foster care.

More recently some of this growth in fostering, and a greater emphasis on adoption of children in care, has been motivated by financial, rather than ideological, factors. While family provision is undoubtedly the best for the majority of children, there is a small minority who would benefit from placement in home-styled, small children's homes. As family placement is cheaper than institutional care, this option is very often not available to these children. Similarly, there may be a push for adoption as a cheaper option to supported fostering. In my experience, adoptive parents have higher expectations and are less supported by statuary services than foster parents. A factor in adoptive breakdown is often their deep disappointment and hurt over the very difficult behaviour that these children bring to a family.

Fostering is not without its problems. Berridge and Cleaver first drew attention to the very high rate of foster family breakdown in 1987 (see also Wolkind and Rushton 1994). Thoburn and Rowe (1991) found that with fostering of older children (i.e. not infants) one in five placements break down within five years of placement.

The growth of fostering services in Britain has been rapid and radical in recent years. The Kent study by Hazel (1990) challenged the view that troubled adolescents were unfosterable within families. She found that extra support to foster families enabled these adolescents to remain living with families. This study, along with concern over disruption rates, has led to the development of a number of specialist fostering agencies with a range of extra support services in place in order to prevent fostering breakdown. This provision includes extra support and training of foster parents, educational provision for those children who are excluded from mainstream schooling and psychotherapy. There are many such fostering placements now in existence, with very few employing fully trained child psychotherapists. Although there are no published outcome studies as to the effectiveness of these specialist organisations on the prevention of foster family breakdown, one would hope that an integration of services to the child may be effective in supporting family placements of fostered children.

The radical aspect of such services is not only that children previously considered unsuitable for family placement are living in alternative families, but that there has been a move away from state-run foster care. There has been a mushrooming of independent sector fostering, whether as charities, non-profit-making organisations or even as small businesses. This is challenging the traditional role of local authorities, who now increasingly buy in fostering services rather than provide their own for troubled children.

This is a controversial area and the question of monitoring standards and evaluating services is only just being considered. There is much debate over the change of philosophy this involves. Arguments are raised as to whether children in care are seen as merely elements within a market economy, with foster care a commodity to be purchased. Counter arguments are that small, single-purpose agencies are better equipped to keep the needs of the child to the fore, rather than being lost in the busy, often overly bureaucratic, anonymity of local authority care.

It is clear that in Britain alternative care for children is undergoing rapid political and economic changes, with virtually no use of long-term institutional placements and a fast growth in independent foster organisations. However, the child's needs remain as Bowlby described – for long-term consistency and continuity of parental care and affection. Attachment research brings the hope that children damaged by disruption of this care may be helped to construct meaningful, coherent narratives of their life experiences in order to be enabled to develop secure adult attachments and, in turn, provide secure attachment experiences for their children. In many cases the only chance for this hopeful outcome is long-term intensive psychotherapy.

References

Ainsworth, M. (1962) 'The effects of maternal deprivation: a review of findings and controversy in the context of research strategy', *Deprivation of Maternal Care: a Reassessment of its Effects*, Public Health Papers no. 14, Geneva: World Health Organisation.

—— (1971) 'Individual differences in strange situation behaviour of one-year olds', in H. R. Schaffer (ed.) *The Origins of Human Social Relations*, London: Academic press.

Bebbington, A. and Miles, J. M. (1989), in M. Rutter and L. Hersov (eds) *Child and Adolescent Psychiatry*, London: Blackwell Scientific Publications.

Berridge, D. and Cleaver, H. (1987) *Foster Home Breakdown*, Oxford: Basil Blackwell.

Bion, W. R. (1962) *Learning From Experience*, London: Heinemann.

Boston, M. and Szur, R. (1983) *Psychotherapy with Severely Deprived Children*, London: Karnac Books.

Bowlby, J. (1952) *Maternal Care and Mental Health*, Geneva: World Health Organisation Monograph.

Fonagy, P., Steele, M., Steele, H., Moran, G. and Higgitt, A. (1991) 'Measuring the ghost in the nursery: an empirical study of the relation between parents' mental representations of childhood experiences and security of attachment', *Bulletin of Anna Freud Centre* 14: 115–31.

Gibbons, J. (1995) 'Development after physical abuse in early childhood', in C. Sellick and J. Thoburn (1996) *What Works in Family Placement*, Essex: Barnado's.

Hazel, N. (1990) *Fostering Teenagers*, London: National Foster Care Association.

Henry, G. (1988) 'Doubly deprived', in D. Daws and M. Boston (eds) *The Child Psychotherapist*, Maresfield Library, London: Karnac.

Hodges, J. (1984) 'Two crucial questions: adopted children in psychoanalytic treatment', *Journal of Child Psychotherapy* 10(1): 47–56.

Hopkins, J. (1990) 'The observed infant of attachment theory', *British Journal of Psychotherapy* 6: 460–71.

Hoxter, S. (1983) 'Feelings aroused in working with severely deprived children', in M. Boston and R. Szur (eds) *Psychotherapy with Severly Deprived Children*, London: Karnac Books.

Hunter, M. (1991) 'Psychotherapy with two children in local authority care', in M. Boston and R. Szur (eds) *Extending Horizons*, London: Karnac.

—— (1993) 'The emotional needs of children in care: an overview', *Journal of Association for Child Psychology and Psychiatry*, Review section 15(15): 214–18.

Klauber, T. (1998) 'The significance of trauma in work with parents of severely disturbed children and its implications for work with parents in general', *Journal of Child Psychotherapy* 24(1): 85–107.

Lanyado, M. (1998) 'Memories in the making: the experience of moving from fostering to adoption for a five year old boy', *Journal of the British Association of Psychotherapists* 34, 3.

Main, M. and Soloman, J. (1986) 'Discovery of an insecure disorganised-disoriented attachment pattern', in T. Brazelton and W. Yogman (eds) *Affective Development in Infancy*, Norwood, NJ: Ablex.

Main, M., Kaplan, N. and Cassidy, J. (1986b) 'Security in infancy, childhood and adulthood: a move to the level of representation', in I. Bretherton and E. Waters (eds) *Growing Points of Attachment Theory and Research*, Monograph 50, Society for Research in Child Development.

Robertson, J. and Robertson, J. (1952) 'A two year old goes to hospital', in M. Ainsworth (1962) *Deprivation of Maternal Care: A Reassessment of its Effects*, Public Health Papers no. 14, Geneva: World Health Organisation.

Routh, C., Hill, J., Steele, H., Elliott, C. and Dewey, M. E. (1995) 'Maternal attachment status, psychosocial stressors and problem behaviour: follow-up after parent training courses for conduct disorder', *Journal of Child Psychology and Psychiatry* 36(7): 1179–98.

Rutter, M. (1972) *Maternal Deprivation Reassessed*, London: Penguin.

Sellick, C. and Thoburn, J. (1996) *What Works in Family Placement?* Essex: Barnado's.

Smith, C. (1997) 'Foster care as private enterprise or community responsibility?', paper given at International Foster Care Conference, Vancouver.

Spitz, R. A. (1946) in Ainsworth, M. (1962) 'The effects of maternal deprivation: a review of findings and controversy in the context of research strategy', in *Deprivation of Maternal Care: a Reassessment of its Effects*, Public Health Papers no. 14, Geneva: World Health Organisation.

Thoburn, J. and Rowe, J. (1991) 'Evaluating family placements', in C. Sellick and J. Thoburn (eds) *What Works in Family Placement?* Essex: Barnado's.

Tizard, B. and Hodges, J. (1978) 'The effect of early institutional rearing on the development of 8 year old children', *Journal of Child Psychology and Psychiatry* 19: 99–118.

—— (1990) 'Ex-institutional children: a follow-up study to age 16', *Adoption and Fostering* 14(1): 17–20.

Winnicott, C., Shepherd, R. and Davis, M. (eds) (1990) *D. W. Winnicott: Deprivation and Delinquency*, London: Routledge.

World Health Organisation (1992) *ICD–10*, Geneva: WHO.

Wolkind, S. and Rushton, A. (1994) 'Residential and foster care', in M. Rutter and L. Hersov (eds) *Child and Adolescent Psychiatry*, London: Blackwell Scientific Publications.

Further reading

Alvarez, A. (1992) *Live Company*, London: Routledge.

Boston, M. and Szur, R. (1983) *Psychotherapy with Severely Deprived Children*, London: Karnac Books.

Fonagy, P., Steele, M., Steele, H., Moran, G. and Higgitt, A. (1991) 'Measuring the ghost in the nursery: an empirical study of the relation between parents' mental representations of childhood experiences and security of attachment', *Bulletin of Anna Freud Centre* 14: 115–31.

Henry, G. (1988) 'Doubly deprived', in D. Daws and M. Boston (eds) *The Child Psychotherapist*, Maresfield Library, London: Karnac.

Hopkins, J. (1990) 'The observed infant of attachment theory', *British Journal of Psychotherapy* 6: 460–71.

Hunter, M. (1991) 'Psychotherapy with two children in local authority care', in R. Szur and S. Miller (eds) *Extending Horizons*, London: Karnac.

—— (1993) 'The emotional needs of children in care: an overview', *Journal of Association for Child Psychology and Psychiatry*, Review section 15(15): 214–18.

21 Delinquency

Peter Wilson

Introduction

Delinquency is a term that has different meanings and usages. Most commonly, a juvenile delinquent is defined as someone who has transgressed the law: 'a young person who has been prosecuted and found guilty of an offence that would be classified as a crime if committed by an adult' (Graham 1991). This definition has the virtue of precision. Its limitation however is that is does not take into account the full extent of behaviour or attitude. In psychodynamic terms, delinquency carries a much broader meaning: it relates to a more fundamental concern about responsibility and honesty, both in relation to oneself and to others. The essence of delinquency lies in its failure of duty to meet both the legal and moral requirements of the prevailing social order. The word itself draws its source from the Latin *linquere* – to leave, forsake or abandon. The delinquent is unable or unwilling to do that which is owed to the group, community or society. Delinquency is thus not an activity confined to a criminal minority, but refers to a tendency that is integral to the development of all social relationships.

There can be few children for example who do not break rules, who do not tell an untruth, who do not take what is not theirs, who do not defy those around them. All children, from time to time, do what they are not supposed to; they try the forbidden and test the limits. In the interests of their growth and curiosity they break new ground, often ruthlessly and regardless of constraints and consequences. There is in the very process of becoming social an anti-social necessity. Delinquency in this sense is part of being a child and adolescent.

The nature of delinquency and child and adolescent development

Delinquency expresses itself in three major ways: through stealing, deception and physical or verbal violence. All constitute an attack on or an abandonment of the other; all, as it were, 'leave' the other. The spectrum of delinquent activity is wide. Stealing covers many activities: 'borrowing', shoplifting, taking and driving away, robbery and burglary. Deception includes a broad repertoire of lies from the periodic white lie to systematic deviousness, duplicity and fraud. Violence consists of fighting, bullying, intimidating, physical and sexual abuse, assault, torture or murder. Many of these activities are not criminal (and thus not delinquent in the legal sense); they are, however, in one way or another, dishonest and offensive (and thus delinquent in the psychodynamic sense). The degree to which these activities become problematic is in part determined by the requirements of the law, but also by the sanctions and prohibitions of the social group – whether this be the family, the peer group, the community or society at large. Some groups turn a blind eye to certain forms of theft; others collude with different kinds of deception or condone various forms of violence. Delinquency is thus relative to the tolerance of the group.

To a large extent, delinquency, as a failure in social adaption, is a mental health issue. Mental health refers essentially to the capacity to function effectively and creatively in the social group. It consists of the ability to initiate and sustain mutually satisfying relationships. Crucial to children's development is their ability and readiness to develop sufficient self-control and conscience to guide their behaviour within the rules of the group. Mental health problems and more severe mental disorders and illnesses reflect, in varying degrees, impairments of these abilities. Delinquency is one particular form of such impairment. Some delinquents behave in a disruptive and aggressive way which is excessive and impervious to modification by the normal range of social sanctions; their behaviour gives rise to disapproval and is associated with significant suffering and disturbance in personal functioning. In psychiatric terms, these young people are classified as having a conduct disorder; an indication of the extent and problematic nature of their delinquency.

The conditions that are likely to determine the development of mental health or of delinquency are now well documented in the literature on risk and protective factors (Farrington 1996, 1997; Utting *et al.* 1993; Wadsworth 1979). These can be grouped broadly into those pertaining to the inborn characteristics and personal resources of children, and those relating to familial and societal circumstances. In the first group, a number of genetic and early physical pre- and perinatal factors (e.g. physical abnormalities, premature birth) can be identified that produce vulnerabilities in infants. Inherent temperamental differences are of key importance pointing to whether or not children are overly sensitive, cranky or regressive/progressive in their basic tendencies. The personal resources of children – intelligence, ego resilience, social skills development – determine whether they are able to comprehend and adapt to what is happening in their lives and thus gain a sense of self-efficacy and control over events.

Familial and societal factors cover a broad range of circumstances. Major risk factors in the family include parental psychopathology and criminality, discordant family relationships and divorce, inconsistent parental supervision, harsh and erratic punishment, physical abuse and neglect, and lack of emotional warmth. Set against these are a range of protective factors, most notably the establishment of secure infant attachment and bonding, the provision of authoritative and consistent parenting, a basic belief in the family in the value of education and residential stability. The degree to which mothers can cope with adversity is critical; this in turn is dependent on the stability of their marriages or partnerships and the presence of significant care networks in their families or neighbourhoods.

Psychoanalytic thinking (e.g. Bion 1962; Bowlby 1951; Freud 1965; Winnicott 1960b) emphasises the significance of infant and early childhood experience and attachment. The role of the family in ensuring sufficient emotional containment of children is crucial to the provision of a sense of inner safety and coherence. This lays the foundation of basic trust and positive expectancy. Children feel essentially nourished, understood and affirmed; they are enabled to think and to learn, with a readiness to enter into relationships and to accept the constraints necessary for socialisation. Later experiences of feeling held and valued within a reliable family environment that establishes clear expectations and boundaries are necessary for the development of self-control and the establishment of ideals and of a moral sense. Children's capacity to benefit from school and community opportunities is greatly influenced by these primary family experiences. In contrast, where such favourable conditions do not prevail, children are less likely to be equipped to process adequately and make sense of their experience. The impact of maltreatment – whether it be physical, sexual or emotional neglect or abuse – is essentially traumatic, overwhelming children with sensations, tensions and feelings they cannot assimilate and exposing them to primitive anxieties over which they cannot achieve mastery – fears of annihilation, loss of control, disapproval and rejection. Children feel betrayed by parental failure to safeguard their safety and integrity. In response, they become resentful and on guard, without faith in those around them and disinclined to comply with their social requirements.

Delinquency represents an attempt to defend against these anxieties and give expression to this resentment. Delinquents find ways of ridding themselves of tension, through various projective mechanisms, and rendering others prey to the very feelings of anger, fear and confusion that they themselves find so intolerable. Campbell (1996) emphasises that 'it is the reliance upon action to project painful thoughts and feelings outside of himself and into the environment that is a fundamental characteristic of the delinquent's psychological defences'. He also draws attention to the delinquent's tendency to master traumatic experiences through sexual fantasy. This contains elements of excitement and risk (Stoller 1975) that both serve a defensive purpose and give expression to sadistic and revengeful wishes. Galway (1991) refers to deficiencies in the internal capacity to contain anxiety, and in more disturbed young people, a lack of an 'internal container altogether'; they are unable to make use of fantasy or the development of the capacity to think in order to process experience. As a result their behaviour is more determined by the impulse to act and by a need to seek containment externally through provocation and manipulation.

It is clear that mental health or delinquent outcome is dependent on the interplay of multiple factors within the child, family and environment, and in relation to the severity of the child's circumstances. The extent to which children are resilient, and thus able to rise above negative circumstances or manage to mitigate the effect of these circumstances, is a major variable. Horowitz (1987), for example, refers to the complex interrelationship between children's inherent vulnerability and the 'facilitativeness' of their environment: resilient children in adverse environments may make remarkable progress whilst vulnerable children in more facilitating ones may not.

Adolescence and the circumstances that surround it have a further determining effect on the development of delinquency. The peak age for all offending in England and Wales is eighteen for males and fifteen for females (Home Office 1995). There are numerous environmental risk factors that can lead to delinquent activity, including disadvantaged neighbourhoods, community disorganisation and neglect and availability of drugs. Poverty, poor schooling and unemployment also play their part. Young people's internal experience of adolescence, however, is of key significance in determining how able they are to cope with these adversities. Ordinarily, adolescence is an exciting, if at times alarming, time of growth and discovery. For those adolescents, however, whose early experiences have been unfavourable, the process of adolescence can be very unsettling. They are less able to negotiate adequately the developmental tasks of adjusting to the impact of puberty and negotiating separation and individuation (Laufer and Laufer 1984); their adolescent state does not excite them; they are fearful of their physical growth and sexuality and of taking responsibility by themselves for their actions. A great deal of delinquent behaviour in adolescence can be seen as a breakdown in the capacity to deal with these anxieties and to fill a developmental void (Greenberg 1975) inherent in the process of the separation. Some adolescents become extremely overwhelmed and disorganised, breaking down severely in suicidal and psychotic type behaviour. Others are more able to 'manage', drawing on the adolescent tendency to find expression through 'a language of action' (Osorio 1997) and veering towards a delinquent outcome.

According to the severity of negative childhood experiences and adolescent turbulence, the degree of delinquency becomes more marked and problematic. Most young people whose delinquent behaviour is persistent and extreme experience the world as fundamentally uncaring, withholding and untrustworthy. They harbour within them a sense of injustice and outrage and an abiding resentment that leads to a contempt and disregard for others. The delinquent act is intended to attack and confound those perceived to be responsible for their difficulties. In effect it carries its own sense of justice – the delinquent feels emboldened to take what he perceives to be his, and to deceive and violate those whom he believes have betrayed and abused him. There is in all of this an exhilarating and powerful mixture of despair and hope – the delinquent determined both to 'leave' the ungiving or hostile other and yet engage and register protest. Winnicott (1965) emphasised the essential purpose of the delinquent act as a positive, self-affirming protest. He viewed 'the anti-social tendency' as a consequence of and response to 'environmental failure'; it represents a testing of the environment and a way of 'staking a claim' on what has been hitherto being withheld. He expressed his position most clearly in the following passage:

> First I must try to define the word psychopathy. I am using the term here (and I believe I am justified in doing so) to describe an adult condition which is uncured delinquency. A delinquent is an uncured anti-social boy or girl. An anti-social boy or girl is a deprived child. A deprived child is one who had something good enough, and then no longer had this, what ever it was, and there was sufficient growth and organisation of the individual *at the time of the deprivation* for the deprivation to be perceived as traumatic. In other words, in the psychopath and the delinquent and the anti-social child there is logic in the implied attitude 'the environment owes me something'.
>
> (Winnicott 1965)

Child psychotherapy and delinquency

Child psychotherapists face major problems in working with delinquents. Many of the factors that give rise to delinquency fall beyond the reach of psychotherapy: little can be done through psychotherapy to change inherent personal characteristics or environmental factors. In relation to inner experience, many delinquents are unable or unwilling to acknowledge their suffering or learn through self-exploration in a therapeutic relationship. They are mistrustful and defiant and unable to hold in mind ideas and thoughts without defensive recourse to action. In adolescence, their need to preserve privacy and defend against dependency additionally works against therapeutic enquiry. In view of these difficulties, the issue of motivation is complicated. Some delinquents for example feel little remorse or concern about their behaviour and thus see no reason to change. As Eissler (1958) puts it,

> the technical difficulty in treating a delinquent arises from his total lack of desire to change. His symptoms are painful not to him but to others in his environment. He has no need or motive to reveal to his analyst what is going on in him. Further more, he sees the analyst as representative of that society against which his aggressions are directed and therefore meets him with distrust and fear.

On the other hand, beneath their antagonism or indifference, many delinquents feel anxious, confused and ashamed of their destructiveness. They are sometimes painfully conscious of their failings in their social, family and vocational lives, and yet they feel helpless in their predicament and unable to stop or comprehend their delinquency. Such acknowledgement of vulnerability is a potential source of motivation; it is however, difficult for them to bear and invariably defended against through attacking those who offer care and interest.

Child psychotherapists need to take in account these various factors that complicate motivation for change and improvement. They need also to be realistic about the extent of their contribution, set alongside other initiatives in the field, tackling the problem of delinquency (Sheldrick 1985). These include vocational and educational training, diversionary programmes in the Youth Justice System (NACRO 1988; Jones 1987) and a range of psychosocial treatments, such as problem-solving skills training, parent management training, family therapy. Many of these have a behavioural and cognitive focus and have been positively evaluated (Kazdin 1997). Psychodynamic child psychotherapy has been less well evaluated and needs more outcome research, despite methodological problems, to counter criticism (see, for example, Rutter 1985).

Despite these difficulties, however, child psychotherapy can be of considerable value to many delinquents in helping them to acknowledge and understand better their internal experience, and thus gain a greater sense of self-control. In many respects, the practice of child psychotherapy with delinquents is no different from that with more neurotic or psychotic young people. Basic to the process is the establishment of a secure setting in which sufficient stability is ensured to enable young people to feel safe enough to explore and discuss their difficulties. The endeavour is to create an experience for them in which they can learn about themselves through the therapeutic relationship and from observations, clarifications and interpretations (Wilson and Hersov 1985). The fundamental purpose is to improve their understanding of the anxieties that interfere with their development and contribute to their delinquency.

The establishment of these basic conditions is especially important in working with delinquent young people, whose need for clear boundaries, reliability and predictability is central. Beyond this, however, there are three issues that need to be addressed in particular in order to deal with the mistrust and hostility of delinquents and their equivocal motivation to change. The first concerns the establishment of *a working alliance*, the second, *the management of transference*, and third, the *adaptation in approach* to different types of delinquency.

Establishment of a working alliance

Without the establishment of a working alliance (Meeks 1971) there can be no prospect of collaborative or explorative work. In view of the many resistances inherent in delinquency, it is incumbent on child psycho-therapists to reach out – to convey in some way an appreciation of the delinquent's behaviour and underlying difficulties and to engender a sense of direction and hope in the possibility of change. This requires their willingness to take a more proactive and supportive approach than is customary. Some writers (Miller 1983), drawing on the work of Aichhorn (1965), suggest that psychotherapists adopt a relatively forceful, almost omnipotent position, in order to capture the imagination of otherwise indifferent and hostile delinquents who nevertheless seek leadership and guidance. Whilst this approach may be effective in certain circumstances with some adolescents, it carries with it considerable dangers, not least in compromising the stability of the therapeutic setting and building un-necessary expectations and inevitable disappointments. What is paramount, however, particularly in the early stages of therapy, is to find ways of engaging delinquents' curiosity about themselves and their circumstances.

The maintenance of a working alliance is of central importance through-out the course of therapy. It is dependent on mutual trust and as such is vulnerable to pressures within the therapeutic relationship. Delinquents may attack the alliance in many ways, and child psychotherapists may overly protect it at the cost of therapeutic progress. It is not uncommon during psychotherapy, for example, for young people to continue their delinquent and criminal activities both within and outside the therapy. They may conceal what they are doing or seek to manipulate child psycho-therapists to accept and condone their delinquent behaviour. Child psychotherapists need to hold a difficult tension between alliance and non-compliance with these delinquents' manoeuvres; this corresponds with the delinquents ambivalence about being caught and found out. Much depends on child psychotherapists' insight into their own relation to delinquency and to authority; it is through this that they can best hold the balance within themselves between moral censure of, and indulgent collusion with, delinquents' activities.

The management of the transference

Whereas transference (Freud, S. 1914) is always a powerful phenomenon in therapy, its impact in the psychotherapy of delinquents is especially force-ful. In the transference, young people re-enact childhood experiences inten-sified in their revival in adolescence. They convey through their behaviour that which is familiar to them. They bring into the therapeutic relationship aspects of how they themselves felt in the past and of how they perceived others who were involved with them. A teenage girl, for example, who has endured sexual abuse by her father as a child is likely to feel, in the reliving in the transference, her own childhood sensations of terror and excitement as well as the fears of a domineering and invasive father. In psychotherapy, she may find herself, in the growing dependency of the therapeutic relationship, having similar sensations as well as anticipating abuse from the psychotherapist. She may retreat from the therapy, or, alternatively, re-immerse herself in the entanglement of her past in the therapeutic relationship. She may find ways to seduce or provoke the therapist into bullying her – both to repeat the past experience and to master anxiety, through turning a passive experience into its active counterpart. She may reverse the past experience and attempt to dominate the psychotherapist, rendering him or her both harmless and as abused as she had felt. It is likely, too, that she may act out outside the therapy through violent behaviour, prostitution or theft in order to relieve this intolerable tension and to be apprehended and punished.

The value of such transference experience is that it opens up possibilities for the understanding and working through of central anxieties that underlie the delinquency. The above picture, however, gives some indication of the volatile and potentially disruptive nature of this experience. Unless the transference can be properly managed, it can become anti-therapeutic. Much depends on child psychotherapists' capacities to withstand the impact of these powerful and conflicting feelings and to provide some degree of containment so that they can be perceived and understood. The key therapeutic task is to resist the young person's implicit invitation to repeat the past – for example, for the psychotherapist to behave like a dominant or abusive father, or to become overwhelmed by feelings of helplessness. The child psychotherapist's ability to find ways of responding that are different from what the young people expect and which do not meet the dictates of the transference is essential. Ultimately, it is through the child psychotherapists' behaviour that they convey their understanding of the meaning of the young person's delinquency and provide the safety and boundary that the delinquent needs. Such behaviour, sustained by the child psychotherapists' own insights, constitutes interpretation and serves as a stimulus and basis for further verbal forms of communication and understanding.

Adaptation in approach

There are many individual differences between delinquents, and psychotherapeutic work clearly needs to be adapted to address these differences, taking into account historical and personal circumstances and based on careful assessment and diagnosis. Various attempts at classification have been made of delinquent and criminal people (e.g. Galway 1991); for the most part these have attempted to identify the degree of persistence and extremity of the offending behaviour and the neurotic or psychotic basis underlying the delinquent personality. For purposes of clarification, delinquent young people can be broadly divided into three main groups: those that are impulsive, explosive and/or compulsive. These categories are not intended as diagnostic categories, but rather as guides to consider the predominate elements of the delinquent behaviour in question and to make the most appropriate response. None, of course, is intended to be seen as exclusive of the others.

The impulsive delinquent

Impulsive delinquents are young people who are largely dominated by the sheer pressure of their wishes and desires. Their behaviour is demanding, insistent, grabbing in nature. They take things on impulse, and steal without apparent remorse or concern. They lie frequently and are often aggressive, bullying if they can get away with it, and at times violent if cornered or threatened. There is a sense in which their delinquency is 'mindless' – defensive, reactive, without thought or regard for others, and with little comprehension of the consequences of their actions. Delinquency of this kind has many causes. In some young people, there may be genetic factors, as in hyperkinetic syndrome, as a result of which they have inherent difficulty in focusing their attention or controlling their impulsive behaviour. In others, early abusive or neglectful childhood experiences may have left them with inner feelings of chaos and terror and with limited resources to manage their anxiety. Anna Freud's (1965) developmental perspective on the nature of lying and stealing is of particular relevance. Some of these young people, because of their immaturity, are less able to distinguish between inner and outer reality or between ideas of what is 'mine' and 'not mine'. In terms of their functioning they are more likely to react to intolerable realities through regression to infantile forms of behaviour and wishful thinking.

The therapeutic response to these delinquents needs to address their basic difficulties in controlling their impulses and tolerating frustration as well as the underlying anxieties that propel them into such trouble. Systematic behavioural and cognitive approaches are useful in enabling them to develop problem-solving skills, build social competencies and clarify their thinking in relation to the consequences of their actions. These approaches can be carried out either individually or in groups, in different settings in school, special educational establishments or in the community in various diversionary schemes. The involvement of the family in supporting these therapeutic interventions through family therapy or parent management training is important. Child psychotherapists have a significant contribution to make in working to understand the anxieties of these young people, particularly those who have some rudimentary capacity for self-reflection and a wish to change. Despite the apparent randomness and remorselessness of their behaviour, many feel fundamentally very frightened and confused and desperate that they cannot control themselves or indeed what happens to them. Child psychotherapists may have to adapt to their needs, through being relatively more structured, focused and supportive in their approach. In view of the need of these young people to feel held within a consistent and comprehensive system of care, it is important that child psychotherapists do not work in isolation – but maintain regular liaison with other practitioners involved with the young person – for example, teachers, social workers, youth workers.

The explosive delinquent

By contrast, explosive delinquents function at a higher level of organisation; their personalities are more structured, less buffeted by impulse and more coherent in relation to others. For most of the time they appear to behave normally and get along well enough with others. The problematic area of their delinquency resides in their periodic outbursts of violence and revengeful preoccupations; the latter can lead to acts of theft, deception and intimidation with no apparent regard for their victims. At the core of this kind of delinquency is often a major narcissistic disturbance, in which the young people are highly sensitive to perceived rejection or humiliation. The causes of such disturbance are complex, but are frequently associated with what Greenberg (1975) has described as a 'symbiotically warped' mother–infant relationship. In this, vulnerable young people have experienced, as children, an accumulation of narcissistic injuries in response to their mother's extreme ambivalence: that is, they have been subjected both to the mother's often engulfing and sexualised over-involvement and yet sudden and unpredictable withdrawals of affection, indifference and hostility. This perplexing intimacy can have a highly disturbing effect leaving them feeling as children and as adolescents helpless, valueless and confused. There is engendered from such experience a deep sense of hurt and anger that constitutes what Kohut (1972) refers to as 'narcissistic rage'. This vulnerability is intolerable and is for the most part defended against through compensatory grandiose or idealising fantasies. When these are challenged, whether through direct criticism or rebuke, or through actual or perceived betrayal (e.g. in an idealised relationship), the rage may erupt and find expression in acts of violence.

The extent of the denial in this kind of delinquency is extensive, often fortified by a sense of righteous justification that allows for no recognition of wrongdoing. The violent outbursts are troubling, but experienced as episodic and 'forgettable'. Cognitive and behavioural therapeutic approaches that have a useful structuring and guiding effect for impulsive delinquents are largely irrelevant for these delinquents. Anger management techniques may be helpful, but they do not meet the depth of the underlying disturbance. Long-term psychodynamic therapy can, in some cases, be effective in reducing the extremity of behaviour and preoccupation. This psychotherapy needs to be based on an understanding of narcissistic psychopathology and to proceed on the basis of building an essentially supportive and affirming relationship. Once this is established, there exists the opportunity of re-experiencing and working through elements of the early narcissistic hurt and rage in the transference, and thus of greater integration and control. The work of Kohut (1972) in treating narcissistic personality disorders through mirror transferences is of particular relevance.

The compulsive delinquent

Compulsive delinquents are those whose behaviour is repetitive and chronically destructive both to themselves and others. It is behaviour that combines both impulsive and explosive elements but is relatively more controlled and sustained. Behind this behaviour is an attitude of contempt that derives from a basic fear of dependency and dread of humiliation. These delinquents are often clever, streetwise, well resourced in terms of social skills and competence; they are adept at controlling others through seduction and manipulation, and are callous and sadistic in their attacks on others. Their overriding purpose is to get what they want as quickly and immediately as possible, regardless of the rules or sensibilities of others. To this end, they are able and willing to defy and undermine others through concealment and duplicity.

At the source of this kind of delinquency is again a fundamental narcissistic disturbance drawn from comparable early infantile circumstances as described in relation to the explosive delinquent. There is additionally a complex overlay of more neurotic conflicts that give rise to a sense of guilt which, though denied, has a powerful unconscious influence on behaviour. It is this factor, together with a fear of omnipotence (a sense of limitlessness, of there being no bounds to what they might get away with), that gives rise to the self-destructive and compulsive nature of their delinquency. This takes the form not only of theft, deception or fraud, but also of activities that are self-punishing – for example: the burglar who repeatedly breaks into houses until he is caught; the boy who takes and drives away cars until eventually he crashes.

Delinquency of this kind is perhaps the most difficult to deal with in psychotherapy; it is habitual, a way of life that for many may be 'successful' enough. Nevertheless despite this, many such young people experience a pervasive sense of unease that can lead to a desire for change. They are frightened of their destructiveness, of their potential loss of control, of their sense of being bad and unwanted. Many express a strong need for a relationship and to be understood.

In the following example, an account is given of the psychotherapy of a young person whose delinquency contained impulsive and explosive elements, but whose life was built upon deception and compulsive delinquent activity. The fundamental task of the psychotherapist was to establish and maintain a working alliance that could allow for moments of experience that were genuine and non-delinquent and that could be used for exploration and gradual integration.

Case illustration: Paul

Paul was a fifteen-year-old boy, tall, well built and always dressed stylishly. He was referred for psychotherapy by his mother who had decided she could no longer tolerate his behaviour. The school had complained to her for sometime about his stealing from other pupils, his tendency to bully and sexually pester girls. In recent months he had got into trouble with the police. He had been questioned about a number of car thefts in the neighbourhood; matters had come to a head recently when he had been caught driving a stolen car. His mother felt she could never trust him.

Paul lived alone with his mother. Paul's father had left the family home when he was aged six. There had been numerous violent marital arguments when Paul was a small child and he had at times been victim of his father's violence. His relationship with his mother had been very close and it was clear that in many ways she was very proud of him. However she had also been preoccupied with her own design business and had had several relationships with other men. This, Paul had resented; he had, for example, stolen money from the wallets of his mother's boyfriends. His father had remained a constant presence in his life, though always elusive and unpredictable. Paul remained loyal to him and looked up to him, although he never could be sure where his father was or what he did. 'He comes and goes in big cars and flash suits.'

Paul was seen in once-weekly psychotherapy for just over a year. His attendance was erratic although this improved towards the end. The therapy terminated because of his family moving to another area; this was premature and progress was by no means complete. Enough was accomplished however to help him understand his delinquent behaviour better and to begin to try to change his ways.

Paul made it clear from the outset that he was happy to come to therapy. He said that he knew he needed to sort himself out. His mother worried too much but he could well understand her feelings. He loved his mother and he did not want to upset her. He also wanted to do well and 'go into the design business' with her. He intended to go to college and get down to studying. He understood that I knew the extent of his mother's concern and of his delinquency and police involvement. He acknowledged that he was 'in a bit of trouble' but he was quick to point out that he had learnt his lesson and was about to change.

In all of this, his tone was assured, grown-up, conciliatory. He smiled a lot and it seemed that his overall purpose was to disarm and circumvent me as much as he could. To some extent, the early sessions moved along well enough as he began to talk about his feelings towards his parents, his memories of having felt frightened and confused as a child and his wish to know more about his father. He talked, too, at the beginning about his interest in cars and achievements in computer design. There remained however a lack of depth or connectedness. Despite his apparent sincerity, I felt as if he were play-acting, almost in mockery of the therapy. His attitude was flippant, he turned up late for sessions with poor excuses, he hinted at various criminal activities – but never explicit, always keeping me guessing. At one level, it seemed clear that he was attending therapy to be 'good' and to get out of trouble with the police. The degree of control and manipulation, however, in the way in which he maintained distance in the therapeutic relationship, indicated a more profound level of fear of dependency in the transference. His mockery seemed an effective way of rendering me powerless, feeling as foolish and duped as he did.

Throughout, Paul's delinquency was a feature of the therapy. This was something I needed constantly to keep in mind whilst always remaining open to his underlying vulnerability and possible search for help. It was an achievement in itself that Paul attended therapy, albeit at times irregularly, and that he opened up the opportunity to talk about aspects of his life. Nevertheless, there was much in what he said that was false and in denial of his difficulties. This became particularly noticeable when he talked about his relationship with girls. On the one hand, he said he had a steady girlfriend whom he would never leave; on the other hand, he talked of other girls whom he had 'had' – seemingly oblivious of his effects on them or indeed on his girlfriend.

A turning point occurred in psychotherapy towards the end of the third month. Its impetus was a telephone call from Paul's mother informing me that he had been arrested with someone else for a burglary in a large house in the neighbourhood. Paul attended his subsequent session in his usual breezy manner without making any reference to this information. Eventually I informed Paul of what I knew. Paul's initial reaction was to smile, shrug it off; it wasn't really him who was involved, it was his friend. His mother, he said, fretted too much; she wasn't well. I stayed silent for a while and then said simply, 'I am listening; but I am wondering why I don't feel convinced about what you're saying.' Paul smiled again and picked up a pen on the desk. He mimed at smoking it like a cigarette and asked uncertainly what I was getting at. I repeated what I had said and added I thought that Paul was kidding himself as well as his mother and me about what he was up to. Paul was at first quiet, but then, suddenly and violently, threw the pen across the room and got up to walk towards the door. He swore at me, accusing me of being a flash Harry, a twisting bastard, a bully who 'couldn't give a toss'. As he opened the door I simply but firmly said 'stay – don't leave this'. Paul hung about but eventually walked over to the pen, picked it up, put it back in its proper place and slumped back into his chair. Suddenly he cried – at first in anger at me for not caring, and then at the police and at his mother for messing him about and his father for never being around. He sat in his chair for several minutes and said nothing. He then looked directly at me and said 'I am well and truly messed up, I hate it, I don't know what to do'.

This was an extraordinary moment in therapy, quite uncharacteristic. It touched on something genuine in Paul that for the most part he sought to conceal. There were other comparable experiences later in the therapy, but this first moment served as a central reference point – to understand the desolation and vulnerability that underlay his delinquency. Following this, he became more open to exploration of his feelings, not least his sense of betrayal by his mother and father. He was able to gain some understanding of his excitement in invading the privacy of the house that he had burgled; it had belonged to a woman who was a friend of his mother. He also acknowledged that he had been relieved to be caught. He felt bad and he deserved it. Throughout he conveyed a sense of yearning for a relationship – wanting in the moment of burglary to be close to and inside his mother – and in his taking and driving away cars, seeking to be alongside his father. The reality of his impending court experience and sentencing together with his experience of therapy had a moderating effect on his delinquency.

Summary

This chapter has drawn upon a broad definition of delinquency, encompassing a wide range of activities, some of which are criminal, all of which are designed to attack and confound other people. Delinquency represents an inability or unwillingness to relate to others with respect and honesty. Although integral to development and to mental health, it becomes problematic according to its persistence and extremity and to the extent that it disturbs the social group. Numerous risk and protective factors exist to determine a delinquent outcome. Psychodynamic thinking emphasises the importance of early childhood experience, in particular the traumatic impact of childhood maltreatment. Delinquent behaviour is understood in relation to the failure of the environment to provide sufficient care and emotional containment for children to develop the capacity to process and master anxiety. It is seen as a necessary expression, defensive against anxiety and purposeful in evoking a compensatory response from the environment.

In the face of considerable complexity and perplexity, child psychotherapists are faced with considerable therapeutic difficulties, not least delinquents' antagonism, mistrust and equivocal motivation to change. Their responsibility is to find ways of engaging with young people to enable them to overcome their resistances to change and to make sense of the inner experience. This requires a capacity to develop an effective working alliance with young people, to manage the therapeutic potential of the transference and to adapt therapeutic approaches to meet the needs of the different kinds of delinquents. Child psychotherapists need to appreciate the depth of narcissistic disturbance that resides at the centre of much delinquent behaviour and to ensure a secure therapeutic setting in which delinquents can feel contained and facilitated to think. The main struggle in the psychotherapy of adolescents is about trust – to acknowledge and explore what is genuine and authentic. It is that which child psychotherapists search for and delinquents avoid, but need to find.

References

Aichhorn, A. (1965) *Delinquency and Child Guidance: Selected Papers*, New York: International Universities Press.

Bion, W. R. (1962) *Learning from Experience*, London: Heinemann.

Bowlby, J. (1951) *Maternal Care and Mental Health*, Geneva: World Health Organization.

Campbell, D. (1996) 'From practice to psychodynamic theories of delinquency in adolescence', in C. Cordess and M. Cox (eds) *Forensic Psychotherapy: Crime, Psychodynamics and the Offender Patient*, vol. II, London: Jessica Kingsley.

Eissler, K. R. (1958) 'Notes on problems of technique in the psychoanalytic treatment of adolescents: with some remarks on perversions', *Psychoanalytic Study of the Child* 13, New York: International Universities Press.

Farrington, D. (1996) *Understanding and Preventing Youth Crime*, Joseph Rowntree Foundation/York: York Publishing Services.

—— (1997) 'A critical analysis of research and the development of antisocial behaviour from birth to adulthood', in D. M. Stoff, J. Breiling and J. D. Maser (eds) *Handbook of Antisocial Behaviour*, New York: Wiley.

Freud, A. (1965) *Normality and Pathology in Childhood*, New York: International Universities Press.

Freud, S. (1914) 'Remembering, repeating and working through', *Standard Edition*, Vol. 12, London: Hogarth.

Galway, P. (1991) 'Social maladjustment', in J. Holes (ed.) *Textbook of Psychotherapy in Psychiatric Practice*, London: Churchill Livingstone.

Graham, P. (1991) *Child Psychiatry: A Developmental Approach*, 2nd edn, London: Oxford University Press.

Greenberg, H. (1975) 'The widening gyre: transformation of the omnipotent quest during adolescence', *International Review of Psychoanalysis* 2: 231–44.

Home Office (1995) *Aspects of Crime: Young Offenders 1993 Statistics* 1, London: Division of Home Office Research and Statistics Dept.

Horowitz, F. D. (1987) *Exploring Developmental Theories: Toward a Structural/Behavioural Model of Development*, Hillside: N.I. Erlbaum.

Jones, D. W. (1987) 'Recent developments in work with young offenders', in J. Coleman (ed.) *Working with Troubled Adolescents*, London: Academic Press.

Kazdin, A. E. (1997) 'Practitioner Review: Psychosocial treatment of conduct disorder in children', *Journal of Child Psychology and Psychiatry* 38(2): 161–78.

Kohut, H. (1972) 'Thoughts on narcissism and narcissistic rage', *Psychoanalytic Study of the Child* 27, New York: International Universities Press.

Laufer, M. and Laufer, M. E (1984) *Adolescence and Developmental Breakdown*, New Haven: Yale University Press.

Meeks, J. E. (1971) *The Fragile Alliance: An Orientation to the Outpatient Psychotherapy of the Adolescent*, Baltimore: Williams and Wilkins.

Miller, D. (1983) *The Age Between: Adolescence and Therapy*, London: Jason Aronson.

NACRO (1988) *Diverting Juveniles from Custody*, London: NACRO.

Osorio, L. C. (1977) 'The psychoanalysis of communication in adolescents', in S. C. Feinstein and P. L. Giovacchini (eds) *Development and Clinical Studies*, Vol. 5, New York: Aronson.

Rutter, M. (1985) 'Psychosocial therapies in child psychiatry: issues and prospects', in M. Rutter and L. Hersov (eds) *Child and Adolescent Psychiatry: Modern Approaches*, 2nd edn, Oxford: Blackwell.

Sheldrick, C. (1985) 'Treatment of delinquents', in M. Rutter and L. Hersov (eds) *Child and Adolescent Psychiatry: Modern Approaches*, 2nd edn, Oxford: Blackwell.

Stoller, R. (1975) *Perversion: The Erotic Form of Hatred*, New York: Pantheon Books.

Utting, D., Bright, J. and Henricson, C. (1993) *Crime and the Family: Improving Child Rearing and Preventing Delinquency*, London: Family Policy Studies.

Wadsworth, M. (1979) *The Roots of Delinquency*, London: Martin Robertson.

Wilson, P. (1991) 'Psychotherapy with adolescents', in J. Holmes (ed.) *Textbook of Psychotherapy in Psychiatric Practice*, London: Churchill Livingstone.

Wilson, P. and Hersov, L. (1985) 'Individual and group psychotherapy', in M. Rutter and L. Hersov (eds) *Child and Adolescent Psychiatry: Modern Approaches*, 2nd edn, London: Blackwell.

Winnicott, D. W. (1960a) 'Classification: is there a psychoanalytic contribution to psychiatric classification (1959–64)', in D. W. Winnicott *The Maturational Processes and the Facilitating Environment*, London: Hogarth.

—— (1960b) 'The theory of the parent infant relationship', in D. W. Winnicott (1965) *The Maturational Processes and the Facilitating Environment*, London: Hogarth.

—— (1965) *The Maturational Processes and the Facilitating Environment*, London: Hogarth.

Further reading

Cordess, C. and Cox, M. (eds) (1996) *Forensic Psychotherapy: Crime, Psychodynamics and the Offender Patient*, London: Jessica Kingsley, Vol. I, chapters 2, 7, 8, 10; Vol. II, chapters 7, 17, 18, 20, 23.

Holmes, J. (1991) *Textbook of Psychotherapy in Psychiatric Practice*, London: Churchill Livingstone, chapters 14, 15, 19.

Freud, A. (1965) *Normality and Pathology in Childhood: Assessments of Development*, New York: International Universities Press, chapters 4 and 5.

22 The violent child and adolescent

Marianne Parsons and Sira Dermen

Introduction

In this chapter, by violence we mean unacceptable use of physical aggression in response to perceived provocation. To dwell briefly on the qualifying words 'unacceptable' and 'perceived': 'unacceptable' derives from society's norms and refers to external reality, 'perceived' derives from the individual's experience and refers to internal reality. Often an act of violence, while unacceptable, will strike us as comprehensible, because we can trace a pathway from provocation to execution. That a bullied child one day lashes out at his tormentor does not tax the imagination. By contrast the violence of an adolescent boy who rapes and batters the elderly woman who has befriended him is profoundly disturbing.

The psychotherapist's task is not to justify the unacceptable; it is to discover the meaning of the act from the point of view of the subject. It is important to bear in mind that this may be as opaque to the perpetrator as the outside observer. It may, however, emerge gradually in the course of psychotherapy (which will neither exclusively concentrate on the offence nor ignore it). When we consider the perpetrator's internal world, we begin to understand that all manner of objectively 'harmless' or even 'friendly' overtures are, for him, deadly provocations. Someone who befriends a troubled youngster, invites him into her house and feeds him, yet fails to be available to him in the middle of the night when he is wandering the streets alone and depressed, runs the risk of becoming a tormentor, someone who tantalises him seemingly for her own gratification.

We are all capable of reacting violently in extreme circumstances when our very survival (physical or psychological) is at stake. In the above example, the tragedy for the friendly elderly woman, and also the adolescent, is that her experience of the extreme bears little relation to his.

Violence is a huge subject and can be approached from many directions. We have already gestured towards the social dimension. That all societies sanction violence under certain circumstances goes without saying. Equally, many writers have drawn attention to society's turning a blind eye to violence it does not sanction, such as child sexual abuse, domestic violence, abuse of the vulnerable in institutions, etc. In what follows we will limit ourselves to considering violence perpetrated by an individual, rather than in groups or gangs.[1] However, even when we confine ourselves to understanding an individual's violence by addressing his internal world, the subject is too vast to be adequately covered within the limits of this chapter. Rather than offer a compendium of factors which contribute to the psychodynamics leading to violence, we have chosen to focus on one area which we find central in clinical work.

Our main thesis is that violence is the most primitive (physical) response to a perceived threat to the integrity of the psychological self. The ultimate danger the violent individual defends himself against is *the experience of helplessness in the absence of a protective internal object*. This, for him, spells annihilation. Because of failures in his earliest nurturing, the violent individual lacks an adequately flexible protective membrane which would allow him to register anxiety as a signal of impending threat and mobilise appropriate defences. He has developed instead a rigid protective barrier (more like an impenetrable fortress). This renders him powerful, invincible and independent (in fantasy) and extremely vulnerable to the slings and arrows of ordinary intercourse (in reality). Thus rigidly fortified, he is always unprepared for danger; any threat which penetrates his barrier is experienced as traumatic and triggers the most primitive defences of flight or fight.[2]

The developmental perspective

We will consider those aspects of development that are relevant to our thesis outlined above, including the development of aggression, defence and mastery, the self, ways of relating and the conscience. In order to understand what can go wrong, we need to consider the usual paths of development. This is a vast and complicated matter and for the purposes of this chapter we will have to paint broad brushstrokes without filling in the finer details. (For fuller accounts, see Colarusso 1992; Edgcumbe 1976; Freud, A. 1949, 1972; Stern 1985; Tyson and Tyson 1990.)

It is important to note that aggression is a natural part of life and a major source of energy. Without it we would not be able to assert or protect ourselves actively or progress from dependence towards independence (Winnicott 1963); but it is a powerful force which, without appropriate control and deflection, can get out of hand. Although we appreciate that aggression is innate and that genetic influences may contribute to increased aggressive behaviour in some individuals, our particular emphasis is to account for its dangerous eruptions in terms of early environmental failures and the way they are carried in the child's internal world.

The earliest form of mental aggressiveness concerns the infant's need to get rid of intolerable feelings (Edgcumbe 1976) in order to achieve a sense of internal balance, safety and well-being. When a tiny baby feels hungry or frightened he has no resources for making himself feel better and has to rely on his caregivers. If his needs are not adequately met, his distress, helplessness and sense of frustration will become overwhelming. He will yell and cry, kick and flail his arms. This constitutes the earliest mode of response to an overwhelming experience, namely a bodily one. The crucial thing from the point of view of development is the nature of the mother's response. Good-enough mothering will give the baby sufficiently often an experience of not yelling and flailing into a vacuum, but of having elicited a response which alleviates his distress. This is more than the meeting of a need; it is the meeting up with an empathic and receptive object. It lays the foundations for the capacity to tolerate vulnerability because helplessness is associated with a protective object.

Abstract language can scarcely capture the overwhelming nature of the infant's experiences of these extreme danger situations. The words we resort to are annihilation, disintegration, fragmentation. It is up to the mother to prevent or relieve the infant's pain and anxiety by acting as a protective shield (Freud, S. 1920; Khan 1973) against both internal and external dangers. The prolonged absence of the mother's protective function exposes the baby to unmanageable amounts of anxiety. In such extreme states the baby may resort to pathological defensive behaviours such as avoidance, freezing and fighting (Fraiberg 1982), each of which set in train a deviant course of aggression and of patterns of relating. The baby's perception of the world as a safe place and his capacity to develop internal adaptive resources will be put in jeopardy.

However, if the mother is able to act adequately as a protective shield, keeping her baby safe until he gradually develops the resources to do this for himself, the baby will develop a sense of basic safety and trust, and will form a secure attachment to her. He will begin to internalise her ways of looking after him and will gradually be able to tolerate small amounts of anxiety and frustration as he learns that she will do something to make him feel better. The mother's empathy with the baby and her active attunement to his physical and emotional needs help him not only to feel loved, but also to develop a capacity to be attuned to his own internal states. Over time he will come to recognise and tolerate his needs and to differentiate between shades of feeling, so that not every internal state has the same preremptory quality. A space opens up for thought and reflection. Both the tolerance of need and the receptivity to one's internal states require a good-enough experience of dependence, without which the child will develop a false or precocious independence – a trait commonly met in violent individuals, who may use their minds instrumentally but seldom for self-reflection.

As the baby gets older and begins to develop a sense of self-agency (Stern 1985), the good-enough mother intuitively recognises both that he can tolerate more frustration and also that he wants to exercise his curiosity and do more things for himself. She continues to 'feel with' the baby (Furman 1992), but gives him more space to begin to learn how to manage his own feelings and experiences without immediately managing them for him. The mother adapts herself, letting go in degrees her initial total preoccupation with the baby, as he begins to internalise her protective function. Repeated experiences of amounts of optimal frustration in the context of empathic mothering help the baby to learn that he can survive feelings of helplessness without being overwhelmed, and promote the development of healthy aggression. As the mother very gradually lets the baby separate and individuate from her, he gains more confidence to explore his environment and to extend his natural urge to relate to others. She encourages his developing relationship with his father who offers an importantly different style of relating and limit setting with more of an emphasis on goal-related activities (Colarusso 1992).

As the child becomes more mobile, he can begin to move physically away from his mother. Increasingly, the mother has to say 'no' and stop him from doing things in order to protect him from dangers of which he is not yet aware, or to protect herself and others from his behaviour. The toddler thus has to face the reality that he is not all-powerful and will not be unconditionally gratified. This painful blow to his previously omnipotent sense of himself arouses enormous frustration and often results in the temper tantrums typical of the so-called 'terrible twos'. The parents' handling of their frustrated angry toddler is crucial – the question is how to contain the child's frustration calmly and control his aggression without increasing his fear and without abusing the child's sense of an active self. The toddler in a tantrum can feel overwhelmed and out of control, and he needs the continuous presence of the adult to help him to regain his composure. Being angrily controlled or left alone in such a state leaves the child at the mercy of unmanageable panic and does not help him to learn ways of containing his frustration and aggression. The parents' ability to treat the child with respect and enable him to feel a 'somebody' (Furman 1992), while imposing restraints on him, offers the child a model for internalisation whereby he can develop self-respect and accept limits. This, in turn, lays the foundation for being able to respect others who will not always comply with his wishes. In the absence of a good-enough experience of 'no', all future limits are experienced as the mere exercise of power, which the child deals with by alternating between compliance and defiance, a dynamic characteristic of violent patients.

So far we have emphasised the parents' impact on the child's development. We need now to reiterate that psychic development proceeds from an interplay of internal and external factors. Environmental influences will be experienced and made sense of by the child according to his particular developmental level, each level characterised by different modes of mental functioning and unconscious fantasy. For example, the baby will experience getting rid of painful feelings in terms of vomiting or defecation; the angry toddler who is left by his mother will imagine that her disappearance has been brought about by his wish to get rid of her. In this mode of functioning magical thinking holds sway, whereby to wish is to bring about; there is no clear distinction between reality and phantasy or between internal and external events.

During healthy toddlerhood the child begins to assert more independence by actively doing more things for himself and wanting to do them his way, but he also wants to please his mother because his sense of well-being is dependent on her love for him. Here he faces a major conflict – one of ambivalence. He hates his mother when she does not gratify him, but when she comforts and provides for his needs he loves her. In the state of hatred, his sense of loving and being loved disappear. Good-enough mothering gradually helps the child to recognise that the hated and loved mother are the same person, and that the mother who may sometimes be angry with him also still loves him. As he integrates his loving views of the mother with the angry and hostile ones, he also develops a sense of trust that his affectionate relationship with his mother will endure during moments of anger and during separation from her. In the absence of such integration, omnipotent and magical ways of thinking will persist unmodified, the power of love to tame destructiveness will be diminished, and the child's belief in the enormity of his aggression will be unchecked. Violent patients often speak of their sense of being irremediably evil.

The parents' capacity to recognise, tolerate and manage their own frustration and aggression is crucial to the child's healthy development. They give the child repeated opportunities to see that aggression may be held in check, expressed in an assertive but not damaging way or channelled into other activities. They show the child that the use of language is usually more appropriate than the physical expression of aggression. They open up the possibility for reparation and forgiveness which facilitates the development of a healthy and non-punitive conscience. Also, very importantly, the parents' good-enough tolerance of their own aggression will allow them to perceive their child's aggression as that of a child, enabling them to respond appropriately as an adult instead of reacting on the basis of their own childlike needs and impulses. Thus, the parents' patterns of dealing both with their own and their child's aggression help the child to develop an understanding of his aggressive feelings and a capacity to process and manage them. All this promotes the child's natural urge for mastery of his feelings and anxieties which, in turn, enhances his self-esteem and sense of well-being.

While human development is too complex to allow of certain prediction, some parental attitudes and behaviours promote violence in children, the most obvious being parental violence towards the child or a violent relationship between the parents. The most straightforward route to the forming of a violent temperament is through identification with a violent parent, but it is not the only one. Sometimes a parent may not be physically violent towards the child, but will act on unconscious hatred in less obvious ways. For example, one mother frequently left her son unprotected from physical danger because of her unconscious death wishes which arose from the displacement on to him of her hatred for her younger brother (see clinical example: Charles, this chapter). At the other extreme we find parents who are too fearful or guilty about their own aggression. The effects on the child are less obvious, but in practice this leads to a failure of authority and consequent lack of safety for the child. Some parents turn to the child, inappropriately using him as a partner, out of dissatisfaction with their own relationship. This prolongs the child's sense of being special, plays havoc with his relinquishment of omnipotence and grossly interferes with his capacity to separate effectively. Some parents have difficulty in setting appropriately benign but firm limits for their child for other reasons; for example, out of anxiety about the child's frailty or their over-investment of him as a narcissistic extension of themselves. If a child is not allowed to experience, and then helped gradually to relinquish, omnipotence and grandiosity age-appropriately in toddlerhood, he will not learn to tolerate frustration and set his own limits on his behaviour and become a person capable of sharing and relating to others with concern and respect.

Let us consider the common sight of a mother struggling with a screaming, demanding child in the supermarket. If the mother leaves him to go on and on screaming, the child's sense of exclusion will increase. She may eventually, out of her own frustration or sense of humiliation, give him a sweet or a smack to shut him up. Either way, she has not empathised with his feelings and helped him to manage them, but she has acted on the basis of her own needs. Typically, this will be out of failures in her own upbringing whereby she herself was not related to on the basis of her own needs or helped to learn how to manage frustration. The effect is that her child will not be able to develop a sense of himself which can integrate and master both his omnipotence and helplessness. Getting the sweet may feel like gratification, but it is a hollow gift in that the child is being fobbed off in order to be kept quiet. He is not being given the experience of containment and help to manage his frustration. Getting the smack is not only punishment, it also provides the needed contact with the mother. However, instead of providing recognition of the child's real dilemma, the contact generates mutual excitability. Such interaction, if repeated sufficiently often, lays down a pattern for future relationships where aggression is sexualised. This sado-masochistic mode of relating, with its mixture of punishment, humiliation, control and excited contact with the other, forms a blueprint that becomes particularly intractable and gets passed down the generations. Instead of gaining a view of relating based on negotiation and give and take, the child learns that there are two protagonists – the attacker and the attacked, the controller and the controlled – and his sense of identity will necessarily encompass both aspects. In order to escape from the position of being attacked, humiliated and controlled, he may identify with the aggressor and take on that role.

The child's identification with the parents' modes of relating combines with his identification with their standards and values to form the basis of his conscience. One aspect of the conscience determines what is and is not acceptable and forgiveable, another determines the conditions under which the person feels loved and appreciated. The conscience therefore provides standards for behaviour and a means of regulating self-esteem. It is a fallacy to think that children and adolescents who behave violently do not possess a conscience. What we discover as therapists is that they have a peculiarly harsh and primitive one which offers little in the way of forgiveness or self-worth. In effect it creates an internal source of danger that is so punitive that it can only be dealt with by fight or flight – that is, by defying or evading its persecuting authority. This is a consequence of the lack of an internalised protective membrane. The vulnerable or dependent part of the person feels as helpless in relation to his punitive conscience as the child originally felt in relation to his external object.

There are a number of different pathways for the intricacies of the development of the conscience and its relationship to the self, and we will restrict ourselves to just a few of the dysfunctional ones common in violent patients. One pathway is that the child forms an ideal picture of himself as tough and invincible in order to counteract feelings of being helpless and utterly vulnerable. Some patients describe this in terms of being the 'iron man' or the 'dictator', which gives them a sense of an idealised self that they have to live up to and also a tyrannical model of both internal and external control. Tyranny as the only available mode of control contrasts sharply with the more tolerant conscience. This contrast highlights one of the differences between a rigid barrier and a flexible protective membrane. The benefit of a healthy conscience is that, while effectively exercising appropriate controls and offering satisfactions from mastery, it also makes less rigid and unforgiving demands on the self and other. Another dysfunctional pathway is that of the child who, out of fear of his own or the parents' uncontrollable aggression, retreats from all conflictual situations, especially competition, and becomes compliant. He gains self-esteem from living up to his ideal of himself as 'good' whilst perceiving others as aggressive. This type of child does not learn to differentiate between shades of angry feelings (ranging from mild irritation to murderous rage), nor does he aquire ways of asserting himself appropriately. He may, if faced with an extreme situation, suddenly explode with violent fury.

Whilst the child is young and relatively weak physically, he can feel somewhat assured that an adult will restrain him bodily if his aggression gets out of hand. Once he reaches adolescence, however, he has more physical strength to overpower and damage others. Alongside this increase in physical strength, the adolescent's sexual and aggressive urges become more powerful and also give rise to much anxiety and confusion. Also, the adolescent is struggling against the wish to remain like a child and against the fear of becoming an independent adult, and he is trying to find an identity that will make him feel good about himself. The desperate need not to be abnormal, ubiquitous in adolescence, arouses heightened fears of humiliation which severely test his capacity for mastery and the effectiveness of his conscience. It is not uncommon, for example, for an adolescent to build up an image of himself as tough, potent, active and 'not a push-over' as a defence against age-typical regressive wishes or passive anxieties.

For those young people whose earlier development was disturbed and who have arrived at adolescence with inadequate resources for self-protection, mastery and a healthy conscience, violence may become the way in which they shape their identity. There are some adolescent boys with a history of being picked on at school, who, at some point, decide to fight back. One patient expressed this as 'one day the worm turned'. He insisted that he was not a bully and in fact hated bullies. Whenever he fought he saw himself as protecting the weak and exploited. Such a patient has an uneasy relationship with his physical aggression which troubles his conscience. By contrast an adolescent who revels in persistent violence is much more chilling and hard to engage in therapy (see clinical example: Tom, this chapter).

We have described some typical developmental pathways in order to understand how they have gone astray for the violent individual. Our major point concerns the construction of a rigidly fortified barrier in a desperate attempt to compensate for the lack of a flexible protective membrane, internalised by the child in healthy development as a result of good-enough mothering. It is not clear how or when this rigid barrier becomes established. Our view is that, although it has its roots in early infancy, the barrier itself takes a long time to solidify and is probably not firmly in place until mid- or late adolescence.

Implications for clinical work

The purpose of this section is not to advocate modifications of standard psychotherapeutic technique, but working with patients who act out violently presents us with specific hazards, chief amongst these are doing, saying or being something which acts as a provocation to the patient. One ignores at one's peril the fact that the patient's perception of danger is different from ours. On the other hand, if we are so careful not to offend that we cannot risk ever saying anything that may cause pain or disturbance, we are hardly in the business of doing therapy. The daily craft of psychotherapy has been described as walking on a tightrope, and this is particularly relevant to working with violent patients. Fear, danger and safety – whether the patient's or the therapist's – are central issues. Ultimately, the only and best safeguard is good technique grounded in the psychotherapist's own psychoanalysis. The therapist's awareness of her own sadism, frustration and narcissistic vulnerability is particularly crucial.

The therapist working with violent youngsters has the difficult task of combining two contradictory perspectives: provision of safety, and understanding that her efforts to reach the patient will inevitably represent a danger situation for him. Where helplessness is the central danger, the capacity to experience oneself in need of help cannot be taken for granted. An interpretation which reaches the patient's vulnerability runs the risk of being experienced as a puncturing of his protective barrier and may provoke a violent reaction in the room.

The violent child desperately attempts and fails to find some sense of safety and stability. Being unable to process and contain his anxieties, he cannot think, only act. The child psychotherapist needs to respect the child's desperate attempts to cope as the only way he has found so far to protect himself from unmanageable anxiety. It is to be expected that the patient is simply unable to do anything other than experience the therapist as undependable as well as dangerous. The therapist will have to earn the patient's trust, and this is likely to take an extremely long time. In the meantime, the therapist may well understand the child's difficulty in allowing himself to become attached and needy of her, but to interpret this to him in the early stages of therapy may be experienced as a humiliating attack.

It is up to the child psychotherapist to think and process what is happening in the room in the way the child cannot. She needs to address his bodily enactments as concrete expressions of his emotional states – that is, provide one of the functions of the protective shield – in order to help the child to begin to process them for himself. This has to be done in a very careful way so as not to be intrusive, patronising or humiliating.

The following clinical examples, of a six-year-old and a seventeen-year-old, highlight some of the difficulties of working with violent children and adolescents and give a feeling of what the experience is like both for the therapist and the patient.

Clinical example: Charles

A six-year-old boy was referred for five-times-weekly analysis because of severe aggressive outbursts, an inability to relate to peers, and alarming swings between infantile behaviour and pseudo-mature language. In his first session he behaved initially like a toddler, crawling on the floor, flinging the toys over his shoulder aimlessly and naming the toys in a babyish voice. When the therapist said she knew he was very unhappy sometimes and that she was there to help him understand his worries so that he could be happier, Charles said in quite a different voice, 'Well, shall I tell you about my worries then? I don't like school, I have a devil inside me, and I get cross with my mummy.'

Such direct communications were extremely rare and fleeting, and were invariably followed by infantile and aggressive behaviour. He suffered from extreme fears of abandonment, perceiving himself as a 'devil' whom his parents hated, a pattern repeated in the transference relationship. He seemed hell-bent on proving that the therapist must hate him and want to be rid of him.

His physical attacks on the therapist were very violent. At times he behaved like a wild animal: he would spit and bite, hit and kick, hurl toys at her. When lunging at the therapist he used every bit of his body as a weapon. At first these attacks seemed unprovoked and unpredictable, but the therapist came to understand that she herself was the source of danger. Careful interpretations, instead of containing his anxiety, actually heightened it and fuelled more violent attacks. She felt shaken, helpless, overwhelmed. She had to set limits for her own safety and to safeguard her capacity to continue working with him; she was also convinced that allowing him to hurt her or the room would confirm his view of himself as unstoppably evil. Setting limits was a good deal more a case of dodging missiles and thinking on her feet than implementing a programme. When she could not dodge the physical assaults she had to restrain him physically. What was so hard about this was that she was in an aroused state which she recognised as bordering on wanting to be sadistic towards him. This had to be watched carefully. When holding him she tried to talk to him, saying she knew this was awful and that he felt controlled and trapped by her, but she needed to keep them both safe. She would also say that she knew he would be scared of her and might not want to come to the next session, and that he would fear she didn't like him any more.

It seemed wholly inadequate to understand these physical attacks as manifestations of rage. Rather, they were driven by panic. They were enactments of his internal chaos. He could only enact because of his inability to process his emotional experiences in symbolic form, either through play or words. There was, however, a very primitive attempt to hold himself together by an identification with a devilish object. He became phobic of the therapist and would either resist coming to the room or run out of the building where he had to be kept safe from dashing in front of cars in the street. Or he would come to the room and attempt to defecate there. When taken to the toilet he would smear his faeces and want the therapist to clean him up. This demonstrates his predicament: he needed the protective intervention of the very person he feared.

Attempts by the therapist to help him organise his chaos by verbalising his fears and fantasies had the effect of making his emotional experiences yet more concrete. As his anxiety increased, so did his bodily enactments. The therapist had to show that she could survive his attacks and would not reject him, frequently referring to her need to keep them both safe until he could manage this for himself. A therapy 'language' then had to be found to communicate with Charles in a way that made words meaningful yet safe. The therapist's ability to understand and speak of his enactments as 'body talk' facilitated a shift towards symbolic communication. She gradually began to talk about his 'spilly feelings', but only at times when he was relatively calm and not when he was actually 'spilling' out his chaos.

As his experiences with the therapist were sufficiently contained, understood and described in a way that he could hear, Charles began to be able to play. This offered a displacement from 'body talk' for the expression of his anxieties and fantasies. Gradually he became obsessed with building gold mines, nuclear power stations and dams, which expressed his concerns about anal explosions and dangerous substances leaking out and destroying everything. One day he built a dam and spoke with mounting anxiety about the dam breaking and destroying the nearby town. The therapist understood the imminent approach of a dangerous 'spilly' situation, but did not interpet this directly, recognising that her words would be experienced by Charles as referring to a concrete reality. Instead, she addressed it in displacement by talking of his fear of the town getting destroyed because the water could not be contained, and verbalising the wish to keep it safe. She suggested that they could make special valves in the wall of the dam to let out small amounts of water at manageable intervals to prevent the possibility of flooding. Charles was noticeably relieved and kissed her. She then said that she understood how frightened he got that his feelings would spill out, like the water in the dam, and that she was going to try to help him find ways of managing his 'spilly' feelings so that they did not flood him.

Initially everything spilled out of him – bodily contents, feelings, words. He lacked any sense of safety and containment, which the therapist had to provide. However the aim was not just to keep him safe, but to enable him to internalise the protective function initially provided by the therapist. The first step was to help him recognise an impending danger (approach of spilly feelings) which would then allow him to prepare himself by using anxiety as a signal. The next step was to help him to find appropriate defences to deal with anxiety. Developing some symbolic capacity to play and use words meaningfully were the necessary condition of this process, enabling him to do the equivalent of letting out small amounts of water to prevent flooding.

At a later stage, when his analysis was threatened by his parents, Charles reverted to concrete enactments aroused by the danger of losing his therapist by trying to climb on the banisters outside the therapy room. Such self-endangering behaviour escalated towards the end of sessions. Interpretations (such as his fear of being dropped by the therapist, his anger that she was not safely holding on to him and his analysis) again proved fruitless. To prevent him from falling downstairs, he had to be physically restrained again. Over time the therapist realised that this was turning into an excited battle for him, so she decided instead to stand in front of the therapy room door to prevent him from escaping towards the banisters. Charles erupted into a tantrum, throwing himself around the room and screaming, but he did not attack the therapist with any force. She tried to stay calm, telling him it was very important that he did not get hurt. She said she knew that he got wobbly at the end of the session because he was worried that she wanted to say goodbye, and added that perhaps he needed to know that she wanted to see him tomorrow (referring here with some delicacy to his fear that his object wished him dead). Finally the orgy of extreme emotions subsided and Charles fell to the floor in a heap, clinging to her ankles and lovingly repeating her name, 'My ***, my ***'. He could then leave the sessions calmly.

This case report highlights some of the elements that arise in clinical work with violent patients. Although Charles is physically aggressive towards the therapist, she can tolerate the aggression sufficiently to remain receptive to the underlying internal state of panic and chaos. She realises that his capacity to symbolise is limited at best and fails entirely at times of pressure – particularly when in the grip of what might be called separation anxiety, which in his case collapses into terror of being annihilated. Thus, what looks like a child attacking his therapist is understood as a child terrified that the therapist is out to kill him. She is prepared to act to keep him and herself safe, but talks to him the while. She has also recognised that close physical contact, instead of making the child feel safe, can generate excitement. The alternative action of barring his exit from the room leads to the danger of his feeling trapped. She understands a great deal more than she interprets, having observed that addressing his feelings can heighten his anxiety, because he hears her words as concretely bringing about the very danger situation he dreads. It is only after she judges that he feels safe that she addresses his fear that he will spill out.

This case illustrates why experiences of humiliation are so universally the trigger to violence in older children and adolescents. In the absence of symbolisation, being humiliated is not an emotional experience, it is a body-feeling of substances spilling out.

While working with a child as young as Charles is taxing, physically and emotionally, it provides an invaluable opportunity to understand the sheer life and death nature of the anxieties which trigger violence. Charles has not yet fortified himself with an impenetrable barrier. With the violent adolescent the picture is much harder to read. The underlying helplessness is scarcely observable and the youngster has had the resurgence of sexual and aggressive urges of puberty to contend with. Our next example demonstrates the different difficulties in working with an adolescent with a rigidly protective barrier already in place.

Clinical example: Tom

Seventeen-year-old Tom had no compunction about his violence, and indeed gloried in it. His whole sense of identity was shaped by violence.

Tom was referred for once-weekly psychotherapy following an attempted rape on a girl who looked like someone who had ditched him for another boy. He tried to carry out his careful plan to lie in wait for a suitable girl and then rape her at knife-point. He got as far as holding the knife to her throat, but, unable to proceed with the rape, he demanded money instead. He returned to the same spot the next day determined to carry through his plan fully this time, but the police had been alerted to the incident of the day before and were there to pick him up.

Tom described being treated dismissively and violently by his mother and father. He would escape to his grandparents' house to seek refuge from his parents' beatings. In therapy he denied any hatred towards his parents, shrugging his shoulders as if his history had no power to effect him. Later, his intense sense of grievance that his younger brother had received the attention and care he had been denied became manifest. He had been bullied as a child at school, and now revelled in getting into fights. He had plans to become a powerful political leader. He had fiercely racist opinions and felt completely morally justified in terrorising boys from ethnic minorities whom he described as 'keeping themselves to themselves, taking our jobs, always getting their way, and having their own shops'. It seems that he felt justified in attacking the ethnic minorities because, in fantasy, they represented the recipients of constant access to limitless supplies and had no impediments to indulging in their regressive wishes. His earliest experiences of feeling unacknowledged and unprotected by his parents, especially mother, were carried as an unprocessed trauma which could only be enacted.

He had no wish to give up his violence towards boys, but felt helplessly besieged by fantasies of violently raping a woman. These fantasies disturbed him greatly because he feared that he would enact them again and get punished. He hoped that therapy would somehow get rid of the fantasies. It gradually became clear that his sexual fantasies were linked to warded-off feelings of murderous rage towards his mother whom he experienced as humiliating and castrating. The rape fantasies stopped when he had his first sexual relationship soon after therapy started. Significantly, this was with an older woman who was in a position of authority over him.

The experience of being in the room with Tom was very different from being with Charles. With Tom, the therapist felt a pervasive leaden barrenness that was very hard to bear. The sessions felt interminable and lifeless, but something boiled dangerously underneath the surface. It felt like being at the edge of a volcano, where the bleak grey ash could make one forget the raging power liable to erupt at any moment.

Tom came regularly to his sessions from a long distance and seemed to want help, but his fear of trusting the therapist made it very hard for him to engage in the therapeutic process. He was polite, but mostly silent. Unlike most adolescents who are silent in therapy and tend to avert their gaze, Tom invariably stared at the therapist in an expectant and disconcerting way. He found the silences very awkward, too, and wanted the therapist to take the lead by asking questions. However, if she did so she ran the risk of making him feel forcefully intruded upon. She voiced her dilemma that both her words and her silence caused him anxiety, and acknowledged what an unsafe position he was in.

As the therapist tried to explore his discomfort in the room with her, it emerged that he found all verbal communication difficult. He felt he had nothing interesting to say and consistently felt nobody noticed him. The therapist addressed the terrible loneliness of this, suggesting that it was very hard for him to feel he was a 'somebody' worthy of notice. It was as if he was invisible. He agreed and said that the only thing he could talk about that would always make an impact was his racist political opinions. It did not matter whether the reaction was positive or negative. All that mattered was that he got an intense reaction. The therapist linked this urgent need to get through to people with his helpless isolation of never having felt acknowledged by his mother. She wondered if the only way he felt he could make an impact on someone was by force, that is, by his forceful political views or physical violence. This seemed to reach him. He responded by saying for the first time that he felt helpless and vulnerable sometimes.

Tom's violence can be understood in terms of identification with the aggressor, as well as his unconscious need to blot out his vulnerability. It was characteristic of this adolescent that, while allowing the therapist the briefest of glimpses into his extreme neediness, he had organised himself around a complete denial of any regressive wishes. He presented himself as an immaculately besuited adult with none of the typically adolescent anxieties about growing up. The capacity to acknowledge regressive wishes implies an internalised protective object who can be relied on. Without such an internal presence Tom could only deal with his regressive wishes by repudiating them and externalising them on to the ethnic minorities whom he then murderously attacked for being like greedy children who got everything they wanted.

Like Charles, Tom also had no sense of safety. This accounted for his 'tough guy' behaviour. The toughness prevented him from feeling vulnerable and fortified a rigid internal barrier as a substitute for the missing protective function. The absence of Tom's internal protective membrane was dramatically illustrated when he spoke of having no fear of physical danger and being able to fend for himself. When he was beaten up by a gang of other boys he was only concerned about the fact that his clothes were torn and he made light of the severe bruising of his body. The holes in his shirt can be understood as concretely equated with damage to his very self, which was far more dangerous for Tom than damage to his body.

In this profile of an adolescent we see how violence offers a false solution which bypasses age-appropriate conflicts and developmental tasks rather than tackling them. With a violent and negating mother and no age-appropriate allowance for omnipotence in early childhood, the smallest slight was experienced as the most devastating trauma. It was only when his sense of being both dismissively unacknowledged and also intruded upon by the therapist could be meaningfully addressed and worked on, that he could begin to recognise some of his own helplessness and vulnerability. Underneath the presentation of himself as all-powerful there was a frightened and humiliated child whose only way of protecting himself from an overwhelming sensitivity to feeling a rejected nobody was to act violently. Coldly calculated violence shaped Tom's identity specifically so that he would not experience the threat to his psychic survival and the anxieties this mobilises. The excitement of being violent also offered a powerful antidote to other buried feelings such as fear, depression and dependency.

Further clinical issues

The clinical examples above show the importance of establishing a safe setting in the patient's as well as the therapist's mind so that the therapeutic work can proceed. This is no easy matter. From the child's point of view, the therapist is someone to be feared because she represents for him the original unprotective parent as well as an externalisation of the child's primitive conscience. The therapist needs to be especially careful not to compound this by seeming in any way dismissive or punitive. From the therapist's point of view, she has to deal with the impact of the child's very primitive anxieties which will inevitably trigger her own. In practice, the twin dangers are that she may either defend against her own anxieties by denying that she is with a patient who could well attack her, or be so afraid of this possibility that she cannot be receptive to the patient's needs. It is worth bearing in mind that the patient will find it intolerable to be at the receiving end of the very defences he relies upon: for example, failing to be receptive to the patient will be experienced as putting up an impenetrable barrier against him. This is a major provocation to the patient. Additionally, the therapist will have to contend with the arousal of her sadism when attacked. She may respond to this by wishing to control or get rid of the patient. Since the work proceeds slowly and acting out is inevitable, she will also have to deal with feeling useless, helpless and guilty.

We have already noted the crucial importance of the therapist's own psychoanalysis and self-awareness. Supervision is also vital for providing a setting where the therapist's state of mind can be acknowledged and contained.

The child psychotherapist's concern is with the whole child and not exclusively with his violence. This is not an easy perspective to hold on to when the referring agency's preoccupation is, quite understandably, with the curbing of the child's dangerous behaviour. Therapy with such patients will require careful management. Putting the appropriate structure in place is crucial both to free the therapist for her proper task and also to provide the necessary communication with those who are responsible for the child (such as the child's carers, teachers, social workers). For the child psychotherapist to expect she can do it all is not only unrealistic, but it runs the risk of her either feeling she has to do everything omnipotently herself or feeling overwhelmed with helplessness in relation to the concerns of external agencies. In extreme cases, it may have to be recognised that psychotherapy is not possible until the child is in a safe-enough environment. This may involve recommendations for more suitable placement.

Conclusion

This chapter argues the limitations of an exclusive preoccupation with aggression in working with violent youngsters. We suggest instead that violence be understood as an attempted solution to a trauma the individual has not been able to process, and we define this trauma as helplessness in the absence of a protective object. In arguing for this orientation we may be thought to be condoning violence, treating the perpetrator as victim. On the contrary, our position is that the youngster is both a perpetrator (in the external world and in his ideal image of himself) and also a victim (having been failed at a point of maximum helplessness and lacking an internalised protective membrane). He enacts this disjunction, causing harm to others and inviting punishment unconsciously from the law. The job of the child psychotherapist is to resist collusion either with the values of his ideal self (violence) or the demands of his harsh conscience (sadistic punishment); rather, it is to understand his predicament, something he cannot do himself. In the task of neither condoning nor judging the youngster, we have found the ideas summarised in our main thesis crucial. It has enabled us to establish emotional contact with patients who find it singularly difficult to communicate effectively with others, or indeed with themselves, without resorting to violence.

Notes

1 For a psychoanalytic account of adolescent group violence, and an exploration of the distinction between a group and a gang see Hyatt Williams (1997).
2 In this formulation we are referring to what has been called 'self-preservative' as opposed to 'sado-masochistic' or 'malicious' violence. However sado-masochistic violence will be addressed later in the chapter. For a discussion of this differentiation see Glasser (1998).

References

Colarusso, C. A. (1992) *Child and Adult Development: a Psychoanalytic Introduction for Clinicians*, New York/London: Plenum Press.

Edgcumbe, R. (1976) 'The development of aggressiveness in children', *Nursing Times* April (RCN Supplement): vii–xv.

Fraiberg, S. (1982) 'Pathological defences in infancy', *Psychoanalytic Quarterly* 51: 612–41.

Freud, A. (1949) 'Aggression in relation to emotional development: normal and pathological', *Psychoanalytic Study of the Child*, Vol. 3/4, New York: International Universities Press.

—— (1972) 'Comments on aggression', in *Psychoanalytic Psychology of Normal Development*, London: Hogarth Press, 1982.

Freud, S. (1920) 'Beyond the pleasure principle', *S.E.* 18, London: Hogarth.

Furman, E. (1992) *Toddlers and their Mothers*, Madison CT: International Universities Press.

Glasser, M. (1998) 'On violence: a preliminary communication', *International Journal of Psychoanalysis* 79(5): 887–902.

Hyatt Williams, A. (1997) 'Violence in adolescence', in V. Varma (ed.) *Violence in Children and Adolescents*, London: Jessica Kingsley.

Khan, M. (1973) 'The concept of cumulative trauma', *Psychoanalytic Study of the Child*, Vol. 18, New York: International Universities Press.

Stern, D. N. (1985) *The Interpersonal World of the Human Infant*, New York: Basic Books.

Tyson, P. and Tyson, R. L. (1990) *Psychoanalytic Theories of Development*, New Haven: Yale University Press.

Winnicott, D. W. (1963) 'From dependence towards independence in the development of the individual', in D. W. Winnicott *The Maturational Processes and the Facilitating Environment*, London: Hogarth Press, 1979.

Further reading

Campbell, D. (1996) 'From practice to psychodynamic theories of delinquency in adolescence', in C. Cordess and M. Cox (eds) *Forensic Psychotherapy: Crime, Psychodynamics and the Offender Patient, Vol. 1, Mainly Theory*, London: Jessica Kingsley.

Chiland, C. and Young, G. (1994) *Children and Violence*, New Jersey: Jason Aronson.

Varma, V. (ed.) (1997) *Violence in Children and Adolescents*, London: Jessica Kingsley.

Winnicott, D. W. (1947) 'Hate in the countertransference', in *Through Paediatrics to Psycho-Analysis*, London: Hogarth Press, 1978.

—— (1962) 'Integration in child development', in *The Maturational Processes and the Facilitating Environment*, London: Hogarth Press, 1979.

—— (1969) 'The use of an object and relating through identifications', in *Playing and Reality*, Harmondsworth: Penguin Books.

23 Sexual abuse and sexual abusing in childhood and adolescence

Ann Horne

Prologue

Case study: Wayne

Wayne was four years old when his new 'stepfather' first abused him sexually. His natural father had left six months previously, following a relationship with Wayne's mother characterised by absence, frequent drunkenness and unpredictable violence. Wayne's mother also had a serious drinking problem and said she was unaware that her new partner had a previous conviction for the sexual abuse of an infant. The nursery reported their concerns to Social Services when Wayne became preoccupied with the genitals of other children whom he would invite into the toilet with him. His attempts to remove another child's trousers led to complaints to his mother but no apparent action other than her rage with Wayne. The realisation of his mother's partner's conviction, together with her reluctance to give up the relationship, led to Wayne's being removed into care. He was placed with temporary foster parents in a family where he was the youngest, and then with another family when the first found his sexually inviting behaviour towards the foster father too provocative and his attempts to insert objects in his anus too disgusting. Disclosure interviews were indecisive; there were no corroborating witnesses; no prosecution followed. No referral was made to any service for therapeutic work.

Wayne returned to his mother at the age of six when she separated from this partner. His behaviour became strange: at home he would defecate in corners of his room and hide soiled underpants in corners or amongst clean garments. At school he spoke little and had no resources for engaging with other children. He could be goaded into silly and often dangerous behaviour. He stood on his desk and removed his clothes; he hid in the teacher's cupboard. Frequently he ran out of the class and the school worried about their capacity to keep him safe. An ongoing curiosity about younger children was equally worrying: his peers dealt with it by calling him 'Jayne' or 'pervert'; his teachers were more wary, monitoring his opportunities for being with smaller children. His mother found him unmanageable at home – angry with her, oppositional and often running away. Mother's complaints led to a referral at age eight to child guidance where sterling efforts were made to engage the family, but mother's unreliability meant that no solid work could be undertaken. By now, many agencies were involved and concerned. A new partner arrived; a new baby was born. The social work network hoped that a 'father' would help. Mother turned up at Social Services when Wayne was ten: she wanted rid of him before he broke up her current relationship. She saw him as malicious, deliberately trying to destroy her and 'evil'.

Wayne went to stay with a foster family who found him 'unlikeable'. A change of placement was made to an experienced family where Wayne settled, although he was still exhibiting severe learning and behavioural difficulties in school. The illness of the foster mother's mother led to the former's frequent absence and distraction and Wayne, now aged twelve, was moved again. This placement broke down after three months. After much co-ordinated work with the foster family and Social Services, Wayne was sent to a residential home from which he attended a weekly boarding school. Contact with the family was disorganised with Wayne frequently running from school to home and from home to school. A preoccupation with soiled underwear (women's) was hard for the school to handle. Wayne at thirteen was accused of 'interfering sexually' with his four-year-old sister and a neighbour's three-year-old boy on a home visit. At this point he was finally referred to a specialist clinic in London for assessment, advice and treatment.

Introduction

There may be those who object to one chapter covering the work of the child psychotherapist with sexually abused and abusing children and young people. The one group, after all, is victimised by the other. Several therapists have told me of how they feel unable to work with young abusers and link this to the intensity of feeling experienced in their work with abused children: anxiety that this outrage might spill over, be uncontainable, in work with the latter group seems common. There is also an interesting but intellectually flawed position which sees work in this area as of necessity polarised – either one helps the victims or one is, by treating the abuser, somehow condoning the acts committed. It becomes an almost impossible task to try to integrate the developmental trauma that is a feature of both groups into one's internal picture and to hold in mind the abuser as both offender and victim.

It may be that part of the process at work is the impact of the act of abusing on the mind of the therapist – with *both* groups of young people. Both touch the therapist's 'perverse core' (Chasseguet-Smirgel 1985). Our basic tenets of morality are challenged in a most disturbing way (Freud, S. 1913). Both, equally, engage the network surrounding the child/adolescent in what can too often become an exercise in non-communication, contradiction and split functioning – sometimes it feels like a war zone. It is vital, therefore, to give thought to the re-enactment of abuse and the mirroring of the internal world of victim and offender (Davies 1996) which occur all too easily amongst those involved in this work. Central to this process is making space for thought: the process of memory, recollection and thinking is attacked so easily in child and network, and in the often disbelieving outside world. It is, after all, not so long ago that Butler-Schloss strove to convince the public of the presence of sexual abuse in Cleveland (Butler-Schloss 1988).

Prevalence and definition

From the research surveyed by Kolvin and Trowell (1996), key areas in the definition of sexual abuse are:

(a) direct acts – molestation, penetration and force all appear on a spectrum of greater or lesser psychological damage
(b) indirect acts – e.g. enforced watching of pornography; genital exposure
(c) exploitation – the balance of power between abused and abuser is an important factor.

Each of these factors needs to be weighed when thinking of the impact of abuse on children.

Prevalence is an inexact science, not least because of differences in definition. Apart from clear-cut incidents, there are times when clinical judgement may indicate abuse but evidence and witnesses be lacking. Under-reporting is also likely to be a feature. Estimates, such as that by Smith and Bentovim (1994), that 15–30 per cent of women are likely to have experienced some form of undesired sexual contact during childhood, may therefore be cautious. The rate for men – less frequently considered in the past but now fortunately gaining attention – seems to be a little less than half of that for women:

about 20,000 to 40,000 16 year old boys will have experienced sexual abuse involving bodily contact at some time.

(Flood 1994)

It is even more difficult to ascertain the prevalence of organised or ritual abuse, in part because there is resistance to taking on board further depths to the human psyche and to hearing the unbearable. That it exists is not in doubt and, as Trowell notes, increased recognition will follow increasing awareness (Trowell 1994). The detailed clinical reports given by Sinason demonstrate the different depth of fear and the desperate psychological measures required of children subjected to such abuse (Sinason 1994).

Recovered memory and false allegations

The issues surrounding 'false memory syndrome' and recovered memories tend to be less problematic in child psychotherapy than in work with adults. Any abuse tends to be more available – further detail may be recovered but rarely abuse which comes as any surprise to those working with the child. Children are usually referred for therapy following disclosure or where some investigation has been pursued in relation to sexualised or otherwise worrying behaviour. It was Wayne's misfortune, in the introductory vignette, that, following the initial Social Services intervention, no referral was made to Child Mental Health services.

It can, however, happen that a child in therapy makes allegations of abuse. Mostly, children's allegations are true: indeed, concern tends to be over the non-reporting of abuse rather than about the 2 per cent of allegations which turn out to be false. In a review of the literature on false allegations, Adshead (1994) gives a helpful context when she states:

> children very rarely make up malicious false allegations of their own accord: in 98 per cent of allegations, children are *not* deliberately setting out to make trouble for adults. . . . False allegations appear to be much more likely when adults initiate them (such as in custody disputes), and these appear to be the majority of allegations.
>
> (Adshead 1994: 59)

Indeed, Goodwin found that false retractions (where a child withdraws a claim of abuse yet that abuse is later found to be corroborated) were as common (Goodwin *et al.* 1978).

Displaced allegations are not unknown in this work, where the child, usually when he feels safe in his situation (perhaps in a good foster home), accuses a safe adult of acts which another adult figure committed. Allegations are also made against therapists. Ironside (1995) provides a painful, important and thoughtful comment on the meaning of the 'disclosure' when false allegations are made by a child about his therapist. The experience of early trauma and the defences marshalled against this are noted as influences in the child's concrete thinking and re-enactment, and helpful comment is given on the varied responses triggered in the network in three case examples. The capacity to continue to think becomes vital as therapy is disrupted and therapist attacked by an unthinking system. Regaining a position in which thought becomes available once more is vital in such a scenario.

Thinking developmentally about the impact of abuse

When one returns to theories of normal development in children (see Chapter 3), it is possible to see many points at which an experience of trauma can leave the child ill-equipped to grow emotionally and meet the world with confident curiosity. A fuller account is given in Chapter 19, together with protective factors, to which the reader should refer. It is important to keep in mind the resources – inner, psychological and external – available to the child in coping with experiences which are overwhelming to the immature sense of self, and to reflect on the strategies to which the child must have recourse in order to survive. A sense of developmental insult is the strongest legacy of the sexual abuse of children.

We know that the consequences of sexual abuse are more traumatic when the abuse has involved body contact:

> Abuse involving penetration, abuse which is perpetrated by a father/ step father or other trusted adult, or abuse which involves violence or force, are all likely to be particularly damaging. Repeated abuse which endures over a long period is also associated with a more serious impact.
>
> (Flood 1994)

It is clear from our knowledge of normal emotional development that the body not only is the first 'self' or 'ego' for the child, but also that its changes have constantly to be incorporated into the changing sense of identity finally established by late adolescence (see Chapter 3). Keeping in mind the importance of early, in-tune relationships for the healthy psychological development of the child, and our knowledge of the drive for engagement and attachment present in the infant, the impact of abuse on what should be positive and essential aspects of the child's experience cannot be under-estimated. It therefore follows that:

> an act of child abuse bisects the line of normal development and disrupts the natural timing of the biological clock and turns the oedipus complex upside down. Incestuous wishes are gratified with parents, siblings or adolescents or adults who are perceived as sibling or parental substitutes.
>
> (Campbell 1994)

Although a clear distinction is made in psychoanalytic theory between perpetrators of incest and of paedophilia, it is important to keep in mind that, for the child, the incestuous relationship may be one involving the principal caring person in that child's life, the only person to whom the child feels special, and so add to the difficulty in recognising right and wrong and in talking about it. Indeed, it can in many ways be easier to deal with abuse by an outsider whom one can hate, than by a loved person where love and hate are then difficult to integrate.

To this one would add that we do not yet know enough about the impact of abuse when the child is a pre-verbal infant. The importance of an adult who believes the child's disclosure and takes immediate action to ensure the child's protection is a known protective factor in relation to recovery from the trauma and the capacity to resume a developmental path. For the pre-verbal child, beginning to gain a sense of body ego, which becomes corrupted, and with no recourse to language, the situation is critical unless an attuned adult can make sense of other cues about distress. Equally, the role of mothers in abuse is only beginning to be explored (Welldon 1988; Gurisik and Horne, in preparation): Smith and Bentovim (1994) propose that as much as 5–15 per cent of child sexual abuse is at the hands of women; Sinason (1996) provides a vivid comment on what the child experiences as abusive in her descriptions of pubertal and pre-pubertal boys who are made to share a bed with their mothers.

If the abuse happens within the family, the capacity to make and use attachments and object relationships is severely damaged, and the sense of normality is turned upside down. Adults blame children for their seduction; children are made responsible for the adults; boundaries between parents and children become totally muddled; ideas of 'loving' and 'caring' are confused. The capacity, then, for any Oedipal resolution (see Chapter 3) and for making use of other adults and identifications is limited. Equally, the ego ideal, developing in toddlerhood, is corrupted and the protective function of shame damaged (Campbell 1994). The sense of control, fairness and conscience that should develop in latency is inhibited and often a cruel and punitive conscience, driven to seek punishment, results. It becomes impossible to distinguish rules and to take in from peers and other adults. Indeed, learning is disrupted (Sinason 1991): how can one 'take in' in a meaningful way or even use any orifices for hearing, seeing, talking when all are rendered unsafe.

The integration, in adolescence, of this traumatised body–self into the adolescent identity may become a matter of impossible conflict. Within the development of girls there comes a recognition of the permeability of the body, preparation for intercourse and pregnancy. Attacks on this body (self-mutilation, eating disorders) and the body products (babies/children) are one response to overwhelming, indigestible memories of sexual trauma (Welldon 1988). For boys, the boundariedness of the body has been violated, leaving a fear of feminisation, or homosexual fears (which may be dealt with by violence – *vide* Chapter 22) at a time when fluidity of sexual feeling and object choices is a normal, expected possibility. Equally, the role of the penis at adolescence can become a matter of conflict – how can it be used in a potent, creative and penetrative way that does not become destructive or abusive.

The defences available to the child to deal with abuse will depend on the maturity of the child at the time of the abuse, as well as on the capacity of the adults to hear and act on any disclosure. Where there has not been suitable intervention at the time, this may result in the child growing older but resorting to a repertoire of very primitive defence mechanisms, normally found in much younger children. Issues about the body will be re-enacted through the body: the young child may repeat his sexual anxiety by trying to interest other children in his body and explore theirs – as Wayne did in the prologue to this chapter. The older child may put himself in dangerous situations with no internalised sense of self-preservation. In adolescence, the young person may turn to abusing others or seek a repeat of the original abuse by prostitution: the 16-year-old rent boy feels in control of the older men whom he seduces, but is, in fact, repeating his abuse with a veneer of being in control. The 14-year-old girl who has turned to prostitution and to encouraging others in this is both assuming a false control over her compulsion to repeat and creating other victims as safe locations for her sense of powerlessness.

The choices in such an extreme are to identify with the aggressor and become an abuser, repeating the cycle and making someone else into a victim; to externalise the abuse; or to adopt a victim role as a way of feeling that at least this choice is under one's control. The final choice is suicide. For many children, a 'splitting' process takes place as they try to deny what has happened: the memory of the abuse sinks to the bottom of the pre-conscious memory to enable the child to continue to function. This, however, leaks gradually into the conscious mind (Trowell 1992). One young man, abused at boarding school, described it as 'having a fire in my head. I close a door on it and it's OK for a while. Then it burns through again and I close another door – but it doesn't go away.' This 'splitting-off' process is an attempt to deal with the experience of powerlessness and humiliation only too common in victims of abuse: sexual abuse by an adult or parent-substitute is, after all, an abuse of a relationship of power and responsibility. Such denial is also often used in the service of retaining some sense of being parentable. All children have to deal with the conviction that their parents have failed them – at the least, by not protecting them. For some, an identity as 'disgusting' and 'bad' is preferable to the dramatic loss and abandonment to be faced in acknowledging the failure in parenting.

It is the memory of humiliation and powerlessness that is unbearable and needs to be evacuated or located elsewhere. One can see, in many adolescent abusers, the flashback memories of their own abuse being turned into the fantasy of abusing a weaker, more vulnerable victim as a way of getting back in control. The leap from memory/fantasy to action, denying any space for thought, results in acting-out with the body in a repetition of the abuse.

The clinical task in individual psychotherapy with sexually abused children

Preliminary issues for the therapist

The therapist working with the sexually abused child has first to face personal issues: in a sense, the fact of the abuse cannot be mended. We work often in NHS teams where 'treatment' and 'cure' are concepts used daily. Yet trauma cannot be undone; the now sexualised child cannot turn back from adult awareness and the experience of being a child has been corrupted. The challenge to omnipotence in the clinical team is great and may be one of the reasons why the work is so stressful.

> Bridie, a thoughtful fourteen-year-old, had been abused while at primary school over a number of years by her babysitter, a boy of sixteen. Thinking about ending her weekly therapy (appropriately) she said, 'It's like taking a walk through the forest. The hunters have laid traps for the wild animals – dug holes and covered them over, so that you can't see them on the pathway. I can't fill in the traps but I have learned to walk round them and not fall into them.'

The therapist is also faced with internal conflict over the need, therapeutically, to hear the child's story and give it full acknowledgement, while struggling with a wish not to do so. Such stories are disturbing, not simply in content but also in the realisation that we are all, as human beings, capable of perverse and unimaginable acts. It is imperative, in work with sexually abused children, to have a venue for sharing feelings aroused in the work – somewhere to take them where space is given for thought. Without this, there is not only a danger of the re-enactment of sadistic and abusive elements in the therapy – a process unconsciously sought by the child – but of exhaustion and burn-out in the therapist who, like the child, becomes overwhelmed and rendered impotent by the abusive experience.

The most immediate expectation of the abused child is that the adult – any adult – will wish to repeat the abuse. This has to be allowed into the transference relationship where the therapist must be available to be perceived as a potentially abusive adult (Sinason 1991). It challenges our professional identity as belonging to the 'good guys', those who listen and help mend, but such work cannot achieve anything unless the potential to abuse is addressed in the transference.

When beginning work with a sexually abused child, the clinician should give thought to issues of confidentiality. It is usual to explain this to children in terms of privacy, and to talk of breaching it only when issues of safety are paramount. For the abused child, this can become very confused with the enforced secrecy that is inevitably part of sexual abuse. The abuse of power in the sexually abusive relationship will have involved secrecy and threats of what would follow any disclosure – usually threats of loss of parents and parental affection. It is useful, therefore, in preliminary meetings with child and carers to go over the ground carefully together in relation to what is confidential, and it will be necessary from time to time to ascertain together what can be told to the outside world.

Finally, there are often severe issues for the clinic team. Sexually abused children have a capacity for acting-out that can take in the whole clinic setting. The need to evacuate memories and anxieties may, from time to time, be dealt with by running from the room, screaming and attempts at seduction of therapist and clinic staff (as a way of taking control). This can be terrifying and humiliating for the therapist, and enraging for both therapist and team as children appear to try to break all the careful treatment boundaries. Five major issues must be addressed within teams, in the interest of the progress of therapy:

(a) There must be an agreed understanding of the processes at work – that the child has recourse to the body, in a primitive way, as a way of avoiding thought and memory. The therapist and team, therefore, need to be able to think in the face of the child's overwhelming anxiety.

(b) The breaking of boundaries is a repeat of the perversion of boundaries between adults and children that has already taken place. It is helpful if the team has a strategy, supportive of the therapist, for children who insistently challenge the boundaries – e.g. comments about return to the room; not engaging in prolonged conversation with an out-of-session child. These should be clear and sustained approaches.

(c) The team needs to hold together and be aware of the danger of splits and recriminations that would repeat the unheld and scapegoated early experience of the child. It is too easy in clinics for comments to be made about each other's clinical practice and competence when what is needed is thought and mutual support. It is easy for the anger felt by all at the predicament of the child and the relentlessness of the challenging work to be acted out amongst team members. Some understanding of the countertransference of the whole clinic – receptionists and cleaners included – helps enormously in containing this and enabling the team to function together.

(d) It is essential that a team member be appointed to liaise, meet and think with the external network – a case manager. This will involve work with the parents/carers (vital) but also with the social workers, guardians *ad litem*, teachers and other professionals involved in the care of the child; it will also entail attendance at planning and review meetings. The aim is to free the therapist to be simply that – the child's therapist. This will be attacked and it takes great resistance on the part of teams to keep the lines of communication open but the boundaries firm and clear.

(e) Finally, all team members, including child psychotherapists, need a thorough knowledge of their employing Trust's Child Protection Procedures and of the recommendations of their local Area Child Protection Committee. This should be an automatic part of the induction of any new staff member.

Key themes in the process of therapy

The early process with abused children often involves great care in building basic trust. The presence of an attentive, non-abusing adult in an intimate relationship like therapy is, to the child, extremely risky. Expecting the therapist, in the transference, to be another abusing adult, yet hoping that it might not be so, the child experiences swings of hope, sudden trusting intimacy and equally sudden re-enactment of terror and the invitation to abuse. The process of coming to therapy itself can be interpreted as merely a repetition of abuse as the child struggles with ambivalence.

> Wayne took care to keep his therapist at a distance. Card games allowed him to show her that he felt he was 'tricky', untrustworthy, but a small sense of hope emerged when he carefully showed her how the tricks were done – a glimpse of the wish to be understood. He dismissed any sign of his competence, rubbished himself and her, struggled to draw and tore up his work. He wondered if she could look at horror videos – bear his internal world. Recounting one gruesome story, he suddenly saw a connection to his own experience and dashed to the far end of the room, shaking. Calm interpretation of his suddenly expecting the therapist to be like the video mother (attacking and annihilating) allowed him to return to his seat, but he remained fearful and dashed out at the end of the session.

Technical aspects remain vital with such young people. The defences that they have organised must be respected. They can be noted, verbalised and slowly explored but it will take time before sufficient ego solidity is gained to allow real questioning.

For the first few months Wayne found the process of attending for fifty-minute sessions desperately persecutory. Arriving felt like being locked away by his father, when anything could happen; leaving – no matter how carefully the therapist tried to prepare and warn him – was a repetition of abandonment. After much thought, his therapist gave him control of the last ten minutes of the session: he could choose at what point he left within this ten-minute space, although the therapist would always remain in the room for his full time and he would wait in the waiting room with his escort until she emerged to say good-bye. He rarely used this control, although he occasionally drew attention to the fact that it was now 'me to choose' time. Much later in his therapy he reflected on this and on the impotence he had felt as a child. He could now recognise states of anxiety and think rather than act.

Such strategies, while they collude briefly with the defence, give space for thinking seriously about the necessity for that defence. Space for thought takes time to achieve, as does any capacity for reflection. It is, after all, an Oedipal achievement to be able to take up a position of observing oneself and reflecting on that (Britton 1989) and Oedipal resolutions are few in seriously abused children. The process between therapist and child, whereby the therapist seeks space for reflection, takes time to internalise and recognise as safe. Even when much has been achieved, there will be regression at times of high anxiety to action rather than thought.

Attending to one's countertransference comes as a matter of course in child and adolescent work. However, the depths of feeling aroused in working with abused children, the rage and sadism unconsciously provoked and the profound and paralysing helplessness felt in the countertransference, make this more essential than ever. For therapists in this work it is vital to have individual or group supervision, or a regular clinical workshop to which one can take the experiences (Morice 1995; Trowell 1997).

When therapy is well-established, when more mature ego functioning has been achieved and a greater sense of integration is present, it is possible to arrive at three important themes:

(a) *Damage*: 'Who am I and who can I possibly be sexually?' is an issue for all abused children. Fear of pregnancy, of menstruation and of internal damage (possibly exacerbated by paediatric internal examination for police purposes) arises frequently in work with girls. Such concerns, while taken up in relation to their internal meaning, may also require external advice and intervention that can be secured, with permission, via the case manager. In boys, fear of feminisation and passivity must be addressed to enable fluidity of sexuality in adolescence. For both, there is otherwise a danger of foreclosing on any prospect of adolescent and adult sexuality.

(b) *The sense that the mother wished this to happen.* All children – even these for whom the circumstances of the abuse meant that parental failure to protect was understandable – have to deal with the sense that their mothers wished the abuse to happen and colluded with it (Trowell 1992). This internal, early-Oedipal revengeful object comes into the transference for attention in the context of the Oedipal wishes of the child. Working through is essential not only for Oedipal resolution but also in preparation for adolescent and adult sexual roles.

(c) *The child's view of his own role and responsibility* – the sense children feel of having been the seducer in an Oedipal drama replayed. This can be exacerbated by the child's awareness of betrayal by his own physiological reactions – the body is, after all, programmed to respond to sexual invitation (Sinason 1996). The child may also, as the only possible position available, have adopted a pose of enjoying or seeking the abuse as a defence against humiliation and impotence. Or the child's wishes for a loving relationship (frequently present in sibling incest) have been granted. It takes a lot of time to reach the loss of intimacy, of feeling special to the abusive attachment figure. All of this must be analysed before work can be completed.

Court

It is often very difficult to explain to colleagues why one is reluctant to provide court reports for children in therapy. The intimacy and confidentiality of the relationship, the delicacy of the transference – everything can end up frustratingly being construed as 'preciousness' on the part of the therapist. Yet – as will be evident in the section on 'Networks' – such external intrusions arrive frequently, often as a result of requests for Access Orders and Residence Orders that the court must hear.

It is possible to negotiate a position, with the child, of providing information via the case manager that allows another professional – either case manager, expert witness or *guardian ad litem* – to present a child-centred case to the court. Greater sophistication and understanding of children's needs amongst judges and barristers has helped in this process. Nowadays, this should be achievable. Nevertheless, it occasionally becomes necessary to appear in court. There can be a danger that the therapy begins to focus on the therapist's need to explain to the child, or even that the therapist's anxiety about court appearance interferes with the therapy, and helpful supervision is a great aid here. With the child, there will inevitably be a regression to former anxieties in the transference relationship. The idea of adults working together and planning together may, on the other hand, offer a practical interpretation to the child that Oedipal boundaries can be held and can work.

Forgetting and returning: an experience of normality

With the child, one seeks a 'good-enough' resolution that enables the abuse to be confronted and articulated, responsibility located, the internal sense the child makes of him or herself to be less persecutory and the defences to be more appropriate, allowing development to continue more on track. Indeed, for many sexually abused children and young people, there is a need thereafter to have an experience of forgetting (Alvarez 1989; Lanyado 1991) and a sense of returned normality. The door should be left open, however, for a return for therapeutic input: when the next developmental challenge comes along (e.g. a first boyfriend, a first equal sexual relationship, the birth of a child), the abused young person often needs to touch base again to rethink 'Who am I now?' and to accommodate the memory of the abuse into his or her evolving identity.

Working with adolescents who sexually abuse children

Assessment

It has long perturbed those working in the area of child sexual abuse that research consistently shows us that 50 per cent of abusers have themselves been abused. What, then, about the 50 per cent who say they were not abused? Are they simply unable to recall their own abuse? The recent discoveries by the research team at Great Ormond Street Children's Hospital, London, develop our understanding further (Hodges *et al.* 1994; Lanyado *et al.* 1995). It has become clear from this work that trauma, especially violence, is a key factor in the early lives of young abusers. The experience of continuing and often unpredictable violence, with concomitant feelings of rage and helplessness and with no attendant adult to make sense of or make safe the situation, is frequent in the histories of adolescents who abuse other children:

> It took Wayne ten months to talk of his terror at his father's drunken violence. His distress at remembering was evident, and he could say how afraid he was that talking of it would make him remember more. He was locked in a cupboard under the stairs while his father beat and raped his mother. He soiled himself in his fear and was beaten on his release. He wanted to murder his father. Patchy memories grew as he gained a sense that he had deserved better. He recalled his parents

drinking together and his uncertainty as to whether this would end in laughter or violence: both were possible and he could not predict which would occur by the end of an afternoon's drinking. His ambivalence towards the unprotecting, weak and yet colluding mother was unbearable. The smell of alcohol, he said, made him physically terrified. He had hit his first foster father when he came to tuck him in bed with beer on his breath. It took him a long time to recall that his sexually inviting behaviour towards this man had been his only strategy to preclude the violence that he was certain would come from him. He struggled in therapy with the knowledge that his therapist would not violate him and the uncertainty that she might change, or that he himself might be violent to her. His notion of adult sexuality was bound up with fantasies of violence. He presented fantasies of revenge for small slights, threatening and trying to shock the therapist, and drew cartoons of blood, bodies, graves and sadistic violence. His key worker was essential at this time in escorting him safely and in containing his terrifying anxieties on the way to therapy.

This experience of impotent helplessness in the face of unpredictable violence may emerge in the assessment of young abusers; it may, however, take some time to reach and marks an important point in therapy when it occurs.

It is also important at the initial stage to gain a differential diagnosis of the young person and his acts. Campbell (1994) includes in this the victim's story: the victim's feelings provide an important indicator both of the degree of the young abuser's dangerousness and of the unmanageable feelings that he is trying to decant outside him. Wayne's sister expressed unease at his attentions but also conveyed a sense of puzzlement and playfulness at her brother's actions. It was his invitation to her to touch his genitals that led to her conviction of inappropriateness and disclosure to her mother. Ali, a 16-year-old Kurdish refugee, who had experienced horrendous ethnic violence in his homeland and who was regularly physically abused by his father at home, approached the women he assaulted diffidently but left them with feelings of terror and intrusion.

Within the young person's recounting of his actions, it is helpful to get a sense of where responsibility for the offence is located – is this a young person with a clear idea of responsibility or is the child blamed for being seductive, seeking a sexual relationship? The rationalisations used in this description are helpful in assessing where, developmentally, the abusing adolescent places himself. Primitive defences of denial or projection indicate concerns about the survival of a basic sense of self. Guilt and fear often feature in an assessment; shame may only emerge (indeed, only be possible) after months of therapy. Fantasies should be explored, if at all possible, and their relation to ideas of sexuality, violence and being violated. Fantasy often begins as a reaction to flashbacks and the beginnings of fantasising with its quality of rehearsal is important, as is the impact of masturbation and how the fantasy then changes. Beliefs about children can also be reached, giving clues about the young person's own experience, but also indicating whether sexually abusive acts are indicative of part-object rather than whole-object relationships, and whether they contain information about power and compliance.

Wayne's abuse of his sister happened when he was left baby-sitting for her and the neighbour's 3-year-old son who was sleeping over with them. He described his enormous loneliness and worry at his mother and stepfather being out for the evening, and had terrifying flashbacks of waiting for his drunken parents to return and being locked away from them in a state of fear. His relief when the children crept downstairs to join him was great. When they began somersaulting in their nightwear, he became – unaccountably to him – angry at their freedom and also sexually aroused. He touched his sister's exposed body and genitals, and those of the neighbour's child, and invited both children to look at his. At this point his sister said, 'Dirty!' and he angrily put them to bed, shut them in their room and could not understand why he wept as he masturbated alone downstairs.

A good psychosocial history is essential, preferably one covering at least three generations of the family: identifications, vulnerabilities, family myths, scripts and stories. Much serious abuse is transgenerational. That said, the frequent breakdown in attachments in the histories of such young people means that it may take an enormous effort to get a relatively clear picture of the early years in particular. Masses of paperwork may well make its way to the clinic; the therapist often has to piece together a story that has never been seen as a whole or as a developmental, sequential history before. For these adolescents, continuity of experience may not have been available – the pressure in them and in the network has been *not* to connect, that it is dangerous to bring things together.

Wayne's mother's drinking and her inability to protect him were not unconnected to her own abuse by her stepfather. Never close to her mother, she told no one but ran away from home several times in her early teens. Towards the end of her clinic sessions, she wondered if her mother had hated her or if she, too, had been abused and could not bear to remember. Wayne's father, she recalled, had been 'knocked about all the time by his Dad'. She considered therapy for herself, but, as yet, has not taken up the offer.

Finally, the assessment should cover the adolescent's capacity for engagement in therapy. This involves considering whether thinking can be tolerated and links may be made; whether a capacity for basic trust can be developed; whether the abusing is defensive against psychotic breakdown; whether there is more than simple denial of responsibility and harm; and – most importantly – whether the network will hold this young person while he represents a risk to society. Taking the support structures into consideration is vital: Is a therapeutic residential setting necessary? Will the foster parents cope and support therapy? Can care staff in a children's home be consistent and understanding enough to deal with a person who is both victim and risk? Planning supportive intervention with the network and clarifying what is basically necessary if therapy is to proceed as a treatment of choice are an essential part of the assessment.

This is obviously work that cannot be done quickly. Several sessions will be necessary to build up a picture of the adolescent's functioning and psychological position. The Great Ormond Street team interspersed open-ended psychotherapy sessions with semi-structured interviews and standard questionnaires over twelve sessions (Hodges *et al.* 1994; Lanyado *et al.* 1995); the Portman Clinic in London, where work with such young people has been going on since 1933, offers up to six assessment sessions. There is a containment in knowing that one is taken seriously, particularly when the adolescent has a sense of fear about his own potential for hurt and for retribution. There is also a terror of abandonment – described poignantly by Lanyado in her case study (Lanyado *et al.* 1995) and evident in Wayne's description of what happened when he abused his sister – which also should be addressed.

Issues in the therapy

The externalisation of humiliation and powerlessness on to the victim for observation and, if more fixed, for enjoyment is repeated in the transference relationship in the therapy. There is a fine line between exploring this, being felt to collude and in being an abuser. Lanyado provides a vivid case example of this process (Lanyado *et al.* 1995: 235). In the transference, one can gain a sense of whether this is a process of externalisation or whether projection, with a sense of an object, is involved, and how near this has grown to sadism.

For all workers with abusing young people, the need to reach the victim behind the aggressor is prime (Lanyado *et al.* 1995; Woods 1997). This is one reason why a psychoanalytic approach may ultimately offer long-term benefit, if appropriate. Cognitive methods do not always approach this, and too confrontative a style, one which does not hold 'abused' in mind, has been known to end in the suicide of the young person. Where there is a mature ego and stronger sense of self, cognitive approaches offer possibilities. With young people like Wayne, however, where there are atolls of functioning in a sea of anxiety and dysfunctionality, much ego structuring has to occur first.

Woods describes three key factors that he has noted in working with adolescent abusers: the sexualisation of the therapeutic relationship, the re-enactment of trauma and anxieties and acting-out around boundaries (Woods 1997). While these may well be experienced in work with the abused but non-abusing child, his comments on the need to mobilise the network are very apt and reflect experience with Wayne:

> Wayne found that his sister's presence on home visits both made him feel guilty and tantalised him. He was able to say that he did not feel she was safe with him. After much discussion, he agreed to the therapist's talking to the case manager who would alert and help the network. The next home visit was put on hold while plans were made to ensure contact was supervised. Wayne expressed fury with the therapist at his next session – which he had been reluctant to attend – then suddenly reflected on his own position, when little, and his rage and sadness that 'no one did anything'.

Guilt is often accessible with abusing adolescents, as is a sense of imminent retribution that parallels their earlier abuse, but it takes time to reach a sense of shame. This can emerge when being heard as a victim is certain for the young person, and when he can then begin to address what he has done. This is a risk time for depression – as is the growing admission of early abused impotence – and needs a holding structure. There is also a risk of harm when the young person begins to trust attachments as he may well lack appropriate defences:

> In the waiting room before therapy, Wayne began to engage in conversation with an older male patient. His need for a benign father

was recognised by his escort who brought it to the therapist's attention
delicately in front of Wayne, allowing scope to address both the wish
and the need to protect himself.

In creating a space for thought, inserted between fantasy and the immediate
rush to activity, the therapist makes use of technical strategies normally
helpful in work with adolescents where preventing humiliation has to be
kept in mind: taking up anxieties in the displacement, splitting the age-
appropriate concern and capacities from the infantile worries.

Wayne began to talk of a school friend who was uncertain whether his
girlfriend liked him or not. For several weeks ideas about sexuality and
the risks of denigration, engulfment and loss of individuality were
explored in the displacement of 'the friend'. More recently he has begun
to talk of a girl whom he likes, and to draw Valentine cards for her,
opening the way to integrating his concern for his friend with his own
anxieties.

Thought also involves the capacity to integrate, to connect things together
and bear their being together.

Thoughts on networks

Throughout this chapter, networks have been mentioned. Constant attention has to be paid to developments within the network surrounding abused
and abusing children and young people. In part, this is to ensure that all
workers have access to support, the work being stressful. Partly, however, it
is because things frequently go strangely wrong. Decision-making suddenly
becomes difficult; placements break down through lack of input to foster
parents and children are further abandoned; mothers who have been
sentenced for their part in abuse suddenly become possible carers for their
children again with no intervention or assessment; social workers go silent
and the therapist hears from the child that he or she is being moved again;
good social workers are removed suddenly from the case with no warning to
the child; therapy becomes perceived as a process which is not effective
speedily enough, or which keeps the child a victim, and review meetings
suggest it should stop forthwith; the therapist is decried for not being able
to state categorically that an adolescent is no longer a risk. Every therapist,
social worker and foster parent can probably add to the list. As if in an *Alice
in Wonderland* world, one moves around the triangle of victim–rescuer–

abuser, taking up each position in turn (Jezzard 1992, personal communication). What, therefore, gets into the system?

Three factors may help in thinking about this. First, Kolvin and Trowell (1996) point to a mirroring process that takes place in networks around abuse: different agencies or different professionals will find themselves adopting the position of different family members and identifying with them. Such identifications are helpful in bringing transference feelings into the discussion, but only when it is clear that it *is* transference that is being experienced. Otherwise they can militate against any sense of an integrated position – particularly regarding being clear about the risk presented by the young patient and the structures necessary to help. Thus with abusing adolescents there can be a split between those who see the young person only as a victim and those who see a dangerous perpetrator. It is essential that both views are held at the one time, and that these should be held in common by all the workers involved, or different parts of the structure will pull against each other. This trend can often be seen in professionals' meetings in relation to abused children. The danger occurs when one partial perspective prevails, to the detriment of the child.

Second, one can also see the process as being a reflection of the dysfunctional family system itself – the system being more than the sum of its parts. The secrecy, denial, abuse, collusion and misapplication of power are then unconsciously replicated in the support system which, like the family, may also experience difficulty in seeing the situation, hearing the evidence and acting in the child's interests.

Finally, in all such work there is a propensity for those engaged in the network to re-enact the internal world of the child (Davies 1996). The defences and projections used by the child will find themselves, again unconsciously, lodged in the network where, unless the process becomes conscious, they will be harmful. Amongst these there will inevitably be the child's expectation of abuse. There can also, however, be deep empathy for the child's wish to be parented, to have parents who can parent, and often an ill-placed desire to return home a child who is ready to be victimised once more by a family that is not yet ready or able to be different. If the therapist is to be able to work, a colleague who has a clear understanding of such dynamics and processes is an essential partner in the process.

Epilogue

After twenty-two months of therapy Wayne is able to connect fantasies of harming smaller children to times when he feels small, despairing and victimised. His stronger ego can recognise this and preclude his acting on it. While understanding his mother's position more – he has had several helpful joint meetings with her at the clinic – he does not wish to live at home although he is a welcome weekend visitor. He is planning a college course on building and working with computers – a new preoccupation with a different kind of 'insides', which makes him smile. He has found a capacity for work and concentration in school that he enjoys and can accept his teachers' praise. Suicidal thoughts have gone, although his sense of shame remains and he is overwhelmed by his sister's continuing affection for him. Relationships with girls remains an area for work, encompassing adolescent sexuality and his sexual future. Although he knows that he is now in control of the degree of risk he might present, he is aware of work remaining to be done and will continue in therapy for some time.

References

Adshead, G. (1994) 'Looking for clues: a review of the literature on false allegations of sexual abuse in childhood', in V. Sinason (ed.) *Treating Survivors of Satanist Abuse*, London: Routledge.

Alvarez, A. (1989) 'Child sexual abuse: the need to remember and the need to forget', *The Consequences of Child Sexual Abuse*, Occasional Papers No. 3, London: Association for Child Psychology and Psychiatry and Allied Disciplines.

Britton, R. (1989) 'The missing link: parental sexuality in the Oedipus complex', in R. Britton, M. Fieldman and E. O'Shaughnessy (eds) *The Oedipus Complex Today: Clinical Implications*, London: Karnac

Butler-Schloss, E. (1988) *Report of the inquiry into child abuse in Cleveland 1987*, London: HMSO.

Campbell, D. (1994) 'Breaching the shame shield: thoughts on the assessment of adolescent child sexual abusers', *Journal of Child Psychotherapy* 20(3): 309–26.

Chasseguet-Smirgel, J. (1985) 'Perversion and the universal law', in *Creativity and Perversion*, London: Free Association Books.

Davies, R. (1996) 'The inter-disciplinary network and the internal world of the offender', in C. Cordess and M. Cox (eds) *Forensic Psychotherapy: Crime, Psychodynamics and the Offender Patient. Vol II: Mainly Practice*, London: Jessica Kingsley.

Flood, S. (1994) 'The effects of child sexual abuse', *Young Minds Newsletter*, Issue 18, June 1994.

Freud, S. (1913) 'Totem and taboo', *SE* 13, London: Hogarth Press.

Goodwin, J., Shad, D. and Rada, R. (1978) 'Incest hoax: false accusations, false denials', *Bulletin of the American Academy of Psychiatry and Law* 6: 269–76.

Gurisik, E. and Horne, A. (eds) (in preparation) *Silent Mothers of Sexually Abused Children: Psychoanalytic and Legal Perspectives*, London: Jessica Kingsley.

Hodges, J., Lanyado, M. and Andreou, C. (1994) 'Sexuality and violence: preliminary research hypotheses from psychotherapeutic assessments in a research programme on young offenders', *Journal of Child Psychotherapy* 20(3): 283–308.

Ironside, L. (1995) 'Beyond the boundaries: a patient, a therapist and an allegation of sexual abuse', *Journal of Child Psychotherapy* 21(2): 183–205.

Kolvin, I. and Trowell, J. (1996) 'Child sexual abuse', in I. Rosen (ed.) *Sexual Deviation*, 3rd edn, Oxford: Oxford University Press.

Lanyado, M. (1991) 'Putting theory into practice: struggling with perversion and chaos in the analytic process', *Journal of Child Psychotherapy* 17(1): 25–40.

Lanyado, M., Hodges, J., Bentovim, A. *et al.* (1995) 'Understanding boys who sexually abuse other children: a clinical illustration', *Psychoanalytic Psychotherapy* 9(3): 231–42.

Morice, M. (1995) 'A community group for abused children', in J. Trowell and M. Bower (eds) *The Emotional Needs of Young Children and their Families*, London: Routledge.

Sinason, V. (1991) 'Interpretations that feel horrible to make and a theoretical unicorn', *Journal of Child Psychotherapy* 17(1): 11–24.

—— (1994) *Treating Survivors of Satanist Abuse*, London: Routledge.

—— (1996) 'From abused to abusing', in C. Cordess and M. Cox (eds) *Forensic Psychotherapy: Crime, Psychodynamics and the Offender Patient. Vol. II: Mainly Practice*, London: Jessica Kingsley.

Smith, M. and Bentovim, A. (1994) 'Sexual Abuse', in M. Rutter, E. Taylor and L. Hersov (eds) *Child Psychiatry: Modern Approaches*, London: Blackwell.

Trowell, J. (1992) 'Child Sexual Abuse', talk given to British Association of Psychotherapists.

—— (1994) 'Ritual organised abuse: management issues', in V. Sinason (ed.) *Treating Survivors of Satanist Abuse*, London: Routledge.

—— (1997) 'Child sexual abuse', in Hon. Mr Justice Wall (ed.) *Rooted Sorrows: Psychoanalytic Perspectives on Child Protection, Assessment, Therapy and Treatment*, Bristol: Family Law.

Welldon, E. (1988) *Mother, Madonna, Whore: The Idealisation and Denigration of Motherhood*, London: Free Association Books.

Woods, J. (1997) 'Breaking the cycle of abuse and abusing: individual psychotherapy for juvenile sex offenders', *Clinical Child Psychology and Psychiatry* 2(3): 379–92.

Further reading

Association for Child Psychiatry and Psychology (1989) *The Consequences of Child Sexual Abuse*, Occasional Papers No. 3, London: ACPP.

Kolvin, I. and Trowell, J. (1996) 'Child sexual abuse', in I. Rosen (ed.) *Sexual Deviation*, 3rd edn, Oxford: Oxford University Press.

Lanyado, M., Hodges, J., Bentovim, A. *et al.* (1995) 'Understanding boys who sexually abuse other children: a clinical illustration', *Psychoanalytic Psychotherapy* 9(3): 231–42.

Sandler, J. and Fonagy, P. (1997) *Recovered Memories of Abuse: True or False?*, Psychoanalytic Monograph No. 2, Monograph Series of the Psychoanalysis Unit of University College, London and Anna Freud Centre, London: Karnac.

Sinason, V. (1998) *Memory in Dispute*, London: Karnac.

24 Gender identity dysphoria

Barbara Gaffney and Paulina Reyes

Introduction

Charlie was sixteen when she was referred for psychotherapy because of extreme distress about being a girl. She would cry inconsolably at the time of her monthly periods and it would take her some days to overcome her feelings of horror at her body's reasserted femaleness, so at odds with her own sense of male identity. She had felt she was a boy ever since she could remember and when she first heard about the existence of 'sex-change operations' she clung to that as the only solution to her predicament. Her conflict had come to a head during the pubertal changes accompanying adolescence. With the onset of the menarche she had started having suicidal feelings, which caused extreme concern in her parents and affected her otherwise good school life. By the time the therapist met Charlie, she was extremely distrustful of anyone who tried to explore her feelings about identity and her concepts of femaleness and maleness, and their meanings for her. From this description of Charlie's feelings we get a vivid illustration of gender identity dysphoria.

In Charlie, and other children and teenagers like her, we encounter one of the most basic and painful of possible alienations, that of psyche and body, where the body is felt so alien to the sense of self that it cannot act as the physical container for the psyche. Such young people find themselves in a radical dissociation that does not allow them to integrate their sense of identity with their bodies; such feelings inhibit interaction with the social environment. The body is felt constantly to be negating the child's sense of who he or she is and later on the arrival of pubertal bodily changes are experienced as an attack to the very core of the sense of identity.

Changing definitions and terminology

In nineteenth-century Germany there was an upsurge of interest in sexual behaviour, and atypical sexual behaviour in particular became an object of study in the medical literature. This was an important social change from previous eras when so-called sexual deviance was exclusively dealt with by the judiciary.

Freud's ideas revolutionised even further the understanding of human sexuality, particularly with the publication of his monumental works *The Interpretation of Dreams* (1900) and *Three Essays on Sexuality* (1905), where he put forward the idea that sexuality was not only determined by inheritance, biochemistry and other organic factors, but also by life's experiences from infancy onward. Additionally, Freud developed an extremely important insight about the bisexual nature of human sexuality. By this he meant that men and women have both masculine and feminine tendencies which arouse conflicts in the establishment of sexual identity. This conceptualisation also emphasised that all sexual behaviour forms part of a continuum stemming from an ever-present neonatal bisexual potential.

The appearance of the diagnostic category of 'transsexualism' was not the result of a theoretical breakthrough. Rather, it appeared on the scene as the result of the development of a surgical treatment for what was thought at the time to be an extreme form of transvestism. The first known case of sex change is that of Christine Jorgensen, reported by Hamburger and his colleagues in 1953. Although Hamburger had called the condition 'genuine transvestism' to distinguish it from other types of cross-dressing, the label 'transsexualism' was soon applied, and the surgical treatment came to be called 'sex reassignment surgery'.

The term 'gender dysphoria' emerged out of a consensus in the 1960s about the diagnosis of transsexualism, and it was often used to indicate the extreme affects, in particular depressed affects, experienced by transsexual patients, who were found to be much more distressed by the incongruity between their gender identity and their anatomical sex than, for example, transvestites.

The relative independence of gender and sex

In the 1950s, John Money and colleagues at Johns Hopkins University conducted studies that led them to differentiate between a set of feelings, assertions and behaviours which define maleness and femaleness, which they called 'gender role', as distinct from the biological characteristics which define a person's sex. Money (1955a) did extensive work to prove his thesis that sex and gender are not necessarily directly interrelated. He referred to well-documented cases of children born with adrenogenital syndrome whereby they are genetically, gonadally and endocrinologically female and have the internal structures of females, though their external genitalia are masculinised. Depending on the degree of external masculinisation, these children had in the past been either designated correctly as female or sometimes incorrectly as male; however, by the age of five years they firmly believed themselves to be of the sex to which they had been assigned, therefore implying that nurture was stronger than nature in determining gender identity, that sex and gender do not necessarily exist in a one-to-one relationship. Money later (1955b) defined the term 'gender role' as a set of feelings, assertions and behaviours that identified a person as being a boy or a girl. In the cases above, 'gender role' was in the vast majority consistent with their rearing more than with their biological make-up.

The concept of gender identity

Later in the 1960s John Money expanded his longitudinal studies to include boys born without birth defects but who presented with gender role incongruity, that is with extreme effeminate behaviour. After many years of research he concluded that 'gender identity' and 'gender roles' were even more complex than he had anticipated and that 'gender dysphoria' related to complex and multiple physiological and psychological causes. By this he meant that children with 'gender identity development disorder' were a very distinct group and very entrenched in their identification with the opposite sex (Money 1994).

A study group on 'identity' at the University of California in the mid-1960s was the first to use the concept of 'gender identity'. Robert Stoller, a physician and psychoanalyst member of this group, defined this as:

> a complex system of beliefs about oneself: a sense of one's masculinity and femininity. It implies nothing about the origins of that sense (e.g. whether the person is biologically male or female). It has, then, psychological connotations only: one's subjective state.
>
> (Stoller 1968)

One further development also established by Stoller (1968) was that of the term 'core gender identity' to designate the child's awareness of being either a boy or a girl, which develops during the first year of life. In his view this 'core gender identity' is the product of the interaction of three variables: the infant–parent relationship, the child's perception of his external genitalia, and the biological force that springs from the biologic variables of sex.

It is also important to differentiate from the above definitions 'sexual orientation', which refers to erotic object choice, so that a person may know that they are a man or woman but have a choice of same-sex sexual partner. Stoller differentiates between transvestite and transsexual boys, defining the first group as being fetishistic: they become sexually excited when wearing women's clothes and they first go through a phase of clear-cut masculinity. Transsexualism, on the contrary, starts early, even appearing by the end of the first year, and 'it more completely possesses the boy's gender'.

Possible causes and incidence of gender identity disorder (GID)

The struggle of the therapeutic professions to find a causality for cross-gendered identification has been long and difficult. One of the many studies conducted by Money over a period of more than forty years concerned children who were biologically hermaphrodites and who had been at birth assigned to either one sex or the other depending on their degree of masculinisation. Out of thirty children, only five had a gender role identity or an erotic orientation that was different from their assigned sex. Money and his colleagues concluded that psychosexuality was neutral at birth and determined almost entirely by socialisation. They identified the critical period for the development of gender identity as before twenty-seven months of age.

Stoller indicated that he could find no evidence that there was any genetic, constitutional or biochemical abnormality in most transsexuals. According to Stoller (1976), transsexualism was the result of a mother–infant symbiosis wherein the father was either psychologically or physically absent. He described the cases of three young boys whom he saw at the ages of between four and five because they insisted that they were girls and had feminine gestures. Stoller described the mothers as 'neuter' in their appearance and demeanour. They had been boyish young women, and all were unhappy with their marriages. The fathers were busy with their own lives and not attentive to the children, so the boys lacked male role models.

The idea that socialisation can produce a permanent gender identity was challenged in 1979 by Imperato-McGinley, amongst others, who reported the case of thirty-three people in a village in the Dominican Republic with a rare hormonal disorder. At birth, nineteen of them had been labelled as girls, but as the townspeople later came to understand the disorder, they labelled them 'penis at 12' children. These children had lived as girls until puberty, when their voices had deepened and their phalluses enlarged and became sexually functional. After this momentous change they had all managed to change to a masculine identity.

Richard Green undertook a longitudinal study of a population of children who appeared to be at risk for a transsexual adult life (Green 1987). He reported a fifteen-year follow-up of a sample of fifty 'feminine boys' who exhibited a high degree of cross-gender behaviour. These boys were matched with a control group of fifty boys of comparable age, ethnicity and parental education. The major finding of the study to date is that 'feminine boys' are more likely to mature into homosexual or bisexual men than are most boys. Only one boy in the study had a transsexual outcome. These findings certainly suggest that not every feminine boy grows up to cross-dress, but they do not tell us much about the genesis of transsexualism. Green carefully tested Stoller's assertions that mothers who spent too much time holding their boys may have made them feminine, but Green's data did not support this hypothesis. He was able to show that feminine boys spent less time with their fathers, but it is not clear whether this was a cause or a consequence of their feminine behaviour.

The incidence of childhood cross-gender identification has not yet been definitely established. Zucker *et al.* (1985) and Green (1968) both state that cross-gender behaviour is uncommon among the general population of boys, and there is even less epidemiological research regarding girls to be able to make a statement.

Coates and Spector Person (1985) have shown that children with gender identity disorders also present separation anxiety, depression and emotional and behavioural difficulties. In a number of cases of children referred to the Gender Identity Unit at the Portman Clinic, London, learning difficulties are also present and school refusal. In a small percentage of cases, child sexual abuse has been associated with a gender disorder. Suicidal attempts in adolescents are frequent and in some cases this is how they come to professional attention.

It seems possible that hormonal imbalances may modify the foetal brain at a critical period during its development. There have been studies of hereditary and genetic factors which could also play a part in influencing gender specific behaviour; however, these factors by themselves are not considered sufficient to produce gender identity disorder (Michael and Zumpe 1996).

One can therefore say that no physical causes of gender identity disorder have yet been found. A number of authors (see Money (1992) and Coates (1990)) agree that many biological and socio-psychological factors need to be present at the same time and work together during a critical period to produce a real gender identity disorder.

The incidence in the general population is very low, and of those boys who do present with effeminate behaviour an extremely small proportion will grow up to become transsexual. At present there are no definite studies about girls with cross-gender behaviour and more research needs to be done in this area.

As the causes of gender identity disorder (GID) are unclear and multifactorial, the primary therapeutic aim should not be to alter the child's gender identity disorder as such but to try to facilitate the child's development by addressing any associated emotional, behavioural and relationship difficulties.

Psychoanalytical views of GID

From the psychoanalytical literature there seem to be two distinct views about the causality of GID, some writers linking it to a pre-Oedipal wish to merge with the mother, leaving no Oedipal conflict for the boy between the desire for the mother and the fear of retaliation from the father. In the view of these authors, psychotherapy or psychoanalysis would not be able to effect change, because psychoanalytical treatment is based on the resolution of unconscious conflict. The main representative of this non-conflictual view is Stoller (1975), who thinks that a behavioural approach should be the treatment choice.

Other writers link GID to early object loss, abandonment and/or abuse, whereby the symptoms represent a compromise solution due to intra-psychic conflict and the gender identity disorder is a defence against anxiety. These authors think that if those conflictual issues are addressed in the therapy, the child may be able to find more benign defences and overcome the cross-gender identification. Two representatives of these views are Coates and Bleiberg and colleagues.

Bleiberg *et al.* (1986) link gender identity disorder, in a particular sub-group of boys, to early maternal object loss. They found that therapeutic work which centres on issues of separation, loss, abandonment and concerns about trust in parenting and caring figures brings positive change in gender identity.

Coates *et al.* (1991) describe familial influences on GID in boys – mother–son dyad, father–son relationship and marital and family dynamics – concluding that the cross-gender fantasy allows the child to manage traumatic levels of anxiety. They consider it a rare disorder that appears before the pre-Oedipal phase due to an interaction of biological, developmental and psychological factors. Temperament, family traits and state, and severe stress lead to the occurrence of massive anxiety in the child during a developmentally sensitive and vulnerable period. They have found that early therapeutic intervention, before the boy reaches the age of five, plus work with the family, can reverse cross-gender identification.

Treatment

The Gender Identity Development Clinic

Working as child and adolescent psychotherapists in the Gender Identity Development Clinic, we have had a unique opportunity to see several teenagers and children with difficulties in gender development, and sub-sequently been able to explore and begin to understand with them the many interacting influences in their development of a sense of self. The Gender Identity Development Clinic was started in 1989 by Dr Domenico Di Ceglie, Child Psychiatrist. Initially situated in the Child Psychiatry Department in a general hospital, St George's, the clinic is now based at the Portman Clinic, London. Dr Di Ceglie's vision of establishing a specialist multidisciplinary team, aiming to keep open the possibilities for children's gender development and to support a facilitating environment, followed from his understanding of the distress of a teenager with gender dysphoria whom he saw in psychotherapy. She let him know that she wished someone could have understood how she had felt and could have helped her when she was a young child. This wish for help was in order not to suffer her predicament alone and in secrecy. Perhaps, in addition, it raised the question as to whether, had she received help when younger, it may have enabled her to feel at home with her biological gender.

There is a range of children and adolescents seen at the clinic. These include children and adolescents who have expressed gender dysphoria, children whose parents are concerned by their cross-dressing and enduring gender-dissonant behaviour (Green 1987; Zucker *et al.* 1985) and teenagers who cross-dress (either wishing to be of the opposite sex – transsexual, or wishing for comfort or sexual arousal – transvestic fetishistic) (Bradley 1998). The clinic is involved in the establishment of national guidelines as to the treatment, hormonal and surgical, of gender identity disorder. The psychiatrist and social worker have been instrumental in setting up an independent self-help parent group called Mermaids.

Through media contact, the clinic is engaged in trying to increase public knowledge of the existence and plight of these children, whilst also bearing in mind the dangers of voyeurism. From the basis of some understanding of the internal dilemmas, social tensions and medical procedures involved in the life of the adult transsexual, the clinic offers to see children in a family where a parent has undergone sex reassignment surgery (Green 1978). Children born with inter-sex disorders are also seen. The different needs of these children and their families are only briefly referred to in this chapter.

Technique and treatment is adapted according to the limitations of geographical distance and in response to the available resources of the family and child. A variety of work is undertaken at the clinic: assessment of the child with a diagnostic formulation and treatment recommendation with referral back to local resources; supervision or network meetings with professionals doing direct work at a local level; and treatment based at the clinic. The assessment includes a developmental history, looking in particular at the gender identity development of the young person over time and their acceptance or dysphoria as regards the reality of their biological body, as well as the usual aspects of any assessment.

Treatment includes family work, individual work, network meetings, liaison with school and other agencies so as to provide a facilitating environment for the child and not deprive them of ordinary developmental influences. This is all in conjunction with the availability of a medical assessment, which could include recommendation for hormonal intervention in late adolescence after careful evaluation by a paediatric endocrinologist. Decisions about irreversible surgical procedures are left to adulthood (Royal College of Psychiatrists 1998). The weekly team meeting has a co-ordinating and containing function which is especially important in work where intense feelings are provoked in therapist and network.

The work of the child psychotherapist

The clinic exists within a given historical and social context at a time when there are changing understandings of gender and sexuality from moral, social, political and medical perspectives. This evokes internal passion and conflict. Questions about gender, identity, masculinity/femininity provoke the nature–nurture debate (Golombok and Fivush 1994). The development of surgical techniques and hormonal knowledge has given rise to the possibility of improved, if imperfect, sex reassignment interventions. There is a growing social awareness of transsexualism, linked both with intolerance of difference and an increasing social acceptance of diverse life styles. This is the social context of the work at the clinic which impinges in many ways on the treatment of children and adolescents seen there; such young people undoubtedly suffer, provoking the question of which is primary and which secondary to the disorder (Coates and Spector Person 1985). One example of this occurred during an assessment following a teenager's self-referral. The mother, who attended at her teenage daughter's request, painfully castigated the therapist for 'perverting' her child and encouraging disabling surgery, eventually weeping with sorrow when the therapist spoke of her mourning of the feared loss of her daughter. The teenager, Orla, verbally attacked the therapist for not providing immediate relief through hormone treatment and surgery, whilst critical that the therapist might try to change her mind. The therapist continued to try to establish a way of thinking about this fear of being unheard, deprived or overwhelmed.

Since the clinic team began work in 1989, the psychotherapists have adapted and applied their skills in direct individual work and in family work in a variety of ways, always questioning what is possible. For the young person who feels in conflict with his/her own body, the realities of his/her biological gender especially confronts him/her soon after starting at school, and again in adolescence, provoking increased and intense distress.

Families arrive with varied expectations, despite the clinic mostly receiving referrals from other mental health professionals and also sending out an introductory leaflet with the first appointment letter. Engagement is an important first step, together with the need for careful diagnostic history-taking, including a developmental history with particular reference to separation anxiety (Coates 1985) and the clinical presentation of the following:

- statements about their perception of themselves as boys or girls
- cross-dressing
- persistent preference for toys stereotypically used by the other sex
- interest in cosmetics and jewellery for boys; refusal to wear skirts for girls
- preference for female roles for boys and male roles for girls in play acting

- preference for friends of the other sex
- female mannerisms in boys and vice versa
- avoidance of rough and tumble play for boys.

Engagement can entail voicing the child's gender dysphoria for the first time in a family. William, an eight-year-old, gradually moved from talking about not liking school to talk of bullying and name calling, and then to revealing to his parents his secret feminine fantasy life. In contrast Olwyn, aged eight, came to the clinic brittle but overt in her silence, refusing to go to school unless accepted in male clothing, and the family complained of the school's resistance to accepting her male attire. The therapist attempted to engender some curiosity and exploration, wondering if the family's support reflected a premature foreclosure. Some parents question whether to allow their child to cross-dress, so risking ridicule and social isolation and a damaging developmental path, or to fight their child's wishes and feel distanced.

The approach of the team is that treatment and amelioration of behavioural and emotional problems can be addressed, but that atypical gender identity may remain unchanged (Di Ceglie 1995) – indeed it may be a solution to a greater problem and aetiology remains uncertain (Money 1994). There is an attempt to foster a facilitating environment for each child.

Adolescents who refer themselves to the clinic may be seeking support for a decision that they feel they have already made, or to understand unbearable inner terror. They can be very sensitive to how the therapist views them: are they seen as ill, mad or suffering from a biological mistake from birth?

The adolescent attending the clinic may hope to find a place where he feels recognised and not alone, but may also bring a terror of feeling 'mad', out of control, or of losing a sense of self (Hurry 1990). Powerful issues about hope and despair, suicide or the possibility of a future need to be addressed. The therapist's own bodily awareness will be challenged. As therapists, we have found ourselves struggling with what therapy is possible. Sometimes we simply aim to keep a neutral space within which to explore and understand; at other times, the best we can offer is management and support, so concrete and desperate is the young person. Is this a collusion – or a facilitating intervention at a critical time in the child or adolescent's development?

James came questioning that he might be mad in thinking of gender reassignment and, if so, should end his life. He requested further appointments to consider what the best decision for him might be. He then requested support whilst living in an ambiguous gender role awaiting medical rectification of what he viewed as a biological mistake from birth. He dropped out of school and wanted to start college in a female role. If gender identity is felt to be a psychological solution to a greater threat to psychic integrity, then the psychotherapist must proceed with great caution and work with what is possible for that individual (Limentani 1977). James could not entertain the thought of sexual contact with a male until after surgery, adamantly stating that he was not gay and furthermore would despise this. In the past he had felt in love with a boy but saw himself as female in relation to him.

In contrast, David came to the clinic relieved that, after two suicide attempts, he had finally told a local therapist of his wishes for sex reassignment. He now saw a future for himself as a transsexual. With few friendships and remaining very close to his mother, David felt she would oppose his sex reassignment. He had arrived at the clinic to explore his distress and gender dysphoria. He hated his genitalia, shaved his legs and face vigorously, and had long hair. He saw men as aggressive and difficult to understand. What seemed important for David was that these concerns could be talked about for the first time. This was a great relief. Through therapy there has been a lessening of his brittle stereotyped identifications as reflected in his move away from pursuing a transsexual outcome to taking time to think about himself in occasional therapy. He made a career change, starting a drama course so as to discover varying possible identifications and enact feared emotions (Waddell 1992).

Fiona, an older adolescent, came to the clinic after finding she could not sustain living a dual gender, being known differently to different people. After several difficult sessions, she began to bring to her therapist drawings which she had done during her earlier adolescence. These expressed something of her terror of disintegration and ravaging aggression, and captured a central, enduring, integrating, but also watchful, angry and persecuting, eye. She requested once-weekly therapy, unsure of how she would proceed whilst waiting for a paediatric assessment and seeking somewhere to live in a male role.

It is in the work with younger children that there is likely to be more fluidity, less rigidity and the possibility of more profound change. Dr Susan Coates, a psychiatrist and psychoanalyst at the Childhood Gender Identity Clinic, St Luke-Roosevelt Medical Centre, New York, does not accept children for treatment beyond the age of five or six as, from the clinic's longstanding research, treatment beyond this age is seen as ineffective in preventing a transsexual outcome. Very few children who cross-dress become transsexual, and contact with mental health professionals seems a significant influence (Money and Russo 1979). Dr Coates reconceptualises GID as a disorder of attachment, a reaction to early maternal depression and early trauma: there is a stereotypic identification which is brittle, rigid and without aggression. In boys, a feminine identification is a solution to the search for the 'lost' mother. She suggests a multi-factorial aetiology and a probable constitutional factor. It is interesting to consider this in relation to research into gender differences in babies in reaction to maternal depression, where boys have been found to have difficulty in regulating emotional states and to be more dependent on their mothers when faced with the 'still face', unresponsive mother experiment, while girls are more self-comforting. Male babies are therefore more vulnerable in relation to maternal depression.

Both girls and boys with gender identity disorder are seen at the clinic, but very few under five have been referred. The children can be distant, self-sufficient and mistrustful, tending to keep their inner lives hidden and not immediately accessible to individual psychotherapy. Lawrence, aged six, poignantly conveyed his dilemma through family assessment sessions. He did not wish to speak of his dysphoria, but had brought with him a list of six requests regarding wished-for changes to become female – hair, clothes and, finally, an operation. Lawrence had made this list following a dream where he had felt compelled to tell his parents of his wish to be female. Lawrence had friends of both sexes, but he was gradually being rejected by his peer group and called gay. He spent the sessions drawing mermaids and brought with him various Barbie dolls and purses from home. His ability to symbolise in drawings and to play were hopeful indications that he might be able to benefit from therapy. He made a lot of eye contact with the therapist and began to talk about his drawings. His parents, however, wanted immediate answers to concrete questions – such as, What do we do about cross-dressing? – so an extended occasional assessment was offered, including information about possible adult outcome for the parents, in the hope that more in-depth work could be worked towards.

William, aged eight, presented with a longstanding, well-established gender identity disorder which had become a cause for concern when he began to refuse to go to school. His headteacher spoke of William being bullied and teased by name-calling such as 'poof'. Initially, the family was reluctant to speak of William's gender disorder behaviour, perhaps seeing him as troublesome. Family sessions were held over a couple of years. William's father often worked away. His early care had been shared between mother and paternal grandmother after mother returned to work when he was five months old. His mother felt that he was a sensitive, difficult-to-please baby and there were many reports of separation anxiety. As he grew older, he seemed to prefer his grandparents' care. After grandmother's sudden death when he was aged five, William had been unable to tolerate her loss but he concretely identified with her, repeating in detail her ways of cooking and cleaning and criticising his mother. William revealed the comfort and early tactile gratification he gained by touching the silky female clothes he choose to wear. He talked with embarrassment and pleasure. His absorption with external appearances suggested an identification with what he felt to be a vain preoccupied mother (Henry 1974).

In family sessions, using a geneogram initially, these painful feelings were gradually approached by William and his mother. William revealed his fantasies of being and wishing to be a girl; he began to mourn the loss of his grandmother; and his father became engaged with his son in a more lively manner, both on advice from the therapists and after his own and his son's fear of explosive rage was explored. As William became increasingly able to trust the therapists, he asked to be seen once on his own when he recounted an incident before his grandmother's death where he had been naughty towards her. His parents did not know of it – William felt fearful of rejection, guilty and responsible for her death. His fear of his loss of self-control, the imagined power of rage and a dread of abandonment underlay many other difficulties and could then be approached in other areas. He longed to be accepted by the other boys but could see no way in: for example, to engage in football might mean no one would pass the ball to him but to seek or ask for the ball seemed to be an act of aggression. William gradually let go of his feminine identification and could countenance age-appropriate activities away from his family. He successfully negotiated a move to a new school.

Through this work both therapists, male and female, attempted to hold in mind various possibilities so as to enable the child and family to tolerate uncertainty in this area of gender identity development. The imagined disastrous outcomes which William's defensive feminine identification attempted to avoid were spoken about with the gradual establishment of a secure base in therapy. William's atypical behaviour – wishes and fantasies which incurred social difficulties for him, and which he felt would possibly mean rejection and ridicule – was something enduring. For William it was a way of holding on to something which had meaning in the development of his sense of self, for his own intrinsic integrity (Wilson 1998). William, with the support of his family and therapy, seemed to have discovered other possibilities.

Thoughts on girls

Both boys and girls presenting gender dysphoria have been brought by their parents or sought referral themselves as adolescents to the clinic. There are fewer references in the literature to work with girls (Bradley 1980), and so we would like to make some observations from our perspective as female psychotherapists. As the baby begins to develop a sense of self, for a baby girl her sense of gender identity is the same as that of her mother, the first object of love and one from whom she is trying to separate and individuate. For the girl and for the boy there is a different pathway to an independent identity and to a choice of sexual partner, at both Oedipal and pre-Oedipal stages. The infant negotiates how to have a coherent sense of self as an autonomous agent, with her own thoughts and actions, and be independent of the primary object, the mother; yet she has an attachment to, interest in and need of the mother. The infant's sense of basic integrity of mind and body, and sense of psychic survival, are at stake. This underlies subsequent developmental tasks such as negotiating 'I can't have bisexuality' and the Oedipal dilemmas. Psychoanalytic views of female subjectivity are interestingly explored in the work of Jessica Benjamin (1990) and Chodorow (1978). Could gender dysphoria in some girls reflect an anxiety about the mother's/female integrity? The masculine identification could reflect both a move to find a pathway to the mother in identification with the father and a protection of the mother.

Case example: Toshiko

Toshiko was three years old when her mother sought help because she was refusing to wear girl's clothes, insisted that she wanted to be a boy and had behavioural difficulties. The parents had split up during the pregnancy and also mother's father had died after a long illness. Following the birth, Toshiko's mother had been depressed and had damaged her back, forcing her to have surgery and then to lie flat for months. Maternal grandmother had looked after the little baby. Father maintained contact with Toshiko but mother always spoke badly of him. A year later, when finally the mother was able to start looking after the little girl, they were not able to establish a loving relationship as Toshiko behaved in a tyrannical and angry manner while showing severe separation anxiety. By the time the therapist met them, Toshiko had been displaying a strong dislike for girl's clothes since she had been able to express herself; her mother was not able to say anything positive about Toshiko and felt persecuted by her behaviour. Mother by then had a new partner who had recently moved in, exacerbating Toshiko's sense of insecurity. Toshiko was already showing an interest in wearing his clothes. That summer they went on holiday abroad. Mother longed for them finally to be like other families, but to her disappointment and anger Toshiko had become even more obsessed with clothes, insisting on changing several times a day depending on what she saw other little boys to be wearing.

During the assessment interviews, Toshiko presented as an unhappy and distrustful child. Any comment from the therapist or suggestion of using the play material was greeted with a refusal. The therapist experienced in the countertransference how rejected Toshiko felt, that any opening felt a ploy to take her away from her mother, which of course she refused, and even after several meetings Toshiko refused to spend any time with the therapist let alone freely interact with her. It was also felt that Toshiko was unable to use her imagination creatively and to play on her own for any period of time because she constantly kept an eye on her mother through fear of losing her. At the same time Toshiko seemed to feel that she had no free access to her mother, adding to her frustration. The therapist felt that, by trying to create a space for thinking about her, she was perceived by Toshiko as a threat to her very existence: the only solution perceivable by Toshiko, albeit an unsatisfactory one, was to become someone else, a boy.

It was not possible to continue working with Toshiko. We can only hypothesise, from these observations, that she felt that she had no real access to the inside of her mother's mind, while at the same time she felt she had to protect herself from the projections coming from her mother. Toshiko felt psychologically homeless.

Case example: Orla

Orla, an older adolescent mentioned earlier, referred herself to the clinic, giving a thoughtful written account of various familial and psychological factors shaping her sense of being a male trapped in a female body. At interview she came with photographs showing herself, aged two, in male clothes with short hair, in a family context where for generations the women had long hair. Her family reported her as a young tomboy, which to Orla implied a biological origin to her discomfort. In addition she described how she perceived females. Her petite mother had been mistreated by her unpredictable husband. Orla's older brother had been favoured and also had been violent and frightening to her for as long as she could recall (he was later diagnosed as mentally ill). Orla had not been protected by her mother who was physically ill at times. Orla became increasingly protective of her mother who relied greatly upon her. It was only in respect of her gender that Orla was anything but an ideal support in her mother's eyes.

Orla despised her female body for it represented weakness and vulnerability. She found her breasts intolerable, binding them out of sight. She longed to be tall, male and potent. As she spoke of her turmoil the therapist felt increasingly aware of her own delicate and feminine body and dress. Every so often Orla would stop to apologise, saying it was nothing personal, as if attempting to undo a feared attack upon the therapist whom she felt could not withstand it.

Orla's longing for a biological explanation for her gender dysphoria was reflected in her bringing photographs and family recollections from when she was under two years old. She could find no psychological solution to her dilemma in being either a feminist or a lesbian; she despised femininity and loathed her female body. The reality of her body was recognised and investigations were offered by the paediatrician. Orla was intensely distressed and close to despair following the biological investigations which showed nothing unusual and confirmed her as female. She continued to see her therapist and did not act upon suicidal thoughts. She had been in danger of excluding herself from home and from further education for fear of disapproval and rejection (as well as her envy of the apparent secure identity of others). Colleagues from the team met with her mother and the educational network. Orla started at a new college and requested a referral to a service nearer to home for more frequent psychotherapy. This work extended over some time and involved much active reaching out by the therapist with phone calls and letters.

Some reflections

The experience of working with children and adolescents in the clinic can be intense and distressing with a strong countertransference to process: the horror of the sense of dislocation within and without; the shock of descriptions of attacks upon the body; the overwhelming anxiety which engenders fear about survival from one session to the next; the struggle to find a way in. These reflect some of the experiences that we have come to hear of as the daily life of such children and adolescents. Reflecting on our work, it became apparent that we adapt and modify psychoanalytic psychotherapy – we feel ourselves to be 'a bit of this and a bit of that', leading us at times to question our experience and whether we are proper psychotherapists. This dilemma and questioning, which confronts one's professional identity, could be understood as a reflection of the internal world of the children and adolescents we have seen at the clinic.

References

Benjamin, J. (1990) *The Bonds of Love*, London: Virago.

Bleiberg, E., Jackson, L. and Ross, L. (1986) 'Gender identity disorder and object loss', *Journal of the American Academy of Child Psychiatry* 25(1): 58–67.

Bradley, S. J. (1980) 'Female transsexualism: a child and adolescent perspective', *Child Psychiatry and Human Development* 11: 12–18.

—— (1998) 'Developmental trajectories of gender identity disorder in children', in D. Di Ceglie (ed.) *A Stranger in my Own Body: Atypical Gender Identity Development and Mental Health*, London: Karnac.

Chodorow, N. J. (1978) *The Reproduction of Mothering: Psychoanalysis and the Social-isation of Gender*, Berkeley CA: University of California Press.

Coates, S. (1990) 'Ontogenesis of boyhood gender identity disorder', *Journal of the American Academy of Psychoanalysis* 18(3): 414–38.

Coates, S. and Spector Person, E. (1985) 'Extreme boyhood femininity: isolated behaviour or pervasive disorder?', *Journal of the American Academy of Child Psychiatry* 24: 702–9.

Coates, S. Friedman, R. and Wolfe, S. (1991) 'The etiology of boyhood gender identity disorder: a model for integrating temperament, development, and psychodynamics', *Psychoanalytic Dialogues* 1(4): 481–523.

Di Ceglie, D. (1995) 'Gender identity disorders in children and adolescents', *British Journal of Hospital Medicine* 53(6): 251–6.

Freud, S. (1900) *The Interpretation of Dreams*, SE Vols 4 and 5, London: Hogarth.

—— (1905) *Three Essays on Sexuality*, SE Vol. 7, London: Hogarth.

Golombok, S. and Fivush, R. (1994) *Gender Development*, London: Cambridge University Press.

Green, R. (1968) 'Childhood cross gender identification', *Journal of Nervous and Mental Disorders* 147: 500–9.

—— (1978) 'Sexual identity of thirty-seven children raised by homosexual or transsexual parents', *American Journal of Psychiatry* 135: 692–7.

—— (1987) *The 'Sissy Boy Syndrome' and the Development of Homosexuality*, New Haven CT: Yale University Press.

Hamburger, C., Sturup, G. K. and Dahl-Iversen, E. (1953) 'Transvestism: hormonal, psychiatric, and surgical treatment', *Journal of the American Medical Association* 152: 391–96.

Henry, G. (1974) 'Doubly deprived', *Journal of Child Psychotherapy* 3(4): 15–28.

Hurry, A. (1990) 'Bisexual conflict and paedophilic fantasies in the analysis of a late adolescent', *Journal of Child Psychotherapy* 16(1): 5–28.

Imperato-McGinley, J., Peterson, R. E., Gautier, T. and Sturla, E. (1979) 'Androgens and the evolution of male-gender identity among male pseudo-hermaphrodites with 5-alpha reductase deficiency', *New England Journal of Medicine* 300: 1233–7.

Limentani, A. (1977) 'The differential diagnosis of homosexuality', *British Journal of Medical Psychology* 50: 209–16.

Michael, R. P. and Zumpe, D. (1996) 'Biological factors in the organization and expression of sexual behaviour', in I. Rosen (ed.) *Sexual Deviations*, London: Oxford University Press.

Money, J. (1955a) 'Hermaphroditism, gender and precocity in hyperadrenocorticism: psychological findings', *Bulletin of the Johns Hopkins Hospital* 96: 253–64.

—— (1955b) 'An examination of some basic sexual concepts: the evidence of human hermaphroditism', *Bulletin of Johns Hopkins Hospital* 97: 301–19.

—— (1992) 'The concept of gender identity disorder in childhood and adolescence after 37 years', *Proceedings of the Conference on Gender Identity and Development in Childhood and Adolescence*, London: Conference Unit, St George's Hospital.

—— (1994) 'The concept of gender identity disorder in childhood and adolescence after 39 years', *Journal of Sex and Marital Therapy* 20(3): 163–77.

Money, J. and Russo, A. (1979) 'Homosexual outcome of discordant gender identity/role in childhood: longitudinal follow-up', *Journal of Paediatric Psychology* 4: 29–41.

Royal College of Psychiatrists (1998) *Guidelines for the Management of GID in Children and Adolescents*, London: Royal College of Psychiatrists.

Stoller, R. (1968) 'Male, childhood transsexualism', *Journal of the American Academy of Child Psychiatry* 7: 193–201.

—— (1975) *Sex and Gender Vol. I Splitting: A Case of Female Masculinity*, London: Hogarth Press.

—— (1976) *Sex and Gender Vol. II The Transsexual Experiment*, London: Hogarth Press.

Waddell, M. (1992) 'From resemblance to identity: a psychoanalytic perspective on gender identity', *Proceedings of the Conference on Gender Identity and Development in Childhood and Adolescence*, Conference Unit, St George's Hospital Medical School, London.

Wilson, P. (1998) 'Development and mental health', in Di Ceglie (ed.) *A Stranger in my Own Body: Atypical Gender Identity Development and Mental Health*, London: Karnac.

Zucker, K. J., Bradley, S. J., Doering, R. W. and Lozinski, J. A. (1985) 'Sex typed behaviour in cross-gender identified children: stability and change after one-year follow-up', *Journal of the American Academy of Child Psychiatry* 24: 710–19.

Further reading

Di Ceglie, D. (ed.) (1998) *A Stranger in my Own Body: Atypical Gender Identity Development and Mental Health*, London: Karnac.

Hurry, A. (1990) 'Bisexual conflict and paedophilic fantasies in the analysis of a late adolescent', *Journal of Child Psychotherapy* 16(1): 5–28.

Loeb, L. R. (1996) 'Childhood gender identity disorder', in I. Rosen (ed.) *Sexual Deviation*, London: Oxford University Press.

25 Eating disorders

Niki Parker

Introduction

Every day there is something else in the news about eating disorders. In 1997 when, before her untimely death, the Princess of Wales publicly admitted to having anorexia and bulimia and stated that she had attempted suicide, she made these painful and at times disgusting illnesses almost glamorous. In June of the same year we heard, as had been stated in the past, that there is an organic reason for this illness, this time that reduced blood flow between the temporal lobes of the brain triggers the symptoms. Later that year Dr Dee Dawson, who runs an eating disorder clinic in London, told the Girls School Association that they should regularly weigh pupils to catch them when they start losing weight as 2 per cent of their pupils were likely to have an eating disorder, rising to 5 per cent in the sixth form. Eating disorders can be headline news and their aetiology is the subject of much debate and controversy.

This chapter describes the treatment of several different forms of eating disorder, including anorexia, bulimia, and the issues involved for a young woman who kept herself significantly overweight. The treatments are described from the perspective of a child and adolescent psychotherapist working in a Child and Adolescent Mental Health Service (CAMHS) in the community. As such, my theoretical framework for thinking about these patients is a combination of psychoanalytic training and experience, and of working in the multidisciplinary team.

The clinical symptomatology

Anorexia

Anorexia usually starts in early adolescence and is seen predominantly in girls. Boys, however, are also affected. The first known description of anorexia (made by Avicenna, a Persian philosopher in the eleventh century) was of a young prince who had melancholia and the symptoms of anorexia nervosa (Sours 1980). The family dynamics surrounding eating disorders are important; it is however difficult to know if what is observed in the eating-disordered young person and her family originates *before* the illness or after.

The sufferer from anorexia goes on a diet, but dieting does not stop when a reasonable weight has been achieved. The diet goes on until she is well below normal weight for her age. She might eat vegetables and fruit, and drink diet drinks with very low calories, to disguise her starvation diet. She might take slimming pills, and continue a punishing exercise routine as long as she is able. She thinks about food all the time, has a comprehensive knowledge of how many calories every morsel of food contains and takes pleasure in feeding others in her family or friends. She does all this without taking in anything more than a minute amount of food herself. She looks horrifically emaciated to others but cannot see this for herself. This bizarre pattern of behaviour can continue until she starves to death. Anorexia is a very dangerous illness.

It seems that in Westernised societies an ideal body image is sought by women, men, and even children. Exercise, body-building and jogging are ways (alongside restricting food intake) to achieve the goal of the desirable body image. Sixty per cent of the female population in this country is on a diet at any time (Orbach 1978), but do not develop these illnesses. However, self-starvation, or bingeing and vomiting seems to be on the increase in industrialised countries, particularly amongst girls, and eating disorders have certainly become much more socially acknowledged and visible.

The tenth revision of the International Classification of Diseases and Related Health Problems (*ICD-10*) and American Diagnostic and Statistical Manual of Mental Disorders, *DSM-IV*, list the same main symptoms and manifestations of anorexia. Anorexia actually means loss of appetite. (I would agree with those who say that this is not really the right term because sufferers *have* appetite but *ignore* the hunger messages from their stomach.) This refusal to eat leads the sufferer first of all to diet, then seriously to undereat, with the result that some or all of the following symptoms become true:

- denial of the seriousness of being underweight or of distorted eating habits;
- terror of fatness;
- body image distortion;
- loss of three or more menstrual cycles or delayed onset of menarche.

Someone with anorexia weighs 15 per cent below expected weight for age and height. However, only *ICD-10* refers to Quatelet's Body Mass Index, which is calculated by dividing the weight in kilograms by the square of height in metres. This index takes account of the fact that a given weight loss is more or less significant according to build. *ICD-10* also stresses that *the fear of becoming obese* is the main defining criterion rather than *body image distortion*. Halmi has pointed out that this latter concept is no longer as central as originally considered (Halmi 1995).

DSM-IV defines subtypes of eating disorders, such as exclusive starvers (restricters), those who starve and purge but do not binge (purgers), and those who binge. It may, however, be premature to distinguish between those whom they call 'restricters' and those referred to as 'bulimic anorectics', as these may just signal different phases or different indices of severity that may alternate over time in individuals.

A clear discussion of anorexia is given by Steinhausen who states that there has been an increase in anorexia over the last fifty years. It is found equally in urban and rural communities, affecting predominately females; it is an illness which spans all social classes. In undeveloped countries, it seems that it is an illness of the rich (Steinhausen 1994). However, some comparative studies in developing countries do not show this pattern, as Szmukler and Patton point out. Many studies have not compared like with like and ensured that the research structure was absolutely equivalent in each place (Szmukler and Patton 1995).

Steinhausen also reports that there is a significant amount of disturbed communication in sufferers' families of origin. He notes, in these families, a higher incidence of weight problems and physical illness as well as affective disorders, especially depression and addictions such as alcoholism. Hsu, from twin studies, suggests that anorexia has a heritability factor, whereas bulimia does not (Hsu 1990). Sociocultural explanations emphasise the high value placed in Western societies on slimness, youthful appearance and attractiveness in women. Particular groups at risk are athletes, runners, gymnasts and ballet dancers. Precipitating events, from which the onset of the eating disorder in an organised form can be dated, are usually external. Life events involving separation and loss, disruptions of family life – such as divorce, new environmental demands – such as exams or group pressure about girl/boyfriends, and sometimes physical illness, all play their part.

In summary, Steinhausen's paper suggests the following contributory interacting factors that can lead to eating disorders: a young person who has little feeling of self-worth, who is compliant and perfectionist, where there is a loss or stress within the familiar external environment. These factors combine with all the ordinary physical and emotional demands of puberty and adolescence where the body and fantasy life can feel alarmingly out of control at times (Lanyado 1999). These ordinary developmental preoccupations with control over body size and shape lend a certain apparently age-appropriate internal logic to the sufferer's rationale for the eating disorder. However, when the body is starving, the symptoms become self-perpetuating and a deadly vicious circle is set up because the chemical changes induced by starvation affect mental processes. When a previously starving anorectic patient has eaten to a goal weight, it becomes possible to engage in meaningful dialogue again.

Developmentally, anorexia seems to start most frequently just as the young person is in transition to adolescence, with its unexpected and apparently uncontrollable explosion of physical, social, psychological and sexual changes. It has been noted that young people who are vulnerable to this eating disorder have often been compliant and perfectionist children who are educationally ambitious – hence the clusters in girls' grammar schools or colleges. Childhood sexual abuse and depression are found in some histories of those presenting with eating disorders. For excellent accounts of how it feels to struggle with anorexia from the point of view of the sufferer, the reader is directed to Bruch's *The Golden Cage*, Sours' *Starving to Death in a Sea of Objects* and Malan's excellent book with three case histories, *Anorexia, Murder and Suicide* (Bruch 1978; Sours 1980; Malan 1997).

Bulimia

The sufferer from bulimia is less visible since she does not seem under-weight. The illness was first classified psychiatrically as an ominous variant of anorexia by Russell (1979) although it was described clinically by psychoanalytic writers before this time. As with anorexia, the sufferer is also consumed by a preoccupation with food: however, she goes through a cycle of bingeing followed by vomiting what she has taken in. As with anorexia, there are physical sequelae to this behaviour in the biochemical make-up of the body, as well as damage to teeth and bones. The physical symptoms follow the psychological disturbances in both illnesses (Russell 1995).

Both *ICD-10* and *DSM-IV* define bulimia as fear of fatness while main-taining normal appearance and normal weight. In addition to the cycle of bingeing and vomiting, many sufferers have irregular periods, use laxatives excessively, have a feeling of lack of control over eating behaviour and persistent over-concern with body shape and weight. Other commonly associated behaviours are mood disorder (especially depression), impulsive and self-destructive behaviour, such as cutting the body, overdoses and misuse of drugs.

Bulimia affects an older age group of people who have often been over-weight as children. It is a hidden eating disorder in that the sufferer keeps her weight within normal limits. However, it is known that food is a constant preoccupation and that the sufferer feels full of guilt and self-disgust about her eating behaviour. The cycle of bingeing and vomiting becomes well established and very difficult to break. Sufferers may have started by being anorectic and continued with a bulimic cycle rather than take the risk of a normal relationship – with food and other people.

As described above, anorexia and bulimia can be associated with cutting, suicidal and psychotic behaviour as part of the more complex picture. In his study of a consecutive series of 112 normal-weight bulimic women, all stemming from the same urban catchment area, Lacey notes the prevalence of self-damaging and addictive behaviour in normal-weight bulimic women, including alcohol or drug abuse, stealing, overdosing and self-cutting. He identified a core group of multi-impulsive bulimics who might be likely to give a history of sexual abuse (Lacey 1993). This suggests that it is something about these patients' underlying mental state (which in psychoanalytic terms would be seen as 'borderline', with the person veering from very self-destructive to more realistic behaviour) that must be attended to rather than the various alarming symptoms with which this results.

Theories of causation

A number of causes of eating disorders have been cited over the years by different clinicians. Bruch (1979) suggests a sense of personal ineffectiveness; Selvini Palazzoli (1963) notes a failure in the parents to regard the developing child as an individual in their own right; Crisp (1980) describes an intense fear of becoming physically and emotionally mature together with food phobia; Lieberman (1995) suggests that a family who has an anorectic person are more than normally concerned with appearances; Orbach (1985) gives the feminist societal explanation.

In the special edition of the *Journal of Family Therapy* dedicated to eating disorders (1995), there is an interesting discussion about the rise of feminist, psychoanalytical and societal explanations of eating disorders. Attention is drawn to the fact that, historically, different treatment approaches have been heavily weighted towards 'male and medical' – the male doctor treating the female patient in a medical setting. The main definitions do tend to come from medical sources; however, there has been much clinical discussion in the psychoanalytical literature about these conditions. Most *definitions* therefore have focused on the historical, societal and medical symptoms, or the family context and the outside world, rather than defining unconscious issues and motivations. Child and adolescent psychotherapists have written detailed clinical accounts of their work with these patients which illustrate how effective psychoanalytic work can be in understanding and helping this group of patients (Daws 1993, 1997; Henry 1997; Likierman 1997; Miller 1997; Parker 1993; Segal 1993; Tustin 1958).

In his introductory chapter to the *Handbook of Eating Disorders*, Russell emphasises how the illness has developed over time in response to the societal context (Russell 1995). In the same book, Dare and Crowther, in an important chapter discussing psychoanalytic views of the aetiology of eating disorders, argue that 'The understanding of the patient is sufficient. The claim to constitute an ultimate aetiological theory is an irrelevant burden' (Dare and Crowther 1995). They discuss how the classical Freudian psychoanalytic theories have not been particularly helpful in reaching an understanding of eating disorders, being based as they are on a 'one-person psychology'. Dare and Crowther emphasise the importance of object relations theory, in a societal context, which is based on a 'two-person psychology' that takes into account the difficulties of separateness as well as relatedness.

The developmental tasks of puberty and adolescence and their implications for eating disorders

When a parent says goodbye to an eleven-year-old on the first day of secondary school, it is hard to realise how quickly this new institution will seem to transform their child into a young adult on the brink of college or work. The primary school child, who has been emotionally close to his or her parents in so many of the intimate details of life, will become metamorphosed into a sexually mature young adult with a large area of privacy which the parents have to respect as best as they can. An extraordinarily complex development will have taken place – physically, emotionally, sexually, socially and intellectually. In an observable, external way, childhood has ended – although of course many of the internal conflicts and issues of infancy and childhood remain active within the adult despite the appearance of physical maturity.

These issues reverberate around the adolescent renegotiation of the Oedipus complex (see Chapter 3) which have been predated by the quality of the early mother–infant relationship. In particular, Stern draws attention to the earliest forms of non-verbal communication between mother and infant, where attunement and intersubjectivity play such an essential role (Chapter 7 in Stern 1985). This is inevitably also a crucial factor in the mother–infant *feeding* relationship. Perhaps for the group of young people who have eating disorders, as distinct from other adolescent problems, difficulties in separation from the family follow early problematic patterns of feeding and weaning.

The transition from childhood to adulthood can be one of the hardest to negotiate in family life. No wonder there are often such difficulties with it. An eating disorder can be one way of putting a stop to this anxiety-provoking separation from home. A young person, while protesting she is in control of her life and does not need her parents to have anything to do with her life (adding that it is her business how, what and where she eats), is making the developmental process go into reverse, causing as much worry as a baby who is refusing to be fed. These conflicts arise and become established in the spiral of control, starvation and lying that eating disorders entail.

Growing up is something to be survived through the minefield of normal emotional and physical development (Hindle and Smith 1999). For a girl, the development of a mature female body is difficult enough if things have always gone well enough between her and her parents. Her body is preparing to contain the next generation at a time when her mother may be experiencing the first intimations of the menopause and feeling vulnerably that she is approaching the 'biological scrap heap'. This is Darwinian dynamite — about survival of the species. If there are still many issues to be addressed from childhood that have not been adequately worked out between her and her parents, amongst other difficulties, the issue of rivalry between females can be potent.

Female sexual rivalry: the old and the young lioness

Over time, I have recognised a useful organising concept in thinking about eating disorders, particularly anorexia: the difficulty for a mother to let go of her daughter — and for the daughter to leave her mother. This is the transition when the mother can feel biologically defunct whilst her daughter is the new nubile female in the home. This rivalry of the old lioness with the young lioness is rarely noted although the parallel issue in male rivalry is often mentioned.

Liekerman (1997) posits that during her adolescent development a girl has to prepare her inner world to contain a baby and that her full feminine identity is forged at this time. To this important idea it must be added that the rivalry with the mother has to be addressed in order to achieve personal, sexual and physical identity. In addition, in order to separate safely from mother, it is necessary to be able to express anger at her *safely*. This can be difficult for parents to cope with. Infected by the heady brew of adolescence present in the family, parents may start to act out their unresolved adolescent issues alongside or in rivalry with their children. The whole of this is of course vastly complicated by sexual abuse, if present.

In addition, socially, adolescence is the time to join with the group and obey group mores rather than parental rules. This commonly leads to conflict between parents and offspring about friends, time to come home, money, clothes, how to wear hair, when and where to pierce ears — and other places on the body, sexual behaviour and relationships, issues to do with drugs — legal and illegal. If the family is not a safe place for all these conflicts and heated debates because it is not safe to express anger for all kinds of reasons, it might be easier to retreat to an earlier stage of development and get the issues addressed in terms of a younger child.

Another dimension of the problem relates to peer social pressures during puberty and adolescence. Young adolescent girls do not always feel ready to face the interpersonal and social pressures from girls, as well as boys, despite their outwardly apparent maturity. The issues of rivalry in the group and with others girls are linked with those of rivalry with the mother. Questions of sexual orientation and sexual experimentation are around — have the others really done the things they say they do? The young person needs to feel secure enough to be able to face this exciting and frightening scene let alone participate in it.

So, the task of adolescence is to grow up and leave home. It is a time when young people have a second chance to sort out the things that have not been worked out between them and their parents, and in this respect it can become an enormously creative and exciting period of personal development (Lanyado 1999). It is an opportunity to experiment with an identity as a young adult, at the same time having a safe base to which to return. Similarly, a toddler in Mahler's 'practising stage' makes the first forays into the world and can retreat to his or her parents when the world is overwhelming (Mahler *et al.* 1975). What is remarkable in the eating disordered adolescent is how she has managed to be treated as a baby in making her parents worried about her food intake, whilst announcing at the top of her voice that she is fine and wants to be left alone. Although she is now adolescent, she *is* the Mahlerian toddler who is not satisfied by her parents' efforts at refuelling. Stern (1985) develops this concept by stating that it is not only 'refuelling' that is taking place; he argues that the child and parent need to share a *new* experience. Is this a clue as to what is being reworked with these eating disorders in adolescence where such intense attention has to be paid to the young person's feeding relationship – attention of the kind that would ordinarily only take place in the intensity of the mother–infant feeding relationship, and during the common conflicts over food that take place during the toddler stage?

Eating disorders at a community Child and Adolescent Mental Health Service (CAMHS)

There does seem to be agreement that the best outcomes are when the treatment can begin early with younger children who have less entrenched patterns of eating disorder, and that there is a better prognosis where blame for the eating disorder has not become an issue in the family dynamics (Le Grange *et al.* 1992). As the prevalence of eating disorders becomes more widely recognised, there are a growing number of referrals of children. However, in the main, my experience is with adolescents.

At any time, a significant proportion of my caseload involves adolescent girls and young women who have starved themselves until their periods stop. Each one has seemed to have a different reason driving her to this extreme and dangerous behaviour. Some of them have added bulimia to the self-harming activities, some cut or scratch their bodies, and some have attempted suicide as well. This is a category of extreme and dangerous behaviour, distressing for those who are nearest to the young women. They attempt to keep the behaviour secret, but it becomes obvious to all as they become thinner and more emaciated. In effect, they are doing the opposite of what is expected of them, namely, to allow biological development to take its course and to take their place in society – a woman's place in society rather than a child's.

I am struck by the relatively high level of this kind of referral. In my own experience the referral often comes from the school nurse, as she is the person who is trusted by pupils – and the sufferer has often been drawn to her attention by a friend, rather than coming independently. Other cases can come from the GP, or hospital – when someone emaciated has been admitted.

Addressing this frightening situation starts with the family. Some members of the family say 'it' has nothing to do with them – and the young person will assert 'it' has definitely nothing to do with anyone but her – it is her business and no one else's. Nevertheless, it is very important to join with the family and attempt to enable communication to be established about the forbidden subject, *without blame*. Le Grange *et al.* have noted that patients whose families criticise them have a poorer prognosis (Le Grange *et al.* 1992).

Our clinic team has found that with severe cases, a period as an in-patient in the local paediatric ward, working towards a goal weight, can serve to support the family in changing its approach to long-established ways of far from optimal communication. It is important that the parents should not feel deskilled when their offspring starts to eat once others have become involved. Hopefully, hospital could be the place where the issues can begin to be spoken and thought about instead of being acted on through the eating disorder. Some talking and thinking can then take place in the family sessions. Family therapy continues in the community clinic, with the addition of individual once-weekly psychotherapy when the sufferer has reached a weight where she is mentally able to think about the situation. Monitoring weight is important. Sometimes this is done by the practice nurse at the GP surgery, or by the co-therapist working with the family. When the reality of anorexia is spoken about in individual sessions, I find that the eating disordered person knows the catalogue of risks – death, osteoporosis, kidney problems, infertility – but is still driven to diet or vomit what she has eaten. It is as if she knows intellectually but not emotionally – as if she has become detached from her feelings and is unaware of the powerful effect of her non-verbal communions to her loved ones – that is, that she is starving herself to death. Malan comments that eating disordered behaviour is a defence against feelings and relationships (Malan 1997).

Some clinical examples – or, those who have taught me

I always try to look at what the meaning is to the individual of the symptom that brings them to my room in the Child and Adolescent *Mental* Health Service. No one wants to come to a place like this – 'I'm not mental – why do I have to see a shrink?' they ask me. What causes someone to attack her own body, undermine the most basic means of survival and lie about it to her friends and family? It does seem mad, yet it is not a mysterious thing out of the blue, but something to be understood in context.

It is important to think about eating disorders as an *acted* rather than spoken communication, typical of what Tonnesman refers to in her paper as the 'normative adolescent crisis' (Tonnesman 1980). In this important paper, Tonnesman draws on thinking from Freud to Winnicott, via Anna Freud, Ernest Jones, Blos, Bowlby, Erikson and Heimann, to consider this in-between period of development. Tonnesman argues that if there have been failures at earlier times, it is vital to seize the moment to re-enact the past failure in order to be able to master that failure in the present and thus be able to continue and fulfil one's potential as 'a self within a personal history'. If this is not possible, there is what Tonnesman calls 'foreclosure of adolescence', and the individual is doomed to repeat experiences and remain stuck. The therapist's task can be seen as attempting to provide an emotionally balanced context so that the young person can establish a link with a traumatic past experience, be able to re-enact it in the present and become free. In other words, the therapist has to listen with inner and outer ears to the transference–countertransference relationship, to understand, contain and resist unneccesary acting out, and most importantly *survive* what is brought to the session. Each sufferer's experience is different, and the personal meaning of the symptom is different in every case.

Case example: Anita

Anita told me that she had started dieting at Christmas, aged sixteen, when she looked in the mirror while she was buying clothes. There she saw a young woman who was not the pre-pubertal girl that she wanted to see, and she started to control the curviness of her body. She spoke of herself as Daddy's girl, and had been a star footballer as a child. She still wanted to be a footballer. Anita's parents had met and married as adolescents. Her mother had negotiated the transition from her family of origin by a denial of separation – establishing a relationship with her husband without separating from her parents and discovering her identity first. Anita tended to 'act' feelings for the family, as opposed to talk about them. For example, she 'acted' enormous rivalry by standing up to her father on her mother's behalf, by shouting at and physically fighting him. She said that she took money from where her father kept it, as if it was hers of right. She described her parent's relationship as including her father's mockery of her mother because she was overweight. Sexual issues were not mentioned in the family. Whilst Anita never disclosed sexual abuse it remained a possibility in my mind. Unresolved Oedipal feelings were powerfully present. It was as if, in her family, the resolution of the Oedipus complex had not occurred in early childhood and was still being acted out during adolescence – as seen in Anita's special relationship with her father, the use of his money as if it was hers, and the combined denigration by father and daughter of mother.

Her mother admitted to ineffectual dieting and hating her overweight appearance. I wondered about the feelings of this woman, who was denigrated at home, for the daughter who was treated as 'special' by her husband. Whilst Anita and her father did come to real blows at times, there was an edge of excitement to these fights which mother could not help but be aware of. Anita was attractive, despite being underweight, and was not dangerously emaciated. From Anita's account it seemed that mother's way of responding to her daughter's budding sexuality was to support Anita in a search for what, I thought, were unsuitable and possibly dangerous jobs – letting her go to interviews which were clearly linked with the sex industry. Instead of protecting her daughter, she let her go to these interviews unsupervised. Through this behaviour I felt that mother was acknowledging a sexual rival in her daughter and putting her at risk. They were acting out Anita's transition to womanhood in a very dangerous way for the girl. Here the young lioness and old lioness were in a battle. I felt that the looking in the mirror, which precipitated the eating disorder, was for Anita a traumatic moment – as if she was recognising in herself, for the first time, a potential sexual partner for her father.

Very soon after our first meeting, Anita impulsively went to Spain for two months, keeping in touch with me by letter and postcard. It seemed that the possibility of a trusting relationship with a woman who wanted to listen to her was daunting. She stayed with a cousin whom she knew was physically abused by her husband and who, although she had previously come to England to try to escape from this abusive relationship, had decided to go back to him and the abuse. This further illustrated what I came to understand as a family pattern to repeat the past and not to be able to risk and negotiate appropriate developmental transitions.

Despite this strong family pull towards repeating destructive relationship patterns, Anita came back to see me when she returned from Spain. The once-weekly therapy consisted of my listening to accounts of the interviews in London for modelling jobs of various kinds. I found that I acted out a protective role by giving advice about the dangers of some of these jobs and trying to get her to take someone else with her. Sometimes her mother did accompany her. In addition, and as a counter-balance to these interviews, I felt that it was important to encourage her to recognise more fully her academic achievements and potential – she had been a good student who had opted out of school.

Eventually she started to talk about the detail of her abuse of food and laxatives, and told me about the angry and violent scenes she took part in at home. She also told me about the different boyfriends who became very distressed at her starving herself. In the transference–countertransference relationship, I felt at first like an observer rather than a voyeur, then was entrusted with the disgust Anita felt at what she was compelled to do in terms of bingeing and vomiting and laxative abuse. This was just a glimpse behind a façade she kept for the world.

After ten months, Anita got an office job and, because we could not find a suitable therapy time, her therapy came to an end. Like many others of her age group she did not keep her last appointment. She cut off our relationship – a sudden separation, perhaps the only way she saw possible. However, she did write and thank me for the work we had done together. In my view, the year's treatment had not been enough to work as deeply as I would have liked on the Oedipal issues she was struggling with. However, there had been important changes in the way she lived her life. I thought that we had made a start, but we had not really experienced together what was under the surface. But she had kept coming to her sessions and this in itself showed a clear commitment to change and development which had not been present before. Our time together could be seen as being of value in that she now had a suitable job which used her intelligence and not purely her good looks, and her weight had not become dangerously low. In addition, she had moved out of her parent's house and had not committed herself to an exclusive relationship before discovering her identity, in the way her mother had.

On the negative side, she had become bulimic, therefore able to keep her eating disorder more secret, and none of the issues in her family of origin had been directly addressed in treatment (although moving out of her parent's house was clearly highly significant in Anita's emotional development). I was concerned, in the course of her treatment, to discover sexual abuse in the wider family, as well as another anorectic relative. Her father never attended the clinic, her mother only intermittently, not allowing herself to become involved in this opportunity to sort things out between herself and her daughter. Any freeing-up of their relationship had seemed to come through Anita's efforts. It seemed that Anita had learned, by sampling once-weekly psychotherapy, another way of addressing her serious difficulties, one to which she can return later.

I find that the timing of referral is often when the young person is facing important exams and a subsequent separation from parents and peer group. The time available for therapy is then a matter of months.

Case example: Fiona

Fiona was brought by her boyfriend. I knew from the school nurse that she caused concern to her teachers because of her extreme lack of confidence in her work and anxiety over exams. Yet she was a popular pupil and a school prefect. She had disclosed bulimic laxative abuse to the school nurse and while in therapy she described how regularly she cut herself with a razor on her arms and thighs after her father had shouted at her.

When my psychiatrist colleague met with the parents and sister, it was almost impossible to address emotional issues in the family. It was particularly difficult to acknowledge feelings of anger. Fiona was full of self-hatred. She reported how she had been bullied in primary school, but had been unable to tell her mother because she felt her mother was too fragile and would not have been able to deal with it. Fiona felt bad about herself and had low self-esteem, so she felt in some ways appropriately punished by the bullies. I found myself wondering how this bullying at school might have echoed something that was going on at home at the time. As with Anita, the family was unwilling to continue to attend the clinic.

Fiona also had a mother who felt she was overweight and who was profoundly critical of how she herself looked. It was interesting how, when family sessions were terminated, this lady would still bring her eighteen-year-old daughter regularly to the clinic to see me – even though they lived close to the clinic. It was difficult for Fiona to tell her mother that she preferred to come to the clinic on her own. Interestingly, when, during therapy, the cutting and bulimia started to diminish, she was able to tell her mother about these self-destructive acts, and to request that she came to the clinic on her own. A more appropriate relationship with distance and intimacy was established between them.

So, as with Anita, this was a significant first step. I say it is a 'first step' because we had not begun to work at any depth about the issues. However it was valuable because she had been able to ask for and keep a weekly confidential time for herself, mother and daughter had become more able to communicate using language rather than actions, her symptoms had subsided and she took up a place in a local Teacher Training College. We had started a process of thinking and talking that would help her to express herself verbally rather than act out issues of sexuality, anger, rivalry and control. She said she would find a counsellor when things felt difficult again.

Fiona and Anita are examples of how the work in a community CAMHS such as ours can offer a service as a first step. While still at school they were both able to find a way of thinking about their experiences, rather than acting the attack on their internal parents, through a relationship with a listening adult. They both recognised the possibility of finding such a relationship again in the future and this suggested some real internal change as a result of the work we had done in the transference relationship.

Case example: Tammy

Tammy was significantly overweight and seemed to feel the disgust about herself that I associate with bulimia sufferers. For her, the central issue was the difficulty of separating from her mother. Her father had left the family on Tammy's fifth birthday during a dramatic scene vividly remembered by Tammy ten years after the event. He had a second family with a younger woman in a house not far away from Tammy's home, but never divorced Tammy's mother. It seemed that Tammy's parents were acting out non-separation. Her mother had allowed her father to keep a front door key and visit regularly, and clearly had difficulties in letting go of this relationship. Tammy attacked herself in two main ways. She attacked her mind – she was academically bright but unable to attend school – and she attacked her sexuality by over-eating and by blurring her body shape.

The issue of blurred or weak boundaries (as seen in the arrangements over father's keys to the house which allowed open access to the family he had rejected) was further acted in the household arrangements where Tammy's bedroom formed the passageway for her sexually active sister to reach *her* bedroom. Tammy was mother's youngest daughter and mother played an active part in preventing an age-appropriate transition and separation from her, keeping Tammy tied to her and home in an infantile way. Whilst Tammy denied and was consciously unaware of any anger with her mother to whom she felt close, her anger was expressed self-destructively. As with many of these young people, there was powerful suicidal rumination. She carried a bottle of paracetamol with her and attempted to compose a suicide note to her mother. She had shared this idea with her paternal grandmother who said that Tammy's mother would kill herself if Tammy committed suicide. She could acknowledge that she was angry with her father whom she felt had abandoned her just when, at the age of five, she thought she was the apple of his eye. She felt hurt and denigrated in her own right, but also confused at what was to do with her and belonged with her mother. It seemed to me that her mother's attack on Tammy was in order to deny her any differentiation. Un-cannily, even their birthdays were on the same day. We met for a year, with mother seeing my colleague, the psychiatrist, and continuing to deny her own part in her daughter's difficulties. There was some progress at home in that, with great difficulty, Tammy eventually demanded a bedroom where she could close the door. Her treatment ended when she gradually managed to separate sufficiently from her mother to attend college. The psychoanalytic view, in this instance, would be that Oedipal and pre-Oedipal issues have only been partially negotiated in the past and that these have resulted in significant measures of non-separation. This leads to what could be thought of as a 'double dose' of non-separation.

Case example: Becky

Becky is possibly the person who has taught me most about this difficult work, and I have written in more detail elsewhere about our work together (Parker 1993). Aged fifteen, she was referred by her mother who rightly thought she was anorectic. She came from a family where there were issues of transgenerational sexual abuse, and psychiatric instability and illness. Both parents abused substances – father was alcoholic and mother abused the use of slimming pills. Becky also disclosed sexual abuse. After her initial hospitalisation, and alongside family therapy, she attended first for once-weekly and then for twice-weekly psychotherapy, for six years. She abused drugs and became bulimic in the course of therapy. She hurtled through self-destructive, exciting and sexualised defences (which included anorexia and bulimia) against her intense inner emptiness, anger and despair, and was only halted when she became pregnant. Her daughter was born during therapy and proved to be a vital ally in her recovery. Becky was able to think and talk more clearly about her feelings during the third year of therapy when she was able to say (when her relationship with her violent boyfriend broke down) 'I want to diet but I know it is mad.'

Within the clinic, work with Becky and her family helped to underline the importance of meeting regularly to discuss the different tasks of the multidisciplinary team in our work with different members and aspects of the family. We found that family conflicts were all too readily enacted within the team if we did not have sufficient open discussion of our work. This could lead to polarisation and splitting within the team with colleagues 'taking sides' over issues in a manner which reflected Becky's family's defensive ways of dealing with conflict.

Becky taught me that, at times, as her therapist I was the only person to keep in mind the real threat to her survival, the reality of which, her parents were unable to face. This is an extermely difficult countertransference issue which I have experienced with other young women with eating disorders. (For a fuller discussion of these countertransference issues, see Parker 1993.)

Conclusion

The therapeutic task, when working with these young people, is to find out the reasons behind the symptom of the eating disorder. As described above, these can be issues of the rivalry of 'the old and young lioness', and unreached Oedipal issues, with or without real sexual abuse, combined with all the ordinary conflicts and distresses that adolescence presents – physically, sexually and socially.

It is important (although, as illustrated above, it may be difficult) to make every effort to join with the family in their struggle with their eating disordered offspring so that the age-appropriate separation, appropriate distance between the generations and self-actualisation of the young person can begin to take place. Once-weekly therapy can provide young people with a space in which they can struggle with the trauma in their lives during the developmentally turbulent teenage years, and learn to think rather than act. Whilst some sufferers will need hospitalisation and possibly treatment at centres that specialise in helping the most severe eating disorders, many are helped by treatment at the local CAMHS. Early intervention is vital because of the life-threatening potential of the symptoms. In this respect, public recognition of the seriousness of this condition has greatly helped young people to be referred for help sooner rather than later.

References

Bruch, H. (1978) *The Golden Cage: The Enigma of Anorexia Nervosa*, New York: Vintage Books

Crisp, A. H. (1980) *Let Me Be*, Hove/Hillsdale: Lawrence Ehrlbaun.

Dare, C. and Crowther, C. (1995) 'Psychodynamic models of eating disorders', in S. Szmukler, C. Dare and J. Treasure (eds) *Handbook of Eating Disorders: Theory, Treatment and Research*, Chichester: Wiley.

Daws, D. (1993) 'Feeding problems and relationship difficulties: therapeutic work with parents and infants', *Journal of Child Psychotherapy* 19(2): 69–83.

—— (1997) 'The perils of intimacy: closeness and distance in feeding and weaning', *Journal of Child Psychotherapy* 23(2): 179–99.

Halmi, K. (1995) 'Current concepts and definitions', in G. Szmukler, C. Dare and J. Treasure (eds) *Handbook of Eating Disorders: Theory, Treatment and Research*, Chichester: Wiley.

Henry, G. (1997) 'Reflections on some dynamics of eating disorders: "no entry" defences and foreign bodies', *International Journal of Psycho-Analysis* 78(5): 927–41.

Hindle, D. and Smith, M. (eds) (1999) *Personality Development: A Psychoanalytic Perspective*, London: Routledge.

Hsu, L. K. G. (1990) *Eating Disorders*, London: Guilford Press.

Lacey, H. (1993) 'Self-damaging and delinquent behaviour in bulimia nervosa. A catchment area study', *British Journal of Psychiatry* 163: 190–4.

Lanyado, M. (1999) '"It's just an ordinary pain": thoughts on joy and heartache in puberty and early adolescence', in D. Hindle and M. Smith (eds) *Personality Development: A Psychoanalyic Perspective*, London: Routledge.

Le Grange, D., Eisler, I., Dare, C. and Hodes, M. (1992) 'Family criticism and self-starvation; a study of expressed emotion', *Journal of Family Therapy* 14(2): 177–92.

Lieberman, S. (1995) 'Anorexia nervosa: the tyranny of appearance', *Journal of Family Therapy* 17(6): 133–8.

Likierman, M. (1997) 'On rejection: adolescent girls and anorexia', *Journal of Child Psychotherapy* 23(1): 61–80.

Mahler, M., Pine, F. and Bergman, A. (1975) *The Psychological Birth of the Human Infant* (reprinted 1985), London: Karnac.

Malan, D. H. (1997) *Anorexia, Murder and Suicide*, Oxford: Butterworth-Heinemann.

Miller, L. (1997) 'Mother-daughter and absent father: Oedipal issues in the therapy of an eleven year old girl with an eating disorder', *Journal of Child Psychotherapy* 23(1): 81–102.

Orbach, S. (1978) *Fat is a Feminist Issue*, New York/London: Paddington Press.

—— (1985) 'Accepting the symptom: a feminist psychoanalytic treatment of anorexia nervosa', in D. Garner and P. Garfinkel (eds) *Handbook of Psychotherapy for Anorexia and Bulimia Nervosa*, New York: Guilford Press.

Palazzoli, M. S. (1963) *Self-starvation: From the Intra-psychic to the Transpersonal Approach to Anorexia Nervosa*, Haywards Heath: Human Context Books.

Parker, N. (1993) 'How far is near enough: a waiting game', *Journal of Child Psychotherapy* 19(2): 37–51.

Russell, G. F. M. (1979) 'Bulimia nervosa: an ominous variant of anorexia nervosa', *Psychological Medicine* 9: 429–48.

—— (1995) 'Anorexia Nervosa through time', in G. Szmukler, C. Dare and J. Treasure (1995) *Handbook of Eating Disorders: Theory, Treatment and Research*, Chichester: Wiley.

Rutter, M., Taylor, E. and Herzov, L. (1994) *Child and Adolescent Psychiatry*, 3rd edn, Oxford: Blackwell Scientific.

Segal, B. (1993) 'Attachment and psychotic processes in an anorexic patient', *Journal of Child Psychotherapy* 19(2): 53–67.

Stern, D. (1985) *The Interpersonal World of the Infant: A View from Psychoanalysis and Developmental Psychology*, New York: Basic Books.

Steinhausen, H. (1994) 'Anorexia and bulimia nervosa', in M. Rutter, E. Taylor and L. Hersov *Child and Adolescent Psychiatry*, 3rd edn, Oxford: Blackwell Scientific.

Sours, J. A. (1980) *Starving to Death in a Sea of Objects*, Northvale, New Jersey/London: Jason Aaronson.

Szmuckler, G. I. and Patton, G. (1995) 'Socio-cultural models of eating disorders', in G. Szmukler, C. Dare and J. Treasure (eds) *Handbook of Eating Disorders: Theory, Treatment and Research*, Chichester: Wiley.

Tonnesman, M. (1980) 'Adolescent re-enactment, trauma and reconstruction', *Journal of Child Psychotherapy* 6: 23–44.

Tustin, F. (1958) 'Anorexia Nervosa in an adolescent girl', *British Journal of Medical Psychology* 31(3–4): 184–200.

Further reading

Dare, C. (1993) 'The starving and the greedy', *Journal of Child Psychotherapy* 19(2): 3–22.

Dare, C., Eisler, I., Colahan, M., Crowther, C., Senior, R. and Asen, E. (1995) 'The listening heart and Chi square: clinical and empirical perceptions in the family therapy of anorexia nervosa', *Journal of Family Therapy* 17(6): 31–57.

Journal of Child Psychotherapy (1993) 19(2): Special Edition on Eating Disorders.

Journal of Family Therapy (1995) 17(6): Special Edition on Eating Disorders.

Malan, D. H. (1997) *Anorexia, Murder and Suicide*, Oxford: Butterworth-Heinemann.

Sours, J. A. (1980) *Starving to Death in a Sea of Objects*, Northvale, New Jersey/London: Jason Aaronson.

Szmukler, S., Dare, C. and Treasure, J. (eds) (1995) *Handbook of Eating Disorders: Theory, Treatment and Research*, Chichester: Wiley.

26 Psychotherapeutic work with child and adolescent refugees from political violence

Sheila Melzak

The psychological consequences of impunity

Community leaders, healers and clinicians with long experience in work with survivors of human rights violations highlight the importance of acknowledging the psychological consequences of impunity, i.e. that such crimes are often not acknowledged by the perpetrators, and that the perpetrators are certainly not acknowledged under the law and punished (Rojas 1996). In my opinion, this lack of acknowledgement can reinforce the tendency of victims to deny and avoid acknowledgement of their own experiences, making them feel empty, ashamed, guilty, confused, invisible, inaudible and expendable. Part of the work of the psychotherapist therefore involves 'bearing witness' (Blackwell 1997) to these abuses and to their consequences by acknowledging, 'holding' (Winnicott 1960) and slowly 'working through' (Freud, S. 1914) the extreme, complicated and painful emotions until they become bearable. Clearly, painful memories and feelings are not easy to acknowledge. Survivors try to put memories out of their minds or try to protect their children and partners who, in turn, try to protect the survivor. The consequence can be profound and damaging family secrets that transmit the consequences of human rights abuses to the next generation.

Introduction and context

> I disapprove of what you say but I will defend to the death your right to say it.
>
> (Voltaire, quoted in Tallentyre 1906)

The children, adolescents and parents whose stories feature in this chapter have all experienced human rights abuses as defined by international legislation. Such abuses are not new. We know, moreover, that a significant proportion of adults receiving mental health care and treatment or in prison have experienced human rights abuses during childhood. This raises many questions about vulnerability, resilience, mediating factors and preventive mental health work with populations who have experienced neglect, abuse and scapegoating. I assume that at the heart of every individual survivor of violence there is a conflict which could be expressed as 'Am I entitled to life?' or 'Am I expendable?'

One frame of reference is not sufficient if we are to think appropriately about therapeutic interventions. A multi-dimensional approach is necessary, embracing psychoanalytic, historical, phenomenological, social, political and philosophical perspectives, and the inequalities of rights and power. We need to enter into the academic and community debates about the universality of human rights, and we also need to think about terms such as truth, responsibility, impunity, compensation, reconciliation and justice.

I work as a community child and adolescent psychotherapist in a human rights organisation, a charity based in London, the Medical Foundation for the Care of Victims of Torture. Although we have some paid clinical staff, much of the clinical work is carried out by experienced clinicians who work as part-time volunteers. My work involves direct assessment and treatment of children, parents and families, and the co-ordination of the children's team, including the management and supervision of clinicians carrying out direct work with children, adolescents and their carers within the Medical Foundation. Teams at the Medical Foundation have clearly separate functions as well as sometimes overlapping with other teams who carry out psychotherapeutic work – for example, the adult psychotherapy team, the group psychotherapy team and the family therapy team. There are also two intake teams and a front-line team. The Director of the Medical Foundation, Helen Bamber (who worked with unaccompanied Jewish refugee children taken during the Second World War to concentration camps in Germany and then sent to Britain) is very supportive of work with unaccompanied asylum-seeking children and adolescents who have survived political violence and who are not being parented.

One aspect of my work involves training, supervision and consultation with those in the community who work with refugee and asylum-seeking children and their families – teachers, social and health workers, lawyers and advisors from various statutory and voluntary organisations and workers from the refugee communities. This is essentially *applied* child psycho-analytic work, in which the theory and principles involved in understanding child development from a psychoanalytic perspective and in working psycho-therapeutically with children are applied to the needs of children in different contexts within the community.

The legal context and practice

Although the *UN Convention on the Rights of Children* (1991) and the 1951 *UN Declaration on the Rights of Refugees* have been signed by Britain and other European countries, it is clear that for most the maintenance of their boundaries by immigration legislation has a greater priority than keeping to legal human rights agreements. This results in most of the 27 million people seeking asylum each year remaining near to their countries of origin, usually in the Third World (Summerfield 1993; Van Beuren 1994).

Clearly, this also results in divided families and communities, and separated and unaccompanied children and adolescents, all of whom have to struggle with the emotional impact of their experiences of death, violence, scapegoating, confusion and secrecy, separation, loss, change and exile. Such emotional struggles, which might ideally be carried out in an atmosphere of security and genuine asylum, are, in fact – given our current asylum legislation – experienced in a context of further uncertainty and insecurity. This makes the necessary internal, emotional work difficult and often impossible, and has serious implications for the well-being of asylum-seeking children and adolescents.

An important aspect of our work at the Medical Foundation concerns writing reports in support of the asylum claims of young refugees. This is part of the process of bearing witness and acknowledging with the child the level of violence and loss he has experienced, and the consequences of these experiences both for the child and for the community. Working with the child to prepare such reports sometimes begins the process of the 'working through' (Freud, S. 1914) of complex past experiences by slowly putting feelings, especially unwanted feelings, into words. This makes even extreme and terrifying feelings and memories available for review and transformation.

Implications of the external world

If we assume that the developing mind of the child is modulated both by the internal and the external world, it is important to understand how children during different phases of development make sense of their experiences and the specific impact on the developing mind of extreme external events. This is no easy process. Faced with the most destructive human acts and their consequences, it is a natural tendency to turn away, to close our eyes and to cover our ears, as Louis Blom-Cooper (1985) described in his introduction to the Beckford report. This tendency not only makes working together difficult, as the Beckford Inquiry showed, but also inhibits careful and reflective thinking. Additionally, the presence of refugees and asylum seekers in a community seems to highlight pre-existing difficulties between agencies in that community – between health, education and social services, or between the statutory and the voluntary sector. An easily identifiable group, as are children from different cultures for whom English is not a first language, can be scapegoated as the cause of social problems that in fact they only highlight. It may be quite unclear to some agencies whether these children are victims and survivors, or, in fact, perpetrators. It can also be a huge threat to a newly-arrived refugee community in exile, feeling powerless when the children fail in school or are 'accommodated'. In this situation, statutory agencies become perpetrators in the minds of certain sections of that refugee community. In order to focus on the experiences of refugee children, and the way that child psychotherapeutic knowledge can be used both in direct clinical work and in work in the community, I will tease out some of the themes that highlight the external and the internal worlds of this group of children.

Themes from the external world

The external world of children and adolescents seeking asylum in Britain (with or without parents) can be described in a few concepts, each of which characterises a complex network of events that can potentially cause significant stress in the child's development.

Repression and war

Asylum-seeking children come to Europe to seek safety from countries at war or from repressive societies where any dissident voice is dealt with by violence, arrests, torture, and murder (often public executions). Various psychological techniques are used, specifically designed to terrify and divide the population so that constructive collective opposition is not possible. The target of this kind of psychological warfare is the civilian population – usually women and children (Summerfield 1993; Van-Beuren 1994). Social values are attacked. There is often looting, general violence and murder on the streets alongside a breakdown of the society and its social institutions. Many people are murdered; others are forced to consider a life in exile, separated from family, culture and friends. Each repressive country and culture will develop its own style of repression and social control and in working with asylum seekers and refugees we need to inform ourselves about these specifics. It is also important to understand that repression is not confined to a style of government practised in the Third World, but that it also occurs in European countries where refugees seek safety, but where they are marginalised, have almost no rights and usually have no way to re-establish their pre-existing social position. They often experience institutional and direct prejudice, racism and xenophobia. Cecile's story highlights the assaults on her safety both in her home country and also in her flight to exile:

> Cecile comes from a French-speaking African country with a strongly repressive government that can tolerate no democratic debate and no criticism. It maintains its power with an army financed and supplied with guns by Western countries with strong economic interests in the resources of Cecile's country. Cecile is the eldest girl in a family of five children, three girls and two boys. Cecile, as a child, had no under-

standing of politics but, as she entered adolescence, she began to realise that her beloved, lively, thoughtful mother was involved in a political group, determined to raise awareness of the huge economic differences between the minority of wealthy and the majority of poor in their society (and in the community) and determined to fight against these huge disadvantages and, in particular, disadvantages and abuses perpetrated against women. In common with many girls and women, Cecile felt passionately that she had, since her birth, been seen by her father as a disappointment and a second-class citizen by virtue of the fact that she was female. As she grew up she could not fail to realise that her society was not a safe place. Her social life outside school was severely restricted.

As in many families referred to us, Cecile had two parents with totally different political beliefs, with allegiances to two totally different political parties. Her father left the family home when the government began to target members of her mother's group and he was terrified of losing his social position by connection and implication.

Men in army uniforms entered Cecile's home on several occasions. They shouted, beat the females in the family and raped them all, including Cecile's younger sisters. Being quite unable to hold these events within her mind, one of the two small girls became psychotic.

It was after several of these violent and overwhelming intrusions into her home that Cecile's mother decided that, as an adolescent girl, Cecile was particularly vulnerable to the government's repressive activities and raised money to send Cecile to Britain where she believed that her daughter would be safe.

It is clear that, while she is physically safe, Cecile feels very frightened about her own and her family's future. She has been accommodated by Social Services (by no means a routine event for unaccompanied young asylum seekers separated from their main carers) and has an involved foster carer. She attends college and wants to enter higher education.

She is terrified of being physically attacked again in Britain, thinks often about her family and finds the unwanted memories of the violence she experienced often on her mind. She is still terrified of being overwhelmed by the feelings of terror and helplessness and rage that she unconsciously splits off from these memories. After several months in Britain she is unable to carry out the requirement of her asylum claim, that she tell her history of persecution to her asylum lawyer, as she becomes too distressed. She still has dreams about being raped and murdered, and tries to avoid sleep. Without her family and culture to reflect her identity back to her, she sometimes feels that she does not know who she is.

She comes weekly for psychotherapy, which she clearly finds sometimes to be a relief and sometimes a burden. She wants to come and to put some of her memories into the past. Only by discussing the political, social situation in her country in some detail, and the issues of human rights, can she become in touch with her enormous murderous rage towards the government of her country, towards the soldiers, and towards her father. It still puzzles and bothers her that this intermittent awareness brings her such relief, as she is still ashamed of all strong emotions. Our work will continue.

Violence

Refugee and asylum-seeking children will all have seen or experienced violence. Some will have experienced physical violence personally, some violent war situations, some forced to watch their parents being arrested, tortured or beaten. Others will have only heard about violence to their community, but they will have all been exposed to some level of violence, and to adults attempting to assert their power and resolve conflicts by using violence and being intolerant of difference. All of them will have experienced psychological violence due to the loss of familiar adults, siblings and friends, and all will have been excluded from the decision-making process by which they have come to seek asylum in Europe. This is always an adult decision, whether children and adolescents arrive with parents or adult substitute carers, or unaccompanied.

The sense that children and adolescents are able to make of violence and concomitant extreme experiences, which may include seeing dead and mutilated human bodies and violent acts such as rape and murder, clearly depends very much on the sense that adults close to them are able to make of these events. A crucial mediating factor in the lives of refugee children is whether or not they have access to adults who themselves are able to develop an explanation that integrates many layers of meaning.

Scapegoating

After experiencing in their own country the scapegoating that leads families to seek asylum, all adolescent refugees inevitably experience further scapegoating and prejudice in exile. In addition to becoming part of the marginalised minority group in exile, they experience racism, xenophobia and bullying in school on account of disability, not speaking English, skin colour. A favourite form of abuse in London schools is 'mother-cussing' (where adolescents attempt to humiliate their peers by calling their mothers prostitutes). This has particular effects on refugee children raised in communities with very traditional values, whose mothers have been raped or murdered. Physical fights often ensue. The victims are blamed, especially when they don't have the language (technical or emotional) to give an account of their own experiences, as Abdel's story shows:

> Abdel is a fourteen-year-old Somali boy who sought asylum in Britain when he was nine. His parents had been murdered during the clan fighting. His mother was beheaded during the machine gunfire and Abdel was found clinging to her dead body. His mother's sister took in Abdel and his brothers. They settled in an area of Somalia far from Abdel's home. As the fighting moved nearer, they were forced into exile – first to a refugee camp in Kenya and later to Britain. In Britain, Abdel's aunt tried to make a home for her own children and for Abdel and his brothers in inadequate accommodation and with little money. The combined stresses of assimilating her own traumatic experiences alongside the ongoing practical and financial difficulties wore her down. When she was eventually unable to care for her nephews they were taken into foster care. In school, Abdel has been exposed to extremely cruel verbal abuse about his mother, and he feels that the only reasonable response to this abuse is physical aggression. He often becomes involved in fights and has been suspended several times.

In our psychotherapeutic group for adolescent boys, the majority have lost at least one parent through organised violence. They often raise the issue of racist and xenophobic abuse at school and how best to manage their anger whilst keeping to the school rules. Loyalty, protection and respect towards parents, and towards the memory of lost or dead parents, is a fundamental aspect of the identity of children raised in traditional cultures, whatever the religion.

In addition to the importance of individual and group therapy, Abdel's case highlights the need for work with schools on policy, practice and curriculum issues (Rutter 1996). Such work includes oral history, the development of awareness of others and of feelings, including extreme and difficult emotions connected with violence and loss, and work on difference, prejudice, racism and conflict (Kriedler 1984; Bolloton and Spafford 1996, 1998).

The promotion of preventative mental health work in the environments where children and adolescents spend a significant proportion of their waking hours is a very appropriate concern for child and adolescent psychotherapists. It fits clearly within our models of applied child psychoanalytic theories where we raise questions about 'good-enough environments' and 'holding' in connection with the development of good-enough self-esteem, the capacity to think and learn and to manage frustration, and the capacity to make relationships with adults and peers and to develop a mature morality. Internal representations and identifications with aggressive, competitive, prejudiced and violent adults can be modified and transformed, not only through intensive individual child psychotherapy, but also through warm relationships with thoughtful adults working together in the children's interest. This implies the need for child psychotherapists to work closely with other professionals such as social workers, youth workers, play workers, refugee workers and leaders.

Loss

Leaving home, extended family, climate and a familiar cultural world inevitably brings about separation and loss. The issue is not whether or not separation and loss has occurred, but whether mourning is possible. Relevant questions are:

(a) Has a mourning process begun?
(b) If so, has it become arrested or frozen in some way?
(c) Is it ever possible to mourn massive and traumatic losses completely?
(d) What are the developmental costs of incomplete mourning?
(e) What strategies do children and adolescents use to avoid the experience of emotional pain and other associated extreme emotions?
(f) Is it possible to remain in a state of continuous and unresolved mourning?

Families and part-families travelling into exile have no real idea about whether they will ever return to their home country or whether the social and political situations that brought about their persecution might change. Uncertainties about whether forced or voluntary return is possible, desirable, or to be feared are compounded by restrictive asylum legislation. The longer that asylum seekers remain in exile, the more they and their home society have the potential for change, and the wider the difference between the remembered communities of the past and present social relations in exile. In this context, mourning can be a protracted process with no resolution. This is further complicated by other issues. Family members living in different continents separated by wars and corrupt regimes often lose touch with each other. People disappear and are killed, but there is no way of knowing if they are alive or dead, so no mourning rituals can be carried out.

Significant numbers of children and adolescents arrive in Britain alone (600 in 1996 and a further 600 between January and April 1997). These unaccompanied or separated children and adolescents have been sent to Europe for their physical safety, much in the same way that European children were evacuated during the Second World War. Some may know that their parents have disappeared, been imprisoned or died. Others have been told nothing about why they have had to leave and experience exile as a rejection.

Thus losses are profound. They are both concrete and abstract (e.g. loss of a way of life, a culture). Often parents are lost and no substitute parental care is arranged, forcing children and adolescents to take care of themselves without any preparation or guidance for this. In these confusing circumstances, some will lose their sense of identity. Some try to cope with these feelings of being lost by holding on firmly to their own cultural identity in its most traditional form. Others become very Westernised and rapidly abandon their own culture and traditions. Surprisingly few of these separated children break down completely, though they cope at considerable cost. They have all, to a greater or lesser extent, lost their childhoods and experience the fundamental loss of a sense that adults can keep them safe. Ardit's story illustrates the impact of such profound losses:

Ardit is a sixteen-year-old Albanian boy from Kosova. Our weekly work is likely to be brief and it is informed by a perspective on human rights violations and on psychoanalytic child development. Ardit arrived in Britain seeking asylum a few months ago with a friend, another adolescent boy, but without parents and family. He knew no one in Britain but wanted to travel as far as possible from a country where his people, the Kosovan Albanians, had been persecuted for generations – and certainly throughout his life – by the Serbs who felt it was reasonable to retaliate thus for perceived past injustices. One day soldiers came and took away Ardit's father who had been campaigning for social and economic rights for his people. Ardit went to the barracks to ask where he was. Aged fifteen, he was imprisoned, questioned and severely beaten for several weeks. His hands were so damaged that some fingers had to be amputated. His father has disappeared and may be dead; his mother wanted him to be safe and, against her wish to keep her family together, sent him into exile, far away from siblings and extended family. He has been fostered and attends college.

Our weekly meetings give him an opportunity to explore the consequences of violent events that have led to so many changes in his life. He has time and space to acknowledge and mourn his several losses and separations, including a lost childhood, lost family and community, and the loss of an adolescent relationship with his father. Repeated nightmares about his own prison experiences have evolved into dreams about meeting his father surrounded by guards and being unable to speak with or rescue him. One aim of our work is to link experiences and feelings that have been separated under the impact of violence – disconnections caused by overwhelming experiences that are difficult to think about and process. In a recent session we talked again about his feelings towards the perpetrators of his abuse. Ardit spoke quietly and the interpreter translated: 'It would not be enough for them to say sorry, to acknowledge their crime. I would like them to feel the fear that I felt in Kosova and the pain that I felt in prison and that I feel now. I know where they are, but my father has disappeared, I miss him very much.'

Our work together will explore his feelings, which include rage, revenge, fear, guilt and shame, and also moral issues concerning justice and injustice. These are significant themes for an adolescent who has grown up in a repressive society and seen daily violations of human rights. Why is the world like this and what can he do about this when he becomes a man?

With a father and a mother lost in his home country, Ardit was clearly bereft of parental care; but even some asylum-seeking children who are accompanied by parents or substitute parents may also have completely lost parental care. Those children living with parents who functioned well as parents at home but who change profoundly as a result of torture, loss, enormous change and the stresses of life in exile, I call 'psychologically unaccompanied'. They are especially vulnerable. Many parents are unable to explain to themselves the series of social and political changes that led to violence, scapegoating and eventual exile, so they are in no way equipped to explain these events to their children. Many parents are not only angry with their home country, but also with the country of exile for their loss of position and status and their inability to find adequate housing, work and income. It is difficult for children either to understand these events or the strong feelings of their parents. Such children also have to deal with the anxiety about the change in their parents and with their feelings of grief, fear and rage that the reliable containing parent is no longer present.

Each family member's perception of the traumatic events is likely to be very different, depending on their level of developmental maturity and their individual experience of violence. Some parents neglect and emotionally abuse their children in exile by being emotionally unavailable or by unconsciously placing strong expectations on their children to take on the role of lost loved ones whom they cannot bear to mourn. This style of parenting, a consequence of the parents' difficulties in mourning, may result in children who have no real sense of themselves and who demonstrate a false self (Winnicott 1960).

Change

We thrive on secure attachments. However well prepared we are, change is always connected to losses which are painful and need time for adjustment, but unplanned change brings separation, loss and shock for which there has been no opportunity for preparation. As part of the process of assessment of any asylum-seeking child it is helpful to think about the number of changes he has had to deal with since he left his home country and to discuss with him which were the most difficult, what was felt about the change at the time and now, and what helped him to feel better. Whether the child's strategies are good-enough or not depends both on his internal resilience and on the capacity of the people in his external world to promote that resilience, to help him to reflect on the changes and their consequences and to find ways to make connections between old and new situations.

Culture

Cultural identity is complicated. People may feel connections to a variety of cultures and also criticise and disown certain aspects of their own culture. It is important to keep in mind that cultures develop and change, depending many factors, for example on whether the community is part of a significant social group or part of a minority group living in exile. Working with refugee children means forming relationships with children who have some differences and some similarities between their world view and that of the therapist. It is important that the differences are understood and respected. As child psychotherapists, we need to inform ourselves about the political situations that lead our refugee clients to come into exile, and also about their culture and belief systems. This information is available from the British Refugee Council and from the Minority Rights Group.

Resilience and protective factors

In trying to help traumatised children, it is important to know what factors can foster the development of their resilience to help them face the adversity in their lives (Emanuel 1996). There seem to be five main factors whose presence is important in the development of resilience in asylum-seeking children:

1   *Belonging*: having a parent or a parental substitute.
2   *Thinking*: being enabled to reflect on one's experiences, past and present, both the 'difficult to understand' and the truly overwhelming experiences.
3   *Active problem-solving*: after prolonged experiences of helplessness and powerlessness, being enabled to make real choices that affect the present and the future and to think about past events where almost no active involvement was possible.
4   *Being able to make use of natural healing processes* (such as play, dreams, community processes and rituals) in order to make sense of and work through complicated feelings connected with extreme events.
5   *Being able to make use of community healing processes*: sharing, remembering and being sustained by family and community stories, legends and values that connect with altruism, empathy, hope and commitment.

Child psychotherapists spend too little time discussing survival and resilience; the processes described above can help us to explore the child's real links to the refugee community and to the community of exile.

The internal world and therapy: validation, clarification and interpretation

In addition to the impact of violence, loss and change, all asylum-seeking children have experienced a breakdown of orderly society and of reasonable authority. This may have a profound effect on their expectations and on their capacity to make sense of new and different societies and institutions. They are likely to be suspicious, fearful and mistrustful, and to overreact to unexpected situations. Significant themes in the child's internal world include issues around secrecy, bereavement, trauma and problems of memory. Psychotherapeutic work needs, initially, to conceptualise and then work with the material that emerges, always bearing in mind the distinction between unconscious and conscious material.

Separate work with children and also with parents is often necessary, as asylum-seeking family members characteristically try to protect each other from the 'truth' of their own mixed feelings, especially from their anger, envy, jealousy and rage. Children will especially protect parents whose level of emotional investment in their children has changed. The clinical work is often long term as the losses are numerous and overwhelming. Individuals often feel that putting their feelings into words will result in a flood of unbearable pain that could potentially incapacitate not only them personally but also every family member. Parents often say, 'If I cry I am afraid that the tears will never stop, so I try to stop myself from thinking and feeling.' This strategy can often lead to psychosomatic complaints. Our therapeutic task is to 'hold' these difficult feelings, to acknowledge their roots, and eventually to enable them to be bearable. Our work is not to help people to forget, but to enable the past to be experienced as the past, not as a continual intrusion into the present, and thus to enable living in the present and some thinking about future possibilities.

Secrecy

> Keeping secrets is a way of keeping power.
>
> (Aristotle)

The theme of secrecy is one that is particularly helpful to consider when trying to conceptualise the experiences and needs of young refugees. Many have to keep a series of political, familial and personal secrets in order to survive physically and psychologically. Once they arrive into exile and safety, some children, especially those who arrive unaccompanied, are unable to generalise about whom they might trust. Putting a lot of their emotional energy into keeping various secrets (for fear that if they reveal their secret their own life or the lives of family members would be at risk) restricts the energy available for thinking, for the work of mourning, for adjustment to a changed personal and social situation, and for development in general. In addition to political secrets, there are family secrets. Children may protect vulnerable parents upon whom they depend by keeping secret the fact that the parent cries all the time, is violent or is absent (physically or emotionally). Similarly, children may hide the fact that they have to take on the adult responsibilities at home – doing the cooking, cleaning and taking care of siblings and parents.

Personal secrets are also important. Adolescents who are trying to be independent find it particularly difficult to bear regressive symptoms, such as bed-wetting and encopresis; and symptoms of trauma and bereavement such as flashbacks, night terrors and eating difficulties can make children and adolescents feel that they are losing control and going mad. Personal secrets can also include feelings of guilt, shame and anxiety about actions and thoughts in the past or the present, as well as feeling the burden of responsibility for remembering what human rights abuses have been perpetrated against your people. These secrets may be held in the conscious or unconscious mind, or find expression somatically via bodily pain, which may mark actual physical injury or memories of abuses to significant people in the young person's life. Children are most at risk in families where parents are unable to discuss not only past but also the present problems of their children. Children, in an act of loyalty, protect parents and deny themselves (Melzak 1992).

Bereavement and loss

Mourning is rarely a straightforward process for refugees because they face so many ongoing uncertainties. Losses may be denied for many years, with both parents and children holding on to a fragile hope that these losses are not permanent. The asylum-determination process is very long, and families often have to wait many years to hear from the Home Office whether they can be given refugee status and remain in exile. With only temporary status, people are not entitled to family reunion, so news about refugee status can mean being reunited with the family. Also, if relatives are lost through disappearance, it is impossible to know if they are alive or dead. Clearly this period of uncertainty is too long for a child's mind to understand. Family splits can arise when the children live in the present by adapting to the values of the culture of the country of exile, but the adults are locked in the past and hold on to strict interpretations of their original culture's belief system as a form of mourning their enormous losses. This interferes with open family communication between adults and children. In this context, child-centred family meetings can begin to build bridges of communication between family members.

Parents may lose their sense of authority if they cannot support the family at the standard they enjoyed in their own countries. Much work and support may be needed to re-establish parental authority when parents are used to different models of childcare and discipline from those in Britain. Many refugee parents become afraid to set firm limits on their children (who often have special problems with respecting authority after life in a repressive society), because they are anxious that children will be taken into care by the authorities if they use their traditional physical punishments. In some families the impact of pervasive losses is defended against in various ways which affect the child's development, and delicate long-term therapeutic work is required to facilitate individual and family mourning, and to enable children and adolescents who have lost their sense of self to regain and reclaim a sense of identity.

Trauma

Trauma results from overwhelming experiences of feeling helpless, powerless and hopeless, being unable to make sense of the world or to protect oneself. Refugee and asylum-seeking children are likely to have experienced an accumulation of overwhelming events. Even in these circumstances most children are able to make use of the protective, mediating factors in their environment to enable them to develop resilience; but for a relatively small group of children the capacity to learn and socialise is seriously limited as a direct result of their experiences of human rights abuses. Many writers refer to the phenomenon of 'psychic numbness' where survivors are unable to think about small (or large) present difficulties without the symptoms of the original traumatic events emerging. This process may or may not be defended against.

In therapeutic work with these children, the most useful models refer to the disintegrating and disconnecting effects of trauma and to the role of the therapist in enabling integration and synthesis of past and present experiences, memories and feelings. Even fairly benign teasing may arouse strong feelings because of previous experiences, such as the sudden loss of parents. Some children may remember difficult experiences but lose connection with the accompanying emotions, like Ahmed, who laughed loudly whilst telling me about his cousin being shot and killed next to him. Psychotherapeutic work involves the reconnection of memories with the original painful and difficult affects. Recovery from the consequences of trauma can occur within the context of a safe, healing relationship (Herman 1992) where remembrance and mourning can take place. Only then will some integration of the trauma and an awareness of the commonality of the experience of human rights abuses be possible.

Emanuel (1996) suggests that in working with traumatised children:

> the psychotherapist's primary function . . . is to help them to make sense of their emotional experience. This involves initially receiving and containing the emotions surrounding it by attending to the fragments presented and to the emotions evoked by them in the therapist . . . The child has to learn to label or name the elements of his emotional experience before thought about the relationships between the elements is possible.

He refers to Greenacre, and to Hopkins who notes the importance of helping people 'not only to accept the reality of traumatic events and the feelings which they engendered, but to become able to grieve about the damage done to them and to express appropriate anger about this' (Hopkins 1986). This requires an extremely painful mourning process about what has been lost as well as what can never be regained. In fact, no traumatic event can be wholly assimilated and vulnerability will always remain (Greenacre 1953).

The potential for retraumatisation is high. It is not an uncommon event that adolescents who report being imprisoned and tortured in their own countries are not believed when they apply for asylum in Britain. In fact 5 per cent of unaccompanied young people who entered Britain in 1996 were detained in prison (Smith 1998). There is a similar potential for retraumatisation in many schools where there is no attempt to be democratic and which are rife with bullying, racism and xenophobia.

Memory, forgetting and remembering

In our work with child survivors of human rights violations, one of the main tasks is to acknowledge with the child the reality of his memories of an accumulation of abusive events and his connected feelings of violent rage, terror, helplessness and hopelessness. These feelings are sometimes extremely painful and humiliating for an adolescent to bear, especially in situations where close family members were, in their presence, hurt or killed, or arrested and subsequently disappeared. The child may feel a profound sense of his own failure, a feeling that involves denial of his profound helplessness in the face of organised violence, guns and soldiers. Another central therapeutic task is to think with the child, at his own level of understanding, about the specific effects and meaning of these traumatic events for him at the particular phase of his development when they occurred. After this process of acknowledgement, 'working through' may begin.

By listening carefully to the accounts of survivors' experiences in concentration camps during the Second World War, Langer was able to describe in detail the problems of remembering and forgetting (Langer 1991). To save their own lives, survivors were forced to participate against their will in actions that surprised and horrified them at the time, let alone later when living in a society not at war. He describes the changes in their language and affect to a more concrete, emotionally disorganised communication when they talked about their Holocaust experiences. They spoke of the past as if they were in the present. Sometimes, children find this reliving unbearable and will bring into play all kinds of defensive strategies so as not to remember the feelings connected with overwhelming memories, or the memories connected with strong feelings. This begs the question as to whether child survivors of human rights abuses need to acknowledge their experiences (verbally or non-verbally) in order to move forward in a good-enough way. My answer to this question has political, historical and child-centred dimensions. There are significant numbers of asylum-seeking children whose capacity to learn and socialise is profoundly restricted both by their past experience of violence and also by their present social position in exile. Such children certainly need attention, and some need psychotherapy, but their social environment also needs attention. All children need the opportunity to enhance their self-esteem and their capacities to reflect, acknowledge difference and resolve conflict if they are to be able, via the school curriculum, to think about their own history and the histories of their classmates, including those involving abuses of power, exploitation, war and violence.

Children who have a basic resilience rooted within their family history, and who have adult care and support, are able to address these traumatic issues. For other children, key aspects of their experience become repressed – a process which is reinforced by an environment that does not want to listen. Such children are likely to demonstrate their difficulties in partial remembering and partial forgetting via learning and social difficulties. The difference in capacity to cope lies, not in the degree of violence experienced, but in the presence or absence of mediating and protective factors that can enable children to remember, to acknowledge and then to forget. These issues can best be illustrated in the histories of two boys who experienced similar human rights abuses in Zaire:

Olivier is the youngest boy in a family of seven children. His mother died from illness when he was six and the children were subsequently cared for by their eldest sister. Olivier was present (aged nine) when his father was arrested and imprisoned as a result of his leading role in a democratic political party in opposition to the oppressive and auto- cratic government of Zaire led by Mbutu. Olivier visited his father in prison and saw him with broken legs after torture. On his release, Olivier's father continued to produce political leaflets criticising the government. Olivier was at home on the day that soldiers burst into the house and shot his father. When Olivier went into the room, his father was dead and his eldest sister had fainted. As education was not free in Zaire, Olivier and his siblings could not attend school from that time. A few days after his father's murder, soldiers again came to the house and (perhaps believing that children are to blame for the sins of their fathers) forced Olivier's adolescent siblings to have sexual inter- course with each other. Two of the siblings seemed to go out of their minds as a result of this experience and were taken away by friends. The two other adolescent siblings disappeared in the chaos. Olivier was left with two sisters, one older and one younger. Friends eventually helped the small family to come to Britain. They have never received any information about the rest of the family and do not know if they are alive.

Though the family has experienced a series of overwhelmingly terrifying and outrageous experiences involving a series of violent events, losses and changes, and though they have had to adjust for the sake of safety to a complete change in their social position and status and are now part of a minority group, they are coping. Olivier has friends, attends school and does well, and, most importantly, is able to reflect on his experiences in Zaire and in Britain. Now a young black refugee who sometimes stutters when he speaks, and who is humorous, thoughtful and sensitive, he is able both to protect himself and also to communicate his needs and concerns. Like most refugee students, he experiences racist and xenophobic bullying in school, but is able to make appropriate links between this and the violent scape- goating his family experienced in Zaire. In general, Olivier has no problems with memory, though for a brief period when the family was threatened with deportation he had repeated nightmares about being shot by Mbutu on arrival in Zaire.

In a recent meeting of our fortnightly adolescents' group we were talking about injustice and abuses of power in Britain and in the home country of each young person in the group. Olivier strongly identifies with his father's democratic values and told the group about an incident that none of us had heard about before. In the broken disorganised Zairean society there were no medicines available. There was looting and murder on the streets. Olivier described how his sister's small baby suddenly became ill and he was asked to hold the baby on the short journey to the doctor. The child died in his arms. The group was stunned and Olivier said, 'I was mad! I felt mad!' Annie Ellisson, my co-worker, asked Olivier if he meant crazy or angry and he quickly replied, 'Angry, angry. If I told you all the things I've seen, all the things that are in my head, you would be very, very angry like me!'

I write this example to illustrate two issues. One is the importance, in both individual and group work, of the role of the therapist as an effective listener who can contain the young people's feelings and experiences of loss, violence and injustice, extreme sadness, rage, terror and confusion. This enables both the remembering and also the kind of healthy forgetting that facilitates life in the present. The second issue is to demonstrate the resilient way a boy can cope with events that have left him vulnerable, but able to function and develop. It is a real strength in Olivier that he can talk about, think about and use others to help him to make sense of his experiences. I see this resilience as rooted in his strong positive memories of his family and, especially, in his clear, firm identification with his father. Our work with Olivier has offered him some support during his adolescence in a country where he feels safe but where he also feels continuously a stranger. Our main therapeutic tasks have been to give him time and space to mourn his numerous losses, to reflect on the consequences for him of trauma and separation, and to think about the extent to which, as he develops into adulthood, he wants to identify with his memory of his dead father.

In contrast:

Pascal is a boy with many developmental difficulties which originated prior to his experience of political violence in Zaire, but which were certainly amplified by his experiences of this violence and also of being in exile. His experiences of political violence were very similar to those of Olivier. Pascal's father belonged to the same democratic political party as Olivier's father, and was equally brave and effective in his attempts to highlight the exploitation of the poor. Like Olivier, Pascal was nine when his father was arrested, and the arrest of both fathers occurred at about the same time in the social history of Zaire. Pascal witnessed with terror, but perhaps also excitement, the looting and murder on the streets of the capital, Kinchasa. The differences in Pascal's story are that:

(a) His mother was encouraged by his father to travel to Britain with his three young siblings for their safety after soldiers entered the family home.
(b) Pascal and his older brother were left with their father.
(c) Pascal's father disappeared after his arrest, and only after years (and a change of government in Zaire) did they find out that he had been killed. Pascal and his family thus lived for two years with enormous uncertainty both about his father and about whether they would gain asylum.
(d) After the arrest Pascal and his brother stayed with friends who could not manage Pascal's difficult behaviour. He was then taken to stay with a family he did not know.
(e) Pascal came to Britain with a stranger who had been paid to escort him and to leave him at immigration.

Once in Britain, Pascal joined his mother and young siblings but found the much reduced economic situation of his family and the absence of his father to be an almost intolerable change. He dealt with the sequence of changes, separations and losses, and with his experience of the breakdown in adult authority, by hostility towards his teachers and, intermittently, his mother, and by an idealised longing for his father, hoping his father would return and make everything as it had been during the best family times in Zaire.

For the first four years of his life in Zaire, Pascal had been in and out of hospital because of a chest disorder. His mother usually stayed with him in the hospital. When Pascal was about five his mother become pregnant again and, because it was a difficult pregnancy, Pascal's maternal grandmother offered to take care of him. She lived in the countryside, more than a day's journey from Kinchasa. Pascal thus had a different childhood from his older brother. There was no primary school in the countryside, only nursery-level care. Pascal had a great deal of freedom, exploring the neighbourhood, which he knew like the back of his hand (even now he can make a detailed map of the area), and playing by the big river; but at the same time he was constrained by his grandmother's fundamentalist Christian beliefs and rural superstitions, and also by her strong physical punishments for any of his transgressions.

At first, Pascal loved life in the countryside, but he soon missed his close family and felt angry and excluded. His father's infrequent visits did not make up for these feelings. He expressed a strong wish to return to Kinchasa, but for more than two years the situation there was considered too chaotic and dangerous. Then, even though the social and political situation was worsening, Pascal's grandmother felt too old to care for him and he had to return to Kinchasa. However, his father was often away, his mother was terrified and trying to cope with child-care, and Pascal (now eight) was functioning like a much younger child. He had no real conception of the political upheavals in Zaire or of his father's work in relation to these. He thought, rather as cartoons and comics will have us believe, that good superheroes will always win by destroying the forces of evil. Perhaps to protect the political activists and the innocence of children, no one explained what was going on, either to the children or even to the women in the community. Already an angry boy, Pascal must have begun at this time to identify with the powerful men in uniforms who were similar to the powerful superheroes in his comics and in his internal world. This identification was reinforced by the persistence of his early magical thinking processes. When his father was arrested by soldiers who turned up at the house, Pascal was playing with his new football (a present from his father) in the yard. When I later asked him about this, Pascal (now twelve) said, 'You'd better ask my mum or my big brother.' When I reminded him that his mother had not been there, he said that he only remembered the soldiers arriving and later running into the empty house and finding his brother in tears. He implied that little children did not need to think about these things – he had been nine at the time.

Unlike Olivier, Pascal did not have any understanding of the realities of the world in which he lived and he had no real capacity to reflect, as reflection had been avoided by his carers and may even have been discouraged. Thus Pascal was subjected to a series of unplanned changes to which he reacted with rage, terror and physical aggression. The various separations early in his life meant that he did not trust any adults to hold his interests in their minds or to make sense of the world for him. He was often solitary, and narcissistically seemed to use other people (both children and adults) to meet his current needs, not to share and identify with them.

When I began weekly psychotherapy with Pascal (essentially he needed developmental help which will be long term) he had just begun secondary school in Britain. He could not manage to be at home or with his siblings and often ran away. He looked very sad, frightened and confused, though he often talked in an aggressive way. He was clearly not ready for secondary school either emotionally or intellectually, but he had to go. Like all traumatised people, he found any new experience an enormous stress as it reawakened feelings of helplessness, terror and rage. The school was large and he was one of the youngest and smallest students. Even though the school was sensitive to refugee students and their needs, Pascal could not cope with rules developed for large groups of children. He had been told not to play with his football inside the school but that he could play outside during breaks. One of the senior masters agreed to keep the ball safe. However, at the start of one lunch break when Pascal asked for his ball, the teacher was too busy to retrieve it. It is unclear whether the teacher explained the situation or if he simply told Pascal to wait. Pascal became angry at the injustice of not getting his ball back, and moaned that it was all unfair. This must have irritated the teacher, who told Pascal to go away; Pascal refused and the master became angry. Pascal must have felt furious and terrified. He wanted his ball and did not want to lose face. He kicked the master between his legs and was suspended from the school. This incident, during his first week at school, made the school doubt that they could manage him. Pascal is clearly very bright and responds well to very small group and individual tuition but he is unable to hold his feelings for long. Once aroused, he acts as soon as he feels his verbal explanations are not being accepted. After nine months of several similar incidents, Pascal was expelled. Psychotherapeutic work with Pascal has centred on helping him to think before he acts and to reflect on his feelings (and those of others) in different situations. Some of this work includes the kind of interactions that mothers have with young babies – labelling feeling states and connecting them with experiences. Another therapeutic task is to enable him to remember various aspects of a situation in which he eventually acted out aggressively.

The first year of his treatment comprised such work, interspersed with long and fantastic imaginary sagas acted with dolls, puppets or plasticine, or depicted in drawings in which each episode ended in violent death and destruction. Pascal reacted to each tragedy, not with despair, but with a bemused shrug of inevitability. He clearly could not imagine any other ending. It was only after a year of weekly treatment, after Pascal had been expelled and was waiting for a new school and after the news of his father's death, that he began to give up his fantasies of omnipotent superheroes, magical rescues and inevitable destruction, and could listen to comments that I had frequently made over a long time. These were broadly on three themes: that all stories did not have to end in death, destruction and disaster; that real men are not superheroes – they can be brave, caring and wonderful, as well as horrible, frightening and cruel – but real men are fragile and feel pain, and once they are dead they cannot come alive again; and that some people really are worth trusting, but trust is something that develops slowly and has to be earned. It was in this context that Pascal could begin to mourn the loss of his father.

Pascal is one of the relatively small proportion of refugee children for whom the psychotherapeutic techniques of clarification, validation and confrontation are insufficient to facilitate forward development, and for whom interpretation of unconscious conflict is necessary. Pascal longed for his father, but was also furious with him for leaving him with his grandmother and for leaving him to go to prison. Pascal was so angry and omnipotent that he thought his father's death was his fault. Interpretive disentangling only became possible after a long period of building a therapeutic alliance, reflecting back his comments, naming feelings and reconnecting them to the experiences from which they originated. Eventually, he felt ready to relinquish some of his omnipotence and magical thinking.

Working together: conclusions

Child psychotherapeutic work with child and adolescent survivors of political violence must be informed by detailed knowledge about the external world of these children (both the political and social situation in their country and the restrictions that these impose on personal freedom) and about the political and practical situation of families and unaccompanied children and adolescents seeking asylum in Britain, given the current restrictive asylum laws in Europe which are interpreted in very xenophobic ways.

I believe it is important to apply child psychoanalytic ideas in training and supporting adults who work with and care for children – teachers, social workers, lawyers, health workers and members of the refugee communities.

With the ongoing support of a child psychotherapist's focus on the developmental needs of children, the adults in contact with refugee children can increase their understanding of the child's experience of trauma, loss and change and promote the factors that facilitate the development of resilience.

Children who need only involvement, validation, clarification, explanation and clear authority do not need direct help from child-centred mental health workers; but the significant adults in their lives may need some help in assessing and disentangling the child's experience from their own response to these experiences, and time to assess what the child's special needs might be in school and at home. Consultation with a child psychotherapist, in this context, can give time and space to clarify the special needs of asylum-seeking children. In my workplace, a child psychotherapist runs a regular fortnightly consultation group for adults who work with refugee children and adolescents. This provides the opportunity to discuss the children's needs and to address the institutional problems they raise.

Those children for whom unconscious feelings, conflicts and confusions profoundly interfere with their development will need direct child psychotherapeutic intervention. This may be quite brief, as with Ardit, or long term, as with Pascal.

Involvement with the mental health needs of refugee children makes us all 'political' in terms of thinking about children's rights and human rights, as well as the abuses of these rights. Work with refugee children involves daily contact with vulnerable children and young people who are marginalised in this country and who do not receive their basic right to parental care and education. Awareness of the dire situation of such vulnerable children, coupled with the knowledge gleaned in long, child psychotherapeutic trainings, will hopefully galvanise our profession to campaign to improve the situation of children whose basic needs for development (as set out by the United Nations in its *Convention on the Rights of the Child* (1991)) are not met, and to think together with others about how these needs might best be met in our community.

References

Blackwell, D. (1997) 'Holding, containing and bearing witness: the problem of helpfulness in encounters with torture survivors', *Journal of Social Work Practice* 11(2): 81–9.

Blom-Cooper, L. (1985) *A Child in Trust: the Report of the Panel of Inquiry into the circumstances surrounding the death of Jasmine Beckford*, London: London Borough of Brent.

Bolloton, W. and Spafford, T. (1996) *Teaching Refugee Children: a Guide to Resources*, London: Newton English Language Service.

—— (1998) 'Refugee children in the U.K.: the current situation', in S. Scott and P. Gibbon (eds) *Meeting the Individual Needs of Children from Minority Ethnic Groups*, London: Intercultural Education Partnership U.K.

Emanuel, R. (1996) 'Psychotherapy with children traumatised in infancy', *Journal of Child Psychotherapy* 22(2): 214–39.

Freud, S. (1914) 'Remembering, repeating and working through', *SE*, Vol. 12, London: Hogarth Press.

Greenacre, P. (1953) *Trauma, Growth and Personality*, London: Hogarth Press.

Herman, J. L. (1992) *Trauma and Recovery*, New York: Basic Books.

Hopkins, J. (1986) 'Solving the mystery of monsters: steps towards the recovery from trauma', *Journal of Child Psychotherapy* 12(1): 61–71.

Kriedler, W. J. (1984) *Creative Conflict Resolution*, Glenview IL: Scott Foresman and Co.

Langer, L. L. (1991) *Holocaust Testimonies: The Ruins of Memory*, New Haven CT: Yale University Press.

Melzak, S. (1992) 'Secrecy, privacy, survival, repressive regimes and growing up', *Bulletin of the Anna Freud Centre* 15: 205.

Rojas, B. P. (1996) 'Breaking the human link: the medico-psychiatric view of impunity', in C. Harper (ed.) *Impunity: An Ethical Perspective*, London: World Council of Churches Publications.

Rutter, J. (1996) *Refugees in the Classroom*, Stoke on Trent: Trentham Books.

Smith, T. (1998) *Children behind Bars*, London: British Refugee Council.

Summerfield, D. (1993) *Addressing the Human Response to War and Atrocity: Major Themes for Health Workers*, London: Medical Foundation for Victims of Torture.

Tallentyre, S. G. (ed.) (1906) *The Friends of Voltaire*, London: Smith Elder.

United Nations (1951) *United Nations Convention Relating to the Status of Refugees*, UN Treaty Series, Vol. 189: 137.

United Nations (1991) *United Nations Convention on the Rights of the Child*, London: Children's Rights Development Unit.

Van Beuren, G. (1994) 'The international protection of children in armed conflicts', *International and Comparative Law Quarterly* 43.

Winnicott, D. W. (1960) 'Ego distortion in terms of true and false self', in D. W. Winnicott (1965) *The Maturational Processes and the Facilitating Environment*, London: Hogarth Press.

27 Autism: clinical and theoretical issues

Judith Edwards and Monica Lanyado

Autism is of a totally different order to the other clinical topics addressed in this section. Children who have been deprived, traumatised or abused, in the main, nevertheless are capable of some degree of relatedness to other people – although these relationships will frequently be deeply conflicted and painful. Children with autism, on the other hand, can be totally or partially unable to make this vital link with another human being, lacking, as it seems, the rudimentary capacity and will to reach out for or feel any curiosity about human contact. They exist in a world of their own, which has developed its own private and idiosyncratic ways of operating. Anything which disturbs this universe arouses intense fear, panic and at times rage. They develop rituals in their lives which have to be adhered to almost as a desperate matter of life and death – in a manner which goes way beyond ordinary children's need to feel in control of their lives.

The emotional isolation of children with autism from their parents is a tragic consequence of their inability to relate and, in this isolation, they create a form of emotional self-starvation as all the ordinary processes of development which need to take place within the intimacy of parent–child relationships cannot take place (see Chapter 3). Their language may be non-existent, or consist solely of repeating the words of others without any sense of meaning. The words 'I' and 'you', if they are used at all, may be used interchangeably. They may avoid all eye contact with others, treating people in the same way as they treat inanimate objects, such as a chair or an item of clothing. It is hard for us, who live in a world which has meaning and understanding in it, to imagine ourselves in the stark world which they inhabit. The therapeutic task is to experience in the countertransference the particular quality of the child's internal world, then slowly and gradually to draw the child away from the barren and stultifying, but nevertheless safe, world that he or she has created, into a world in which relationships, rather than meaningless rituals and totems, are what sustains life.

The problem of aetiology and diagnosis

There are many difficult issues that need to be addressed, not least of which is the accuracy of the diagnosis of autism and the tremendous variations in its severity. Both of these inevitably affect the outcome of any therapeutic or educational intervention. The difficulties of diagnosis lead to disagreement between clinicians about whether there is brain damage present for all children with autism, and, if so, to what extent and how specific this brain damage is. What cognitive and emotional functions would specific brain damage have to affect to result in the types of behaviours typical of children with autism? Sometimes no specific brain damage can be detected with current technology. In other cases, there is identifiable brain damage and deficit, but this does not mean that the secondary effects of the brain damage cannot be ameliorated, as described by Sinason (see Chapter 28). If we accept the idea of multiple causation, what is it that constitutes this particular vulnerability? We have some indications about hypersensitivity across the sensory modalities: many autistic children seem painfully sensitive to sound, light, touch and smell. This painful sensitivity and susceptibility to being overwhelmed may lead to autistic avoidant patterns, which may also be seen as protection for a vulnerable self.

As child and adolescent psychotherapists, we cannot ignore the large grey area of organic/psychological overlap that exists in which an understanding of the aetiology of autistic disturbance may be vital in helping us to frame realistic treatment goals for our patients. However, as a profession, we also have a growing body of clinical evidence that some of these children and young people can be helped. They are helped through a careful combination of observation and assessment in a containing therapeutic setting, a knowledge of current infant development research, the sound and practical use of the transference and countertransference relationship, and a special adaptation of therapeutic technique which takes account of how severely limited these children are in being able to communicate with and receive communications from others. This chapter will present an overview of the ways in which this work has developed in contemporary practice, followed by discussion of the theories which this clinical experience has generated.

There has been much debate about the role of parenting in the aetiology of autism, but the contemporary view within the psychoanalytic world is that the emotional distance between the child with autism and his or her parents may be the awful result, not the cause of, autism. In any event, it is important to have a multi-factorial perspective. Nowadays, as a vital part of the treatment plan, parents of children with autism are usually offered very regular help alongside their child in order to maximise the improvements in communication that may be possible through treatment, and also to help them in the very difficult day-to-day management of family life, which can be ruled by their child's rituals and demands (Klauber 1998).

As already indicated, autism can be mildly or severely present for any particular child, but certain underlying features are terrifyingly uniform in their structure. The sheer repetitiveness and persistence of these features is a measure of how limited these children's emotional lives are. Imaginative and creative play can be non-existent in some children, and very restricted in others. For many children with autism, the capacity to think symbolically has not developed. They are children who often cannot play, although they can spend hours spinning toy car wheels without a thought or idea in their heads.

Case example: Peter

Four-year-old Peter had been developing normally until he was eighteen months old when his mother suffered a traumatic loss. From this time on, he became unpredictably aggressive in his behaviour, developed rituals over which he threw inconsolable tantrums if stopped, and gradually lost his ability to communicate meaningfully with his parents. When Peter came for his first therapy session, he entered the room like a nervous and tense animal exploring a new space. He was an angelic looking, chubby little boy with beautiful, but expressionless, large brown eyes. He carried an empty plastic washing-up liquid bottle, which he clutched to him all the time as other children would clutch a special teddy. When he finally noticed the box of small toys that had been put out for him, he took each toy, one at a time, smelt it and then threw it on to the floor until he had emptied the box. Later in the session, when he spotted another empty washing-up liquid bottle which was available for water play, he promptly dropped the bottle he had brought into the room with him, and clutched this new bottle with exactly the same determination as he had the old. He did not look the therapist in the eye, nor speak to her throughout the session. It was as if she did not exist. Although he talked to himself as he examined the room and its contents, and his words were perfectly formed, these words were strung together in a nonsensical manner and seemed to be used for the sound that they made (which appeared to soothe him) rather than because they had any meaning. When the therapist tried to say anything, simply to try to make contact, her words were drowned by a rising tide of noisier and noisier words, ending up in a loud ear piercing squeal.

During the course of his three-times weekly treatment which lasted for nine months, Peter would regularly try to strip off down to his underpants at the start of the session, and spend the rest of the session half naked, playing with the constant flow of water from the running tap. At home, he could spend hours just staring at the water, licking it, watching the bubbles it made, sensuously feeling it and drinking it. Throughout this time, he was totally cut off from the therapist. He was gradually persuaded to keep his clothes on more and play with the water less, but this was always with the attendant risk that he would have a screaming tantrum. He could rapidly end up in a terrified state in which he could not be comforted. Whilst Peter was able to make some headway in his therapy, and became more communicative – often singing appropriate snippets of nursery rhymes or adverts by now, to convey his thoughts and feelings, his tantrums, when he could not be understood or could not have his way, became so severe and at times so frighteningly violent for his parents that they could not cope. In addition, the fact that mother was heavily pregnant and father's work meant that he was away from home a great deal and so could not become involved in the help the clinic offered to the mother, or be much involved with him at home, contributed to the weekly treatment being broken off. Peter was rediagnosed as 'mentally handicapped' and he went to a residential community.

It is necessary to note that although there was a change of official diagnosis of Peter at this stage, it does not mean that he was not still suffering from the secondary handicap of autism. This change of diagnosis is a common occurrence when these children improve, especially if the diagnostician did not see the child at the time of the initial referral to the psychotherapist. It is also important to put Peter's illness in the context of his family relationships. Mother's initial traumatic loss of her grandmother to whom she was very close, when Peter was eighteen months old, seems to have precipitated his withdrawal and this loss was reactivated for both of them with mother's new pregnancy. Father's inability to support mother in her distress because of the demands of his work further complicated this picture. With hindsight, it was not surprising that the treatment broke down at this stage.

Peter illustrates not only many of the common features of how children with autism behave, but also the terrible heartache for the families – and the despondence of professionals – when the family's capacity to cope becomes overwhelmed by the scale and intensity of the child's problems. Peter was never able to play with the water in an imaginative way as, for example, ordinary children would – making tea, sailing boats, bathing dolls, and so on. He was totally fixed on the physical qualities and sensations that the water running from the tap produced. His eyes were gripped by the colours and ripples it made as it moved, his tongue and mouth loved to feel and taste it, his ears loved the splashing noise it made, he revelled sensuously in the sheer wetness of it, and he did this for months in therapy without any change in his routine. Tustin drew attention to these sensation dominated states (Tustin 1992). When Peter seemed occasionally to become minimally more aware of the presence of the therapist, she would firmly but cautiously try to attract him away from the water by introducing her own playfulness as a way of trying to draw him into a more exploratory kind of play. But these windows in his autistic behaviour did not occur often, and required great vigilance on the part of the therapist, and then great ingenuity in her therapeutic response. Alvarez described this 'reclaiming' role of the therapist (Alvarez 1992).

The concrete use of words as sounds, rather than a means of communication, is also common. In addition, Peter would repeat the therapist's words in an echolalic manner, using exact imitation of her intonation as he repeated, for example, 'Do you want to come in now Peter?' when she met him in the waiting room at the start of the session. Later in treatment he would ask to go to the toilet by saying (again in the therapist's intonation), 'Do you want to go to the toilet Peter?', by which she knew that he was actually asking her to take him to the toilet. This use of echolalia illustrates how difficult it can be for these children to use 'I' and 'you' correctly, as well as the hopeless muddle they can be in about who is who when making any attempt at communication. (For further discussion of echolalia and the development of verbal interchange in the development of children with autism, see Rhode 1997.) The direction of this phrase when the therapist said it to Peter, that is from one person to another, had lost its significance and the phrase became a string of noises that were uttered in connection with going to the toilet, like some incantation. The person-related quality of the question was obliterated.

The problem of how to communicate across the space that exists when the separateness of people's minds is comprehended is something which ordinary children take in their stride (see Chapter 3). To varying degrees, children with autism cannot bear this separateness and either obliterate it by their autistic behaviour, or become utterly terrified by it. Tustin's understanding of autism vividly conveys this traumatic, ripped apart and wounded sense of separateness, and she uses this as a basis for understanding many of the manifestations of autism. Tustin also explains the autistic child's use of objects, such as Peter's use of the washing-up liquid bottle (Tustin 1992). This is very different from an ordinary child's use of a transitional object, such as a teddy bear, which is thoroughly imbued with the child's imaginative life and is very definitely not interchangeable with any other teddy!

Peter's sensuous involvement with the water possibly indicated that he had not been able to integrate his separate sensuous experiences of the water

– sound, light, taste, and touch – into a more sophisticated and complex concept of a substance that combined all these separate qualities of water.

In contrast to Peter, five-year-old Molly made a remarkable recovery from her cut-off autistic state, with very little therapeutic impact.

Case example: Molly

For practical reasons, Molly and her mother were only able to have once-monthly parallel consultations with the therapist and her colleague. Molly was reported as not having 'been right' from birth. Shortly before Molly's birth, and for several years afterwards, there were severe problems in her parents' marriage which left her mother feeling very isolated, but determined to keep up a pretence that all was well. Mother described herself as being very cut off and depressed in the first weeks of Molly's life, and said that Molly had felt like a 'plank of wood' in her arms. As mother recovered and became more able to sort out the problems in the marriage, she realised that her daughter needed specialist help. Often with this type of presentation of autism, in which the child is very remote, unable to relate to adults and children and virtually without any speech, the child will be seen by many paediatric specialists in a search for physical explanations for their communication problems – such as deafness or brain damage. As for so many parents, the diagnosis of autism had come as a terrible shock to Molly's mother and she welcomed the opportunity to work with an adult therapist whilst Molly was seen by a child therapist.

During the first four monthly sessions, Molly was like a little automaton, a lifeless doll with whom it felt totally impossible to make any contact whilst she played monotonously with the sand, endlessly pouring it from one container into another and back again. Her experienced therapist had severe doubts that she could be helped, particularly on such an infrequent basis. However, the work with her mother enabled a process to get started between her and Molly during the gaps in treatment. There suddenly opened a 'window' in her autistic presentation through which the therapist was able to find a way to make contact with her.

She arrived for her fifth session, and, having previously been oblivious of the therapist's presence, on this occasion stood in front of her, clutching a doll (which was unusual), and looked deeply into the therapist's eyes. This felt quite electrifying and the therapist was reminded of the Sleeping Beauty awaking from her hundred-year sleep. The doll was of the kind that needed a battery to make it speak, but the battery was missing and there was a cavity in the doll's body where it should have been. Although it was by no means clear that this little girl would understand, the therapist took a chance and talked about how Molly was rather like the doll with the missing battery. She added that maybe the fact that she and her mother came to the clinic could help her to come alive as the doll could 'come alive' with the battery. Amazingly, Molly seemed to grasp the flavour of this interpretation and very clearly said 'Yes'.

Although Molly could not sustain this remarkable contact with the therapist and retreated to her sand play for most of the rest of the session, she had managed to peep out of her autistic protective shell (Tustin 1992) for long enough to discover that the world outside was not as terrifying as she had feared. Her mother, in the concurrent session, also reported an incredible change in Molly saying 'It's as if she's seeing me as a person for the first time'. She had also stopped soiling and wetting. This kind of dramatic reawakening is rare, but offers wonderful opportunities to see behind the walls of autism. Some authors have written fascinating autobiographical accounts of autism (see Williams (1992) for an adult account of recovery from childhood autism, and see Hocking's account (1990) of her life with her autistic son).

Molly's new awareness of other people had disadvantages as she became very anxious about being separate from others, particularly her mother. If one is separate from, that is, not within the same body and mind as the people one depends on, how can they know your needs, feelings and thoughts? It is only through actively trying to communicate with others across the gap of separateness that this is possible. But, whilst this is being learnt, life can feel precarious. Molly demonstrated this by becoming unable to move around the therapy room unless the therapist moved with her. She seemed to be frightened that if the therapist did not do this they would lose their relatedness – which was still a very concrete experience for her. At first, she would suddenly grab the therapist's arm, as if it were a walking stick, and certainly not human, and pull her across the room. Later, she would stand motion-less and silent next to the therapist, almost willing her to move to where she (Molly) wanted to move. When the therapist grasped what this behaviour was about and spoke about it, Molly beamed at her. This eventually developed into Molly saying, 'You come too'. Two months later, when Molly had become quite intoxicated with all she was discovering and learning as she emerged from her autistic state, she was able to move around the room as her interest took her. When the therapist reminded her of how she had needed her (the therapist) to 'come too' in the past, Molly actually roared with laughter.

Eight months into treatment, Molly became fascinated with birds which she could watch landing and flying off from the fire escape outside the therapy room. After watching them with great concentration for a while, she said 'Can't jump' in a don't-be-silly sort of voice, which seemed to refer to the fact that she couldn't 'jump' off and fly like the bird. The therapist commented that she seemed to be saying that she knew that if she tried to jump or fly she would fall to the ground. She added that Molly hadn't understood this before. Molly was pleased with this and moved on to making kites, which she attached to the fire escape railings. This led to further discussion of the fact the she had weight – and that in the past she had felt that if she wasn't tied to her mother like the kite was tied to the railings she would just float away. It was very similar to talking to a two-year-old child discovering these concepts – and it seemed as though Molly had been like a dormant seed behind her autistic shell, which now that it had found that the light and air were not dangerous, indeed were good for it, simply unfolded along natural developmental paths (see Chapter 3).

Over the two years that Molly and her mother continued to be seen for monthly consultations, she continued to develop in her language and play like an ordinary child. However, there was a 'ceiling' which she seemed to reach after this time, and, when she stopped treatment, she clearly still had what could be described as learning difficulties for which she needed a special classroom assistant – but within a normal school setting.

As children with autism grow chronologically into adolescents and young adults, the concern of their parents and professionals involved in their care will be how to maximise potential and integrate them appropriately into manageable life situations.

Case example: James

James, an adolescent boy who had emerged from an autistic state as a young child following two years psychoanalytic psychotherapy treatment, was re-referred at sixteen, when his post-autistic obsessionality, ritual preoccupations and difficulty with appropriate boundaries had precipitated him into a state which he called a breakdown. (This material is discussed more fully elsewhere (Edwards 1994, 1999).) This occurred at a point where the impact of ordinary adolescent development, when young people in general may feel anxious and unsure of their identity, had intersected with his particular post-autistic difficulties over boundaries, space and separation.

One of James's principal anxieties, apart from a host of worries about his physical health, was that he would be swallowed by a black hole – which Frances Tustin discovered to be an archetypal fear of children with autism (Tustin 1992). While at times of most acute concern he would launch into a spate of hand-flapping rituals which seemed almost unstoppable, he was able over time, when the three-times weekly therapy he had requested was under way, to step back and think about his anxieties rather than endlessly reiterate them or try to shake them away through his flapping hands.

James's history was that he had been premature and had been in an incubator for several weeks. The trauma of this separation had caused this particular child, constitutionally vulnerable and 'naked to the wind' (Meltzer *et al.* 1975), to withdraw into a terrified autistic state where he denied separation and thus relationship, which implied separate life. When he finally came home, he refused eye contact and could only be fed facing away from his mother. While he developed normally physically, he also developed autistic rituals, played obsessively, rather than symbolically, particularly with keys, cars and electric switches, and by school age was assessed as being in need of special educational provision. His parents had older children and it was through their patient persistence, and their experience previously as successful parents, that they could help him, in partnership with education and health professionals, to relate at least in part, rather than turning completely from the external world. One of his early articulated fears was of 'leaking down': one might hypothesise about this in relation to being tube fed in an incubator, where the life-preserving equipment designed to ensure survival might feel in a persecutory way to be draining life away.

James's second psychotherapy treatment lasted two years, and was ended by him when transport arrangements became difficult and confusing. Although this was a premature step and more could have been achieved if he had been able to persist in thinking rather than resorting to a defensive flight from confusion, much had already been gained in the contained and consistent space of the therapy and the therapist's mind. One of his favourite jazz pieces, 'On Solid Ground', had become a metaphor for his increasing sense of solidity and self. As he announced in one session, rather grandly, ' I don't have keys now, I have thought.' In his last session, James said ,'You know, you've got a good mind.' His therapist responded that James had discovered that he too had a good mind, and that he could now use it. He had indeed made progress both socially and academically, attending the same college as his older sister. His parents, too, noted his increased confidence: that he seemed more located in time and space (being for the first time able to calculate and read time), and that in place of the black hole, something more solid had begun to form. Several years later James was able to separate from his parents, embark on independent living and hold down a job, none of which had been thought possible previously. While he was still obsessional and sometimes depressed, life had become manageable. In cases such as this, improved functioning is the aim, rather than 'cure', which would be an unrealistic goal.

Discussion

Freud (1911) and Mahler (1961) originally posited what was then termed a 'primary autistic state' as a normal part of infant development: an undifferentiated, fused sense of union with the mother before the infant gradually became differentiated and achieved a sense of self. Researches in infant development, however, have revealed that far from this being the case, human infants come in a sense pre-programmed, hardwired to relate, and from the first days of life develop a self–other awareness, a sense of others' minds (Brazelton *et al.* 1974; Stern 1985; Trevarthen 1977). In one of two final papers written by Frances Tustin (1994), she talked of the 'perpetuation of an error' and acknowledged the impact of child development research in its impetus for a change in thinking and in techniques on the part of psychoanalytically oriented child practitioners. She says, 'This revised view will bring about a significant re-orientation in our approach to the treatment of autistic children.' Autism is now seen as a serious developmental aberration rather than as a regression to a ' normal' infantile state.

Not only did the facts emerging from child development research afford new insights into the life of the human infant, but they also, through theory of mind experiments, led to an increased understanding of children with autism in their apparent lack of the idea about the minds of others – the ordinary 'folk wisdom' about other peoples' minds that we take for granted. In an experiment adapted from a previous study, three psychologists presented a group of autistic children with a small scenario using dolls (Baron-Cohen 1988). Sally puts a marble into her basket and goes out of the room. Enter Ann, who removes the marble from Sally's basket to her own. When Sally returns, where will she look for her marble? The normal child of four years old has no difficulty in realising that Sally will look for the marble where *she* put it, though three-year-olds find this more problematic. The control group of Down's syndrome children mostly got this right (and were able to follow the researcher's instructions and questions), but the group of children with autism, even from older age groups, mostly made a wrong prediction and thought Sally would go to Ann's basket (Baron-Cohen 1988). While the experimenters themselves saw these results as demonstrating a cognitive deficit, psychoanalytic workers would be thinking much more about processes of identification. The capacity to 'put yourself in another's shoes' has emotional as well as cognitive components. It has also been argued that the cognitive deficits exemplified in the 'Sally–Ann tests' are the *result* rather than the cause, of the autistic child's inability to understand the emotions of others (Hobson 1989). (For a more elaborated discussion of these issues, see Alvarez 1992.)

Research into early infantile development and theory of mind has led to an expansion of 'classic' psychoanalytic technique, with the need for the therapist to become more active in 'reclaiming' an area of consciousness lost sight of, or never achieved, by the child with autism (Alvarez 1992). In 1984, the Tavistock Autism Workshop was set up by Susan Reid in order to provide a forum for the understanding of the theoretical, clinical and technical issues when treating these children, for both students and senior practitioners from Great Britain and abroad. This workshop, which was joined by Anne Alvarez as co-convenor in 1991, eventually became the first psychoanalytically oriented multidisciplinary team assessing and treating children on the autistic continuum, both locally and extra-contractually. Research projects have been set up and continue, and, for the first time in the history of the profession, the video camera has been used in the recording of sessions in order to provide frame-by-frame analysis of autistic phenomena, as well as providing an invaluable teaching tool. Professionals from both Britain and abroad join this team, and in this way the current thinking and dilemmas posed in treating these children are disseminated, much in the way that the original methods of infant observation and analysis eventually spread from core training schools to centres round the world (see Chapter 15). Building on the pioneering work of Melanie Klein and Frances Tustin, and Donald Meltzer and his colleagues, there has occurred a substantial evolution in thinking, which has been importantly documented, not only for professionals, but for the interested general reader (Alvarez 1992; Rustin *et al.* 1997; Reid and Alvarez 1999).

In 1930, Melanie Klein published her account of the treatment of four-year-old Dick, an autistic boy whose difficulties she saw as being the result of a withdrawal from his own aggression into a hermetically sealed state which cut him off from his capacity to learn and to be creative. She described his lack of affect, his echolalia and the apparent purposelessness of his behaviour. (Tustin (1983) discussed this paper in the light of the development of theories about autism and differential diagnosis.) McDougall and Lebovici describe in fascinating detail the analysis of a nine-year-old psychotic boy during the 1950s. Their account provides some follow-up of the boy's progress, together with notes on his mother's subsequent analysis (McDougall and Lebovici 1989). Kanner's significant paper in 1944 further elaborated the associated symptoms which together constitute the condition which he called 'Early Infantile Autism'. In this paper, documenting and describing eleven children, he noted the characteristic features which have become known as the 'Autistic Triad': difficulties in socialising, *and* in language, *and* in symbolic play. Kanner's paper indicated both organic and environmental factors as being aetiologically significant, and while over the succeeding years there have been swings in each direction, from notions of 'refrigerator parents' to notions that the environment had no significance, most psychodynamic and organic thinkers now accept multiple causation. This is in line with an evolution generally in thinking about development: that it is not linear, but is the result of complicated interactional patterns where, as Alvarez notes in *Live Company*, one can trace the 'awesome power of an effect to become a cause in itself' (1992: 187). She talks of the need for a 'double helix' understanding, 'where heredity and environment twist around each other in interacting spirals'. This of course underlines the importance of working with both the child and the family, so that the traumatising effects of the diagnosis of autism and autistic behaviour on the family system can be slowly and gradually deconstructed, and more benign cycles of interaction may eventuate over time (Reid and Alvarez 1999).

Diagnostic categories

Within the overall group of children with autism there exist sub-groups (Wing and Attwood 1987). While some children are actively withdrawn, there are those who seem rather more *un*drawn, than withdrawn – indifferent to others because of a deficit in their ideas about human beings, or 'internal objects'. Tustin talked of 'shell-type' autistic children, actively withdrawn as the term suggests for the sake of protection (Tustin 1990). Others may have never embarked on an interactional journey with other human beings, and these children, treated more recently as the boundaries of psychodynamic work are pushed further in terms of possibility and effectiveness, require a particular approach in order to be reached and drawn into relationship (Alvarez 1992; Reid and Alvarez 1999). Not all autistic children are alike, and it is the task of the therapist to assess where they are on the continuum of autism and what possible mix there may be in each case. Are they hiding or are they lost? It will be evident that techniques used will differ accordingly, as a parent would treat differently the child who is lost from the one who is, however determinedly, actively hiding away.

While we have been considering autism as a pathological reaction, it is also important to bear in mind situations in which it may be in some ways a logical, if not a healthy, solution to a situation which would be intolerable and beyond endurance. Reid's observational and clinical work with autistic children is an example of where infant observation can give a close-up (and chilling) picture of the early development of the autistic defences in situations where it may indeed seem to be the best alternative. Reid describes an initially healthy baby, where maternal handling resulted in an increasingly withdrawn autistic state. In this instance, ordinary defences were no longer sufficient (Reid 1997).

Autism may, in addition, be seen as a retreat and protection from psychosis, as can be seen in Rhode's description of ten-year-old Daniel (Rhode 1997), where his terror of being taken over and flayed by a 'Cruella de Ville' was a projection of his own aggressive and destructive rage at being separated from the mother and the feeding breast. During the persistent and patient work undertaken in this treatment, Daniel was able to move from a closed autistic state to face his psychotic terrors. The question of what is unlocked when autistic defences are loosened remains to be debated in each case. For Molly, at a later phase of treatment, there was a delightful stage of 'psychological birth' when she could revel in her separateness from her mother because of her awareness of their ever-developing lively relationship. For Peter, the growing awareness of his separateness from his mother felt like a psychological catastrophe. This was possibly the result of a combination of his emotional rawness and terror of separateness which any parent would have found extremely difficult to help him cope with, and the fact that his parents were psychologically not able to 'meet' him as he emerged from his autistic defenses. Tustin discusses these issues of psychological birth and psychological catastrophe (Tustin 1992).

The issues of differential diagnosis are complex, and there can be an oscillation and interplay between autistic and cut-off schizoid states of mind. Schizoid mechanisms can be used to ward off autistic fears, and, conversely, a child such as Molly may emerge from autistic shell-type states either towards post-autistic obsessionality (such as James at sixteen) or towards more disturbed psychotic or schizophrenic episodes, involving hyperintrusiveness or destructive symbiosis (such as Peter as treatment progressed): the kind of child that Tustin described as 'confusional' and 'entangled'.

Psychosis and schizophrenia are not recognised as diagnostic criteria before the age of six (Kolvin 1971; Kolvin *et al.* 1971; Kolvin *et al.* 1971a, 1971b), and before this age a child will usually receive the diagnosis of 'atypical autistic'. There are, as will be evident, different points of view on this whole question of diagnosis. As Rhode (1997) says: 'At this very detailed level of work, and in considering prognosis, it may be more useful to think in terms of feeling response elicited by the child and the balance between various ways of coping than in terms of immutable descriptive categories.'

Concluding remarks

It can be seen that, in its deepest manifestations, autism represents a turning away from the world, a denial of separation, in some cases a refusal *or* inability on the part of the child to join the mainstream of separated life and growth, the time–space continuum of everyday life with its beginnings and endings, sleepings and wakings. This profoundly shut-off state, and related states on the autism spectrum, can cause extreme difficulty not only for the child, but also for the family as they attempt to deal with a life denying state of mind and become traumatised by it in their own turn. As we have indicated in this chapter, there is an ongoing theoretical and technical debate which continues to refine psychoanalytic thinking and inform psychodynamic practice in order to help these children and their families.

References

Alvarez, A. (1992) *Live Company: Psychoanalytic Psychotherapy with Autistic, Border-line, Deprived and Abused Children*, London/New York: Tavistock/Routledge.

Baron-Cohen, S. (1988) 'Social and pragmatic deficits in autism: cognitive and affective?', *Journal of Autistic and Developmental Disorders* 18(3): 379–402.

Brazelton, T. B., Koslowski, B. and Main, M., (1974) 'The origins of reciprocity: the early mother–infant interaction', in M. Lewis and L. A. Rosenblum (eds) *The Effect of the Infant on its Caregivers*, London: Wiley Interscience.

Edwards, J. (1994) 'Towards solid ground: the ongoing psychotherapeutic journey of an adolescent boy with autistic features', *Journal of Child Psychotherapy* 20(1): 59–83.

—— (1999) 'Towards solid ground', in S. Reid and A. Alvarez *Autism and Personality: New Perspectives from the Tavistock Autism Workshop*, London: Routledge.

Freud, S. (1911) 'Formulations on the two principles of mental functioning', *Standard Edition*, Vol. 12, London: Hogarth Press.

Hobson, P. (1989) 'Beyond cognition: a theory of autism', in G. Dawson (ed.) *Autism: Nature, Diagnosis and Treatment*, New York: Guilford.

Hocking, B. (1990) *Little Boy Lost*, London: Bloomsbury.

Kanner, L. (1944) 'Early Infantile Autism', *Journal of Paediatrics* 25(3): 211–17.

Klauber, T. (1998) 'The significance of trauma in work with the parents of severely disturbed children, and its implications for work with parents in general', *Journal of Child Psychotherapy* 24(1): 85–107.

Klein, M. (1930) 'The importance of symbol formation in the development of the ego', in *The Writings of Melanie Klein, Volume 1*, London: Hogarth Press (1975).

Kolvin, I. (1971) 'Studies in the childhood psychoses. I: Diagnostic criteria and classification', *British Journal of Psychiatry* 118: 381–4.

Kolvin, I., Garside, R. F. and Kidd, J. S. H. (1971) 'Studies in the childhood psychoses. IV: Parental personality and attitude and childhood psychoses', *British Journal of Psychiatry* 118: 403–6.

Kolvin, I., Ousted, C., Humphrey, M. and McNay, A. (1971a) 'Studies in the childhood psychoses. II: The phenomenology of childhood psychoses', *British Journal of Psychiatry* 118: 385–95.

Kolvin, I., Ousted, C., Richardson, L. M. and Garside, R. F. (1971b) 'Studies in the childhood psychoses. III: The family and social background in childhood psychoses', *British Journal of Psychiatry* 118: 396–402.

McDougall, J. and Lebovici, S. (1989) *Dialogue With Sammy: A Psychoanalytic Contribution to the Understanding of Child Psychosis*, London: Free Association Books.

Mahler, M. (1961) 'On sadness and grief in infancy and childhood: loss and restoration of the symbiotic love object', *Psychoanalytic Study of the Child*, 17: 332–51.

Meltzer, D., Bremner, J., Hoxter, S., Wedell, H. and Wittenberg, I. (1975) *Explorations in Autism*, Strath Tay, Perthshire, Scotland: Clunie Press.

Reid, S. (1997) 'The development of autistic defences in an infant: the use of a single case study for research', *Infant Observation* 1(1): 51–79.

Reid, S. and Alvarez, A. (1999) *Autism and Personality: New Perspectives from the Tavistock Autism Workshop*, London: Routledge.

Rhode, M. (1997) 'Going to pieces: autistic and schizoid solutions', in M. Rustin, M. Rhode, A. Dubinsky and H. Dubinsky (eds) *Psychotic States in Children*, Tavistock Clinic Series, London: Duckworth.

Rustin, M., Rhode, M., Dubinsky, A. and Dubinsky, H. (1997) *Psychotic States in Children*, London: Duckworth.

Stern, D. (1985) *The Interpersonal World of the Infant*, New York: Basic Books.

Trevarthen, C. (1977) 'Descriptive analyses of infant communicative behaviour', in H. R. Schaffer (ed.) *Studies on Mother–Infant Interaction*, London: Academic Press.

Tustin, F. (1983) 'Thoughts about autism with special reference to a paper by Melanie Klein', *Journal of Child Psychotherapy* 9(2): 119–31.

—— (1990) *The Protective Shell in Children and Adults*, London: Karnac.

—— (1992) *Autistic States in Children*, London: Routledge.

—— (1994) 'The perpetuation of an error', *Journal of Child Psychotherapy* 20(1): 3–23.

Wing, L. and Attwood, A. (1987) 'Syndromes of autism and atypical development', in D. Cohen and A. Donnellan (eds) *Handbook of Autism and Pervasive Developmental Disorders*, New York: Wiley.

Williams, D. (1992) *Nobody, Nowhere*, London: Doubleday.

Further reading

Alvarez, A. (1992) *Live Company: Psychoanalytic Psychotherapy with Autistic, Border-line, Deprived and Abused Children*, London/New York: Tavistock/Routledge.

Journal of Child Psychotherapy (1994) 20(1): Special Issue on Autism.

Reid, S. and Alvarez, A. (1999) *Autism and Personality: New Perspectives from the Tavistock Autism Workshop*, London: Routledge.

Tustin, F. (1992) *Autistic States in Children* (rev edn), London: Routledge.

28 The psychotherapeutic needs of the learning disabled* and multiply disabled child

Valerie Sinason

Introduction

It has been an historic triumph that in the last decade of the twentieth century we can agree that learning disabled children have psychotherapeutic needs. The Anna Freud Clinic has long upheld the treatment needs of blind children (Burlingham 1963; Wills 1968) or diabetic children (Fonagy *et al.* 1989), whilst individual analysts or child psychotherapists have underlined the therapeutic needs of severely deprived children (Boston and Szur 1983), autistic children (Tustin 1991; Reid 1991; Alvarez 1992), physically disabled (Fraiberg 1977; Hoxter 1986) or dying children (Judd 1989).

However, with the honourable exception of Maude Mannoni in France (1970), it is only in the last ten years that there has been any internationally consistent awareness of the therapeutic needs of the learning disabled child (Sinason 1992). Fear and guilt about the existence and nature of learning disability have all too often led to what Bicknell has aptly termed 'the horticultural approach' in which the severely learning disabled child is fed and watered adequately, but with little cognitive or emotional understanding (Bicknell 1983).

The prevalence and nature of learning disability

Mild learning disability

The total prevalence of learning disability is 20–30 per 1000 of the population. Eighty per cent of the total number are mildly disabled. This means that their acquisition of developmental skills may be slow, although even, and in childhood they would be placed in schools for those with moderate learning disabilities They are at the lower end of the ordinary range of distribution of human intelligence. The majority of these belong to Social Class 5. They are more likely to experience poverty, parents with a psychiatric history, large numbers of siblings, inadequate housing and chronic unemployment. The children in this category will therefore have features in common with severely deprived children. In addition, they are more vulnerable because of their learning disability.

Severe and profound learning disability

Severe and profound learning disabilities, in contrast, are spread evenly across all social classes. However, the prospective ameliorating factors of an easier external environment are offset by the impact on the child and his family of a more severe mental or multiple disability. A severe learning disability is usually accompanied by other disabilities such as epilepsy, cerebral palsy, etc. Emotional disturbance, not surprisingly, increases according to the level of severity of the handicap. If we consider the depleting effects of even a minor ailment like a cold, it is not hard to understand why the daily burden of something irreparable makes the individual more vulnerable to disturbed intrapsychic processes.

Treatment provision

We are looking at a child population that faces both external and internal trauma and distress. What provision do we have? Chris Oliver *et al.* (1987) looked at one category of emotional disturbance in disabled children and adults in their area. They found that, of 596 self-injuring children and adults, only twelve were receiving any treatment at all. Of those twelve, eleven were receiving psychological treatment and one received psycho-analytic psychotherapy.

Derek Ricks, the late Consultant Paediatrician in learning disability at University College Hospital, pointed to one difficulty in providing suitable treatment, namely, the difficulty in assessment:

> A major obstacle to diagnosing psychiatric disorder in the learning disabled is the extent to which their everyday behaviour in response to stress may in many respects resemble the symptomatology of major illness.
>
> (Ricks 1990: 531)

Faced with a child who is banging his head and unable to speak or use sign language, many unsupported workers have given up thinking about the emotional meaning of the child's actions and have dismissed the behaviour as being part of the handicap.

Where residential workers or teachers have realised a child is distressed, they have all too often faced a disabled response from their local clinic or hospital. 'You can't treat learning disabled children with psychotherapy.' Many despairing referral letters describe such encounters where the referrer has been told 'They can't make use of therapy because you need a certain level of intelligence.'

It was in 1904 that Freud suggested 'a certain measure of natural intelligence' was a prerequisite for analysis. However, the work of the Tavistock Clinic Mental Handicap Workshop (Stokes 1987; Sinason 1986, 1992) has pinpointed the need for 'emotional' rather than cognitive intelligence, further validated by Stern's work (1985) on the intersubjective state. Autistic children (Elmhirst 1988) and severely learning disabled children (Sinason 1986, 1991, 1992) are able to understand the meaning of time and the therapeutic task and make good use of it.

Prerequisites for accommodating psychotherapeutic needs

In order to have a space for considering the therapeutic needs of disabled children who are emotionally disturbed or distressed there are certain essential practical and emotional prerequisites.

The clinical worker has to face the meaning of 'difference'

Although we are all disabled in different ways there is a major qualitative difference in the psychic experience of severe learning disability. To deny the emotional experience of this difference is to handicap any possible treatment. This means coming to terms with the guilt of not being learning disabled. It means giving up defensive myths such as 'ignorance is bliss' or 'children with Down's syndrome are friendly' (Sinason 1986, 1992). It also means giving up mad hopes for cure. Emotional disturbance might be treatable but the actual organic handicap is not.

The agreement of the child's multidisciplinary team

Where a child is so severely disabled that he would not function without the aid of others, the therapist becomes one more person in a large extended family of professionals who will stay with that child for life. The basic team might consist of speech therapist, psychiatrist, psychologist, social worker, teacher, paediatrician and physiotherapist. In addition, there might be a special escort who takes the child from home to school or from school to hospital. If the child is lucky there might be an art, music, drama or movement therapist; there might be a key worker if the child lives in a residential establishment. Above all, there might also be the parents.

They have had to deal with the disappointment that their child was not normal and, however loving and however much they have since bonded, their original hurt and loss will be highlighted on different occasions. For example, when another child leaves home, or moves to secondary school, it will highlight the handicap of the other. The parent has also had to face sharing his child with a range of professionals.

Therefore, unlike therapy with other children, for any treatment to take place for this group, the co-operation of the whole team is needed. A child who needs help to wash, dress, feed or toilet himself is not in a position to agree to a commitment to treatment by himself. The therapist needs to rethink very carefully therapeutic boundaries for this shared client.

The agreement of the therapist's clinical team

Some of the most emotionally disturbed, severely and profoundly learning disabled children are referred for self-injurious behaviour. They punch their heads, poke their eyes and bite themselves and their workers. Some are incontinent and encopretic. Some make bizarre noises or movements.

Can the setting make adequate physical and emotional allowance? Will the other staff in the centre mind the particular nature of the noise? Is there support for the receptionist if transport difficulties mean a child has to wait to be collected? Receptionists need to understand the language and non-verbal cues of patients when their escorts are late in picking them up.

The physical suitability of the setting

Is there a ramp for wheelchair access? Is the lift large enough to take a wheelchair if there are no ground-floor therapy rooms? Is there a disabled toilet? Are the fire doors too heavy for a disabled person in a wheelchair to push by herself? Is the therapy room large enough for a wheelchair?

Without that, workers bringing an opposite sex physically or multiply disabled patient in a wheelchair have a difficult dilemma. Having a ramp, a disabled toilet and a therapy room that a wheelchair has access to are essential prerequisites. Otherwise, a patient knows he has not been thought about. The environment can be just as handicapping as the handicap.

Help with incontinent or smearing patients

This issue does not just apply to emotionally disturbed learning disabled patients. Other patients smear faeces or are incontinent too. Will the therapist get any help with cleaning such primitive disturbing mess? In addition to the usual physical tidying-up time that is needed (Elmhirst 1988), something more substantial is needed.

The support of administrative staff is crucial. One colleague (Gordon Greener) helped me by cleaning my room when I was worn down after working with a severely mentally ill, learning disabled patient who had smeared blood and faeces over herself and the room. Gordon Greener used to work in a hospital setting 'So I was more aware of the physical side of a patient's needs and difficulties.' This is not a regular occurrence, but it matters that the environment can meet with such needs. Similarly, in another context, the head porter (Michael Shaw) has been willing to be on guard duty outside a therapy room as a protection to treatment when the patient is violent, and has changed parking restrictions to allow escorts bringing disabled patients to park as closely as possible.

Reliable transport

The referrer and the referred might agree that therapy would be helpful, but if there is no transport available it is not a viable proposition. With the break-up of the Inner London Education Authority the future of special transport in London is uncertain. Schools that have their own buses are not necessarily able to use them for one child's therapy times. Escorts are few and far between. A violent or severely multiply disabled child sometimes needs two escorts as well as a driver. That involves a great deal of staff time and a great deal of expense. One key worker who might agree to bring a child may then change jobs a few weeks later.

Establishing the importance of unbroken treatment is an essential pre-requisite and it must be noted that some centres manage great distances and difficulties for the sake of their clients' treatment. The head of one LEAP (Lifelong Education for Autistic People) centre took a whole minibus of his clients on a shared outing to one clinic when he was short of staff so that one patient had access to the treatment he needed.

Support for the worker

A workshop or supervision is essential when taking on emotionally disturbed children (or adults) with severe learning disability. The work involves getting close to great grief of a kind I have only otherwise experienced when working with severely abused or dying children. Underneath the appeasing 'happy' smile (Sinason 1988) of the disabled child there is often devastating loneliness and rage.

Assessment of whom?

With this client group, I have increasingly come to look on assessment for therapy as an assessment of myself. Do I feel I have something to offer this client? Can I bear to be with her weekly for years with, for example, no verbal speech and no symbolic play? Before we begin to consider the countertransference there are issues to do with the therapist alone. The therapist who does not mind an incontinent child might not bear a child who is attacking himself more openly. Self-injury is a painful sight.

Similarly, a therapist who manages active disruptive children excellently might be worn down by the chronic depression of some severely disabled disturbed children. A therapist needs to be able to manage an infantile transference of the most powerful kind. Sometimes, a severely brain-damaged patient cannot even begin to think a thought, let alone speak one, without the therapist voicing the possibilities that might exist in her mind.

Where a patient has only a mild learning disability it is possible for one staff member to provide a psychotherapy assessment and seek out a colleague to offer treatment. However, where there is a severe handicap accompanied by severe emotional disturbance, I think the assessment needs to be carried out by the person who will offer the treatment.

Assessment by whom?

A multidisciplinary assessment is the most helpful, where resources allow it. In a workshop held jointly by the Tavistock Clinic Learning Disability Workshop and the Wolfson Centre, it was agreed (McConachie and Sinason 1989) that a multidisciplinary assessment minimised unnecessary extra journeys for family and escorts. Where a child had major medical problems as a result of the disability, it was considered important to have a medical colleague as part of the assessment team. If the family find it hard to travel because of the nature of their child's handicap, can the assessment be done during a home visit? A joint psychological and psychotherapeutic assessment that includes the possibility of an observation at home is ideal.

Cognitive and projective psychological tests, together with the psychotherapy assessment, provide the fullest picture of the inner world of the prospective patient. Differentiating between organic deficit and emotional attacks on thinking processes is something that can be helpfully thought about as a result of this assessment procedure.

What choices of treatment or staff are there?

Is there a choice of individual, group or family (or extended family) treatment? Sometimes staff resources dictate what therapeutic response is available. I have found groups successful with mildly and severely learning disabled children and adolescents. Individual work has been the treatment of choice for profoundly multiply disabled patients.

Why has the referral been made?

The majority of our referrals come with a note stating that the referrer is about to change jobs. Residential workers often find it difficult to deal with the fact that they are free to leave, change their job, whilst their client remains in the same setting. Unlike day-school teachers who can say good-bye when a class moves up to another colleague, residential workers or teachers at boarding schools often have to face leaving before the referred child or adolescent does. Whilst such referrers often correctly anticipate the trauma of loss their departure will cause, they are not always in a position to gauge correctly the management support for psychotherapy in the remaining staff. Network meetings are then essential to establish the basic structure for treatment.

Sometimes, the referral is the passing on of a case that a particular team or area found too hard or dangerous to handle. The majority of such cases are those where workers are concerned about the possibility of sexual abuse but there is no adequate legal proof. Seventy per cent of all referrals made in one year concerned sexual abuse, with self-injury being the commonest consequence in females and violence in males.

The child's needs: therapy or a new school/home/family/court case?

Sometimes a child is referred for therapy when his real need is for something quite different. Some severely learning disabled children and adolescents have such depleted lives that a referral is made as a way of communicating that fact.

Materials for the therapy room

In addition to the standard equipment provided for most children in therapy (see Elmhirst 1988) certain additions are useful when working with severely learning disabled or multiply disabled patients.

For patients with no verbal language and little sign language (or patients with sign language but with a therapist who has not learned it) it is helpful to have extra physical means of communication. I have found shopping catalogues useful as they detail most of the material objects that a child or adolescent has in his daily life. Clockwork musical toys have a double use. They allow the mute patient to control a sound whilst showing something that slows down. This slowing down process is often used symbolically to explore the handicap itself. Many patients will try and find the moment where the retardation begins. For patients who are humiliated by their lack of ability to write, I have found a typewriter a useful piece of equipment.

The anatomically correct dolls have been useful for both disabled children and adults, as have large teddy bears and teenage dolls (Sinason 1988). At St George's Hospital Medical School Department of Psychiatry of Disability, Professor Sheila Hollins and I have developed colour picture books for disabled adolescents and adults on sexual abuse. These books, *Jenny Speaks Out* and *Bob Tells All*, tell a story in pictures so that a profoundly disabled individual can follow the theme with no literacy skills needed. We have found that just having these in the room with patients with little or no speech facilitates an environment in which it is concretely understood that painful issues can be thought about.

Consent, privacy and confidentiality

Where a child or adolescent has no speech or little sign language and requires the support of family and a team to manage functioning throughout a day, including washing, feeding and toileting, there needs to be careful thinking concerning the meaning of confidentiality, consent and privacy. It may be necessary to share physical information (soiling or wetting in the therapy room, epileptic fits) whilst keeping mental processes confidential. A child may be brought to a clinic in a wheelchair because he or she has problematic behaviours but without any personal wish to be there.

Prerequisites as containment

Bion (1970) has delineated the way that absence is a prerequisite for thinking. Without the ability to recognise and experience and manage absence there can be no symbolic thinking. However, to manage absence there has to be a good experience of being contained. Bion (1953), in describing Melanie Klein's thoughts on projective identification, shows how containment can be provided by the mother when she can deal with the fears the baby projects into her.

The nine months of pregnancy provide a way for parents to become accustomed to the presence of the important 'other' and make emotional changes needed to accommodate the new being. Where a child has been born with a deficit and has therefore faced an absence that is hard to symbolise, I think that the setting needs a similar incubation period to provide the containment that is needed. For this client group then, the pre-thinking is as important a part of answering the psychotherapeutic needs as the therapeutic containment of the sessions themselves. Hanna Segal's definition of the crucial aspect of containment – the therapist's understanding – can, I think, be extended to the pre-therapy period:

> The psychoanalytic setting, with its regularity of time and place, the supporting couch, and so on, is one of the factors in this containment. But the crucial factor is the analyst's understanding. It is when the patient feels understood that he feels that what he projected into the analyst's mind can be processed by that mind. He can then feel mentally contained.
>
> (Segal 1991: 53)

The key findings from therapy

(a) The most important finding is that learning disabled children and adults of all levels of disability can make use of psychoanalytical psychotherapy. They have feelings and fantasies about their disability let alone other issues in their lives.

(b) In a research project involving all the patients I was treating we found (Bichard *et al.* 1996) that, compared with a contrast group who were matched for IQ and emotional problems, our therapy controls improved significantly. Unsurprisingly, three years' therapy provided greater improvement than two years', and two years' greater than one year!

(c) The key issues in therapy are differentiating the primary disability, the organic deficit, from the secondary handicap (Sinason 1992), the depleting ways that the original disability is defensively exaggerated to hide the fear and shame of the real difference.

(d) There are small technical variations in treatment. We found from 1980, as those working with autistic patients (Alvarez 1992) also now comment, that more affective colouring is required in the therapist's verbal speech. Additionally, it is important to provide an environment in which curiosity and anger, the two most taboo states for learning disabled people, are allowed space.

(e) To deal with these issues mutatively there are five themes that have to be tackled (Sinason 1992): the disability itself, loss, dependency needs, sexuality and, most profoundly of all, the fear of being murdered. All patients, however disabled, have heard on radio or television discussion about amniocentesis. It is unbearably difficult to differentiate between stopping someone like you being born (and hailing it as a medical triumph) and killing someone like you now you are born, especially when you face societal deathwishes so unremittingly. The annihilating pre-Oedipal mother takes on a terrible hue of reality here.

Clinical example of an assessment of a profoundly multiply disabled adolescent

This young woman was abandoned at five years of age and went through a myriad of short and long-term placements until reaching the caring residential home that referred her. Her IQ was under 30. She was paralysed from the waist down and had blinded herself in one eye through her eye-poking. She was doubly incontinent, had no verbal speech and little sign language.

As the lift-doors opened I felt a sudden shock. On the wheelchair, covering her eyes with twisted fingers, a mass of black hair looking the only healthy sign of life, sat Maureen. Her back was curved, a breast was falling out of the loose T-shirt just under her neck and her useless legs had thinned into matchsticks. Maureen had clearly registered my shock as she was now covering her eyes with both hands. For a moment I had a stupid cowardly wish to cancel that knowledge. Then my intelligence returned. After I had introduced myself to Teresa, the worker, and Maureen, I commented to Maureen that she had come out of the lift with her eyes covered, perhaps because she knew that when new people saw her for the first time they got a shock at how handicapped she was. Her hands then came down, and two brown eyes, one very vivid and one dull from self-injury looked at me.

I knew then in that moment that Maureen possessed a high level of emotional intelligence. Inside the room, Teresa gently pushed Maureen next to a table full of paper and pens and various objects. Maureen did not look. I asked Teresa to say why Maureen had been referred. Teresa gently said that everyone was very proud of Maureen for being so brave when she had gone through so much; having no use of her legs, not being able to speak. However, Maureen cried for hours and was clearly very distressed and nobody had been able to do anything about that, and that was the main reason why she had been referred. I said that Teresa had mentioned those things in her letter and she had also mentioned one other matter, that Maureen was most distressed at Christmas time because that was when her mother had abandoned her.

To Teresa's surprise, and my own, Maureen reached out quickly from her wheelchair and picked up a baby doll. Then she picked up a mother doll and made it knock the baby doll away. She quickly covered her eyes again. I said she was showing us her key worker was right – she was sad at being rejected and now she was seeing a strange woman and would I knock her away too. Without any further exploration I let her know that I had a once-weekly vacancy and it was hers if she would like to come.

(Taken from Sinason 1992)

Discussion

From this small extract we can see how, expecting the shock of rejection (a re-enactment of family abandonment) and, unconsciously, annihilation, Maureen exacerbated her primary disability with a range of secondary handicaps that gave her the illusion of controlling whether she is rejected or not. However, these behaviours tragically alienated the staff who tended her. During six and a half years of therapy her functioning improved dramatically.

Mildly, severely and profoundly multiply disabled children and adolescents can make good use of psychoanalytic therapy and it is an essential step in their human rights that all training schools should make space for this work and allow such cases to be training cases. Learning about the shades of silence from one profoundly multiply disabled child improves one's therapeutic ability with all patients!

Note

* Linguistic Note: 'Learning disability' is the current British term for what was previously known as 'mental handicap' or 'special needs' and before that 'retardation' or 'backwardness'. The psycholinguistic process of euphemism is at work here (and indeed in most countries), changing the terms of the client group every few years in the hope that the 'bad thing' – the difference – will go away if we change the words.

References

Alvarez, A. (1992) *Live Company*, London: Routledge.

Bichard, S., Sinason, V. and Usiskin, J. (1996) 'Measuring change in mentally retarded clients in long-term psychotherapy. I The draw-a-person test', *NADD Newsletter* 13(5): 6–11.

Bicknell, J. (1983) 'The psychopathology of handicap', *British Journal of Medical Psychology* 56: 167–78.

Bion, W. (1953) 'Attention and Interpretation: Seven Servants', *Four Works by Wilfred Bion*, New York: Aronson, 1977.

—— (1970) *Attention and Interpretation: A Scientific Approach to Insight in Psychoanalysis and Groups*, London: Tavistock.

Boston, M. and Szur, R. (1983) *Psychotherapy with Severely Deprived Children*, London: Routledge and Kegan Paul.

Burlingham, D. (1963) 'Some problems of the ego development in blind children', *Psychoanalytic Study of the Child* 18: 197.

Elmhirst, S. I. (1988) 'The Kleinian setting for child analysis', *International Review of Psycho-analysis* 15(5): 7.

Fraiberg, S. (1977) 'Congenital sensory and motor deficits and ego formation', *Annual of Psychoanalysis* 5: 169–94.

Fonagy, P., Moran, G. S. and Higgett, A. (1989) 'Psychological management of children with problems of diabetic control: a psychoanalytic perspective', in S. Pearce and J. Wardle (eds) *The Practice of Behavioural Medicine*, Oxford: OUP.

Hoxter, S. (1986) 'The significance of trauma in the difficulties encountered by physically disabled children', *Journal of Child Psychotherapy* 12(1): 87–103.

Judd, D. (1989) *Give Sorrow Words: Working with a Dying Child*, London: Free Association Books.

Mannoni, M. (1970) *The Child, his 'Illness' and the Others*, London: Tavistock Publications

McConachie, H. and Sinason, V. (1989) 'The emotional experience of multiple handicap: issues in assessment', *Child Care, Health and Development* 15: 75–8.

Oliver, C., Murphy, G. H. and Corbett, J. A. (1987) 'Self-injurious behaviour in people with learning disability: a total population study', *Journal of Mental Deficiency Research* 31: 147–62.

Reid, S. (1991) 'Review of *The Protective Shell in Children and Adults* by Francis Tustin', *Journal of Child Psychotherapy* 17(2): 106–9.

Ricks, D. (1990) Chapter 41 in H. Wolff *et al.* (eds) *University College Hospital Textbook of Psychiatry*, Part 7, London: Duckworth.

Segal, H. (1991) *Dream, Phantasy and Art*, The New Library of Psychoanalysis 12, London: Routledge.

Sinason, V. (1986) 'Secondary learning disability and its relationship to trauma', *Psychoanalytic Psychotherapy* 2(2): 131–54.

—— (1988) 'Dolls and bears: from symbolic equation to symbol. The use of different play material for sexually abused children', *British Journal of Psychotherapy* 4(4).

—— (1990) 'Individual psychoanalytical psychotherapy with severely and profoundly disabled patients', in A. Dosen, A. Van Gennep and G. J. Zwanniken (eds) *Treatment of Mental Illness and Behavioural Disorder in the Mentally Retarded*, Logon: The Netherlands.

—— (1991) 'Interpretations that feel horrible to make and a theoretical unicorn', *Journal of Child Psychotherapy* 17(1): 11–24.

—— (1992) *Mental Handicap and the Human Condition: New Approaches from the Tavistock*, London: Free Association Books.

Stokes, J. (1987) 'Insights from psychotherapy', paper presented at International Symposium on Learning Disability, Royal Society of Medicine, London 25 February 1987.

Stern, D. N. (1985) *The Interpersonal World of the Infant: A View from Psychoanalysis and Developmental Psychology*, New York: Basic Books.

Tustin, F. (1991) *The Protective Shell in Children and Adults*, London: Karnac Books.

Wills, D. (1968) 'Problems of play and mastery in the blind child', *British Journal of Medical Psychology* 41: 213.

Further reading

Sinason, V. (1992) *Mental Handicap and the Human Condition: New Approaches from the Tavistock*, London: Free Association Books.

Appendix
Further information

(i) The work of the Child Psychotherapy Trust (CPT)

The Child Psychotherapy Trust is a registered charity dedicated to improving the lives of emotionally damaged children and adolescents by increasing their access to child and adolescent psychotherapy services. One of the most important tasks in order to achieve this is to raise the number of child psychotherapists available throughout the UK, particularly outside London. The Trust works closely with the Association of Child Psychotherapists (ACP) to promote the benefits of child psychotherapy and child mental health in general. Where possible, the Trust raises funds to support trainees in clinical training and to support some projects and regional development work. The Trust undertakes public relations and lobbying activities on behalf of and in conjunction with the ACP.

The Trust has produced leaflets and a video as a part of a series that aims to raise awareness of children's emotional and mental health needs. As a part of the Trust's *Your Child's Emotional Health* campaign, information such as this is being taken to major exhibitions and conferences in the UK and, where possible, presentations are made to the delegates. Amongst others, the campaign has been promoted at the Community Practitioners and Health Visitors' Conference and Community Health Council Conference.

Leaflets on the following subjects are currently available from the Trust in this expanding series: 'Your new baby, family and you', 'Separations and changes in the early years', 'Tempers and tears', 'Crying and sleeping', 'Attending to difficult behaviour', 'Sibling rivalry', and 'Divorce and separation'. These leaflets, written by experienced psychotherapists, are designed to address the common preoccupations, anxieties and queries of parents and young children. They are designed to help parents and all who work with children and families to think and make more sense of children's behaviour and what lies behind the interactions between children and their caretakers. Among those consulted on the leaflets are The Community Practitioner's and Health Visitor's Association, The Royal College of Nursing and The Royal College of General Practitioners.

There is a lot to be done to achieve an equitable child psychotherapy service throughout the UK. The Trust's priorities are to convince commissioners to purchase training posts, and to raise awareness of the benefits of psychotherapy as part of the solution to the inner turmoil of so many of our children.

Further details are available from:

> The Child Psychotherapy Trust
> Star House, 104–108 Grafton Road
> London NW5 4BD
> Tel: 0171-284 1355; Fax: 0171-284 2755;
> email: cpt@globalnet.co.uk

> The Child Psychotherapy Trust in Scotland
> 13 Park Terrace
> Glasgow G3 6BY
> Tel: 0141-353 3399; Fax: 0141-332 3999

(ii) Addresses of the ACP, training schools and observational studies courses in the UK

> Association of Child Psychotherapists
> 120 West Heath Road
> London NW3 7TU
> Tel: 0181-458 1609; Fax: 0181-458 1482

Training schools

> The Anna Freud Centre
> 21 Maresfield Gardens
> London NW3 5SH
> Tel: 0171-794 2313

> Birmingham Trust for Psychoanalytic Psychotherapy
> 96 Park Hill
> Mosely, Birmingham B13 8DS
> Tel: 0121-449 9552

> The British Association of Psychotherapists
> 37 Mapesbury Road
> London NW2 4HJ
> Tel: 0181-452 9823

> The Scottish Institute of Human Relations
> 56 Albany Street
> Edinburgh EH1 3QR
> Tel: 0131-556 0924

The Society of Analytical Psychology
1 Daleham Gardens
London NW3 5BY
Tel: 0171-435 7696

Training Office
The Tavistock and Portman NHS Trust
Tavistock Centre
120 Belsize Lane
London NW3 5BA
Tel: 0171-435 7111

Observational studies courses

These courses are formally linked to Universities, to the Tavistock Child and Adolescent Psychotherapy Training, the Anna Freud Centre or the British Association of Psychotherapists. In addition, a number of members outside London run seminars for colleagues who wish to enlarge their therapeutic skills and learn more about psychoanalytic work with children and young people. For further information, please contact the ACP.

Paul Barrows, Observational Studies Course Tutor
Knowle Clinic Child and Adolescent Service
Broadfield Road
Knowle, Bristol, BS4 2UH
Tel: 01179 724227

Marta Smith, Observational Studies Course Tutor
Department of Child and Family Psychiatry
St James University Hospital
Leeds, Yorks LS9 7TF
Tel: 01132 433144 x 4292

Merseyside Psychotherapy Institute
c/o Department of Child and Adolescent Psychiatry
Alder Hey Children's Hospital
Eaton Road
Liverpool L12 2AP
Tel: 0151-228 4811

Andrea Watson, Oxford Observational Studies Course Tutor
12 Rectory Road
St Clements
Oxford OX4 1BW
Tel: 01865 243491

MSc Course Tutor
Anna Freud Centre
21 Maresfield Gardens
London NW3 5SH
Tel: 0171-794 2313

Introductory, Diploma and Masters Courses Secretary
British Association of Psychotherapists
37 Mapesbury Road
London NW2 4HJ
Tel: 0181-452 9823

Index